D1241249

STAGES ON LIFE'S WAY

Lectori benevolo!

As a specimen of Kierkegaard's beautiful handwriting the Royal Library in Copenhagen courteously furnishes this photographic reproduction of the first page of

The Stages on Life's Way:
Lectori Benevolo!
etc.

STAGES
ON LIFE'S WAY

BY

S. KIERKEGAARD

TRANSLATED
BY WALTER LOWRIE

Introduction by Paul Sponheim

SCHOCKEN BOOKS • NEW YORK

First SCHOCKEN edition 1967

Reprinted by arrangement with Princeton University Press

Library of Congress Catalog Card No. 66–14875

Manufactured in the United States of America

CONTENTS

INTRODUCTION
BY PAUL SPONHEIM

IN 1936, Princeton University Press and the American-Scandinavian Foundation published David Swenson's translation of Sören Kierkegaard's *Philosophical Fragments.* From that event dates the deluge of Kierkegaardiana in English. The task of translation dominated the first decade, that of exposition the second, and the work of interpretation has really only begun in the third. What accounts for this prodigious outpouring? Is there any reason to expect its continuance? Surely a central fact to be faced in finding answers to these questions is the tendency to link Kierkegaard's name with the existentialist protest in philosophy and the dialectical theology of Barth, Brunner, and the Niebuhr brothers. *Stages on Life's Way* seriously challenges these apparent executors of Kierkegaard's estate and pleads pungently for the reader who, tired of shouting the name, will let the man speak. It is fitting that this edition makes that speech available to a wide audience.

It is also fitting that introductory comments lead the reader into this book, for this work is by no means transparently intelligible. Difficulties of two sorts exist. There is, first of all, the intricate literary scaffolding employed by the author to support his thought. Even if one gets past this problem, ambiguities within the thought itself combine to constitute a dilemma for the interpreter.

I

The subtitle Kierkegaard gave the *Stages* informs us that studies by "sundry persons" lie ahead. That claim will win little dispute: Hilarius Bookbinder binds into a book contributions by such opaque characters as William Afham ("Byhim") and Frater Taciturnus ("Brother Silent"). Printed here is some man's (Quidam's) diary found in a lake—or is it the word of the silent one? Through it all, characters in a dizzying array clash with each other. What is the author about here? All this could be simply spectacular fireworks fired by a runaway imagination. But it is worth noting that Sören Kierkegaard thought otherwise. What he said on the subject clusters around the phrase "indirect communication."

Kierkegaard's statements concerning indirect communication are not equally clear or completely consistent, but beneath them all lies a conception of man as being at once caught in the tissue of temporality and yet required to choose the content of the time of his days. As Kierkegaard put it in *The*

Sickness unto Death, man is a synthesis of necessity and possibility. He cannot escape the concrete immediacy of his life. He is caught in a web woven by his biography and those of other men. Still, the loose phrase of common coin, "accidents of biography," is too loose. That outside the self presses in upon the self necessarily, but it does so as possibility. It is the self's own choice which determines the pattern the push of time will find in his actual existence.

As *Stages* shows, Kierkegaard felt that this issue of choice was almost wholly ignored in his time. Indeed, the Hegelians seemed rather to repudiate than to ignore individual choice, as they celebrated the ceaseless parade of the Idea through its course of thesis, antithesis, and synthesis. Surely patterns are discernible in history, but they describe and do not strictly predict. Patterns evolve from the piecing together of the products of personal choice—of inner acts of selves. To be sure, the product of such an act "enters the order of things . . . which digests, so to speak, the free actions and coordinates them in its eternal laws." [1] But "with what one calls the inward work philosophy has nothing at all to do, but the inward work is the true life of freedom." [2]

The religious community of Copenhagen seemed to conspire with the philosophers in turning man away from the call to choose for himself. After all, did not the truth stand secure in the nineteen centuries of Christian history, and available every seventh day in the pulpits of the city? Does the doubt—or the faith—of one individual matter before all the saints of God? Why not let the six days run their course so long as the seventh surely follows? This silent conspiracy found open expression in Kierkegaard's own teacher at the University, Hans Lassen Martensen, who would "go beyond" Hegel to a strange blend of idealistic philosophy and Christian tradition. With Hegel at least one knows where one is!

The trouble with that time was not trivial. In the *Concluding Unscientific Postscript,* Kierkegaard offered the diagnosis that the "misdirection of speculation . . . must not be something accidental, but must lie far deeper in the whole tendency of the time—it must indeed lie in the fact that one had with such great knowledge altogether forgotten what it is to *exist* and what *inwardness* means." [3] The requirement of choice and the alternatives

[1] Kierkegaard, *Either/Or,* translated by David Swenson, Lillian Swenson, and Walter Lowrie (2 vols.; Princeton, N.J.: Princeton University Press, 1944), II, 147. In quoting Kierkegaard reference will always be made to the existing English translations, though the reader will notice some alterations for which the author of this introduction must assume responsibility.

[2] *Ibid.*

[3] *Concluding Unscientific Postscript to the Philosophical Fragments,* translated by David Swenson and Walter Lowrie (Princeton, N.J.: Princeton University Press, 1944), p. 216.

of choice must be made clear. But the form in which the remedy is made available may control the chances for any cure. If the prescription becomes a pompous pronouncement, the spirit of the age is altogether capable of swallowing such a pill whole and regurgitating it as one more bit of objective truth supported by the authority of the ceremonial seriousness of its sponsor. Rather let the alternatives stand clearly forth for themselves and by the intrinsic conflict of their claims evoke in the reader the activity of choice. So all of Kierkegaard's books come "without authority," and many without an author. *Stages* provides a particularly striking example of this art of "indirect communication," which Kierkegaard exercised so persistently.

II

If Kierkegaard would have the alternatives speak for themselves, it is perhaps best that they do so. However, it may be useful to gather a few references to other works in which such dialogue occurs. A skeletal identification of the alternatives is needed to support those references. That will require some few paragraphs about the "aesthetic, the ethical, the religious," and their interrelationships here and elsewhere.

The first of Kierkegaard's major works to be published, *Either/Or* (1843), corresponds to the first two-thirds of the *Stages*. Already in this earlier work, published when he was thirty, Kierkegaard shows a sure hand when it comes to indirect communication. The papers contained in the two volumes were found in the drawer of a desk acquired from a second-hand furniture dealer. The authors (A and B) of the two sets of papers had known each other, and their views clash as openly as the title suggests in the letters of the second author (Judge William of the *Stages*) to his brilliant young friend. Still, Judge William does not seem to know the specific papers of A which make up Volume I. All this is rather like the *Stages,* where the drunken banquet speakers stumble upon the married bliss of Judge William, whose observations about marriage in turn respond to the attacks launched from the banquet table without explicitly recognizing them. In the *Postscript,* Kierkegaard claims that "in connection with the truth as inwardness in existence . . . the law is: the same, and yet changed, and still the same." [4] He has followed that rule well.

The substance of the books joins the form in being "the same, and yet changed, and still the same"—in constituting a "repetition," as Kierkegaard would say. In both works the aesthetic emerges in a wide variety of forms. The aesthete refuses to choose to be himself—to affirm his identity and to

[4] *Ibid.,* pp. 254–55.

reveal it. But his refusal may flee life in a dreaming absorption in the Idea or immerse itself in every chance change of fashion. The sketch is the same and yet not the same. In the *Stages,* the aesthete is presented in a more decisive garb. The "either/or" has become visible in opposed life stances.

In the ethical stage, one seeks no decaying good, but rather that which holds good for the self in every moment of time. That is, one chooses one's own real self. In *Either/Or,* Judge William puts it so:

> But what is it I choose? Is it this thing or that? No, for I choose absolutely, and the absoluteness of my choice is expressed precisely in the fact that I have not chosen to choose this or that. I choose the absolute. And what is the absolute? It is myself in my eternal validity. Anything else but myself I can never choose as the absolute, for if I choose something else, I choose it as a finite thing and do not choose it absolutely.[5]

While no one else can choose for the self, the self's choice of itself brings it into relationships to others. In *Either/Or,* Judge William wrote of the duty of every man to be revealed, and hence of the duty of every man to enter marriage, with its goal of mutual disclosure. Now, in the *Stages,* he extols the miracle of mutuality, in which each partner completes the other and every good is twice blessed. In the *Postscript,* Kierkegaard says that the new note in the *Stages'* description of the ethical is the appreciation of time. The sheer act of choice is placed more clearly as part of the process of time in which "a woman's beauty increases with the years." [6]

Something else in the *Stages* is different. The Judge is older now and sees more difficulties. He finds that marriage requires faith, "honesty toward God and one's wife," and he speaks of God's existence as that which sustains the mutuality of marriage. Moreover, he develops more fully than in *Either/Or* the suggestion that there might be an exception to the universal goal of marriage. The category of the exception does not really fall within Judge William's concern, but it is, of course, the dominant theme of the book's last part—Quidam's diary and the comments by Frater Taciturnus. Thus, the chief advance of the *Stages* over *Either/Or* is attained in the addition of the religious stage to the other two. According to the *Postscript,* the advance is a significant one:

> The aesthetic stage is very briefly indicated, and it is presumably in order to lay the accent quite emphatically upon the religious that the

[5] *Either/Or,* II, 179–80.

[6] *Concluding Unscientific Postscript to the Philosophical Fragments,* p. 265.

author has called the first part *A Recollection*. By pressing the aesthetic back, the ethical and particularly the religious are brought to the front.[7]

The religious stage in the *Stages* represents a kind of repetition too. Quidam's diary constitutes a striking formal parallel to the Diary of a Seducer in *Either/Or*'s presentation of the aesthetic stage. And *Either/Or* closes with a sermon by a country parson entitled "The edification implied in the thought that as against God we are always in the wrong." But the *Stages*' presentation of the religious stage, linked as it is with the note of a religious exception to marriage, gives new life particularly to two other earlier works (dating from 1843), *Repetition* and *Fear and Trembling.*

Repetition takes with the *Stages* the theme of a broken engagement—broken because there is no possibility for the sharing marriage requires. In *Repetition,* it is a young man's poetic spirit, which renders the beloved's image more precious than her actuality, which constitutes the obstacle. In the *Stages,* it is the state of being shut in by melancholy that bars the way to the openness of marriage. In *Repetition,* the young man takes Job's dilemma as his own. In his case, he cannot marry, though he still loves. In a somewhat surprising ending, the young man is said to experience a reintegration of his personality upon hearing that the girl has married another. The *Stages* more consistently leaves the issue in doubt and has Frater Taciturnus judge Quidam for even supposing that such a result as that found in *Repetition* would alter matters. The *Stages* also makes clear that the question at hand is that of a religious exception to the ethical universal—marriage. It involves, in the words of *Fear and Trembling,* a "teleological suspension of the ethical" duty to tell the truth and ultimately to reveal oneself in marriage. In *Fear and Trembling,* Johannes de Silentio ("John the Silent," cf. Frater Taciturnus) employs the Abraham-Isaac story to put the question: "May there be such a thing for an individual as an absolute duty to God which is other than and higher than his duty to the ethical universal?" Ethically considered, Abraham wills to commit murder, and the issue of the story, Johannes emphasizes, does not alter matters.

A comparison of the *Stages* and *Fear and Trembling* already suggests that the religious stage is not fully stated in the *Stages*. In fact, the *Stages* makes that point itself. Quidam deals with a religious possibility, but lays no claim to the actuality, acknowledging that he "cannot understand the paradigm." One can hardly do more than to say with Frater Taciturnus that Quidam is "in the direction of the religious." And the Frater himself

[7] *Ibid.*

stops short of really delineating the religious, for he fails to speak of the forgiveness of sins, which lies outside his task and, he concedes, his understanding. But it had already fallen within the scope of Kierkegaard's activity as an author. In 1844, he had published *The Concept of Dread,* which ponders the state of dread out of which sin emerges—though always by the leap of choice. And in that same year appeared *Philosophical Fragments or a Fragment of Philosophy,* which sought to chart the systematic consequences of the supposition that, going "beyond Socrates," man does not have the truth even vaguely in recollection but must acquire it in time.

Then, in 1845, came the *Stages* and, in the following year, the crowning center of Kierkegaard's work, the *Postscript.* At one time Kierkegaard intended that the *Postscript* would conclude all his literary activity. In a final note in this work he acknowledges that he is the author behind the pseudonyms, and already the title page carries his name as "responsible for publication." The *Postscript* proved to be center rather than climax. But it does mark a turning point in the production, for the rest of the authorship is dominated by religious literature. In the *Fragments* and the *Postscript,* Kierkegaard had introduced as the decisive advance over Socrates the God in time, the God-Man. In these works the reader meets head on the paradoxical claim that one gains an eternal happiness in time in relation to that which can come to be in time only against its own nature. The religious works following the *Postscript* develop this theme further. These last works lie beyond the immediate setting of the *Stages* and can only be mentioned here. Perhaps chief among them are *The Works of Love* (1847), *Christian Discourses* (1848), *The Sickness Unto Death* (1849), and *Training in Christianity* (1850).

Still later falls the final episode in the literary production, and the one to which so much attention has been directed. From December, 1854, until his death in October, 1855, Kierkegaard kept up a steady attack on the Church through newspaper articles and pamphlets. The notes of resignation and suffering already present in the *Stages* and more completely developed in the *Postscript* are totally in control here—and now the emphasis falls on external suffering. These pieces, with their exaltation of martyrdom, seem in sharp contrast to the discussion of the religious stage in the *Stages* and its immediate companions in the authorship, where so much stress is placed on the impossibility of any external expression of religious truth. Similarly, these last outpourings reject pseudonymity, and, in reissuing *Training in Christianity* in 1855, Kierkegaard exclaims, "Take the pseudonymity away!" [8]

[8] *Attack upon "Christendom,"* translated by Walter Lowrie (Princeton, N.J.: Princeton University Press, 1946), p. 55.

III

Does any significant unity characterize a literary production so diverse? That question might be put concerning Kierkegaard's intentions with his works. What has been said here concerning indirect communication and choice already implies an affirmative answer, albeit a modest one. Can more be said? Kierkegaard himself said more on two occasions particularly. These two responses are strikingly different and may serve to reintroduce the topic of the contemporary appropriation of Kierkegaard's legacy.

On the one hand, it could be claimed that Kierkegaard would simply let the life views clash so that the discord would force the reader to an authentic decision—*any* decision. This is a reading of Kierkegaard which is attractive to the existentialists, with their emphasis on the need for choice and the absence of any justification for any particular choice. It seems odd to argue from authority for the absence of authority, but if one will do so and will specify Kierkegaard as the authority, the *Postscript* is the place to go. There, Kierkegaard, while acknowledging that he has produced the pseudonyms, denies any responsibility for their views:

> So in the pseudonymous works there is not a single word that is mine, I have no opinion about these works except as a reader, not the remotest private relation to them, since such a thing is impossible in the case of a doubly reflected communication.[9]

The last phrase gives the clue to the flaw in this interpretation of Kierkegaard's work. The disclaimer is issued in the name of "a doubly reflected communication." Kierkegaard gives these works life—they are fully free to be themselves. But that is not to say Kierkegaard had no purpose in granting them independence. The rejection of pseudonymity in the final phase of the authorship need not force one to believe that he had no personal interest in the earlier works. He came to think that pseudonymity ill served his purpose. Kierkegaard's papers make clear that he once felt the pseudonyms made it possible for the age to hear the "I" again, "and a personal I." [10] But later the conviction came that "a pseudonym is after all also an impersonal thing." [11] Beyond that, Kierkegaard has claimed a very pointed personal purpose in the whole churning production. In 1848, he wrote *The Point of View for My Work as an Author* as a "report to his-

[9] *Concluding Unscientific Postscript to the Philosophical Fragments,* p. 551.

[10] *Sören Kierkegaards Papirer,* ed. P. A. Heiberg and Victor Kuhr (11 vols., Copenhagen: Gyldendals, 1909–48), VIII, 2 B 88, p. 183 (translation mine).

[11] *Ibid.,* X, 2 A 393 (translation mine).

tory." Indirect communication is still affirmed, but as a way of meeting the reader on his own ground, in order then to move him on to the higher ground of the Christian faith. The basic support available to Kierkegaard's argument is the fact that he "accompanied" the publication of the pseudonymous aesthetic works with "edifying" discourses in his own name.

The discourses do stand as fact, though the question of any substantive unity among them or between them and the rest of the production remains a separate matter. Kierkegaard even concedes that he has overstated the case for a subjective unity of intention when he writes quaintly that the explanation in *The Point of View* "assumes a little too much in the direction of consciousness." [12] To that admission he joins the confession of his faith that Providence has been at work directing the whole toward its goal. What may that goal be said to be, and how great is the distance to be traversed to reach it from the territory of the *Stages?*

At this point the other class of claimants to Kierkegaard's legacy becomes eloquent. Karl Barth has said that the theme in his watershed work on the Epistle to the Romans was his insistence that Kierkegaard's word about the infinite qualitative difference between God and man be taken absolutely seriously. The other dialectical theologians link Kierkegaard's name to the rhythm of paradox running through their work. With respect to the authorship, this view requires that the truth of Christianity—"Religion B" in the language of the *Postscript*—be set apart from all that goes before, including the general category of the religious with which the *Stages* is concerned.

Again a disagreement must be registered. While Kierkegaard does most surely speak of the difference between God and man, he warns against a view in which "God becomes so endlessly exalted that there is absolutely no real relationship at all between God and the individual man." [13] His real concern is not metaphysical contrast—though that is his interest in the category of the comic—but religious relatedness: "If the difference is infinite between God, who is in heaven, and you, who are on earth: the difference is infinitely greater between the Holy and the sinner." [14] Even at the height of his utterances regarding paradox, it is still the inward choice to which Kierkegaard appeals, though that choice is set in relationship to a very specific other external to the self—the Christ:

Man is granted a choice. . . . Man not merely *can* choose . . . he

[12] *The Point of View for my Work as an Author,* trans. Walter Lowrie, ed. Benjamin Nelson (New York: Harper & Row, 1962), p. 73.

[13] *Sören Kierkegaards Papirer* X, 1 A 59 (translation mine).

[14] "The High Priest," trans. Walter Lowrie. A discourse from 1849, published in *Christian Discourses* (New York: Oxford University Press, 1961), p. 368.

> *must* choose. . . . For in such a way God holds himself in honor, while he also has a fatherly concern for man. If God has condescended to be that which *can be chosen,* then man also *must* choose—God does not let himself be mocked.[15]

If the role of human choice is affirmed, the essential thrust of the ethical is at hand. So it is that in no work other than the *Postscript,* with its stringent statement of the paradox, Kierkegaard declares concerning the *Stages:*

> There are three stages: an aesthetic, an ethical, and a religious. . . . But in spite of this triple division the book is nevertheless an either-or. The ethical and the religious stages have in fact an essential relationship to one another.[16]

Where then does the advance in the religious stage lie? A final quotation from the *Postscript* is needed:

> Had *Either/Or* proposed to make it clear where the difficulty lies, the entire work would have had to have a religious orientation. . . . The difficulty is, that the ethical self is supposed to be found immanently in despair, so that the individual by persisting in his despair at last wins himself. He has indeed used a determination of freedom: to choose himself, which seems to lesson the difficulty. . . . When I despair, I use myself to despair, and therefore I can indeed by myself despair of everything; but when I do this, I cannot by myself come back. In this moment of decision it is that the individual needs divine assistance, while it is quite right to say that one must first have understood the existential relationship between the aesthetic and the ethical in order to be at this point; that is to say, by being there in passion and inwardness one will doubtless become aware of the religious—and of the *leap.*[17]

Nor should one suppose that the aesthetic is wholly repudiated in the religious. The ethical choice is a choice of one's self—yet that self is not some supra-temporal substance, but the process of life in its highly specific, local character. The *Stages* recognizes this by stating that the problem is to combine the gift of love (the aesthetic immediacy) and the task of

[15] "What We Learn from the Lilies of the Field and the Birds of the Air," trans. David Swenson and Lillian Swenson. Discourses published in *The Gospel of Suffering* (Minneapolis, Minn.: Augsburg, 1948), pp. 228–29.

[16] *Concluding Unscientific Postscript to the Philosophical Fragments,* p. 261.

[17] *Ibid.,* pp. 230–31.

resolution (the ethical universal) in a synthesis. Beyond this book, Kierkegaard speaks often of faith as a higher or second immediacy. In the double movement of repetition one does get back to the concrete, the temporal. That is why Kierkegaard says the stages can be structured by asking what meaning time has for each.

From this assessment of the interrelationships in the authorship, the *Stages* emerges as a key work. It can usefully chart a course between extreme interpretations of Kierkegaard on either side. A closer look at this book might bring about a reading of Kierkegaard generally in something approximating his own terms, rather than as the grandfather of such strange kinfolk as Sartre and Barth. Even entering this caution may backfire, of course, for there is risk in bringing the banners of this day into the discussion at all.

An opposite error, but one bearing the same stultifying result, would be to read the *Stages* as an exercise in biography. It is that, of course, though the facts seem to reach us here with a fairly generous dose of interpretation. The dreaming young man, the melancholy Quidam, the impasse of the engagement, and much more mirror even in close detail a life dominated by the figure of a brooding father and the untroubled immediacy of Regina. It is worth noting that Kierkegaard also had glimpses of the glory of the free life of openness which Judge William extols. A persuasive case can be made for the suggestion that a revelatory act of confession on the part of the father so healed the breach between him and his son that the son could follow the course marked out in *Either/Or:* "He repents himself back into himself, back into the family, back into the race, until he finds himself in God." [18] And the result of Kierkegaard's decisive religious experience of Easter week, 1848, falls into place: "My shut-in-ness is broken—I must speak." [19]

Speak he surely did, and to do overmuch with a biographical matching game would be to do other than to let him speak now. What shall the outcome of his discourse be? Surely Kierkegaard is right when he says that only the reader knows that—but not even he does so beforehand. That stimulation and reflection will result—of that there is little doubt. And if men should manage to be more authentically themselves as a result, that would be more than a little part of the way Kierkegaard would have the reader go. To help him (Kierkegaard would want, of course, to read "you") on his way to such a result, Kierkegaard left the book without an ending.

[18] *Either/Or,* II, 180–81.
[19] *Papirer,* VIII, A 640 (translation mine).

STAGES ON LIFE'S WAY

STAGES ON LIFE'S WAY

STUDIES BY SUNDRY PERSONS

Collected, forwarded to the press and published

by

Hilarius Bookbinder

Copenhagen

1845

[April 30]

CONTENTS

LECTORI BENEVOLO!

FORASMUCH and whereas there ought to be honesty in all matters and more especially in the realm of truth and in the bookworld, considering also that some eminent professor or a man of high station might take umbrage if a bookbinder, instead of sticking to his trade, were to mingle without justification in the ranks of the literati, which effrontery moreover could only occasion severe condemnation of the book, and possibly have the effect that many, ashamed of the bookbinder, would not even read the book—therefore there follows here the book's veracious history.

Several years ago a literatus well known to me sent a considerable number of books to be bound, *item* several quires of manuscripts which were to be stitched in quarto. As this was in the busy season of the year, and as the literary gent did not press for them, being as he always was a kind and accommodating person, the books, to my shame be it said, remained in my shop well on to half a year. And since it is as the German says, *"Heute roth morgan todt,"* and as the parson says, "Death has no respect for class or age," and as my deceased wife put it, "We must all take that road, but the good Lord knows best when it is needful, and then it comes to pass by God's help,[1] as it also comes to pass that even the best men must go hence," so in the meantime the literatus died, and his heirs, who were in foreign parts, received the books through the probate court, and through the same court I got payment for my work.

As a hard-working man and a good citizen who honestly gives to everyone his due, it never occurred to me but that I had sent back everything to the literary gent, when one day I find a small packet of manuscript papers. I vainly pondered over who could have sent them to me, what was to be done with them, whether they were to be bound, in short over all such thoughts as can occur to a bookbinder on such an occasion, or whether the whole thing was a mistake. Finally there comes an illumination to my poor wife now deceased, who was always a rare and faithful helper and support in the business, that the packet must have

[1] cf. *Papirer,* III, A 201.

lain in the big basket in which the books of the literary gent came. I myself also came to this opinion, but now so long a time had elapsed, no one had thought of requiring the return of the packet, so, thought I, it surely cannot contain anything of great value, and I left the papers lie, after I had bound them in colored boards, so that they might not "lie and fly about the shop," as my poor wife used to say.

In the long winter evenings when I had nothing else to do I sometimes took up the book and read parts of it for pleasure. But I cannot say that the pleasure was great, but I had my pleasure in sitting and speculating what it might all be about. And since a great part was written in a well practised calligraphy, I had my children transcribe a page of it now and then, so that by imitating the fine characters and the swing of it they might get practice in handling the pen. Sometimes, too, they had to read it aloud for practice in reading handwriting, which very inconceivably and inexplicably is entirely neglected in school instruction, and presumably would long continue to be neglected were it not that now Mr. J. Levin,[2] as one reads in the newspapers, has sought to supply this need and has taught me to verify my poor wife's saying, that "the reading of handwriting is necessary in various situations in life and ought never to be neglected in schools," and indeed what is the use of one being able to write when one cannot read what one writes, as Henrich says in the comedy,[3] that he can write German well enough but cannot read it.

My elder son had now reached his tenth year when last summer I thought of having him enter upon a more serious course of instruction. And by a respectable man there was recommended to me as especially capable a personally not unknown to me seminarist and candidate in philosophy whom I often had heard to my genuine edification in the Church of our Saviour at evensong. Although he had not passed his examination and had entirely given up the thought of being a parson from the time he discovered he was a finely fibered soul and a poet (to use his own words), he nevertheless had a deal of learning and delivered good sermons, but in particular he had a splendid voice for the pulpit. Our agreement was that in return for the midday meal he should in-

[2] Who in 1846 published an "Album of present-day Danish handwriting by men and women. For use in reading in the schools."

[3] Not Henrich but Peer, in Holberg's comedy *Jacob von Tyboe,* Act I, Scene 4.

struct the boy in the most important branches of learning for two hours daily.

It was a real bit of good luck for my humble house that the aforesaid seminarist and candidate in philosophy became teacher to the boy, for not only did he make great progress, but I came to be indebted to that worthy man for something much more important, as I shall now relate. One day he noticed the book bound in colored boards which I had used for the instruction of my children, he read a little of it, and thereupon he begs the loan of it. I say to him just what I meant: "You may quite well keep it, for since the boy now has one who is himself able to write copy for him, I do not need it." But this he was noble enough, as I now perceive, not to want. So I lent it to him. Three days later (I remember this as if it was yesterday), it was the 5th of January of this current year, he comes to our house and desires to speak with me. I thought that possibly he wanted to open a little loan, but no! he hands me the well-known book and says: "Dear Mr. Hilarius, you presumably did not know what a glorious gift and boon providence bestowed upon your house in this book which you so recklessly would give away. Such a book is worth its weight in gold when it gets into the right hands. It is by the printing of such useful books that one contributes to good and profitable advancement in learning among the children of men in these times when not only money but faith becomes scarce among folks. And not only this, but you, Mr. Hilarius, whose desire it has always been to benefit your fellowmen also in some other way than as a bookbinder, and to honor as well the memory of your departed wife by some good deed or another of unusual merit, you to whose happy lot it has fallen to be able to do this, will by this undertaking be able to earn a sum by no means inconsiderable when the book is disposed of." I was deeply moved and became still more so when he lifted up his voice, and with uplifted voice continued: "For my part I desire nothing, or next to nothing; in consideration of the expected capital gain I require only $10 down and a half-pint of wine at midday on Sundays and holidays."

So then it has been done as the worthy seminarist and candidate in philosophy counselled me—if only I were as sure of the large capital as he is of the $10 I gladly paid him, so much the more as he pointed out that my merit was the greater for the fact that it was not one book but several books I published, presumably by several authors. For my learned friend supposes that there must have been a brotherhood, a society, a club, of which the caput or leader was the literatus, who for this reason preserved the writings. About this I myself have no opinion.

That a bookbinder should desire to be an author could only awaken justifiable resentment in the literary world and contribute to bring the book into discredit; but that a bookbinder stitches, forwards to the press and publishes a book, that he "also in another way than as a bookbinder seeks to benefit his fellowmen," no sensible reader will take amiss.

And herewith be the book and the bookbinder and the undertaking humbly recommended.

Christianhavn, January 1845.

Your obedient humble servant,

Hilarius Bookbinder.

IN VINO VERITAS

A RECOLLECTION

Subsequently related

by

William Afham

Such works are mirrors: when a monkey peers into them, no Apostle can be seen looking out.

Lichtenberg

PREFATORY NOTE[1]

WHAT a pretty employment it is to prepare for oneself a secret, how seductive the relish of its enjoyment, and yet how dubious an advantage it sometimes is to have enjoyed it, how readily it may disagree with one! For if anyone thinks that a secret is personal property, belonging exclusively to the depository, he is in error, for here applies the saying, "Out of the eater comes forth meat"; but if anyone thinks that in enjoying it one is only exposed to the difficulty of not betraying it, he is in error too, for one is at the same time under obligation not to forget it. It is even more distasteful, however, to recollect partially and turn one's soul into a depot for damaged wares. So in relation to others let forgetfulness be the silk curtain which is drawn in front of the stage, and recollection the vestal virgin which retires behind the curtain. Behind the curtain too there is forgetfulness, if it is not recollection of the right sort, for with that all forgetfulness is excluded.

Recollection must not only be exact, it must also be happy; on being sealed, the wine of recollection must have conserved the bouquet of the experience. As the grape may not be pressed at every season, since the weather at the time of the vintage has a great effect upon the wine, so neither may an experience be recollected or recalled at every season and under all conditions.

Recollection is not by any means identical with remembrance. Thus one can remember an occurrence with precision without recollecting it. Memory is merely a minimal condition. By means of memory the experience presents itself to receive the consecration of recollection. The distinction is discernible in the difference so easily observed between youth and old age. The old man loses his memory, generally it is the faculty which is lost first. Yet the old man has a poetic quality, in the estimation of primitive peoples he is prophetic, God-inspired. But recollection indeed is his best faculty, his consolation which consoles him with poetic far-sight. On the other hand, childhood has memory and retentive apprehension in a high degree, with no recollection whatever. Instead of saying that old age does not forget what childhood apprehends, one might perhaps say that what the child remembers the old man recollects. The old man's spectacles are ground for seeing near at hand. When youth wears spectacles the lens is ground for seeing at a distance,

[1] *Forerindring* means no more than prefatory note; but *Erindring* is recollection, and thus the title is linked with the subject of the following disquisition.

for youth lacks the power of recollection, which consists in removing, putting at a distance. However, the happy recollection of old age, like the happy apprehension of childhood, is the gracious gift of nature, which encompasses with partiality the two most helpless, yet in a certain sense the happiest, periods of human life. But for this reason recollection also, as well as memory, is sometimes only the depository of casual occurrences.

Although the difference between memory and recollection is great, they are often confused. In human life this confusion gives opportunity for studying the depth of the individual. For recollection is ideality, but as such it involves effort and responsibility, which the indifferent act of memory does not involve. Recollection seeks to assert man's eternal continuity in life and to insure that his earthly existence shall be *uno tenore,* one breath, and capable of being expressed in one word. Hence he declines to have his tongue compelled to engage again and again in the tittle-tattle which apes the tittle-tattle of life's content. This is the condition for immortality, that life be *uno tenore*. Strangely enough, Jacobi is the only one, so far as I know, who has remarked upon the dreadfulness of thinking oneself immortal.[2] It seemed to him at times as if the thought of immortality, if he were to hold on to it for more than a single instant, must cause him to lose his mind. Was this because Jacobi was nervously weak? A strong man whose hands have become thick-skinned merely from pounding the pulpit or the professor's desk every time he advanced a proof for immortality feels no such dreadfulness, and yet he understands all about immortality, for to have a thick skin signifies in Latin to understand something thoroughly. However, when one confounds memory and recollection the thought is in fact not so dreadful. First of all, because one is courageous, manly, robust, and in the second place, because one does not really think the thought. Thus there is certainly many a man who has written recollections of his life in which there is not a trace of recollection. And yet the recollections would be his investment for eternity. In recollection a man draws a check upon eternity. Eternity is humane enough to honor every draft and to regard everyone as solvent. But eternity is not responsible if a man makes a fool of himself and remembers instead of recollecting, and consequently forgets instead of recollecting, for what is remembered is also forgotten. But again memory makes life unconcerned. Unconcernedly one passes through the most ludicrous metamorphoses; even at

[2] Fr. H. Jacobi, *Werke* (Leipzig, 1819), Vol. IV, 2, p. 68: "Just as little could I bear the prospect of *continuing everlastingly in being.*"

an advanced age one still plays blindman's-buff, still takes risks in life's lottery and can still become what one is due to become, notwithstanding one has already been an incredible number of different things. Thereupon one dies—and so one becomes immortal. And, after all, by having lived in such a way should not one have insured oneself of possessing abundant material for recollection throughout a whole eternity? Yes, if eternity's ledger were not quite different from a scrapbook in which one scribbles whatever comes into one's head. But eternity's accounting is of a very particular sort. One might adduce several examples of it as a school exercise—not, however, as a way of reckoning with a view, to social advantage. One man talks day in and day out in Parliament, always about what the age requires, yet not tiresomely like repetitious Cato, but interestingly and piquantly, keeping abreast of the instant and never saying the same thing, *item* in society he draws upon his resources and deals out from the store of his eloquence, now with scant measure, now with a liberal hand, being applauded constantly with clapping, once a week at least there is something to be read about him in the daily paper, even at night he profits somebody (his wife, namely) by talking in his sleep about what the age requires, as if he were speaking in Parliament; another man keeps silent before he speaks and carries the thing so far that he never comes to the point of speaking—they live the same length of time, and here the question is in order about the answer to the problem: who has the most to recollect?

A man pursues one thought, one only, occupied with that alone; another is an author in five sciences and "is interrupted in his important activity [it is a journalist who is speaking] just when he was about to reform veterinary science"[3]—they live the same length of time, and here the question is in order about the answer to the problem, who has the most to recollect?

Properly speaking, only the essential is the object of recollection, although, as was remarked, the recollections of old age are sometimes fortuitous, and the same observation applies to analogous instances of recollection. The essential is not simply essential in itself, but it is such by reason of the relation it has to the person concerned. He who has broken with the idea cannot act essentially, cannot undertake anything essential—unless it be to repent, which is the only new ideality open to him. Outward criteria notwithstanding, everything he does is unessential. To take a wife is indeed something essential; but he who has once dabbled in love can smite his forehead and lay his hand upon his heart,

[3] In the *Postscript* S.K. (like repetitious Cato) six times pokes fun at the sciences in general by aligning them with veterinary science.

or upon his r——, as an expression of sheer seriousness and solemnity, it nevertheless is only tomfoolery. Although his marriage might be important to a whole nation and was rung in with the pealing of bells, and although the Pope were to perform the ceremony, it nevertheless is nothing essential to him but is essentially tomfoolery. The outward rumpus has nothing to do with the case, any more than the fanfare and the presentation of arms can make the drawing of the lottery an essential act on the part of the boy who draws the lots.[4] For the blowing of trumpets has nothing to do with acting essentially. — But neither can one forget what has been recollected. What is recollected is not indifferent to recollection as what is remembered is indifferent to memory. What is recollected one may throw away, but it comes back like Thor's hammer, and not only so but it has a longing for recollection, like a dove which however often it is sold to another can never remain in the possession of the other, because it always flies home. [But the analogy with the bird goes further,] for the thing recollected was hatched by recollection, and this is a secret and hidden brooding, in complete solitude, undisturbed therefore by any profane cognizance—so it is that the bird will not brood over its egg when any stranger has touched it.

Memory is immediacy and comes immediately to one's aid, whereas recollection comes only by reflection. Hence it is an art to recollect. Like Themistocles[5] I wish to forget, as the opposite of remembering. But to recollect and to forget are not opposites. The art of recollecting is not an easy one, because at the instant recollection is taking shape it may assume a great variety of forms, whereas memory merely fluctuates between remembering right and remembering wrong. Take homesickness for example. What is it? It is due to recalling something which is remembered. It is brought about most simply by being away. The art would be to be able to feel homesick notwithstanding one is at home. Expertness in the use of illusion is requisite for this. To live on in an illusion where it is ever twilight and never dawns [is only too easy], and to reflect oneself out of all illusion is not so difficult as to reflect oneself into illusion, allowing it to affect one with all of illusion's power, in spite of the fact that one does it knowingly. To bring back to oneself the past by enchantment is not so difficult as to remove from oneself by enchantment the object nearest to one for the sake of recollecting it.[6] This

[4] In Rome until recently a priest presided at the drawing of the weekly lottery, and a chorister in a cotta (as an assurance of innocence) thrust his hand into the bowl to draw the lots.

[5] cf. Cicero, *De Oratore,* II, 351.

[6] See *Repetition,* S.V.², III, p. 198.

properly is the art of recollection, employing reflection raised to the second power.

To achieve a recollection requires acquaintance with contrast in moods, situations, environments. An erotic situation in which the snug aloofness of country life is the essential point may sometimes be best recollected or recalled in a theater, where the environment and the noise force the contrast into evidence. Not always, however, is the direct contrast the most favorable. If it were not in bad taste to use a human being as a means to an end, a favorable contrast for recollecting an erotic relationship might perhaps be found by getting oneself into a new love affair —just for the sake of recollecting. — The contrast can be carried out to the extremest limit in reflection. The extremest point of the reflection-relationship between memory and recollection is attained when memory is used against recollection. Two people might for opposite reasons be unwilling to see again a place which recalls an event. The one does not remotely suspect the existence of anything called by the name of recollection, but he is afraid merely of memory. Out of sight, out of mind, thinks he; if only he does not see, he has forgotten. The other definitely desires to recollect, hence he does not want to see. Only for disagreeable recollections does he make use of memory. He who, though he may be expert in memory, does not understand this truth, may still have ideality, but he lacks experience in using *consilia evangelica adversus casus* [*sic*] *conscientiae*.[7] He would regard such counsel as a paradox and shrink from enduring the first pain, which nevertheless is always to be preferred, just as is the first loss. When memory is again and again revived it enriches the soul with a mass of detail which distracts recollection. Thus repentance is recollection of a fault. Regarding the thing from a purely psychological point of view, I really believe that the police help the criminal not to come to repentance. By dint of the continual recording and repeating of his life history the criminal attains such dexterity in recounting his story by rote that the ideality of recollection is extruded. It requires great ideality to repent really, and especially to repent straightway; though nature may also help a man, and the tardy repentance, which has little to do with memory, is often the most real and profound. — The condition of all productivity is to be able to recollect. If one would be productive no longer, one has only to remember the very things the recollection of which would make him productive, and with that production is rendered impossible, or will become so distasteful that one gives it up the sooner the better. Fellowship in recollection,

[7] Using the evangelical counsels of perfection to relieve a scruple of conscience.

properly speaking, does not exist. A kind of quasi-fellowship is a species of contrast which the recollector employs in his own interest. The recollection is sometimes most effectually enticed to come forth when one appears to confide in another, merely to harbor behind this confidence a new reflection wherein the recollection comes into being for one's own delectation. So far as memory is concerned, people can well unite for mutual assistance. In this respect banquets and birthday celebrations, love-tokens and dear keepsakes, are serviceable, like turning down the corner of a page in order to remember where one left off and to be able by means of the dog-ears to be sure of having read the whole book through. The wine press of recollection every man must tread alone. In and for itself this is far from being a curse. Inasmuch as one is always alone with one's recollections, every recollection is a secret. Even though several persons were interested in that which for the recollector is the object of his recollection, he is still alone with it, the apparent publicity is merely illusory.

What I am propounding here serves to recall to me the recollection of thoughts and thinking processes which many a time and in many ways have preoccupied my soul. The reason for making these remarks here is that I now feel in the mood to desire to set free for recollection an event one time experienced, the desire to record what already has been lying perfected in memory for some time and partially so in recollection. What I have to remember amounts to little, and to that extent the labor of memory is light; but on the other hand I have had difficulty in getting it in shape for recollection, just for the reason that for me it had become something quite different than for the gentlemen who took part in it, who presumably would smile at seeing any importance whatever attributed to such an insignificance, a frolicsome whim, a wild idea, as they themselves would have called it. How small a part my memory has in the matter I can perceive from the fact that I sometimes feel as though I had not experienced it, but had poetically invented it.

I know full well that I shall not soon forget that banquet, in which I participated without being a participator; but nevertheless I cannot make up my mind to let it go without having assured myself of a careful *ἀπομνημόνευμα*[8] of that which for me was really *memorabile*. — I have sought to promote the erotic understanding of recollection, while on the other hand I have done nothing for memory. The situation for recollecting is formed by contrast, and already for a considerable time I have sought to weave the object of my recollection into the contrasted

[8] A memoir.

environment. In the splendidly illuminated hall in which the banquet was held the inebriating sea of light with its many reflections produced a fantastic effect. Recollection, however, craves a contrast which is not fantastic. The exalted mood of the participants, the noise of the festivity, the foaming delight of the champagne, are recollected best in a place which is quiet, remote and forgotten. The exuberance of expression which swelled to expression in the moods of the speakers is recollected best in peaceful security. Every attempt to come to the aid of memory directly could only be amiss and would punish me with the disagreeable tang of mimicry. — So I have chosen an environment well calculated for contrast. I have sought the solitude of the forest, but not at a time when it too is fantastic. Thus the stillness of night would not have been favorable, for that also is under the dominion of the fantastic. I sought the peace of nature at just that time when it is least emotional. Hence I chose the illumination of late afternoon. If the fantastic is present at that hour, the soul has only a remote presentiment of it, and on the other hand there is nothing milder, more peaceful and more quieting than the feeble glow of late afternoon. As a sick man who has been won back to life seeks preferably this assuaging refreshment, and as one spiritually exhausted from much suffering seeks preferably this relief, so did I for an opposite reason seek to achieve the opposite.

In Gribs-Forest[9] there is a place called the Nook of Eight Paths; he alone finds it who worthily seeks it, for it is not indicated upon any map. The very name seems to involve a contradiction. For how can the junction of eight paths constitute a nook? how can that which implies travel in all directions accord with what is lonely and concealed? And what the solitary man shuns is named after the junction of only three paths: triviality—how trivial then must be the junction of eight paths! And yet it is so: there actually are eight paths, but very solitary paths. Though it is apparently remote, hidden and lonely, one is quite near the hedge of the enclosure, which is called Hedge of Ill Luck. So the contradiction in the name merely makes the place more solitary, as contradiction always does. The eight paths, the much traffic, are merely a possibility, a possibility for thought, since no one frequents these paths except a tiny insect which hurries across them *lente festinans*; no one frequents them except that cursory traveller who is continually looking about him on all sides, not in search of anyone but with the aim of avoiding everyone, that fugitive whom only the death-dealing bullet overtakes—which explains indeed why the stag now is still, but not why it was so restless; no one

[9] Gribs-Skov is an extensive forest north of Copenhagen. The Knook of Eight Paths was one of S.K.'s favorite resorts.

frequents them except the wind, of which no man knows whence it cometh and whither it goeth. Even the man who lets himself be deceived by the beguiling suggestion wherewith morbid reserve seeks to capture the wayfarer, even he who followed the narrow footpath which entices one into the recesses of the forest—even he is not so solitary as one is on the eight paths along which no one travels! It is in fact as if the world were extinct and the survivor confronted by the embarrassment of having no one to bury him; or as if the whole tribe had wandered away by the eight paths and left one of the members behind. — If it is true as the poet says, *bene vixit qui bene latuit,*[10] then I have lived well, for my nook was well chosen. Certain it is too that the world and all that therein is never appears to better advantage than when it is seen from a nook and one must take a look at it by stealth; certain it is too that all one hears in the world or is able to hear sounds most enchanting and delicious when heard from a nook where one give ear to it by stealth. So I often have resorted to my retired nook. I knew it before, long before, but now I have learned not to need the night in order to find quiet, for here it always is quiet, always beautiful, but most beautiful, as it seems to me, now when the harvest sun holds a vesper service, and the sky turns a languishing blue; when the creatures take breath after the heat, when coolness is released, and the leaves of the meadow shiver voluptuously, while the forest rustles; when the sun thinks of the evening when it will cool itself in the ocean, when the earth prepares itself for repose and thinks of thanksgiving, when before their parting the two come to an understanding with one another in the tender fusion which darkens the forest and makes brighter the green of the meadows.

O friendly spirit which inhabitest these places, thanks be to thee for always protecting my quietness, thanks for those hours passed in serious recollection, thanks for thy hiding place which I call mine! There quietness increases as the shadows lengthen, as the silence grows—what a formula of enchantment to conjure with! How inebriating is quietness! For hastily as the drinker may raise the cup to his lips, his inebriation does not increase so rapidly as that of quietness, which grows every second! And what is the mere drop contained in the intoxicating cup in comparison with the infinite sea of silence from which I drink! And what is the seething of wine in contrast with the spontaneous ebullition which seethes more and more powerfully! But also what vanishes so quickly as this inebriation, if someone is merely heard to speak! And what more vexatious than the situation when suddenly one is wrested

[10] He has lived well who was well hidden.

out of it—worse than the awakening of the drunkard it is when in silence one has forgotten speech, become shy at the sound of words, stammering like one the ligament of whose tongue has never been loosed, rendered weak like a woman who is taken by surprise, too faint to be able at the instant to be capable of deceiving with language! Thanks be to thee then, thou friendly spirit, who didst keep away surprise and interruption, for the excuses of the intruder help but little. —How often have I reflected upon this! In the human swarm no one is guilty who is innocent; but the quiet of solitude is holy, hence whatever disturbs it is guilty, and the chaste companionship of silence when it is violated brooks no excuse nor is helped by it, any more than offended modesty is helped by explanations. How it has smarted when it has happened to me and I see one standing there with a gnawing pain in his soul, ashamed at the offense of disturbing a solitary! In vain will penitence seek to fathom what it is—the guilt is ineffable like silence. Only he who has unworthily sought solitude can be profited by a surprise, as when a loving pair lacks even the power to shape a situation. If such is the case, one may do a service to Eros and to the lovers by showing oneself, although his service is a riddle to the lovers, as their debt to him is: that they put their heads closer together in wrath at the intruder, to whom, however, they owe it that they do so. But if it is two lovers who worthily seek solitude, how bitter an experience it is to surprise them, how justly might a man curse himself, as every beast was accursed which came near to Sinai! Who does not have this feeling, who is there, when he sees while remaining himself unseen, who might not wish to be like a bird which soars voluptuously over the heads of the lovers, to be like a bird whose screech is an omen for love, to be like a bird which glides through the bushes, beguiling to behold, to be like nature's solitude which tempts Eros, like the echo which confirms the feeling that one is alone, like the distant noise which gives security that the rest are going away and leaving the lovers behind! Oh, the best wish is surely this last, for one becomes solitary on hearing the others vanish. The most solitary situation in Don Juan is that of Zerline: it is not that she *is* alone; no, she *becomes* alone; one hears the chorus vanishing, and with the notes which die away at a distance solitude become audible, and solitude comes into being. Ye eight paths, ye have led all men away from me and brought back to me only my own thoughts.

So hail to thee in parting, thou delightful forest; hail to thee, thou unappreciated hour that makest no pretension for thyself, unlike the early morning, unlike the evening, unlike the night, but art humbly content to be thyself, content with thy rustic smile! As the labor of recollection is always blessed, it has in addition this blessing, that it becomes a new recollection which in its turn enthralls; for he who has once understood what recollection is, is caught for all eternity and at the same time captivated; and he who possesses a recollection is richer than though he were in possession of the whole world; and not only the woman with child, but above all the person with a recollection, has the blessing of being in an interesting situation.

IT was about ten o'clock in the evening of one of the last days of July when the participators assembled for that banquet. I have forgotten the day of the month and even the year; such things are the concern of memory, not of recollection. The only thing that properly concerns recollection is mood and what pertains to mood; and just as a generous wine gains by passing over the line because the watery particles evaporate, so too does recollection gain by losing the watery particles of memory—yet by this the recollection no more becomes a mere fancy than does the generous wine.

The men who participated in the banquet were five in number: Johannes, nicknamed the Seducer, Victor Eremita, Constantine Constantius, and two more, whose names I cannot precisely say I have forgotten, but whose names I never learned to know. It was as though these two possessed no proper name, for they were constantly indicated by an epithet. One was called the "young man." He was certainly not over twenty-some years of age, slenderly built and graceful, with a decidedly dark complexion. The expression of his face was thoughtful, but even more pleasing was his amiable and attractive bearing which gave evidence of a purity of soul in perfect harmony with the almost womanly and vegetative softness and transparence of his whole figure. But this outward beauty one would be inclined to forget, or to keep it merely *in mente,* when contemplating a youth who, being brought up—or, to employ a more tender expression, coddled up—exclusively by thought, nourished by the content of his own soul, had had nothing to do with the world, had neither been aroused and inflamed, nor rendered disturbed and uneasy. Like a sleep-walker he had within himself the law of his behavior, and his amiable, kindly attitude was not concerned with others, but merely reflected the fundamental disposition of his soul. The other was called the "Ladies' Tailor," that being his occupation. Of him it was impossible to get an integral impression. He was dressed in the very latest fashion, curled and perfumed and odorous of *eau de Cologne.* At some moments he did not lack an air of solid assurance, but the next moment he assumed in his gait a certain dancing air of festiveness, a certain hovering motion, which was definitely limited, however, by the robustness of his figure. Even when he was most malicious in his speech, his voice constantly had something of the ingratiating tone of the shopkeeper, the sweetishness of gallantry, which I am sure was highly distasteful to him and only gratified his spirit of defiance. When I think of him now I understand him better than when I saw him alight from the carriage and found myself unable to suppress a laugh. Some contrariety, however, is still left unresolved. He has enchanted and bewitched himself, by the sorcery of his will he has transformed himself into a figure almost foolish, but with it he is not entirely content, and hence reflection now and then peeks out.[11]

When I think of it now it seems to me almost absurd that five such men should be able to arrange a banquet. Presumably nothing would have come of it if Constantine had not been one of the party. At a coffee-house where they sometimes met in a private room the matter had once been broached, but the proposal had completely fallen through when the question was raised as to who should take the lead. The young man declared himself unqualified, the Ladies' Tailor had no time. Victor Eremita excused himself, not indeed by saying that he had married a wife or that he had bought a yoke of oxen and must go to prove them, yet even though he was ready to make an exception and come, he would decline the honor of taking the lead, being able to "show just cause why. . . ." Johannes regarded this as the right word spoken in good season, for to his mind there was one only able to serve a banquet, and that was the magic cloth which spreads itself and serves the dinner when one merely utters the word, "Spread!" It was not always, he said, the most correct thing to enjoy a young girl in haste, but a banquet he could not wait for, and generally he was tired of it a long while in advance. However, if this were to be taken seriously, he proposed one condition, that it should be so arranged as to be accomplished all of a sudden. To this all were agreed. The surroundings should be fashioned anew, and everything subsequently destroyed, indeed one might well be pleased on rising from the table to hear the preparations for destruction. Nothing should remain over; "not so much," said the Ladies' Tailor, "as there remains of a gown when it is made over into a hat"; "nothing at all should remain," said Johannes, "for nothing is more unpleasant than a piece of sentimentality, and nothing is more disgusting than to know that somewhere or other there is an external setting which directly and impertinently gives itself out to be a reality."

[11] We must suppose that the three named characters are not described for the reason that Johannes the Seducer was sufficiently known from his "Diary" in *Either/Or*, and that Victor Eremita, as the reputed author of the last part of the *Stages*, and Constantine Constantius, who is one of the two principal figures in this part, sufficiently reveal themselves in the sequel. But the same might be said of the "young man," who is contrasted with Constantine in the *Repetition*. Evidently S.K. had a special fondness for the "young man," who represents that side of his own character which he considered the best or the most amiable.

When the conversation had thus become animated, Victor Eremita suddenly arose, struck an attitude beside the table, making a gesture of the hand like one in command, stretching out his arm like one who lifts a goblet, and as though flourishing the goblet he said: "With this goblet, the fragrance of which already befuddles my senses, the cooling heat of which already inflames my blood, I hail you, dear pot-companions, and bid you welcome; and with the same goblet I drink to your health after eating, being assured that everyone is sufficiently sated merely by the talk about the banquet, for the good Lord satisfies the stomach before the eye is satisfied,[12] but imagination acts inversely." Thereupon he thrust his hand into his pocket, brought out a cigar-case, took out of it a cigar and began to smoke.

When Constantine Constantius protested against his highhandedness in thus transforming the projected banquet into a sheer illusion, Victor declared that he did not in the least believe it could be carried out, and in any case a mistake had been made in talking about it in advance. "To be good, a thing must be at once, for 'at once' is the most divine of all categories and deserves to be honored as in the Latin language is the word *ex templo,*[13] because it is the starting point of the divine in life, so that what does not occur at once is of the evil." However, he did not care to dispute about it; if the others were inclined to speak or act differently, he would not say a word, if they wanted him to develop his views further, they must give him leave to make a set speech, for to occasion a discussion he regarded as ungracious.

Accordingly the permission was granted, and as the others exhorted him to begin "at once," he spoke as follows: "A banquet in and for itself[14] is a difficult business, for even though it be arranged with all possible taste and talent, there is still something else essential to it, namely, luck. By this I do not mean what the anxious housewife might be most likely to think about, but something else which no one can absolutely make sure of: a happy concord of moods and of the subordinate features of the banquet, that fine ethereal touch upon the chords, that inward music, which one cannot bespeak in advance from the town band. Hence it is a risk to begin, for if the thing goes wrong, maybe from the very beginning, it is possible at one banquet to start off in such a way that it will take a long time to recover. Habit and thoughtlessness are the only fathers and godfathers of most banquets, and it is due to

[12] cf. Eccles. 1 : 8.

[13] Might be interpreted, "from the temple," but it means "on the spot," or "at once."

[14] S.K.'s way of poking fun at what he regarded as Kantian jargon about "the thing-in-itself."

a lack of critical sense that the absence of idea is not noticed. For the first thing, there ought never to be women present at a banquet. Parenthetically be it said that I never have liked the word 'ladies,' and now since Grundtvig[15] in his most Grundtvigian fiddle-faddle has *grundwichtiglich* employed this word—but that has nothing to do with this subject. Only in the Greek fashion can women be employed as a chorus of dancers. Since at a banquet the essential business is to eat and drink, woman ought not to be included in the company, for she cannot acquit herself properly, and if she does, it is exceedingly unaesthetic. Where a woman is present the business of eating and drinking ought to be reduced to insignificant proportions. At the very most the eating and drinking must be a little feminine occupation just to give the hands something to do. In the country more especially such a small repast (which may even be appointed at another hour than that of the important meals) may be extremely charming, and, if so, this is always attributable to the other sex. To do as the English do and let the other sex retire before the real drinking begins, is neither one thing nor the other, for every constructive plan ought to be a whole, and the very way I seat myself at the table and take hold of the knife and fork stands in relation to the totality. So too a political banquet is unaesthetic because of its ambiguity. One wants to reduce the essential elements of the banquet to an insignificance, and again one would not have it thought that the speeches are delivered *inter pocula*. So far we are doubtless in agreement, and our number—in case anything should come of the banquet—is well chosen, in accordance with the fine rule: neither more than the Muses, nor less than the Graces. I require now the richest abundance of everything that can be thought of. Even though not everything is actually present, the possibility of it, which is more seductive than the sight, must be immediately at hand, hovering over the table. From banqueting off matches, or, like the Dutch, off a loaf of sugar which all lick by turns, I beg to be excused. My requirement, on the other hand, is difficult to satisfy, for the meal itself must be calculated to awaken and incite that inexpressible desire which every worthy member of the party brings with him. I require that the fruitfulness of the earth shall be at

[15] Disparaging references to Grundtvig occur parenthetically in many of S.K.'s works, from his first book to his last. In religious disposition as well as in his attitude to the Christian faith S.K. was the polar opposite of Grundtvig. The many followers of Grundtvig in the Denmark of today are magnanimous enough to forgive S.K.'s jibes. And they may well be magnanimous, for it is Grundtvig who has triumphed in the Denmark of today. Not only are the admirable *Folkerhøjskoler,* and the social reform they have brought about, due to his initiative, but the spirit of worship, of religion, in the Church of Denmark is prompted by and reflected in his rollicking hymns.

our service, as though everything were sprouting the very instant when appetite desires it. I require a more exuberant abundance of wine than Mephistopheles procured by boring holes in the table. I require an illumination more voluptuous than that of the gnomes when they heave up the mountain upon pillars and dance in a sea of flame. I require what most excites the senses, I require that delicious refreshment of perfumes which is more glorious than anything in the Arabian Nights. I require a coolness which voluptuously kindles desire, and then appeases the desire already satisfied. I require the ceaseless animation of a fountain. If Maecenas could not sleep without hearing the splash of a fountain, I cannot eat without it. Do not misunderstand me: I can eat stockfish without it, but I cannot eat at a banquet without it; I can drink water without it, but I cannot drink wine at a banquet without it. I require a staff of servants, well chosen and good looking, as though I were seated at the table of the gods; I require chamber-music, strong and subdued, and I require that at every instant it shall be an accompaniment to me; and as for you, my friends, the requirements I make in this respect are incredible. Behold! By reason of all these requirements, which are just as many reasons against it, I hold that a banquet is a *pium desiderium,* and, regarding it in this light, I am so far from being inclined to talk about a repetition that I assume the thing cannot be achieved in the first instance."

The only one who had taken no real part in this conversation or in defeating the banquet was Constantine Constantius. But for him the whole thing would have ended in mere talk. He had reached a different conclusion and believed that, if one were to take the others with a trump, the idea might well be realized. Then some time elapsed and both the banquet and the talk about it were forgotten, when suddenly, one day, the participants received from Constantine a card of invitation to a banquet that very same night. As the password for the occasion he fixed upon *In vino veritas,* because, though speeches were to be allowed as well as conversation, no speeches might be made except *in vino,* and no truths were to be heard except such as are *in vino,* when wine vindicates the truth and the truth vindicates the wine.

The place was chosen in a wooded region a few miles from Copenhagen. The hall where they were to eat was newly decorated and rendered entirely unrecognizable. A small room separated from the hall by a corridor was arranged for the orchestra. Shutters and curtains were disposed at every window, and behind them the sashes were thrown open. Constantine had it in mind that driving thither in the dusk of the evening they might get an inkling of what was coming. Even though one knows that one is driving to a banquet and imagination endeavors for an instant to deal with the voluptuous thought, the impression made by natural surroundings is so powerful that it must prevail. That this might occur was Constantine's only fear; for while there is no power which knows so well how to beautify all things as does imagination, neither is there any power which can so profoundly disturb everything when it fails one upon coming into contact with real life. Driving on a summer evening does not deflect imagination from luxurious thoughts, but has exactly the contrary effect. Even though one may not see or hear it, imagination spontaneously constructs a picture of the evening's longing for cosiness, thus one sees men and maidens making their way home from labor in the field, hears the hurried clatter of the hay wagon, and interprets the faraway lowing from the meadows as longing. Thus it is the summer evening elicits an idyllic mood, refreshes even the aspiring mind by its quietude, induces even the fleeting fancy to abide with autochthonous nostalgia upon the earth as the place from which it came, teaches the insatiable mind to be satisfied with little, making a man content, for in the evening hours time is standing still and eternity is lingering.

So the invited guests arrived in the evening, for Constantine had come out somewhat earlier. Victor Eremita, who was dwelling in the country not far off, came on horseback, the others in a carriage; and just as their carriage drew up, a Holstein wagon swung through the gate, bearing a jolly crew of four mechanics, who were entertained in the common-room, to be ready to act at the decisive moment as a demolition corps—just as in the theater, for an opposite reason, the firemen are on hand to extinguish a fire at once.

So long as one is a child one has sufficient imagination, though it were for an hour in the dark room, to keep one's soul on tiptoe, on the tiptoe of expectation; but when one is older imagination easily has the effect of making one tired of the Christmas tree before one has a chance to see it.

The folding doors are thrown open; the effect of the radiant illumination, of the coolness which encountered them, of the infatuating fragrance of perfume, of the elegance of the table-arrangement, overwhelmed for an instant the guests who were on the point of entering the room, and when at the same moment strains from the ballet of Don Juan reached them from the orchestra, they were transfixed and for an instant stood still as if in reverence before an invisible spirit which encompassed them, like a man whom admiration has awakened and who has risen to his feet to admire.

Who is there that knows the happy instant, who has comprehended the delight of it and has not sensed that dread lest something might suddenly occur, the most insignificant thing, yet with power to disturb it all! Who has held in his hand the magic lamp and yet has not felt that swooning of delight at the thought that one only needs to wish? Who has held in his hand that which beckons[16] and has not learned to keep his wrist supple so as to let it go at once?

Thus they stood close to one another. Only Victor stood somewhat apart, absorbed in his own thoughts; a shudder passed through him, he almost trembled; then, collecting himself, he saluted the prognostication in these words: "Ye secret, festive, seductive strains which tore me from the cloistered seclusion of my tranquil youth and beguiled me by a sense of loss, like a recollection, most terrible, as if Elvira had not been seduced at all but only desired to be! Immortal Mozart, to whom I owe all! But, no, not yet do I owe thee all; but when I have become an old man, if ever I do, or when I am ten years older than now, if ever I come to that, or when I shall die, for of this at least I am certain, then I will say, Immortal Mozart, to whom I owe all! Then the admiration which is the first and only one I have known I will suffer to break out with all its might, suffer it to slay me, as it often has threatened to do. Then I have set my house in order,[17] then I have remembered my beloved, then I have confessed my love, then I have completely verified the fact that I owe thee all, then I belong to thee no more, no more belong to this world, but only to the solemn thought of death!"[18]

Just then the orchestra played that invitation in which pleasure exults most prodigiously, storming the very heavens as it soars triumphantly above Elvira's sorrowful words of thanksgiving; and then with a quick apostrophe Johannes repeated the words, *"Viva la liberta"*—*"Et veritas,"* adjoined the young man; "But above all," said Constantine, interrupt-

[16] In dealing with S.K. one must keep one's wrist very supple. I suppose that he employs this circumlocution to describe the rod of witchhazel the dowser uses to discover water, because he is thinking of Regina, whom he once held in his hand, like a bird, who beckoned him to pleasure in this world—and then, when he had let her go, continued to "beckon from another world."

[17] 2 Kings 20:1.

[18] Compare the apostrophe addressed to Mozart at the beginning of *Either/Or,* in the chapter on the erotic element in music, pp. 49 *ff.* in the Danish edition, in my *Kierkegaard,* pp. 349 *ff.*

ing them, "above all *in vino*," thereupon taking his seat at the table and inviting the others to do likewise.

How easy it is to give a banquet, and yet Constantine has affirmed that he would never again take the risk! How easy it is to admire, and yet Victor has affirmed that he will never again give word to his admiration, because a discomfiture is more dreadful than to be invalided in war! How easy it is to desire when one has a wishing-rod, and it is sometimes more dreadful than to perish from want.

They took their seats at the table. That same instant the little group was launched half-way out upon the endless ocean of enjoyment, as though with a single bound. Everyone had all his thought, all his desire, set upon the banquet, his soul freely afloat for the enjoyment which was proffered overflowingly and with which the soul overflowed. The practised driver is recognized by the fact that he knows how to let the champing team start with a single bound, and how to hold them evenly together; the well-trained steed is recognized by the fact that by a single leap he rises with absolute decision. If one or another of the guests was perhaps not quite on a par, Constantine proved himself a good host.

So then they dined. Soon conversation had woven its beautiful garland about the guests, so they sat there crowned with it. At one moment the conversation seemed to be in love with the food, then with the wine, then again with itself; at one moment it was as though it was on the point of signifying something, then again it meant nothing at all. Now a fanciful notion came to development, that gorgeous fancy which blooms but once, that tender fancy which straightway closes its petals; then there was heard an outburst from a banqueter, "These truffles are superb!" then a shout to the host, "But this Château Margaux!" Now the music was drowned by the noise, now it was heard again. For one instant the company of servants stood still *in pause* at the important moment when a new course was to be served or a new wine was ordered by the name of its vintage; and then they were all busy again. Now silence intervened for a second, then the reanimating spirit of the music descended upon the guests. Now an individual with an audacious thought threw himself in front of the other talkers, and they all followed him as their leader, almost forgetful of the food, and the music followed in their rear as it follows an exulting host; then in turn there was heard only the tinkling of glasses and the clinking of plates, and the work of eating proceeded in silence, supported only by the music, which joyously took the lead and again recalled conversation. — So they dined.

How poor a thing is language compared with the unmeaning yet significant combination of clangorous sounds in a battle or at a banquet, which not even a theatrical rendering can reproduce, and for which language possesses but a few words! Yet how rich is language in the service of the wish, compared with its use for the description of reality!

Only once did Constantine abandon the rôle of omnipresence in which his presence was hardly noticed. At the very beginning he got them to sing one of the old drinking-songs, "to recall the pleasant times when men and women banqueted together." The effect of this proposal was sheer burlesque, as perhaps Constantine intended; but that spirit almost got the upper hand, for the Ladies' Tailor wanted them to sing "The Night I get into the Bridal Bed, falderi, faldera." After a few courses had been served Constantine proposed that the banquet should be concluded by every man making a speech, with the precaution, however, that the speakers be not permitted to flutter around too indefinitely. Accordingly, he made two conditions: first, that there were to be no speeches till after the meal; second, that no one might speak until he had drunk so much that he could perceive the power of the wine or was in that state in which one says much which in other conditions one would rather not say—without implying that the coherence of the speech or of the thought needed to be interrupted constantly by hiccups.[19] Hence before speaking everyone should solemnly declare that he was in this state. It would not be possible to prescribe the precise quantity of wine required, seeing that the saturation point might be so different. Against this Johannes made a formal protest. He never could get drunk, and when he had reached a certain point he became more and more sober the more he drank. Victor Eremita was of the opinion that the experimental reflection involved in watching how drunk one got would prevent one from getting drunk. If one were to get drunk, it must be accomplished by "immediacy." Then there was divers talk about the diverse effect of wine upon consciousness, noting in particular that in the case of very reflective individuals the consumption of a great deal of wine might be expressed, not by any strange impetus but, on the contrary, by cool discretion. As for the content of the speeches, Constantine proposed that they should deal with love, or with the relationship between man and woman. No love-experiences, however, might be told, though such affairs might perfectly well lie at the basis of the particular view one maintained.

[19] Alluding to the situation in which Aristophanes found himself in Plato's *Symposium.*

The conditions were accepted. All the just and reasonable demands a host makes upon his guests were fulfilled: they ate and "they drank and they drank largely," as the Hebrew tongue expresses it—which being translated means that "they made merry."[20]

The desert was served. If Victor had not yet found his requirement fulfilled of hearing the splash of a fountain (which fortunately for him he had forgotten again since that conversation), at least champagne now sparkled abundantly. The clock struck twelve. Then Constantine enjoined silence, drank to the young man with these words, "*Quod felix sit faustumque,*"[21] and bade him speak first.

The young man arose and declared that he perceived the power of the wine, a fact which was also partly visible, for the blood throbbed violently at his temples, and his outward appearance was not so beautiful as before the meal. He spoke as follows:

"If there be truth in the words of the poets, dear boon companions, unhappy love is indeed the bitterest grief. If any proof be needed, listen to the tale of the lovers. They say that it is death, certain death, and the first time they believe it as long as a fortnight; the second time they say that it is death, the third time they say that it is death, and finally some day they die . . . of unhappy love. For that it is love they die of there can be no doubt, and that it takes love three times to take the life out of them is just like a dentist taking three times to get a firm molar pulled out. But if unhappy love is certain death, how happy I am then who have never loved and may manage presumably to die some day . . . not of unhappy love. But perhaps this is precisely the greatest misfortune—how unhappy then I must be! The significance of love must presumably (for I speak as a blind man about colors), must presumably be its bliss, and this is expressed again by saying that the cessation of love is the death of the lover. That I can understand as a thought-experiment which sets life and death in relationship with one another. But if love is to be regarded merely as a thought-experiment, the lovers are ridiculous who go ahead and actually fall in love. If on the contrary it is to be regarded as something real, then reality must corroborate what the lovers say about it. But who ever heard or perceived in real life that such things came to pass, though one may hear it said that they do? In this I already perceive one of the contradictions wherein love involves a person; for whether to the initiates it seems different I do not know, but to me it

[20] Gen. 43: 34.

[21] The formula with which the Romans would often introduce a speaker: "Whatever is happy and of good omen."

seems to involve a man in the strangest contradictions. No other relationship between human beings demands so much ideality as love, and yet it is never discernible. This already is enough to make me afraid of love, because I am afraid it might have power to make me too talk into the air about a bliss I do not feel and about a pain I do not feel. I say this here because I have been bidden to talk about love, in spite of the fact that I am not versed in it, I say it here in an environment which is as congenial to me as a Greek symposium; for otherwise I have no desire to speak about it, no desire to disturb anyone in his happiness. Perhaps in the eyes of the initiated these thoughts are mere foolishness and cobwebs of the brain, perhaps my ignorance is to be accounted for by the fact that I have never learned nor wished to learn from anyone how one gets to be in love, and that I have never, because it was smart, challenged a woman by a glance, but I have cast my eyes down, unwilling to abandon myself to an impression before I have clearly made out what is the significance of that power under the dominion of which I am about to let myself fall."

Here he was interrupted by Constantine, who remonstrated that by admitting he never had had any love-experience he debarred himself from making a speech. The young man declared that at any other time he would gladly comply with a command enjoining silence, since he had often enough been sensible of the tedium of talking, but here he would stick up for his rights. Precisely the fact of having no love-experience was also a love-experience in a way, and he who could affirm this of himself was especially entitled to talk about Eros, because he could be said to have, through his thoughts, a relation to the sex as a whole and not merely to particular individuals. He was given permission to talk, and he continued as follows:

"Since my right to speak has now been put in doubt, this doubt may well serve to exempt me from your laughter, for I know very well that as among rustics no one is considered a proper man who hasn't a tobacco-pipe, so among males no one is considered a real man who has not been tried in love. If anyone wants to laugh, let him laugh—to me the thing of chief importance is thought. Or has love perhaps the privilege of being the only thing one is not to think about in advance but only afterwards? If so, what would happen in case I, the lover, were to begin afterwards to reflect that it was too late?[22] This, you see, is the reason why I choose to think about love beforehand. Lovers also, it is true, will say that they have thought about love beforehand, but it is

[22] The same word, *bag efter,* means both afterwards and too late.

not so. They assume that it is essential to man to fall in love; but this is not to think about love, but to assume it for the sake of bethinking themselves how to find a sweetheart.

"Whenever my reflection seeks to grasp love, all I retain in my hand is contradiction. Sometimes indeed I feel as if there were something I had missed, but I cannot tell what it is, and on the other hand my reflection here again shows me at once the contradiction. So then, to my way of thinking, love is the greatest contradiction it is possible to think of, and at the same time it is comic. The one corresponds to the other. The comic is always implied in the category of contradiction—a theme which I cannot develop here. But what I would point out here is that love is comic. By love I understand here a relationship between man and woman, and I am not thinking of Eros in the Greek sense, as it is so beautifully extolled by Plato;[23] but he has so little to say of love for women that it is mentioned only in passing, and it is regarded even as imperfect in comparison with love for young men. I say that love is comic for a third party—more than that I do not say. Whether it is for this cause lovers always hate a third party, I do not know; but this I know, that reflection always is a third party, and hence I cannot love without at the same time being myself in reflection a third party. This surely cannot seem strange to anybody, seeing that everybody has in fact doubted everything,[24] and for my part I only try to doubt about everything that has to do with love. But on the other hand it does seem to me strange that people have doubted everything and again found certitude, yet never whisper a word about difficulties which have been shackles to my thought, so that I have sometimes wished longingly for liberation—by help of him, be it noted, who first has thought these difficulties, and has not had it suggested to him in sleep to doubt and to have doubted everything, and again I say, had it suggested to him in sleep to explain and to have explained everything. So give me your attention, dear boon companions, and if you yourselves are lovers, do not interrupt me and do not hush me up because you don't want to hear the explanation; rather turn away and hear with averted face what I have to say, what I now desire to say, once I have begun.

"In the first place, I find it comical that all men are in love and want to be in love, and yet one never can get any illumination upon the ques-

[23] In Cap. 9 of the *Symposium* the goddess of love towards women is called "the vulgar Aphrodite," whereas "the heavenly Aphrodite" is the goddess of love towards young men.

[24] S.K. constantly poked fun at Hegel and his followers, who supposed they were following Descartes by beginning with universal doubt.

tion what the lovable, i.e. the proper object of love, really is. I make no attempt to define the word love, for with that we get nowhere, but no sooner is the subject broached than we are confronted by the question what it is one loves. To this no other answer is forthcoming than that one loves the lovable. For if one answers with Plato[25] that one should love the Good, one has overstepped with a single stride the boundary of the erotic. But then perhaps one gives answer that one should love the Beautiful. If I were to ask whether 'to love' means to love a beautiful landscape or a fine painting, one would perceive at once that the erotic is not related as a species to the genus which comprises universally everything that can be loved, but that it is something entirely *sui generis*. Accordingly, if a lover, wishing to express adequately how much love there dwelt in him, were to talk in this fashion, 'I love beautiful landscapes and my Lalage[26] and the beautiful dancing girl and a beautiful horse, in short I love all that is beautiful,' then Lalage, if in other respects she was content with him, would certainly not be content with his panegyric, even if she was beautiful; and suppose now that Lalage was not beautiful, though he loved her nevertheless. Again, if I were to bring the erotic into relation with that differentiation of which Aristophanes[27] talks when he says that the gods divided man into two parts, as one serves a flounder, and that these separated parts yearningly seek one another, there again I stumble upon a difficulty I cannot fathom: namely, how far I am justified in appealing to the authority of Aristophanes, who in the continuation of his address thought further,[28] and, because there is no reason for stopping there, thinks it might occur to the gods, for their still greater amusement, to divide man into three parts. 'For their still greater amusement'—is it not true, as I say, that love makes a man ridiculous, if not in the eyes of others, at least in the eyes of the gods? However, I will assume that the erotic has its potency in the relationship between the masculine and the feminine—what then? If the lover were to say to his Lalage, 'I love thee because thou art a woman, I could just as well love every other woman, just as well love the ugly Zoe,' the beautiful Lalage would be insulted. What then is the lovable? That is my question, but the fatality is that no one has been able to tell me. The individual lover stoutly believes for his part that he knows the answer, but to another

[25] *Symposium,* Cap. 24.

[26] One of Horace's *Odes* (I,22) has given currency to this Greek name by which he designates his lady-love.

[27] Plato's *Symposium,* Cap. 24.

[28] Like the philosophers who, as S.K. complains, were boastful of "going further."

man he is not able to make himself intelligible, and he who listens to the talk of several lovers will ascertain that no two of them say the same thing, although they all talk about the same thing. I need say nothing of the perfectly foolish explanations which end by letting a man run his nose against the door, that is to say, end by saying that it is the sweetheart's pretty feet or the beloved man's much admired mustache which properly is love's object; but even when one hears a lover talk in a lofty style, he hears him first recount several particulars, but finally he says, 'her whole lovable nature,' and when his declamation has reached its climax he says, 'that inexplicable something which I do not know how to account for'—and this sort of talk is supposed to be especially pleasing to the beautiful Lalage. But it does not please me, for I don't understand a word of it, but find that it contains a double contradiction: first, because it ends with the *inexplicable*; and second, because it *ends* there. For he who would end with the inexplicable had best begin with it and say not a word more, so as not to become an object of suspicion. If he begins with the inexplicable and says not a word more, this is no proof of his impotence, for in a negative sense this after all is an explanation; but if he begins with something else and ends with the inexplicable, this is proof of his impotence.

"So then we have love—to this corresponds the lovable, and the lovable is the inexplicable. That goes in one ear and out of the other, it can no more be understood than the inexplicable way love has of seizing its prey. Who would not be alarmed if all around one, time and again, people were suddenly falling down and dying, while no one was able to account for it? But this is precisely the way love pounces down in the midst of life—only no one is alarmed by it, since the lovers regard it as the greatest happiness, but rather one is prompted to laugh, for there is a correspondence between the comic and the tragic. Today one talks with a man and can understand him fairly well; tomorrow this man speaks 'with tongues' and with strange gestures—he is in love. In case the purport of love were to fall in love with the first comer, it would be easy to understand why no one could explain it more exactly; but since the purport of love is to fall in love with one only, the one only person in the whole world, it seems as if such a prodigious act of segregation and choice must contain in itself a dialectic of reasons which one might decline to hear, not because it explained nothing, but because it would be too prolix to listen to. But, no, the lover is not able to explain anything. He has seen hundreds and hundreds of women, he perhaps has reached a certain age, he has felt nothing, suddenly he sees *her,* the only one, Catherine! Is it not comic that this thing, love, which is to transform and beautify the whole of life is not like a grain of mustard seed from which there grows a great tree, but is even smaller than that, is at bottom nothing at all; for there is not a single antecedent criterion that can be alleged (as if, for example, there was a certain age at which the phenomenon occurred), and there is not a single reason that can be alleged why he chose her, her alone in the whole world—and this not at all in the same sense in which 'Adam chose Eve, because there was no other.'[29] Or is not the explanation which the lovers give equally comic, or rather does it not serve precisely to throw into sharp relief the comic character of love? They say that love makes blind, and by this they explain the phenomenon. In case a man going into a dark room to fetch something were to reply to my advice that he carry a light by saying, 'The thing I am seeking is only a trifle, therefore I carry no light'—ah, then I could understand him perfectly. On the other hand, when the same man takes me aside and confides to me in a mysterious manner that the thing he went to fetch was of the utmost importance, and therefore he could do it blindly—ah, I wonder how my poor mortal head might be able to follow the high flight of this speech. Even if for fear of offending him I might refrain from laughter, as soon as his back was turned I could not help laughing. But at love nobody laughs; for I am prepared to encounter the same embarrassment as the Jew who after he had concluded his story said, 'Does nobody laugh?' However, I have not, like the Jew, left out the point, and though I myself laugh, my laughter is far from meaning offense to anybody. On the contrary I despise the fools who imagine that they have such good reasons for their love they can afford to laugh at other lovers; for since love never can be explained, the one lover is as ridiculous as the other. Moreover, I find it just as foolish and supercilious for a man to look around proudly upon a group of girls in order to find one who is worthy of him, or for a girl to toss her head proudly and sort out the men; for such people are busying themselves merely with finite thoughts within an unexplained hypothesis. No, what engages my thought is love as such, it is that which appears to me ridiculous, and hence I fear it, lest I become ridiculous to myself or ridiculous in the eyes of the gods who fashioned man thus. For if love is ridiculous, it is equally ridiculous whether I get a princess or a serving-maid, for the lovable, as we have seen, is the inexplicable. Hence it is I fear love, but in this again I see another proof that love is comic, for my fear is of such a strangely

[29] Musäus, *Volksmärchen der Deutschen* Vol. III, p. 219. cf. *Either/Or,* S.V., II, p. 34.

tragic sort that it is a precise illustration of the comic. When men are tearing down a wall they hang out a sign of warning, and I keep out of the way of it; when a fence is being painted they put up a notice; when a coachman is about to run over a man he shouts, 'Look out!'; when there is a case of cholera a soldier is stationed in front of the house, etc. What I mean is, that when there is danger, the danger can be pointed out, and one happily avoids it by giving heed to the signs. So as I am afraid of becoming ridiculous by falling in love, I naturally regard it as dangerous—what am I to do then to avoid it, or what am I to do to avoid the danger that a woman might fall in love with me? Far from me be the proud thought that I am an Adonis with whom every woman falls in love (*relata refero,*[30] for I don't understand what it means), the gods preserve me! But since I do not know what the lovable is, I cannot possibly know how to behave in order to avoid this danger. Moreover, since qualities which are precisely opposites may constitute the lovable, and since in the last resort the inexplicable is the lovable, I am in the same situation as that man about whom Jean Paul tells that when he was standing on one foot he read a sign saying, 'Fox-traps set here!'—and now the poor fellow does not dare to raise the one foot or to put the other down. I will not love anybody before I have fathomed the thought of love, and that I am not able to do; on the contrary, I have reached the conclusion that love is comic. So I am unwilling to love; but, alas, by this precaution the danger has not been avoided, for since I do not know what the lovable is, how it attacks me, or how it attacks a woman with reference to me, I cannot be sure of knowing whether I have avoided the danger. This is tragic, in a sense it is profoundly tragic, even though no one is concerned about it or is concerned about the contradiction so bitter to a thinker, that there is something which exercises its power everywhere and yet cannot be grasped by thought, something which is capable of attacking from behind the man who is vainly trying to think it. But the tragic aspect is deeply grounded in the comic traits which I have pointed out. Perhaps everybody else will invert the thing and will not find comic what I find comic, but rather will find the comic in what to me is tragic. But even this shows that I am in the right to a certain degree, and that the reason why, if I am to become a sacrifice, I must be a comic or a tragic sacrifice is sufficiently clear, viz. my resolution to reflect about everything I do, and not to imagine I am reflecting upon life when what I say of the most significant problem is 'Never mind.'

[30] I report only what has been told me.

"Man consists of soul and body—about this the wisest and best of men are agreed. If then we assume that the potency of love is discoverable in the relationship between the feminine and the masculine, the comic will appear again in the reversal which takes place for the fact that the loftiest psychic experience expresses itself in the most sensuous terms. I am thinking here of all the exceedingly strange gesticulations of love and of its mystic tokens, in short of all the freemasonry which is in perfect continuity with that primary incomprehensibility. The contradiction in which love here involves a man is this, that the symbolism signifies nothing whatever, or, what comes to the same thing, that no one can tell what it is supposed to signify. Two loving souls assure one another that they will love one another to all eternity; thereupon they embrace one another and seal with a kiss the eternal covenant. I ask any thinker whether such a thing as that has ever entered his mind. And such a confusion is constantly occurring in love. The loftiest psychic experience finds its expression in the extremest contrary, and the sensuous is supposed to indicate the loftiest psychic feeling. Suppose that I were in love. It would then be of the utmost importance to me that the loved one should belong to me for all eternity. That I can understand, for essentially what I am speaking of here is the Greek erotic, the love of beautiful souls. So when the loved one has assured me of this, I would believe it, or insofar as there was any doubt left I would endeavor to combat it. But what happens? For if I were in love, I would doubtless behave like the others, I would seek some other assurance than that of believing her word, which after all is clearly the only assurance. Here again I am confronted by the inexplicable. When Cockatoo,[31] clinging to his perch for all he is worth, begins to believe he is a duck that has swallowed the wrong way and regurgitates the word 'Mariana,' then everybody laughs. Perhaps the spectators discover the comic trait in the fact that Cockatoo, who doesn't love Mariana, should be on such terms with her. But suppose now that Cockatoo was in love with Mariana, would not then that be comic? To me it appears equally comic and that the comic element consists in the fact that love has become commensurable and is to be regarded as commensurable with such an expression. Though such an incommensurable expression had been customary from the beginning, the case is not altered, for the comic has from eternity a prescriptive right to consist in contradiction, and here is a contradiction. There is not anything really comic in a marionette, for there is no

[31] A figure in Overskou's comic play, "Capriciosa" (*Comedies,* III, 184).

contradiction in the fact that it makes extraordinary movements, since in fact someone pulls the strings. But to be a marionette in the service of some inexplicable power is comic. The contradiction is that no one sees any rational reason why it should get a twich now in one leg, now in the other. When I cannot explain to myself what I am doing, I don't want to do it; when I cannot understand the power to whose sway I am about to commit myself, I don't want to commit myself to its sway. And if love is an enigmatic power of this sort which binds together the extremest opposites, who guarantees me that it may not suddenly result in confusion? However, I am not so much concerned about this. But I have already referred to the fact that some lovers find that other lovers behave ridiculously. What their laughter really means I am unable to conceive; for if love obeys a law of nature, it is surely the same for all lovers; and if it is a law of freedom, those laughing lovers must be able to explain all their actions, which, however, they are not able to do. To some extent I can understand it better as a general principle that the one lover regularly laughs at the other, finding the other ridiculous but not himself. If it is ridiculous to kiss an ugly girl, it also is ridiculous to kiss a pretty one, and the notion that doing a thing one way is any justification for laughing at a person who does it another way is nothing more than superciliousness and a complot, which does not, however, avail to set such a snob outside the category of the ridiculous, which is determined by the consideration that nobody can say what it means to kiss, although it is assumed to mean that the lovers desire to belong to one another for all eternity, yea, what is still more amusing, it is supposed to give them assurance of this. In case a man sitting at his ease were to lay his head on one side, or shake his head, or kick out his foot, and were to answer the query why he did it by admitting, 'I don't really know myself, I just happened to do it, another time I do it differently, for it is involuntary'—ah, then I would understand him. But in case he were to say, as in fact the lovers say about those gesticulations, that perfect bliss consisted in this, how could I not find it ridiculous, as I found also the other case ridiculous, though in another sense, to be sure, until the man checked my laughter by explaining that his movements did not signify anything. Thereby the contradiction which is of the essence of the comic is resolved; for it is not ridiculous to explain that the insignificant has no significance, but to explain that it has the utmost significance surely is ridiculous. With regard to involuntary actions there is primarily present the contradiction that involuntary actions are not expected in a free rational being. Thus if one were to suppose that the Pope at the instant when he was about to place the crown upon Napoleon's head was seized with a cough, or that the bride and groom at the solemn moment of the wedding began to sneeze, the comic element emerges clearly. The more any given occasion accentuates the freedom of a rational being, the more comic the involuntary becomes. So it is in the case of the erotic gesticulations, where the comic element comes to the fore a second time, owing to the fact that the lovers would explain the contradiction by attributing to it absolute significance. It is well known that children have a great sense for the comic, as is proved by the fact that children always respond to this appeal. Now children as a rule will always start to laugh at lovers, and if they are induced to recount what they saw, surely nobody can help laughing. Perhaps this is because the children have left out the point. It is strange then that when the Jew left out the point nobody would laugh, whereas here, conversely, when one leaves out the point everybody laughs. But since no one can tell where the point is, it is naturally left out. The lovers explain nothing, the people who praise love explain nothing, they are intent only, as the Constitution of the Realm commands, to say everything that might be pleasant and lovable.[32] But the man who thinks accounts for his categories, and the man who thinks about love thinks also at once of the categories. However, in the case of love people do not do that, and we still lack a bucolic science, for though in a pastoral lyric the poet may make an attempt to let love come into existence spontaneously, the conventions are all smuggled in again by means of a person who teaches the lover how to love. — So then I found the comic element in the erotic reversal whereby the loftiest experience in one sphere does not find its expression in this sphere but in the polar opposite of another sphere. It is comic that the high flight of love (the desire to belong to one another for all eternity) constantly ends like Saft[33] in the pantry; but still more comic it is that this conclusion of the affair is supposed to be its highest expression.

"Wherever there is contradiction the comic is also present. This is the cue I am constantly following. If it should prove disconcerting to you, dear boon companions, to follow me on this path, then follow with averted face, in fact I myself am speaking like one with a veil before his eyes, for as I see only enigmas, I am unable to see, or rather

[32] The reference is to Section 26 of the ancient constitution of the absolute monarchy, which was abrogated only three years later by the revolution of 1848: "All that can be uttered or written about an absolute sovereign Christian hereditary monarch to his best advantage, so and in all points shall be construed and interpreted in the best and most gracious sense what is said about the all-powerful King of Denmark and Norway."

[33] The glutton in Oehlenschlager's comedy, *Sovedrikken.*

I see nothing. What is a consequence? In case it cannot in one way or another be brought under the concept of identity along with that whereof it is a consequence, it becomes ridiculous, notwithstanding it is currently regarded as a consequence. So for example when a man would take a bath, jumps into the tub and while he is still a bit confused comes out of the hot water, gropes for the bath-rope to steady himself, but makes a mistake and grasps the cord which releases the cold shower, which now with obvious motivation and with the readiest possible compliance descends upon him in a cold stream—the consequence then is thoroughly correct. The ridiculous thing is that he grasped the wrong rope, but there is nothing ridiculous in the fact that a shower operates when one pulls the cord. Rather it would be ridiculous if the shower were to fail—as if for example (to prove the correctness of my proposition about the contradictory), as if a man were to nerve himself in preparation for enduring the shock, and with the ardor of bold resolution were to pull the cord . . . and no shower came! The lovers want to belong to one another for all eternity. They give expression to this in that strange way they have of embracing one another with the intensity of the instant, and all the pleasure of the bliss of love is supposed to consist in this. But all pleasure is selfish. The pleasure of the lover, to be sure, is not selfish with respect to the loved one, but in union they are both absolutely selfish, inasmuch as in union and in love they constitute one self. And yet they are deceived, for at the same instant the genus triumphs over the individual, the genus is victorious whereas the individuals are reduced to the position of being in its service. This I find is more ridiculous than what Aristophanes found so ridiculous. For the ludicrous aspect of the halving of man consists in the contradiction which Aristophanes does not sufficiently emphasize. In looking at a man one would surely think that he was a whole, all by himself, and that indeed is what one thinks, until one sees that under the obsession of love he is only a half which runs after its other half. There is nothing comic in half an apple, the comical would only emerge if a whole apple were a half apple; in the first case there is no contradiction, but surely there is in the latter. If people took seriously the saying that woman is only man's half, she would not be comic in love. The man, however, who has enjoyed civic prestige as a whole man becomes comic when he begins to run about and thereby betrays that he is only half a man. The more one thinks of it, the more laughable it becomes; for if the man actually is a whole, he does not become a whole in love, but he and the woman make one and a half. What wonder then that the gods laugh, and that they laugh especially at man! I return, however, to my consequence. Now when the lovers have found one another, one would surely suppose that they were a whole, and herein should be manifested the truth that they desire to live for one another to all eternity. But, behold, instead of living for one another, they begin to live for the race, and they have no suspicion of it! — What is a consequence? In case a consequence when once it has resulted cannot be traced back into that out of which it resulted, it is a ludicrous sort of consequence, and they to whom it occurred are ridiculous. Now in case those separated halves have found one another, this surely should mean perfect satisfaction and repose, and yet there ensues upon this a new existence. That the finding of one another should constitute a new existence for the lovers is comprehensible, but not that from them there dates also a new existence for another being. And yet this resulting consequence is greater than that whereof it is a consequence, and yet the conclusion such as this the lovers attained in finding one another must surely be an indication that no further consequence was thinkable. Does any other pleasure supply an analogy to this? On the contrary, the satisfaction of every other pleasure denotes a point of rest, and even though there supervenes a *tristitia*[34] which indicates that all desire is comic, yet such a *tristitia* would be a simple consequence, although no *tristitia* witnesses so powerfully to the antecedent comic as does the *tristitia* of love. On the other hand, it is an entirely different question in the case of such a prodigious consequence as that about which we are here speaking, a consequence about which no one knows whence it comes or whether it comes, whereas if it comes it comes nevertheless as a consequence.

"Who is able to comprehend this? And yet for the initiates what is the highest pleasure is at the same time the thing of greatest moment; it is so momentous that the lovers even assume new names which are derived from the consequence—which, strangely enough, has retroactive force. The lover is now called Father, and the loved one, Mother; and to their ears these two names are the most beautiful. And yet there is one to whom these names are even more beautiful. For what is so beautiful as filial piety? To me it seems the most beautiful thing of all, and fortunately I am able to understand the thought involved in it. We are taught that it behooves a son to love his father. That I understand, I do not even suspect any contradictions, I feel myself blissfully bound by the beautiful ties of filial piety. I believe that to owe life to another is the highest debt, I believe that this debt can neither be settled

[34] Sadness or dejection—alluding to the ancient dictum: *Omne animal post coitum triste.*

nor fathomed by any reckoning, and hence I find that Cicero is right in saying that as against the father the son is always in the wrong,[35] and it is filial piety precisely that teaches me to believe this, teaches me not even to wish to penetrate the hidden, but rather to remain hidden in the father. It is quite true, I am glad to be another man's greatest debtor, but conversely, before I resolve to make another my greatest debtor, I would want to be clear about the thing myself, for to my thinking there is no comparison between being another man's debtor and making a debtor of another man so that in all eternity he is not able to liberate himself from the debt. So then what filial piety forbids the son to consider, love bids the father to consider. And here a contradiction again emerges. If the son is an eternal being like the father, what does it mean to be a father? I may indeed smile to myself at the thought of being a father, whereas the son is most profoundly moved when he thinks of his relationship to the father. I understand perfectly what Plato[36] so well said, that an animal will produce an animal of the same species, a plant, a plant of the same species, and so a man will give birth to a man; but by this nothing is explained, thought is not satisfied, only a vague feeling is aroused; for an eternal being cannot be born. Whenever the father regards his son in the aspect of his eternal essence, which is the essential way of regarding him, he cannot but smile at himself, not being able to conceive in any way all the beauty and significance he has for his son in filial piety. If on the other hand he regards his son in the aspect of his physical nature, he must again smile, because the notion of fatherhood is altogether too lofty an expression for this. Finally, if it were thinkable that the father had influence upon the son, that the father's nature was a postulate from which the son's nature could not liberate itself, the contradiction comes from another side; for then the thought is so dreadful that there is nothing on earth so dreadful as to be a father.[37] There is no comparison between putting a human being to death and giving life to a human being; the first merely decides his fate in time, the other, in eternity. So here then there is a contradiction, one fit both to laugh and to weep over. Is paternity an imagination (though not in the sense in which

[35] cf. the title of the sermon which concludes *Either/Or*: "As against God we are always in the wrong." cf. IV, A 256. This whole passage breathes the spirit of filial piety so characteristic of S.K., but as usual there is no thought of the mother. Note that this feeling is too sacred for satire.

[36] Rather, Aristotle, *Ethics,* II, 6.

[37] In S.K.'s youth this in fact was his melancholy conception of his solidarity with his father.

Magdalene says this to Jeronymus[38]), or is it the most dreadful of all realities? Is it the greatest benefaction, or is it the highest enjoyment of pleasure? Is it something that merely comes about, or is it the loftiest task?

"Behold, for this reason I have renounced love, for to me my thought is all in all. If love be the most blissful pleasure, then I renounce the pleasure, without wishing to offend anyone or to envy him; if love constitutes the condition for performing the greatest benefaction, then I disavow all claim to such an opportunity, but my thought is safely preserved. I am not without an eye for the beautiful, my heart is not unmoved when I read the songs of the poets, my soul is not untouched by sadness when I dreamily reflect upon those conceptions of love, but to my thought I will not be unfaithful, and what would it avail anyway, when for me there is no blessedness where my thought is not safely preserved to me, where I, if I were in such a place, would yearn in desperation for my thought, which I dare not desert to cling to a wife, since to me it is my eternal essence, and so is of still greater value than father and mother and of still greater value than a wife. I perceive indeed that if anything can be holy, it is love, that if in any circumstances unfaithfulness is base, it is in love, that if any deceit is detestable, it is in love; but my soul is pure, I have never looked upon any woman to desire her, I have not fluttered about undecidedly until I blindly plunged or swooned away into the most decisive relationship. In case I knew what the lovable is, I should know to a certainty whether I had been at fault by tempting anyone, but as I do not know that, I can only say definitely that I am not conscious of having willed it. Suppose I were to let myself go, suppose I fell to laughing, or suppose I drooped under the dreadfulness of it—for it is impossible for me to find the narrow way which the lovers tread so easily, as if it were the broad way, undeterred by trying doubts, which they surely have thought of, since our age has in fact thought everything through, and consequently can easily understand my assertion that to act 'immediately,' i.e. unreflectively, is nonsense, and so that one must have thought all possible reflections through before acting—suppose I were to let myself go. Have I then irretrievably offended the loved one if I laughed, or cast her immediately into despair if I drooped? For I comprehend very well that a woman cannot be so thoroughly reflective, and a woman who found love comic (as only gods and men can find it, and hence woman is a temptation which is meant to entice men to be ridiculous), such a

[38] In Holberg's comedy, *Erasmus Montanus,* III, 6.

woman would betray a suspicious amount of antecedent knowledge and would understand me least of all, but a woman who comprehended the dreadfulness would have lost her lovableness and still would not understand me, she would be annihilated, as I by no means am so long as my thought preserves me.[39]

"Does nobody laugh? When I began by wanting to talk about the comic side of love, you perhaps expected to have a laugh, for you are a laughing lot, and I myself am a friend of laughter,[40] and yet perhaps you are not laughing. The effect was a different one, and yet it proves precisely that I have talked about the comic. If nobody laughs at my speech—very well, dear boon companions, then laugh a little at me, it will not surprise me; for what I have occasionally heard you say about love I do not understand—presumably you are initiates."

Thereupon the young man sat down. He had become almost more beautiful than before the meal. Now he sat gazing in front of him without concerning himself with the others. Johannes the Seducer wanted at once to make objections to the young man's speech but was interrupted by Constantine, who warned against discussions and ruled that now only speeches were in order. This again gave rise to a discussion about what order they were to speak in, which Constantine again checked by inviting himself to speak, in consideration that they would recognize his competence to command the others to speak in turn.

Constantine spoke as follows:

"There is a time to keep silence and a time to speak, and now, it seems to me, is a time to speak briefly, for our young friend has spoken very long and very strangely. His *vis comica* has brought us to the pass of fighting *ancipiti proelio*,[41] for his speech was of as doubtful a character as he is himself, whom you now see sitting there, a puzzled man, not knowing whether he ought to laugh or weep, or whether to fall in love. Indeed, if I had had foreknowledge of his speech, such as he insists upon having about love, I would have forbidden him to speak, but now it is too late. So now I bid you, dear boon companions, "that ye merry and jovial here shall be";[42] and if this is not a mood that

[39] S.K. is obviously reflecting here upon his experience with Regina—for the first time it is obvious in this book, but by no means for the last time. At this point the reader may be apprised that this "young man" is the same "young man" that appears later in "Guilty?" "Not Guilty?" The first "young man" is S.K. before he had fallen in love, the other "young man" is in the throes of breaking his engagement.

[40] cf. *The Point of View*, English edition, p. 125.

[41] A doubtful battle.

[42] From Scribe's opera, *Brama og Bayaderen*, Act I, Scene 1.

comes by bidding, I bid you then to forget each speech as soon as it is delivered, washing it down with a single gulp.

"And now for woman, the subject on which I would speak. I too have pondered, and I have fathomed her category; I too have sought, but I have also found, making a peerless discovery which I impart to you herewith. She can only be rightly construed under the category of jest. It is man's part to be absolute, to act absolutely, to give expression to the absolute; woman has her being in relationships. Between two such different beings no genuine reciprocal action can take place. This incongruity is precisely what constitutes jest, and it is with woman jest first came into the world. It follows, however, as a matter of course that man must know how to keep himself under the category of the absolute, for otherwise nothing comes of it, that is to say, there comes of it something only too universal, that man and woman tally with one another, he as a half-man and she as a half-man.

"Jest is not an aesthetic but an imperfect ethical category. Its effect upon thought is like the effect upon one's frame of mind at hearing a man who begins a speech, and after reciting a phrase or two with the same eloquence, says, 'Hm'—and then dead silence. So it is with woman. One aims at her with the ethical category, one shuts one's eyes, one thinks of the absolute in the way of requirements, one thinks the thought of man, one opens one's eyes, one fixes one's glance upon the demure little miss upon whom one is experimenting to see if she meets the specifications; one becomes uneasy and says to oneself, 'Ah, this surely is jest.' For the jest consists in applying the category, in subsuming her under it, because with her the serious never can become serious; but precisely this is jest, for if one might require seriousness of her, it would not be jest. To put her under a vacuum pump and pump all the air out of her would be cruel and would not be in the least amusing, but to pump air into her, to pump her up to supernatural size, to let her suppose she has attained all the ideality a little miss of sixteen years can imagine she wants to have—this is the beginning of the performance, and the beginning of a highly entertaining performance. No young man has half so much imaginary ideality as a young girl. But 'there is a rebate on that,' as said the tailor, for all her ideality is illusion.

"If one does not regard woman in this way, she may do irreparable harm; with my interpretation she becomes harmless and amusing. There is nothing more dreadful for a man than to catch himself in the act of twaddling. With this all genuine ideality is brought to naught; for to have been a knave is a thing one can repent of, not having meant one word of all one said one can regret, but to have meant all one said, and lo, it turned out to be twaddle—even repentance turns away from that in disgust. It is different with woman. She has a prescriptive right to be transformed in less than twenty-four hours into the most innocent and pardonable galimatias; far be it from her candid soul to want to deceive anyone, she meant all she said, now she says the contrary, but with the same lovable frankness, for she is ready to die for the contrary. In case a man in all seriousness surrenders himself to love, he can say that he has lots of assurance, if only he can get any assurance company to take the risk, for a material so inflammable as woman must always make the insurer suspicious. What has he done? He has identified himself with her: if on New Year's Eve she goes off like a rocket, he goes with her, or if that does not occur, he has nevertheless come into pretty close affinity with danger. And what does he stand to lose? He can lose everything; for there is only one absolute opposite to the absolute, and that is twaddle. He is not to seek asylum in a society for persons morally depraved, for he is not morally depraved, far from it, he is merely reduced *in absurdum* and rendered beatific by nonsense, he has made a fool of himself. Between man and man this situation can never occur. If in this fashion a man fizzles out in nonsense, I despise him; if he dupes me by his shrewdness, I have merely to apply to him the ethical category and the danger is very insignificant; if the thing is carried too far—well, then I put a bullet through his head. But to challenge a woman to a duel—what is that? Who does not know? It is jest—as when Xerxes gave orders to have the sea scourged. When Othello murders Desdemona, he gains nothing, even assuming that she really had been guilty; he had made a fool of himself in the first instance, and he remains a fool. For even in murdering her he only draws attention to the consequence of an act which originally makes him ridiculous, whereas, on the contrary, Elvira can always be pathetic when armed with a dagger to revenge herself. Shakespeare's interpretation of Othello as tragic (even without regard to the unfortunate catastrophe that Desdemona was innocent) is only to be explained, but at the same time is absolutely justified, by the fact that Othello was a colored man. For a colored man, dear boon companions, who cannot be supposed to represent *esprit,* dear boon companions, who also becomes green in the face when he is angry (which is a physiological fact), a colored man can well become tragic when he is betrayed by a woman, just as the woman has the whole pathos of tragedy on her side when she is betrayed by her husband. A man who becomes red in the neck might perhaps become tragic, but a man of whom one ventures to require *esprit* either doesn't become jealous, or he becomes comic when he does, and most of all when he comes running up with a dagger. What a pity that Shakespeare has not produced a play on such a theme, where the challenge implied in a woman's unfaithfulness was rejected by irony; for not everyone who can perceive the comic aspect of this situation or even can describe it is endowed with the talent for dramatizing it. But one has only to imagine Socrates accidentally discovering Xanthippe *in flagrante*—I say "accidentally" because it would be essentially unsocratic to imagine Socrates being profoundly concerned about Xanthippe's fidelity, or that he might even spy upon her. I believe that the subtle smile which changed the ugliest man in Athens into the handsomest must for the first time have been transformed into a roar of laughter. It is inconceivable that Aristophanes, who sometimes liked to hold Socrates up to ridicule, never thought of letting him run out upon the stage shouting, 'Where is she? where is she? that I may murder her,' viz. Xanthippe, the unfaithful Xanthippe. For whether Socrates was made cuckold or not is a question of no importance, for anything Xanthippe would do in that respect would be labor lost, like snapping one's fingers in one's pocket, and Socrates remains the same intellectual hero even with the horn upon his forehead. But that he might become jealous, that he might want to murder Xanthippe—alas, then would Xanthippe have power over him as the entire Greek state and the death-sentence did not have . . . to make him ridiculous. Hence a cuckold is comic in relation to his wife, but can be regarded as tragic in relation to other men. The most obvious illustration of this is the Spanish notion of honor. However, the tragic element here is essentially this, that the injured husband can get no real satisfaction, and that the smart of his suffering is meaningless—and that is dreadful enough. To shoot a woman, to challenge her to a duel, to show contempt for her, only makes the poor man more ridiculous, for woman is the weaker sex. This consideration is brought forward everywhere and brings everything to confusion. If she does something great she is more admired than a man would be, because people did not suppose they might venture to require it of her; if she is deceived, she has all the pathos in her favor, whereas when a man is deceived, people have a little sympathy and a little patience so long as he is present, only to laugh at him when he is gone.

"One had better be prompt, therefore, to regard woman as a jest. The entertainment is peerless. Let one regard her as a fixed quantity and make a relative quantity of oneself. One is not to contradict her, far from it, that would only be to play into her hands. Just because she is unable to set limits to herself, she shows off to the best advantage, seriously speaking, when one contradicts hei a bit. One is never to doubt what she says, far from it, every word must be believed. With a rapturous look of blissful intoxication one must dance attendance upon her with the mincing step of an idolatrous worshipper—one falls upon one's knees, one pines, one raises one's eyes to her, one pines, one breathes again. One is to do everything she says, like an obedient slave. Now comes the spice of it. It requires no proof that a woman can talk, i.e. *verba facere*. Unfortunately, she does not possess sufficient power of reflection to insure her against self-contradiction for any considerable time, say a week at the maximum, if the male does not help her regulatively by contradicting her. So the consequence is that in a short while the confusion is in full swing. If one had not done what she told one to do, the confusion would have passed unnoticed, for she forgets again as promptly as she is prompt to talk. But since her adorer has done everything she wanted and been entirely at her service, the confusion is palpable. The more gifted a woman is, the more amusing. The more gifted, so much the more imagination has she. The more imaginative, so much the more potent is she at the instant, and so much the more does confusion reveal itself the next instant. This amusement is rarely witnessed in life because such blind obedience to a woman's whim is very rare. If it is to be found in the languishing shepherd, he hasn't wit enough to perceive the amusement.

"The amusement, as I have said, is priceless; indeed I know that, for sometimes I have not been able to sleep at night, merely for thinking what new confusions I might live to see, wrought by my lady and by my humble zeal to serve her; for no one who bets on the lottery can have experience of more extraordinary combinations than the man who has a passion for this game. For one thing is certain, that every woman possesses this possibility of flying up and being transfigured into nonsense, with an amiability, a nonchalance, an assurance, befitting the weaker sex. As a true lover one discovers in one's lady every imaginable charm. Thereupon finding that one has some talent for this, one does not let it lie fallow as a mere possibility but develops it into virtuosity. I need say no more, nothing more can be said in general terms, everybody understands what I mean. Just as one man finds his amusement in balancing a cane upon his nose, in swinging a glass of water in a circle without its contents flying out, or in dancing among eggs, and other similar exercises which are as entertaining as they are profitable—so and not otherwise has the lover in commerce with his lady the most incomparable amusement and the most interesting study. With respect to erotic situations one is to believe her absolutely—not only that she is faithful, for one soon tires of that game, but one is to believe absolutely in all those outbursts of indefeasible romanticism from which presumably she would perish if one did not apply a safety-valve through which the sigh and the smoke (which is the air of romanticism)[43] stream forth to the delectation of the adorer. One has to raise her to the pinnacle of a Juliet—the only difference being that no one has thought of touching a hair of Romeo's head. With respect to intellect one has to credit her with everything, and if one has been fortunate enough to find the right woman, in a trice he has on his hands a brooding authoress, and one must admiringly shade one's eyes with the hand to see what the little black hen[44] is going to lay next. It is inconceivable that Socrates did not choose this part instead of scolding Xanthippe—well, after all, he wanted to keep in practice, like the horse-trainer who, though he has the best trained horse, knows how to tease it in such a way that there may be reason sufficient for breaking it in again.[45]

"I should like to speak a little more concretely in order to illuminate a special and rather interesting case. Much is said about woman's fidelity, but not often wisely. Regarded from a purely aesthetic point of view, it belongs among the theatrical properties of the poet, as a phantom which crosses the stage in search of the loved one, or the phantom which sits by the spinning-wheel awaiting the loved one—for when she has found him or he has come, then aesthetics has lost interest in it. Her unfaithfulness, which can be brought into the closest connection with her foregoing faithfulness, is essentially regarded from an ethical point of view, and then jealousy makes its appearance as a tragic passion. There are three cases, and the situation is favorable to woman, inasmuch as two of them are instances of faithfulness and only one of unfaithfulness. Inconceivably great is her faithfulness so long as she is not sure of the loved one, and just as inconceivably great when he declines her fidelity. The third case would be that of infidelity. Now if only one has enough *esprit* and detachment to think, one will find in what has already been said ample justification of the category 'jest.' Our young friend, the very beginning of whose speech misled me for a moment, made as if he wanted to start out with this theme but sprang back affrighted at the difficulty. Yet the explanation is not difficult if one really is serious in putting death and unhappy love in conjunction, if one has seriousness enough to hold this thought fast—and one ought to have at least as much seriousness as that . . . for the sake of the jest. All this sort of talk originates of course with a woman or with a womanish male. One

[43] An allusion to Wessel's comedy, *Kjerlighed uden Strømper* ("Love without Stockings"), Act III, Scene 3.

[44] An allusion to Holberg's comedy, *Den Studenløse,* Act II, Scene 1.

[45] Diogenes Laertius, II, 37, reports that Socrates appealed to this analogy.

recognizes it at once, for it is one of those absolute outbursts which, uttered with aplomb at the instant is sure of great applause at the instant; although it is a matter of life and death, it is intended for instant enjoyment, like an omelet soufflé; although it concerns a whole lifetime, it lays no obligation whatever upon the dying person but only obliges the auditor to hasten that very instant to the aid of the dying. If a man were to deliver such a speech, it would not be in the least amusing, for he would be too despicable for anybody to laugh at him. Woman, on the other hand, is a genius, she is lovable for that quality, and is amusing from first to last. So then the lady dies of love. That is certain—for has she not said she would? Here lies her pathos; for woman is man—at least she is man enough to say what hardly any man is man enough to do.[46] She is a real man! When I say this I have passed upon her an ethical judgment. Do ye likewise, dear boon companions, and thus understand Aristotle.[47] He remarks justly that woman cannot well be used in tragedy. That indeed is obvious, she belongs in the pathetic and serious *divertissement,* in the half-hour farce, not in the five-act drama. Accordingly she dies. But for all that, might she not be able to love again? Why not?—in case anyone can bring her to life again. If she comes again to life she is in fact a new person, and a new person, another person, begins anew, loves for the first time, there is nothing remarkable in that. O death, great is thy power! Not the most violent emetic, not the strongest laxative could effect so clean a sweep.

"The confusion is marvellous, if only one is on the lookout and does not forget. A deceased person is one of the most amusing figures one can encounter in life. How strange that it is not more frequently employed on the stage, in real life one now and then sees such a thing. Even a man who has one time been taken for dead is essentially a comic object of interest, but a person actually deceased contributes to our amusement all that one can reasonably require. Be on the lookout. The fact is, my attention was first drawn to this one day when I was walking in the street with an acquaintance. A pair passed us by. Judging from the look of my acquaintance I inferred that he knew them and asked if it were so. 'By Jove,' he replied, 'right well do I know them, especially the lady, for she was my deceased.' 'Your deceased what?,' I enquired. 'By Jove, my deceased first love. Yes, it's a strange story. She said, 'I am dying,' that very instant she departed—in death of course, I hadn't

[46] In view of this whole passage one must remember S.K.'s experience with Regina: she had declared she could not live without him—she already was engaged to Fritz Schlegel.

[47] *Poetics,* Cap. 15.

even time to take out insurance on her life, it was too late; dead she was and dead she remained; and now I rove about, as says the poet, seeking in vain the loved one's grave to offer her the sacrifice of a tear.' So spake that dejected man who was left behind in the world all alone, though it comforted him nevertheless to find that his deceased love had got so far along, if not by the help of another, at least in the company of another. It is a good thing for the girls, thought I, that they don't have to be buried every time they die. In that case too the parents, who hitherto have regarded male children as the most expensive luxury, might easily find the girls still more expensive. A simple case of infidelity is not nearly so amusing—I mean, when a young woman falls in love with another man and says to her husband, 'I cannot help it, save me from myself.' But to die of sorrow because she cannot endure to have her lover separated from her by a journey to the West Indies, to have to put up with his departure, and then upon his return not only not to be dead but to be joined forever to another—that is really a strange fate for a lover. What wonder then that this dejected man sometimes comforted himself with the refrain of an old song: Hurrah for me and you, I say, that day is ne'er forgotten![48]

"Forgive me now, dear boon companions if I have spoken too long, and now drain a glass to love and woman. Fair is she and lovely when regarded aesthetically—that no one can deny. But since it so often is said, I too will say: one should not remain standing, but 'go further.' So regard her ethically, and the thing becomes a jest. Even Plato and Aristotle[49] take it that woman is an incomplete form, that is, an irrational quantity, which perhaps some time in a better existence might be brought back to the male form. In this life one must take her as she is. What this is will soon appear, for she too is not satisfied with the aesthetic sphere, she 'goes further,' she would be emancipated—that she is man enough to say. Let that come to pass, and the jest will be beyond all bounds."

When Constantine ceased speaking he instantly commanded Victor Eremita to begin. He spoke as follows:

"Plato, as you know, gave thanks to the gods for four things, and the fourth was that he was contemporary with Socrates. An earlier

[48] cf. *Forlovelsen*, p. 71, a letter to Emil Boesen written from Berlin after S.K. had broken his engagement, where this same refrain is quoted (inexactly) from a song which can be found in Caen's *Folker-Visebog*, II, p. 18 (Copenhagen, 1849).

[49] Aristotle, *Politics*, I, 13, ascribes to woman "incomplete reflection"; Plato, *Timaios*, Cap. 14, lets men who in their former life were imperfect become women in the next.

Greek philosopher[50] had already expressed his gratitude for the first three of them,[51] so I conclude that they were worth it. But I, alas, supposing I were desirous of expressing my gratitude like those Greeks, cannot very well give thanks for privileges which are denied me, and so I will muster all the powers of my soul to express gratitude for the one boon which was accorded me: that I became a man and not a woman.

"To be a woman is something so strange, so mixed, so complex, that no predicate expresses it, and the many predicates one might use contradict one another so sharply that only a woman can endure it, and, still worse, can enjoy it. The fact that she actually has less significance than man is not what constitutes her misfortune, even if she were to come to know it, for after all this is something that can be endured. No, the misfortune is that, owing to the romantic way in which she is regarded, her life has become meaningless, so that one moment she has the utmost significance and the next moment none whatever, without ever coming to know what her significance really is—yet this is not the whole of her misfortune, for the worst of it is that she can never come to know it because she is a woman. For my part, if I were a woman, I had rather be a woman in the orient where I would be a slave, for to be a slave, neither more nor less, is at any rate something definite, in comparison with being hurrah boys and nothing whatever.

"Even if the life of a woman did not present such contrasts, the distinction which she enjoys and which is rightly assumed to belong to her *qua* woman, a distinction which she does not share with man, already indicates the meaningless of her life. This distinction is that of gallantry. Now gallantry consists quite simply in construing by means of fantastic categories the person towards whom one is gallant. Hence gallantry showed toward a man is an insult, for a man deprecates the application of fantastic categories to him. On the other hand it is a tribute to the fair sex, a distinction essentially due to her. Alas, alack! If it were only a single cavalier that was gallant, it would not be so serious a matter, after all. But such is by no means the case. At bottom every man is gallant, he is instinctively gallant. Accordingly, this signifies that nature itself has bestowed this perquisite upon the fair sex. On the other hand, woman instinctively accepts this homage. Once more a misfortune; for if only one woman here and there were to accept it, a different explanation might be given. So here again we have the irony of life. If there is to be truth in gallantry, it must be reciprocal, and

[50] Thales of Miletos, according to Diogenes Laertius, I, 33.

[51] That he had been created a human, not an animal; a man, not a woman; a Greek, not a barbarian.

gallantry would then be the current rate quoted on the bourse for the difference between beauty and strength, cunning and might. But this is not the way of it, gallantry is essentially woman's due, and the fact that she accepts it instinctively may be explained as an instance of nature's tender care for the weak, for those who have had a hard deal, to whom an illusion gives more than adequate compensation. But this illusion is precisely the calamity. Not infrequently nature comes to the aid of an ill-favored man by consoling him with the belief that he is the most beautiful. Thus nature has made good the deficiency, the man possesses in fact even more than he could reasonably desire.[52] But to possess this in a vain conceit, not to be enslaved to wretchedness, but to be fooled into a conceit, is in fact a still worse mockery. In the sense of being ill-favored it cannot be said that woman suffers from nature's neglect, yet she does suffer in another sense, inasmuch as she never can free herself from the illusion with which life has consoled her.

"If one will analyze a feminine existence in its entirety so as to bring out the decisive factors, every feminine existence must make a perfectly fantastic impression. Woman has turning-points in her life of a sort entirely different from those man may be said to have, for her turning-points are in every case ups and downs. In Tieck's romantic dramas one sometimes runs across a character who aforetime was a king in Mesopotamia and now is a green-grocer in Copenhagen. Precisely as fantastic is every feminine existence. If you will call the girl Juliana, then her life is as follows: 'aforetime Empress in love's far-reaching realm of exorbitant speech, and titular Queen of all the exaggerations of tomfoolery—now Madam Petersen at the corner of Bathhouse Street.' A girl when she is a child is considered of less account than a boy. When she is a little older one does not quite know what can be made of her. Finally there comes the decisive period which makes her a sovereign despot. — Man approaches her adoringly, he is a suitor. Adoringly—for every suitor is an adorer, it is not the device of an artful deceiver. Even Jack Ketch, when he lays aside the *fasces* to go a-wooing, even he bows the knee, notwithstanding he has it in mind at the earliest possible opportunity to play the part of private executioner at home, which he takes so much for granted that he does not think of making the excuse that public executions are becoming so rare. The man of culture behaves in the same way. He kneels, he adores, he construes the beloved in the most fantastic categories, and thereupon he very quickly forgets his kneeling posture, and even whilst he knelt he knew full well that it was

[52] This is the "over-compensation" with which analytical psychology has made us familiar.

fantastic. If I were a woman, I had rather be sold by my father to the highest bidder, as in the orient; for a bargain has some sense in it. What a misfortune to be a woman! And yet the misfortune essentially is that when one is a woman one doesn't comprehend this. If she laments, it is not over the former situation but over the latter. If I were a woman, I would first of all decline to be wooed and would resign myself to being the weaker sex, if that is what I am; but I would take heed, as the thing of chiefest concern to a proud person, that one does not go beyond the bounds of truth. This is of small concern to her. Juliana is in the seventh heaven, and Madam Petersen puts up with her fate.

"So I thank the gods that I became a man, not a woman. And yet how much I forego! Poetry, from the drinking-song to the tragedy, is the deification of woman. All the worse for her, and for him too who admires, for if he doesn't take care, he will suddenly, just as sure as he stands there, draw a long face. The beautiful, the sublime, man's noblest exploits, are due to woman, for she inspires him, woman is the inspirer. How many a lovelorn shepherd has played this theme upon his flute, and how many a shepherdess has harkened to it! Verily my soul is devoid of envy and is only grateful to the gods; for after all I had rather be a man, and be a little less exalted, and be that in reality, than be a woman, and be an indeterminate quantity, and be made blissful by a vain conceit; I had rather be a concretion which means something than an abstraction which means everything. It is quite true therefore, as I said: through woman ideality came into the world—what would man be without her. Many a man became a genius through a girl, many a man became a hero through a girl, many a man became a poet through a girl, many a man became a saint through a girl—but he didn't become a genius through the girl he got, for through her he became only Privy-Councillor; he didn't become a hero through the girl he got, for through her he only became a general; he didn't become a poet through the girl he got, for through her he only became a father; he didn't become a saint through the girl he got, for he didn't get any, and he wanted only the one he didn't get, just as each of the others became a genius, became a hero, became a poet, through the girl he didn't get.[53] If the ideality of woman were in itself inspiring, then surely the inspiration must be the woman to whom a man is united for life. But actual existence gives a different account of it. That is to say, in a negative relationship woman makes a man idealistically productive. So understood, she is inspiring, but to assert this directly and without qualification is to be guilty of a

[53] The autobiographical character of this passage hardly needs to be pointed out. S.K. frequently asserts that he became a poet through the girl he didn't get.

paralogism which one would have to be a woman to overlook. Or who has ever heard of anyone becoming a poet through his wife? So long as the man does not have her she is an inspiration. This is the residual truth in the imaginary conceit of poetry and of woman. The fact that he does not possess her denotes perhaps that he is still fighting for her. In this way a girl has inspired many a man and made him a knight. But who has ever heard of anyone becoming valiant through his wife? Or else the fact that he does not possess her means that he cannot get her. In this way a girl has inspired many a man and awakened his idealism, in case she happened to have something worth while to contribute. But a wife who has ever so much to contribute hardly awakens idealism. Or else the fact that he does not possess her means that he is in pursuit of the ideal. He perhaps loves many, and to love many is also an unhappy love affair of a sort, and yet his soul's ideality consists essentially in this striving and yearning, not in the fractions of lovableness which taken all together constitute the *summa summarum* of the contributions of the several individuals.

"In fact the highest idealism a woman can awaken in a man is the consciousness of immortality. The force of the proof which she gives consists in what one might call the necessity of a rejoinder. As one says of a theatrical piece that it cannot end without one or another making a rejoinder, so, says ideality, life cannot be all over at death, I require a rejoinder. This proof is often employed directly in obituary notices. That seems to me as it should be, for if it is to be used in obituary notices, it must be used positively. For example: Madam Petersen has lived a certain number of years, until in the night between the 24th and the 25th 'it pleased providence' etc. On this occasion Mr. Petersen is seized with an attack of reminiscences of the period of courtship—to express myself very concisely, nothing but *Wiedersehen* consoles him. In the mean while, for this blessed *Wiedersehen* he prepares himself by taking a second wife, for maybe the second marriage is not anything like so poetic as the first, but at any rate it is a good reprint. This is the positive proof. Mr. Petersen is not satisfied with requiring a rejoinder; no, *Auf Wiedersehen* in the other world. It is well known that a spurious metal sometimes assumes the luster of the genuine article; this is the brief glamor of silver plate. For the spurious metal this is tragic, for the spurious metal must resign itself once of all to being spurious. It is not so with Mr. Petersen. Ideality is every man's due by right. When I laugh at Mr. Petersen it is not because he, being the true metal, had only a single glint of silver, but because this silver glint betrays the fact that he has become spurious metal. So it is that Philistinism looks most ridiculous when it is arrayed in idealism and affords an apt occasion to say with Holberg,[54] 'Isn't the cow, too, all dolled up?' The fact is that if a woman awakens in man ideality and therewith the consciousness of immortality, she always does it negatively. The man who actually became a genius, became a hero, became a poet, became a saint, through a woman, grasped at the same instant immortality. If the idealizing inspiration were positively present in woman, it must be the wife, and only the wife, who awakens the consciousness of immortality in the man. Actual existence expresses exactly the opposite. If she is really to awaken ideality in the husband, she must die. In Mr. Petersen she does not awaken it, for all that. If then by her death she actually awakens ideality in the man, she does in fact perform all the great things poetry tells of her—but note well that what she did in a positive way did not awaken ideality. Meanwhile, the longer she keeps on living, the more doubtful does her significance become, for she actually has begun to want to be something positive. The more positively the proof is presented, the less does it prove, for then the longing will be for something experienced, the content of which may be assumed to be drained off, inasmuch as it has been experienced, lived through. The proof becomes most positive when the object of longing is the marital cooing in corners—'that time when we were in the Deer Park together.' In the same way one can also get a longing for an old pair of slippers in which one used to be so comfortable, but this longing is no proof of the immortality of the soul. The more negatively the proof is presented, so much the better; for the negative is higher than the positive, it is the infinite, and so the only really positive proof.

"Woman's significance is wholly negative, as compared with that her positive significance is nil, indeed it is even pernicious. This is the truth which existence has hidden from her, while it consoles her with a vain conceit which surpasses everything that can enter into any man's brain, and with fatherly care has so arranged it all that language unites with everything else to confirm her in the conceit. Even when she is conceived of as the very opposite of inspiring, as the one from whom all depravity issues—whether it be that sin came into the world through her, or that it is her infidelity which is the ruin of everything—the conception is always gallant. For on hearing such talk one might think that woman was capable of becoming infinitely more guilty than man—which after all is a prodigious appreciation of her. Alas, the situation is in reality quite different. There is a secret way of reading this verdict

[54] Act II, Scene 2, of the comedy *Barselstuen* ("The Lying-in Room").

which woman does not understand; for the very next instant existence as a whole accepts the very same conclusion as the state, which makes man responsible for his wife. People condemn her in a way they never have condemned any man, for he gets only a real sentence, and with a woman the thing ends, not with getting a milder sentence (for then her life would not be all illusion), but by quashing the case, leaving the public, i.e. existence, to pay the costs. At one instant she is supposed to be in possession of all possible cunning, the next instant they laugh at the man she deceived, which surely is a contradiction, and even over Potiphar's wife there hovers the possibility of being able to give the impression that she was seduced. Thus woman has a possibility such as no man has, a prodigious possibility, but her reality is in inverse proportion to that, and the most dreadful thing of all is the sorcery of illusion in which she feels happy.

"So let Plato thank the gods that he was contemporary with Socrates, I envy him; let him give thanks for being a Greek, I envy him; but when he gives thanks that he became a man, not a woman, I join in that with my whole heart. If I had become a woman and could understand what I now understand—how dreadful! If I had become a woman and consequently could not even understand that—how much more dreadful!

"But if such be the case, it follows that one had better keep out of any positive relationship with her. Wherever woman is involved one has that inevitable hiatus which renders her blissful because she does not notice it, but kills a man if he discovers it.

"A negative relationship to a woman may exalt a man to infinity. Let that always be said in honor of woman, and it may be said without any qualification; for essentially it does not depend upon any particular quality of the woman, upon her loveliness, or upon the lasting quality of her loveliness; it depends upon the fact that she appears at the right instant, when ideality is acquiring the power of vision. It is a brief instant, and then she would do well to vanish again. For a positive relationship to woman reduces a man to finiteness in the greatest conceivable degree. The highest thing, therefore, a woman can do for a man is to come within his range of vision at the right instant, but that, after all, she cannot do, it is the kindness of fate—but then comes the greatest thing she can do for a man, and that is, to be unfaithful to him, the sooner the better. The first ideality will assist him to reach an ideality of a higher power, and then he is succored absolutely. It is true, this second ideality is bought with the sharpest pain, but it is also the greatest bliss; it is true, he cannot by any means wish it before it has come to pass, but afterwards he thanks her for it; and since after all, humanly speaking, he has no great reason for being so very grateful, all is for the best. But woe unto him if she remains faithful.

"So I thank the gods for the fact that I became a man, not a woman; then in the next place I thank the gods that no woman with a lifelong tenure constrains me constantly to think too late.

"What a strange invention marriage is! And what makes it still stranger is the fact that it is regarded as an 'immediate' step. And yet there is no step so decisive, for there is nothing so self-willed and domineering in relation to a human life as is marriage. A thing so decisive as that, one is to do, not reflectively, but 'immediately'! And yet marriage is not a simple thing but something extremely complex and ambiguous. Just as the meat of the turtle savors of all kinds of meat, so has marriage a savor of everything; and as the turtle is a slow-moving beast, so also is marriage. A love affair is a simple thing after all—but marriage! Is it something pagan or something Christian or something pious or something worldly or a little of everything, is it the expression of that inexplicable erotic sentiment, that concordant elective affinity of souls, or is it a duty or a partnership or expediency or use and wont in certain lands, or is it a little of all that; is one to engage the town band to play the music, or the organist, or a little of both; is it the parson or the police magistrate who is to make the address and inscribe their names in the book of life—I mean the parish register; does marriage play raucous music upon a comb, or does it listen to that whisper which sounds like the whisper of 'fairies from the caves of midsummer-night?'[55] And such a complex piece of music, such a complicated passage, more involved than any other, every Benedick thinks he has performed when he got married, and thinks he is performing it when he lives as a married man! My dear boon companions, should we not, in default of other wedding gifts and congratulations, should we not give to each married couple one NB as a demerit for repeated inattention, and two NB's to marriage? It can be fatiguing enough to give expression to one simple idea, but to think something so complex and bring unity out of it, to express something so complex in a way that gives each individual element its due and so that everything is present at the same time—yes, verily, he is a great man who can do that. And yet every Benedick does it, and he does it, as he says, 'immediately,' without the need of reflection. If it is to be done 'immediately,' it must be by virtue of a 'higher immediacy,' as they call it, which has permeated reflection

[55] Quoted from Oehlenschläger's *Aladdin*.

entirely.[56] But about this there is not a whisper. To ask any married man about it is a waste of time. The man who once has perpetrated a folly is pursued by the consequences. The folly is to have got into all this, the revenge is that now when it is too late he perceives what he has done. One moment he struts, becomes pathetic, and thinks that he has done something extraordinary in getting married, now he puts his tail between his legs, now it is in self-defense he praises marriage, but a thought-unity which holds together the *disjecta membra* of the most heterogeneous conceptions of life I wait for in vain.

"To be an upright Benedick is fudge, to be a seducer is also fudge, to want to experiment with a woman for the sake of amusement is also fudge. The two latter methods essentially imply on the part of man just as big a concession to woman as does marriage. The seducer wants to avenge himself by deceiving, but the fact that he deceives, that he wants to deceive, that he likes to deceive, is also an expression of his dependence upon woman, and the same is true also of the experimenter.

"If any positive relationship to woman is to be thought of, it must be so thoroughly reflected that by reason of so much reflection it would not become any relationship to her. To be an excellent husband, and yet in secret to seduce every girl; to seem to be a seducer, and yet to cherish secretly within one's heart all the glow of romanticism—that would be something, and in such a case the concession made in the first potency would be obliterated by the second. Man, however, possesses his true ideality only in a reduplication. Every immediate existence must be annihilated, and the annihilation must constantly be insured by a false expression. Such a reduplication woman is unable to grasp, to her it makes man's nature unpronounceable. If a woman could live and move and have her being in such a reduplication, no erotic relationship with her would be thinkable, and her nature being what it notoriously is, the erotic relationship is disturbed by man's nature, which constantly lives and moves in the annihilation of the very thing in which she lives.

"So I perhaps am preaching the monastic life and am called with good reason Eremita? Not a bit of it. Away with the cloister. After all, that too is only an 'immediate' expression for spirit, and spirit cannot be expressed 'immediately.' It is a matter of indifference whether somebody uses gold or silver or paper money, but the man who never pays out a farthing unless it is false will understand what I mean. The man for whom every direct expression is only a *falsum* is better insured than

[56] Perhaps some reader may need to be told that all this about "immediacy" is satirical comment upon Hegelian theory and terminology.

if he entered a monastery, he continues to be a hermit even though he rides day and night in an omnibus."

Hardly had Victor finished than the Ladies' Tailor sprang to his feet, upset a bottle of wine standing in front of him and began as follows:

"Well-spoken, dear boon companions, well-spoken, the more I hear you talk, the more I am convinced that you are co-conspirators; I hail you as such, I understand you as such, for conspirators understand one another from afar. And yet what do you know? What is your bit of theory worth to which you give the semblance of experience, your bit of experience which you revamp into a theory? And after all, you now and then believe in her for an instant and are captivated for an instant. No, I know woman on her weak side, that is to say, I know her. I shun no terror in the pursuit of my studies and shun no measures calculated to confirm what I have understood. For I am a madman, and one must be mad in order to understand her, and if one was not mad before, he must be so when he has understood her. As the robber has his haunt near the noisy highway, and the ant-lion his funnel in the loose sand, and the pirate his hiding-place near the roaring sea, so have I my *maison* of fashion in the midst of the human swarm, seductive, irresistible to a woman, as the Venusberg is to man. Here in a *maison* of fashion one learns to know her practically and from the bottom up, without any theoretical fuss. Oh, if fashion meant nothing more than that a woman in the heat of desire were to throw off all her clothes, well, that would be something. But that is not all of it, fashion is not undisguised sensuality, not tolerated debauchery, but a contraband trade in indecency licensed as decorum. As in heathen Prussia a marriageable girl wore a bell which served as a signal to the men, so likewise is the existence of a woman of fashion a perpetual bell-ringing, not for debauchees but for lickerish voluptuaries. It is believed that fortune is a woman—oh, yes, it is changeable, to be sure, but it is changeable in something, for it is able to give much, and to that extent it is not a woman. No it is fashion that is a woman, for fashion is changeable in nonsense, is logically consistent only in becoming more and more crazy. One hour in my *maison* is worth more than a year and a day outside of it, if one wants to learn to know woman. I say in my *maison,* for it is the only one in the capital of Denmark, no one thinks of competing. Who would dare to risk competition with one who has sacrificed himself completely and continues to sacrifice himself as high priest of this idolatrous worship? No, there is not a distinguished company where my name is not mentioned first and last, there is no middle-class company where my name when it is mentioned does not inspire holy awe like the name of the King, and there is no costume so crazy that, when it is from my *maison,* it is not accompanied by whispers as it walks through the salon; and there is not one lady of gentle birth who dares to pass by my *maison,* and not a single girl of the bourgeois class who passes it by without sighing and thinking, 'If only I could afford it!' Well, she was not in the least deceived. I deceive no one; I furnish the finest, the most costly stuff at the lowest prices, indeed I sell below cost, so I am not eager to win a profit, no, I lay out large sums yearly. And yet I will win, I *will* to win, I am ready to spend my last farthing in bribing and underselling the organs of fashion so that my game may be won. To me it is a rapture beyond compare to bring out the most costly fabrics, to cut them up, to clip pieces out of genuine Brussels lace to make a fool's motley; I sell at the cheapest prices genuine material of the latest fashion. You think perhaps that it is only at particular instants she wishes to be in the fashion; far from it, that is what she wants all the time, and that is her one and only thought. For woman has spirit, but it is about as well employed as was the fortune of the Prodigal Son; and woman possesses reflection in an indescribably high degree, for there is nothing so sacred but in the same breath she finds it commensurable with finery in dress, and the proudest expression of finery is fashion. What wonder she finds it commensurable, for indeed fashion is the holy, and there is no detail so insignificant that she does not know how to relate it to finery in dress, and the most senseless expression of finery is fashion. And there is nothing, nothing whatever in all her attire, not the least ribbon, concerning which she has not a definite view of its relation to fashion and does not instantly detect whether the lady who passed her has noticed it. After all, for whom does she dress, unless it is for other ladies? Even in my *maison,* where she comes indeed to be shown what fashion is, even there she is in fashion. Just as there is a special bathing-costume and a special riding-habit, so also there is a particular kind of dress which it is *moderne* to wear in my *maison.* This costume is not so careless as the negligée in which a lady likes to be surprised early in the forenoon. The point then is her femininity and the coquetry involved in letting herself be surprised. The costume at the tailor's, on the other hand, is calculated to be careless and a bit frivolous without her seeming to be embarrassed by it, because the fashion tailor stands to her in a different relation than the cavalier. The coquetry now consists in displaying herself thus before a man who by reason of his position dare not claim the lady's feminine favor, but must be content with the chance perquisites, which accrue to him abundantly, but without her thinking of it, and without it ever occurring to her to want to be a lady in the eyes of a dressmaker. The point therefore is this, that femininity is in a way left out, and coquetry is nullified by the patronizing superiority of the distinguished lady, who would smile if anyone were to hint at the possibility of such a relationship. In her negligée on the occasion of a social visit she makes an attempt to conceal herself and betrays herself by the concealment; in my *maison* she exposes herself with the utmost nonchalance, for it is only a tailor—and she is a woman. Now her shawl drops a little and exposes her a little—in case I don't know what that means and what she wants, my renown is in jeopardy. Now she purses up her lips aprioristically, now she gesticulates aposteriorically, now she sways on her hips, now she looks at herself in the mirror and sees my admiring phiz behind her, now she lisps, now she minces, now she hovers, now she trails her foot lightly, now she sinks languidly into the armchair, while I in a humble posture offer her a flask of salts and by my adoration cool her heat, now she strikes at me roguishly with her hand, now she drops her handkerchief, without the slightest motion she lets her arm hang indolently, while I bow deeply and pick it up and tender it to her and receive a little patronizing nod. So it is a woman of fashion behaves when she is in my *maison*. Whether Diogenes made any impression upon the woman who in a rather indecent position was lying prostrate in prayer when he enquired whether she supposed the gods could not see her from behind, I do not know; but this I know, that if I were to say to her kneeling ladyship, 'The folds of your gown do not fall in a fashionable way,' she would be more afraid of this than of offending the gods. Woe to the scum, the Cinderella, who does not understand this. *Pro dii immortales,* what then is a woman when she is not in the fashion? *Per deos obsecro,* what is she when she is in the fashion?!

"You wonder whether it is true? Well, just put it to the test: at the moment his sweetheart sinks blissfully upon his breast and whispers incoherently, 'Thine forever,' as she hides her face against his bosom, let the lover say to her, 'Dear Kitty, your curls are not in the fashion.' Perhaps men don't think about this, but the man who knows it and has the reputation of knowing it is the most dangerous man in the kingdom. What blissful hours the lover passes with his sweetheart before the wedding, I do not know, but the blissful hours she passes in my *maison* he has no inkling of. Without my royal license and sanction a wedding is an invalid act, or at least it is a very plebeian affair. Suppose the moment has already arrived when they are about to meet in front of the altar, suppose she is marching up with the best conscience in the world, knowing that everything was bought in my place and was tried on in my presence, and I rush up and say, 'But, my God! gracious lady, the myrtle wreath is all awry!'—perhaps then the ceremony would be postponed. But men know nothing about this sort of thing, one must be a *modiste* to know it. It requires such prodigious reflection to keep track of a woman's reflection that only a man who sacrifices himself to that task is sufficient for it, and then only in case he has a native gift. A man is fortunate therefore if he never takes up with any woman, in any case she doesn't belong to him, even if she doesn't belong to any other man, she belongs to that phantom which is formed by the unnatural intercourse of feminine reflection with feminine reflection, i.e. fashion. For this reason a woman ought always to swear by fashion, then her oath would have some force, for fashion after all is the one thing she is always thinking about, the one thing she is able to think together with and in everything else. From my *maison de mode* has gone out to the world of elegance the glad tidings for every lady of distinction that fashion commands the use of a special sort of headdress when one goes to church, and again that the headdress must be somewhat different for high mass and for evensong. When the bells are ringing the equipages begin to draw up at my door—for it has also been proclaimed that nobody can properly adjust the headdress but me, the arbiter of fashion. I rush out to meet her with a low bow and lead her into my salon. While she vegetates languidly I adjust everything as it should be. The work is finished, she has looked at herself in the glass. Swift as a messenger of the gods I hasten on before her, I have opened the door of the salon and bowed, I hasten to the door of the *maison,* I fold my arms upon my breast like an oriental slave, but encouraged by a gracious curtsy I venture even to throw her an adoring and admiring kiss—she takes her seat in the carriage, ah! she has forgotten her prayer-book, I make haste and hand it to her through the window, permitting myself to remind her once more to hold her head a little to the right and to rearrange things herself a little if in alighting her headdress should become a trifle disordered. She drives away and is edified.

"You think perhaps that only ladies in high society do homage to fashion. Far from it. Just look at my seamstresses, upon whose toilet I spare no pains in order that the dogmas of fashion may be emphatically proclaimed from my *maison*. They compose a chorus of nitwits, and I the high priest go before them as a shining example, prepared to squander everything if only by the help of fashion I may make every woman ridiculous. For when a seducer boasts that the virtue of every woman is vendible to the right bidder, I don't believe him, but I do believe that before long every woman will be satanized by the crazy and defiling self-reflection of fashion, which depraves her more thoroughly than if she were to be seduced. I have put it to the proof more than once. If I am not able to accomplish it by myself, I egg her on by the help of the female slaves of fashion who belong to her own class. For as one can train rats to bite rats, so is the bite of a satanized woman like that of a tarantula, and it is dangerous above all when a man takes part in it. Whether I am serving the devil or serving God, I do not know, but I am in the right, I will be in the right, I will it, I will it as long as I have a single farthing left, I will it until the blood spurts from my fingers. The physiologist draws the form of a woman to show the dreadful effect of corsets, and alongside of this he draws the normal form. That's all very well, but only the one drawing has the validity of truth—for they all wear corsets. Describe in this way the miserable stunted extravagance of the fashion-mad woman, describe the insidious self-reflection which consumes her, and describe the womanly modesty which knows about itself last of all; do this well, and with that thou hast passed judgment upon woman, and in reality hast passed a damning judgment. If ever I discover such a girl, contented and humble, who is not yet depraved by indecent intercourse with women, she shall fall nevertheless. I entangle her in my toils, now she stands at the place of sacrifice, i.e. in my *maison*. With the most disdainful look a haughty nonchalance can arm itself with I take her measures, she is ready to perish with fright, a peal of laughter from the adjoining room where my trained assistants sit annihilates her. Dressed up in the fashion she looks as crazy as a lunatic, as crazy even as one who could not be admitted into a lunatic asylum. Then she departs from me full of bliss, no man, nor even a god, could terrify her, for she is indeed in the fashion.

"You understand me now, you understand why I call you co-conspirators, though at a great distance from me. You understand now my interpretation of woman. Everything in life is a matter of fashion, the fear of God is a matter of fashion, and love, and hoop-skirts, and a ring in the nose. So with all my might I will abet the lofty genius who desires to laugh at the most ludicrous of all animals. Since woman has reduced everything to fashion, I by the aid of fashion will prostitute her as she deserves. I give myself no rest, I, the Ladies' Tailor; my soul chafes when I think of my task, she must yet come to the point of wearing a ring in her nose. Therefore seek no sweetheart, forego love as you would shun the most dangerous neighborhood, for also your sweetheart would have to come to the point of wearing a ring in her nose."

Thereupon Johannes the Seducer spoke as follows:

"Esteemed boon companions, is Satan plaguing you? You talk like undertakers, your eyes are red with tears and not with wine. You move me almost to tears, for an unfortunate lover is very sadly situated in life. *Hinc illae lacrymae*. Now I am a fortunate lover, and my only desire is to remain such constantly. Perhaps this is a concession to woman, which Victor is so much afraid of? Why not? It is a concession. The fact that I undo the wire of this champagne bottle is also a concession, that I let its foam spurt into the goblet is also a concession, that I raise the goblet to my lips is also a concession—now I have drained it—*concedo*. Now, however, the goblet is empty, so I make no more concessions. Thus it is with the girls. If some unlucky lover has bought a kiss too dearly, that only proves to me that he knows neither how to help himself to a dish nor to abstain from it. I never buy it too dearly, I leave that to the girls. What is the meaning of this? To me it means the most beautiful, the most delicious, and pretty nearly the most persuasive *argumentum ad hominum;* but since every woman at least once in her life possesses this primitive power of argumentation, why should I not let myself be persuaded? Our young friend would like to *think* the thing. In fact he can buy what the confectioner calls a 'kiss,' just to look at it. I want to enjoy. No nonsense! Hence an old song says about a kiss, *Es ist kaum zu sehen, es ist nur für Lippen, die genau sich verstehen*[57]—which understand one another so perfectly that reflection is impertinence and folly. The man who is twenty years old and does not comprehend that there is a categorical imperative: Enjoy thyself—that man is a fool. And he who does not seize the opportunity is a Wesleyan Methodist.[58] But you are unfortunate lovers, hence you want to remodel woman. God forbid it. I like her as she is, exactly as she is. Even Constantine's notion that she is a jest implies a secret wish. I, on the other hand, am gallant—and why not? Gallantry costs nothing and brings in everything and is the condition of all erotic enjoyment. Gallantry is the Freemasonry of sensuousness and sensuality as between man and woman. It is a primitive language of nature, like love's language in general. It is not made up of sounds but of masked desires which are constantly changing their rôles. I can understand very well that an unfortunate lover is ungallant enough to want to convert his deficit into a bill of exchange on eternity. Yet at the same time I do not understand it, for to me woman possesses abundant intrinsic value. That I will

[57] It is hardly to be seen, it is only for lips which understand one another perfectly.

[58] Literally, a Christianfelder, Christianfeld being the name of a town in South Jutland where the Moravian Brethren were numerous.

assert of every woman, and it is true, but it is certain also that I am the only one not deceived by this truth. As to whether a deflowered woman is worth less than man is an item not to be found in my price list. I do not pluck broken flowers, I leave that to married men for a decoration at Shrovetide. Whether Eduard, e.g., would think it over and fall in love again with Cornelia,[59] or would recite his love affair by heart, I leave to him. Why should I get mixed up in other people's affairs? What I thought of her I explained to her at the right time, and she truly has convinced me, convinced me to my absolute satisfaction, that my gallantry was well placed. *Concedo. Concessi.* If a new Cordelia comes under my eye, I shall enact comedy 'Ring No. 2.'[60] But you are unfortunate lovers and conspirators and are more deceived than the girls, in spite of the fact that you have abundant talents. But resolution, the resolution of desire, is the gist of living. Our young friend always remains on the outside, Victor is an unpractical enthusiast, Constantine has purchased his common sense too dearly, the Ladies' Tailor is a madman. What's the good of all that? Though the four of you were after one girl, it would come to nothing but wind. Let one have enthusiasm enough to idealize, taste enough to take part in the festive enjoyment of clinking the glasses, sense enough to break off, to break off as absolutely as death, madness enough to want to enjoy again—then one is the darling of the gods and of the girls. But what's the use of talking here? I don't want to make proselytes, nor is this the place for it. I enjoy wine, to be sure, and I enjoy the abundance of the banquet, but let me have a girl for my company, and then I talk. So I thank Constantine for the banquet and the wine and the excellent appointments, the speeches, however, were not much to boast of. But in order that it may not end thus I will speak in praise of women.

"As he who is to speak about the divine must be inspired by divinity in order to speak worthily, so that divinity itself teaches what one is to say, just so it is with women. For woman is further even than the deity from being the whim of a man's brain, a day-dream, something one happens to think of all by oneself and can dispute about *pro et contra.* No, only from her does one learn how to talk about her. And the more women one has learned from, so much the better. The first time a man is simply a learner, the second time he has already been coached, just as in a learned disputation one can use the last opponent's complements

[59] In "The Seducer's Diary," which concludes the first part of *Either/Or,* Cordelia is the young woman seduced by Johannes, and Eduard her former suitor.

[60] The reference is to a comedy by Fr. L. Schröder (following Farquhar) which in a translation by Fr. Schwartz had a short run in Copenhagen in 1830.

against the next. Nevertheless there is no lost time. For the notion that a kiss is a smacking of the lips, that an embrace is an exertion, is no more absurd than that this lesson is exhausted like the proof of a proposition in geometry which remains the same though the letters are altered. Such notions only apply to mathematics and ghosts, not to love and to women, where every new experience is a new proof and demonstrates in another way the truth of the same proposition. It is my joy that the female sex, far from being more imperfect than man, is on the contrary the most perfect. However I will clothe my speech in a myth, and for woman's sake whom you have so unjustly offended I shall be glad if it may prove a judgment upon your souls for the fact that sensual pleasure is brought before your eyes but flees from you like the fruits from Tantalus, because you have fled from it and have offended woman. For only thus is she offended, though she is exalted high above offense and everyone is punished who ventures to offend her. I do not offend anyone. The idea that I do is the invention of married men and is a slander, whereas on the contrary I appreciate her much more than does the married man.

"Originally there was one sex, that of the man—so the Greeks report. Gloriously endowed was he, so that he reflected honor upon the gods who created him, so gloriously endowed that the gods were in the position in which a poet sometimes finds himself when he has expended all his forces upon a poetic creation: they became envious of man. Yea, what was worse, they feared him, lest he might bow unwillingly to their yoke. They feared, though it was without reason, that he might cause heaven itself to totter. So then they had conjured up a power they hardly thought themselves capable of curbing. Then there was concern and commotion in the council of the gods. Much had they lavished upon the creation of man, that was magnanimous; now everything must be risked, for everything was at stake, this was self-defense. So thought the gods. And it was impossible to revoke him, as a poet may revoke his thought. By force he could not be compelled, or else the gods themselves might have compelled him, but it was precisely about this they had misgivings. He must then be taken captive and compelled by a power which was weaker than his own and yet stronger, strong enough to compel. What a marvellous power that must be! Necessity, however, teaches the gods to surpass themselves in inventiveness. They sought and pondered and found. This power was woman, the miracle of creation, even in the eyes of the gods a greater miracle than man, a discovery for which the gods in their naïveté could not help patting themselves on the back. What more can be said in honor of her than that she should be able to do what even the gods did not think themselves capable of doing, what more can be said than that she was able? How marvellous she must be to be capable of it! This was a ruse of the gods. Cunningly the enchantress was fashioned; the very instant she had enchanted man she transformed herself and held him captive in all the prolixities of finiteness. This is what the gods wanted. But what can be more delicious, more pleasurable, more enchanting, than this which the gods as they were fighting for their own power devised as the only thing that could decoy man? And verily it is so, for woman is the unique and the most seductive power in heaven and on earth. In this comparison man is something exceedingly imperfect.

"And the ruse of the gods succeeded. However, it did not always succeed. In every generation there were some men, individuals, who became aware of the deception. They perceived her loveliness, it is true, more than did any of the others, but they had an inkling what it was all about. These are what I call erotics, and I reckon myself among them; men call them seducers, woman has no name for them, such a type is for her unmentionable. These erotics are the fortunate ones. They live more luxuriously than the gods, for they eat constantly only that which is more precious than ambrosia and drink what is more delicious than nectar; they dine upon the most seductive fancy which issued from the most artful thought of the gods, they dine constantly upon bait. Oh, luxury beyond compare! Oh, blissful mode of living! They dine constantly upon bait—and are never caught. The other men set to and eat bait as the vulgar eat caviar, and are caught. Only the erotic knows how to appreciate bait, to appreciate it infinitely. Woman divines this, and hence there is a secret understanding between him and her. But he knows also that it is bait, and this is a secret he keeps to himself.

"That nothing more marvellous, nothing more delicious, nothing more seductive can be devised than a woman, the gods vouch for, and the necessity which sharpened their invention; and in turn it vouches for them that they risked their all and in the forming of her nature set heaven and earth in commotion.

"I leave for a moment the myth. The concept of man corresponds exactly to the idea of man. One therefore can think of a single man existing and nothing more than that. On the other hand, the idea of woman is a generality which is not exhaustively exemplified in any single woman. She is not *ebenbürtig* with man but is later, is a part of man, and yet more complete than he. Whether it be that the gods took a part of him while he slept (fearful of awakening him if they took too much), or that they divided him in equal parts so that woman is a half

—in any case it is man that was divided. So it is only as a subdivision she is related to man as his mate. She is a deception, but that she is only in her second phase and for him who is deceived. She is finiteness, but in her first phase she is finiteness raised to the highest power in the delusive infinity of all divine and human illusions. Not yet is the deception—but one more instant and a man is deceived. She is finiteness, and so she is a collective term, to say one woman means many women. This the erotic alone understands, and hence he is so prompt to love many, never being deceived, but sucking up all the voluptuous delights the cunning gods were capable of preparing. Therefore woman cannot be exhaustively expressed by any formula but is an infinity of finitudes. He who is bent upon thinking her idea is like one who gazes into a sea of nebulous shapes which are constantly forming, or like one who is bewildered by looking at the billows with their foaming crests which constantly elude him; for her idea is only a workshop of possibilities, and for the erotic these possibilities are the never-failing source of enthusiasm.

"Thus the gods fashioned her, delicate and ethereal as the mists of a summer's night and yet plump like a ripened fruit, light as a bird in spite of the fact that she carried a world of craving, light because the play of forces is unified at the invisible center of a negative relationship in which she is related to herself, slim of stature, designed with definite proportions and yet to the eye seeming to swell with the wave-lines of beauty, complete and yet as if only now she were finished, cooling, delicious, refreshing as new-fallen snow, blushing with serene transparency, happy as a jest which causes one to forget everything, tranquilizing as the goal whereunto desire tends, satisfying by being herself the incitement of desire. And this is what the gods had counted upon, that man upon catching sight of her should be amazed as one who gets a sight of himself in the glass, and yet again as if he were familiar with this sight, amazed as one who sees himself reflected in perfection, amazed as one who sees what he never had an inkling of and yet sees, as it appears to him, what must necessarily have occurred to him, what is a necessary part of existence, and yet sees this as the riddle of existence. Precisely this contradiction in his amazement is what elicits his desire, while amazement eggs him on nearer and nearer, so that he cannot desist from looking, cannot cease to seem familiar with this sight, without, however, quite daring to approach, although he cannot cease to desire.

"When the gods had thus forecast her form they were fearful lest even they might not be able to express it. But what they feared most was woman herself. They did not dare to let her know how beautiful she was, fearing that she might spoil their ruse if she were cognizant of it. Then was the crown placed upon the work. The gods made her perfect, but then they hid all this from her in the ignorance of innocence and hid it from her once more in the impenetrable mystery of modesty. She was perfect, and victory was assured. An enticing thing she was, at one moment she enticed by avoiding a man and betaking herself to flight, she was irresistible for the fact that she herself was resistance. The gods were jubilant. And indeed no allurement has been discovered in the world equal to woman, and there is no allurement so absolute as that of innocence, and no temptation so fascinating as that of modesty, and no deception so incomparable as woman. She knows nothing, and yet modesty contains an instinctive presentiment, she is separated from man, and the wall of modesty is a more decisive separation than the sword of Aladdin which separated him from Gulvare[61]—and yet the erotic, who like Pyramis lays his ear against the separating wall of modesty, has a presentiment, remotely sensed, of all the lust of desire behind it.

"So it is that woman tempts. As food for the gods men present the most glorious things, they have nothing more glorious to offer. In the same manner woman is show-fruit, the gods know nothing to compare with it. She *is,* she is here, present, and yet she is infinitely remote, hidden in modesty, until she betrays her hiding place, by what means she does not know, nature itself is the sly informer. She is roguish as a child at play who peeks from his place of concealment, and yet her roguishness is inexplicable, for she herself is not aware of it and is always inscrutable, inscrutable when she hides her eyes, inscrutable when she emits a glance as her messenger, which no thought, still less a word, is able to follow. And yet a glance is the interpreter of the soul —where then is the explanation when even the interpreter speaks unintelligibly? Placid is she as the stillness of the evening hour when no leaf is stirring, placid as a consciousness which is not yet aware of anything, the movements of her heart are as regular as if it did not exist, and yet the erotic who listens with stethoscopic precision discovers the dithyrambic beat of passion as an unconscious accompaniment. Careless as a puff of wind, content like the deep sea, and yet full of longing, as the inexplicable depths always are. Brothers, my mind is assuaged, indescribably assuaged; I conceive that my life too expresses an idea, even if you do not comprehend me. I too have found out the secret of ex-

[61] An allusion to Oehlenschläger's *Aladdin.*

istence, I too am in the service of something divine, and to a certainty I do not serve for naught. As woman is a deception on the part of the gods, this is the true expression of the fact that she wants to be seduced, and as woman is not an idea, therefore the truth is on the side of the erotic who wants to love as many as possible.

"What rapture it is to relish the deception without being deceived, only the erotic understands. How blissful it is to be seduced, only woman knows. I know it from women, though I have never given time to anyone to explain this to me, but have taken my revenge and served the idea by a breach as abrupt as death; for a bride and a breach[62] correspond to one another as female and male. Woman only knows this, and knows it by means of her seducer. No married man comprehends such a thing; she never speaks to him about it. She puts up with her fate, she has a presentiment that thus it must be, that only once can she be seduced. Hence she is never really angry with her seducer. That is, if he actually did seduce her and expressed the idea. A broken marriage vow and things like that are of course galimatias and no seduction. So it is not so great a misfortune for a woman to be seduced, and she is lucky to be so. A girl who is admirably seduced may make an admirable wife. If I were not so good at seducing (though I feel deeply my inferiority in this respect), and if I wanted to be a married man, I would always choose a seduced woman, so that I might not have to begin by seducing my wife. Marriage also expresses an idea, but in relation to this idea that particular thing [i.e. innocence][63] is a matter of complete indifference which in relation to my idea is the absolute. A marriage therefore ought never to be planned to begin as if it were the beginning of a story of seduction. This much is certain, that for every woman there is a corresponding seducer. Her good fortune consists in encountering precisely him.

"By means of marriage, on the other hand, the gods conquer. Then the aforetime seduced woman walks through life by the side of her husband, looks sometimes longingly backward, puts up with her fate until she has reached life's limit. She dies, but not in the same sense that men die; she is volatilized and resolved again into the inexplicable element from which the gods formed her, she vanishes like a dream, like a provisional form the time for which is past. For what is woman but a dream?—and yet she is the highest reality! So it is the erotic under-

[62] A grim pun. For *en Brud* means a bride and *et Brud,* a breach or break, differentiated only by the common and the neuter article.

[63] cf. the motto of "The Seducer's Diary" in *Either/Or: Sua Passion predominante è la giovin principiante.*

stands her and leads[64] her and is led by her at the moment of seduction —outside of time, where she belongs as an illusion. With a husband she becomes temporal, and he through her.

"Oh, marvellous Nature, if I did not admire thee, she would teach me to do so, for she is the *venerabile* of existence.[65] Gloriously hast thou fashioned her, but still more glorious for the fact that thou didst never make one woman like another. In the case of man the essential is the essential and therefore always the same; in the case of woman the accidental is the essential, hence the inexhaustible variety. Brief is her glory, but the pain I quickly forget as if I had not even sensed it, when the same glory is proffered to me again. Yes, I too perceive the uncomeliness which may make its appearance later, but she is not thus with her seducer."

They rose from the table. Only a hint from Constantine was needed; the participants understood among themselves with military punctuality when it was time for "Right about! Face!" With the invisible wand of command, which in his hand was as elastic as a wishing-rod, Constantine touched them once again in order by a fleeting reminiscence to recall the banquet and the mood of sheer enjoyment which had been in a measure suppressed by the reasoning processes of the speakers, and in order that, as in the phenomenon of resonance, the tone of festivity which had vanished might return again to the guests for the brief instant of an echo, he gave the parting salute with a full glass, he emptied it, he flung it against the door in the wall behind him. The others followed his example and performed this symbolic act with the solemnity of initiates. The pleasure of breaking off was thus given its rights, this imperial pleasure which, though briefer than any other, is yet emancipating as no other is. With a libation every enjoyment of the table ought to begin, but this oblation wherewith one flings the glass away into annihilation and oblivion and tears oneself passionately away from every remembrance as if one were in mortal danger, this libation is made to the gods of the underworld. One *breaks* off, and it requires strength to do it, greater strength than to cut a knot with the sword, because the difficulty of the knot bestows passion, but the strength required for breaking off one must bestow upon oneself. In a certain outward sense the result is the same, but in an artistic respect there is

[64] *Fører* means to lead—*forfører,* to lead astray, seduce. This is not a mere pun: S.K. contended that Don Giovanni was not so much the seducer as the seduced—all the women wanted to seduce him.

[65] cf. "nature's *venerabile*" in *Enten/Eller* (*Either/Or*), Vol. I, p. 416.

a heaven-wide difference whether one leaves off (comes to an end) or breaks off by an act of freedom, whether it is an accident or a passionate decision, whether it is all over like the ballad of the schoolmaster when there is no more of it or is brought to an end by the imperial sword-stroke of pleasure, whether it is a triviality everybody has experienced or that mystery which escapes the majority.

It was a symbolic act of Constantine's when he threw away the goblet, and in another sense this throw was a decisive blow, for at the last blow the doors were thrown open and one saw, like him who has presumptuously knocked at the portal of death and sees when it is opened the puissance of annihilation, so one saw that crew of destruction prepared to lay everything waste—a memento which in a second changed the participants into fugitives from that place, and in the same second transformed as it were the whole environment into a ruin.

A carriage stood ready at the door. At Constantine's invitation they took their places and drove away in good spirits, for that tableau of destruction in the background had imparted a new elasticity to their souls.

A mile from the starting-place the carriage halted. Here Constantine took leave of them as host, informing them that there were five carriages at their service, so that each might follow his own inclination, drive whither he would, alone, or, if he would in company, and with whomsoever he would. So it is that a rocket by the force of powder rises as a single shoot, stands for an instant still, collected as one entity, then disperses to all the winds.

While the horses were being hitched the nocturnal guests strolled a little way along the road. The fresh morning air purified their hot blood by its coolness, to the refreshment of which they abandoned themselves completely, whereas upon me their figures and the groups they formed made a fantastic impression. For that the morning sun shines upon field and meadow and upon every creature which at night found rest and strength to arise jubilant with the sun—with this we have a sympathetic and wholesome understanding; but a nocturnal party beheld by morning illumination, in the midst of a smiling rustic environment, makes an almost uncanny impression. One begins to think of ghosts which are surprised by the dawn of day, of elves which cannot find the crevice through which they are accustomed to vanish because it is visible only in the dark, of unfortunates for whom the difference between day and night has become obliterated by the monotony of their suffering.

A footpath led them through a bit of field to a hedged garden, behind which a modest country house betrayed itself in the distance. At the end of the garden next the field there was an arbor formed by trees. Noticing that there was someone in the arbor, they all became curious, and with the searching look of observers the besiegers closed in around this friendly hiding-place, looking as tense as the emissaries of the police when they are bent on outwitting somebody. Like emissaries of the police—well, I must confess that their outward appearance made possible the confusion that the emissaries of the police might be seeking them. Each had taken up his position to peek in, when Victor drew back a step and said to his neighbor, "Why, my God! it's Judge William and his wife!"

They were surprised—I do not mean the two whom the foliage concealed, that happy pair, too much absorbed in domestic pleasures to be observers, too confident of their security to believe themselves the object of anyone's attention, except that of the morning sun which peeked in upon them with delight, while a gentle breeze rocked the boughs above them, and while the rural peace like everything else around them protected this little arbor. The happy married couple were not surprised and noticed nothing. That they were married people was clear enough, it was to be seen at a glance, alas, when one stands in a relation of consanguinity with an observer.[66] Although nothing, nothing in the wide world, nothing evident, nothing hiddenly evident, nothing hidden, has any notion of wanting to disturb the happiness of the lovers, nevertheless when they are sitting alongside of one another they do not feel themselves thus secure; blissful they are, and yet it is as though there were some power that wished to separate them, so closely do they cling to one another, and yet it is as though there were an enemy at hand against whom they must protect themselves, and yet it is as though they never could be sufficiently assured. It is not thus with married people, and not thus with that married couple in the arbor. How long they had been married it was not possible, however, to determine precisely. The way the wife busied herself with the tea-table did seem to indicate the assurance acquired by long practice, and yet she showed an almost childish eagerness in this occupation, as if she were a recently wedded woman in that intermediate state where she does not yet know definitely whether marriage is play or earnest, whether being a housewife is a business or a game or a pastime. Perhaps she may have been married for a considerable time but did not as a rule preside at the tea-table, perhaps she did so only here in the country, or perhaps she did it only that morning, which may possibly have had a special significance for them. Who can

[66] S.K. himself, being a constant and acute observer, frequently remarks upon this trait, and even likens himself to a detective.

decide? All reckoning is to a certain extent futile when it has to do with one who possesses originality of soul, for this prevents time from leaving its mark. When the sun shines in all its summer splendor, one thinks at once that it must be to celebrate some solemn occasion or another (it cannot surely shine thus for daily use), or that this is the first time it shines so brightly, or at least one of the first times (it surely could not be repeated during a long course of time). So thinks he who sees it only once, or sees it for the first time—and it was the first time I saw the Judge's wife. He who sees this sight every day may think differently—supposing he really sees the same thing. However, that is properly the Judge's business.

So then our amiable housewife was occupied: she poured boiling water into two tea cups (presumably to warm them thoroughly), she emptied that out, set the cup on a tray, poured in the tea, served the condiments, so all was ready—was this play or earnest? In case someone is not ordinarily a tea-lover, he ought to have sat in the Judge's place, for at that moment this drink seemed to me most inviting, and only the inviting look of the kind lady herself seemed more inviting.

Presumably she had not had time to talk until this moment, now she broke the silence, and as she passed the tea she said, "Be quick now, dear, and drink while the tea is hot; after all, the morning air is rather cool, and so the least thing I can do is to be a little careful of you." "The least?" rejoined the Judge laconically. "Well, or the most, or the only thing." The Judge looked at her inquiringly, and while she was helping herself she continued, "You interrupted me yesterday when I was about to say this, but I have thought it over again, many a time I have thought it over, and especially now—you know well enough what has suggested it to me—anyway it is certainly true that if you hadn't married you would have become a much greater person in the world." With the cup still on the tray the Judge sipped the first mouthful with obvious delight and felt refreshed—or was it perhaps joy in the lovely woman. I believe it was that, but she seemed only to rejoice that it tasted so good to him. Then he put the cup on the table beside him, took out a cigar and said, "May I light it at your samovar?" "With all my heart," she replied, taking a glowing coal with the teaspoon and handing it to him. He lit his cigar and put his arm about her waist while she leaned against his shoulder, he turned his head the other way to blow out the smoke, then his eyes rested upon her with all the devotion a look can express; he smiled, but this smile of joy had a little ingredient of sad irony; finally he said, "Do you really believe that, my girl?" "Believe what?" said she. He was silent again, the smile predominated, yet his voice was perfectly serious when he said, "Then I forgive your former foolishness since you yourself have forgotten it so quickly, for you speak like one of the foolish women—what sort of a great person would I have become in the world?" His wife seemed for an instant embarrassed by this rejoinder, but she promptly collected herself and elaborated her point with feminine eloquence. The Judge looked straight ahead of him, he did not interrupt her, but as she went on he began to thrum on the table with the fingers of his right hand, he hummed a tune, the words of the ballad were momentarily audible; just as the woven pattern in a piece of damask in one aspect is visible and again disappears, so did the words fade again into the humming of the ballad's tune: "Her husband went out to the forest and cut him the cudgels white." After this melodramatic address, i.e. the wife's explanation of her cause accompanied by the humming of the Judge, the dialogue began again. "You still are unaware," he said, "that the Danish law permits a man to beat his wife, the only trouble is that it doesn't specify on what occasions it is permissible." His wife smiled at the threat and continued, "But why can't I ever get you to be serious when I speak of this? You don't understand me. Believe me, I mean it honestly, it seems to me a very pretty thought. Of course, if you were not my husband, I shouldn't dare to think it, but here now I have thought it, for your sake and for my sake, so please be serious, for my sake, and answer me honestly." "No, you can't get me to be serious, and no serious answer do you get. I must either laugh at you and make you forget it as I have done before, or else thrash you, or you must stop talking about it, or I must find some other way of keeping you silent. You see it's a joke, and that is why there are so many expedients possible." He arose, pressed a kiss upon her forehead, put her arm in his and disappeared in a heavily wooded path which led away from the arbor.

The arbor remained empty, there was nothing more to be done here, the corps of occupation retreated without any booty. None of them seemed pleased with this result; however, the others[67] contented themselves with some malicious remarks. They turned back but missed Victor. He had rounded the corner, skirted the garden and reached the rural edifice. Here the door of a garden-room stood open on the side of the lawn, and a window facing the street was open also. Presumably he had seen something which attracted his attention. He entered the door, and just as he was leaping out through the window he encountered the others who had been searching for him. Triumphantly he holds up a

[67] i.e. *not* the sympathetic reporter of this scene.

packet of papers and shouts, "A manuscript written by the Judge! If I have published the other one,[68] it is no more than my duty to publish this too." He thrust it into his pocket, or rather he meant to stick it into his pocket, but when he had bent his arm and already had the hand and the manuscript half-way in his pocket, I stole it from him.

But who then am I? Let nobody ask. If it has not occurred to anybody to ask, I am relieved, for then I am over the worst of it. Besides, I am not worth asking about, for I am the most insignificant of all things, it makes me quite bashful to have people ask about me. I am "pure being"[69] and therefore almost less than nothing. I am the pure being which is the accompaniment of everything yet never observable, because I am constantly *aufgehoben*. I am like the line above which is written the task for the pupil to reckon out, and below it the answer—who cares about the line? I myself am not capable of doing anything whatever,[70] for even the idea of stealing the manuscript from Victor was not my own whim, but even this whim of "borrowing" the manuscript, as the thieves say, was borrowed from Victor. And now in publishing the manuscript I again am nothing whatever, for the manuscript was written by the Judge, and I as editor am in my nothingness only a nemesis upon Victor, who surely meant to get his revenge by publishing it.

[68] Victor Eremita appears on the title page of *Either/Or* as the pseudonymous editor, who therefore was responsible for the publication of the letters of Judge William which constitute the second half of that book.

[69] Here we have a satire upon Hegel which might apply as well to Kant.

[70] The Lutheran dogma of the total impotence of man was frequently the subject of S.K.'s reflection. He takes it seriously; but cf. a passage in the *Efterskrift*, pp. 450-474, where the comical aspect is also made the subject of reflection. But "to be nothing, less than nothing" was his own poignant experience in religious conversion.

VARIOUS OBSERVATIONS ABOUT MARRIAGE IN REPLY TO OBJECTIONS

by

A Married Man

Motto: "The deceived is wiser than the not-deceived."

[Plutarch (*De gloria Atheniensium,* 5) reports that Gorgias uttered these words with reference to spectators at the theater.]

MY dear Reader,

In case thou hast not time and opportunity to spend half a score of the years of thy life in travelling around the world to see everything the globe-trotter gets to know, in case thou hast not talent or occasion by many years of practice in a foreign tongue to become familiar with the distinctive character of national individuality as this is revealed to the student, in case thou dost not cherish the intention of discovering a new astronomic system which shall supplant both the Copernican system and the Ptolemaic—then go and get married; and in case thou hast time for the first, talent for the second and a notion of doing the last, then go and get married all the same. Even if thou didst not manage to see the whole terrestrial clot or to talk in many tongues or to be knowing about the heavens, thou wilt not regret it; for marriage is decidedly the most important journey of discovery a man can undertake, every other sort of acquaintance with life is superficial in comparison with that acquired by a married man, for he and he alone has thoroughly fathomed the depths of life. Yes, it is true, no poet will ever be able to say of thee as the poets say of the crafty Ulysses that he saw many cities of men and learned to know their dispositions,[1] but the question is whether he would not have learned just as many things and just as pleasant if he had stayed at home with Penelope. If no one else holds this opinion, my wife does, and so, if I do not err egregiously, does every wife. Such a majority is a little more than a simple majority, and so much more that he who has the wives on his side will eventually have the husbands. Yes, it is true that on this expedition the company of travellers is small, that it is not as in the case of a five- or ten-year expedition a numerous party, which also, be it observed, remains ever the same; but then for marriage is reserved a peculiar sort of acquaintanceship, which is the most marvellous of all, where as a rule every new event which comes about is the most welcome.

So all honor be to marriage, and honor too to everyone who speaks in praise of it. If a beginner may be so bold as to take the liberty of expressing his opinion, I would say that the reason it seems to me so marvellous is that everything turns upon insignificant things which the divine element in marriage transforms however into significance for the believer. And then again all these insignificant items have the remarkable characteristic that nothing can be evaluated in advance and nothing exhaustively comprehended by a cursory estimate; but while

[1] The first line of the *Odyssey*.

judgment is at a standstill and imagination is in a fix and calculation reckons amiss and sagacity is in despair, the married life goes on and is transformed from glory unto glory, the insignificant becomes ever more and more significant, by means of the miracle—for the believer. But a believer one must be, and a married man who is not a believer is the most tiresome customer, a real skeleton in the closet. Nothing is more odious when occasionally one sets out in company with others to be diverted by beholding demonstrations and experiments in natural magic, nothing is more odious than to have an obstinate fellow along who is incredulous about everything although he is never able to explain the tricks. However, one can stand a nuisance like that, it doesn't often happen that one sets out on such a quest, and moreover one may reap some advantage from such a crusty spectator by seeing him take part in the game. Generally the professor of magic picks upon him and lets him hold the light, entertaining the rest of us by his sagacity, just as the dunce in a play entertains us by his stupidity. But such a surly churl of a married man ought to be put in a sack like a parricide[2] and thrown into the water. How distressing it is to see a woman expending all her lovableness to convince him, and to see him, after he had received the initiation which entitles him to be a believer, bent only upon spoiling the whole thing—yes, spoiling the whole thing, for, jesting aside, marriage is after all in so many ways like an experiment in natural magic, and truly a marvellous experiment. It is disgusting to listen to a priest who doesn't himself believe what he says, but it is still more disgusting to see a married man who is not a believer in the order to which he belongs, and it is the more revolting because the hearer can desert the priest, but the wife cannot desert her husband; she cannot, she will not, she doesn't wish to—and even this fails to convince him.

People usually talk only about a married man's unfaithfulness, but what is just as bad is a married man's lack of faith. Faith is the only thing required of him, and faith makes amends for everything. Let understanding and sagacity and refinement add up, reckon out and describe how a married man ought to be—there is only one trait which makes him amiable, that is faith, absolute faith in marriage. Let expertness in living determine precisely what is required of a married man in the way of fidelity—there is only one fidelity, one honesty, which is truly amiable and comprises all in itself, that is, honesty towards God and one's wife and one's order which has no wish to deny the miracle.

[2] As was prescribed by an ancient Roman law.

So this is what gives me confidence when I elect to write about marriage. For though I make no claim to any other proficiency, I can hold my own in one respect, namely, in conviction. That I have conviction I know of myself, and I know it from my wife, which to me is a criterion of the greatest importance; for though it is seemly for a woman to be silent in the congregation and not to meddle with science and art, yet what is said about marriage should be of such a sort that it meets with her approval. It does not follow that she is to appraise everything critically, that kind of reflection does not suit her, but she must have an absolute veto, and her approval must be respected as satisfactory security. My conviction then is my one legitimation, and again the guarantee for my conviction is the weight of responsibility under which my life lies like that of every other married man. True, I do not feel this weight as a burden but as a blessing; true, I do not feel this bond as bondage but as liberation; but yet it is there—the bond, no, the innumerable bonds by which I am securely tied to life, as the tree is by the manifold ramifications of its root. Suppose that everything were to be changed for me—great God, if that were possible, suppose that I were to find myself in bondage by being wed, what then were Laocoön's misery compared with mine! For no one serpent and not ten of them could so compress and so alarmingly and so tightly wind about a man's body as the married life which binds me in a hundred ways, and so—in this event would fetter me with a hundred chains. Observe then (if this may be regarded as a guarantee) that whereas I feel glad and content and give thanks without ceasing for my earthly good fortune, I also sense the horror which in this way may appall a man, the hell which reveals itself when a married man, *adscriptus glebae,* would tear himself loose and discovers thereby only how impossible it is, would sever one chain and discovers thereby only that there is another chain more elastic which binds him indissolubly—in case this is a sufficient negative guarantee that what I have to say does not consist of idle thoughts conceived in a spare moment, or of ingenious cobwebs of the brain calculated to catch other men, then do not disdain what I have to say.

I am very far from being a learned man, I make no claim to that, it would put me to embarrassment if I were foolish enough to affect any such thing. I am not a dialectician, not a philosopher, but, with such meager opportunities for learning as I have, I have respect for science and for all that persons of superior talent propound in explanation of existence. But on the other hand I am a married man, and when it is a question of marriage I fear nobody. I would confidently and cheerfully assume the professor's chair if that were required of me, though what

I have to say is not altogether appropriate to that place. I maintain my thesis buoyantly against all the dialecticians of the world, Satan himself shall not be able to wrest from me my conviction. Let captious *chicaneurs* heap together all the objections against marriage, they will nevertheless have to throw up their hands. One quickly divides these objections into two parts: one sort is answered best, as Hamann declares, by saying bah! and the other can be disposed of by argument. In all other respects I am rather thin-skinned, I cannot well put up with having people laugh at me. This is a weakness which hitherto I have not been able to overcome. But if anyone would laugh at me because I am a married man, I am in this respect invulnerable to laughter, in this respect I feel a courage which is almost in contrast with the habitual life of an assistant judge who goes from his home to the law court and from the court to his home, constantly occupied with documents. Suppose I were to find myself in a circle of clever pates who were in conspiracy to render marriage ridiculous and to make a mock of holy things—arm them with all wittiness, point their mocking darts with the sting which is whetted by an ambiguous relationship with the other sex, dip the darts in the malice which is not stupid but acquired by devilish shrewdness—and I am not afraid. Wherever I am, even if it were in the fiery furnace, when I have to talk about marriage I am aware of nothing, there is an angel with me, or rather I am far away, I am with her, with her whom I still love constantly with the blissful resolution of youth; I have still, although married for a considerable number of years, I have still the honor of fighting under the victorious banner of a happy first love alongside of her by reason of whom I feel the significance of my life, feel that it has significance and manifold significance. For what for the rebellious are fetters, and for slavish minds are hard duties, are for me titles and dignities which I would not exchange for those of the King: King of the Wends and of the Goths, Duke of Schleswig, etc. Whether, after all, these titles and dignities will have any significance in another life, whether like much else they are forgotten in a hundred years, whether there is any way of excogitating and defining exactly how by means of memory such facts can compose the content of an eternal consciousness, I do not know. I honor the King, as does every good married man, but I would not exchange my titles for such as his. Such for my part am I, and that every other married man is the same is something I would gladly believe, and verily, whether any individual be far from it or near, my wish is that he may be even as I am.

Behold, I wear inwardly upon my breast the ribbon of my order, love's chain of roses, its roses verily are not withered, verily its roses wither not, even if they alter with the years, they do not fade, even if the rose is not so red, it is because it has become a white rose, but faded it is not. And now for my titles and dignities—what is so glorious about them is that they are so evenly apportioned, for only the divine justice of marriage is constantly able to give tit for tat. What I am through her, that she is through me, and we are neither of us anything by ourselves but only in union. Through her I am a man, for only a married man is a genuine man,[3] every other title to honor is as nothing compared to this which in reality is the assumption underlying all titles. Through her I am a father; every other dignity is merely a human invention, an artifice, which is forgotten in a hundred years; through her I am head of the family, through her I am defender of the home, its breadwinner, the children's protector.

When one has so many dignities, one does not become an author for the sake of attaining a new dignity. I have not the least desire for a dignity I dare not lay claim to, but I write in order that he who is as happy as I am, if he reads this, may be reminded of his good fortune; that he who doubts, if he reads this, may be won over, if it were only a single individual, I am glad even of that; I demand but little, not because I am easily satisfied, but because I am indescribably content. When one has so many employments, all of them so dear, and writes as opportunity offers, one must wish that the man who might possibly profit by it may not be put out by deficiency in form, and must deprecate all criticism. For a married man who writes on marriage is surely the last person to write for critical appreciation. He writes as opportunity offers, and is often distracted by dearer occupations. For though I might be something to many by being an author, I greatly prefer to be as much as possible to my wife. I am her husband by marriage; that is to say, by marriage the *corso* was opened to me, the career which is my Rhodes[4] and my dance-floor. I am her friend, oh, that I may be that in sincerity of heart, oh, that she may not feel the want of anything more sincere! I am her counsellor, oh, that my wisdom were on a par with my willingness! I am her comfort and her cheer—not yet summoned in that capacity, it is true, but, oh, that if once I am requisitioned for that service, my strength may be equal to my readiness to serve! I am her debtor, my accounts are honestly kept and the accounting is a blissful labor. And in

[3] An outrageous pun: *Aegtmand* means married man; *aegte Mand* means genuine man.

[4] *Hic Rhodus, hic salta.* In one of Aesop's fables a boastful fellow relates that at Rhodes he had made a prodigiously long jump. A bystander says, "Here is Rhodes, now jump."

the end, as well I know, I shall become a recollection of her when death separates us. Oh, that my memory may be trustworthy, that it may preserve to me everything when it is lost, an annuity of remembrance for the days that remain, that it may bring back to me even the most insignificant things, and that I may say with the poet when I am concerned for today, *et haec meminisse juvat,* and when I am concerned for the morrow, *et haec meminisse juvabit!* Alas, one must as a judge from time to time digest with loathing the *vita ante acta* of a criminal, but one can never tire of the *vita ante acta* of the beloved, nor does one need the precision of the printed page in order to remember. It is doubtless true that pleasure stimulates labor, and so it does the work of remembrance. It may be, as sentimentality puts it, that at death there will be found the image of the loved one upon the lover's heart, but matrimonially put there awakens in the lover a decision of the will lest the thing run wild in endlessness. The lover says indeed that an instant with the beloved is heavenly bliss, but marriage, wishing all joy to the lover, fortunately has a better knowledge of the situation. Suppose it to be true that the first ebullient enthusiasm of love cannot be carried through quite in that way, yet marriage knows how the best in love can be carried through. In case a child has received from his parents a fresh copy of his lesson-book and before the year is over he has as it were consumed it, would this be an indication that he was to be praised for his zeal and earnestness? So it is with marriage. The married man who from God in heaven has received his copy—ah, as beautiful as a gift of God can be—and has read out of it daily, every day throughout a long life, and behold, when it is laid aside, when night has come and the reading must cease, it was just as beautiful as when he received it—was not then this honest prudence, which was in direct proportion to the lover's pleasure which prompted him to read again and again, was not this just as praiseworthy, just as strong an expression of love, as the strongest expression love has at its command?

It is only about marriage I desire to write. To convince an individual is my hope, to have done with those who speak against marriage is my purpose. So marriage is the only string[5] I play upon, but that is so composite that, without exactly boasting of virtuosity, which ordinarily is required of one who has but a single string, I dare venture to make myself heard, not precisely as an artist before a numerous public, but rather as a strolling musician who takes up his position before the door of a simple house and calls no one away from his work, although there

[5] Not long after this book was published the bitter experience S.K. had with the *Corsair* put, as he said, "a new string upon my instrument."

is in his music when it is heard in the midst of labor something attractive. For I do not mean that what I have to say is devoid of elegance. Several passages I owe to my wife, although I do not talk with her quite as I write here; but everything that comes from her has a certain charm which is woman's dowry. I have often marvelled at it. As one who writes only indifferently well, when he sees his manuscript reproduced by a calligraphic artist must be amazed; as one who has sent a crabbed sheet to the press, when he receives a neatly printed copy hardly dares to recognize it as his own, so it often has been with me in my domestic life. What moves obscurely in her, I express as well as I can, and then she marvels that it was precisely this she wanted to say; so I say it as well as I can, and she appropriates it. But then comes my turn, when I behold with amazement that my thoughts, my words, have acquired an animation, a heartiness, a charm, so that I can say justly it is not my thought. The misfortune is that the lovable finery in which these words and thoughts are dressed almost entirely disappears when I would rehearse them and can no more be expressed than I can describe her voice here on this paper. Here, however, she is to a certain extent co-author, and a literary partnership of this sort seems to me quite a pretty thing when one would write only on marriage. I know that she approves of my making use of what I owe her, I know that she forgives me for employing the opportunity of saying one thing and another about her which otherwise I could not manage to say except in solitude, for how much she means to me I cannot say to her directly, for fear my laudation might be vexatious to her and perhaps almost disturb our good understanding. As an anonymous author and as one who takes the greatest precaution to preserve his anonymity I have insured myself against an offense which I hope delicacy even would forbid, against the danger that my domestic life might become the object of anybody's curiosity.

All honor be to marriage, and honor to everyone who speaks in praise of it. What I have to say does not consist of new discoveries; it would indeed be precarious to make a new discovery about the oldest institution in the world. Every married man knows the same things I do. The leading thoughts are the same, like the consonants in Hebrew; but while these remain unaltered one can find pleasure in adding new vowels and so reading it again. Of course this must be understood *cum grano salis,* and it must not be supposed that in doing this I do it with the thought of the malicious mocker who said that love and marriage have the same consonants and only differ in the vowels, and this again is like a well known passage in the book of Genesis where it is related that Esau kissed

Jacob,[6] and the learned Jews, not being able to credit Esau with such an affectionate disposition, and not daring to alter the consonants, merely indicated other vowels, so that it read, "he begged him." Such an objection one answers best by saying bah! Every other objection is all the more welcome the more openly it is expressed, for a consistent objection is a feeler after the truth and comes very opportunely to one who has the explanation at his fingertips.

[6] Gen. 30:4.

LOVE can boast of having its own god. Who is there that does not know his name? And how many there are who believe they gain much by calling their relationship after his name an erotic relationship! Eros, the erotic feeling, and everything that goes with that, has a claim to be regarded as poetic. On the other hand, marriage is not favored in this way, is not of such lofty extraction; for though it is said that God established marriage, it is commonly the priest that says this, or, if one will, the theologian, and they both of them speak about God in a sense entirely different from that of the poet.

The consequence is that all the cosiness, all the fragrance, which one has along with Eros is liable to disappear, for it is characteristic of Eros that it can be entirely concrete in the individual, whereas the thought of God is on the one hand so serious that the pleasure of love seems to disappear when the God who is the father of spirits must be the one who joins together in matrimony, and on the other hand this thought is so generic that one seems to disappear before one's own eyes as a naught, though desiring to have a teleological purpose by which one is defined in relation to the highest being. The clearness, the transparency, and on the other hand the roguishness, the demi-obscurity, in the relation of Eros to the lover, is something the God of the spirit cannot easily acquire in relation to marriage. The fact that He is involved in the affair is in a certain sense too much, and precisely on that account His presence signifies less than that of Eros, who is present wholly and undividedly for the lovers. A purely human relationship illustrates this. If His Royal Majesty lets a chamberlain appear in his stead as godfather, it may perhaps heighten the festive mood of the party, but if the King himself were to appear, it would perhaps make them ill-at-ease. It is only in connection with marriage one remembers that there is no distinction of rank which makes one class to be nearer to God than another. It is by no means an easy task to think God as the God of the spirit, and then to think Him into marriage in such a way that the thought does not become an introduction of so general a character that it has no tendency at all to conduct *in* (introduce), and in such a way that the conception does not become so spiritual that it instantly conducts *out* again.

If one would be content with the poetic explanation of love (which is essentially pagan, for to refer love to a divinity is merely the pretty playful seriousness of immediacy), or if one would let marriage shift for itself, or (if that won't do) would let it be something which comes afterwards, then perhaps one discovers no difficulty—but that way of discovering no difficulty puts a man who is accustomed to think in a difficult position. Eros as a matter of course does not claim any faith and cannot become the object of faith, and it is this which makes Eros so serviceable to poets; but a God of the spirit who is the object of a spiritual faith is in a sense infinitely remote from the concretion of love.[7]

In paganism there was a god for love but none for marriage; in Christianity there is, if I may venture to say so, a God for marriage and none for love. For the fact is that marriage is a higher expression for love. If the matter is not regarded in this way, everything is brought to confusion, and one either remains unmarried—a scoffer, a seducer, a hermit—or one's marriage is a bit of thoughtlessness. The difficulty is that so soon as one thinks of God as spirit, the relation of the individual to God becomes so spiritual that the physico-psychical synthesis wherein the strength of Eros lies readily disappears from sight, as if one were to say that marriage was a duty, to get married a duty, that this is a higher expression than love because duty means a spiritual relationship to God, who is spirit. Paganism and immediacy do not think of God as spirit, but when once this conception is given, the difficulty is to preserve the characteristic qualities of the erotic in such a way that the spiritual does not burn them up and consume them but burns in them without consuming them. So marriage is threatened from two sides: if the individual has not put himself in a relationship of faith to God as spirit, paganism haunts his brain as a fantastic reminiscence, and then he cannot enter into any marriage; or, on the other hand, he has become entirely spiritual, and so neither in this case can he marry. Even if both the former and the latter of these were wed, such a love affair and such a wedding is not marriage.

Now even though paganism had no god for marriage, and though marriage is a Christian idea, there is something to tie to after all in the fact that Zeus and Hera had a special predicate as the guardians of marriage: Τελείος and Τέλεια.[8] It must be left to the philologists

[7] These paragraphs do not make easy reading. S.K. is wrestling with the difficulty which made marriage impossible for him. He presents here to the psychologist the profoundest data of self-analysis, and I have not endeavored to make his meaning clearer than he has made it—like Schrempf, who paraphrases several pages, and so presents the German reader with just as much (or as little) as he himself has understood.

[8] τέλος means the end, the purpose, the final cause, and is used in the language of the mysteries for the perfection of the initiate. S.K. uses the word here in the sense of the fulfilment of the ideal of man in so far as he is a synthesis of body and soul. In this sense only is it "the highest τέλος"; for "the absolute τέλος" which he emphasizes in the *Postscript* is immeasurably higher than all the relative τέλοι with which it is

to explain this expression more precisely; I do not hide my ignorance, and knowing for my own part that I lack the necessary erudition, I am not disposed to boast of a spiritual falcon-eye which would warrant me in heaping scorn upon classic learning and classic culture, which remains when all is said and done the pithy pabulum of the soul, far more nutritive than green food or the speculator's guess as to "what the age demands." To me it is important only that I be allowed to apply these words Τελείος and Τέλεια to married people—Jupiter and Juno I leave out of account, not being inclined to make a fool of myself by wanting to solve the historico-philologic difficulty.

Marriage I regard as the highest τέλος of the individual human existence, it is so much the highest that the man who goes without it cancels with one stroke the whole of earthly life and retains only eternity and spiritual interests—which at the first glance seems no slight thing but in the long run is very exhausting and also in one way or another is the expression of an unhappy life. That the highest τέλος, if marriage be so regarded, is not exhaustively expressed by a suite of finite "wherefores" everybody can readily perceive and it need not be argued. The highest τέλος always embraces the particular determinants which compose it as its predicates, and so rigidly does it embrace them that they possess what significance they have only as immanent to it and are devoid of significance so soon as they attempt to be independent; for a detached thought which would be its own complete self is comic and scatterbrained. This is said to avoid misunderstanding. The main point is that marriage is a τέλος—not, however, as a blind urge of nature (a notion which verges on the mystery cults), but for free individuals. For if it is a τέλος, it is not something "immediate" but a work of freedom, and as belonging to the realm of freedom it proposes a task which can be realized only by a resolution of the will. Now the signal is given: all the objections which sneak like solitary figures upon the outskirts of social life will now, if they are shrewd, converge upon this point. I know well that here the battle is to be fought, and this shall not be forgotten, even if for a little while I appear to forget it in order hypothetically to take a little look around.

The difficulty is this: love or the state of being in love is entirely "immediate"; yet at the same time being in love is something which looks forward to being absorbed in matrimony or in the resolution, the will to marry. That is to say, the most instinctive or "immediate" of all things is to be at the same time a resolution of the freest kind, a thing

contrasted and which doubtless include marriage. It was the absolute τέλος which hindered him from attaining the very high τέλος of marriage.

which because of its immediacy is so inexplicable that it must be referred to a divinity is to come to pass at the same time by virtue of deliberation and of a deliberation so exhaustive that a resolution results from it. Moreover, the one must not follow after the other, the resolution must not come sneaking along behind, but it must occur at the same time, both must be together at the instant of decision. If the deliberation has not exhausted the possibilities of thought, I form no resolution, I act either by the inspiration of genius or by force of a whim.

If the individual makes the venture, that is to say if his being in love is not merely a state of mind but actually a union with the beloved, though without his having any other expression for being in love than simply being in love,[9] if in making the venture he is only blissfully moved and urged on by the impetus which he takes to be a trade wind that will carry him without hindrance along the luminous path with his lady-love beside him—this is not by any means to say that marriage will result the next moment. "The next moment"—for as this man is only "immediately" determined, there is bound to come sooner or later a next moment. Marriage implies a resolution, but a resolution does not result directly from the immediacy of being in love. Either nothing more is needed but the prompting of love, which like a magnet points constantly to the same point; or the resolution must be at hand from the beginning. If the resolution is to come later, something else may come to pass instead. What is there to insure against it? Love, somebody answers. All right, but this is precisely love's critical moment when it cannot therefore come to its own aid; for the fact that the breeze of immediacy does not fill the sail of love indicates that a change of wind is to occur whilst immediacy is about to be brought to a standstill as it were in a dead calm. The other possible consequence of love's immediacy is . . . seduction. Who will say that the seducer at the first instant was a seducer? No, he became that at the second instant. When a man talks about love as immediacy it is not possible to decide whether it is a knight or a seducer that is speaking, for it is the next instant which decides this. To marriage this does not apply, for there the resolution is present from the beginning.

Let us take for example Aladdin.[10] What youth with desire and aspiration in his heart, what maiden with longing in her heart, has read Aladdin's command to the spirit in the fourth act (where he gives orders

[9] *Kaerlighed* means love, in all its reaches, even to the highest; *Elskov* is the more "immediate" and sensuous passion; *Forelskensen* is the state of being "in love"—in this passage it is very embarrassing that our language makes no distinctions of this sort.

[10] The reference is to Oehlenschläger's play of that name.

for the nuptials) without being inflamed and almost set on fire by the poet's enthusiasm and the fire of the words? Aladdin is a knight, to depict such a love is moral, says somebody. No, it is poetic, and the poet by his happy thought and by the profound wealth of his presentation has forever demonstrated that he is absolutely a poet. Aladdin is entirely immediate. His wish therefore is of such a sort that the next instant he can be a poet. The only thing that concerns him is "that beloved and long-desired nuptial night," which confirms him in the possession of Gulnare—hence the palace, the nuptial hall, the nuptials.

Prepare a lordly wedding, turn the darkness into day
With incense-perfumed torches in the spacious nuptial hall.
A corps of comely maidens shall perform an airy dance,
While the others shall delight us with the cittern and sweet song.

Aladdin is himself almost overwhelmed, he is fainting in the swoon of anticipated delight. Not without a certain tremor in his voice does he inquire of the spirit whether he is able to perform this, he conjures him to answer sincerely, and in this word "sincerely" is to be heard as it were the dread which immediacy experiences in the face of its own good fortune.

That in which Aladdin is great is his wish, the fact that his soul has the pith to desire. If with a view to this point I were to make any criticism of a masterpiece, which here could only be an enamored expression of envy, it would be that it never is clearly and strongly enough brought out that Aladdin is a justifiable personality, that to wish, to be able to wish, to dare to wish, to be foolhardy in wishing, resolute in grasping, insatiable in aspiring, is a quality of genius as great as any other. Perhaps one may not believe this, and yet in every generation there are born perhaps not more than ten youths who possess this blind courage, this intensity upon the inordinate. Eliminate these ten and give to every other man full warrant to wish, it becomes in his hands little more than a begging-letter; his nose becomes pale, he wants to reflect, he would like indeed to wish, but now it is a question of wishing the right thing—that is to say, he is a bungler, not a genius like Aladdin, who is the favorite of the spirit for the reason that he is rude. The fulfilment of his wish must therefore not be made to appear an accidental favor, so as not to provide the bunglers with the pretext that if they were sure of a certain fulfilment, they too would wish. Falsehood, falsehood! Here already there is a reflection. No, even if Aladdin had no wish fulfilled, he would rank high for the wish, for the potency of desire, which in the last resort is of more value than any fulfilment.

Great is Aladdin! He celebrates the wedding, it is true, but he does not wed. Verily no one can more heartily congratulate him and more sincerely rejoice in him than I; but if I were able, as the poet gives him the spirit of the lamp, to give him a spirit of resolution, if I were able by daily intercessory prayer to procure for him the one thing I think he lacks, a spirit of resolution which in intensity and concretion corresponds to what his wish is in boundless extension and abstraction (for his aspiration is indeed boundless and is as hot as the burning sand of the desert)—ah, what a husband Aladdin might have been! Now one is not able to say anything of the sort; my enemies on the other hand, robbers who lie in wait for their prey, coolly appropriate Aladdin. The seducer fortifies his soul with Aladdin's immediacy, and so he seduces, and then he says: "Aladdin too was a seducer, that I know from a very reliable source, he became a seducer the morning after the wedding." If it were not in fact the very next morning but a few years after the wedding, makes no real difference and only proves, if it were a few years later, that Aladdin had become small. Here the seducer is in the right: if it is to be all over with immediacy, then the thing to do is to break off hastily (and precisely for this reason it is a moral task to present the figure of a seducer[11]); and if this is not to be the case, the resolution must have been present from the beginning, and so we have a husband. The enthusiasm of the poet is enlisted by immediacy, the poet is great by reason of his faith in immediacy and in its power to prevail. The married man has permitted himself to entertain a doubt, an innocent, a well meant, a noble, a lovable doubt; for verily he is far from wishing to offend love or to do away with it: as certainly as the immediacy of love does not constitute a husband, just so certainly on the other hand is a wedding where love has been left out (for whatever reason) no marriage.

By venturing out and being borne along by the blissful and irresistible prompting of love, the lover is indeed carried into the arms of his lady-love, with her he is carried perhaps much further along, but marriage he does not attain; for if that union of the lovers is not from the beginning a marriage, it never becomes such. If the resolution were to come along tardily in the rear, the idea would not be expressed. Maybe the lovers live happily, possibly they do not bother about the objections, yet in a way the enemies are right. Everything depends upon the idealities. Marriage must not be a fragmentary thing which comes about in an occasional way, something which happens to the lovers after they

[11] As S.K. had already done in "The Diary of the Seducer," which concludes the first part of *Either/Or*.

have for some time been living with one another, and so the enemies are right in a way. They for their part stand for an ideality which belongs to the realm of evil, demoniacal ideality. From the objections which are raised one can easily perceive whether the speaker is merely a *chicaneur* or has demoniacal ideality. One may be quite right in not wishing to have anything to do with the objections, not wishing to be disturbed by them, but one must have a good conscience and an unbroken covenant with the ideas. To be content with being well off, being happy, etc., is perdition when this happiness is founded upon thoughtlessness, upon cowardice, upon a worldly-minded deification of existence. To have preserved one's covenant with the ideas, even though one were to become unhappy, is heaven compared with such a pitiable situation—such is my opinion too. Hence I dare to talk; as a married man I do not put my tail between my legs, I dare to talk with enemies, and not with friends only. I know that as a married man I am τέλειος, but I know what is demanded of such with respect to the idea. No haggling, no compromise, no grounds of consolation offered by one husband to another, as though husbands, like women in a harem, were life-prisoners who have something to themselves which they dare not confess before the world, as though love were the glittering finery one lets the poet turn outward for display, and marriage the shabby side which one turns inward. No, let it be an open fight; the idea of marriage is sure to win. With humility before God and with deference to the divine majesty of love I hold up my head far above all witticisms and do not bow it in the face of any objection.

We grant that the enemies are right in stating the whole difficulty, and that the synthesis which constitutes marriage is difficult, but we do not grant that they are right in representing this as an objection, still less in avoiding the difficulty in the way they do. When an opponent states the whole difficulty of the objection in order to deter us by fear, we need to have the courage to say with Hamann, "That's exactly how it is." This is a good answer aptly made. Here too the answer is to come, but I demand that the question be postponed for a few minutes till we have oriented ourselves a bit by a few general considerations about marriage as the highest τέλος.

In paganism there was a punishment inflicted upon bachelors, while those who produced many children were rewarded;[12] in the Middle Ages it was counted a perfection to be unmarried. These are the extremes. As for the first case, there was no need of inflicting a punishment,

[12] Such was the case in Rome under the Empire—and now again under the Duce of Fascism.

for existence always holds up its own end and knows how to punish the man who would emancipate himself. In this case the man who would emancipate himself is the one who will not marry. Stress must be laid upon the fact that he *will* not. As marriage is a resolution, so also is its opposite, a resolution not to marry. Such only can be the subject of this discourse. For to fool life away, seeking after the ideal (as though all such seeking were anything but stupidity and presumption), without comprehending what either love or marriage means, without even comprehending the innocent enthusiasm which reminds youth that time is fleeting, time is fleeting—so to fool life away means an existence devoid of idea. And so it is also with the fastidiousness of picking and choosing (as though all such choosing were anything but an expression of the fact that the chooser is not pure), and then getting nobody—which is life's objective expression for this subjective choosing. That marriage in contrast with such foolery is absolutely preferable is something so definitely sure that it is almost an offense against marriage to affirm it. No, the objection that is to have any significance must vindicate its claim to consideration by a negative resolution. The resolution of marriage is a positive resolution, and properly the most positive of all. The opposite is also a resolution which resolves not to realize this task. Everyone who not only remains unmarried but remains so without a resolution—his course through life it is not worth while to follow. Every human existence which would not be twaddle (and no man should wish to be that) dare not forego the universal,[13] except by virtue of a resolution, whatever the reasons may be which prompt him to make this resolution, which with respect to the decision not to marry may be very various—but here it is not in place to go into them, lest attention might be distracted from the main point.

The resolution not to will to get married exhibits of course an ideality, but not such an ideality as does the positive resolution. Only in relation to time and circumstances can it become clearer to the individual that he has made a resolution when he has made the negative one, whereas the positive resolution made in compliance with a universal opinion may have been made easily enough. One can indeed succeed in getting married, as it is called, without having made a resolution, in spite of the fact that a resolution has been made, but a resolution and a resolution are widely different things. A resolution which is determined upon without

[13] In the second part of *Either/Or,* which was written when S.K. had resolved to forego marriage, he regarded it as "the universal," and the universal meant to him the moral rule. Hence the effort in *Fear and Trembling* to justify his position as "the exception"—like Abraham, etc.

more ado in continuity with others, and is decided by virtue of the fact that the next neighbor and the opposite neighbor have also resolved upon it, is properly no resolution; for whether there be such a thing as poetry at second hand, I do not know, but a resolution at third hand is no resolution. As compared with such marriages, which display neither love nor marriage in the most favorable light, the negative resolution appears at an advantage. But such marriages are not marriages at all, but mere mimicry.

All of a man's ideality consists first and last in resolution. Every other ideality is an insignificance, to admire it is childish, and the person thus admired, if he understands himself, will feel offended. So only of a positive or a negative resolution can there be any question here. The positive resolution has the great advantage that it consolidates life and reassures the individual in his own mind, whereas the negative holds him *in suspenso*. A negative resolution is always much more laborious than a positive one, it cannot become habitual, and yet it must always be maintained. A positive resolution is secure in its happy result, for the universal, which is the positive factor in it, assures that happiness will come and gives assurance to happiness when it does come. A negative resolution, even when the result is happy, is always ambiguous; it is deceptive like good fortune in paganism, for good fortune *is* only when it *has been*. That is to say, only when I am dead can I know whether I *have been* fortunate.[14] Thus it is with the negative resolution. The individual has declared war upon human existence, hence there is no instant when he is through with it, he cannot, like one who has made a positive resolution, learn to understand day by day more deeply the original ground of his resolution. A negative resolution does not support him who made it, but he has to support it; and however far it goes, even if good fortune favors him, even if the most important results come from it, he dare not deny the possibility that suddenly everything may receive a different interpretation. By reason of his negative resolution he now exists hypothetically or in the conjunctive mood, and it can be said of a hypothesis that it is never finished until it has explained all phenomena. For even by a false hypothesis one can provisionally make out a good deal, until the phenomenon comes along which overthrows the hypothesis; and in the case of the conjunctive "if" the reply is, "Yes, if." A positive resolution has only one anxiety, the fear of not being true to itself; a negative resolution is always exposed to a double danger: that of not being true to itself, which is like that of the positive resolution, but with this differ-

[14] Solon's saying to Croesus: "Call no man fortunate till he is dead." Herodotus, I, 32.

ence, that all this fidelity is without reward, a withered glory, and unfruitful as the life of a celibate; and then another temptation, the suspicion that this fidelity by which one is true to oneself may be rewarded at last by repentance. Whereas the positive resolution joyfully recruits its strength by repose, joyfully arises with the sun, joyfully begins where it left off, and joyfully beholds everything thriving about it, as a married man does, joyfully beholds with the new day a new proof of that which needs no proof, for a positive resolution is not a hypothesis which has to be proved. On the other hand, he who has made the negative resolution sleeps uneasily at night, expects that the terror will suddenly erect itself against him, that he has chosen wrong, he wakes up exhausted to behold about him the golden heath, he is never refreshed in strength because he is constantly hovering.

Verily the state has no need to impose a punishment upon bachelors, life itself punishes him who deserves punishment, for he who makes no resolution is a wretched creature of whom it may be said in a tragic sense, "He cometh not into judgment."[15] It is not because I am envious of the man who will not marry that I speak thus, I am too happy to envy anyone, but I am jealous in behalf of human existence.

I return to the foregoing thesis that resolution is man's ideality. I will now seek to show what must be the nature of the resolution which cultivates most thoroughly the individuality, and I cheer my soul by the reflection that such precisely is the nature of marriage, which, as has been said, I am disposed to regard as the synthesis of love and resolution.

There is a phantom which is often enough astir when it is a question of making a resolution, and that is *probability*—a contemptible fellow, a bungler, a peddling Jew, with whom no freeborn soul will have any dealings, a ne'er-do-well who had much better be sent to the house of correction than overshrewd men and women, since it tricks people out of something more than money and money's worth. Every man who in the matter of resolve has not got further and never gets further than to resolve by the aid of probability is lost to ideality, whatever else he may become. When in making a resolution a man does not meet up with God, has never formed a resolution in which he made a bargain with God, he might just as well never have lived. But God always deals *en gros,* and probability is a commercial paper which is not quoted in heaven. It is important therefore that in resolution there should be a factor which overawes probability and renders it speechless.

[15] John 5:24.

There is a spook which the man about to make a resolution runs after as a dog runs after a shadow on the water, and that is the *upshot,* an indication of extreme misery, a dazzling delusion of perdition—woe to the man who is on the outlook for that, he is a lost soul! As the man who looked upon the bronze cross in the wilderness was sound in health although he was bitten by a serpent, so he who fixes his glance upon the upshot is bitten by a serpent, wounded by the earthly mind, lost both for time and for eternity. If at the instant of resolution a man is not irradiated by the clarity of the Deity in such a way that all spooks formed by the mists of drowsiness vanish away, then his resolution amounts to only a greater or less forgery—let him take what comfort he can in the upshot. It is therefore so exceedingly important that the matter the resolution deals with should be of such a nature that no upshot may venture to bid for it at the auction, because what is being bought is bought *à tout prix.*

What is said here applies to every resolution in which the eternal is a factor and concludes the sale, and not merely to the resolution of marriage when for the first time it presses love to its bosom and concludes it in the faithful embrace of resolution. This applies to every resolution which has the eternal within it, and to that extent it applies also to the negative resolution, insofar as it is negative towards the temporal but turns positively towards the eternal. This, however, is precisely what causes it to hover. On the other hand, in the resolution of marriage love is deposed from the position of suzerain and has precisely the power of drawing down the man of resolve—not to the earth, oh, far from that, but down to the side of the loved one in temporal existence. The act of resolution is the ethical act, it is freedom. The negative resolution has this same character, but bare and naked as freedom is in this case; it is as though it were dumb, with a difficulty in utterance which is hard to overcome, and in a general way there is something hard in its nature. Love, on the other hand, promptly sets the thing to music, though it is true that this composition contains a very difficult passage. For the bridal pair who, at this sacred moment, or when they think of it afterwards, do not find that it is nonsensical for the priest to say to the lovers that they "shall" love one another, and on the other hand do not find that it is capitally said—such a bridal pair lacks an ear for the music of marriage. Delicious as it is to be sensible of the whisper of love, this precious witness at the wedding, just so heartily welcome is that impertinent word which says, "Thou shalt love her." How dithyrambic is this wedding formula, how presumptuous almost, which is not content with love but calls it a duty. What wonder that the resolution which answers to such an address appears to some a hard saying! That love is not content with being sure of itself but in its audacity has recourse to this, "Thou shalt!" That marriage has a resolution which expresses the one and only wish, has a duty which is the eyes' delight and the heart's desire! Have courage, therefore, dare boldly, have courage to will the difficult, and so in turn the difficulty proves a help. For difficulty is not a morose man, not a *chicaneur,* but an omnipotence which will make it so very good. Whereas the man who in his eternal resolution conducts himself negatively towards the temporal is lonely at the instant of resolution, even if he is very great, even though he were a Prometheus, is chained, not to a mountain, but held captive by the temporal as by a chain—the married man, on the other hand, when again he opens his eyes (supposing that he has closed them in the eternity of resolution), finds himself standing again where he was before, always in the same place, alongside of the beloved, just where he would prefer to be, feeling no want of the eternal, for it is with him in time.

The negative resolution has reference only to the eternal, the positive has reference to both the temporal and the eternal—and man in fact is at once temporal and eternal. The ideality of the true resolution consists therefore in a resolve which is just as temporal as it is eternal, which is, if I may venture to say so, both signed and countersigned—a precaution which is taken in the case of government bonds and which even the bank takes with its bigger checks. The true idealizing resolution accordingly has this characteristic: it is signed in heaven and then it is countersigned in time. And not only this, but again and again as life goes on the married man is constantly getting new and newer endorsements, each one of them as precious as the other. Every married man understands what I mean. How could I believe anything else of him—that he regards reluctantly the additional assurances as burdensome? The right sort of a married man understands that the wife is the principal endorser and that everyone in the group that is growing up under the eyes of marriage is a new and ever new certificate. Oh, blessed security! Oh, wealthy man! Oh, reassuring bliss! To possess one's whole wealth in one single security, which cannot vanish from one's sight as does the eternal resolution from the sight of him who assumes a negative position to the temporal! The latter individual is either an unfortunate or a rebel—and a rebel also is an unfortunate. He is an unfortunate man who goes through time with his eternal resolution but never gets it countersigned—on the contrary, wherever he goes it is protested, he is an outcast from the race, and even though he is consoled by the eternal, he is yet remote from joy, in tears, perhaps in gnashing of teeth; for he who in eternity has not on a wedding garment is cast out, but in earthly life the wedding garment is literally the wedding garment.

The true idealizing resolution must be just as sympathetic as it is autopathic. But the man who is negative in relation to the temporal has no outlet for his sympathy, which accordingly, instead of being a refreshment to him when it pours out the benediction of its abundance and when it recruits itself anew, becomes to him a torment which consumes his soul because it is unable to express itself. To be suffocated is dreadful, but to have sympathy and not be able to let it draw breath is quite as dreadful. For I assume that the man has sympathy, otherwise he would not be worth talking about. Sympathy is an essential quality of man, and every resolution which overlooks this is not in the largest sense an idealizing resolution, and neither is that in which sympathy fails to find an adequate opportunity for expression. Suppose the bachelor is a fool and wastes his sympathy upon dogs and cats and foolery; suppose the hermit who made the negative choice is a noble soul, suppose his sympathy seeks and finds tasks much greater than that of having a wife and children, he nevertheless has no joy in it. If the dew of heaven might not fall upon the grass and might not have joy at seeing the flower refreshed by its delicious moisture, if it were to spread over the wide ocean and evaporate before it reached the flower, would not that be dreadful? If the milk in the mother's breast were to flow abundantly, but there was no babe; if the wasted milk were as precious as the milk of Juno after which the Milky Way is named, ah, how sad! And so it is also with a man whose sympathy does not get leave to see a wife grow green like a tree which is planted in the blessed enclosure of sympathy, does not get leave to see the tree blossom and bear fruit which ripens under the care of sympathy! Unhappy the man who has not this expression for his sympathy, and the still more glorious expression for everything his sympathy expresses: that all this is his responsibility. This contradiction is sympathy's most blissful pleasure, a bliss which makes him as it were go mad for very joy. Suppose an unhappy man who does not possess through the resolution of marriage a good understanding with the temporal—suppose he cares for the sick, feeds the hungry, clothes the naked, visits the prisoner, comforts the dying; I praise him, he shall in no wise lose his reward, but neither is he in divine madness an unprofitable servant, his sympathy constantly seeks its deepest expression but finds it not, seeks it far afield, as in fact his solicitude wanders from house to house, whereas the married man finds opportunity in his own house, his home, where it is bliss for him to want to do everything, and a still greater bliss, a divine *poscimur,*[16] that he is and remains without merit.

The true idealizing resolution must be just as concrete as it is abstract. In the same degree that a resolution is negatively formulated, in that same degree it is sheerly abstract. But say what you will about a resolution, there is nothing between heaven and earth so concrete as marriage and the marriage relationship, nothing so inexhaustible; even the most unimportant things have their importance, and whereas the matrimonial obligation is elastic enough to span a whole lifetime (like that ox-hide which measured the whole circumference of Carthage[17]) it closes just as elastically around the instant, and around every instant. There is nothing so piecemeal as marriage, and yet there is nobody that can less endure a divided heart than marriage; God Himself is not so jealous. Every relationship of duty can after all be approximately exhausted by definitions, every labor, every business, in short, everything a man ordinarily occupies his time with, has its time; but the married life evades every such definition. Woe unto him who finds this a burden, even the idea of being sentenced for life gives no adequate notion of the pain of his punishment; for the life-sentence is an abstract expression, but such a matrimonial criminal feels every day the horror of being sentenced for life. The more concrete a man becomes in ideality, the more perfect the ideality is. The man who will not marry has as a consequence discarded the most idealizing resolution. Moreover, it is an inconsistency for a man to will not to marry, and then to resolve upon some positive aim in temporal existence. What interest can he have in the idea of the state, what love for the fatherland, what civic patriotism with regard to all that affects the social weal and woe? A man who will not let marriage have its realization! The more abstract it is, so much the more imperfect is ideality. Abstraction is the first expression of ideality, but concretion is its essential expression. This is expressed by marriage. In the stage of love the lovers wish to belong to one

[16] Horace, *Odes,* I, 32, 1: "it is exacted of us." S.K. often recalled Luther's saying at the Diet of Worms: "I can do no other." In this passage he is thinking, not of the "unprofitable servant" who is cast into outer darkness (Matt. 25: 30), but of the saying recorded in Luke 17: 10: "When ye shall have done all those things which are commanded you, say, We are unprofitable servants, we have done that which it was our duty to do." The thought in this passage becomes coherent when we know that S.K.'s "only" objection (as he said in one place) to the institution of monasticism was that the monk felt he was doing something meritorious which made him superior to other men.

[17] Virgil, the *Aeneid,* I, 365 *ff.,* which tells of the clever ruse of Dido, who bargained for as much land as could be covered by an ox-hide, and then cut the hide into strips which measured the whole circumference of Carthage.

another *eternally,* in their resolution they resolve to be *everything* to one another; and this prodigious abstraction finds its concrete expression in what is so unimportant that no third party dreams of it. The highest expression of love is that the lover feels himself as nothing in the presence of the beloved, and this feeling is mutual, for to feel oneself as something conflicts with love. The resolution has no word by which to express itself, for words are almost too concrete; the vow is silent or is expressed in that immortal "Yes"—and this abstraction finds expression of such a sort that if all the stenographers were united, they would not be able to describe what goes on in a week of married life.

This is the happiness of marriage. I do not mean this in the sense in which one speaks of a particular married pair as happy. No, it is simply the happiness of being a married man. For what life is happier than that of the man for whom everything has importance? How could time be long to him for whom every instant has importance? And how secure this happiness feels itself! For indeed there is an old proverb which says that *Ehestand* is *Wehestand,*[18] and as such indeed does marriage proclaim itself. How sure then it must be of itself that it dares to invite others to try it! Is there any other institution in life, any other relationship, which begins in this fashion? Alas, all other beginnings are only too ingratiating and are silent about the difficulties. Figaro,[19] to excuse himself for the letter he had written to the Count, says to the Countess that she is the only lady in the realm against whom he would with assurance venture to permit himself to take such a step. So likewise I believe that marriage is the only institution which with assurance dare say of itself that it is a worry. On the part of the others it would be an imprudence to let such a thing be known.

The true idealizing resolution must be just as dialectic with reference to freedom as to fate. Nothing ventured, nothing resolved. Now then the resolution is formed. The more abstract it is, the less dialectic it is with reference to fate. Hereby the ideality of the resolution acquires a certain untruthfulness, it readily becomes proud, supercilious, inhuman, and more particularly all the arguments of fate are regarded as legally invalid. The more concrete the resolution is, the more it comes into relation with fate or divine providence. This yields the ideality of humility, meekness, gratitude. But a married man who puts all his life

[18] Musäus, *Volksmärchen der Deutschen,* Gotha 1826, Vol. II, p. 70: "The married state is a mournful state."

[19] *Figaro's Marriage,* translated into Danish by N. T. Brunn, 1817, Act II, Scene 2. Figaro had sent a letter to the Count warning him that a lover was seeking a rendezvous with the Countess. Figaro says to the Countess, "There are but few, my lady, of whom I would have ventured to say that—for fear my guess might be right."

and soul into it is surely the one who risks most of all. He ventures out from love's hiding-place with the beloved, taking the beloved with him —and what may not happen! He knows not, if he were to indulge in such reflections his hair might indeed become gray in a night; he knows not, but this he knows, that he may lose all, and he knows this, that he cannot in any way avoid the issue, for the resolution holds him fast there where love chains him, but also holds him undismayed there where love is groaning. There is an old saying which perhaps has fallen a bit into discredit, no matter, it runs as follows: "What will a man not do for the sake of wife and children?" Answer: "He does everything, everything." And what does one do against fate? Who can fathom its secret? A man bares his arm, he labors, he struggles, he suffers, ah, there is nothing a man will not endure! The more positive a man's resolution is, the more declinable he himself becomes, and only a married man is declined by fate in all *genera, numeri* and *casibus.*[20] — Externally regarded there are hundreds upon hundreds who have risked more than a married man, have risked riches and lands, millions upon millions, have lost thrones and principalities, fortune and well-being, and yet the married man risks more. For he who loves risks more than all such things as that, and he who loves in as many ways as it is possible for a man to love risks most of all. Suppose then that the married man is a king, a millionaire—no need of that, no need of it, everything else only confuses the clearness of the reckoning—let him be a beggar, he risks most of all. Suppose then that the courageous man takes part in the hero-dances in the ballroom, or dances upon the tumultuous sea—no need of that, no need of it, for daily use there is no need of it; in the theater perhaps it might be needed, but it would go ill with mankind if life and the good Lord did not have several reserve batallions of heroes who are not applauded although they risk more. A married man takes a risk every day, and every day the sword of duty hangs over his head, and the journal of accounts is kept open as long as marriage lasts, and the protocol of responsibility is never closed, and the responsibility arouses more enthusiasm that the most glorious epic poet who has to bear witness to heroes. Well, it is true, he does not take the risk for nothing. No, it is an even wager, he risks all for all, and if marriage with its responsibility is an epic, it is also by reason of its happiness an idyl.

Thus marriage is the beauteous mid-point and center of human existence, giving a reflection as deep as the thing is high which is

[20] Gender, number and case.

disclosed by it: a revelation which in cryptic form discloses the heavenly. And this is what every marriage does, just as the quiet lake reflects as well as the ocean, provided the water is not turbid. To be a husband is the most beautiful and the most significant task. The man who has not become such is an unfortunate one whose life either did not permit it or whom love did not visit, or he is a suspicious character who had better be taken into custody. Marriage is "the fullness of time." The man who never married is an unfortunate, either to an observer or to himself—in his eccentricity he will find time a burden. Such is marriage. It is divine, for love is the miracle; it is of the world, for love is nature's profoundest myth. Love is the unfathomable bottom which is hidden in obscurity, but resolution is the victor which like Orpheus fetches love out to the light of day, for resolution is love's true form, its true transfiguration, hence marriage is holy and blessed by God. It is civic, for thereby the lovers belong to the state and the fatherland and the concerns of their fellow citizens. It is poetic, ineffably poetic, as love is, but resolution is the conscientious translator who translates enthusiasm into reality, and this translator is so precise, oh, so precise! Love's voice "sounds like that of fairies from the grottoes of midsummer-night," but resolution has the earnestness of perseverance which resounds through the fleeting and the transitory. Love's gait is light as the feet which dance upon the meadow, but resolution holds the tired one till the dance begins again. Such is marriage. It is childishly joyful and yet solemn, because it has constantly before its eyes the miracle. It is unassuming and retiring, though festivity dwells within it, but as the tradesman's door is shut upon the street during divine service, so is that of marriage always shut because divine service is constantly going on. It is troubled by concern, but this concern is not uncomely, since it is due to an understanding and a sense of the deep pain in the whole of existence—he is uncomely who knows not this concern. It is serious and yet tempered by jest; for not to will to do all is a poor jest, but to do one's utmost and then to understand that it is little, little, nothing in comparison with love's wish and resolution's desire, is a blissful jest. It is humble and yet bold, yea, such boldness is found only in marriage, because it is fashioned out of man's strength and woman's weakness and is rejuvenated by the child's freedom from care. It is faithful, verily if marriage were not faithful, where would faithfulness be found? It is secure, composed, snugly at home in existence, no danger is a real danger but only a temptation. It is content with little, it knows also how to use much, but it knows also how to be beautiful in frugal circumstances, and knows how to be no less beautiful in abundance. It is content and yet full of expectation, the lovers are sufficient to one another and yet exist only for the sake of others. It is commonplace, yea, what is so commonplace as marriage, it belongs entirely to the temporal, and yet the memory of eternity accompanies it and is forgetful of nothing.

This must suffice as a plea for marriage. It doesn't occur to me at this moment to say more; another time, perhaps tomorrow, I may have more to say, but "always the same thing and about the same,"[21] for only gypsies, robber gangs and swindlers follow the adage that where a person has once been he is never to go again. At any rate, it appears to me to be enough, and the only additional remark I would make is that if marriage were merely half as good a thing as it is, it would for all that be well pleasing to me; and I am the more ready to conclude because I feel that it is not a eulogy upon myself I have been pronouncing but rather a judgment. However, one can be a happy husband without having attained perfection, if only one has this aim in view and is sensible of one's imperfection. Here I have wanted only to peg the price up a bit; for when one has to do with bores who seize every occasion to grumble, with freebooters who ravage with fire and sword, with spies who lurk at the door, with street-loungers who would rush from the street right into the house, then one authoritatively imposes respect for holy things and plays blindman's buff with them a bit, knowing that they stand at the street door, the blind door of marriage, and collect there, but in that way can get to know nothing about marriage.

Now for the objections. Even if a married man cannot formulate them so sharply as a *chicaneur* can, yet he knows very well where the shoe pinches, and in rendering an account of marriage he knows how to include such things, or at least he has acquired a general aptitude for taking a hint. To elaborate the objections in detail would be a waste of time, even if one had a talent for doing that. However, this much is certain, that everyone who raises objections is always a person to be pitied. Either he has sown his wild oats and thereby hardened himself, or he is befuddled in his understanding. In the case of every objection which is due to the latter cause the first reply to be made is that "Bah!," *à la* Hamann. One lets the man talk as long as he wants to, then inquires whether he has finished, and thereupon utters that magic word. When one has thus closed the door on him there is a second reply to be made. The sophist Gorgias is reported to have said with reference to tragedy that it is a deception wherein the person deceived is evidently better off

[21] As Socrates said about his teaching.

than the person not deceived, the deceived is wiser than the non-deceived.[22] The last observation is an eternal truth and makes an apt reply whenever the understanding runs wild in its own conceits and is deceived precisely by the fear of being deceived. Yes, verily, for remaining in the blissful deceit of love and of illusion and of the miracle a very different sort of wisdom is required than for running from house to house stark naked and half mad from sheer common sense. So queer appears the contradiction. Distraction of mind is sometimes due to lack of memory, and yet there are instances of a man becoming *distrait* because he has too much memory.

If the objection is to be fundamental, it ought in aiming against marriage to aim first against love, for the first should always be first. This seldom occurs. The enemies who aim against love are the less mischievous and only very rarely get a hearing. As soon as the understanding would make an attempt to explain or to think love, the ludicrous is in evidence, which is best expressed by saying that the understanding becomes ludicrous. The matter assumes a different aspect, however, in relation to the character of the speaker. If he is a depraved man who ends a dissolute life by wanting to heap ridicule upon that which has always known how to evade his profane touch, though he has dabbled a good deal in so-called love, in this case a reply of any sort is superfluous. However, a more admissible form of objection can be conceived, it is so admissible that one may be inclined to pity the erring one and explain his error. He must be a youth who actually is pure in relation to the erotic, but a youth who, like a child too early wise, has skipped one stadium of the soul's development and happened to begin life with reflection.[23] Such a case is conceivable in our reflective age, a man of this sort may even be regarded as a legitimate instance, inasmuch as all the talk about reflection, the deification of it, the assumption of its necessity which is enforced by the maxim of doubting everything,[24] is in this case expressed by the fact that he (more serious than many a light-minded systematic philosopher who would like to make a hit by writing a book about doubting everything) gets the desperate idea into his head of wanting to think the erotic, to think himself into it, i.e. think himself cut of it. Such an individual is an unhappy individual, and inasmuch as he actually is pure I cannot think without sympathy of his misfortune.

[22] The motto printed after the title-page of this section. Plutarch, *De gloria Atheniensum,* 5.

[23] Such was precisely the case with S.K.—and with "the young man" who spoke at the Banquet.

[24] A shot aimed at the followers of Descartes.

He is like the Valkyrie who has lost her swan-skin[25] and now sits forlorn, attempting to fly but attempting it in vain in spite of all her efforts. This youth has lost the immediacy which carries a man through life, the immediacy without which love is impossible, the immediacy which is constantly taken for granted and constantly carries a man a step further; he is excluded from the benefit of immediacy for which one never can get to the point of properly expressing one's thanks, because the benefactor always hides himself.

As it is distressing to behold the misery of that Valkyrie, so also it is distressing to behold the thought-struggle of such a man, whether he suffers dumbly or by demoniac virtuosity in reflection knows how to hide his nakedness by the adroit word.

All love is a wonder, a miracle—what wonder then that the understanding is brought to a standstill while the lovers are prostrate in adoration before the sacred sign of the wonder. With respect to what we are here talking of, as in all cases, one should take heed to the expressions one uses. There is a category which means "to choose oneself,"[26] a somewhat modernized Greek category; it is my favorite category and applies to the individual life as a whole, but must never be applied to the erotic, as when one speaks of choosing one's lady-love, for a lady-love is a gift of the deity; and as the chooser who chooses himself is assumed to be in existence prior to the choice, so, if the word is to be used in the same sense in both connections, we must assume that the lady-love is also in existence prior to the choice. If then one uses this expression, "to choose," in the sense of proposing someone as the beloved, instead of accepting the beloved as given, an erring reflection can at once have something to hold on to. The youth then resolves love into loving the lovable object which he has to *choose*. Poor chap, that is an impossibility; and not only that, for after all who would dare to woo if wooing is to be understood in this sense? and what manikin would dare to dote in such a way upon himself that he does not sense the truth that he who woos must first have been moved to woo by the deity and that all other wooing is foolish effrontery? I decline to woo in this way, I had rather thank the deity for the gift. He chooses better, and to give thanks is more blessed. I do not want to become ridiculous by wanting to begin with a senseless critical discourse about the beloved, saying that I love her for this reason, and for that reason, and finally for the reason . . . that I love her. Rightly used such a discourse delivered before the lovers themselves

[25] Helene, in Hertz' *Svanehammern,* Dramatic Works, Vol. VI, pp. 195 *ff.*—a play produced in 1841.

[26] A category which S.K. emphasizes in the second part of *Either/Or.*

may be highly entertaining, by assuming in a purely humorous way that the whole content of love is equivalent to this or that insignificant trait, as if a husband were to say to his wife that he loves her because her hair is blond. Such talk is a humorous jest which has long lost sight of all the pompous importance of reflection. I render unto the deity the things that are the deity's, and this every man ought to do. But he does not do it when he denies the deity the sacred tribute of admiration and wonder. Precisely when the understanding has been brought to a standstill it is in place to possess the courage and the heart to believe in the miraculous, and to return, constantly strengthened by this vision, to reality, not with the purpose of sitting still and wanting to fathom the miracle. However, a fruitless effort after a sharp and well maintained critique which brings down desperation upon the head of the reflecting one, and perhaps thereby saves him, I greatly prefer to a loquacious sort of reflection, a tire-woman who wants to attire love and knows more than the miracle does. Verily love is a miracle, not the latest news of the town, and its priest is a worshiper, not a street wench.

In paganism accordingly they ascribed love to Eros. Since the resolution of marriage adds the ethical element, that half coquettish ascription becomes in marriage a purely religious expression for the fact that one received the beloved from the hand of God. As soon as God exists for consciousness, the miracle is present, for otherwise God cannot be present. The Jews expressed this by saying that he who beholds God must die. This was merely a figurative expression, the adequate and true expression is that one loses one's reason, as does the lover when he beholds the beloved—and at the same time . . . beholds God. True enough, I have been a married man for no inconsiderable time, and perhaps people may laugh at my enthusiasm. Let them laugh! A married man is always in love, and, if not, he never comes to understand love. The knight of reflection, the knight of the sorrowful countenance, goes further;[27] he would fathom the synthesis implied in love. He does not notice that there is a veil hung before his eyes and that again he stands before the miracle. God creates out of nothing, but here, if I dare say so, He does more by clothing an instinct with the beauty of love, so that the lovers see only the beauty and are unaware of the instinct. Who would lift the veil? Who would dare to do that? The ideal beauty is the veiled beauty, and surely the moon shining through the veil of the clouds is only half as beautiful, and the heavens dream only half as yearningly through the curtain of flowers, and the sea by its half-transparency tempts only half

[27] As all the Hegelians professed to do.

so strongly as the beloved one, as the wife, through the veil of modesty. I rave? I am only a poor wretch of a husband? So you may think. But what am I to say about the mystery which was a mystery to me and is and remains such throughout the years? For I have no notion that any explanation is to come, I cannot even comprehend the odious presumption that the veil of nature is more precious than the veil of virtue.

So there he goes, that poor fellow whom reflection, as it ever does, reduces to beggary; he goes further, his fanaticism makes him more unhappy, his wealth makes him poorer. He is brought to a standstill by what he would likely call the consequences of love. And who is not brought to a standstill here? It is as though the natural course of existence were at a standstill while the divinity creatively intervenes. Oh, blessed capacity for wonder! Who does not give thanks for beholding the divinity here, that he may not like the tired warrior of reflection sink into melancholy? Who does not give thanks with joy over existence —not as though the child were a wonder of a child, an infant prodigy (vanity! vanity!), but it is a wonder, a miracle, that a child is born. He who will not perceive the miracle here must (in case he is not utterly shallow) say like Thales[28] that for love of children he will have no children—the most melancholy saying (for therein is implied that it is a greater crime or misfortune to give life to a man than to deprive a man of life), or it is the most baneful self-contradiction.

So love is vindicated as a miracle, and everything pertaining to love pertains to the miracle. Love then is to be regarded simply as a given fact. Every attempt of reflection to explain it, however flattering it is or however offensive, however reckless or however dull, is as a matter of course condemned as false. — There remains the further question, how this immediate experience (love) can find a corresponding expression in an immediacy which is attained through reflection.[29] Here it is that the decisive battle is to be fought.

Now, however, I would call attention to another aspect of the matter. Love is commonly only too much extolled. Even a seducer has impudence enough to want to take part in it. But with this the instant or brief period of love is regarded as woman's culmination, and hence the thing to do is to let go of her. The objections then take another direction, and the gallant's flattering adoration of the sex ends with insult.

28 According to Diogenes Laertius, I, 26.

29 "Immediacy after reflection" is an ideal which hovered before S.K.'s eyes, and which he did in some measure attain, along with the simplicity which is the product of much reflection.

I was differently brought up in the Christian religion, and far as I am from being able to approve of the indecent attempts to emancipate woman, all pagan reminiscences seem to me equally foolish. My short and simple opinion is that woman is quite as good as man—and with that enough has been said. Every more prolix performance upon the theme of the difference between the sexes, and every deliberation as to which sex has the preeminence, is an idle intellectual occupation for the unemployed and for bachelors. One recognizes a well brought up child by the fact that he is delighted with what he gets, and so likewise one recognizes a well brought up husband by the fact that he is joyful and grateful for what providence has allotted him—in other words, he is in love. One sometimes hears a married man complain that marriage gives him so much to attend to; how much more then he must find to attend to if at the same time he is shameless enough to want to be merely his wife's critic and censor, who every other minute of the day torments her with his hollow pretentions, that she should smile thus, hold her head thus, curtsy thus, dress thus, pronounce her words thus, or else wants to be both husband and at the same time critic and censor. As a matrimonial critic I am a perfect tyro. I have had no frivolous preparatory studies of the foppish period, which sometimes are more poisonous than people think. In a certain sense the story of my love affair is short: I was busy about my own affairs and attended to my studies; I have not sampled the girls at balls and promenades, in the theater and at concerts, I have not done it frivolously, neither have I done it with the stupid seriousness of a marriageable male who is pleased to think that it must be an extraordinary girl who is to be good enough for him. Being thus inexperienced, I learned to know her who now is mine; I never loved before, my prayer is that I may not love again later; but if for an instant I were to think what to me is unthinkable, that death might deprive me of her, that there might take place in me such an alteration that for a second time I should be consecrated as a husband, I am convinced that my marriage has not spoiled me or made me more apt to criticize, to sort and to sample. What wonder we hear so much foolish talk about love, since we hear so much talk about it—which in itself is an indication that reflection is everywhere forcing its way in to disturb the quiet and more modest life where love preferably makes its abode, because such a life in its modesty is so close to godly fear.

In view of all this I perceive clearly that the aesthetic critics will without more ado declare me incompetent to engage with them in such an argument, and all the more when I make no concealment of the fact that though I have been married eight years I do not yet know definitely, in the aesthetic sense, what my wife looks like. To love does not mean to exercise criticism, and marital fidelity does not consist in a detailed critique. This ignorance of mine, however, is not due entirely to my lack of culture, for I too can perceive the beautiful, but it is in this way I behold a picture, a statue, not a wife. In part I have her to thank for this, for if she had taken any sort of vain delight in being the object of a love-maker's critical adoration, who knows if I might not have become a love-maker, and ended as usual as a peevish critic and husband? I do not find myself in the least capable of moving easily and with the facility of routine in the employment of technical terms which connoisseurs spout out so readily. I do not require this dexterity, I attend no banquets with the connoisseurs. To put it very mildly, such connoisseurs seem to me like the men who sit and exchange money in the court of the temple, and repulsive as it must be to the man who in an exalted mood would enter the temple to hear the clatter of coins, just so repulsive it is to hear the noise of words like slender, plump, buxom, etc. When I read these words in the writings of a primitive poet where they spring from the originality of feeling and the vernacular idiom I take delight in them, but I do not profane them, and as for my wife, I do not know to this day quite certainly whether she is slender. The joy I find in my love is not that of a haggler, nor is it the hot unhealthiness of a wily seducer. If with regard to her I were to express myself in such terms, I am convinced that I should fall into twaddle. If I have abstained from this hitherto, I presumably am saved for the remainder of my life; for the presence merely of a tiny baby makes love more shy than it naturally is. I have often thought of this, and hence I have always found it unseemly for an older man who has children to marry a very young girl.

Precisely because love is everything to me, all the outcome of criticism is nonsense. So if I were to extol the feminine sex, I would do it only humoristically; for all this slenderness and plumpness, and the eyebrow and the flash of the eye, do not constitute love, still less a marriage, and only in marriage does love find its true expression, apart from this it is seduction or coquetry.

There exists a small book by Hen. Cornel. Agrippa of Nettesheim: *De nobilitate et praecellentia foemenei sexus ejusdemque supra virilem eminentia.*[30] In this little work the strangest things are said in praise of

[30] The author was a German humanist of the sixteenth century, whose book ("On the nobility and excellence of the feminine sex and its superiority over the male sex") was brought out in 1529. The verse referred to in the text is the first line of a poem which was added by a friend to adorn the complete edition of the author's works which was published in 1600: "Cease with vain eloquence to praise the masculine sex."

woman in the most naïve way. That the author has proved what he set out to prove is not exactly my opinion, although he writes in good faith and is also good-natured enough to believe that he has proved it; but on the other hand I approve entirely of the verse with which the book concludes, deprecating all loquacious (*vaniloquax*) praise of man. When with complete and absolute conviction of the happiness of love and marriage one reads these naïve arguments, to everyone of which is attached a highly pathetic *ergo* or *quod erat demonstrandum,* whereas the real pathos is to be found in that conviction which requires no proof, the whole thing produces a purely humorous effect. I will explain this a little more precisely. Before the Twenty-eighth of May Society[31] a speech was once delivered by a scientific young man who in his enthusiasm for the natural sciences was inclined to believe that every new discovery, and so in particular the latest invention, that of making soap from flint, brings God closer to us and convinces us of His goodness, wisdom, etc. If this speech is to be regarded as a serious attempt to get closer to God, it appears to me a perfectly wretched one. It is quite a different case, however, when an individual who is a millionaire in the matter of faith and "better" than the Bank of England, noticing that reflection shows symptoms of wanting to prove something with regard to this matter, were to prevent the production of this proof by making the assertion that now one could even wash one's hands with soap made of flint. He might conclude his speech somewhat in this fashion: "Look, now I am washing my hands; in case this proof is not convincing, I despair of being able to produce any."[32] In the little book mentioned above the statement is made by way of proof that in the Hebrew tongue woman is called Eva (life), and man Adam (earth)—*ergo*. As a jest introduced in the course of an *altercatio* where everything is absolutely determined and attested by the seal of the notary public and of God such a thing may be capital. So again when this author produces as another proof the fact that when a woman falls into the water she floats on top of it, whereas a man, on the contrary, when he falls into the water, sinks—*ergo*. This proof may also be employed in another way, for it helps in some measure to explain the fact that in the Middle Ages so many witches were burnt.

It is several years since I read that little book, but I got a lot of entertainment out of it. The drollest things are brought forward in the most

[31] A society which Tschnerning attempted to establish in 1831 to celebrate the introduction on that date of the Provincial Chambers. The society was prohibited by the Royal Chancellery, but the anniversary was celebrated during the 'Thirties.

[32] S.K. constantly derided the attempt to *prove* the existence or the attributes of God.

naïve fashion from natural science and philology. Several of them have impressed themselves upon my memory, and while I never talk to my wife about her being slender, etc., which certainly would displease her and would be a flat failure on my part, yet sometimes, though I say it of myself, I am very proficient in such arguments and reflections as do give her pleasure, presumably because they prove nothing at all, and just for this reason are a proof that our marriage stands in need of no long-winded demonstration, but that we are happy.

Apropos of this, I have often wondered that no poet seriously tries to present a married couple engaged in conversation. If once in a while they are presented (and in this case they have to be a happy couple), they talk like a pair of lovers. Generally they are only subordinate characters, and so far along in life that they can serve as the father and mother of the lovers whom the poet prefers to present. If a marriage is depicted, it must at least be an unhappy one if it is to be taken into consideration. So different are these two things: love must be happy and be imperiled from without; marriage, to be poetic, must be imperiled from within. I regard this as a dolorous proof that marriage is very far from enjoying the appreciation it deserves, for it appears as though a pair of married people were not so poetic as a pair of lovers. Let the lovers talk with all the froth of love's passion, as young men and maidens like to do, but the married people are by no means a sorry lot. I take it that he is a sorry husband who does not become a humorist through his marriage, in the same sense that he is a sorry lover who does not become a poet; and every married man, I take it, becomes somewhat humorous, has a dash of it, just as every lover becomes somewhat poetical. I appeal to my own case for evidence, not so much with reference to the poetic as to a sense of humor, a dash of it, which I owe solely to my marriage. In the case of love much of the erotic has an absolute significance; in marriage this absolute significance alternates with the humorous view of things, which is the poetic pronunciation of the quiet and contented security of married life. I will adduce an example, and I beg the reader to be humorous enough not to regard it as a proof of anything.

In company with my wife I made a little summer excursion in the southern part of Seeland. We journeyed just as we pleased, and as my wife wished to get a notion of what certain people call loitering along the highways, we put up at all sorts of taverns, sometimes spending the night in one of them, but above all giving ourselves plenty of time. In the taverns one had opportunity to take a look about. Now it happened strangely enough that in five taverns in succession we found on the wall an advertisement which thus pursued us so steadily that we were unable to ignore it. The notice was to the following effect: an anxious paterfamilias expressed in the most complimentary terms his thanks to an experienced and skilful practitioner who with the hand of an artist had easily and without any pain relieved the paterfamilias and his entire family of several bad corns and thus restored them to social life. The personnel of the family was specified, and particularly a daughter, who, like an Antigone, since she belonged to this unfortunate family, was not exempt from the family taint. After we had read this advertisement at three stopping-places it is no wonder that it became a subject of conversation. I expressed the opinion that it was tactless of the paterfamilias to tell on the young girl, for even if it was notorious that she had been entirely healed, it might make a suitor hesitate, which was not at all necessary, for corns might be reckoned among the infirmities one could learn to know after the wedding. I beg a poet to tell me whether the theme of this conversation (which I perhaps was not equal to carrying out as humorously as one might) is not humorous; but I would ask him further whether it is not certain that only in the mouth of a husband such a theme is proper. A lover would feel hurt, because this bad corn, even when it is extracted, has an exceedingly disturbing effect upon an aesthetic fanciful intuition of the beautiful. Such a jest in the mouth of a lover would surely be unpardonable. Now even though my conversation, by reason of my lowly talent, was a simple everyday chat, I know all the same that it amused my wife, it amused her that such a casual circumstance was treated as an aesthetic absolute, as e.g. in the query whether this might not be an adequate ground for divorce, etc. And sometimes when in my drawing room there is carried on by a connoisseur or by an over-shrewd little miss a grandiloquent discourse about love and slenderness, and about the importance of the lovers learning to know one another thoroughly, so that in choosing one can be sure of choosing a faultless mate, then I get my word in, playing really into my wife's hand, and I say, "Yes, that is the difficulty, it is very difficult —now in the case of corns, how is anybody to be sure whether one has them, or has had them, or whether one may not get them?"

But enough of this. Humor finds its support in the security of marriage, which, being founded upon the experience of living together, has not the uneasiness of love's first bliss, though its bliss is far from being less. And now when I as a husband, a husband for eight years, rest my head upon her shoulder, I am not a critic that admires or misses some earthly beauty, neither am I an enthusiastic youth that celebrates her bust in song, yet all the same I am moved just as profoundly as the first time. For I know what I knew and what I convince myself of again and again, that in this breast of my wife there beats a heart, quiet and lowly, but steady and even; I know that it beats for me and my welfare and for what pertains to us both; I know that its quiet, tender movement is uninterrupted, while I, alas, am busy with my affairs, while I, alas, am distracted by the multifarious; I know that at whatever hour and under whatever conditions I have recourse to her it has not ceased to beat for me. And I am a believer: as the lover believes that his lady is life to him, so in a spiritual sense I believe, what also is to be found in that little book, that, as scientists teach, the mother's milk is a saving remedy for one who is sick unto death, I believe that this tenderness which struggles unceasingly to find an expression more and more heart-felt, I believe that this tenderness which was her rich dowry as a bride, I believe that it bears interest abundantly, I believe that it will double itself if I do not dissipate her fortune; I believe that this tender glance, if I were sick, sick unto death, in case it rested upon me—ah, as if she herself, not I, were the dying warrior—I believe that it would recall me to life, in case God in heaven will not exercise His power, and if God will exercise His power, then I believe that this tenderness will bind me again to life as a vision which visits her, as a dead man over whom death cannot prevail, until again we are united. But until then, until that time when God exercises His power, I believe that by means of her I imbibe peace and contentment in my life and many a time am saved from the death of despondency and the sore travail of vexation of spirit.[33]

So does every husband talk, and better than this insofar as he is a better husband, better insofar as he is a more talented one. He is not like the youthful lover, his expression has not the passion of the instant —and what an offense it would be in the flash of a passionate instant to want to express thanks for such a love. He is like that honest accountant who in his time nearly became an object of suspicion; for when by reason of a misapprehension the strict auditor came to his door and demanded to see his account-books, he replied, "I have none. I keep the accounts in my head." How suspicious! But honor to the old man's head, his accounts were all right! A married man expresses himself perhaps even a bit humoristically when he talks to his wife about all he owes her; but this humor, this offhand way of giving thanks, this way of making a receipt without paper but in the ledger[34] of remembrance, is a

[33] Eccles. 1 : 13,14.

[34] In Danish the word is *Hovedbog,* literally "head-book," which recalls the "honest accountant."

sure proof that his accounting is reliable and that his marriage possesses in abundance the daily bread of sound assurance.

By this I have already indicated in what direction I am disposed to seek womanly beauty. Alas, even honest men have helped to give currency to the tragic mistake which reckless young girls accept, unfortunately, with only too much eagerness, without reflecting that it means despair: that woman's only beauty is the first beauty of youth,[35] that she

[35] [The following note—one of the seven furnished by S.K., and by far the longest—is by far the most difficult thing I have ever had to translate. I suspect that it was for this reason Schrempf omitted it without comment. One might also be tempted to omit it because it has so little to do with the text. On the other hand it is highly characteristic of S.K., who later published a similar appreciation of an actress in a little work entitled *The Crisis, or a Crisis in the Life of an Actress*, and wrote, though he did not publish, a eulogy of Pfister as an actor. The difficulty did not deter me, but I confess that for the first time I am dubious about my translation. Ordinarily the translator of S.K. finds a safe control in the assurance that what this author wanted to say he must have said in the best possible way. But how can I know precisely what he wanted to say about the egregious (or egregia) Madame Nielsen, when I have not had the pleasure of seeing or hearing her? I cannot believe that this eulogy so intricately expressed is good writing in Danish. It clearly is intolerable in English.]

Precisely because it would be very hazardous, yea, even misleading, in view of the proposition that woman's beauty increases with the years, to call to mind performances of histrionic art, since there everything is concentrated upon the instant and the differences have to be essential, I see with all the greater joy a beautiful truth which is so precious to me corroborated amidst the swift changes of theatrical life. The one actress upon our stage who most fully impersonates the character of femininity, without being confined to one side of it, or being at once helped and hindered by reliance upon accidental traits, or being assigned to one period only of woman's life, is Madame Nielsen. Her figure, which is not directly displayed, her voice, which does justice to the piece, the hearty spirit by which she enlivens the ensemble, the pensive dejection which inspires so much confidence in the spectator, the tranquillity with which she grasps a situation, the self-assured greatness of soul which disdains all adventitious aids, the even quality of her sonorous voice, which does not storm like a tempest, does not provoke tension by failing coquettishly to make itself audible, does not drift wildly into bombast, does not pretentiously keep one in expectancy, does not break out violently, does not gasp after something unutterable, but true to itself, prompt every instant, above all reliable—in short, the whole rendition is concentrated upon what one may call the essential feminine. Many an actress has been great and been admired because of her virtuosity in the presentation of an accidental aspect of the feminine, but this admiration, which also properly finds expression in all sorts of applause, is from the beginning the rightful prey of time, when the "accidents" [meaning also perquisites] vanish away upon which the triumphant rendition reposed. Since Madame Nielsen's *forte* is the essential feminine, her compass comprises the essential even in the less important rôles (as a lady-love in vaudeville, as a mother in an idyl, etc.), the essential in the exalted characters, and the essential also in the depraved, which although womanly depraved belong essentially to the sex, so that one is not made uncomfortable by the unseemly, nor distrustful because of exaggeration, nor inclined to account for the depravity by the upbringing, by the force of circumstances, etc., for precisely in the ideality of the presentation one perceives the depth and the primary character of the depravity. But like her compass, so also is her triumph essentially not the short-lived triumph of the instant, but the triumph which consists in the fact that time has no power over her. At every period

blooms but once, that this instant is the season of love, that one loves but once. That one loves but once is true, but woman's beauty increases with the years, and so far is it from falling off that there is about the first beauty something dubious in comparison with the subsequent beauty. Who, unless it were a madman, has ever beheld a young girl without a certain sense of sadness, because the fragility of life is here made evident in terms of the strongest contrast—vanity as fleeting as a dream, beauty as fair as a dream. But fair as the first beauty is, it is nevertheless not the truth, it is a husk, a mantle, out of which, only in the course of years, the true beauty develops before the husband's grateful eyes.

Contemplate on the other hand the old woman. Thou dost not grasp after her involuntarily, for this is not the fleeting beauty which hastens past like a dream. No, be seated at her side, regard her more closely: she belongs completely to this world by reason of her motherly, solicitous care; her busy time is over, and only solicitude itself remains, with which she hovers like the angels over the Arc of the Covenant. Truly if here thou dost not sense what reality a woman possesses, thou art and wilt

of her life she will find new tasks and express the essential as she did at the beginning of her fine career. And though she were to come to sixty years, she will continue to be a finished actress. I know of no nobler triumph for an actress than that he who perhaps in the whole realm is the one most anxious not to give offense in this case dares to refer, as I do with confidence, to the sixtieth year, which commonly is the greatest age one may mention with relation to an actress. She will perfectly impersonate the grandmother, again producing the effect by the essential, just as her impersonation of the young girl produced its effect without the aid of any extraordinary beauty which would infatuate the reporters, or the voice of a peerless singer which would enchant the connoisseurs, or ability to dance which would arouse the special interest of the public, or a bit of coquetry which every spectator might complacently regard as addressed to him, but with the consecration which is the covenant of pure femininity with the imperishable. Whereas commonly at the theater one is led to think of the vanity of life and youth and beauty and enchantment, in admiring her one feels such confidence because he knows that this will not perish. Perhaps upon others this has a different effect, so that admiration (because there is no reason for haste—and here indeed there is time enough) fails to materialize, and this actress is regarded as belonging to another class, as in fact she does when the requirement is to compete in the instant and to produce an effect, not by durable means, but by ephemeral. Hence perhaps she does not find her admirers among the reporters who register the pulse of the instant, nor among theater fans who must of course have seen this one and that, nor among express messengers who want someone to run a race with them, nor among the jolly fellows who carry people in triumph for a lark, nor among young men who when they can get no other chance for an immature love affair turn to an actress, nor among the superannuated who keep themselves in life by instantaneous excitements, but rather among those who, being themselves happy and content with life, do not feel the need of the theater, do not crave it, whose right hand, as Horace says, does not run hastily into the left for instant applause, whose pen does not get busy at once the very same evening about some detail, but who, slow to speak, rejoice perhaps all the more at seeing the *beautiful* when it is such *in truth.*

ever remain a critic, a reviewer, a connoisseur perhaps, i.e. a despairing man who rushes into the midst of raging despair, shouting, "Let us love today, for tomorrow it will be no more." Not that we shall be no more —that would be sad; but that love will be no more—that is repulsive. So take a little time, sit down beside her. This is not the pleasant fruit of desire. Be on thy guard against every presumptuous thought or against wanting to use the technical terms of the connoisseurs. In case this desire effervesces within thee, sit thou here that thou mayest be tranquillized. This is not the froth of the instant. Wouldst thou in her presence venture to abandon thyself to that, or wouldst thou offer her thine arm for a waltz? So perhaps thou dost prefer to avoid her company—ah, even if the young generation which surrounds her were discourteous enough (so thinks the gentleman of fashion, maybe, who imagines she is in need of his conversation), no, rather, if the young people were gone so astray as to let her sit alone, she feels no lack of their company, feels no sting of offense, she is reconciled with life, and shouldst thou again feel a need of the reconciling word, need of forgetting the dissonances of life, have recourse to her, sit worthily by the worthy—and which then is the most beautiful: the mother who brings to birth by the force of nature, or the decrepit old woman who brings thee to birth again by her solicitous care? Or if thou art not so sore distressed by the turmoil of the world, sit by her side none the less, the worthy beside the worthy; her life too is not devoid of melody, this old age too is *non sine cithara,* and nothing that has been experienced is forgotten, it is all to be heard from the various epochs of life sonorously mingling when this voice touches the strings of recollection. For behold she has attained the solution of life which is called dissolution, yea, she herself is the solution, audibly and visibly. Never does a man's life finish thus, his accounts are commonly more complicated; but a house-mother has only the little happenings, the daily sufferings and the daily joys, but hence also this happiness. For if a young girl is happy, an old woman is happier still. Tell me then, which is the more beautiful: a young girl with her happiness, or an old woman who completes a divine task, who releases (*løser op*) the distressed and for the joyful is the best eulogy upon life by being life's beautiful solution (*Opløsning*)?

Now I leave the old woman, whose company, however, I certainly do not shun. I go backward in time, rejoicing that by God's help I can hope that a good share of my life is before me, but without anything of the cowardice which fears to grow older or fears this for the wife's sake, for indeed my assumption is that woman becomes more beautiful with the years. In my eyes my wife is already far more beautiful than as a young girl. After all, a young girl is a phantom, one scarcely knows whether she belongs to reality or is a vision. And is this to be the loftiest attainment? Yes, let phantoms believe it. On the other hand, as a mother she belongs completely to reality, and mother-love is not like the yearnings and forebodings of youth but is an inexhaustible well-spring of hearty sympathy. Neither is it true that all this was present as a possibility in the young girl. Even if this were so, a possibility is after all less than an actuality. But it is not so. No more than the mother's milk is present in the young girl's breast is this hearty sympathy there. This is a metamorphosis which has no analogy in man. If one can say jestingly that a man is not full-grown until he has his wisdom teeth, one can say seriously that a woman's development is only complete when she is a mother, for only then does she exist in all her beauty and in the beauty of reality. So let that rhapsodical, light, roguish, happy girl bound away over the meadows, making fun of everyone who tries to catch her. Oh, yes, I too rejoice to behold it—but now, now she is caught, imprisoned—it is not I assuredly that caught her (what nonsense and vain foolishness!), assuredly it is not I that hold her imprisoned (how frail a prison!) ; no, she has imprisoned herself, and she sits imprisoned beside the cradle; imprisoned, and yet she is in possession of her full liberty, a boundless liberty by which she binds herself to the child. I am sure she would be willing to die in her nest.

Here only a word in passing. To speak as harmlessly about the matter as possible, I assume that it was the mother's partiality for the child which made the husband a little jealous. Oh, well, good Lord, this jealousy soon vanishes. So now I have mentioned the word jealousy. It is a dark passion, "a monster which defiles the meat it feeds on."[36] Anger also is dark passion, but it does not follow from this that there cannot be such a thing as noble anger. Just so it is with jealousy: in a noble love there is also a justifiable indignation, which truly is both distressed and offended, and above all is a normal condition of the soul, if the dreadful thing has come to pass. I find nothing blameworthy in it; on the contrary, I require of a husband that in this way his soul shall pay the last honors to her who offended him, and to her to whom he accorded, if one will, such immense importance that she is able to offend him. I regard that condition of the soul as love's ethical sorrow over a deceased one. On the other hand, I know that there are demoniac powers in life. I know that there is an unpraiseworthy intrepidity which, being tormented by an evil spirit, would be sheer spirit, and also would like

[36] Shakespeare's *Othello,* Act III, Scene 3, in Schlegel and Tieck's translation: "vor Eifersucht, dem grüngeaugten Scheusal, die besudelt die Speise, die es nährt."

to have the power to remain in a condition quite as objectionable as raging jealousy, power to remain cold, thoroughly iced by the cold passion of wit. For there is a hell in which the heat scorches all life, but there is also a hell in which the cold kills all life.

But I am not jealous even of the mother. A woman's life as mother is a reality so infinitely rich in variety that my love has enough to do day by day in discovering something new. Woman as a mother is never in a situation which might be called the most beautiful or the most interesting; she is always in an interesting situation, and mother-love is soft as pure gold, and malleable in every sense, and yet whole. And the husband's joy is new every day, it is not consumed even though he consumes it, for it is like the food of Valhalla, and even though he does not live upon it, it is certain none the less that he does not live upon bread alone, but also upon the complacent admiration with which he observes the mother's doings—in his own house he has *panis et circenses.*

And how manifold the collisions to which mother-love is exposed, and how beautiful the mother is when her self-denying, self-sacrificing love comes through the trials victoriously! I am not speaking here of what is notorious, conceded, that the mother sacrifices her life for the child. That sounds so lofty, so sentimental, and does not bear the genuine stamp of marriage. It can as well be seen in small things, and appears just as great, just as lovely. When I see it I wonder, and one sees it not rarely even where one would least expect to see it, on the street, for example. Recently I was going along at my businesslike pace from one end of the town to the Court House where I was to pronounce a judicial sentence. It was about half-past one o'clock. Inadvertently my eyes lighted upon a scene on the other side of the street. It was a young mother taking a walk and holding a small son by the hand. This young person was something like two and a half years old. The mother's dress and her appearance seemed to indicate that she belonged even to the more select class, and hence I was surprised at seeing her unaccompanied by either a manservant or a maid. I was soon busy guessing that perhaps her carriage was waiting in another street, or before one of the nearer houses, or perhaps she had to walk only a few paces from the house where she dwelt, or she was . . . etc. Here I cut my guesses short, and I hope the reader will thank me for setting about so seriously to find earnest and thorough solutions. But after all the situation was rather surprising. The boy was a pretty child. He inquired curiously about everything, came to a stop and looked and inquired, "What is that?" I hastily put on my glasses in order to see more clearly and enjoy more thoroughly the lovable manner, the tender motherliness, with which she entered into everything, the loving joy with which she contemplated the little darling. The boy's questions puzzled her—perhaps no one had ever told her what a wise man[37] once said, that to talk with children is a *tentamen rigorosum,* perhaps the circle to which she seemed to belong still supposed that this was no art—what a desperate embarrassment then to be put in a tight place by the little urchin, as also by the loudness of his question, which invited the attention of the passers-by, the scene being enacted in a street so frequented as the Østergade. Embarrassment!—nothing of the sort could I discover; motherly joy was plainly written upon her countenance, and the situation did not disturb it. Suddenly the little one stood still and demanded to be carried. This was evidently contrary to the understanding they started out with, a breach of their agreement, for otherwise a nursemaid would have been brought with them. Here was a difficult situation—yet not for her. With the most lovable air in the world she took him in her arms and went straight on without turning into a side street to avoid observation. In my eyes this was as beautiful and solemn as a procession, and I piously made after them. One and another turned to look, she noticed nothing, did not hasten her steps, being unalterably absorbed in her motherly happiness. I have sat as examining magistrate on commissions of inquiry and thereby acquired a certain expertness in observing faces, but on pain of losing my office I declare that there was not a trace of any awkward constraint, or of any restrained anger, or of any postponed impatience; there was no effort to let the countenance express any reflection upon the well-nigh ludicrous situation. As she would walk in her own room with the little one in her arms, so she walked along the Østergade. Mother-love is willing to sacrifice life for the child; in this collision it appears to me equally beautiful. Was the little one in the wrong, was he perhaps quite able to walk, was it naughtiness on his part —it will not be held up against him when he gets home. And in a different case, what would have made the difference? What else but that the mother had reflected upon herself? There are perhaps few collisions in which even tender parents more readily make a mistake than when the whole thing is an insignificance, but this little insignificance puts them to embarrassment. The child has perhaps a slightly awkward manner, at which one commonly laughs in the home, and the child has not the least idea that it is at fault; then there is a guest present, and the vain mother would like a little flattery, and behold, the child makes his bow a bit awkwardly, and the mother is angry—not at a thing of any

[37] Hamann, *Works,* Vol. II, pp. 424 *ff.*: "To answer the questions of children is a *tentamen rigorosum,*" i.e. a stiff examination.

importance, but the reflection upon herself makes this unimportant thing important. Oh, yes, if the little boy had fallen, had bumped his head, or had perhaps come too close to a carriage, had it been a question of saving the child with danger to one's life, I should indeed have had a sight of motherliness, but this quiet expression of it appears to me equally beautiful.

In its everyday manifestations mother-love is just as beautiful as on the most critical occasions, and really it is in its everyday use that it is essentially beautiful, because there it is in its element; because there, without receiving any propulsion or any increment of strength from external catastrophes, it is set in motion by itself alone, is nourished by itself, and propels itself by its own primitive instinct; unassuming as it is, it is always prompt to do its lovable work. Unhappy the man who has to go out into the world to seek the flower we call thousand-joys, and yet finds it not. Unhappy the man who has at the most a notion that his neighbor cultivates it. Happy the husband if he knows properly how to rejoice in his thousand-joys. If he discovers this flower outside his own domain, this flower which—unlike the gorgeous flower that has the remarkable trait of blooming but once in a hundred years, has the still more remarkable trait of blooming every day and not even closing at night—then he has joy in relating at home what he has seen abroad. Yesterday I related to my wife a little happening which attracted my attention to such a degree that it made me an inattentive and distracted hearer of the sermon, which usually I am not. Perhaps the young mother who was responsible for my distraction did wrong in taking the little child with her to church. Perhaps—but for this I can forgive her, for this surely was because she would not commit the child to a nursemaid in her absence. I base this conclusion upon the fact that she was a mother who goes to church, not a lady who pays a formal visit there. Do not misunderstand me, as though the thing were decided by the length of time one remains in church. Far from it. I believe rather that a poor servant-girl who can hardly get away from the house and with all her haste does not succeed in getting to church any earlier than just in time to hear the priest say Amen, I believe that she can bring home a blessing from her church-going; but a person who in other respects has plenty of time for every sort of thing in life might after all find time to go to church properly. Our churchgoer came accordingly in very good time, and along with her came her little restlessness; yet I am convinced that the sermon and the whole service had no auditor more devout than she. She was shut into the pew, and the irregular member of the congregation was put up on the seat, presumably in the hope that he would sit like a regular member. This pretention, however, seemed not to have occurred to the little one. The mother bowed her head, holding her handkerchief before her eyes while she prayed. Long before she looked up again the little one had jumped down and begun to crawl about in the pew. She continued in prayer, entirely undisturbed. When she had finished her prayer she set him up again on the seat and spoke to him, presumably a few words of admonition. The service began, but the game had begun before the service, and the little one seemed on his way to find pleasure in this up-and-down and down-and-up again. Till now he had been seated at the right of his mother and had another lady on his right, while the mother sat at the end of the pew. Now there was a change of place. First it was ascertained that the door was firmly shut, then the mother moved up and shared fairly with him, so that he had the corner of the pew at his disposition. He made no noise, but like a child that is accustomed to shift for himself he got hold of his mother's parasol as a plaything, and only as he would climb farther along in the pew did he find his way blocked. The mother remained absorbed in her devotions; only when the priest paused did she look down lovingly at the little one in the underworld. With a countenance radiant with joy in the child she turned her glance up again to the priest and now listened to the discourse with wholehearted devotion. To be able to divide her interest so equally, to have joy in the child even when he disturbed her, or at least seemed as if he would disturb her, or at least was somehow in the way, to make no foolish demands upon the child—for many parents require almost more devotion of such a small being than of themselves, and discompose the child and themselves by persisting in scolding him and correcting him and putting him in his place—to be able to divide her interests so equally that at the same time with undivided soul she is absorbed in devotion, this too is a beautiful expression of motherliness. Insignificant—oh, yes, but it is precisely in the insignificant situations that motherliness is essentially beautiful.

However, it is only the married man who has the open eye for the beautiful achievements of motherliness; he has at the same time the genuine sympathy which is fashioned out of seriousness in appreciating the infinite significance of the task, and of joy in existence which prompts him to make discoveries, though the joy does not on this account break out exactly in words and jubilation. Or might it be jealousy alone and evil passions which keep a husband clear-sighted and vigilant; might not faithful love be able to do the same, yea, be able to keep him vigilant longer? Or did not the wise virgins keep vigilant longer than the foolish ones? In this respect a married man is well described in a good sense by the terms with which Shakespeare describes a deceiver:[38] "a finder-out of occasions, that has an eye can stamp counterfeit advantages, though true advantage never presents itself"—that is to say, the married man does this with the quiet joy which shows that he does not pretend to be an adept, and neither does he coin falsely, and he rarely is in the situation of not finding such advantages.

Woman as a bride is more beautiful than as a young girl, as a mother she is more beautiful than as a bride, as wife and mother she is a good word spoken in due season, and with the years she becomes more beautiful. The beauty of the young girl is evident to many, it is more abstract, more extensive. Hence they flock around her, the pure and the impure. Then the deity brings him who is her lover. He sees indeed her beauty, for one loves the beautiful, and that is to be understood as identical with this, that loving is seeing the beautiful. Thus it is that the beautiful passes unnoticed under the nose of reflection. From now on her beauty becomes more intensive and concrete. The wife has no flock of adorers, she is not even beautiful, she is only beautiful in her husband's eyes. In the degree that this beauty becomes more and more concrete, she becomes less and less easy to appraise by the ordinary standards of gauging and sorting. Is she for this reason less beautiful? Is an author less rich in thought for the reason that an ordinary perusal of him discovers nothing, whereas a reader who has made him his sole study discovers greater and greater riches? Is it a perfection in a human work of art that it makes the best showing at a distance? Is it an imperfection in the flower of the field, as in all of the works of God, that for microscopic observation it becomes finer and finer, more and more delicate, more and more charming?

But if a wife and mother is so beautiful in her happiness, or rather if to him to whom she pertains she is a benediction, in her misfortune and in the day of need she is again more beautiful than the young girl. Let her child die, and then behold the sorrowing mother. There is surely no one who greets the babe on its arrival with such joy as the mother, but neither is there any that can sorrow so when again death comes to fetch it away. But a sorrow which is precisely as ideal as it is real is the most poetic sorrow. — Or a husband dies. He leaves nothing behind him, so it is said, except a sorrowing wife. It seems to me he leaves behind him endless wealth. Let a young girl lose her lover, let her sorrow be never so deep, let her preserve his memory, her sorrow nevertheless is abstract like her recollection; to perform that daily requiem which is the vocation of the sorrowing wife she lacks the consecration and the

[38] *Othello,* Act II, Scene 1, where Iago describes Cassio.

epic prerequisites. Verily I have no desire to leave behind me a great and celebrated name, if it is so to be, if in death which is the final thing I must take the final step of seeking separation from her whom I love, my wife, my happiness here upon earth; yet in case I leave her behind me sorrowing, I have left indeed what I shall sorely miss, yea, I have left what last of all I would do without, but I also leave behind what I should be reluctant to do without, namely, a memory which better than the song of the poet or the defiant immortality of monumental bronze many a time and in many a way will preserve a remembrance of me, will take of its own and give it unto me. — Finally let the wife be tried by the hardest fate, let her be unhappily married. What is the brief suffering of the deceived maiden in contrast with this daily torture? What is the pith of her sorrow compared with the wretchedness which laments with a thousand tongues, this misery which none can bear to look upon, this slow agony which none can follow? And presumably it is because none can follow it that one forgets how beautiful, how far more poetic, here again the wife is than the young girl. Great is Desdemona by reason of her "sublime life"; one admires her for this, and yet she is greater by reason of the angelic patience which, if it were to be described, would fill more books than the greatest library contains, although it is of no avail to fill up the bottomless abyss of jealousy, where it disappears as nothing, yet almost incites the hunger of the passion.

But woman is the weaker sex. This remark seems to come rather *mal à propos* in the present context, for it is hardly thus she has shown herself. In fact a silken cord may be just as strong as an iron chain, and indeed the chain which bound the Fenris Wolf[39] was invisible, was something which had no existence at all. And what if it should be so also in the case of woman's weakness, that it is an invisible power which expresses its strength by weakness? If the objectors must be allowed to use this phrase, "the weaker sex," well, let them do so then, after all they have common usage on their side. One must always beware, however, of concluding prematurely that individual instances constitute the rule. Accordingly I do not mean to deny that it may quite well be that a young girl looks queer—and even comic, if one is depraved enough to laugh—when she is thrown into the utmost dismay at her crisis, into a whirlwind which a man can hardly stand up against to keep her from being whirled away. But who says that she must be thrown into that peril? The same girl, quietly, carefully and lovingly treated, would perhaps

[39] The subject of one of the *Diapsalmata* in *Enten/Eller*, Vol. I, p. 21, which is quoted in my *Kierkegaard*, p. 105.

have become a lovable being as mother and wife. At such things one ought not to laugh, for there is something tragic in seeing the storm tear away the peaceful enclosure where it might have been delicious to dwell in security. Woman should not be so strong that the distress of dismay might perhaps be on the side of the man. If he stands firm, woman by his side stands as firm as the man, and in union they both stand more firmly than either of them alone.

The trouble with this objection is that those who talk thus about woman consider her only aesthetically. This again is the same old gallant and insolent, tickling and insulting talk about her having only one instant in her life, or a brief period, which is the first awakening of adolescence. But he who rightly would talk about her strength or weakness must see her when she stands fully armed, and that is as wife and mother. Severe trials of strength, moreover, are not to be required of her, nor attempted by her, and if one persists in talking about strength, the first condition or the essential form of all strength is endurance. In this respect man perhaps cannot hold his own with her. Besides, how much force is required for every feigned movement! But what is devotion but a concealed expenditure of force, an expenditure of force which is expressed by its opposite, by weakness? For example, good taste and carefulness about one's toilet may express itself by an effect of carelessness, which however is not the carelessness which every baker's boy understands. Or, for example, the ripe intellectual fruit produced by much effort has a simplicity, which is not however that which every seminarist admires in his simplicity. If I think of two actors, one of whom plays the part of Don Juan and the other that of the Commandant, in the scene where the Commandant holds the other's hand in his while Don Juan tries desperately to wrest it away, I ask which of them employs the more force. Don Juan is the passive sufferer, the Commandant stands calmly with his hand outstretched. Yet I back Don Juan. If the actor who plays the part of Don Juan were to employ even a half of his force, he would make the Commandant totter; if on the other hand he did not twist and writhe, he would spoil the effect. What then does he do? He employs one half of his force to express his pain, the other half he employs to support the Commandant, and whereas he seems with all his force to wish to wrest himself free from the Commandant's grasp, he holds on to the Commandant lest he totter. So it is in reality (for this is only a foolish tale), so it is in the case of the wife. She loves the husband so dearly that she always wants him to be the master, and this is the reason why he looks as if he were so strong and she so weak, because she employs her strength to support him, employs it in the form of devotion and subjection. Oh, marvellous weakness! Though the gallery believes that the Commandant has the superior force, though the profane extol man's strength and abuse it to humiliate woman, the married man has a different understanding of the situation, and the deceived is wiser than the not-deceived, the deceived is justified rather than the not-deceived.

People measure strength, moreover, in various ways. When Holger Danske[40] squeezed the sweat out of an iron gauntlet, that was strength; but if one had put a sparrow in his hand, I am afraid he would not have been strong enough to take hold of it rightly. I will mention the highest instance. God's omnipotence shows itself great in having created all things, but does it not show itself equally great in the almighty moderation which can permit a blade of grass to grow in its season? To woman the less important tasks are assigned, which demand all the more strength because they are less important. She chooses her task, chooses it joyfully, and finds joy at the same time in endowing man constantly with the more obvious strength. For my part, I believe that my wife can perform wonders, and the greatest deeds I read about I can understand better than that delicate embroidery of hers with which she clothes and beautifies my earthly existence.

When one has got it firmly fixed in his head that woman is the weaker sex, by which the generality of *chicaneurs* mean more precisely that she has a first instant of youth when indeed she exhausts and surpasses all praise, and that therewith it is over, that her strength was an illusion, and that the only real force she retains is that of the scream—why then of course one can make queer things out of it. Jean Paul says somewhere, "To such secants, cosecants, tangents and cotangents, everything appears eccentric, especially the center." Just because marriage is the central thing, woman must be viewed in relation to that, as man also ought to be, and all talk and reflection about each sex for itself is confused and profane, for what God has joined together, what existence has designed the one for the other, thought also should think together. When a male takes it into his head to keep them apart, it doubtless seems to him to recoil upon woman, whereas in fact he himself becomes quite as ludicrous, a male who with a superior air would ignore a relationship to which existence has bound him no less than woman.

If this comes to pass, the "pepper-prentice" (for however much one may have tried his hand in what one is pleased to call the erotic, even if one were a scoundrel or, what one more frequently encounters, a wind-

[40] A legendary Danish hero who is said to have squeezed an iron bar so tightly that the impress of his hand was left upon it.

bag, we are accustomed to call him in our language a pepper-prentice)—the pepper-prentice then makes an appeal to the ethical categories. But this can be regarded at the most as a crotchet; for to employ ethical categories in order to offend woman, or with the wish to offend, is not exactly the sign of an ethical character. Such jumbling together of paganism, which reduces woman platonically to an incomplete form, and Christianity, which vindicates her ethical claim, I have never seen explicitly carried out. So it must be a confused brain in which such a conceit could become so self-important as to wish to be given a more explicit expression.

On the other hand, the objections raised against woman assume an aspect of profound irony, which is not without a tragic and comic effect when it is set forth with a certain good humor, yes, even with sympathy for the sad fate which is supposed to reduce her to sheer illusion. It sticks to the assumption that she is the weaker sex. The tragedy lies in the fact that this is concealed from her by illusion, and outwardly concealed from her by man's gallantry. It is as if the whole of existence were playing blindman's buff with her. Here is a fit task for irony. What a pity the whole thing is a fiction. The highest things are now affirmed of woman with the most flattering phrases, up to—yea, far beyond—the bounds of the fantastic. Everything great in life is due to her. In this poetry and gallantry are unanimous, and irony is of course the most gallant of all, for gallantry is the mother tongue of irony, and it is never so gallant as when it regards the whole thing as a humbug. Woman's existence in the world becomes a mock procession of fools in motley, and irony acts as gallantry's master of ceremonies. The procession reminds one of the crazy schoolmaster in one of Hoffmann's tales, who holding a ruler as his scepter, and bowing graciously to right and left, announces that his general has now returned home after a victory over the Langobards, whereupon he takes a couple of cloves from his waistcoat pocket and hands them to one of the persons present with these words, "Disdain not this slight token of my grace." Irony prostrates itself to the earth and does obeisance with the most submissive air.

The good thing about this objection is that it bears so clearly the stamp of fiction that it cannot offend even the weakest person. On the contrary it is entertaining, even amusing, and one can abandon oneself to it without scruple, unless maybe a little scruple is suggested by observing that it is presented in all seriousness. If the objection makes an attempt to want to explain something in human existence, one can reduce it in a trice to its most general expression, namely, that marriage or any positive relation to woman is an impediment, that she attains her highest reality in unhappy love, and that here her significance is so dubious that she signifies nothing positive, but negatively is an occasion for awakening the unhappy lover's ideality. Thus the objection is reduced to its briefest expression, and thereby also it is reduced *in absurdum*—just as the objection itself makes as if it would let the whole of existence take that same path. But to make the whole content of life so compendious denotes in reality the haste of the devil, the swiftness of a Caesar—not in conquering but in losing. Lightenberg says somewhere that there are some reviewers who with a single stroke of the pen are well beyond the bounds of sound reason; and so also such a hasty thinker seems as if he didn't take the time even to begin the clause which states the conclusion of his premise. What Augustine said about the celibate life, that by its aid *multo citius civitas dei compleretur et acceleraretur terminus seculi,* such a thinker seems to take seriously, but as in jest; for a religious background such as Augustine has one cannot expect from such an objection. But as a worldly view of life it really is "in haste" (as a woman commonly says of her letter), and it smacks of the defect commonly ascribed to a woman's letter, that it consists of . . . postscripts. With Hamann one may aptly shout "Bah!" at this *festinator* (who of course regards a married man as a dawdler)—if only there is time to shout, and the man is not already far away, "so that barely are his coattails left behind in existence."

I return to the subject of love. It stands intact, no thought approaches it, it is the miraculous. The resolution of marriage is so far from wanting to subvert it that on the contrary it presupposes it. But love is no marriage, neither is a resolution alone a marriage. Someone may think then that it is due to the wretched imperfection of life and existence that love alone cannot penetrate so as to force its way through and must therefore accept the convoy of marriage. Far from it. The very reverse is true. Love penetrates the whole of life, and it does this in marriage. It is an insult to love not to let marriage join in, as though love were something so "immediate" that it could not be made taut by a resolution. On the other hand, it is no insult to a genius if we say of him that in proportion to the immediacy of his genius he possesses an equally highborn power of resolution, and that as debtor to himself he assumes the obligations of his talents. It would be an insult to him if one were to say that he is lacking in resolution or that his resolution is not proportionate to his genius. The meaning of this is not that resolution should little by little come to evidence as genius diminishes, so that at last he would be re-clothed with resolution and be a different man from what he was in the time of his genius. On the contrary, the beautiful meaning of it is that resolution is contemporary with genius and in its way is just as great, so that he who by grace received the gift of immediacy has had himself consecrated for it by resolution—and this then is the beautiful meaning of marriage.

It is also easier to demonstrate this in the case of marriage than in the case of genius, because love is itself a later immediacy which enters upon the scene at a time when the will ought to be sufficiently developed to form a resolution as decisive as love understood as immediacy is decisive. So understood, marriage is the deepest, highest and most beautiful expression of love. Love is the gift of the Deity, but in the resolution of marriage the lover makes himself worthy to receive it. To allow the resolution to be lacking, though life were never so paradisiacal, is unseemly, just as unseemly in a spiritual respect as it is for half-grown youths to want to get married.

I shall approach this same subject again and explore it further, but at this point it would perhaps be best to look around a bit, pausing for an instant to consider love at its critical moment. What is here pointed out in the realm of experience should not, of course, and cannot, of course, serve to disparage love, but only to illuminate it. There has always been a great run on love, and as little as "the nannygoat grows weary of nibbling the green shoots" do certain people grow weary of seeking (*sit venia verbo*) and wishing for the miracle of love. But just here is the difficulty, here it is that the devil sows evil seed while the lovers are not thinking of it. Even the seducer allows love to stand as a thing he cannot bestow upon himself (and it is only very young apprentices and Münchausens who talk about making conquests), but the demoniacal spirit within him causes him with demoniacal resolution to resolve to make the enjoyment as short, and in this way, so he thinks, as intense as possible. By reason of this demoniacal resolution the seducer is actually great in an evil sense, and without this resolution he is not actually a seducer. He may for all that be harmful enough, and his life may be thoroughly ruined, even though it is more innocent than that of a real seducer, or acquires a more innocent appearance because the oblivion of time comes in between. Such a man insults love; he is not evil enough to form a demoniacal resolution, but neither is he good enough to form the good resolution—to express the case precisely, he is not good enough to be a husband in the noble sense in which I use that word, in the noble sense that a man is a husband only when he is worthy to receive the gift of the Deity.

If I must mention an example of the misapprehension of love, I will mention Goethe, that is, Goethe[41] as he has represented himself in *Aus meinem Leben*. His personal life is another matter, I refrain from passing any judgment; as for his poetic writings, I do not ascribe to myself sufficient aesthetic culture to appraise them, but there are certain things I can well understand, just as well as a child can, and there is one thing marriage does not understand, even though, as was observed, it is mitigated by jest; marriage does not understand jest, and in addition to the bad resolution of the seducer there is also another opposite to the good resolution, namely, flight and evasion.

In *Aus meinem Leben* there is depicted a being who is not a seducer, he is too chivalrous for that, although this chivalry, so far as concerns *esprit* (ethically understood), is lower than that of the seducer, since it lacks demoniacal resolution, which also is ethical—that is, ethically bad. Such a being, however, finds forgiveness in this world more easily, too easily indeed, for he is really in love—but then by and by this glow cools, he has made a mistake, he withdraws "in a courteous manner," and half a year later he knows how to give reasons, good reasons, to prove that the breach and withdrawal were sensible and almost praiseworthy: after all it was too petty a thing, a little village belle; there was too much passion, that's a thing that doesn't last indefinitely, etc., etc. . . . for this sort of fudge can be drawn out as far as you like. By the aid of the half-year and by the aid of the theory of perspective the *factum* of love has become an accident (this is not only an impiety towards love but a fraud against the ethical and a satire upon oneself) from which one has been lucky to make one's escape. Everything becomes confused before my eyes the moment I reflect that such an existence is supposed to be a poetic life. I feel as if I were sitting in the Court of Conciliation, remote from the hardiness of immediacy and remote from the magnanimity of resolution, remote from love's heaven and remote from resolution's judgment day—as if I were sitting in the Court of Conciliation, surrounded by Philistines and hearing a talented solicitor defending shady conduct with a certain poetic inventiveness. For in case the solicitor himself [like Goethe] were the hero of these vulgar love affairs, one must surely lose patience, ethically speaking. That these are vulgar affairs is not at all the fault of the individuals who played the feminine rôle (all honor to Goethe's presentation of the case, be it *Dichtung* or *Wahrheit*), for so far as I recall there is no reason to suppose that a single one of them gave up tragedy for vaudeville. For

[41] The reference is more particularly to Friederike, in the first book of *Aus meinem Leben, Dichtung und Wahrheit,* Collected Works, Vol. XXVI, pp. 80 *ff.*, and p. 118.

though a little village belle has been so unfortunate as to misunderstand his Excellency, if only she remains true to herself, I know from my childhood's schooling (and I still know no better) that she advances from the idyl to the tragedy. On the other hand, in case his Excellency has been so unfortunate as to misunderstand himself, and furthermore is extremely unfortunate in the way he takes to make it all right again, I know from my childhood's schooling (and I still know no better) that he has left tragedy and the drama behind him and has settled down in vaudeville.

Time has a strange power. In case that poetic figure in *Aus meinem Leben* had recognized beforehand that after all the thing would be over before very long, or having no presentiment of this in advance and having no other way of making it all right again, he had at least been ethical enough to conceive of himself as a scoundrel, then he would have been denounced as a seducer, and the alarm bells would have been rung whenever he approached a village—but now, now he is a knight. Well, not quite a knight, but after all we are not living in the age of chivalry, yet he is something like a knight . . . a dignitary, to whom in an absolute sense applies *aut Caesar aut nihil.*[42] Some time passes, he himself sorrows also over the broken relationship, which, however, with every possible precaution he would prevent from being in any serious way regarded in the character of a breach; he sorrows a little over the poor girl, it is not sham, he really sorrows—yes, really! That however is carrying courtesy rather too far, it is a sympathy and condolence which well may have the effect of only increasing the pain. The breach itself, or to express it more sharply and exactly, the courteous and amicable agreement upon a separation, is precisely the most offensive part of the thing; this last fraud which will not regard any girl whatsoever to whom a man has contracted obligations as a creditor who cannot be put off, this fraud that a bankrupt will not confess his full liability, is really the most revolting part of it, and yet it is by this courtesy he purchased the world's forgiveness. Oh, the sorrowing lover! He does not sorrow over his own instability, over this flare-up, over this promissory note which is valid in the spiritual world, over his sins: such a sorrow as this that poetic figure would presumably call melancholy, for he expressly deplores the fact that the age, and he along with it, had become melancholy by reading English authors, mentioning Young, for example.[43] Yes, why not? When one is so constructed, one may become melancholy at hearing a sermon, if only it has pith, as Young has. But Young is far from being melancholy.

[42] The motto of Caesar Borgia.

[43] *Werke,* Vol. XXVI, pp. 214 *ff.*

Such an existence, which in an essential sense is hardly a paradigm, may nevertheless in an improper sense assume a paradigmatic character, or be paradigmatic for the casual fact that it represents an irregular declension, in accordance with which, however, many lives are fashioned. One dare not say that such people fashion their lives after it, for they are too innocent for that, and their innocence is precisely this, that the thing happens to them, they themselves don't know how it came about. Sometimes such persons are really enthusiasts who are chasing an ideal. As little as he who plays the lottery learns anything by losing, just so little do these men learn anything by their love affairs. This of course does not apply to that poet in *Aus meinem Leben,* he is too great not to learn, too superior not to reap advantage, and if ethically he had been as enthusiastic as he is gloriously equipped by talents, he rather than anyone else would have discovered and solved the problem as to whether there is an intellectual existence so eminent that in the deepest sense it cannot become commensurable with marriage. The answer that one loves several times, that one parcels out one's superiority, is only a disorientation, which neither in an aesthetic nor in an ethical sense fulfils what one might call a moral man's more serious expectations of life. That poet has doubtless learned much—indeed, just as the latest philosophy has made it a term of reproach to talk about "Kant's honest ways," so does Goethe smile with an air of patronizing superiority at Klopstock, because he was so much concerned about whether Meta, his first love, who had married another, would belong to him in another life.

What has such an existence come to then? It does not remain stationary with love, but neither does resolution supervene. The reflection out of which resolution comes into existence in order to lay hold on love takes a false hold, it becomes reflection about love. Hence I have lingered here to point out what will be shown later, that the reflection belonging to resolution has to let love alone and attend to very different things. So that existing poet in *Aus meinem Leben* makes no resolution, he is not a seducer, he does not become a married man, he becomes . . . a connoisseur.

To what extent every poet-existence ought itself to be a poem, as well as the question under what angle of refraction his life ought in this respect to be related to his poetry, I do not presume to decide. However, this much is certain, that an existence such as that in *Aus meinem Leben* must influence the poetic production. In case this is Goethe's own life, it seems to explain why what one most misses in Goethe is pathos. The pathos of immediacy he does not possess, but neither has he pressed on to attain the highest pathos. Every time the crisis presents itself to the existing poet he leaps away. That he does in all possible directions. He relates that he was brought up in a strictly religious way. This is an impression of childhood, and surely not one of the foolish pranks one puts aside in the course of time, inasmuch as in the matter of religion it is a very serious fact that one learns the best things as a child and acquires a postulate for which there is never, never any substitute forthcoming. There comes then a later period of his life when this religious impression almost overwhelms him. That is the crisis, and a perfectly natural one; precisely as an individual is more intellectually gifted, the more difficult the task that is set before him of preserving or recovering the pious faith of childhood. What then does that poet do?—the poet who himself relates in another place[44] that he practised all sorts of exercises in order to accustom himself not to be afraid of the dark, not to be frightened at seeing a corpse or at being alone among the graves at night.[45] He leaps away, he puts a distance between religion and himself, he avoids all contact.[46] Good Lord, though a person were a bit afraid of walking alone in the dark, there would be nothing so dreadful about that; but to draw back, to retreat, when it is a question of remaining true to oneself with respect to the impression of one's childhood, when it is a question of fighting, though it were unto despair, with renunciation of every demand upon life and of the expectation of any position of importance, of fighting for the precious memory of one's parents (for though that poet again and again recalls his mother, can he believe that in her eyes or in his father's it was a casual circumstance that they let religion acquire so great a power over the child?), to fight for a fellowship of faith with the deceased, in behalf of what they regarded as the one thing needful, what he had at one time accepted himself in childish innocence with the devotion of an undivided soul—at this point to leap away! Might not this revenge itself in the fact that pathos is lacking in the poems? In case this poet is Goethe himself, might not this explain the fact that the idolized hero whose most casual utterances and sayings are collected, edited, read, adored like holy relics, that this idolized hero who is called king in the realm of thought—that he, to put it in the mildest terms, is a king without a throne in the eternal realm of religion? In Goethe's sound wisdom there is supposed to be healing[47]

[44] *Werke,* Vol. XXV, pp. 252 *ff.* [45] *Werke,* Vol. XXVI, pp. 305 *ff.*

[46] S.K. knew this temptation well. In an early entry in his Journal, when he was still in revolt against religion, he said, "With a feeling of dim apprehension I have sought to avoid coming into too close contact . . . not to come like moths too near the flame." I, A 75.

[47] So says J. L. Heiberg in *Urania.*

for the errors of the mind and especially for melancholy, which he himself knew how to escape. How strange! Everyone knows from his childhood's schooling that distraction is the most dangerous thing for one who has a disposition to melancholy; yes, dangerous also for one who has no disposition of the sort. How strange that when he has become somewhat older and somewhat more mature (in case he then believes that the wiser man is different from the simple man for the fact that he understands what the simple man understands, and understands it better, and understands somewhat more than the other, and in case he does not believe that the wise man is to be distinguished by the fact that the only thing he doesn't comprehend is what the simple man understands)[48] —how strange he should not know that to leap away from a task is to consign himself and his soul to an earlier or later melancholy. But Goethe knew how to avoid melancholy in another way. So much by way of illuminating the erotic.

Perhaps more competent critics also will agree with me that Goethe's feminine figures are his most masterly figures. But when one looks more closely, the best of them especially are not viewed in the light of true feminine ideality but under the illumination in which they are seen by the equivocal observer who knows how to discover what is charming, knows how to kindle into flame the glowing coal, but also knows how to look upon this conflagration with a proud air of superiority. They are lovable in a high degree, capitally drawn, and yet it is not so much they that are dishonored as femininity that is dishonored in their persons, because the act seems almost justified, or at least innocent, in view of the superior sagacity which knows how to enjoy, knows how to relish, but also knows how to erect a distance between it and him when the pleasure is over.

In the application of this theory of distance the poet in *Aus meinem Leben* is a master. He himself has been so kind as to explain how the thing works.[49] One must remember however that this poet does not wish to be instructive, far from it; he is conscious that the gift is not bestowed upon everybody, it is a distinction of his nature, he is a privileged individual. True, that poet is now a hero, and I who am bold enough to talk about him am a Philistine; but fortunately there are some things even a child can understand, which are equally valid whether a person be a hero or a judge-assessor or a beggar man. So then whenever a life-relationship is about to overwhelm him he must remove it to a distance by poetizing it. How different men's natures are! Or perhaps after all

[48] A favorite thesis of S.K.'s.

[49] *Werke,* Vol. XXVI, pp. 120 *ff.*

they are not so different![50] What does it mean to poetize a life-relationship? The question is not essentially whether one gets a masterpiece out of it or not—alas, in this respect there is a tremendous difference between a hero and a poor assessor as well as the beggar man. To poetize an actual life-relationship by the aid of distance (for which, be it noted, one has to furnish bond as a surety) is neither more nor less than to falsify the ethical element in it and to stamp upon it the counterfeit impression of a casual happening and a mere problem for thought. Oh, yes, when a man has a lightning-conductor like that in his pocket, what wonder he feels safe in a storm! How many a bungler and smatterer has gone by bowing and cringing before that distinction of nature. And yet every man has more or less of that distinction of nature, it is quite simple, it is no more than the ostentatious parade of the natural and pleasure-loving man in defiance of the ethical. Among criminals one often finds this talent for poetizing, i.e. for viewing at a distance in poetic outline the actual life-relationship. Among melancholy men also it is often to be found, but with this distinction, that the aesthetically melancholy find in it assuagement, the ethically melancholy an aggravation. Possibly the cheerful Goethe was a little melancholy, just as the wise Goethe has a fair share of superstition. So this ability to poetize an actual life-relationship is a distinction of nature which on the one hand is not so rare, and on the other hand is very questionable. As a matter of course, not everybody who poetizes poetizes masterpieces. Who would be so foolish as to affirm such a thing? But from the ethical point of view this distinction, that one is a hero, yes, perhaps even the only one who counts as a hero, and the other a bungler, has nothing to do with the case. The ethical is a judge so incorruptible that if even our Lord were to have allowed Himself a little irregularity in the way of creating the world, ethics would not let itself be put out of countenance, although, to be sure, heaven and earth and all that in them is must be regarded as a mighty fine masterpiece.

If that poet-existence in *Aus meinem Leben* is poetic, then . . . good night marriage! It then becomes at the best a refuge for old age. If that existence is poetic, then what is to be done for woman? She too then must try to be poetic. It is unseemly when a man who is tried and

[50] Perhaps S.K. reflected here that, "after all," he had to reproach himself for the fact that the many entries in his Journal which give an account of his breach with Regina were "too poetic" (i.e. designed to spare him), that all the books he had hitherto written were a close approach to poetizing his love-relationship, and that the subsequent chapter of this book is an outright attempt to poetize it—an outrageous attempt, some may think, to combine *Dichtung* and *Wahrheit.* Certainly Judge William could not approve of the "psychological experiment" of Frater Taciturnus.

experienced in the erotic, a discharged veteran, takes a young girl for his wife so as to be rejuvenated a little and to have the best of nursing, but it is disgusting when an elderly lady, an experienced spinster, takes a young man for a husband to assure herself of protection and of a refined titillation, now that the poetic begins to evaporate.

Resolute as marriage is in prohibiting one to serve two masters, it is not any more inclined to like the deserter. It is prettily said by Solomon that "whoso findeth a wife, findeth a good thing, and obtaineth favor of the Lord," or to modernize the expression a little: he who falls in love, to him the Deity has done a good turn; when he marries his lady-love he does a good work, and he does well in fulfilling what he had begun.

What has been said in the immediately preceding paragraph cannot of course be meant as a clumsy recommendation of the resolution of marriage. This more appropriately recommends itself, since, as I have said, it is the only adequate form love can take.

Now it remains to be seen how the resolution can join in, how the reflection which is presupposed in the resolution can reach the point where it coincides with the immediacy of love. As soon as one eliminates love it becomes ridiculous to want to reflect about whether one shall get married or not. This is quite true, but from this it does not follow that one is justified in eliminating love, as one does whenever one attempts to keep the resolution and love apart and wants to make it seem ridiculous to reflect upon the resolution.

The fact that reflection is ridiculous when applied to the question of getting married when there is no love in the case was rightly perceived and profoundly expressed by two wise men of ancient times, but not, as will be seen, with the purpose of putting a weapon into the hands of the mockers. It is related[51] that in reply to one who asked him about marriage Socrates said: "Marry or don't marry—you will rue them both." Socrates was an ironist who ironically concealed his wisdom and truth, presumably in order that they might not become town gossip which everybody could repeat. But he was no mocker. The irony here is capital. For the stupidity of the questioner consists in asking a third party about something one never can learn from a third party. But all are not so wise as Socrates and often reply quite seriously to a stupid question. If love is lacking, reflection cannot reach any conclusion; and if a man is in love, he cannot ask such a question. When a mocker[52] wants to use the Socratic saying, he treats it as a plain assertion, turning

[51] Diogenes Laertius, II, 33.

[52] Like the young S.K. as he depicts himself in the second part of *Either/Or*.

it into something quite different from what it is, namely, a profoundly ironic, infinitely wise answer to a very foolish question. By transforming this answer to a query into a plain assertion one can produce a certain effect in mad comedy, but this is to jest on the Socratic wisdom and do violence to the trustworthy evidence which expressly introduces the story with these words: "Somebody asked him [Socrates] whether he ought to get married or no." To this he replied: "Whether THOU doest the one thing or the other, thou wilt rue it." If Socrates had not been so ironical, he might have expressed himself thus: "As for THEE, thou canst do as thou wilt; thou art and dost remain a dunce." For not everyone who regrets gives proof thereby that now, at the moment of regret, he is a stronger and better individual than at the moment of heedless action. Sometimes regret may be the best proof that the regretter is a good-for-nothing. — It is related[53] of Thales that when his mother insisted he should get married, he replied that he was too young, that it was not yet the fit time; and when later she renewed the appeal, he replied that now it was no longer the fit time. There is something ironic also in this reply which rebukes the worldly sapience that would reduce marriage to a venture like that of buying a house. For there is only one age which is seasonable for marriage, that is, when one is in love; at every other age one is either too young or too old.

It is always pleasant to bring such things to mind; for if frivolity is calamitous in the erotic field, there is also a certain sort of common sense which is even more calamitous. But this one word of Socrates, when rightly understood, is capable of mowing down, like Death with his scythe, the whole prolific harvest of sensible prate which would chat its way into a marriage.

So then I pause here at the decisive point: there must be a resolution superadded to love. But a resolution presupposes a reflection, but reflection is the destroying angel of immediacy. Such is the situation, and if in fact reflection were to come into conflict with love, no marriage would ever result. But that is precisely what it is not to do; and what is more, even before the operation which through reflection attains to the resolution, and is strictly contemporary with it, there comes the negative resolution which holds off every resolution of this sort as a temptation. Whereas in all other cases the destroying angel of reflection goes about shouting death to immediacy, there is yet one immediacy it suffers to stand, that of love, which is a miracle. If reflection comes into conflict with love, this means that one is about to examine whether the loved one corresponds to the ideal abstract notion of an ideal. Every reflection

[53] Diogenes Laertius, I, 26.

in this direction, even the most airy and unsubstantial, is an affront, and a stupidity as well. Even if apparently the lover had the purest enthusiasm for wanting to discover charms, suppose even that he had a voice "so sweet, oh, so sweet!," suppose he had all of a poet's elegance in reflecting so daintily that even the most delicate feminine soul would hear only the pleasing sound and sense only the sweet fragrance of the sacrifice, without discovering the affront—it is nevertheless an attempt to empty love of its content. But as the god of love is blind and love itself a miracle (as the lover himself and even the most vehement reflection must recognize), the lover must be on his guard against this clairvoyance. There is a modesty to which even the most adoring admiration is an affront, a sort of infidelity to the beloved. Even though this admiration were to bind the lover, as he thinks, more indissolubly to her, it already has released him in a way. It is a sort of infidelity because in this admiration a criticism is latent. Beauty, moreover, is vain, and loveliness may vanish. It is therefore an affront to the loved one to want to let all her loveliness consist in the synthesis which underlies love's modesty. On the other hand, there is a feminine loveliness (here again essentially that of the wife and mother) which does not exact this bashfulness; and yet, though it were the face of an angel she had, it is an affront to want to admire this beauty, an affront which already indicates that love has lost its equilibrium. "But," I hear the lover say, "it is precisely in this admiration I feel the sublimity of the loved one, and feel that essentially I have no claim to be loved in return." Ah, he who reckons with infinite magnitudes is none the less a reckoner. Therefore, whether the loved one is the most beauteous of women, or whether she is not thus favored—the only right, brief, pithy, adequate word for the whole content of love is: I love her. And, verily, he who in the first instance had nothing else to say, and later restricted his soul just as laconically to love's true expression, is more faithful to her than one who by the description of the loved one's beauty could entertain men and gods, and do it to such perfection that they would go away overwhelmed and envious.

But what one may dare to see, what one may dare to admire, is the lovable quality of her essential self. Here admiration is no affront, if only admiration will learn from love not to be a vapid chatterbox or a birthday poet but a faint, imperishable murmur of quiet joy. The essential quality of the soul has opportunity to reveal itself only in marriage, which has at its disposition the cornucopia of many tasks, which is the best gift one receives on the wedding day. Even if the loved one, merely to delight him for whom she would sacrifice her life, having no opportunity for greater proofs of devotion, proves it equally well in lesser instances, even if she were to adorn herself merely to please him, and she, the beauty, were now in her lovable finery so beauteous that old men would follow her wistfully as they did Helen when she walked through the halls of Troy[54]—if he with a single nerve of his eye were to see amiss and admire, instead of comprehending love's correct expression, that it was to please him, already he is on a false track, he is on the point of becoming a connoisseur.

So when one imagines a time of love-making, especially the period of engagement, which is thus outside of marriage, things often go amiss because love lacks the essential tasks and hence may sometimes make both the lovers critical. What Bedreddin says of Gulnare's glance[55]

> Calm as the grave which opens to release
> The savéd soul which rises up on high,
> She opens now her lovely lids in peace,
> And turns her placid glance towards the sky—

this could be understood as applying to the whole lovable quality of the soul in connection with the immediacy of love. This immediacy is dim, but calm as the grave which opens, and in such wise does the transfigured woman develop out of love's hiding-place into psychic beauty, and in this transfigured form she belongs to the husband.

In what direction then is reflection to move till it reaches the resolution?—for within the holy-place of love and upon the consecrated ground of immediacy it dare not tread. The reflection turns towards the relationship of love to reality. That he is in love is for the lover the most certain thing of all, and no meddlesome thought, no broker, runs between love and a so-called ideal. This is a forbidden path. Nor does reflection inquire if he is to marry; he is not forgetful of Socrates. But to marry is to enter into a factual situation in relationship to a given reality: marriage is the most extraordinary concretion. This concretion constitutes the task of reflection. But maybe it is so concrete (defined with respect to time, place, environment, the stroke of the clock, seven and one relationships, etc.) that no reflection can pierce through it? In case this is assumed, one has thereby assumed at the same time that no resolution can ever be reached. A resolution, however, is always an ideality; I have the resolution before I begin to act in virtue of this resolution. But how then do I get this resolution? A resolution is always reflective: if one does not give heed to this, language becomes confused, the resolution is identified with an immediate impulse, and

[54] Iliad, III, 146 *ff*. [55] Oehlenschläger, *Aladdin*, Samlede Wærker, Vol. XV, p. 63.

everything that is said about resolution is just as far from being an explanation of it as it is far from being a journey when a man drives all night long but takes the wrong turn, so that in the morning he finds himself at the same place where he started. In a purely ideal reflection the resolution has ideally exhausted reality, and the conclusion of this ideal reflection is something more than a *summa summarum,* in short it is precisely resolution; resolution is the ideality brought about by a purely ideal reflection, it is the earned capital required for action.

"However," someone may say, "that is all well enough, but it will take a long time, and meanwhile the grass grows—such a married man does not indeed become a 'pepper-prentice' or bachelor, but he becomes a veteran past master." Not at all. And moreover the same objection might be raised against every resolution, and yet resolution is universally the beginning of freedom; but one requires of a beginning that it should be in season, and that it should stand also in a proper proportion to that which is to be carried out, that it should not be like an introduction which recapitulates the whole book, or like an address from the throne which takes the words out of the mouth of the whole session of parliament.[56] But pleasure accelerates every labor, and the pleasure of the lover, which remains the same throughout all this labor of reflection, incites him from morning to night, keeps him alert and unchecked in his knightly quest; for verily this expedition of the lover in quest of the resolution is more chivalrous than a crusade against the Turks or than a pilgrimage, more pleasing in love's eyes than every other exploit, because it is concentric with love itself.

So that happy swain (for that a lover is happy goes without saying) pursues his way, led by the hand of his good genius, while the loved one sits waiting for him, confident and blissful, for every time he comes back to her (only to start out again prayerfully upon his quest, until he finds the jewel, the wedding gift, the resolution, the only worthy gift) she has never found him changed, any more than his love has changed, though it were only to the point of becoming admiration.

And the young swain has not many instants to waste upon the quest, every instant he wastes is, as he knows, a bliss he foregoes—this must be a sovereign expedient for learning alacrity. But the good gift of resolution is also his highest gain, the wedding garment without which one is unworthy—this must be a sovereign expedient for learning not to be overhasty, lest in his hurry he hasten away from the resolution.

[56] Perhaps such an experience was possible in the nominal parliament (*Stænderforsamling*) under the absolute monarchy which was abolished by the revolution which came three years later.

Precisely because the resolution, or the resolver, is thus situated, the reflection becomes ideal, and one promptly plunges into a shortcut. And why should not one take a shortcut when it is certain that it leads swiftly to the goal, more swiftly than any other road, but also more surely? It has rightly been remarked that reflection is inexhaustible, cannot be brought to a conclusion, that it is infinite. Quite true, it cannot be brought to a conclusion in reflection—any more than a man, be he never so hungry, can eat his own stomach—and therefore everyone who claims to have done this, be he a systematic hero[57] or a newsboy, must be regarded as a Münchausen. On the other hand, reflection is brought to a conclusion in faith, which is precisely anticipation of the ideal infinity in the form of resolution. Thus the resolution is a new immediacy, attained through the ideally inexhaustible reflection, a new immediacy which corresponds precisely to the immediacy of love. The resolution is a religious life-view constructed upon ethical postulates, which is to prepare the path of love and secure it against every outward and inward danger. Behold, the lovers, being in love, are paradisiacally plucked out as it were from reality and removed as if to remoter Asia, beside the calm Indian seas, or into the midst of the primeval forest where silence dwells and where no trace of man is to be seen; but the resolution knows how to find the way to human society and prepares this safe path, while love attends to no such things but is as happy as a child which lets its parents take care of all troublesome matters. The resolution is not man's strength, it is not man's courage, it is not man's talent (these are only immediate analogies which do not furnish an objective measure for the immediacy of love, since they belong to the same sphere and are not a new immediacy), but it is a religious starting-point. If it is not this, then the resolver has only become de-infinitized in his reflection, he has not plunged with the headway of love into the shortcut but has remained on the road, and such a resolution is so miserable a thing that love must disregard it and rely rather upon itself than trust to the guidance of such a half-educated robber. The immediacy of love recognizes only one other immediacy as of equally noble birth, that is the immediacy of religion; love is too maidenly to recognize any party as privy to it except God. But religion is a *new* immediacy, it has reflection betwixt it and the first immediacy—otherwise paganism would be really religious, and Christianity not. That religion is a new immediacy everyone can easily understand who is content to follow the honorable path of human common sense. And although I imagine I have but few readers, I admit that I

[57] Hegel, of course.

imagine my readers to be such as these, for I am far from wanting to impart instruction to the admired authors who make systematic discoveries *à la* Niels Klim[58] and who have got out of their good skin in order to put on the "real skin."

To penetrate reflection thus until one wins the resolution is not so very difficult, especially when one has as incentive the passion of love; and without passion one never brings reflection to a conclusion, but may very well linger along the road engaged in small talk with Tom, Dick and Harry, with thinkers and dealers in gimcracks, may get to see a lot of things in life and lots to chatter about, like the man who inadvertently lingered so long on board the ship that he got a trip around the world—or, to express myself less jocularly, he who has not passion never sees the promised land but perishes in the wilderness.

Now what the resolution wants is first of all to hold fast to love. In this new immediacy, which extends far out beyond every reflection, the lover is saved from becoming a connoisseur; he is bowed down under the imperative of duty and made to stand erect again in the optative of resolution. By his relationship to love he is saved essentially and renounces the game of critical reflection.

In the next place, the resolution wants to triumph over all danger and temptation. Precisely because the reflection which comes before the resolution is entirely ideal, one single imagined danger will be enough to make the resolver resolve religiously. Let him think of any danger whatsoever, though it were merely that he cannot by thinking anticipate the future. Owing to the fact that he employs the whole power of his thought and the deep concern of his love to think this danger, he *eo ipso* thinks it in so dreadful an aspect that by himself he cannot overcome it. He has run aground: he must either let go of love . . . or believe in God.[59] Thus the miracle of love is elevated to the purely religious miracle, the absurdity of love to a divine understanding with the absurdity of religion.[60] Be of good courage! A simple honest man who has respect for human common sense can well understand that the absurd exists and that it cannot be understood. From systematic thinkers this is luckily hidden.

[58] In a play of that name, by Holberg. The satire is addressed to the Hegelians in general, but in particular to Martensen, the theologian, who in Heiberg's *Perseus* (No. 1, p. 120) spoke of the "true skin," meaning the artistic rendering of reality.

[59] A pathetic reminiscence of his own unhappy love. S.K. once exclaimed in his Journal: "If only I had had faith, I might have married her."

[60] The absurdity of faith is a theme which had already appeared in *Fear and Trembling,* then in the *Philosophic Fragments,* and was to be developed in the *Postscript.*

Finally, in the resolution the lover would put himself in relationship with God through the universal.[61] This is resolution's bath of purification, which is quite as beautiful as that of the Greeks before a banquet or that which Aladdin desired before the wedding. Everything known as earthly vanity, selfishness, malodorous manly spirit, the itch of criticism, etc., is consumed, and in the resolution the husband becomes worthy of the divine gift of love.

In case the lover while he is marching on in quest of the resolution stumbles upon irregularities, recognizing that he has become peculiar, not in the sense that this peculiarity disappears as a matter of course in the washing of resolution, but in such a way that he dare not presume to think of himself as a generic man—in plain English, in case he stumbles here upon remorse. That opens a wide vista, and if he is truly in love, as we assume, he can regard himself as one who is singled out to undergo an examination by existence, for when he is under a crossfire from love and from existence, the examination can readily become all too severe. — However, I will not follow this out here, this sort of difficulty has no place in the generality of deliberations,[62] the resolver does not ordinarily stumble upon such difficulties, he returns home from his expedition like the knight from a crusade, and so:

> But if he returns with feather in hat,
> A jolly good welcome awaits him for that.

So then that happy young swain (for that a lover is happy goes without saying) has found what he sought, like the man in the Gospel he has sold all to buy the field where the pearl was hid, only in this respect does he differ from that man, that in a way he already owned the field when he was selling all to buy it; for in the field of love he found also the pearl of resolution. He returns home from his holy pilgrimage, he belongs to her, he is ready—ready to meet her at the altar where the Church is to declare him a proper husband.

So now we come to the wedding ceremony. Our young swain has not become an older man, far from it; no need of a year and a day to ripen thus. Yet, if he were not properly in love, and if he has no sense of ethical need and no religious postulates in his soul, he does not yet become ripe. This ripeness, it is true, makes him older in a certain sense, but it is precisely the youth of eternity that is bestowed upon him, and thus it is that love too makes a man older.

[61] In *Either/Or,* which was composed when S.K. found himself "incommensurable" with marriage, he bewails the fact that he is an "exception to the universal human."
[62] Yes, but this was S.K.'s case precisely.

That a loving youth is a pleasant sight need not be said, but perhaps it may need to be said that a married man is a still more grateful sight—unless the altar might be a stumbling-block! For it surely is preposterous that one should be accounted a loving youth only when he still has to fulfil his wish by coming to the altar. But the married man is a loving youth, absolutely, his love is unchanged, only it has the sacred beauty of resolution which the youth's love has not. Is my wealth perhaps less considerable because I possess it in one security which is the only safe one? Is my claim upon life less because I have it on stamped paper?[63] Is my happiness the less because God in heaven vouches for it, and that not in jest, like Eros, but in seriousness and truth, as truly as there is a resolution to hold Him fast. Or might perhaps the language which the loving youth knows how to employ be more divine than the married man knows how to understand? Is not the marriage service itself such a "dark saying" that it needs more than a poet to understand it? Is not its language so astonishing that he who understands the half of it might lose his wits entirely? To talk about duty to a pair of lovers!—to understand this and yet be in love, be bound to the beloved by the tightest bond of immediacy! To talk about the curse which rests upon the race, about the difficulties of marriage, about woman's pain and man's sweat—and yet to be in love, and in the immediacy of love to be convinced that only happiness awaits them! To hear this, to see the resolution, to hold the mind intent upon it, and at the same time to be able to see the myrtle crown upon the head of the loved one—verily, a married man, a proper married man, is himself a miracle! To be able to hear the voice of the loved one while the organ plays! To be able to hold fast to the pleasure of love while existence assembles all the might of sober earnestness upon his head and that of the beloved!

And now as to her—for [it is true of her also that] without a resolution there is no marriage. A feminine soul has not and should not have the sort of reflection man has. It is not in this wise therefore she is able to attain the resolution. But starting with aesthetic immediacy, with the swiftness of a bird she attains the religious, and one can say of a woman, as one hardly could say of a man, that it must be a depraved woman who is not made God-fearing by love. As a married couple both are on the common ground of religious immediacy. But man reaches this through an ethical development. A wise Greek[64] has said that daughters

[63] All Continental countries require that documents, to be legally valid, must be written on paper which is stamped for the benefit of internal revenue.

[64] Cleobulus, according to Diogenes Laertius, I, 91.

ought to get married when they are girls in years but women in understanding. This is very prettily said, but one must remember that a woman in understanding is not a man in understanding. The loftiest understanding a woman possesses—and possesses with honor and consistently with beauty—is religious immediacy.

It has often pleased me to reflect how a girl and a young man must correspond to one another in order to be a proper married couple. And, to tell the truth, the man who does not take pleasure in reflecting upon this may have perhaps a sense for the most beautiful thing in the natural sphere, a loving couple; but he has not a sense for spirit, and he has not faith in spirit.

Will someone say that such a thing is seldom to be seen—the sort of marriage, that is, which expresses the idea? Well then perhaps it is just as rare a sight to see a man who, believing, as we all do, in immortality and in God's providence, really expresses the idea in his life.

Woman because of her immediacy is essentially aesthetic, but just because she is essentially this, the transition to the religious is also direct. Feminine romanticism is the very next instant religion. If it is not that, then it is only a sensuous enthusiasm, a demoniacal inspiration of sensuality, the holy purity of modesty is transformed into a dark quality which tempts and incites.

So in woman love is immediate. This is common ground. But the transition in her case comes about without reflection. It comes about in this way: at the moment when on the border of her consciousness there passes her by the thought which man's reflection ideally exhausts, she falls into a faint, her husband hastens to her aid, and although equally moved, but through reflection, he is not overwhelmed, he stands fast, the loved one supported upon his breast, until again she opens her eyes. In this swooning state she is translated from the immediacy of love into the religious sphere, and here again the two meet. Now she is ready for the marriage ceremony—for without a resolution no marriage.

Has anything now been lost? Has the happiness of love become less because its bliss reflects heaven's benediction? Has love become a temporal factor because the lovers wish to belong to one another for eternity, and because this wish has become seriousness? Is the profoundest seriousness when heard as a consonant in the most lovable jest less beautiful than what love "immediately" desires? For he who speaks at the prompting of pure immediacy speaks only in jest. When the lover would risk his life for love, and she, the loved one, says Amen —even if he does risk his life, it is noble, it ought to move stones, woe to him who laughs; but he who ventures and loses "immediately" has not yet understood himself.

There is a picture representing Romeo and Juliet—an eternal picture. Whether in an artistic sense it is remarkable, I leave undecided, whether the forms are beautiful, I do not presume to judge, I lack the requisite taste and competence. The eternal quality of the picture consists in the fact that it represents a loving pair and represents them by an essential expression. There is no need of a commentary, one understands it at once, and moreover no commentary could give an idea of this repose in the beautiful situation of love. Juliet has sunk down admiringly at the feet of the loved one, but from that adoring attitude her devotion raises her up with a glance of heavenly bliss, but Romeo checks this glance, and by a kiss all the longing of love is forever tranquillized. For the radiance of eternity surrounds the instant, and no one who beholds the picture is prompted to think, any more than do Romeo and Juliet, that there is to be a next instant, even though it were merely to repeat the sacred seal of the kiss. Ask not the lovers, for they hear not thy voice; but direct thy question out into the world, asking in what century it occurred, in what land, at what time of day, at what hour by the clock—no one says, for it is an eternal picture.

It is a lovable pair, an eternal theme for art, but a married couple this is not. May I not dare to mention a married couple? May that other be more glorious because something is lacking of the invisible glory marriage possesses? If such were the case, why then should I be a married man? Not every loving pair is a Romeo and Juliet, but it is the beautiful joy of every loving pair to possess this ideal pattern. Not every married couple is perfect, but here it is a question only of the ideal pattern which, if I may say so, sovereignly determines the rank of subordinates.

[Here is another situation:] she does not kneel in adoration, for the difference which is given in the common immediacy of love, i.e. man's strength which gives him the preponderance, holds her upright. She only sinks, she would like to kneel in the admiration of love, but his strong arm holds her upright. She droops, not before the visible but before the invisible, before the exceeding greatness of the impression; then she takes hold of him who already is holding her upright by his support. He too is moved in laying hold of her, and if the kiss were not their mutual support, they might both totter. This is not a picture, there is no repose in the artistic situation. For as one sees her almost sinking in adoration, so does one see from the interrupted attitude the necessity of a new situation where she stands erect by his side, one has a presentiment of a new pattern which is the real pattern of marriage, for a married couple represents an adjacent angle upon the same base. What is it that gives to the first picture that character of unconcludedness? What is it that is sought in the tottering attitude? It is the balance of the resolution, it is the higher immediacy of religion.

A fig then for all objections which merely cancel themselves. Even when the objection says scornfully, *Habeat vivat com illa*[65] it takes the very words out of the married man's mouth, for that is what the married man wishes, and the objection cannot really wish that one should forbear to get married, for then it would have nothing to jeer at, and we should all be as proudly superior as the objector. Thus marriage seems to me the most secure position of all. Love says, "Thine forever"; the marriage service says, "Thou shalt forsake all others and keep thee only unto her"; the objection says, "Keep her." But then there is no objection; for though the objection thinks that the married man becomes ridiculous, this does not prevent him from leaving all (jeering included) and keeping only unto her. Yes, in case the scoffer himself would like to have her, in case he comes forward in pursuit of a hue and cry—but that cannot be, for in this instance it is only the lawful act they would ban, and if even the lawful must "hereafter forever hold its peace," then there is never anybody who has a search warrant for the unlawful.

Since after all I write only as opportunity offers, and as it is not seemly for a married man to be beating the air against objections which for the most part are as light as air, I will now look at the matter from another side.[66]

[65] Corresponding to the formula "to have and to hold," with the addition of the phrase "to live with her."

[66] This is a rather lame excuse for concluding this treatise with a long digression about "the exception" which could hardly have been of much interest to the Judge as a married man but was in fact the poignant experience of S.K., who recognized that in breaking his engagement he had become an "exception to the universal human." In *Either/Or* he dared to entertain the hope that he might be "the exception in a good sense," and in *Fear and Trembling* (verily with much fear and trembling) he sought to justify his exceptional position ("the teleological suspension of the ethical") by appealing to the example of Abraham. The remainder of this chapter is concerned exclusively with the position of "the exception," and it is easy to see that much of it is exquisitely personal. The reader, however, may need to be apprised at the outset that the theme is monastic celibacy, regarded as the exception which has the most plausible claim to justification. The subject is presented in terms so generic that the particular application is not at once plain. This was not in the strictest sense a personal interest; but S.K. was always deeply and sympathetically absorbed with the phenomenon of medieval monasticism; and though he here allows the Judge to argue against it at great length, the verdict is rather doubtful, hardly amounting to more than S.K. was willing to say in his own person, namely, that it involved a certain pride in superior sanctity.

I do not say that marriage is the highest, I know a higher; but woe to him who would skip over marriage without justification. In this narrow defile I take up my position, in order to inspect thoroughly in thought the man who would slip by. It is easy to see in what direction that feigned sally away from life must occur. It must occur in the direction of the religious, in the direction of spirit, in such a way that being spirit makes one forget that one is also man, not spirit alone like God.

The medieval contempt of marriage may, as I imagine, return again in an entirely different form, in the form of an intellectuality which renounces marriage, not on dogmatic or super-moral grounds, but with the daredeviltry of the intellect. The other extreme corresponding to this already finds expression, for it is just because a puffed up intellectuality has missed the ethical point that it can preachify the doctrine of the idolatry of the flesh; but the idolatry of the flesh is one expression of the fact that the flesh has become indifferent with relation to the intellect. The opposite expression is that the flesh is entirely annulled, that the spirit disowns the corruptible body in which it lives, the temporal conditions in which it has its home or temporary abiding-place, this fragmentary existence out of which it would collect itself as a whole. There are various kinds of eccentricity, the theocentric kind has a reasonable claim to be assigned to the place that belongs to it. But in fact speculation is theocentric, and theocentric is the speculator, and theocentric the theory. So long as it goes no further than that, and the theocentric confines itself to being theocentric three times a week from four o'clock till five in the professor's chair,[67] but for the rest of the time is a citizen and a married man and a good fellow like all the others, one cannot say that the temporal has been unfairly dealt with. Such a theoretical digression three times a week, an incidental occupation, may be expected to have no further consequences.

If, on the other hand, one takes seriously the idolizing of intellectuality, and if the individual has sufficient demoniacal ideality to remodel his life in conformity with his experimental resolution (just as the married man does in conformity with his good resolution), in the sense that every objection, every counter-argument of temporal life, is regarded as a temptation, he has with this done all that it is possible for him to do by way of representing himself as an exception. It cannot be denied that for a time at least an individual may venture everything for the sake of his experimental resolution, it cannot be denied that he may even risk his life for it, but he does not thereby gain any justification,

[67] Whether Professor Martensen was lecturing at precisely this hour I do not know.

any more than one can gain a prescriptive right to stolen property. Such a man as he, is then, to be sure, an exception in a certain sense, in the sense that he as a demon has more will power than the generality of men, who (to speak demoniacally) do not quite manage to be evil.

On the other hand, such a man possesses not the least thing that might corrupt a judge to withhold the sentence that he is unjustified, or to move the viscera of compassion when one sees him plunge into the abyss he has prepared for himself. For pure intellectuality is a prodigious abstraction, and from this point of view nothing is to be descried, nothing whatever, not even the remotest hint of a religious idea. The exception is a wanderer, but of a peculiar sort, for he does not wander to America or to another continent beyond the ocean—or beyond the grave—no, he simply disappears. We have allowed his negative reflection to direct itself especially against marriage. It seems as if, for all that, he might have many temporal interests left. But such is not the case. For marriage is central to the temporal, and the individual personality is unable to put itself immediately into relation with the state—unless it might be that a man wanted to sacrifice himself entirely to the state, and so would not marry. But this is a vain contradiction in which he shows no regard for the consequence of his idea, to which however obedience is dearer than the fat of rams. If in relation to his idea he is to be justified in ignoring marriage, his idea must be indifferent to the idea of the state. Here as in all cases one must remember that we have not to do with the casual fact that an individual does not marry, here it is a question only of a man who is not willing to marry. Every individual of rank (if I may so speak) in the world of spirit has resolution, and his rank is in proportion to his resolution.

The infinite abstraction has behind it a *point d'appui,* and the enthusiasm for annihilation is a case of "little risked little gained" in comparison with what is to be gained if only he who renounces the world and makes the *votum castitatis* has a religious background. Such a man as this does not take for nothing the step wherewith he oversteps temporal existence. It is true he does not gaze at the reward, yet he works hopefully in that direction—just as a man who is rowing rows constantly towards the goal, yet constantly has his back turned towards it—thus does he labor himself out of the temporal.

That such conduct is a religious abstraction is quite true, but that a thing of this sort might be so antiquated that it could not return again to haunt us is less true. It is obvious that religion has long been lying fallow; when it begins again to stir with its ideal energy it would not be surprising if it makes the same mistake. To find the true concretion for religion is not easy, since religion has constantly as its presupposition the infinite abstraction and is no simply immediacy.

People sometimes talk perhaps with good intentions and very prettily and very truly about religion, and sometimes, perhaps without noticing that they do so, they take it all back with a single word which shows that what they are talking about is the purely immediate religiousness. I constantly have marriage in view. To get a correct religious expression for marriage, to find the accurate and categorical definition for that which the Middle Ages despaired of defining, and to which the recent centuries (which are proud enough of being far ahead of the Middle Ages—surely not in the way of religiousness but of worldliness) have contributed but little, I still regard as a *pium desiderium*. I believe that a married man does well to think about such things, and then, if he would like to be a bit of an author, to write about such things. And besides, every other subject is preempted, even astronomy.[68]

It cannot be denied that, regarded from a purely religious standpoint, it is a matter of complete indifference whether a man has been married or not. Here opens the infinite abyss of the religious abstraction. To have a double tongue avails nothing. If one is anxiously seeking for guidance in the religious address, one perhaps finds ambiguity more frequently than one would suppose, and more frequently than the speaker himself is aware of. One extols marriage when that is the theme; on the other hand, if somebody dies unmarried—well then, since marriage is not the theme, one talks with an almost humorous accent about its being a matter of complete indifference whether a person is married or not. But what of him who has heard both discourses? For when one will talk in this way it is a great deal more difficult to be a good listener who is eager for guidance and instruction than to be an orator who is "at your service" in every way. One vindicates the significance of the temporal, its ethical significance, one calls it the season of grace, a space for repentance, the allotted time for the decision which decides for eternity; but then a child dies, and one holds a funeral oration, or one refers in a sermon to the distressed parents who have lost the little one, and the speaker deals humorously with all the vanity of the temporal, he talks about the threescore and ten years as trouble and vexation of spirit, about all the waters running into the sea, yet the sea is not full. The Romans were more consistent in letting the little children weep in Elysium because they were not permitted to live. And all the while people are laboring upon the System—good Lord, it would be asking too much

[68] A sly dig at Heiberg, who had recently begun to write as a dilletante on this interesting subject. In the *Prefaces* S.K. makes fun of it.

of a man that he should have a practical life-view proportionate to this prodigious undertaking.[69] And this much too is certain, that it doesn't do to have many fine speeches, with meaning in them all, but not one meaning in them all.

Even if it were so that the religious abstraction is something outworn, something antiquated, something *superseded* (for this last expression I am indebted to the System, which has been so kind as to confuse what I venture to call an eternal development of generations with the repetition of this experience which every generation makes for itself)[70]—suppose it is so, it nevertheless would be appropriate to discuss it here. If it is not exactly an everyday sight to behold a genuine case of love, it is naturally even more rare for one to behold a real marriage. No use haggling over it, that would merely be playing into the hands of the *chicaneurs,* who know how to distil a corrosive substance even from religion. It is a poor defense to pooh-pooh an objection, though it were the purest chicanery, when one has not a good conscience and the knowledge that one is in the right.

The religious abstraction desires to appertain to God alone, for this love it is willing to disdain, renounce, sacrifice everything (these are the nuances); for this love it will not suffer itself to be disturbed, distracted, engrossed by anything else; with regard to this love it is not willing to have any double bookkeeping, all the turnover is to come about constantly with a clear relation to God, who is not related to him [the monk] through any secondary channels. The pride in such an abstraction may be very religiously tempered by humility towards God, but provisionally the abstraction must be regarded as unjustified because its attitude towards what it renounces is altogether abstract. It is not concerned with the wish to comprehend more concretely the beautiful reality of love and the true reality of marriage (for I stick to my theme), it would regard such employment as temptation. This essentially is the inhumanity of that abstraction—which, however, one should be wary of condemning, and above all one should be wary of extolling railroad speculation and the foolery of committees, as if all this hubbub and hurry-scurry constituted the content of temporal existence.

This inhumanity towards man is at the same time presumption towards God. The inhumanity (as has been said) does not consist in willing the highest; that is not at all inhumane, and the proclamations or anathemas from a society which is worldly well-to-do yet spiritually

[69] The completion of Hegel's System upon which his disciples were laboring diligently.

[70] An anticipation of the modern distinction between phylogenetic and ontogenetic.

a Tattertown,[71] where a man is esteemed for being what people generally are, and where moreover the envy of ostracism and the argument of potsherds[72] is constantly used against the better man—all this of course has no significance here. Nor does the inhumanity consist in wanting to base one's life-view upon something accidental by which many are excluded, for the exception in fact does not deny that everyone is able to do the same thing; and all the fudge about its being a great thing, "but not everybody can do it," about what will become of the world [if all are celibates]—all this comes from Tattertown, where people cannot and will not understand that, if this is correct, one must leave the rest to God, who is well enough able [to look after the world] and is not reduced to such a state that He needs the assistance of Tattertown. No, the inhumanity consists in the fact that one will not have any concrete comprehension of that which for the majority of men is their life's reality. But this concrete comprehension is and remains a condition for having even the appearance of being in the right. Presumption towards God is a sort of over-forward comradeship, even if he [the monk] does not understand it as such. He may even be truly humble; but so also (humanly speaking) may a subject have the most loyal enthusiasm for his king and far outstrip those who are neither cold nor hot but are *numerus* and *pecus*,[73] but yet when he seeks an audience he may want to be admitted by another way than that prescribed for subjects. It seems to me there must be something dreadful at being then turned away and hearing the words: "The other way—then we shall see what can be done for you." For he who has really had inwardness enough to comprehend that religion is the highest love—how downcast he must be, how annihilated, when he discovers that he has presumed too much, that he has been too free, has grieved the Spirit, has offended his love. Ah, all the harder in case he has really meant to give his relationship the highest expression.

Such a religious exception will ignore the universal, he will outbid the terms offered by temporal reality. Therewith one straightway perceives that he is unjustified. The case is more complicated when he underbids them. Quite *in abstracto* he recognizes the reality of the temporal, or—to stick to my theme—the reality of marriage; but he is unhappy, unqualified for this joy, for this security in existence; he is melancholy, a burden to himself, and feels that he must be a burden to others. Let there be no passion in condemning; the weaker also has his

[71] *Pialtenborg* was the name given to a lodging house for the destitute in Copenhagen.
[72] In Athens the vote to exile a citizen was written on potsherds.
[73] Meaning the mob—an allusion to Horace's *Letters*, I, 2, 27 and 19, 19.

rights, melancholy also is something real which one does not obliterate with a stroke of the pen. So, after having expressed himself thus about life, he finds comfort in a religious abstraction. Whereas the man who in an unaccustomed way seeks audience with the King almost awakens compassion, it seems that this is different and that it is fitting he should gain a hearing.

Here again the trouble is that he talks quite abstractly about what he would give up. Precisely because he is melancholy he has an abstract notion of what it is that makes life so joyful and happy for others. But what the alien experience is like he cannot know *in abstracto*. Herein lies the deceitfulness which is inseparable from all melancholy. Whatever may be the misfortune with which the melancholy man contends, be it never so concrete, it constantly has for him an admixture of fantasy and hence of abstraction. If, however, the melancholy man is immersed in practical life, this admixture is only a small affair, a little falsification, which does not prevent him from engaging perfectly well in ordinary business and being like other men, even though in the smallest things which he undertakes or experiences he derives a little subsidy from the inexhaustible funds of imagination, for personal use. If on the other hand he is free to regard the whole of human life *in abstracto,* he never really gets to know what it is he foregoes. The joy of life, which he supposes the others have, becomes to him a burden—a double burden, since he already has enough to bear. Here the comical side of melancholy appears; for in relation to life the melancholy man is like the tailor's apprentice Hebel[74] tells about: he wanted to travel by a boat which was towed up the Rhine and was bargaining for the price—then said the skipper that he might come along for half fare if he would walk by the side and help to pull. Alas, so it is with the melancholy man: by relating himself abstractly to life he believes that he is slipping through for half price, but does not observe that he is pulling as hard as the crew, and has to pay out money besides.

What evidently is lacking to both these exceptions is that they have not experienced. It is easy to see from this that no one by his own effort can become a justified exception. First and foremost something must happen. It is to be understood (as I have already said) that I am talking hypothetically, for I do not know whether there is or ever has been a justified exception, but I will come as near to describing it as is possible for me. It must come to pass in a different way, it must be one who has gone along on good terms with life, and then suddenly is brought to a standstill. So then he must have a love affair, a real love affair. There

[74] J. B. Hebel, *Sämmtliche Werke* (Karlsruhe, 1832), III, p. 405.

is indeed an old saying that to the god of love one can offer no resistance; but the man who from the beginning tempers himself by a resolution against reality will always have power to eject the incitement of love or to kill it at birth. As against an immediate existence love is the stronger power, but as against a resolution which has already armed itself in advance against it, such is not the case.

So first I require that he be really in love. A love broken off is enough for a man, but if it is the lover himself who has to break it, this burden is a two-edged sword in his hand, having no hilt, although he must hold on to it, and this operation is just as painful autopathically as sympathetically. Perhaps someone says, "If once the love is assumed, it is an impossibility to get the exception in this way; for in love everything is at stake, it is high play that is ventured, and in love everything is at stake for the loved one, which amounts to doubling the first wager; how impossible then to be willing to skip away, to be willing to lose everything, honor included; it is impossible if one really loves." Rather, if he does not really love, it is impossible for him to become the justifiable exception, in case there be such a thing, but the other is not impossible. Dreadful it is, a horror, but thus it must be. He who would break with reality must at least know what he breaks with. I am far from being cruel. Just so little as I am cruel when as a judge I sit calmly in an inquisitorial capacity and conjure up all terrors to frighten away evildoers from the peaceful enclosure of law and justice, just so little am I cruel in this case. It is possible that he who has bent the branch of happiness down to the ground may hew it off and himself be thrown by its might into mortal torments, like the unfortunate upon whom the death sentence falls, suffering all the more because at the same time he lacerates the loved one; it is possible when he is sailing securely with his good fortune to go below and bore a hole in the ship and bring himself and one more into peril from the sea, it is possible for him to do this if he is really in love, if he is not in love, then it is impossible for him to be the justifiable exception, in case there be such a thing. It is dreadful to give a sword into the hands of a madman, but just as dreadful that happiness was put into his hands when he was such—for he does not need to be entirely out of his mind. What impels him I will not investigate here, I would only describe the psychic situation which must exist if there is to be any question at all of a justifiable exception.

In the next place I require that he be a married man. This is a loss more dreadful than the loss of honor, and the cry of the fatherless child is louder than the ignominy of any disgrace, and more terrible than the loneliness of the betrayed maiden is the melancholy misery of the mother when she is deserted. "It is impossible," says someone, "it is impossible, when he really is thus tied to life, then to break away." Rather, if he is not thus tied, it is impossible for him to become the exception, in case there be indeed such a thing; but the other, on the contrary, is not impossible, though it is so dreadful that it chills the soul and checks the breath of sensibility. He, however, who sits as examining magistrate must not be moved from the truth by any terror, must not cheat justice of a doit, and the exception shall not purchase his justification for a round sum but must pay the last farthing. Though it is doubtful whether falling in love be from God, and whether in the case of love there be need already of presupposing a religious explanation, marriage is absolutely of religious origin. So he who breaks it brings not only every misery upon himself and upon her whom he loves, but he brings life into contradiction with itself, brings God into contradiction with Himself. This is not impossible for a madman—and yet he does not need to be out of his mind. What can impel him I will not set forth nor try to set forth, I merely propound the psychological presuppositions; if these are not present in all their horror, he is not the justified exception.

Now the breach has been brought about. Now I go further. I require that after this he shall love life; if he become hostile to life, then he is unjustified, for the fact that he is an exception does not render less beautiful that from which he is excepted. With an enthusiasm such as no other has he must love what he broke, and with this enthusiasm descry in its every beauty more charm and deliciousness than does he who rejoices in his good fortune; for he who would renounce something universal must know it more thoroughly than does the man who lives securely in it. Behold, when such a man (if there be such a man) would talk about marriage he will have a fervor such as a married man hardly has (I at least am ready to yield to him), he will talk with a knowledge of its quiet joy such as no married man has; for the torment of responsibility for the breach must keep his soul alert and vigilant in the contemplation of what he destroyed, and the new responsibility requires him first of all to know what he did. If such a man (in case there be such a man) would talk about the justification of the exception, then my position is only that of a subordinate member of the force, in comparison with him who is a general inspector; for he must know surely every haunt and nook, every bypath which no one is aware of, he must be able to see irregularities in the dark where another thinks there is nothing to be distinguished from justification.

The breach itself he must sense as unhappiness and dismay, for the suffering lies in the fact that he is brought to a standstill and does not, like an adventurer, romantically renounce the content of life, notwithstanding that without fraud he became a bankrupt whom life itself had brought to ruin. On the other hand he must comprehend the after-pains of the breach as punitive suffering, for although he despairs of discovering the guilt,[75] since he is really in love and really belongs with all his soul to his married life, and even though the pain of breaking away is for him as great, nay, greater, than the pain of desolation for the loved one, yet must the enthusiasm of desperation still find its joy in making to God the same ascription of praise, in subscribing to the same declaration the fortunate make, that the ways of providence are sheer wisdom and righteousness.

He must so comprehend the breach as to understand that he who had found security in life (for the most lovable education is that which moulds a man by a wife's humble subjection, and the most rejuvenating instruction is that of being educated by one's children, and the best refuge is behind the sacred wall of marriage)—that he who had found security is now cast out into new perils and the most awful of mortal dangers. For even if it is established that he could do no otherwise, yet by this step he has ventured out upon the trackless vast of infinite space, where the sword of Damocles hangs above his head if he looks towards heaven, where the traps of temptation try to catch his feet if he looks towards the earth, where no human help is offered, where not even the daring pilot who would be willing to sacrifice his life ventures to put out, because here there is more to lose than life, where no fellow-feeling takes hold of him, yea, not even the tenderest sympathy can descry him, because he has ventured out upon the empty space before which men recoil with a shudder. He is a rebel against the earthly; and the physical, which when it is on good terms with the spiritual is a staff of support, as time is also, has become an enemy; for the physical has become a serpent to him, and time has become the instant of the bad conscience. He supposes that it is so easy to triumph over the physical; yes, that is so when one does not incite it by wanting to destroy it. One does not talk of such things to lovers, for love keeps them ignorant of the danger which only the rebel discovers, love does not know the reason why marriage was instituted—*ob adjutorium, ob propagationem, ob evitandam fornicationem*[76]—and experiences of the cloister could supply a dreadful

[75] Note that the final section of this book, entitled "Guilty?"/"Not Guilty?," reaches no verdict.

[76] Reasons propounded by the earlier Lutheran dogmatics.

commentary to this text. In this way one constructs with psychological accuracy the catastrophe of Faust, who precisely by wanting to be sheer spirit succumbs to the wild rebellion of the physical. Woe to him who is thus solitary! He is deserted by the whole of existence, yet is not without attendants, for every instant an anguishing remembrance, in which all the passion of sympathy burns consumingly, conjures up before him pictures of the misery of her who was destroyed, and every minute the sudden can overwhelm him with its terrors.

He must comprehend that no one can understand him, and must have the constancy to put up with it that human language has for him naught but curses, and the human heart has for his sufferings only the one feeling that he is guilty. And yet he must not harden himself against this, for that very same moment he is unjustified. He must feel how misunderstanding tortures him, just as the ascetic felt every instant the prick of the penitential shirt he wore next his skin—and in fact he has clad himself in misunderstanding in which it is terrible to be, like the apparel Hercules received from Omphale,[77] in which he was burned up.

To resume the essential points: he must not feel himself higher than the universal, but more lowly, he must *à tout prix* want to remain within the universal, because he is really in love, and what is more he is married; he must want to remain within the universal for his own sake, and for her sake for whom he is willing to sacrifice his life, whereas now he beholds her wretchedness, beholds it as one from whom they have chopped off hands and feet, and out of whose mouth they have torn the tongue, thus leaving him without the slightest means of communicating his feelings. Accordingly he must feel himself the most miserable of men, an offscouring of mankind, and must feel it doubly because he knows, not *in abstracto* but *in concreto,* what the beautiful is. So down he sinks, desperate in all his misery, when that single word, the final, the uttermost, the word so utter that it is not contained in human speech—when that word remain unuttered, when he cannot produce his credentials, when he cannot wrench open the sealed despatch which is not to be opened except out there at sea and which contains the orders from God. This is the beginning of becoming an exception, if there be such a thing; if all this is not given, then he is without justification. Whether out of this misery, which certainly is the deepest, the most torturing, where the pain ceases not except for repentance to wield its scourge over him, where all human suffering is personally present to torment

[77] It was his wife Deianeira who sent him the poisoned shirt which impelled him to leap upon the funeral pyre. It is related that he waited upon Omphale, the Queen of Lydia, dressed as a woman.

him, where suffering does not let up, any more than a town ceases to be besieged because the watch is relieved by another, or because the new watch belongs to another and an unfriendly regiment, and so they "relieve" one another, i.e. if one's own pain slumbers, then sympathy awakes, if sympathy slumbers, then one's own pain awakes, and at any instant repentance may be on its rounds to see if the watch is alert—whether out of this misery, I say, a blessedness can develop, whether in this terrible nothingness there can be concealed a divine significance—oh, what faith is needed in order to believe that God might thus intervene in life, i.e. that this might be visible to the passive-active individual, for if it is really God who intervenes, He surely contemplates the salvation of the man thus destroyed—but note that the one who is grasped by God's hand, the elect, at the moment of decision can know nothing of this—all this surpasses my understanding. I do not know whether there is a justified exception, and if there be such a man, neither does he know it, not even at the instant when he sinks down, for if he has the least presentiment of it, he is not justified.

I have not wished to inquire what can prompt a man to become so desperate that he would get possession of spirit by overreaching God rather than receive it in the way it has pleased the Deity to impart it, or how a man might be able to become the object of a divine partiality which out of jealousy employs as its first expression the terrible trial and temptation of seeming to envy the man every joy which life offers. I have wished merely to sketch the psychological presuppositions. Behold then a candidate for the cloister who cannot flatter himself with the encouragement he would have had in the Middle Ages, but who as a figure strange and alien to the contemporary consciousness must buy the hardest suffering at the highest price. My description is like a ready-made garment, the penitential shirt which the exception must wear—I do not think that anyone could fall in love with such a dress, mistaking it for pleasure.

Not that I am cruel. Oh, when one is as happy as a husband can be, when one loves life so dearly, loves it under oath, under repeated oaths, and so dearly that each oath is dearer than the last, because in this love for life one holds fast to her whom I still embrace with the triumphant resolution of first love, holds fast to one's wife for whose sake one is to leave father and mother, holds fast to that which compensates for the loss, that which adorns and rejuvenates my married life, my darling, whose joyfulness, whose cheerfulness, whose innocent mind, whose progress in the good, turn the scanty daily bread into inestimable abundance, make my thanksgiving for my subsistence and my prayers of intercession just as important in my eyes as the prayers of a king for his country—so one is too happy to be cruel. But when one sits as examining magistrate, one is undaunted by anything that would deflect the course of justice, by anything that would lead truth upon a false scent. I do not go around seeking to discover the man upon whom one might put this penitential shirt; on the contrary, I cry out to the rash one, in case he will hear me, not to venture upon these paths. He who makes the venture of his own accord is lost. But for me this is a new proof of the excellence of existence, that it is so hedged about that no one is tempted to want to venture outside, so well defended that merely the thought of the terror must be enough to quash all foolish and frivolous and conceited and unwholesome and weak-kneed talk about wanting to be the exception; for even when all that I have required is granted, I still do not know whether there is such a thing as the justified exception, indeed I would add this most deterrent warning, that he who would be the exception never gets to know definitely in this life if he is such. So then, by the loss of all things, by torments beyond measure—not to be able to purchase for himself a certitude!

On the other hand, what I definitely know, what neither mockery nor envy, any more than the terrifying character of these considerations, can tear from me, is the happiness of my marriage. The terror is now far off, I am no longer sitting as examining magistrate, but in my library; and as a thunderstorm makes the landscape smile again, so is my soul again in the humor to write about marriage, which in a sense is a task I am never through with. A married man is not a scatterbrain, and no more is marriage a thing that can be disposed of in a trice. I have lately been performing a painful function, now I have come home, I am with her, all the powers of existence having united to put me in lawful possession of her, I am with her who shortens for me the dark days and extends to an eternity our happy understanding, who subtracts from my sufferings and is afflicted[78] with me in my adversities and increases my joys. Behold, just now she passed by my door, I understand it, she awaits me, but she will not come in for fear of giving disturbance. Only an instant more, my love, only an instant, my soul is so rich, I am so eloquent at this moment, I would write it down on paper, a eulogy upon thee, my lovely wife, and thus would convince the whole world of the

[78] "Subtracts . . . afflicted with" does not render the play on words: "*Traeke fra . . . drage med.*"

validity[79] of marriage. And yet before long, tomorrow, the day after, in a week's time, I shall cast thee from me, thou scribbling pen. My choice is made, I follow her hint and invitation. Let a poor wretch of an author sit trembling when a thought presents itself in a favorable instant, trembling lest someone might disturb him; I fear nothing, but then too I know what is better than the happiest conceit in a man's brain, and what is infinitely more precious than any secret which a poor author can share with his pen.

[79] "Validity" is a strange term to use in this connection. But in the second part of *Either/Or* the first disquisition of the Judge was on "The Aesthetic Validity of Marriage." Perhaps it was natural for a jurist to use a juridical term, *Gyldighed.* I have been tempted (though without the shadow of authority) to translate it by "value."

"GUILTY?" / "NOT GUILTY?"
A PASSION NARRATIVE

A Psychological Experiment

by

Frater Taciturnus

ADVERTISEMENT

EVERY child knows that Søeborg Castle is a ruin which lies in the northern part of Seeland, about half a mile from the seashore, close to a little town of the same name. In spite of the fact that the castle was destroyed a long while ago, it still maintains itself in the memory of the nation and will continue to, for it has a rich historic and poetic background to live upon. Something of the sort might be said, in a way, of the Søeborg Lake which is contiguous to the castle. Originally it had a length of a couple of miles and a depth of several fathoms to live upon; for this reason it has not yet disappeared, and in spite of the fact that the mainland is encroaching upon it more and more and is constricting it more and more painfully, it will for a long time continue to vindicate its existence as a lake.

Last summer I fell in with an older friend of mine, a naturalist, who had followed the coast from Copenhagen north to this point for the sake of making observations upon marine plants. He had determined to visit the country about Søeborg, which he expected would yield rich results. He proposed that I should make the excursion with him, and I accepted the proposal.

It is not easy to get near the lake, for it is surrounded by a rather wide stretch of bog. Here it is that the border conflict is carried on day and night between the lake and the mainland. There is something sad about this conflict, which is not indicated, however, by any trace of destruction; for what the land gradually wins from the lake is transformed into smiling and exceedingly fruitful fields. But alas for the poor lake which is thus disappearing! No one has compassion upon it, no one feels for it; for neither the parson whose fields border upon it on one side, nor the peasants whose fields are on the opposite bank, are averse to winning one piece of land after the other. The poor lake is abandoned to its own resources on the one side and on the other!

What imparts to the lake a still more shut-in appearance is the fact that the bog is overgrown luxuriantly with rushes. There is nothing to match it in Denmark, so at least said my friend the naturalist. Only at one place is there a small open channel, and here is a flat-bottomed boat in which we two (he for the sake of science, and I for friendship and curiosity) punted our way out to the lake. With difficulty we got the boat started, for the channel has scarcely a foot of water. The thicket of rushes is as dense as a forest to the height of about four yards, and when hidden by it one is as though lost to the world forever, forgotten in the stillness which is broken only by our struggles with the boat, or when a bittern, that mysterious voice in the desert, thrice repeats its cry and then again thrice repeats it. Strange bird, why dost thou sigh thus and lament? Thine only desire after all is to remain in solitude!

Finally we got beyond the reeds, and before us lay the lake, clear as a mirror and sparkling in the radiance of the afternoon. Everything so still! Silence rested upon the lake. Whereas while we punted our way through the thicket of rushes I felt as though I were transported into the midst of the luxuriant fertility of India, now I felt as though I were out upon the Pacific Ocean. I was almost alarmed at being so infinitely far from men, at lying in a nutshell upon a vast ocean. Now there was a confused voice, a mingled cry of all kinds of fowls, and then stillness prevailed again, almost to the point of making me apprehensive when the sound suddenly ceased and the ear grasped in vain for a support in the infinite.

My friend the naturalist took out the apparatus with which he drew up submarine plants, cast it into the water and began his work. Meanwhile I sat at the other end of the boat dreamily absorbed in the beauties of nature. He already had drawn up a good deal of material and began to busy himself with his booty when I begged him to lend me the instrument. Resuming my former place I cast it out. With a muffled sound it sank to the depths. Perhaps it was because I did not know well how to use the apparatus, at all events when I wanted to pull it up I encountered so much resistance that I was almost afraid of proving the weaker of the two. I pulled again, then up rose a bubble from the depths, it lasted an instant, then burst—and then I succeeded. I had the strangest feeling, and yet I did not have the remotest notion what sort of a find it was I had made. Now when I reflect upon it I know all, I understand it, I understand that it was a sigh from below, a sigh *de profundis,* a sigh that I had wrested from the lake its treasure, a sigh from the shy and secluded lake from which I had wrested its secret. If two minutes earlier I had had a presentiment of this, I would not have ventured to pull.

The naturalist sat absorbed completely in his work, he merely inquired casually if I had got anything, an exclamation which did not seem to expect a reply, since with good reason he did not regard my fishing efforts as having any bearing upon science. In fact I had not found what he was after, but something altogether different. And so each of us sat at our respective ends of the boat, each preoccupied with his find, he for the sake of science, I for the sake of friendship and curiosity. Wrapped in oilskin and provided with many seals was a rosewood box.[1] The box was locked, and when I opened it by force the key lay inside—thus it is that morbid reserve always is introverted. In the box was a manuscript written with a very careful and clear hand upon thin paper. There was orderliness and neatness in it all, and yet an air of solemn consecration as if it had been written before the face of God. To think that by my intervention I have brought disorder into the archives of heavenly justice! But now it is too late, now I crave forgiveness of heaven and of the unknown author. Undeniably the place of concealment was well chosen, and Søeborg Lake is more trustworthy than the most solemn declaration which promises "complete silence," for the lake makes no such declaration. Strangely enough, different as happiness and unhappiness are, they sometimes agree in wishing for . . . silence. The administration of the lottery when distributing the prizes of fortune is extolled for being silent about the names of the fortunate ones lest their good fortune might become an embarrassment to them; but the unfortunate who has gambled away all his fortune also desires to have his name passed over in silence.

In the box there were found also several pieces of jewelry, some being of considerable value: adornments and precious stones—ah, precious indeed, too dearly bought, would the owner say, in spite of the fact that he was allowed to keep them![2] It is a valuable find, and I feel that I am under obligation to advertise it. There was found a flat gold ring with a date engraved inside it, a necklace consisting of a diamond cross fastened to a light blue silk ribbon. The remainder was in part of no value at all: a fragment of a playbill, a scrap torn from the New Testament (each apart by itself in an envelope of vellum paper), a withered rose in a silver-gilt pyx, together with other things which only to the owner could have had a value equal to the diamonds of two carats each with which the pyx was adorned.

Herewith the owner of a box found in Søeborg Lake in the summer of '44 is summoned to apply to me by the initials F.T. through Reitzel's Book Shop. In order to obviate betimes any delay I take the liberty of observing that the handwriting of this application must at once betray the owner, as well as that everyone who may do me the honor to write, when he receives no reply, can from this conclude securely that the handwriting is not the right one, for only this can properly claim a reply. On the other hand, for the comfort of the owner be it said, that even though I have taken the liberty of publishing his manuscript, its contents, unlike the handwriting, are of a sort that does not betray any-

[1] It was in a rosewood cabinet S.K. treasured his memorials of Regina.

[2] Alas, they had been returned by the lady for whom they were bought!

body,[3] and be it said that I have not taken the liberty of showing to anyone, not to a single person, either the manuscript, or the diamond cross, or the other things.

* * *

CANDIDATE Bonfils has published a table by the aid of which one can calculate the year when any day of the week and of the month is given. His merits in this respect redound also to my advantage; I have calculated and calculated and finally have discovered that the year corresponding to the dates engraved on the ring is 1751, the memorable year in which Gregory Rothfischer[4] was converted to Lutheranism, a year which, for the man who with a profound eye contemplates Cyclopically the marvellous course of world history, was also remarkable for the fact that precisely five years later the Seven Years War broke out. So one is compelled to go back to a rather remote epoch in time, unless one is ready to assume that an error has crept into the data or into my calculation. If one refuses to do anything under compulsion, one might, for all I care, assume that a poor devil of a psychologist who can count upon but scanty sympathy for psychological experiments and unsubstantial constructions has made an attempt to give them both a little life by adding a touch of romanticism, the fiction that the thing belonged to a past age. For a sketch, however psychologically correct, which does not inquire whether such a person ever lived, is perhaps of less interest to our age, when even poetry has snatched at the expedient of trying to produce the effect of reality. A little psychology, a little observation of so-called real men, they still want to have, but when this science or art follows its own devices, when it looks away from the manifold expressions of psychic states which reality offers, when it slips away in order by itself alone to construct an individuality by means of its own knowledge, and to find in this individuality an object for its observations, then many people grow weary. As a matter of fact, in real life passions, psychic states, etc., are only carried to a certain point. This too delights the psychologist, but he has a different sort of delight in seeing passion carried to its utmost limits.

As for the reviewers, I could wish that my prayer might be understood in all simplicity and entirely in accordance with the tenor of the

[3] In fact, Quidam's Diary, though it reports substantially the story of S.K.'s broken engagement, did not betray him to the public . . . nor "her."

[4] The sagacious reader will not expect to be told who Rothfischer was, for he will recognize that the whole thing is a satire upon Hegel's philosophy of history, which had such vogue in its time.

words as my honest meaning and that the result might correspond with the prayer's desire: namely, that the book may not be the object of any critical discussion, whether favorable or unfavorable.[5] When one may acquire in so easy a way a claim upon a man's gratitude one surely might oblige him.[6]

F. T.

[5] *Erkjende, anerkjende, eller miserkjende.*

[6] S.K. sometimes stipulated with his publisher that his book should not be sent to any reviewer.

The rich peasant in Norway sets a new copper kettle over his door for every thousand dollars more he acquires; and the inn-keeper sets a new mark on the rafter every time the debtor gets somewhat more in debt—so do I set down a new word every time I reflect upon my wealth and my poverty.

Periissem nisi periissem.

Note by the translator. This saying ("I had perished had I not perished") S.K. derived from Hamann (*Schriften*, Vol. III, pp. 151 and 224) and Hamann attributed it to "a Greek." cf. *Papirer* IV, A 123; IX, A 48.

January 3. Morning.

So it was a year ago today I saw her for the first time, that is to say, for the first time with a soul thoroughly resolved. I was not fantastic, not accustomed to intoxicate my soul with big words and brief dreams, hence my resolution did not mean for me that I should want to die if she did not become mine. Neither did I imagine that my soul would be distracted, my life become totally empty, if she did not become mine—I had too many religious presuppositions for that. My resolution signified for me: either her/or else thou wilt never marry. That was the stake I wagered. That I loved her—as to this there could be no doubt in my soul, but I knew also that with respect to such a step there were so many precarious places that for me it became a most difficult problem. An individuality like mine is not light of foot; I cannot say, "If I don't get the one, then I take the other"; I dare not permit myself to go on the assumption which seems to many so natural, that I certainly am good enough, if only the other is worthy of me. In my case the accent had to fall upon another spot, upon the question whether I was capable of giving my life such an expression as a marriage requires. I was as much in love as anybody can be, in spite of the fact that not many will understand that in case deliberation had not permitted me to take this step I should have kept my love to myself. I marry her/or I never marry.

Ought a soldier of the advanced guard to be married? Dare a soldier on the frontier (spiritually understood) take a wife, a soldier on duty at the extremest outpost, who is fighting day and night, not exactly against Turks and Scythians, but against the robber bands of an innate melancholy, a soldier of the outpost who, even though he does not fight day and night, though for a considerable period he has peace, yet never can know at what instant the war will begin again, since he cannot even dare to call this quiet a truce?

Melancholy is my very nature, that is true, but thanks be to the Power which, though it cursed me thus, gave me also one comfort. There are animals which are not provided with weapons against their enemies but upon whom nature has bestowed a cunning by which they are saved nevertheless. Such cunning was granted also to me, a power of cunning which makes me just as strong as anyone with whom I have tried my strength. My cunning consists in being able to hide my melancholy. As deep as my melancholy is, precisely so cunning is my deception. I have trained myself in it and train myself daily. I often think of the little child I once saw on the Esplanade. He walked on crutches, but on his crutches he could hop, skip and run a race almost as well as the best of them. Since I was quite young I have trained myself, since I saw her and fell in love I have put myself through the most intensive training, before there could be any question of forming a resolution. At any time of day I can put off my melancholy, or rather put on my disguise, for melancholy merely waits for me till I am alone. If there is anybody present, whoever it may be, I am never quite what I am. If I am taken by surprise in an unguarded moment, I can in a half-hour wrest this impression away from anybody I have encountered in my practice. My deception is not exuberant mirth. In connection with melancholy this is nature's own deception, which precisely for this cause will make one an object of suspicion even in the eyes of a mediocre observer. The surest deception is sound common sense, passionate reflection, and above all an open countenance and an open-hearted nature. Behind this deceptive confidence and security in life there is a sleepless and melancholy reflection which, in case the assumed attitude becomes unsteady, brings everything to confusion, to the point that the adversary can't make out where he is, till one manages to attain again one's steady attitude. And so in the heart of hearts . . . melancholy. It is true, this remains there and is and continues to be my misery. But I have no desire to overwhelm with this misery any other person. It is certainly not for this purpose I want to marry.

May I perhaps be somewhat sophistical in favor of myself? Certainly I am in love—might it be love's wish which makes me imagine that I am equal to this? But I have trained myself for so many years, and till now it has never failed. After all, my father was married, and he was the most melancholy man I ever knew. But all day he was joyful and composed, he employed an hour of the night to drain, like Loki's wife,[7] the cup of bitterness, and then he was healed again. I do not require so much time, I need only an instant which time and opportunity may present, and then all goes well. From the bitterness of melancholy is distilled a vital joy, a sympathy, a heartiness, which certainly cannot embitter the life of any person. My joy, as sometimes it overflows in my heart, belongs to her entirely, for daily use I labor to acquire for her a competence of joy, only the occasional dark moments belong to me, and she shall not suffer from them.

So the matter stands. Of all the heroes who float before my imagination it is more or less true that they carry deeply hidden a sorrow

[7] She held a cup under the serpent which dripped venom upon the bound body of her husband, and made haste to drink it when it was full.

which they cannot and would not impart to anyone. I do not marry in order to make another person toil like a slave under my melancholy. It is a point of honor, my pride, my enthusiasm, to keep that shut up which should be shut up, to reduce it to the scantiest possible diet; my joy, my bliss, my first, my only wish is to belong to her whom at all costs I would purchase with my life and blood, but whom I will not enfeeble and destroy by initiation into my sufferings.

Either her/or I never marry. More than once a man does not make this violent exertion, to which only the experience of being in love can impart all the glory of enchantment. For I perceive indeed that marriage is for me a difficult problem, an anxious affair, even though it is my dearest wish.

January 3. Midnight.

WHEN a desperate man rushes through a side-street of existence to take refuge in a monastery, he would do well to consider first whether in his situation in life there is not some tie which makes it his first duty to labor at getting another person afloat if this other is salvable. When to accomplish this he has done all that in him lies, then, though he has not become a knight in his lifetime, he may set his hope upon that honor which the Middle Ages suffered to be rendered to the scholastic, that he be buried as a knight. Be still, therefore. The thing is to remain as apathetic and undecided as possible. I am indeed a murderer, I have upon my conscience the life of a human being! But can one then reasonably seek refuge in the cloister? No! The only thing a murderer has to wait for is his sentence; I await a sentence which is to decide whether I am a murderer—for in fact she is still alive. Oh, Horror! If this was an exaggeration, the expression of a momentary mood, if it was the defiant spirit of impotence which wrung this word from her lips and from the lips of her family![8] Oh, profound mockery upon life, if in the whole world were none but I that took this word seriously! My understanding suggests one suspicion after the other; the demon of laughter harps incessantly upon—I know what it wants, it would whirl her away as an abracadabra. Avaunt, thou unclean spirit! My honor, my pride, bid me to believe her; my melancholy spies out the most secret thought in this word, that I shall not be allowed to hide myself from anyone. She as the speaker bears the responsibility of having uttered that dreadful word, it is my responsibility whether I am to take the word literally.

[8] Regina affirmed that she would die if S.K. were to leave her, and her father echoed this word.

I am not an impartial observer, not the counsellor of conscience, I am a participant, i.e. the guilty one. So therefore my imagination is allowed to depict her in all misery and my melancholy to teach the application: Thou art a murderer. If there be any truth in that first word I said to myself at the instant of separation, "She chooses the cry, I choose the pain"—if there be any truth in it, I now do not wish to know, and I cannot know if there be any truth in it.

Ah, would that she might not die, would that she might not wither away! If it were possible [to return to her]—God in heaven, Thou knowest, it was indeed my only wish, if only it were possible, and if only it were not too late!

Yesterday afternoon I saw her on the street. How pale, how suffering, how like a person who summons one to meet her before the judgment of eternity. Her eye so dimmed, and in my soul this shudder because Death is walking over my grave. And yet I would forget no detail of it, not one; only to the faithfulness of an anxious imagination which gives back to me more dreadfully that which was confided to it, only to the memory of a burdened conscience which reinvests the debt at a higher rate of interest, only to such honesty as that will I and dare I entrust myself! — She is dying. And to think that I for an instant could believe in the craftiness of the understanding or all but listen to the demon of laughter—how detestable!

And yet perhaps she was pale only because she saw me. Perhaps! What a base tormentor dwells in this word! Is it not as when a child has long been tormenting a little bird when every instant it wants to die, and then he teases it so that for a second it grasps for life, grasps with its wings for freedom?

But she is dying, I cannot outlive her. But I would not die an instant earlier, lest my death afford her an explanation[9] which even at the sacrifice of my life I would keep from her.

So then be cool, calm, discreet, unchangeable. Strangely enough, when I wooed her I was fearful of being too artful, now I am compelled to be that.

January 5. Midnight.

THE QUIET DESPAIR[10]

WHEN Swift was old he was taken into the madhouse he himself had founded in his youth. There, it is related, he often stood before a mirror

[9] I.e. that he loved her—the secret he sought by every cunning artifice to keep from her . . . and yet revealed in his books!

[10] cf. my *Kierkegaard,* pp. 45 *ff*.

with the persistence of a vain and wanton woman, though not exactly with her thoughts. He looked at himself and said: "Poor old man!"

There was once a father and a son. A son is like a mirror in which the father beholds himself, and for the son the father too is like a mirror in which he beholds himself in the time to come. However, they rarely regarded one another in this way, for their daily intercourse was characterized by the cheerfulness of gay and lively conversation. It happened only a few times that the father came to a stop, stood before the son with a sorrowful countenance, looked at him steadily and said: "Poor child, thou art going into a quiet despair." True as this saying was, nothing was ever said to indicate how it was to be understood. And the father believed that he was to blame for the son's melancholy, and the son believed that he was the occasion of the father's sorrow—but they never exchanged a word on this subject.

Then the father died, and the son saw much, experienced much, and was tried in manifold temptations; but infinitely inventive as love is, longing and the sense of loss taught him, not indeed to wrest from the silence of eternity a communication, but to imitate the father's voice so perfectly that he was content with the likeness. So he did not look at himself in a mirror like the aged Swift, for the mirror was no longer there; but in loneliness he comforted himself by hearing the father's voice: "Poor child, thou art going into a quiet despair." For the father was the only one who had understood him, and yet he did not know in fact whether he had understood him; and the father was the only confidant he had had, but the confidence was of such a sort that it remained the same whether the father lived or died.

January 8. Morning.

A YEAR ago today I saw her at the house of her uncle, where she and I were at the same party. How mysteriously I brood over my love, and how secretly I imbibe love's nutriment! And why so mysteriously? Verily it is not as though love stood in need of any incitement of mystification; but partly it is because I am accustomed from an earlier period to employ mystification, and still more from the period of preparation for this *tentamen rigorosum,* and partly because it seems to me I owe it to her. Surely it is inexcusable for a man to abuse the free intercourse with the other sex, which our institutions now permit, by making love, as it is called. It is impossible to reckon how and to what extent this love-making may disturbingly affect a girl, and disturbingly affect the man to whom she is one day to belong. I know well that love can ignore trifling occasions of disquietude, and yet, if I were in love with a girl, it would always pain me, it would affect me disagreeably, that she had been the object of a love-maker's attention. Far better if she had been in love or married, for not any of the more serious impression of the erotic has nearly so disturbing an effect as this indeterminate sort, which precisely for this reason is described as flirtation. I could wish then that another might be considerate of me, and so shall I be of him, for I am very far from having the hardihood to assume as a matter of course that she shall belong to me. But whether she becomes mine/or she doesn't become mine—what short shrift language can make, and at other times language is in such loving agreement with the prolixity of sorrow—my judgment remains unaltered. If she is to belong to another, I could wish that my thought, quickly slain, might retire within me and leave no outward trace.

Neither am I so reserved because I wish to take her off her guard by some mystification. What good would that do me? I might indeed go on the assumption that I am a capital fellow who surely could make her happy, if only she were good enough. I do not know if such a thought can find place in a lover's head, mine does not harbor it. I feel all too keenly the responsibility and what it would mean to take a girl off her guard by guile—to beguile myself into assuming this weight of responsibility. If at any time she were to become mine, and I must acknowledge to myself that I had used guile with her, I should be as though annihilated, for all my good luck, because what has been done cannot be undone, yea, not even construed differently by the imagination, since even her interpretation would have nothing to say about how different things would have been if guile had not been used. I do not know if guile can ever be compatible with the erotic, but this I know, that when one strives with God and with oneself about *daring* to follow the beckoning of love, about daring to grasp the wish which is the eye's delight and the heart's desire, one is secured against erring in that way. But for this reason I am so cautious, cautious up to the last instant—ah, if within me there were to come a counter-order, that I ought not to have intervened presumptuously to disturb her, and I were then to have not merely the pain of unhappy love, but be obliged to make the retreat of repentance.

However, the fullness of time is approaching. For well on to a year since for the first time I perceived that I was in love with her (for I had seen her before without perceiving this), I have abandoned myself secretly and clandestinely to this love. I have seen her in society, seen her in her room, I have followed her path unobserved. This last was in a way the dearest to me, partly because it satisfied the secrecy of love, partly because it did not distress me with the fear that someone would find it out, which might vex her and too early snatch me unresolved from my school of training. This year, the year of training, has a peculiar fascination for me. Throughout everything else that I undertook was twined love's silken cord, as in the anchor-ropes of the Americans;[11] and whatever else I undertook stood in close relation to it. The anchor-rope can have no presentiment of the storm which is to test it, but I on the contrary imagined many dreadful situations and exercised myself in them, while the pleasure hummed an accompaniment to the labor. A student who is in love reads diligently for his examination, how much more then must I be enthusiastic about undertaking such a course of training, which in quite a different sense was my *conditio sine qua non.*

How expert I became only he can comprehend who understands what it means to undertake nothing, not the very least thing, except by force of reflection, which is as if in order to walk one had to use an artificial leg and could not take a step without it, and at the same time would conceal from people the fact that it was an artificial leg. That at least in the case of reflection can be done successfully. A man has merely to be aware how much he does spontaneously, and then he would know what it is not to do the least thing without calculation. He would know what a difference there is between coming to a merry party and being joyful as a matter of course, and coming, on the other hand, from the utmost gloom of melancholy, and yet coming precisely at the stroke of the clock as indicated in the invitation, and with the sort of merriment prescribed by the society and the environment. In case one is not in love, one must faint by the way.

She went once a week to her singing-lesson, that I knew. I knew where the singing-teacher lived. Far from making any effort to thrust myself into these circles, I wished merely to behold her secretly. Now it chanced happily that there dwelt in the same street a pastry cook, whose shop she passed in going to her lesson. Here I had my waiting-place. Here I sat and waited, here I saw her, myself unseen, here love's secret growth waxed and developed before my eyes, to my great contentment. It was a second rate pastry shop. I could be pretty sure of not being surprised. However, several of my familiar companions took notice of my habit of going there. I made them believe that the coffee was incom-

[11] He doubtless meant the red thread which distinguishes the ropes of the British navy.

parably the best in the whole city, I went so far as to invite them with great pathos to try it. A few of them went there one day and tasted . . . and found it mediocre—as of course it was. I disputed this opinion zealously. The consequence was that once when the question was broached among these friends and several others why I always went to that pastry shop, one of them said, "Oh, well, that's nothing but his usual obstinacy. Once he has affirmed for a mere whim that the coffee is superb he must force himself to drink the stuff only to show that he is right. It's just like him—a clever pate, but the most contentious fellow—and the best way to take vengeance on him, as on Diogenes,[12] is not to contradict him but to pay no attention to him, or, in this instance, to his coffee-house." Another man thought that I had a marked tendency to fixed ideas, and he found it amusing that I really could believe the coffee was good. In fact they were all at fault, for to my taste too the coffee was bad. On the other hand they were not at fault in revenging themselves on me by fulfilling my wish and leaving me in peace with my pastry cook and his coffee. If I had begged them not to come, I hardly could have been so secure. I drank the coffee without paying much attention to it, but here it was I waited, here it was I fed love with longing and refreshed it with the vision, and from thence when the vision had vanished I had much to take home with me. I never dared to sit by the window, but when I sat in the middle of the room my eye was able to command the street and the opposite sidewalk where she went, but the passers-by could not see me. Oh, beauteous season, Oh, lovely recollection, Oh, sweet disquietude, Oh, happy vision, when I embellished my hidden existence with the enchantment of love!

As a child I had a Latin-master[13] in the grammar school whom I often remember. He was very capable, and it is not to be supposed that one learned little from him, but sometimes he was rather strange, or at least rather *distrait*. His distraction, however, did not take the form of falling into a reverie, lapsing into silence, etc., but once in a while he suddenly talked in an entirely different voice and as though from an entirely different world. We read with him among other things the "Phormia" of Terrence. Here it is related of Phaedrio that having fallen in love with a cithern player, the only way he could gratify his

[12] According to Diogenes Laertius, VI, 41, Plato said that the best way to treat Diogenes was to "leave him alone."

[13] Note what Johannes Climacus says of his Greek teacher, quoted in my *Kierkegaard,* p. 32.

love was to follow her on her way to and from the music school. At this point the poet says:

ex advorsum ei loco
tonstrina erat quaedam; hic solebamus fere
plerumque eam opperiri dum inde rediret domum.[14]

The Latin-master, with a teacher's usual gravity, asked the pupil why in this instance *dum* governed the conjunctive. The pupil replied, Because here it means the same as *dummodo*. That is right, replied the teacher; but thereupon he began to explain that one must not think of the conjunctive in an external way, as though it were the particle as such which governed the conjunctive. It was the internal and the psychical which determined the mood, and so here it is the wishful passion, the impatient longing, the soul's expectant emotion. At this point his voice was entirely altered, and he continued: "For in fact, he who sits and waits in this barber shop, as though it were a coffee-house or some such public place, is far from being an indifferent onlooker, but he is a lover who waits for the loved one. Oh, yes, if it had been a porter, a chaise-bearer, a messenger, or a cabby who had waited, then properly this waiting would have to be thought of as a way of passing the time while the girl was at the music school, and this is not thought conjunctively but indicatively—unless perhaps these gentlemen were waiting for their pay, which is a very mediocre passion. Properly, language ought not to permit such an expectation to be expressed by the conjunctive. But it is Phaedrio who waits, and he is waiting, if only she, if at last she, if only she now, soon, soon, might return—and all this is quite properly conjunctive." There was such solemnity and passion in his tone that the pupils sat as though they heard a ghostly voice. He fell silent. Thereupon he cleared his throat and said with the usual gravity of a teacher, "The next."

This is a recollection of my schooldays. I now perceive clearly that my unforgettable Latin-master, though he only professed to teach Latin, could also have undertaken other subjects.

A year ago I accompanied her home at night. There was no one else who could be asked to do this. I walked joyfully beside her, in company with some other girls. I felt happier, however, for this concealment [which the "others" provided], coming so near to reality, yet without being in reality nearer or farther, while the distance of concealment draws the object to itself. If all this were an illusion? Impossible! Why

14 "Opposite that place [i.e. the school] was a barber-shop; here we were accustomed to catch sight of her when she should return home from thence."

do I feel happier in the distance of possibility? For the reasons I have given—everything else is a gloomy imagination; she is indeed the only one I loved and have loved, I will never love any other. But I will not degrade my soul by learning to know her (as the phrase is), by testing and exploring her nature. She is my loved one, and the secret labor of my love is to think everything lovable of her, until I almost perish with impatience. The time and hour may likely be approaching. My soul is resolved.

January 9. Morning.

TODAY a year ago. I count the instants—if only I am granted an opportunity to talk with her, the lot is cast. I have thought the whole thing over afresh: either her/or nothing. Good God! if only this may turn out prosperously! I did not dare to pray for this gift, except with the infinite reservation that I am not praying for her but for what is beneficial to me. In no other way have I ever dared to pray God for anything, nor have I ever wished to pray in any other way. By the short-cut of resignation God and man are doubtless nearest to one another, but this short-cut is an entire journey around existence. In a certain sense I am almost more afraid of her Yes than of her No. Being on intimate terms as I am with silence and gloomy thoughts, a No befits me better. If however it is Yes—indeed, that is my only wish. It does not have to fit in with my other traits; as I have a dark corner of my soul where I am a melancholy inmate, so also shall joy dwell with me when I belong to her, I shall be able to concentrate my soul upon making her as happy as is possible for me. More I do not demand of life but that my soul might have one haunt where joy is at home, one object upon which to concentrate itself to create joy and to rejoice.

As for her, I have not been concerned to put her to the proof or, as the phrase is, to learn to know her. This saying constantly runs in my mind: "Martha, Martha, thou art careful and troubled about many things, but one thing is needful." This one thing needful is here, she is the beloved. So I think that we fit one another: if I am good enough, she certainly is. Dangers I fear not; indeed I almost find joy in the absurd wish that she were unhappy. Truly, the only thing I fear is that without me she might become far happier.

On the other hand, into her environment, her situation in life, I may almost be said to have spied. Fortunately the situation is favorable to me. She and her family live in an almost idyllic tranquillity. Her father is a serious man, and the death of the mother has softened his nature and instilled a kindliness which, in spite of sadness, is open-hearted and inviting. Cheerfulness is not repelled from this house, but enjoyment is not sought outside or in frivolous companionship with Tom, Dick and Harry. The mother's death has helped to unite the children in a more serious bond and taught them to find their pleasure in the home, where the father watches over them all the more carefully for his bereavement and permits himself not ungraciously to be rejuvenated by youth's just demands upon life. This is as I could wish. Her environment is of a sort that favors my project and my future happiness more than a duenna favors the understanding between the knight and his lady-love. I would not venture to tear a girl from an environment habitual to her if I must transplant her into a strange and foreign way of life.

Come then, thou favorable moment! I would talk with her, I would not write nor have recourse to a third party. It is my belief that a sincere love, a hearty conviction, a resolute choice, bestows the brief word and imparts to the very voice an expression, a trustworthiness, which to the person concerned is more convincing and more satisfying than the result of deliberation by kindred and friends, who after all do not know one. What I want can be said briefly, the more briefly the better, if only it is said face to face. If I possessed eloquence, if I possessed the power to infatuate, how anxious I should be lest I might employ these means, and if I were to employ them, I should be the one to pay most dearly for it. I fear no one as I fear myself. Woe unto me in case I were to discover that there had been one deceitful word in my mouth, one single word whereby I had sought to persuade her.[15]

January 11. Morning.

TODAY a year ago. It is a laborious effort after all, well-nigh beyond my strength, to keep the soul upon the apex of resolution. So it is the wood-chopper swings the axe well above his head, and this position redoubles its weight many times; he throws all his strength into the stroke, every muscle swells with the exertion. That is only an instant. Oh, that these instants might be shortened! Oh, that I may not be making a mistake, grasping amiss! If in this almost supernatural state of mind I am not grasping a reality, if this potentiation of feeling were to turn against me in the service of a new reflection, then I am utterly exhausted, perhaps annihilated forever. O time, time, how dreadful it is to have a quarrel with thee! O man, how strangely art thou compounded: to be capable of being so strong, and to be capable of falling before mere

[15] In fact S.K.'s proposal to Regina was so sudden and so brief that the girl could only rush from the room.

nothing! I feel now as strong as a Greek god, but I perceive also that if nothing comes to pass, I am crushed.

Then I met her. We encountered one another as we both were calling upon a family in Princes Street. The lady we sought was with her grandparents in an apartment some floors above; as I had a message for her, the daughter was polite enough to offer to go and fetch her. — So we were alone. Perhaps an opportunity so favorable or a moment so safe might not soon present itself. The grandmother was rather deaf, but very curious, as old people often are. So everything had to be reported to her loudly and clearly, which naturally takes some time. Juliana as she ran out to the stairway had slammed after her the entry door, and so locked herself and her mother out. The situation did not favor any unbosoming of glowing feelings, but it would compel her to use all her powers to insure that no one would notice anything, and if at the worst the others upon joining us should find her a little different than usual, they naturally would explain this as due to the tactlessness of Juliana in leaving us alone, and all the more for the fact that I had to go out to open the door, which would give occasion to a little merriment. The dramatic happens more swiftly than it can be told. A half-minute was enough for me to survey the situation, though I am prolix in recalling it to memory.

Am I sly after all, is there something calculated in everything I undertake? Good God! When I employ my shrewdness precisely out of consideration for her, what more can I do? The word uttered might remain a secret between her and me, no one, not even a devil could chance to suspect that such an instant had been so employed, the word uttered could be dead, powerless, as though it has never been said, if so it pleased her. The situation was precisely of a sort to prevent her from saying to anyone a word such as in another case she might utter in agitation of mind and bitterly regret.

What I said I do not know, but I trembled inwardly, and my voice though calm showed how deeply I was moved. How it was I cannot describe, only it was an indescribable alleviation to give vent to my feelings. I am sure that what I said had the stamp of the inward genuineness of my passion. She remained as if petrified, she trembled visibly, she answered not a word. — I heard footsteps on the stair, the bell rang, I opened the door, laughter helped us out, conversation began; the thing succeeded. My wish was that she would go first and thus avoid following me directly, which might seem suspicious; and by going first she would also secure herself against any questions. Presumably she had comprehended the situation as I did. She went. I remained for an hour's time to distract attention.

Thereupon I went home and appealed to her father in writing, soliciting her hand. At this point every worldly deliberation, every sympathetic and anxious consideration [on the part of her family] in view of so important a step is agreeable to me and is to my notion appropriate. I am far from wishing to avoid it, on the contrary I desire that every difficulty, every doubt, may be definitely faced, that every danger may become clear to her. But my first word, my declaration of love, is to be upheld in its integrity, it is not to be jumbled in among such deliberations as one additional exhibit. I have kept silent so long, and therefore I have a right to utter the word without artifice, without deceit, but just as my feeling prompts when it concentrates the whole strength of a quiet passion in one decisive word and in one decisive instant. That is the impression I would like her to have of me, and that is the impression I myself would like to have, the rest I commit to God—as also this that I have done, though in another way.

Have I overwhelmed her? Have I made too strong an impression? Can a girl perhaps not bear the unexpected and an outburst of passion concentrated in one word? Why was she silent? Why did she tremble? Why was she almost afraid of me? When the city gate has not been opened for many years, it is not thrown ajar noiselessly like an ordinary door which turns on hinges! When the door of silence has long been shut, the word does not sound like the good day and farewell of a tripping tongue; when a man will stake all upon one word, when for a year and a day a man has willed one thing and now is to say it, not to a friend, but to one who holds in her hand the fulfillment of his wish, then is the voice not uninterested like that of the night-watchman who cries the hours, nor interested in the same way as the peasant who counts his turfs. Why am I afraid then, why am I uneasy, why is reflection ready to wound me, as though there were something crafty in keeping silent so long, something demoniac in being able to do so, something sly in seizing the opportunity, something unforgivable in employing the simplest means and the most honest mode of procedure—because maybe this is the most effective?

January 12. Morning.

TODAY a year ago. It is decided. So they did not make my time of probation too long. Well, I needed the relief, for I am greatly fatigued. Oh, thou sinewy and supple athlete, possibility; one tries in vain to deprive thee of power by raising thee from the ground, for thou wilt let thyself be drawn out as long as eternity, and still dost keep thy foothold; one seeks in vain to put thee at a distance, for thou art a man's self. Yes, I know it, it is thou who one day wilt take my life, but not this time. Let me go, thou withered witch whose embrace is to me more loathsome than was that of the witch of the woods to the squire of Roland,[16] shrink to the nothingness thou art, lie there like a shrivelled snake till life again enters into thee, and again thou dost become tough and elastic before my soul, ready to consume my life. At this instant thy power is broken. The time of probation is past—if only it has not been too short, if only they have not hurried her into forming a resolution, if only they have represented to her sufficiently the difficulties of the case.

Be joyful then, my soul! God in heaven, I thank Thee! Now a little day of rest so that I can thoroughly rejoice in her, for I know that I can undertake nothing, nothing whatever, without thinking of her.

The first kiss—Oh, what bliss! A girl joyful in heart, happy in youth! And she is mine. What are all gloomy thoughts but a cobweb, and what is melancholy but a mist which flees before this reality, a sickness which is healed and which is being healed by the sight of this health, this health which indeed is mine since it is hers who is my life and my future. Wealth she does not possess, that I know, I know it well, nor is there need of it, but she can say as an Apostle said to the impotent man, "Silver and gold have I none; but what I have, that I give thee: arise and be strong!"

If yesterday I became ten years older, today I have become ten years younger—no, younger than I have ever been. Is not this a crisis? Is it suspension of the sentence? *Estne adhuc sub judice lis?*[17] Have I indeed become ten years older, I who was almost an old man?—poor girl, who will have to cherish a dead man! Or have I become young, younger than I ever was—enviable lot to be able to be so much to a man.

January 12. Midnight.

EVERYTHING is asleep; only the dead rise at this hour from the grave and live over again. And not even that am I doing, for as I am not dead, I cannot live over again, nor in case I were dead could I live over again, for indeed I have never lived.

[16] Referring to "Rolands Knappe," a fairy tale in Musäus' *Volksmärchen der Deutschen,* Vol. I, pp. 105 *ff.*

[17] Horace, "Ars poetica," 78: *adhuc sub judice lis est*—"the case is still pending."

To keep my nightly occupation as much hidden as possible I take the precaution of going to bed at nine o'clock. At twelve I get up again. No one thinks of such a thing, not even the sympathetic souls who have sympathy enough to censor me for going to bed so early.

Was it an accident which brought us so near to one another? Or what power is it that persecutes me with her whom I flee and yet would not escape? To see her is a terror to me, such as it must be for a sinner to hear the death sentence read, and yet I dare not avoid this sight, any more than I dare seek it, which to her might be equally disturbing. In case I were to know within myself that I had gone a step out of my usual way to avoid her, had remained away from any place where I am accustomed to go, in order to avoid her, I believe that I should lose my reason. Only by enduring and suffering, by submitting to every argument directed against my lacerated soul, do I retain any meaning in my existence. If I were to follow a particular street in search of her, were to take one step, I believe that I should lose my reason, for fear I might have hindered her from helping herself out of this affair. I dare not do anything nor leave anything undone, my situation is like the eternal torture of the damned.

And today was the anniversary of our engagement! She was about to cross obliquely from the street to the footway where I was walking, she could not step up to the curb till I had passed, and a carriage which drove by made it impossible for her to retire to the street. If I had wanted to talk with her the situation was as favorable as it could be. But no, not a word, not a sound, not a movement of the lips, not a doubtful intimation in the eye, nothing, nothing on my part. Great God! If she were a fever patient, if this word of mine were the glass of cold water she craved—and I were to refuse it? So then I am a monster! No, my little maiden, no! we have talked enough with one another! Oh, to think that I am capable in my thought of talking thus about her for whose sake I would venture everything, if only I can be persuaded that it is profitable to her. But why does she persecute me? I am in the wrong; most truly, most certainly I have done her an atrocious wrong. But am I not punished? Have I not a murder upon my conscience? Have I no rights at all? Should she not understand what I suffer? Is it a loving girl who acts thus? And why does she look at me in that way? Because she believes that inwardly this makes an impression upon me. So then she believes there is some good in me. And then to be willing to wound a tortured soul!

I made the instant as long as possible. In such an encounter there is necessarily a halt, because the one must wait till the other has gone by.

So I used my advantage to form a judgment of her appearance and if possible of the state of her soul. I had taken out my pocket handkerchief, and as one holds it out to see what part one will use, so I stood phlegmatically as though I did not recognize her, although I regarded her, and saw her with the exactness of despair. But not a word, not a look which was not as meaningless as nothing. Only within did I burn, for I too have warm blood, perhaps only too warm. Burst, thou heart, so that I fall over dead—there is some sense in that, one can put up with it. Beat tinglingly to the finger tips, if that must be, beat inwardly with the blow of terror upon the heart, but not visibly in the temples, not in the lips, not in the eye—that I will not, I will it not. Why did I become heated, why was I compelled to discover what a power of dissimulation I possess when it serves a good cause?

She was not so pale, but perhaps the fresh air was the cause of this, perhaps she had been taking a long walk. Her glance made an attempt to judge me, but she cast her eyes down, she had almost a beseeching look. A woman's prayers! Who was so irresponsible as to put this weapon into her hand? Who gives a sword to a madman? And yet how impotent he is in comparison with the prayer of the impotent!

As I turned the corner I had to hold myself up by the support of the houses. In case I had then encountered an acquaintance to whom I would say, "So it is, I may appear quite calm and unimpassioned, but on turning a corner I come near fainting"—and in case this acquaintance were an inquisitive person who would watch me secretly, then what? Why then I should be aware of it, for as Caspar Hauser could feel the presence of metal through countless layers of clothing,[18] so I can feel deceit and cunning through every covering. What then? Why, then I would not become dizzy when I turned the corner, but when I had gone some way along the street and the inquisitive person had seen nothing, then I would seek the nearest cross street in order to collapse.

Sleep well now! Sleep well, my beloved! Would to God she might sleep away all her pain and sleep herself joyful and rosy before morning! Have tight-rope dancers who are parents no father- and mother-love, have they no love when they set the child up on the thin rope and walk beneath it in mortal anguish? If then my sentence has not yet been pronounced, that I am a murderer, what worse can come to pass but that she dies? And yet there is no likelihood of that. Either she is the rare exception among girls, and then my behavior is exactly what is needed to insure that she shall not be troubled at being the distinguished in-

[18] This astonishing talent is ascribed to the legendary hero in the tale recorded by Eschricht, *Folkelige Foredrag*, Vol. II, 1, p. 326.

stance, a girl whose apotheosis did not begin with death but with sorrow/or she is—indeed I do not like to say it—she has imagined, etc., and thereupon she becomes sensible etc., i.e. she imagines she has become sensible, etc.—halt! I possess no factual evidence which justifies me in drawing any conclusion. So then I remain in my misery and hold her in honor. But my shrewd common sense, my common sense it is which says this, yes, it says this to vex me, for it never was my wish that she should prove herself to be less than she seems, and neither for her sake nor for mine could I wish to be delivered in this way, i.e. in this way to be proved a fool.

But there is nothing, nothing that can assist me to get a little evidence. In vain I throw myself now upon one side, now upon the other; when one lies upon a bed of torture it pricks on all sides. She may despise—great God! that is what I want, what I labor for, and yet I shudder inwardly at such a living martyrdom.[19] Whether I can endure it, whether I shall not despair utterly, I do not know, but this I know, and this is known to the Power which by its nature is cognizant of the most secret thoughts, it knows that I pulled the cord of the douche.[20] If that will crush me, I know not. — She can consign her soul to patience, can with unscathed conscience don the veil of sorrow—what can I do, how can I hide from myself, where is the hiding-place in which the weary man can collect new strength, where is the couch spread upon which I can slumber quietly and refreshingly? In the grave? No, it is false when the Scripture says that in the grave there is no remembrance—I shall remember her. In eternity? Is there time there to slumber? Eternity! How will she appear when I see her again? Will she come forward accusingly and condemningly? Horrible! Or will she have sweated the whole thing out like a childish prank? Disgusting! And yet not disgusting but something worse, for would not my silence be to blame for the fact that she became such as this? And I precisely it was who feared lest one word from me might make her chatty and tranquillize her in flippancy!

January 15. Morning.

TODAY a year ago. Is this what it means to be engaged? For I know what it is to be in love, but this new experience, to know that the object of love is assured to one, that she is mine, mine forever!

[19] It has not yet been made plain enough that the author of the diary (like S.K. when he broke his engagement) sought to liberate the girl from her attachment by making her believe he was a scoundrel who had been trifling with her affection.

[20] One may still find on the Continent a showerbath which is released by pulling a cord.

"Is this what it means to be a mother," was Rachel's lament when the twins strove together in her womb; and so probably many a man has said to himself when he attained what he had aspired after, "Is this what it means?"

And are there not as it were two natures striving within me? That is: have I become ten years older, or have I become ten years younger?

How strange it must seem to be a young girl, to live one's life off-handishly. I thought that I should be released, that I should be transformed, that seeing myself in love and looking upon her in love, I should behold myself saved, so that I might become like her, a free bird, a youthful song of gladness, that we should grow into one, that our life would be happy for us in union and comprehensible to others in its happiness, like the greeting of a joyous traveller who throws us a kiss as he hastens by.

I understand many things, every reflection I hear or read is as familiar to me as if it were my own. But this life of a young girl I do not understand. Thinking of nothing, and yet being so lovable; living with foolishness and wisdom so jumbled together that one does not rightly know which is which. Imagine a jeweller who had developed to such an extent his knowledge of precious stones that his whole life was in this distinction between genuine and false, suppose he saw a child playing with a variety of stones, genuine and false, mingled together, and having equal delight in both—I think he would shudder inwardly at seeing the absolute distinction resolved;[21] but in case he beheld the child's happiness, its delight in the game, he perhaps would humble himself under it and be absorbed in this "shuddering" sight. So it is that for the spontaneous ("immediate") nature there is no absolute distinction between the ideas which like precious stones refract rays of light in thought and speech, and those which lack this quality, there is no absolute distinction which makes the one the most precious of all things, and the other nothing; makes the one the thing which defines everything, and the other that which cannot even be defined by relation to this.

Lovers ought to have no differences[22] between them. Alas, alack! We have been united too short a time to have differences between us—we have nothing between us, and so we have a world between us, nothing less than a world.

[21] *Haevet*—in German *gehoben*—the trick by which Hegelian logic could "resolve" all distinctions, even the most absolute.

[22] The Danish word *Mellemværende* means literally "something between"—which explains the play on words which follows.

There are moments when I am happy, perfectly happy, happier than I ever could have dreamed of being. This is abundant compensation for my pain. If only she has no foreboding, all is well.

She is silent, quieter at least than she is wont to be, but only when we are alone. Is she thinking? If only she does not begin to reflect!

January 17. Morning.

TODAY a year ago. What is this? What does it mean? I am as deeply moved as the forest in its anxious flutter against the coming storm. What presentiment is this which oppresses me? I no longer recognize myself. Is this being in love? Oh, no! This much I understand well, that my strife is not with her, not with Eros. The clouds gathering over my head are religious crises. My life-view has become ambiguous to me—exactly how, I cannot yet say. And my life belongs to her, but she has no foreboding.

January 17. Midnight.

WHAT I write in the morning is the past and refers to the past year, what I now write, these "Night Thoughts" of mine, are the diary of the current[23] year. The current year! What a terrible mockery of me is implied in this word. In case a man had invented language, I should believe that he had invented this word to deride me. In old times the army employed a very cruel punishment, that of riding a wooden horse. The unfortunate man was held down by weights on a wooden horse with a very sharp back. One time when this punishment was put in execution and the culprit was groaning with pain, up came a peasant who walked on the rampart and stopped to look at the drillground where the culprit was undergoing his punishment. Desperate with pain and irritated by the sight of such a blockhead, the unfortunate man shouted at him: "What are you staring at?" But the peasant replied, "If you can't bear to have anybody look at you, then you can ride around by another street." And just as that riding culprit was riding, so is the current year running with me.

Something must be done for her. My brain does nothing but spin intrigues from morning to night. If before she became mine my conduct was characterized by complete candor, by the most anxious avoidance of everything that might seem to be guile, now I have become all

[23] Literally "the running year." The grim play on words which follows would be intelligible to us without this explanation if we did not forget that "current" means running.

the more intriguing. Who would not regard me as a fool if I were to tell him that now in this current year I am more busied about her than ever before? And yet the difficulty is that I dare not undertake anything, for the remotest suspicion of how much I am busied about her would be absolutely the most dangerous thing, a thing which might entice her out by a hope of the indefinite, and let her be saved, i.e. let her perish from vacillation.

To want to pay in gold for every bit of information, for every word, and not to dare to do it because it is perilous since it might arouse her suspicion and disturb her in her effort to help herself! To have to elicit an utterance *en passant* by a thousand tortuous ways, when one might have communication in abundance but does not dare to, does not dare to for her sake! In case I were to observe absolute silence towards my so-called nearest ones, that also might arouse a suspicion. Hence I have concocted a formula which I recite to them. Only I do not utter it as a formula but declaim it so that they do not observe that it is a formula. This one can learn from a parson. He knows very well that it is an old discarded sermon he is delivering, but he declaims and wipes the sweat from his brow, so that the hearers believe it is a talk. So do the persons concerned believe that I am talking, in spite of the fact that I am only reciting a formula which is so stereotyped that every word has been selected as a result of long deliberation. The opposite method can also be used with effect, namely, to talk in this manner: "Your highly esteemed favor of the 25th inst. *styli novi* duly received and contents noted." There is nothing that renders passion so opaque as the business style of the bookkeeper and the counting-house. This is the best method. I have studied it in my operation upon a case of morbid reserve, and so I know it. One should never press a reserved person importunately. With that the game is lost. But just as a rheumatic man is alarmed by a draught, one can move the reserved patient by a hint carelessly thrown out without being followed up. Or one can waylay him when once he has given a little vent to his feeling. One can straightway judge of his reserve by noticing how hard it is for him to break off when once he has begun. He regrets that he had said anything, he wants to dispel the impression (one keeps silent), now he is suspicious of himself for the fact that this didn't succeed, he would divert the conversation to another subject (one keeps silent), he is vexed at the pause, he betrays himself more and more, if only by the zeal he shows to hide his secret. But when one knows this, one promptly proceeds with the exercises. And the art is to talk a little around the subject (for complete silence is imprudent), and thus to hold a consuming passion supply bridled by the conversation, so that like a rider one can guide it by a thread, and like a jockey make a turn in a figure eight.

It is after all a diversion to intrigue, to hear witnesses and receive evidence, to compare and check, to run the world around, to lie in wait for the instant, and to undertake something, even if nothing is gained by it—but it is unendurable to sit and be with child and bring forth wind,[24] to devise plans each more ingenious than the last, and not dare to employ them because it is even shrewder to let things be, lest one be betrayed; to see these seductive fruits of Tantalus which tempt sympathy by promising everything! To have the passion of a gambler and not dare to budge from the spot—and only to be bound by oneself! To have the soul full of foolhardy courage, the brain full of plans, the word ready—and then to have a pen which can write, and that only with great pains, hardly more than a letter an hour! To have the passion of a fisherman, to know where the fish will bite, and not to dare to throw out the hook; to see the float jerked and not to dare to pull it in, lest the movement might betray something! To have in one's power the person who could tell everything, to have the knife at his throat in case he were to betray anything, and yet not to be able to employ him because for me there is no comparison between revenge upon him and the injury he might do her! Instead of such information, to have to be content with the chance word of a maid or a man-servant, a cabby, a passer-by, and to have to make something out of that because it is a question of one's salvation! To have to "cook soup on a sausage-pin"[25]—but literally to have to cook strong broth on a sausage-pin because it is the most important thing in the world! To have to sit here by night and go over my talk to make sure that the voice has not betrayed anything, that the conversational tone was maintained! Not to dare trust anyone! What is the sense of trusting anybody if one would not trust the girl one loved and whom one could beset with a hundred spying observations! If one were to confide in anyone, to be obliged then to choose him whom one cannot trust—i.e. to confide in him in the form of deception!

The only one from whom I really learn to know anything is very far from being in my service. Yet there is a secret understanding between us. He knows everything, perhaps he is the most reliable of all. Fortunately he hates me. If possible he would torture me. I understand that. He never says anything directly, never mentions a name, but he recounts to me such strange stories. At the beginning I did not understand him at all, but now I know that he talks about her, but under feigned names. He

[24] Isaiah 26: 18.

[25] The phrase means proverbially "to spin a yarn about nothing."

believes that I have imagination enough to understand every hint; that I have too, but also understanding enough to treat it as nothing. Yet I must take into account that he is malicious.

Would she were dead, would that she had died at once, would that she had sunk dead before my eyes at the decisive moment, would that the family had perished with her, would that I had been arrested, would that there had been a criminal trial! Oh, would that this had come to pass! At once I would have appealed to be executed and thus to be exempted from empty prolixities. Human justice is after all mere foolsplay, the three courts through which the case may be carried only make the jest tiresome. The prosecution and the defense are like Harlequin and Pierot, and justice is like Jeronymus or Cassandra, who are led by the nose. Everything here is ridiculous, including the guards who parade at the execution, the only tolerable figure is the executioner. If my appeal were not denied when I myself was willing to pay all the costs, then with that confidant of mine I would have sought out a neighborhood corresponding to my condition of mind and would have required of him what knights are accustomed to require of their faithful squires, that he run the sword through my heart; and indeed it makes no difference whether it is a squire or an executioner, although the latter has the advantage that he need not feel any scruples of conscience. — Then there would have been some sense in the whole thing.

But in this situation there is no sense. I am a scoundrel. Right—if I were the man I seem to be; but I am exactly the opposite. What am I then? A fool, a visionary, an eccentric knight, who would so take to heart the word of a young girl. What! Is it a theological procedure against me as Aristotle[26] requires? Is there no third [possibility]? Was it an idle word? Death and hell! When I examine the declaration of a witness I do it seriously. I employed two months, I have tested it in every mood, she said it[27] in as decisive a way as possible. Is that an idle word? It must be then that a girl in accordance with her nature is renewed also in a spiritual sense and begins all over again.

Behold, now I am well prepared to go to bed, disposed to sleep—I the faithless one. So I will not think at all about anything, and will abhor especially him whose life-view in wishing to defend a girl offends her more deeply than I have done. So in conclusion I will think of thee, immortal Shakespeare; thou art capable of talking passionately. I will

[26] The Danish editors think that the reference is "doubtless" to *Nicomachean Ethics*, II, 8, where virtue is defined as the mean between two extremes.

[27] Namely, that she would certainly die if he left her.

think of the lovable Imogene in *Cymbeline,* when in Act III, Scene 4, she says:

> False to his bed! What is it to be false?
> To lie in watch there, and to think on him?
> To weep twixt clock and clock? If sleep change nature,
> To break it with a fearful dream of him,
> And cry myself awake?

Here even a poet of the first rank would break off, but Shakespeare knows how to speak fluently the language of passion, a language which *sensu eminenti* has the characteristic that if one cannot speak it fluently, one cannot speak it at all, i.e. it has no existence for one. Hence Imogene continues:

> That's false to his bed, is it?[28]

Grant that Imogene is right in saying, "Men's vows are women's traitors," but cursed be the paltry comfort that a woman's oath can deceive no one, because she is incapable of taking an oath or swearing.

January 20. Morning.

TODAY a year ago. I cannot keep my soul fixed upon the immediacy of love. I see indeed that she is charming, to my eyes indescribably charming, but I have no mind to divert the passion of my soul in that direction. Alas, charm is transitory, it is a pity to grasp it incontinently. She shall not have reason to complain that in this regard I led her astray erotically. There is moreover another reason for my self-restraint, for when she is most beautiful I am most unhappy. It seems to me then that she has such an indescribable claim upon life, so then I conceive that everyone has a claim upon life—everyone but me. I could wish that she were ugly, then everything would go better. I wonder if Socrates would not have understood this declaration of being in love with the ugly.[29] After all it is true that like only loves like. If she were unhappy, it would help. But this childlike happiness, this lightness in the world which I cannot understand and with which I cannot sympathize deeply and essentially (because my sympathy with it is through the medium of sadness, which precisely manifests the contradiction)—and my heroic

[28] Of course S.K. quoted the translation by Schlegel and Tieck, which the Germans (not without some show of reason) are inclined to regard as superior to the English of Shakespeare.

[29] Xenophon, *Memorabilia,* 2, 6, 32—a passage to which S.K. strangely made reference in *The Concept of Dread,* II, 2, A.

struggle, my courage and (to mention something good on my side) my lightness in dancing over abysses, of which she can have no conception and with which she can sympathize only unessentially, as with a dreadful tale one reads without being able to think it as real, except through the medium of imagination—what will come of this?

So I have chosen the religious. This lies closest to me, I have put my trust in this. So let beauty be a thing apart, let heaven conserve it to her. If I gain a common point of departure on that road, come then thou smiling and carefree beauty, I will rejoice in thee as sincerely as I can, then braid fresh roses in thy hair, I will handle thee as lightly as is possible for me, as is possible for one who is wont with the passion of thought, facing mortal danger, to grasp the decisive thing.

Yesterday I read aloud to her a sermon.[30] How moving it was! Never has my soul been more shaken, tears were wrung from my eyes, an apprehension of the dreadful is upon me, lower and lower sinks over me the dark cloud of care, I can hardly see her although she is sitting by my side. I wonder what she is thinking, poor girl! And yet let there come what will on that road. What is she thinking? She is hushed, quiet, but entirely tranquil. I wonder if she might ascribe this effect to love, supposing that I was overwhelmed by her. That is impossible, to my eyes it would be the most unseemly thing I can think of. When I humble myself under God—then for her to suppose it was under her! No, such an effect upon me she has not. I have been able and still am able to bear to live without her, if only I may retain the religious. But I have a presentiment that what affected me so deeply were religious crises involved in the attempt to introduce this factor into what I had begun.

Might it be possible, might my whole life-view be at fault, might I have stumbled upon something where the mysterious is prohibited? I do not understand it. I who had become a master in my art, I who (yes, I admit it) proudly ranked myself with the heroes I found in the descriptions of the poets, because I knew I could do what was related of them, I who precisely for her sake and for the sake of this relationship had brought this art to perfection! If a pilgrim who had wandered for ten

[30] In fact S.K. read to Regina some of Bishop Mynster's sermons. She confessed in later life that this surprised her. He remarked with some humor in his Journal (IV, A 79): "My love-relationship is of a singular sort. It is the usual tactics of candidates in theology to begin by being the teacher, or rather spiritual advisor, to the lady of his choice, and to end by being lover and husband. I began by being a lover and ended by being a spiritual advisor. However, it turns out, my conduct was the better, I have not degraded the holy by making it serviceable to my love; I bow myself as much under the religious as I seek to bow another."—Regina in her old age affirmed that he had not talked to her about religion. That of course was impossible to a man so reserved as he.

years, taking two steps forward and one step backwards, if now he were to see the Holy City in the distance and he was told that this was not the Holy City—oh, well, he would walk farther—but if he was told, "This is the Holy City, but thy way of progressing is entirely wrong, thou must wean thyself from this way of walking if thou wouldst be well-pleasing to heaven!" He who for ten years had walked thus with the utmost exertion!

January 20. Midnight.

Is there no third party here? No, all is dark, the lights entirely extinguished. It goes without saying that if anyone were suspicious of me or curious, the best course would be to remain in a dark room. How rewarding it is to be reserved,[31] verily I cannot say that I have lost my reward.

Supposing a third person were to think about my conduct as a lover, or a second person—for as a matter of fact I perhaps am the only one who thinks about it, and that not with a second party. Well, that after all is what I wish and what I strive for. Yet it is a fearsome thing to think it thus in the stillness of the night when the whole of existence seems somehow topsy-turvy and somehow preposterous and hence somehow uncanny. When will the moment come that I am permitted to examine more closely how it stands with me and what I have suffered? — So then, if there were a third party who thought about my conduct as a lover—at any rate I will begin it, and I am able to begin anywhere, the only thing I cannot do is to leave off. There is a contradiction in this whole desperate effort I am making, I seem to myself like a man who would take his *examen artium* and had read outside the subject enough for seven men, but had not read what was prescribed, and so failed to pass. A third person, whether it be the theatrical friseur, a merchant of silk, wool, or linen, a little girl at boarding school, to say nothing of the gentlemen who write novels and romances—a third person would have the answer on the tip of his tongue. The situation is this: I am a depraved man, in a new debauch of sin I have soon forgotten the girl and the relationship. "That is certain, it is only too certain, so we will find a way out." And certain it is—this is precisely my comfort. I am not known to many people, it is true, but if the girl were to go to any of them that know me, there is not a single one who would fail to say this. Whether it be the green-grocer's apprentice over there, all dressed up on a Sunday and engaged to be married, he thinks with abhorrence of such

[31] The word literally means "shut up."

a man; whether it be one of the simpler amateurs of East Street, he feels himself a knight when he reflects upon such baseness; whether it be a husband who worries his wife to death by his marital fidelity, he is indignant at the thought of such falseness. But the girl, so says the third person, sits and sorrows, she is busy with every little remembrance, she listens for his footstep. — But this first is not so, consequently it follows that the second is not so. Would that this conclusion were true! But what is it Aristotle says?[32]

Every word she uttered, every look of hers, I remember as clearly as if it were yesterday, and every hint I get about her, even the most insignificant, is immediately put in circulation between the deliberating thoughts. The most unimportant item becomes the subject of the most enormous effort. There were some in ancient times[33] who held that the vortex is the principle which explains the world. My life is a vortex. What sometimes brings the vortex to a boil is an atom which cannot be seen by the naked eye, a mere nothing. My pride forbids me to disregard the least item, my honor forbids it, and when one is alone with it as I am, one must deal with it scrupulously. What in another case I should allow to go in one ear and out of the other now possesses importance, absolute importance. In case a religious zealot had only one Biblical text he could appeal to, what efforts he would make to prove its genuineness, so that he might see his system erected upon that secure foundation! And a Biblical text after all is something, but a word of hers, a remark about the tea which she didn't know she had uttered, that is a small thing. Yet it might be possible that this implied a secret—this might be possible. Who but I might be able to understand this? But also in my own person I have confirmation that it might be a secret, for to whom could it ever occur that I might be such a man as I am? *Ergo*—yes, it is correct, absolutely correct, this thing is possible. It is possible that she was just as proficient in reflection as I am. Yes, if my honor and my pride, my melancholy, were not screwing me tight in these thumbscrews, I hardly should have felt the force of this syllogism. But I would not have it otherwise. If the situation might be altered, if only this were possible, oh, if this were to come about, then I should know within myself that I have exerted myself to the utmost, that I have done all that understanding and madness can devise, that the alteration did not come

[32] In his *Analytica priora* he shows that the conclusion may be true even if the premises are false. Here it is the converse of this proposition which disturbs Quidam.

[33] In the *Clouds* Aristophanes represented the vortex as the highest deity of the natural philosophers, in view of the theory of Anaximines and others about the circular movement of the air.

about as a new fancy but as the potentiation of logical consistency, I should know within myself that I have done everything to repel her from me, if this might save her, and everything to keep my soul at the highest stretch of desire, in order that I might remain the same. That I am at this instant, heaven be praised, and my hope is that I may be able to sustain this tension as long as may be necessary. After all there is nothing so fortifying as consistency and nothing so consistent as consistency itself. Till now I have not conferred with flesh and blood, the passion of my soul keeps the sail unchangeably taut for the wind of resolution. As sailors say that the ship keeps going unchangeably with the same headway, so I dare say of myself that I stand still unchangeably with the same headway. She has besought me in prayer, it is her prayer which has brought me to despair.

My suffering is a punishment. I accept it from God's hand, I have deserved it. I have often in my youth smiled inwardly at love. I have not derided it, nor sought with hand or mouth to make it ridiculous, it concerned me too little for that. But I have lived intellectually. When in the poets I read the speeches of lovers, I smiled because I could not understand how such a relationship could concern them so much. The eternal, a God-relationship, relationship to ideals, was what moved my soul, but such a middling thing I could not comprehend. Well, now I suffer, I do penance, although it is not in a purely erotic sense I am suffering.

January 25. Morning.

TODAY a year ago. She appears to have no religious postulates. So a metamorphosis may come about. And yet what will my bit of influence amount to in opposition to the spontaneity of childhood? If only I do not acquire too much power over her. If only there does not supervene the unseemly situation which well may occur along this road, that I become a religious instructor instead of her loved one, that I become patronizing to her and do away with the erotic factor, that I become autocratic instead of the beloved, that I consign her feminine loveliness to oblivion and assert myself. Would that I might succeed in lifting her, or rather that she might vault over into the sphere of religious freedom where she will feel the might of spirit and feel herself secure and safe, then all will be well. May she not come to think unreasonably that she owes me something, or imagine such a thing. Even if my melancholy is unable to afford satisfaction to her pretty youthful claim upon life (and God knows if it be not my melancholy which by its exaggerations puts my sympathy to the torture), well then I will regard her love as a sacrifice which she offers. Can love be more highly valued or more dearly paid for? In an intellectual respect I shall always be able to be something to her. Then too we grow older, so there comes a time when youth no longer desires in such a way and when our love has in a peculiar sense the years in its favor. Or is that love so much to be envied which knows no more beautiful period than when the lovers could float out upon the floor in a waltz?

She is reserved, quiet, thoroughly tranquil. When anyone is present she is merry as usual.

January 26. Midnight.

OH, if it were possible, if it were possible! Every nerve in my body tries out as it were, thrusts out feelers before it in existence to discover whether after all it might not turn out thus: that we might come to the point of suiting one another, that up to this time I shall have retained the strength to maintain my soul and my love at the highest tension of the wish *per tot discrimina,*[34] that she has promptly apprehended the situation aright without looking either to the right hand or to the left. Oh, how great a return for all my misery, though in all it were to last but one day and the wedding day were to be the day of my death, what exorbitant pay for all my trouble, for what, comically conceived, I have lightly given away, and what in my tragic suffering I call the forced labor of a convict! Inexpressible bliss! What then are Romeo and Juliet in comparison with an understanding reached through such trials of temptation, in comparison with a victory attained through such dangers, in comparison with the happiest issue from the deepest despair! Great! yea, verily that would be great! If it were to occur in the winter time, I deem that the flowers might spring up for gladness; if it were in summer, I deem that the sun might dance for joy; and at every season the race would be proud of a happiness which made us too happy to be proud of happiness. — But if, but if, if I were to become weary and lose my strength and were to die away from the wish; if she were to become sick and were to waste away, if she be now sick and is wasting away! Or if she could not hold out with me in the desert of expectancy, if she were to long for the more secure life in Egypt, or if she were to marry another! God's blessing be upon her. That to be sure is what in a sense I desired, what I labored for. And yet now I regard it differently. So I have more than one mind. Is that a sign of cleverness or of madness? If she was entirely unchanged, having suffered nothing either in mind

[34] Virgil's *Aeneid,* I, 204.

or body, but she understood me not, understood me not absolutely, if the heart in the young girl's bosom were not to beat so violently as it does in the breast of the faithless man, if young blood were not to rush to her head as it does to mine, if it were to run tranquilly in the veins of the inexperienced girl and not as it does in the cold soul of the man of understanding, if she were not to comprehend my suffering or its degree, were not to comprehend my icy calmness and its necessity in case the word "forgiveness" between us were to be seriousness, the seriousness of the Judgment, not a rampart we each of us fled to in loving jest while faithfulness rejoiced in its victory, if she were not to comprehend absolutely that in our age there is only one way of being an enthusiast and preserving the soul's romanticism in the midst of the laughing hard-headedness of the nineteenth century, and that this is by being just as cold externally as one is inwardly hot, if she were not to understand, not to understand absolutely, that it is a base thing to help by halves, and that it is faithfulness to decline to give a deceptive alleviation, if she, when from heaven there came the intimation, the signal for our happiness, had ceased to mark time and was not in a position to respond to it—what then, what then, what then? Yea, I can endure no more, I sink back again. If only she is saved, it will be right with me. Let her do what she will if only she is outside of me, actually outside of me, belongs to another, has become weary of the whole affair, or never has understood me. In case I am assured of that, whether she were to wish it, or whether she merely let it come to pass (which is something I do not fear, for if I dare to give rein to my passion, it makes place for me everywhere), then what a sophist I should become to prove to her that she has chosen the highest thing.

So I wish her well. In this very second I can think of ten possibilities, yea, of twenty, in spite of my distressful one-sidedness which has a sense only for the possibilities of misfortune, I can think of an interpretation of everyone, and then again of an interpretation, which shall prove to her that she has done the proudest thing. Supposing she were so proud that she dare not admit her love for me, she who however was bound to die of it, suppose she defends herself by making light of me—if only I might venture to speak, I shall not be ashamed of her, I will say calmly "Much have I lost, much indeed, or rather I have been obliged to deprive myself of my dearest wish." Should I fear to admit an unhappy love? Should I alter myself and my judgment of her because she altered towards me? What after all is a human life? It is like grass, withered tomorrow. Perhaps I too shall be dead tomorrow! If a fool were to laugh at me, what does that prove but that I have acted wisely?

If a son of perdition were pityingly to shrug his shoulders at me, what does that prove but that I still dare hope for my salvation in the beyond before God?

But for myself and for us both I wish still again my most blissful wish which is beyond all human measure and passes all understanding. Sleep well, my beloved, sleep well; be with me in my dreams, be with this lonely one, thou heavenly Perhaps, with thine inexpressible bliss. And so to rest:

Zu Bett, zu Bett wer seinen Liebsten hat,
Wer keinen hat muss auch zu Bett.

February 1. Morning.

TODAY a year ago. Certainly in an erotic sense I am not doing her an injury. With her I comport myself as modestly as if she were not my fiancée but simply a girl confided to my care. How could this have a disturbing effect upon her, how could it have the effect of indirect stimulation? Oh, faithless reflection! When a man fixes his eye upon thee, thou faithless one, thou dost appear trustworthy enough and like an experienced warrior who vouches for victory, and no sooner is one's face turned away than thou art seen as thou art, a deserter, a deserter by profession, a deserter to whom it is an impossibility to be faithful to anyone. That she is encompassed by such a reflection she hardly is aware.

She is quiet and reserved with regard to every religious impression. I will touch her a bit poetically, and in a lighter conversation she seems to find pleasure in the theme.

If only she be not proud, for in that case she must misunderstand me entirely. I do not deny that at certain instants there is something which seems to indicate it, in the presence of others I even have been the subject of utterances which might well be thus interpreted.

February 2. Midnight.

GOD created man in His own image, and in requital man created God in his, says Lichtenberg, and it is true that a man's conception of God is essentially determined by the kind of man he is. So it is that I conceive of God as one who approves of a calculated vigilance, I believe that he approves of intrigues, and what I have read in the sacred books of the Old Testament is not of a sort to dishearten me. I cannot conceive of God without this poetic mindfulness of the honest device of a troubled passion. If it were not so, I must become anxious and fearful about myself. The Bible is always lying on my table and is the book I read most, a severe book of edification in the tradition of the older Lutheranism is my other guide[35]—and for all that I have found nothing whatever to deter me from acting towards her as shrewdly as I possibly can, from concocting a plan as shrewd as I can possibly devise, when I have in view not my own welfare but hers. This collision between shrewdness and pure ethico-religious duties abstractly conceived is difficult enough. From great speculative geniuses and admired poets whose utterances at a merry meal are carefully written down and published with the veneration accorded to the evacuations of the Dalai Lama one learns that the devil never reveals himself wholly, and that therefore close reserve is a demoniac trait. This however ignores the contradiction that the Old Testament as a whole furnishes examples abundantly of a shrewdness which is nevertheless well pleasing to God, and that at a later period Christ said to His disciples, "These things I said not unto you from the beginning . . . I have yet many things to say unto you, but ye cannot bear them now"—so here is a teleological suspension of the ethical[36] rule of telling the whole truth. If it happens that there offers himself for poetic treatment an individual who was great by reason of his close reserve, or if such a character is encountered in the course of world history (which speculation in fact has the task of reconstructing), people sneak up to admire—secured by the result, they can well understand him. What a comfort for the man who in his need is seeking guidance—and is not yet secured by the result! Reserve, silence (the teleological suspension of the duty of telling the truth) is a purely formal determinant and may therefore just as well be the form of the good as of the evil. To resolve the collision by annulling shrewdness is really declining to think the collision at all, for there is also a duty which enjoins the use of one's shrewdness. But the very instant a man recognizes this he has *eo ipso* won God for the cause of intrigue (in a good sense). Thereby subjectivity is reinstated in its rights, which must be recognized by every individual who acts and has not confined himself to gossiping about others or poetizing or speculating by the aid

[35] The Danish editors have no doubt that this reference is to Joh. Arnt, *Vom wahren Christentum.*

[36] The possibility of a teleological suspension of the ethical, as in the case of Abraham's resolution to kill his son, was anxiously argued in *Fear and Trembling.*

of the result. Most men do not so much as come out into these spheres,[37] for there are always few who act in an eminent sense. So if one would by an appellation which singles out those who have experienced what every man is permitted to experience—if one would single these men out, one may use the demoniacal as the chief principle of division and divide thus: every individual is demoniacal who through himself alone, without any middle term (implying in this instance silence towards all others), stands in relation to the ideas; if the idea is God, the individual is religious, if the idea is the evil, the individual is in the stricter sense demoniacal. Thus I have understood it, and this has helped me. Fundamentally the thing is easy enough, except for the man who has once helped himself to the buccaneer riches of the System and thereby has been helped again to the beggar's staff. Only when one is so prudent as to want to construct the System without including in it ethics[38] is such a thing possible, and then one gets a system in which one has everything, everything else, and has left out the one thing needful.

Perhaps I do not really love her? Perhaps in general I am too much given to reflection to be able to love? Now I will begin my self-interrogation as follows. I may not have loved her at all? But, my God, whence then all these sufferings? Is it not a sign of love that I think of her day and night, that my life is consumed simply in saving her, that I never think at all whether it is going to be terrible for me, because I think only of her? And yet against me I have language, have her, have the human race against me, I have nothing I can appeal to, nothing to support me. Do I not love her? "Is that love," retorts she and language and the race, "when one deserts her?" That is a colloquy I have not been able, am not able, to endure. Therefore I have resort to Thee, Thou Omniscient; if I am thus guilty, then crush me—ah, no, who would dare to pray in this wise? So then enlighten my understanding that I may see my error and my depravity! Think not that I desire to escape sufferings, that is not my prayer, annihilate me, cancel me from the number of the living, revoke me as a mistaken thought, as an unsuccessful attempt, but let me never be healed in such a way that I cease prematurely to sorrow, exhaust not my ardor, quench not the fire in it, for that after all is something good, though it needs to be purified, let

[37] Ultimately it is the "spheres" of life rather than the "stages" with which S.K. is dealing in this book. The ethical sphere is characterized by action—in an eminent sense.

[38] S.K. constantly complained that Hegel's system had no place for ethics. That was no accident, for ethics, since it has to do with action, the practical life ("existence"), is fatal to a system. S.K.'s dictum was that we can have a system of ideas but not a system of "existence."

me never learn to haggle, I must conquer, even though the fashion of my victory is infinitely different from anything I can think.

What a comfort to have language on one's side, to be able to say as she can, "I have loved him!" If on the other hand my first proposition is false, no conclusion can be drawn from it. But here it is not a question of a couple of paltry propositions which one would unite in a conclusion, but it has to do with the most frightful thing of all, an eternal torment: a personal existence which is unable to unite itself in a conclusion.

Now I will sleep. It well may happen to a lover that he cannot sleep for the disquietude of love; I perhaps remain sleepless because I cannot ascertain whether I love her or no.

February 5. Midnight.

A LEPER'S SOLILOQUY

[*The scene is among the graves at dawn, Simon lebrosus is sitting on a tombstone, he has fallen asleep, he wakes and cries out:*]

SIMON! — "Yes." — Simon! — "Yes, who is calling?" — Where art thou Simon? — "Here. With whom art thou speaking?" — With myself. — "Is it with thyself? How disgusting thou art with thy corrupted flesh, a pestilence to every living thing, avaunt from me, thou abomination, betake thyself to the tombs." Why am I the only one who cannot talk thus and act accordingly? Everyone else, if I do not flee from him, flees from me and leaves me alone. Does not an artist conceal himself in order to be a secret witness of how his work of art is admired? Why cannot I separate that disgusting figure from me and be secretly a witness of men's abhorrence? Why must I be doomed to carry it about and show it off, as if I were a vain artist who in his proper person must hear the admiration? Why must I fill the desert with my cry and be company for the wild beasts and abbreviate the time by my howling? This is no exclamation, it is a question; I put the question to Him who Himself has said that it is not good for a man to be without society. Is this my society? Is this the mate I am to seek—the hungry monsters and the dead who have no fear of contagion?

[*He sits down again, looks about him and says to himself:*]

What has become of Manasseh? [lifting up his voice] Manasseh! — [*He is silent a moment*]. So then he has wandered off to the city. Yes, I know it. An ointment I have discovered, by the use of which all leprosy turns inward so that none can see it and the priest must declare us whole. I taught him how to use it. I told him that the sickness did not therefore cease, that it became internal and that one's breath could infect another and make him visibly leprous. Then he was jubilant, he hates existence, he curses men, he would avenge himself, he runs to the city, he breathes poison upon all. Manasseh, Manasseh, why didst thou give place in thy soul to the devil, was it not enough that thy body was leprous?

I will cast away the remainder of the ointment so that I never may be tempted. Father Abraham's God, let me forget how it was prepared! Father Abraham, when I am dead I shall awaken in thy bosom, then I shall eat with the purest, thou indeed art not fearful of the leper. Isaac and Jacob, ye are not afraid to sit at table with one who was a leper and was loathed by men. Ye dead who sleep here around me, awake, just for an instant, hear a word, only one word, greet Abraham from me because he has a place among the blessed prepared for him who had no place among men.

What is human compassion after all! To whom is it rightly due unless to the unfortunate, and how is it paid to him? The impoverished man falls into the hands of the usurer, who at the last helps him into prison as a slave—so also do the fortunate practice usury and regard the unfortunate as a sacrifice, thinking that they purchase the friendship of God at a cheap price, yea, by unlawful means. A little gift, a mite, when they themselves possess abundance, a visit when it involves no danger, a bit of sympathy which by contrast may season their lavish living—behold, that is the sacrifice of compassion! But if there is danger, they chase the unfortunate out into the desert so as not to hear his cry which might disturb music and dancing and luxurious living, and might condemn compassion—human compassion, which would deceive God and the unfortunate.

So seek then in vain for compassion in the city and among the fortunate, seek it out here in the desert. I thank Thee, Thou God of Abraham, that Thou didst permit me to discover this ointment, I thank Thee that Thou didst sustain me in renouncing the use of it; I understand however Thy loving kindness in that I voluntarily endure my fate, freely suffering what necessity imposes. If no one has had compassion upon me, what wonder that compassion has fled like me out among the graves, where I sit comforted as one who sacrifices his life to save others, as one who voluntarily chooses banishment to save others. Thou God of Abraham, give them corn and new wine in abundance and prosperous seasons, build the barns greater and give abundance greater than the barns, give to the fathers wisdom, to the mothers fruitfulness, and to the children a blessing, give victory in battle, that it may be the people of Thy possession. Hear the prayer of him whose body is infected and impure, a horror to the people, to the happy ones a snare, hear him if for all that his heart was not tainted.[39]

* * *

Simon lebrosus was a Jew. If he had lived in Christendom, he would have found a very different sort of sympathy. Whenever in the course of the year the sermon[40] is about the ten lepers, the priest protests that he too has felt as if he were a leper—but when there is typhus. . . .

February 7. Morning.

TODAY a year ago. She has beheld me overwhelmed by the power of religion, but she has no eye for the religious; she knew me long before our engagement, she has witnessed my customary demeanor as a man of cold common sense, almost a scoffer; she believes that I scoff at everybody except her—suppose then she were proud, I shudder at the thought, this indeed would be seductive food for pride, to be adored (and in this sense she might misunderstand the religious emotions) by one who scoffs at everything else.

In the presence of others her pride is more clearly exhibited. Perhaps it was there from the very first, but I did not have time to discover it. It begins to dawn even upon me. The other day it came about in such an unseemly way that the people present were startled by it. In itself it is a thing of no importance, a young girl may be allowed to take many liberties, perhaps it was merely frolicsomeness. If only I were tranquil within myself, but I am fearful of worse conflicts. And if it is something else than frolicsomeness—I foresee an abysmal misunderstanding. If only she does not believe that these strange symptoms, as they doubtless seem to her, are nothing more than an erotic impression, that it is the case of an adoring lover who worships a goddess. With that she would be taking my religiousness erotically in vain. Truly one humbles oneself under God and the ethical relationship, not under a human being. It is true that my inward man is quite different from my outward, but never have I religiously scoffed at anyone. Religion is my principle of equality, and my soul is not in the least disposed to erotic squabbles as to which of us might be considered rather extraordinary.

[39] This, like the other five stories registered on the fifth day of the month (that being the monthly date on which S.K. was born), must be regarded as autobiographical, even though its significance is obscure. cf. my *Kierkegaard,* pp. 69 *ff.*, 125 *ff.* and 137.

[40] As prescribed by the Gospel for the day, on the 14th Sunday after Trinity, in Denmark and in England, because it was so in Rome.

I am far from desiring any exaggerated tenderness of love, but I would like very much to have her express herself rather more, in order that I might perceive what is going on in her. In spite of all my efforts she regards me, I believe, as a very sharp critic, and this impedes her freedom of utterance.

February 7. Midnight.

WHEN the whale is wounded it betakes itself to the ocean floor and spouts streams of blood, it is most terrible when it is dying. The herring dies straightway, and then is as dead as a herring. But sometimes the whale lies perfectly still, although it is not dead. If sometimes I spout blood in the instant of passion, if when the word breaks forth it is as though I broke a blood-vessel, I too can be perfectly still, but for all that I am not dead. What an enigmatical power has pathos! In a certain sense one can pack it up all together and keep it in a waistcoat pocket, but when passion is kindled into flame, it then is evident that this little insignificance is an ocean of fire.

Now I will begin in another way, I will think of the situation as though I were merely an observer who had to make a report. I know very well that this objectivity will not relieve me, it is not meant to, I simply feel the need of evacuating the almost comical feature which is found in the situation. Having done that, having shaken off the burlesque, I again shall be in mettlesome mood to pull tragically, hoist tragically as a burden the same thing.

Here is the report. It is a young girl who, though otherwise gifted happily with womanly loveliness, lacks one thing: religious postulates. In a religious respect she stands about at the following point (a point which is probably seldom noted in the parson's official protocol, for she is perfectly well able to "read") : in her case God is pretty nearly the picture one forms of a good-natured elderly uncle who for fair words does everything the child wants. One therefore makes a great deal of this uncle. One has at the same time a certain inexplicable reverence for God, which does not amount to more than that. When one sits devoutly in church, this is, in a purely aesthetic sense, a lovable sight. But of resignation, of infinite resignation,[41] of relationship to spirit, of absolute relationship to spirit, there is not a trace. This girl lays claim to religion and talks about it offhand. And as the youthful mind utters presumptuously the first thing that occurs to it (which is indeed a trait of feminine amiability), so in relation to religion does she comport her-

[41] A theme emphasized in *Fear and Trembling.*

self. She loves a man more than she does God, she swears by God, she adjures by God,[42] and yet as for religion she is merely romantic in the little tablet form,[43] and so far as concerns intrinsic religious value she is only a fiat dollar.

Now in case the opposite player who is her partner were simply a sensible man, he probably would respond to this with tit for tat, like the schoolboys who answer one another with, "Dare you say 'by God'." But he is precisely the opposite of this, he is religiously constructed, his romanticism is the greatness of infinity, where God is a mighty God, and seventy years is a stroke of the pen, and the whole of earthly existence is a period of probation, and the loss of one's only wish is a thing one has to be prepared for if one would have to do with Him, because He has a round conception of time and says to the man who seeks Him, "No, it is not yet the moment, wait a little longer." "How long?" "Well, some three score years and ten." "Good God! Why, in the mean while one might die ten times!" "That may well be left to Me, without whom not a sparrow falls to the ground—so then, let it be tomorrow, quite early,"—that is to say, in seventy years, for since a thousand years are to Him as one day, seventy years is precisely 1 hour, 56 minutes and 3 seconds. Thus it is the partner is constructed, in this situation he believes that it is his business not to be offended at God because He is great, but to consider that he himself is lowly, not to squabble with God because He is eternal (for this after all is never a fault, but it is indeed a misery on the part of the temporal being that he is nothing), that it is his business to stand fast, not to want to disturb within himself the only love which is a happy love, not to lose the only admiration which is blessed, not to want to miss the only expectation which stands fast—like his business, which is to stand fast. If then he is so constructed, it follows that if a person is able to bring her relationship to him under a God-relationship, the schoolboy's "by God" becomes absolute, he is bound both in time and in eternity. He has enough discretion not to respect this word in the mouth of every passer-by, but to that girl he is bound—and she has no hesitation in employing the adjuration. The fact that she recites this phrase merely as an interjection by which she will not feel herself in the least degree religiously bound (because on the whole she exists in the dialectic of the wish, the dialectic of the agreeable and the disagreeable) and the fact that he knows it, are of no help to

[42] The fact that Regina had adjured him by God not to leave her was the cause of S.K.'s greatest disquietude.

[43] Whatever that may mean!

him; by virtue of his God-relationship he must honor this demand unto the last farthing.

There is something profoundly comic in this incongruity. Everyone, it is true, is free to swear by God. People then are commonly accustomed to employ ethical categories in judging the swearer, enquiring whether he is of the truth or whether he is a hypocrite. But this procedure is not adequate and it may do much injustice, for such an individual may in fact be merely comic. Otherwise I can make nothing of it. Even when I take a greater instance, this procedure is not adequate. When the Pharisee is depicted in the Gospel as a hypocrite, this is true only insofar as he feels himself better than other men; what he goes on to say, however, is comic, as soon as one thinks about it imaginatively. Let one imagine an individual who talks with God in prayer and now is moved to talk thus: "I fast twice in the week, I give tithes of mint and cummin." That is just as comic as the man who lay in the ditch and believed that he was on horseback. For the Pharisee believes that he is talking with God, whereas, to judge from what he says, it is clear enough that he is talking to himself or to another Pharisee. Similarly, in case an innkeeper were to stand in a church and talk with God in prayer, saying, "I am not like the other innkeepers who only give the prescribed wages, I give good wages and a New Year holiday besides," he is not for all this a hypocrite, but he is comic, since it is clear that he is not talking with God but is talking to himself, *qua* innkeeper, or to one of the other innkeepers. Therefore one should never summon God's aid in behalf of a wish, for thereby one binds oneself absolutely. For if this wish is not fulfilled, God and I are not for this cause quits, but I must stand by my word, I must every instant hold fast to the declaration that this was and is my only wish, so seriously, so eternally my only wish that I ventured to give it religious expression. For if after some time has passed I come with a new wish and send out a message to God again, just as whimpering parents send out a message to the doctor for nothing at all—what then? Then I have made a fool of God, and at the same time have shown that I am a comic individual who, far from being a hypocrite, took it for granted that to *pray* to God was the same as to pat pappa on the chin and say, "Please, please."

Here ends the report; my common sense has received its tribute, I owe it nothing more. Come now and remain with me, my beloved pain! Outwardly she cannot now be mine (or might it be possible; oh, if only it were possible!), but that in a spiritual sense she should not be where I am is a thought that puts everything to confusion for me. Can the one person not understand the other? Is there then no equality in religion?

— Why did I carry her out with me upon the stream? Why was I so at fault as to apply to a girl's existence a standard which only disturbs us both? Yes, now, now it is too late. Even if everything were to turn out happily, so that she does in effect help herself out of her misery, or never has been so very deep in it, yet to me the religious is so completely the true meaning of life that it terrifies me to think that she might be healed only in a temporal sense. When one has not this anxious care it is easy enough to withdraw with senseless glittering glory, like an elect spirit. But in case my (if it may be so called) great standard has disturbed her life, then she in turn holds me by her (if it may be so called) little standard; she with her little standard is for me a prodigious despot, because without her I cannot bring to completion any life-view, since through her I feel sympathy for every man. Without having any particular knowledge of mankind, it has been my comfort, and as it were my victory over life, my repose from the invidious diversities in life, that one might require religion of every individual. And yet I have stumbled upon an individual of whom I do not know whether I dare require it, whether I may not thereby do an injustice. But on the other hand, if there exists one single individual of such a sort, if therefore religion is to go in the same harness with genius and talent, then I am reduced to impotence, for this thought is properly my life-thought, which gives me the frank-heartedness not to envy the distinguished and highly favored, and gives me the tranquillity of mind not to be distracted at the wretchedness of the man who outwardly is more wretched than I.

Furthermore, suppose that in the last resort she more admired than loved me, suppose she cherished the pitiful notion that I was something great. How difficult then it must be for her, who was perhaps intoxicated by the conceited dream that I worshipped her, to overcome such an impression. And again it is my fault that she is humbled in this way! When one has not such an anxious care, one can well understand that it is a temptation to be reckoned among the persons of distinction upon whom the eyes of many are fixed; this is no temptation to me, I wished to be a soldier in the ranks, indistinguishable from the others.

Not even do I dare to give my outward existence a decisive religious expression,[44] for fear she might misunderstand this and venture out upon the sea of infinity. That she is not able to do, at least not yet. What must save her (such was my first thought, and such it is still) is a certain healthiness of the temporal sort. I am convinced that even at the most

[44] I conjecture that he had in mind the monastery.

decisive instant, when I posited the separation between us, she had no conception of resignation. Either the thought, "Now I am dying and then it is all over"—but that is not resignation; or she continued to hope simply in the form of immediacy—but that is not resignation; or she recovered by virtue of her natural healthiness and was inflamed by the desire to grasp the temporal precisely at that moment—but this is not resignation.

So be still. The thing for me is to be as meaningless as possible. Every hint from me would only be disturbing—and what is the most dangerous of all, it might perhaps be a help at the instant. She must, however, be incited, lest the condition of suffering become habitual. The condition of suffering—I do not definitely know, in fact, whether she suffers.

However, reflection is perfectly inexhaustible. It is like Tordenskjold with his famous parade: it uses over and over again the same few troops, but when they have marched past the reviewing stand they turn into a side street, don another uniform, and thus continue the parade . . . of the incalculable forces of the garrison.

February 12. Morning.

TODAY a year ago. She does not listen without attention when I read to her one or another religious work; I myself am being developed more and more strongly in a religious direction. I cannot yet achieve enough freedom from care to give to love a more erotic expression, I never make the least mention of love.

If only I have not erred in planning the thing on so great a scale, if only it does not prove too serious for her, although in fact all moroseness and harshness is foreign to my nature, especially in relation to her who makes me as gentle as can be.

So I talk to her in a rather lighter vein, I converse. Verily this conversation has for me a fascination I never could have guessed. What a pleasure it is when I think of the future, for this conversation will continue to have something so inviting to me, so refreshing to my soul, that I desire no other solace than this. As ever, she is substantially without reflection, but she does not chatter, she says one thing or another as it happens to occur to her. Instantly my reflection lays hold of what was said, by a slight modification it is transposed into my sphere, and thus the conversation alternates between us. Now she gives utterance to something in her immediate fashion, a slight modification, sometimes only a change of modulation, and I am satisfied by the observation and amused by it. She is unable to comprehend how such a saying of hers can amuse me so much; however, she seems quite delighted at the liveliness of the conversation. She finds satisfaction in expressing herself, then is amazed at seeing her utterances the object of so much attention, then I perceive underneath it a little matter of reflection and introduce it—so we are both pleased. I think I am actually discovering that I have some qualities which might make me a perfectly good husband: I have a sense for insignificant things, I have a memory for small matters, I have some talent for interpolating a bit of significance, and all of this is useful in the long run. If only I knew how I might become a perfect pattern of a husband, I would spare neither time nor trouble. But the misfortune is that I have a fundamental defect in my morbid reserve, and to be anything by halves is a bitter pill to me.

February 13. Midnight.

If only something would happen! To keep one's soul in an ecstasy from week to week, to keep the countless reflections on the *qui vive,* to have everything in readiness, in readiness every instant, because one cannot know whether they are to be used, or when they are to be used, or what is to be used!

I have seen her today. She was pale. Oh, when one has a soul full of foreboding, when along with this one has a sense for the ominous, such a pallor may well acquire significance. Macbeth[45] was furious merely because a messenger who came with an unpleasant report was pale; but here indeed the pallor is the report. And yet the physician's report is to the effect that on the whole she is in good health. At least I heard this at the house of the Hansens, where the physician was and where they were talking about her. For on account of the family's connection with her and the presence of the physician I had a suspicion and repeated interrogatively the word I had heard the physician utter just as I entered the room, asking who was in such good health. They were put to embarrassment, and I, not without a certain note of sarcasm, said that I did not wonder at a physician being embarrassed at saying what he so rarely says, that a person is in very good health—"who then is that person?" The physician bethought himself and said, "Ah, it was Fru Fredriksen." "Good Lord," said I, "Fru Fredriksen! Has she been ill? It was she whose husband was sheriff in Scanderborg, and later was transferred here to Seeland. Why that is very curious," etc. Then for a brisk quarter of an hour I conversed with the excellent family, including the physician,

[45] Act V, Scene 3. The messenger reported that the English were creeping towards Dinsinane.

on the subject of the aforementioned lady. It was clear that the situation was as painful for them as it could be. Thereupon the physician departed, and I began to talk about the physician and the many families who had him as their doctor, remarking that I never knew he was the physician of Fru Fredriksen. This I could not say so long as he was present, for it was very possible that he had spoken the truth, but perhaps the family did not know it, and knew on the contrary that it was an evasion he had hit upon. In this fashion one never need be at a loss for material of conversation. But it was about her they were talking, that I am sure, for I know that less than a quarter of an hour earlier the physician had been at her house, and undoubtedly he had come directly from it. So this is the physician's report. On the other hand, I beheld her pale. What a torment to have to observe a phenomenon when the phenomenon itself alters in relation to the observer.

She had once a desire to be something extraordinary, an artist, an authoress, a *virtuosa,* in short, to shine in the world. That might indeed be possible, at least it is psychologically correct that an unfortunate event might be a decisive impulse in this direction. True enough, I never have been able to understand how this occurred to her, how she could so misunderstand herself. Lovable as she was, she had no particular talent. Had it been there, I surely should have discovered it, for my melancholy would have perceived one suffering the more, because I should have understood that she must have a prodigious claim upon life. But a catastrophe may indeed transform a person, and the wish, the aspiration, was perhaps a veridical presentiment in her soul. What wonder that I did not understand it, I who from my earliest youth have constantly lived in the contradiction between seeming to be highly gifted in comparison with other individuals, and being convinced in my own mind that I was good for nothing.

I am free and untrammelled, no servant to any man, to any other woman, or to any situation in life. I lie at the bow of my boat wondering if out yonder a phenomenon might appear. If she were thus to come forward as an object of admiration, that would be just the thing for me, it would be the happiest existence I could imagine: Secretly to see her admired, secretly to risk the last thought and the last farthing in order that the admiration might be jubilant. Impatience already seethes within me! I am able to talk people around, I can lie, prove everything, flatter, shake hands with a journalist, even write articles myself day and night —and admiration after all is for sale to money and shrewdness. I give up everything, my happy lot it is to labor secretly for her. And then when the end is attained, when pain has potentiated the powers of her soul, when fortune and favor and flattery vie with one another to adorn the distinguished one, when her soul swells to overflowing and she marches past me triumphantly, then I dare to behold her calmly, my glance cannot disturb her, for over against me existence has clearly vindicated her.

But after all one must have something concrete to hold on to. I will not so soon again run after anonymous novels, this last made me thoroughly sensible of the ludicrousness of my conceit. If I have not learned anything else from it, I have got a conception of the way reviewers feel. I have never been able to take seriously the work of a reviewer, but it needed only the vaguest suspicion that she might be the authoress (for rumor said that it was by a woman), and with that I set everything in motion to prove that the book was something extraordinary.

February 20. Morning.

TODAY a year ago. No, I can come to no other conclusion but that I am making her unhappy. There is a yawning disproportion between us, she does not understand me, and I do not understand her, she cannot rejoice at that in which I rejoice, nor sorrow for that in which I sorrow. I have begun the thing, however, and I am holding out, but I want to be honorable: I admit to her that I regard her engagement to me as a sacrifice on her part, I have besought her to forgive me for dragging her with me out upon the stream. More I cannot do. Verily I never dreamed that ever I might humble myself before a human being. Well, of course, it is not precisely under her I humble myself, it is under the relationship and the ethical task; however, I have to bring myself to say this to a human being, and in saying this it is not exactly in a jesting mood I say it! Fundamentally this is no great help, for she hardly catches a word of it, and by herself she is unable to explain what it means. But here again we have the disproportion.

February 20. Midnight.

I SAW her today in Hauser Square. Everything as usual. It is lucky that she sees me often. I know in my own heart that I never go out of my way, not so much as a foot-breadth, in order to see her; that I dare not do, my existence must express absolute indifference. If I were bold enough to do it, and if I did not have my hypochondriac sharpness of vision to spy upon myself and to anticipate every possibility, I long ago would have taken up my dwelling in her neighborhood, merely for the sake of compelling her to see me. There is nothing more dangerous for a girl in her situation than to avoid seeing one and thereby to give imagination opportunity to dream.

She must be nettled, lest she go on and become languid, neither one thing nor the other, neither sorrowful nor triumphant. And now this is about to succeed. A correspondence by letter with a friend out in the country (that is to say, with a person I do not trust) is communicated in copy to my initiate (who plagues me by his fidelity); my friend of course received this communication from me under a pledge of the profoundest silence, and on condition of the profoundest silence he in turn confides it in writing to his lady-love in Holbek, and so it goes along famously and at the greatest speed. They sometimes complain of the slowness of the post—when one is so lucky as to have a friend's woman-friend to carry the letter it travels at the greatest speed, I expect she will run on foot to the capital merely to disclose her secret for the information of the person for whom it is intended. After all there is nothing in the world so reliable as a friend of whom one knows to a certainty that he will betray everything that is confided to him—nothing more reliable if only one takes care what one confides. If one were to beseech a friend to say this or that, there is no assurance that he will do it, but when one confides to him under the pledge of secrecy something which one would have come out, one is perfectly secured, for then it is sure to come out. All the same, it is a piece of rare good fortune when such a friend has in turn a friend, and this friend again has a woman-friend —then it goes with the swiftness of light. In this way friendship has assumed the charge of my correspondence.

The more one suffers, the more, I believe, has one a sense for the comic. It is only by the deepest suffering that one acquires true authority in the use of the comic, an authority which by one word transforms as by magic the reasonable creature one calls man into a caricature. This authority is like the self-assurance of the policeman when he lays hand upon his stick without ceremony and permits no back-talk and no obstruction of the street. The man who is struck would retort, he makes a protest, he would be treated with respect as a citizen, he threatens an investigation; at that instant the next rap of the stick follows, with the warning, "Hold your tongue, keep moving, don't stand still." To want to stand still, to protest, to threaten an investigation, is in fact an attempt on the part of the pathetic bungler to count for something serious, but the comic turns the fellow about to show another side, just as the policeman by his impetus gets him turned around, and regarding him from behind makes him comic by the help of his stick.

However, this authority over the comic must be so painfully acquired that one cannot exactly desire to have it. But this comic forces itself upon me especially when my sufferings bring me into relation with another person.

The correspondence above mentioned contains a confidential communication regarding my love affair. Everything is correct, especially the name, the year and the day—the rest is in greater part fiction. I am entirely convinced that she cannot possibly possess a just apprehension of me and of our relationship; I have confused for her the whole thing too much for that, transforming it into a witch's letter which can signify whatever you please. Everything must be left to her, and from me she must at no price acquire an authoritative interpretation, for then she will never be healed. That she may be able to recover herself completely is my highest wish for her, and I will venture everything for it. Merely one single trustworthy word of guidance would be enough to insure that she would retain in quietness an impression of me which she must not have.

My peroration during the two months [since the engagement was broken], my departure from the scene, which certainly was not brilliant but was consistent with the part I played, was calculated to give the impression that I was a depraved man. This is the principle point in my interpretation of the case. For such an interpretation brings it about that her suffering becomes at once autopathic, free from any trace of sympathy, that for her the suffering does not become in the least dialectic, as though she were at fault in any way or had any cause to reproach herself. We must proceed now in the same way. What now in the next place will have the most stimulating effect? I think it is when such a scoundrel is not without a certain sympathy for the poor girl. A rascal properly stands altogether outside the good, but if he becomes impudent enough to wish to communicate with it through an almost chivalrous sympathy—I know nothing more revolting. That confidential falsification of mine bears precisely the stamp of this sympathy. It is written without passion, but in the form of courtesy. To keep the tone exactly right I constantly had in mind when I was writing a person who has or has had a toothache and about the state of whose health one does not inquire without sympathy.

On other grounds I have felt an aversion to writing all this, not indeed on her account, for my hope is that it will be profitable to her, but on account of those through whose hands it passes. And this for a peculiar reason: I am convinced, I wager a hundred to one, that all three of them will say after reading it, "Ah, after all he is not so bad as I thought, he is not without sympathy after all." It is incredible how men are struck with stupidity in regard to the ethical. By being impudent enough to want to be the most despicable of all men, one becomes a perfectly honest man, just about as good as most people are. For, good Lord! so many have had a love affair and left the girl sitting and waiting, but when one has a little sympathy one is a fairly good sort. And yet to be a scoundrel is not so hopeless, salvation is still possible in that case; but to be able to show sympathy in that way furnishes indubitable evidence that the man has lost his own soul.

And now to rest. I withdraw every thought of mine from the effort of intrigue, I concentrate all my thought upon her, upon my anxious care, upon my wish. I will not be disturbed by anything, but also I will do what I regard as my duty. If it may be right for a good cause to become a fool,[46] one may also be justified in being an intriguer—or rather, I fear a subsequent anguish and regret if I have left any means untried. I have no great faith in intrigues—not for the reason that I have failed to calculate everything to the best of my ability, but because the affair is so important to me.

Oh, blended pain! We are more and more separated, there lies a lifetime between us, and it seems to me as though there might now lie an eternity between us, if she completely tears herself loose from me. It is as though I were serving two masters: I do everything to work her loose, to annihilate everything between us, and then I discipline my soul that it may maintain itself upon the apex of the wish, in order that my wish, if its fulfillment in any way were possible, might be just as ardent at the instant when she is lost to me forever as it was when prostrate at my feet she besought me.[47] To wish while one is young is not difficult, rather it is difficult to desist; but to keep the soul fixed upon the wish when secret remorse, when deathly anguish, consumes one's strength is not easy. To cut capers when the horse is young and mettlesome and has breath in its nostrils is not difficult; but when it is weary, when it totteringly supports itself, when at every step it wants to fall—then to cut capers is a thing the horse cannot do. But the spirit giveth life, and as an aged king said, "A king can die, but he cannot become sick," so it is my comfort that I can die, but I cannot become weary. For what is it to have spirit, unless it be to have will, and what is it to have will, unless

[46] Like Brutus, who pretended to become a fool in order to overthrow Tarquinius Superbus.

[47] So in fact did Regina fall at his feet and beseech him not to leave her.

it be to have it beyond measure? For he who does not have it beyond measure does not have it at all.

February 28. Morning.

TODAY a year ago. It needs only courage and endurance, and I shall reach the religious with her. This assurance is life assurance—or, alas, it is only a precaution like making a deposit in the Widows' Fund. In any case I can take part in everything and develop more and more dexterity. Her youth is a claim upon me for every effort, and I am as youthful as I can manage to be. I believe that it is succeeding. A few days ago there was a man who said of us that we were a regular pair of young lovers. Of course, that we are too: she by virtue of her seventeen years, and I by virtue of the artificial leg[48] I use. The deceit is succeeding, as it always does with me. The fact is, I seldom succeed in expressing myself directly, but indirectly and deceitfully I succeed beyond measure. In my case this is a natural disposition, a talent for reflection I was born with. But at the same time I am learning something else, I am learning the comic from the ground up—a young lover with an artificial leg! I appear to myself like Captain Gribskopf.[49] This comic however is my secret, not to be jested with. I am not afraid of exertion, for I take delight in it, but I fear misunderstanding.

February 28. Midnight.

IT is the last straw—she is on the lookout for me, that is evident. So I have been fighting the air, she must have a residual sympathy, a nerve in which I still pain her. She cannot yet have received the confidential communication, it was lucky I thought of sending it. In my look she can discover nothing. My face is no advertisement sheet, or, if it be such, it is for mixed notices, which are so mixed that no one can make anything out of it.

Last Thursday I already was struck by the fact that for a second time, and on a Thursday, I had seen her in Hauser Square. She knows from an earlier time that every Thursday precisely at four o'clock I pass that way, she knows that I have dealings with a man who dwells there. If she is seeking me, I dare bear witness within myself that I have not gone a foot-breadth out of my way to seek her. It is almost

[48] S.K. frequently applied to himself this pathetic analogy.

[49] A disabled veteran with a wooden leg and a patch over one eye who figured in a comic opera in two acts by Stephani the younger, translated by Lars Knudsen with the title *Apothekeren og Doktoren,* Copenhagen, 1799.

maddening, so apprehensive I am about doing anything which might arouse her suspicion, and my apprehensiveness makes me assume that she is just as susceptible to the least impression as I am.

This must be investigated. Five minutes before four I was in Hauser Square and entered the Jewelry shop. My suspicion was correct, she came along two minutes later. She walked slowly, looked about her, and turned in the direction of Tornabuske Street, from which I was accustomed to come. In and for itself it is a capital idea to be seen on the street, where chance can always account for it. But since my separation from her I have opened an incessant warfare against the power men call chance, in order to do away with it if possible. No military force is necessary for that, but especially memory, a memory just as petty as is chance itself. Hastily I sprang out of the shop, ran around by Suhnes Street, and came out of Tornabuske Street precisely at four o'clock as usual.

We met and passed one another by. She was a little embarrassed, perhaps also for the reason that she was a bit alarmed at walking in what was as good as a forbidden path, or a bit exhausted by spying out the terrain. Hastily she cast down her eyes and avoided my glance.

So much is clear, that my machinations are rather fruitless; but so much also is clear, that she has a lot of strength.

There is nothing for me to do. I come every Thursday precisely at four o'clock to Hauser Square. To remain away would be very imprudent. I believe I have never been so precise about time as I am with the stroke of the clock, lest my coming too early or staying away might arouse her suspicion either that I was waiting for her or was avoiding her, which in different ways would prove the same thing, that I concerned myself about her.

March 5. Morning.

TODAY a year ago. No new symptom. When a brighter prospect opens before me as now, when it seems to me that all will succeed, when a joyful thought lodges in my soul, then I hasten to her, I am really young, young as one must be in the days of youth. At such moments I take no circuitous path, I rush with the haste of longing so as to be able to delight myself with her. If it were always so, if I were always able to be thus, it surely would be possible to marry.

How it stands with her in a deeper sense I do not know, nor do I wish to know. I will not force her or take her off her guard, but I am surprised at her cautious reserve, and it is something constrained, it is as if she were fearful of my criticism, lest her utterances might not be clever enough. So difficult to understand has my outward nature made me.

March 5. Midnight.

SOLOMON'S DREAM[50]

SOLOMON'S judgment is well enough known, it availed to discriminate between truth and deceit and to make the judge famous as a wise prince. His dream is not so well known.

If there is any pang of sympathy, it is that of having to be ashamed of one's father, of him whom one loves above all and to whom one is most indebted, to have to approach him backwards, with averted face, in order not to behold his dishonor. But what greater bliss of sympathy can be imagined than to dare to love as the son's wish prompts, and in addition to dare to be proud of him because he is the only elect, the singularly distinguished man, a nation's strength, a country's pride, God's friend, a promise for the future, extolled in his lifetime, held by memory in the highest praise! Happy Solomon, this was thy lot! Among the chosen people (how glorious even to belong to them!) he was the King's son (enviable lot!), son of that king who was the elect among kings!

Thus Solomon lived happily with the prophet Nathan. The father's strength and the father's achievement did not inspire him to deeds of valor, for in fact no occasion was left for that, but it inspired him to admiration, and admiration made him a poet. But if the poet was almost jealous of his hero, the son was blissful in his devotion to the father.

Then the son one day made a visit to his royal father. In the night he awoke at hearing movement where the father slept. Horror seizes him, he fears it is a villain who would murder David. He steals nearer —he beholds David with a crushed and contrite heart, he hears a cry of despair from the soul of the penitent.

Faint at the sight he returns to his couch, he falls asleep, but he does not rest, he dreams, he dreams that David is an ungodly man, rejected by God, that the royal majesty is the sign of God's wrath upon him, that he must wear the purple as a punishment, that he is condemned to rule, condemned to hear the people's benediction, whereas the Lord's righteousness secretly and hiddenly pronounces judgment upon the

[50] This is the third autobiographic enigma registered in this diary on the fifth of the month, and it is by far the most important. For an interpretation see my *Kierkegaard,* pp. 69 *ff.*—where to my chagrin I note that the translation of this passage is too free and has to be corrected here.

guilty one; and the dream suggests the surmise that God is not the God of the pious but of the ungodly, and that one must be an ungodly man to be God's elect—and the horror of the dream is this contradiction.

While David lay upon the ground with crushed and contrite heart, Solomon arose from his couch, but his understanding was crushed. Horror seized him when he thought of what it is to be God's elect. He surmised that holy intimacy with God, the sincerity of the pure man before the Lord, was not the explanation, but that a private guilt was the secret which explained everything.

And Solomon became wise, but he did not become a hero; and he became a thinker, but he did not become a man of prayer; and he became a preacher, but he did not become a believer; and he was able to help many, but he was not able to help himself; and he became sensual, but not repentant; and he became contrite and cast down, but not again erect, for the power of the will had been strained by that which surpassed the strength of the youth. And he tossed through life, tossed about by life—strong, supernaturally strong, that is, womanishly weak in the stirring infatuations and marvellous inventions of imagination, ingenious in expounding thoughts. But there was a rift in his nature, and Solomon was like the paralytic who is unable to support his own body. In his harem he sat like a disillusioned old man, until desire for pleasure awoke and he shouted, "Strike the timbrels, dance before me, ye women." But when the Queen of the South [*sic*] came to visit him, attracted by his wisdom, then was his soul rich, and the wise answer flowed from his lips like the precious myrrh which flows from the trees in Arabia.

March 7. Midnight.

I DID not see her on Thursday. Presumably she has now received the confidential communication. Certainly it was confidential enough, it was entrusted to weakness and dishonesty. Or perhaps she came a little earlier or a little later, I do not know, for I always come punctually, not a minute before and not a minute later, not at a quicker pace at one time than at another. That I dare not do. Only he who has a notion of the shrewdness and cunning required in order to turn the most insignificant things to account will comprehend what such ascetic renunciation means when it is applied to the most insignificant things.

My head is weary; oh, if I might betake myself to rest and lull myself to sleep by sorrowful recollection! Oh, that like a departed spirit I might leave pain behind and remember only what was so beautiful! But I dare not, with that I should be depriving her of her rights. I dare not, for I am living, I am in fact still in the midst of the action. The play is far from being over. Is the play not over? For me verily it is not over, for the later development is so far from being a postlude that the engagement was rather a prelude, and the piece began when it was broken off. And yet there is no action, nothing occurs, in the visible and outward world nothing occurs, and all my effort is to refrain from acting and yet to maintain myself in action *κατὰ δύναμιν*.[51] Why all this? Why do I do it? Because I can do no otherwise, I cannot endure that my life should have no meaning at all. The nothing that I do does after all give a little meaning to it; every other attempt, be it to forget, to start afresh, to clink glasses with a friend and drink the health of a comrade, is impossible for me, although I understand that people then would find that my life had a deep meaning. Perhaps my eye is at fault, but I have never seen a friendship where the one inflamed the other to risk the utmost for an idea which bears on one's personal existence; but I have indeed seen that, because the other, *ὁ ἕτερος*, had not the pudicity which for a time one always has with regard to oneself—I have seen that their comradeship taught them both to chaffer and not to take the world too much to heart. Only the God-relationship is the true idealizing friendship, for God's thought penetrates so as to separate mind and thought, and does not come to an agreement in fudge and nonsense. — I do this nothing and this everything because it is the loftiest passion of my freedom and the deepest necessity of my being. In case Simon Stylites had in any way been able to bring into relation with the thought of God his practice of standing on a high pillar and bending in the most difficult postures and scaring away sleep and courting terror in the crises of trying to balance himself—then in my eyes he did well to do that. His fault was that he did it before the eyes of men, that after all he was a ballerina, that, like her when she bends upon the floor in the most difficult posture, he seeks the applause of the public. That I have never done, but I have indeed done as he did, I scare away sleep and contort my soul.

On my part this is not morbid reflection, for the leading thought in this whole matter is as clear to me as day, namely, to work her loose and to keep my soul upon the apex of the wish. I do not hit upon a new purpose every day, but my reflection may well hit upon something new in relation to the purpose. Would that be called morbid reflection when a man who would be rich in the world holds to this firmly but in the

[51] Potentially—an expression used technically by Aristotle.

form of calculation takes everything into account without altering his first plan? Is this morbid reflection when he holds fast to his resolution but, perceiving that by one method he will not succeed, chooses another? If I had been suffering from morbid reflection, I should long ago have acted in an outward way and broken with my first purpose to keep quite quiet and yet on the alert. Yes, if I merely had to keep awake like one of the wise virgins, had merely to keep my lamp burning, and for the rest might let my soul be without passion, it would be easier, but that I dare not do, for then I would be insensibly changed and would not be maintaining myself unchangeably upon the apex of the wish by the elasticity of passion. This then is what I will: if I am changed, it must be against my will. Praise God, this has not occurred up to date.

March 9. Morning.

TODAY a year ago. No new symptom. Where we are I do not know. I will not be in too great haste to explore.

March 15. Midnight.

YESTERDAY I did not see her. Perhaps after all that encounter in Hauser Square was an accident, or perhaps it was an attempt she ventured to make out of solicitude for me. Perhaps she has got my confidential communication, perhaps it has not had the effect of nettling her but only of depressing, perhaps she chooses at last to languish, to be anesthetized by the soothing alleviation of quiet sorrow. Suppose she were to move out into the country, suppose she were unwilling to live in the old surroundings, could not bear it, but rather would have an emphatic expression for the fact that she was mortified, suppose she were to become a lady's companion in a noble family, or a governess.[52] Great God! to have a creditor of this sort, one who has power of life and death over me! And not to dare to redeem the obligation, and that this precisely must be a man's humiliation, that he dare not do it! Presumably she does not dream what an enormous power she has over me, that she determines the quotation of life-value, that by such a step as that which I now fear she plunges me into the deepest despair. The case stands thus: if I get her worked loose, or if she works herself loose, in short,

[52] Regina had said to S.K. that if he left her, there was nothing for her to do but become a governess. Later, when her husband was made Governor of the Danish West Indies, S.K. slyly remarked that she had carried out her threat, and he often referred to her as "my little governess."

if she becomes herself again, I have got to the point precisely where I can work for my own interest, can be anxiously concerned about my own pain. Before I was engaged to her my life was like a painful inquisition of myself, then I was interrupted and summoned out to the most dreadful decisions; and when I am through with that, if ever I am, then I can begin again with myself where I left off. Now of course I have learned what is even more painful than that. And if this does not come about, if she wilts, I am a beggar, a pauper, yea, a slave who lies in outer darkness.

And yet in fact she let fall a word about wishing she might find a place in the country. And such a word, a word of hers, a caprice, a remark of which she was no more aware than one is aware of what one says in one's sleep, such a word is enough for me. It strikes me that I am like a child of the urchin age which tries its hand at the first problems of practice in the mother tongue, to construct a meaning out of a given word.

Today I heard accidentally from a liveryman that her father had engaged a carriage to drive to a manor house half a score miles out in the country. What is he doing there, he who almost never goes beyond the walls of the capital, except when he rides, and that at the most is the distance of a mile; he who has no connections in the country? Suppose now—the word runs in my mind, and the school exercise begins!—suppose now she actually has resolved, suppose she wills to be mortified, wills to be that openly, wills to despair and to have the characteristic form for despair.

Great God! only not this, everything else, only not this! Cursed be riches and earthly glitter, and to be or to seem to be something great in the eyes of the world! Would I were a pauper, a wretched creature, then the incongruity would be a different one. It is true in fact that in the eyes of the world I am a scoundrel. In the eyes of the world! What are the eyes of the world but blindness? And what is the judgment of the world? I have not found ten men who have the strength to judge severely. Or am I not honored and esteemed as I was before? Do I not enjoy more recognition than before? and is not the qualification, the title, which is required in the eyes of the world just this, that one is a scoundrel or at least has an unusual *ingenium* for becoming one? Give the world the choice between a deserted girl who bows her innocent head with sorrow and seeks a hiding-place in the country where she may repine, and a play actor upon life's stage, a shameless fellow who holds his head high and defies everybody with his proud eyes—the world's choice is promptly made. A man is condemned to lifelong imprisonment for accidental homicide; but I, I have no sentence pronounced upon me. Condemned! I incite people against me, and they cry "Bravo"; I expect that they will slay me, and they carry me in triumph; I shudder, I doubt despairingly whether I have courage and strength enough to bear the condemnation of the world, whether I do not owe it to myself to put myself in a better light, but I do not waver, I pull the cord of the douche—and the judgment of the world is extremely favorable.

But let not this occur, merciful God! let it not occur! I am in despair, I break with Thee, I rush out there, I win her once again, I surrender everything so as with gold to bid defiance to the grandeur of the manor house, I celebrate the wedding and I shoot myself on the wedding day.

At any rate, out there I must hasten, I must see what takes her there. Alas, I dare not make any inquiry of anyone, never that! It is easy enough to impose the vow of silence when one would have nothing more to do with the world, but to have to be silent when one is so deeply concerned!

March 17. Midnight.

A FALSE alarm. Now I have driven twenty miles in sixteen hours, I have been close to death owing to anxiety and impatience—and for nothing. In a ludicrous way my life has been in danger—and for nothing. A lout of a postilion falls asleep, and the horses with him. In a fury I leap out of the carriage and beat the fellow, without taking into consideration that he is a giant compared to me. But what will not one do in such a mood? And the people extol the system of posts, the extra-post. It is a miserable affair. If Richard III would give his kingdom for a horse, I believe I would have given half of my fortune for a team of racers. The postilion throws me to the ground. It would be no use to walk, I must give fair words and a prodigious pourboir—and we started.

The whole thing turns out to be a private affair. There is a farm vacant, and a man in Jutland has a son who wants to have it. His father is an old friend of her father, who is out there now enquiring about the terms.

That a brain can stand that! It is a heaving swell such as there is not in the Atlantic Ocean, for this swell has nothing on either side of it and is the most terrible of all.

March 20. Morning.

TODAY a year ago. No new symptom. Whether this quietness and security is a good sign I do not know, whether in a spiritual sense it is a fertile air and the fair blossom is burgeoning in secret, I do not know, I dare not yet investigate, for fear of doing so too early and thereby interfering with the growth.

March 20. Midnight.

I HAVE no time to think about myself, and yet my inward life is of a sort to give me enough to think about. I am not actually a religious individual, I am only a properly and completely formed possibility of such a thing. With the sword hanging over my head, in mortal danger, I discover the religious crises with a sense of originality as vivid as if I had not known them before,[53] with so vivid a sense of originality that, if they had not been discovered, I must have discovered them. Of that there is no need now, in this respect I can humble and chasten my soul in the way I once consoled a man of rather limited intelligence to whom another said mockingly that he had not invented gunpowder—"there is no need of that," I replied, "for it has been discovered." But it is one thing to learn from a textbook exercises to be memorized, one thing to be able to recite the catechism to the parson, or even to the bishop when he makes his visitation, one thing to be able to preachify like a parson—but an entirely different thing is primitiveness in appropriating. It is well I do not have to teach others. I joyfully pay the school tax and the priest's tithes. Hail to him who is so sure of himself that he dares to take money for giving instruction!

I am good enough as a possibility, but in the catastrophe when I would appropriate to myself the religious patterns, I encounter a philosophic doubt which I will not pronounce as such to any man. It has to do with the factor of appropriation. Placed as I am in the religious catastrophe, I grasp after the paradigm. But, behold, I am not able to understand the paradigm,[54] even though I venerate it with childlike piety which will not let it go. One paradigm appeals to visions, another to revelations, a third to dreams. To talk about this, to kindle the address with imagination and yet retain the assumption, the assumption which bears precisely upon the factor of appropriation on the part of subsequent generations, is easy enough—but to understand it!

When one is able to comprehend the religious need so profoundly that one might even do well to call for the priest, and one has a philo-

[53] One may find in this passage an explanation of the fact that in *The Point of View* (Oxford Edition, pp. 83 *ff.*) S.K. regards his engagement and the breach of it as the occasion of the profoundest religious experience, in comparison with which he ignores the conversion of May 19, 1838, which looms so large in his Journal. During the period of his engagement the Journal was all but silent.

[54] In *Fear and Trembling* S.K. said again and again, "I cannot understand Abraham."

sophic scepticism completely corresponding to it, the prospects are not exactly the best. However, if only I get through this year of mourning when I have to mourn for her (and my year of mourning is not determined astronomically, it may be drawn out to five and even to ten years and my whole life may be determined by her), then I can throw myself into these conflicts, and then surely the thing will succeed. To hold out I am resolved, I will not run away from the conflict, I will not be clever in the use of shrewd devices by which one deceives another, like schoolboys who when they are writing the first pages of the copybook look in the middle of the book, and when they are in the middle of the book look at the last pages of the book, and with the last pages of the book fool the teacher. It is my conviction that the will is the principal thing even in relation to thought, that talents ten times as good without an energetic will do not make so good a thinker as do talents ten times as poor with an energetic will—the superior talents will avail for understanding the many things, the superior will for understanding the one thing. But from the fact that one has will and has the will to hold out it does not follow that one becomes a jubilant saint,[55] who, contemplating the course of life and of the universe and of world history sees and, behold, "It is so wonderful!" Let him contemplate if he will life and world history and behold that it is so wonderful—when I contemplate him I behold that he is an ass, just as he also beats a cancan on the pulpit for the honor of Christianity or becomes so serious that he tickles the people as the priest tickles himself with a pinch of snuff. Stupidity or getting into a sweat and becoming red in the face is no nearer to seriousness (because the perspirerer is too stupid to be able to laugh) than the asinine stare is to religiousness. If I know nothing else, I know this, that the comic ought to be employed to police the religious field. One should not characterize delusion as hypocrisy but as stupidity. By calling a person a hypocrite he is put at an advantage inasmuch as this implies that he has a God-relationship. A pathetic anger and indignation at the malversations of speculation, at the systematic peculation which (like the Roman proconsuls who sucked the provinces dry and enriched themselves) makes the System rich and life poor, and a good comic sketch of a religious enthusiast—that most assuredly is what is needed. A skipper can keep on swearing all day without meaning anything by it, and so can a religious enthusiast be solemn the whole day long without having a wholesome or a whole thought in his soul. That

[55] It is plain from this phrase that S.K. is thinking of Pastor Grundtvig, the religious enthusiast and the speculative philosopher Cf. *Papirer,* V. A 94 and B 102, 4.

Gothic king[56] would not be baptized when he heard that in heaven he would not be united with his fathers, the natives in America feared heaven more than hell and wanted to remain heathen lest in heaven they might be united with the orthodox Spaniards—and so does many an enthusiast, if he does nothing else, make one disgusted with religion.

About this step I dare not yet say within myself "today," but I feel that with respect to what I have ventured I have put myself deeply in debt to her. He who has made another person unhappy is well adapted to hold out in such conflicts. The man who is sentenced for life they put to rasping dye-wood, which is mortally dangerous; but after all he is sentenced.

This too I perceive, that the unmarried man can make greater ventures in the world of spirit than the married man, he can stake everything, being concerned only about the idea, and he is far better prepared for the *discrimen* of decision where one has barely room to stand, let alone to establish an abode. But truly it was not for this reason I would not marry. I too desired quiet joy in life, and her prayer made my one wish my only wish; and even if I had not wished it, I should have done it, because I always believe that obedience is dearer to God than cosmopolitan, philanthropic, patriotic sacrifices upon the altar of humanity, that quietness in the fulfilment of a modest duty is infinitely more worthy and more becoming to every man than luxurious living in the world of intellect and prodigality in concerning onself about the whole human race, as though one were almighty God. Let them talk glowingly about the wrath of God and the consuming fire—there is something else that I fear, and that I fear just as much, namely, that I should compel God to become haughty (*fornem*) towards me, so that I should vanish as an untruth before His haughty majesty. A religious enthusiast would likely find this expression not sufficiently serious, he would likely wish to have me swear in a godly way, as the skipper swears in an ungodly way. It is serious enough for me, and more terrible than the sensuous conceptions of a heated imagination. So soon as I disdain duty God becomes haughty, for only in the performance of duty am I in submissive understanding with His sublime highness, and therefore it is not a haughty majesty. Hence it is not God that makes Himself haughty—that He never does, that is paganism—but it is I that make Him haughty, and this is a punishment. Here is the profound consistency in this relationship, that the man who would approach nearer to God by disdaining the simplest things actually removes God to a distance by

[56] The Frisian king Radbadus.

reason of His haughtiness, a haughtiness which even the most wretched man does not have to experience. In this respect also I am very sharp of hearing, and though it is not heard by many a philosopher who cries out in the world *δόσ μοι ποῦ στῶ*,[57] yet I hear a voice which says, "I will give you *dosmoi,* ye dunces [*dosmere*]!"

No! If I had not believed that I had a divine counter order,[58] I never would have retreated, and if only this order is recalled I shall choose again my wish. God forbid that laborious exertion and tension should weaken my wish before such a thing is permissible! I can understand my counter order, for it passes through repentance. A repentant individual who can employ his whole life for a recantation cannot go forward. It is a perfectly simple protest against a marriage. I have neither visions nor dreams to guide me, my collision is quite simply one between repentance and existence, a collision of suspension with relation to a present actuality. Until that collision is resolved I am *in suspenso,* so soon as it is resolved I am free again. Hence it is that I make every effort to keep myself upon the apex of love. So soon as she is free the religious crises are my task.

To think quite hypothetically, suppose that she were again in possession of herself; suppose that the word about death[59] were an exaggeration, not intended as a pathetic line, but only as one says in the course of conversation, "I am about dying of heat in these small rooms"; suppose she may have meant it but had not understood herself; or suppose she had suffered unto death but had triumphed; suppose I had contributed little to this triumph, or nothing at all; suppose she were to snatch at the defense that she had never troubled about me at all—what then? Then I have troubled all the more about her. Good God! if this were possible! How my soul clutches at every explanation from this angle! Although in some of these hypothetical cases I should be sorry for her sake, I ask nothing more, so then I have suffered most, more I do not ask, I have assumed the rôle of the girl, have been more active in the work of sorrowing, or at least just as active, I ask no more. I did not leave her in order to lead the dance or to play the part of chief lover in a comedy.

[57] The exclamation of Archimedes, "Give me a place to stand," i.e. a fulcrum outside the earth, "and I will move it." The subsequent *"dosmoi"* is simply a transliteration of the first two of these Greek words, which suggests the *"dosmere,"* that is, dunces.

[58] In his Journal S.K. refers several times to the "counter order" which prohibited his marriage. He heard it first, or rather had a presentiment of it, a year and more before he became engaged, and in the midst of an entry in the Journal (II, A 347, Feb. 2, 1839) he exclaimed, "Shall I embrace thee in my arms—or does the order read, Farther"? Like the demon of Socrates this voice guided only by deterring.

[59] That is, her assertion that she must die if he deserted her.

What for her has had no significance, or only perhaps the significance of a temporal decision, has had for me eternal significance. I regret nothing, not a tear, not a single tear I shed for her sake; I am not ashamed of it, for it is not unmanly to be able to weep, but it is womanish not to be able to hide it from everyone. Yea, if there were a mocker who had counted every tear (ah, despicable deed, ah, pitiable delusion of the man who counts the tears which assuage my grief!); suppose the number were great, suppose she were to mention the number to deride me, a man who weeps—I shall not regret it. Though I should die tomorrow, my life was yet an epigram which makes an inscription on my tomb superfluous. I do not regret it; after all she has done me good, done me an infinite good, just by an unconsidered word and an exorbitant utterance.

But, behold, if such were the case, my position becomes difficult in a peculiar way. I had to have a human life upon my conscience in order to be awakened and torn out of the lethargy of melancholy. I humble myself under the seriousness of this thought. But then comes my understanding and says, "No, it is not true, thou didst perceive well enough that it was not a human life, that it was thine own imagination which fashioned this conceit and showed it to thy melancholy, and both agreed that it was indeed possible. But then it was not a human life, it was a word, a word which in the mouth of many another thou wouldst even have laughed at." Yes, in a sense that is true. And yet I regret nothing, not even that I have suffered all this pain, which after all has not yet lamed me, though it would do so were I to talk to anyone about it. In loneliness, in sleeplessness, I have been sensible of it, when in a single second one is able all at once to think together more thoughts than can be written in months, when imagination conjures up dreadful presentiments which no pen dare deal with, when conscience starts up anxiously and provokes terror by optical deceits.

But, alas, all this is only an hypothesis.[60]

March 25. Morning.

TODAY a year ago.

What is the happiest existence? It is that of a young girl of sixteen years when she, pure and innocent, possesses nothing, not a chest of drawers or a pedestal, but has to make use of the lowest drawer of her mother's escritoire to keep all her magnificence: the confirmation dress

[60] At the date of this writing, of course, it was an hypothesis confirmed in part by Regina's engagement to Schlegel.

and a prayer-book! Happy the man who possesses no more than he is content to put in the next drawer.

What existence is the happiest? It is that of a young girl of sixteen years, pure and innocent, who indeed can dance but goes to a ball only twice a year!

What is the happiest existence? It is that of a young girl when, sixteen summers old, pure and innocent, she sits diligently at her work and yet finds time to glance sidewise at him, at him who possesses nothing, not a chest of drawers, not a pedestal, but is only a partner in the same wardrobe, and yet has an entirely different explanation of the case, for in her he possesses the whole world, in spite of the fact that she possesses nothing.

And who then is the most unhappy? It is that rich young man twenty-five winters old[61] who dwells opposite.

When one is sixteen summers old and the other sixteen winters old, are they not equally old? Ah, no! How is that, is not the time identical when it is identical? Ah, no! The time is not identical.

Ah, why were nine months in my mother's womb enough to make me an old man? Ah, why was I not swaddled in joy? Why was I born not only with pain but for pain? Why was my eye not opened for happiness but only to behold this realm of sighs and to be unable to break away from it?[62]

March 27. Midnight.

To clutch an hypothesis is like embracing a cloud instead of Juno, and at the same time it is unfaithfulness towards her. But to employ the hypothesis as an expedient for exercising the soul, ungirding it and giving its energies new elasticity, is permissible, yea, obligatory. Being thus fortified I am again completely hers. If I no longer hold her to my breast, I do nevertheless embrace her, for the work of remembrance in the morning hours and the lifesaving attempt at the hour of midnight constitute as it were an embrace in which she is enfolded. A lifesaving attempt—can it be called such? Though I had everything in readiness, what does this avail if I dare not employ it? Though I were never so willing, what does it avail when I am bound, and to keep myself bound

[61] These data are appropriate to March 1839, the year before the engagement, when S.K. was just less than twenty-six and Regina had recently passed her sixteenth birthday.

[62] This poetic composition was written before the engagement and preserved in the mahogany case (commonly called the rosewood pedestal) where all the mementos of his love were kept. cf. *Papirer,* V. B 97 (30).

is the only thing that possibly may help her a little? If I could get myself afloat, I soon should be in my boat, in case this might in some way be of advantage to her, for it is also possible that what at one time would have saved her has now no importance in her eyes. It is incredible how many ways possibility knows of getting out of a difficulty, especially for one who dare not tread a single one of them—for with that there would be one less way, perhaps several. And yet it is a lifesaving attempt.

How strange a power a single word has when, as in this case, it is not integrated in the coherence of the discourse or the sentence where it is hardly noticed in passing, but when without grammatical connection it stares at one with the provocation of a riddle and the relevance of dread! I am as deeply depressed as if in this word there were a veridical presentiment of actual truth, as if I were to lie in my boat upon that rush-encircled lake[63] one quiet evening, as if I heard her cry—and now to my oars, and I saved her life, but never more shall she be human. Dread and pain and bewilderment had thus been slowly picking the lock of consciousness, and at last despair succeeded in disintegrating the charming essence of this lovable womanliness. Horrible! Dare I not command this thought to flee from me? dare I not pray that this thought be taken from me? No, it is in fact a possibility. And yet if only I were sitting with her, only this, that I might venture to be present, that I might venture all, although it were nothing, this at least would be an alleviation, an alleviation like the tumor which causes a dull incessant pain but not so much suffering. Everything would now be confused for her, she would believe that we were sitting as aforetime in a boat upon this lake where once we rowed together; and then we would exchange, if not the winged word, at least the expressions of insanity and would understand one another in madness, and talk about our love, as Lear would talk with Cordelia about the Court and enquire for news from it. — But to be separated from her, and then if she were to die, that he who was closest to her, the only one, perhaps, who had a whole lifetime, short or long, to mourn for her, that he was the only one who might not be in mourning, or rather that he was prevented from riding in the carriage when the funeral cortège followed her to the grave, although he knew better than anyone that a deceased person is the mightiest of all!

Oh, any expression at all for sorrow, though it be the most painful expression, is after all an alleviation in comparison with having no expression whatsoever. To live as though I were dumb, and to have torments in my soul and speech within it, not as one learns it from a

[63] Evidently that lake is meant where, according to the Advertisement, this document was found, and where, as appears in the sequel, the lovers had been together.

phrase-book but as the heart discovers it; to be as if dumb, yea, as if mutilated, and yet to have sufferings which crave the eloquence of an actor! To have to be distrustful of the voice lest it tremble, to have to be distrustful of the foot lest it go out of its customary way and leave a betraying footprint, to have to be distrustful of the hand lest it seek its place upon the breast and indicate the hidden thought, and lest it stretch out for her. To sit at home in sackcloth and ashes, or rather naked in one's wretchedness, and when one would dress, to have no other clothes but those of joyfulness and merriment in order to hide oneself!

"Where precisely is it you are suffering?" says the physician to the sick man. "Ah, everywhere, dear Doctor," he replies. "But how do you suffer?" continues the physician, "Tell me, so that I can diagnose the disease." No one asks this of me, I have no need of it, I know well how I suffer, I suffer sympathetically. Precisely this suffering it is that is able to shake me. Although in my melancholy I am inwardly convinced that I am good for nothing, so soon as danger comes I have the strength of a lion. When I suffer autopathically I can apply all my will, and melancholy as I am and brought up in melancholy, the terrible finds me prepared for the still more terrible. But when I suffer sympathetically I have to employ all my strength and all my inventiveness in the service of terror to fashion an image of the other's pain, and thereby I become powerless. When I myself suffer my understanding discovers grounds of consolation, but I dare not believe in any of them when I suffer sympathetically, for in fact I am not so precisely acquainted with the other that I can know whether there are present the presuppositions which condition the effectiveness of such consolations. When I suffer autopathically I know where I am, I place signs along the path of suffering so that I may have something to go by; but when I suffer sympathetically I go astray, for I cannot know where the other really is, and every instant I have to begin all over again, and be prepared to be able to think a still more dreadful possibility, the horror of which I must endure in order that I may shirk nothing.

The moment she is free, then indeed I am without sorrow; but at that moment I am at the point where she supposed I was when sometimes she begged me to remember her.[64] Yes, at that moment I shall remember her, but at that moment I shall have found alleviation, I shall be sad and say with Ossian,[65] "Sweet is the sorrow of melancholy!" Then I shall

[64] That Regina should have begged him to remember her was for S.K. one of the most poignant experiences of their parting, and the most ironical.

[65] The poems of Ossian were translated into Danish by Blicher, Copenhagen, 1807-1809.

have peace, for the remembrance of melancholy is blessed and softened and is as happy as the weeping willow when it is swayed by the evening breeze. But not now. I do not fear the whole world, at least I think I do not, but I fear this girl. A glimpse of her as she passes by, and my fate is decided till the next time. Hence she essentially is everything, absolutely everything; if she is free, she essentially is nothing at all. True, she is lovable, but essentially this does not signify anything. I have been in love, but my soul is fashioned of a substance too eternal to despair over an unhappy love; on the other hand I can despair over an unhappy responsibility, over being on unhappy terms with the eternal meaning of life. How dialectically difficult my position is, only he can comprehend who himself is tried. When an inexperienced man reads a legal document through, he can understand it to be sure, but only the experienced lawyer can reconstruct its genesis, only he can read the invisible writing which witnesses to difficulties overcome, only he is capable of knowing about the contributions vanished generations have made to the formulation of this document, he recognizes the signs of border warfare waged by ingenuity against ingenuity, ingenuity in the service of justice and ingenuity in the service of deceit, and for him therefore each individual expression has significance, not just up to a certain point, but absolute significance, and for him such a document is also a contribution to the history of the human race. The inexperienced man can indeed understand it, but he is unable to draw it up, yea, hardly with any confidence can he copy it exactly.

April 2. Morning.

TODAY a year ago. I had determined that either on the first or the second of this month I would examine where we are. I arranged an occasion and the interrogation of circumstance in order to give her feeling an opportunity of expressing itself. What comes of it? In the most free and easy way in the world, in fact with unseemly vehemence which bordered almost upon petulance, she declared that she didn't care for me at all, that she had accepted me out of pity and couldn't in the least conceive what I wanted of her.[66] In short, it was a little improvisation *ad modum* Beatrice in *Much Ado about Nothing*.[67] O melancholy, what sport thou dost make of the melancholic! The poet[68] says truly, *quem deus perdere vult primum dementat*. Now I have been

[66] S.K. in his Journal harks back again and again to this painful episode, describing it as "an attempt at boundless presumption." See my *Kierkegaard,* p. 216.

[67] In his preliminary notes S.K. refers to Act V, Scene 4.

[68] A familiar proverb which can be traced to no poet.

wandering through the valley of the shadow of anxiety, seeking to do everything as well as I could, I have humiliated myself in such a way as I dare not admit before anybody, I have sat in the darkness of death, deeply wounded by the thought that I could not make her happy—and never did I suspect what is the most natural thing, and what now that she says it I can perfectly well understand, that she doesn't care for me at all.

However, it was perhaps only an unpremeditated utterance, an impetuous outburst, perhaps she was vexed, though I cannot comprehend by what. I will not let her provoke me to anger.[69] If only I were perfectly well assured in my life-view, so that I might venture to use force, the whole thing would be a prank. But on the other hand she opens to me a bright prospect. This much is certain, a marriage is for me a difficult problem; I have now learned to understand this much, that if I had so understood myself before, I would not have embarked upon this. And now she seems to have far greater power in relation to me than I in relation to her.

The exploration resulted in an explosion, and I received the corrosive sublimate straight in the face. Just as one who for a long while has been sitting in the dark cannot at once see anything when a strong light shines into the room, so it was with me: although she was sitting by my side, I could not see her. This ideal figure which I embraced with the anxious responsibility of an eternal obligation became in fact something less, something so inconspicuous that I hardly could descry her. My melancholy was as if wafted away by the wind, I beheld what I had before me—heavens and earth! a saucy little miss!

I have to repeat the experiment again to see whether this is seriousness or not. I feel a lack of consistency in her behavior. To be consistent she must put an end to the thing and reject me. But she doesn't seem to have that in mind. What does this signify? We shall see.

April 2. Midnight.

But if she actually were to become insane! As for the danger of death, maybe there never was any serious question of it; at all events she now seems to be past that peril, although there remains always for me the alarming logical conclusion which results from confounding a *cum hoc* with a *propter hoc*. But as for insanity . . . let us see how the thing went.

[69] In fact he was thoroughly angry and "used force," as he admits in the Journal, X, 5 A, 149.

First of all, my retirement as a scoundrel made an essential change in the situation, inasmuch as that would throw her into a pathological emotion of a totally different sort, it would arouse wrath, exasperation, defiance in her mind against me, and more especially her pride would prompt her to venture to do anything which might keep up her spirits. If I had been faithful to her, not only love but the other sides of the soul would have found satisfaction in possessing all in the loved one, and hence in losing all in the loved one; but as I did not prove myself a worthy object of her love, it would require a very rare heroism to disdain the comfort which most readily presents itself: that, namely, of making the unworthy one as unimportant as possible. In this respect I have supported her with all my might, and I believe that if I had not used such prudence (by which at the same time I paid due respect to the common judgment passed upon me), I should have been directly to blame if she had become insane; for to want to be a worthy object of her love, and then to want to behave in such a way, is to propose to her a dialectical problem which is so specifically relevant to the single individual's God-relationship that only by God's help can one hold fast to the problem. Hence it is the duty of the individual to submit, even to contribute, to the opinion that he is a depraved man, in the eyes of all who are concerned in the matter, and especially in her eyes, though in relation to unconcerned parties he may well hold his peace. This I have done.

Psychologically considered, it is possible for a feminine soul to become crazy in two ways. One is by a sudden transition which gets the better of the understanding. One may become blind by the sudden change of light and darkness, the heart may cease to beat by reason of a sudden change of temperature, breathing being impeded by the air which is drawn in. So it is also with the understanding in the case of a sudden transition: reflection is unable to breathe, and the understanding comes to a stop. So in this case insanity is petrifying. There is no proportion, or rather there is an absolute disproportion, between what the understanding is capable of dealing with, and the problem proposed to it. This disproportion expresses the character of the insanity. One instant is decisive for the whole thing—only one instant more, and this would not have occurred.

The other way is when a secret passion exhausts the will, and the sufferer slowly sinks into insanity. In this case the sufferer does not become petrified but becomes distracted by a multiplicity of ideas which displace one another by a natural necessity and stand in no relation to freedom, which at one instant when it was free called up the ideas, but now they unfreely call themselves up.

The first could not possibly be the case with her, for the transition was made as gradual as possible, and besides it must at once have been observable that this had occurred. It is rather the second, which in a way is the most dangerous, we might suppose has set in. For in a certain sense the relationship was made for her as dialectical as it was possible for my reflection to make it. I do not know that I have neglected to bring forward any possibility reflection could suggest, throwing it out always as an aside and so hypothetically that it was left entirely to her to find an explanation. That I did intentionally, and I believe (humanly speaking) that it is the only correct way. Ah, the labor was trying, and it was almost to be feared that I rather would be the one to lose my mind. By nature she was not very reflective, or rather hardly reflective at all, but one can never know what effect an occurrence may have. Merely a tenth part of the reflection-possibilities I set in motion would have been enough to unsettle a feminine brain if she had discovered them herself. But reflection-possibilities must have lost their attraction for her. That is what I wanted, and (humanly speaking) that is the correct thing. Secret sorrow must itself discover and bring forward reflection-possibilities, and then sorrow finds seduction in holding on to them, and this is the earnest money of insanity. Such is not her case. She may call up whatever reflection-possibility she will, it does not acquire the refreshing coolness of novelty, nor the enticing allurement of surprise, it possesses no secret infectious power, for she is already acquainted with it. Moreover, I have brought forward every reflection-possibility as completely as I could. I wanted to give her an impression of a superior reflection. One does that any way one can. So the instant she begins to reflect it will occur to her to say, "Ah, what good does it do me to reflect! If only I could reflect like him—and what good did it do him?" For a feminine soul, reflection is like sweets for the child: a little is tempting, but *en masse* sweets lose their seductiveness.

Furthermore, if sometimes she thinks of me, if she sets her hope upon the possibility that the relationship might be reestablished, a new sort of reflection might sneak in, she herself being the discoverer of such. With a view to this I have labored and am laboring with might and main by keeping my existence entirely unchanged. Perhaps, however, she will draw a conclusion from something she has heard about me or from something she thinks she sees in my outward appearance. Quite so, but at the same instant she will bethink herself that my reflection has exhibited to her so much possibility that she cannot possibly keep pace with it. This cannot humiliate or mortify her, for it is entirely natural that a reflective individual has more and even much more reflection than a girl. If she has not yet, as I hope not, to the point of nausea, formed a concrete conception of what reflection amounts to, it would perhaps be able to tempt her. I do not believe that such is the case now. I have done everything to make reflection loathsome to her (for the omnipotence of reflection when it dwells upon one thought of course becomes omnipotence in dialectical bosh when the one thought is taken away) and to bring it about that every attempt at reflection, the moment she began it, might seem to her fruitless. I have suffered in doing this and suffer from it: a man may suck poison from another and himself die of it; by wresting reflection from another a man may become only too reflective. But if reflection is odious to her, she will be close to a resolution and will not tread the slippery path which may lead to insanity. If she becomes free, she becomes free by reason of her own resolution and not by means of one or another consideration or interpretation which I contrived to suggest to her.

In all human probability she could not become insane for love. Just because she has so little power of reflection the sudden transition would be the most dangerous thing for her. This danger has been obviated, and I have done the best I could with all my might to prevent the delirium of reflection. If then insanity were to set in, it must be due to the mortification of pride at finding herself rejected, which in despair of having a revenge would shut itself up within itself until it went astray. Ah, I know the world's judgment upon me, I perhaps have felt the pain more agonizingly than she; I shudder when I think that by a proud or (what is still more dreadful) by a compassionate glance somebody might give her to understand that she was insulted and thus impart to her the sense of insult. Once it was the custom in olden days, so it is related, that when a prince was being educated there was educated with him a boy of simpler extraction who had to take the floggings. People have talked about the cruelty towards the poor boy who had to take the floggings. To me it seems a far greater cruelty towards the poor prince, who, if he had a sense of honor, must have felt the blows far more forcibly, far more painfully, far more devastatingly, than they were felt corporally. I know also how it tortured me to expose her to this pain, I know that I was willing to do everything to prevent it by giving a false expression to the separation, so that in the eyes of the world I should be the sufferer, for when it is only a question of myself I know just how much pain there is and what I have to do for it. It was not possible, however, to put this through. Several times in our colloquies I let fall jestingly and in a conversational tone a few hints to call her attention to this, but in vain. Only a word from her, and the thing would have been done, though I had prudence enough to broach in a jesting and conversational tone an expedient which for me would have been an indescribable alleviation. More I did not dare to do. Ah, if I had talked about it with all the passion I felt, she would have perceived *eo ipso* in my zeal how much she concerned me, and then again the whole thing would have hung fire, and again she would have allowed herself to employ every means to move me, that is, to torture me, for moved I might not be. It is a comic contradiction to talk with pathos or with the decisive assurance of a systematic philosopher about what one is not convinced of oneself or does not oneself understand, but it is a tragic, a profoundly tragic contradiction to have to talk in vague terms, with jesting hints, in conversational phrases, about a matter which concerns and alarms one in deadly earnest. It is a comic contradiction to be ready to bet fourpence when there is an infinite stake to be won, but it is a tragic, a profoundly tragic contradiction to have to play as if one were playing for counters when one knows only too well how much is at stake. I suppose it would be one of the most dreadful collisions, perhaps the most dreadful of all, if one were to imagine that solicitude for some person made it necessary for an Apostle to talk ambiguously and in a light conversational tone about the truth of Christianity. — But to return to the subject. That insanity might come about in such a way I am reluctant to conceive, not because it is a dreadful thought, for the dreadful is a challenge to my honor to think it, but because it would cast a less favorable light upon her conduct towards me. Every outburst of passion whereby she laid a murder upon my conscience, every such outburst of passion which, until further evidence is forthcoming, my honor requires me to regard as truth, in spite of the protest of the understanding, every such outburst which may be ascribed to exaggeration can after all be easily reconciled with womanly purity and womanly loveliness, but every such outburst, on the assumption that pride was the motive, can only be an unseemly falsehood directed by self-love against me. True enough, I have permitted myself to direct many a falsehood against her, but truly it was for the sake of saving her and was meant sympathetically. Hence I am so reluctant to conceive this horror. Moreover, again I have done everything I could and have done it indefatigably. If my existence were to express something positive, it is conceivable that it might inflame her pride. If I were able to sustain a manly existence, which is such precisely by reason of its relation to the other sex, that is to say, by personal beauty, elegant deportment, an ingratiating nature, courteous ways, etc., then the prejudice in favor of me might be prejudicial to her, it might be an incitement to anger that he to whom the sex conceded competence as a judge had passed such a judgment upon her. But fortunately no man is farther from this than I. If I were an artist, one therefore who has an understanding of beauty and of femininity, if I were a poet, who is in fact the darling of the sex, then that possibly might inflame pride, for the fact that he whom the sex acknowledged had passed such a judgment upon her. If I were a thinker, a scholar, it would be more difficult to imagine how such an existence could be a further trial to offended feminine pride; and yet such an existence would be something after all, and on the other hand the something I am is precisely nothing. With her *in mente* it gratifies me and my genius to keep my whole existence at the critical zero-point between cold and warm, at the critical zero-point between being something and being nothing, between being perhaps wise, and being perhaps, perhaps sottish. Such an existence is entirely heterogeneous with a feminine existence, it cannot even be of any concern to a woman, still less incite her. My derangement of mind is not so great as to inspire her sympathy, but I am just half mad enough for her to say disinterestedly, "Oh, he's so mad," and if an offended pride is concerned about vindicating itself against me, it easily could rise superior to such a queer chap. It requires a good deal of dialectic to conceive of the zero-existence and to sustain it, but then to conceive of this existence as a polemic against oneself demands an uncommon dialectician. A woman rarely possesses much dialectic; she did not have it, if subsequently she has become such an uncommon dialectitian, she is perfectly able to look after herself, and if she has not, then my mode of procedure is correct and well thought out.

This is my diagnosis. To me unfortunately it gives scant comfort—though for me it is always a necessity to make everything clear to myself. If I had been consulted and had dared to say with regard to the condition of the sufferer that it is as I have described, I should be tranquil about the danger of a delirium setting in. Since I am not a physician but am the guilty party, this is of no help to me. The poison works upon me, the poison of reflection which I have developed within myself in order to suck all reflection out of her. I remember that she once said to me that it must be dreadful to be able, like me, to explain everything. She might here have got a notion how little she understood my reflection, for she scarcely apprehended how welcome this utterance was to me, and in what way it was welcome.

However, I have understood that after all she might become insane; my melancholy has also impressed upon me this possibility. Even though the unfortunate one whom insanity has ensnared in its infatuation were to suffer nothing, to have to experience insanity sympathetically in the case of another, staring incessantly at the doubtful reading of an eternal responsibility—ah, the thought of it is enough to drive a man to distraction! And yet if that were to come to pass, I should dare to seek her out, and that would be an alleviation to me—but suppose she were to recover and my problem were to retire again, then surely it would be my turn to go mad. To keep watch by her side night and day, that I can do, but I cannot sleep, and my agony is not overcome by "each night to rest beside my faithful wife," when it is not settled whether she can be my wife.

Now I will extinguish the lights. When everything is dark around me and I am silent I feel better. What is the use of talking. Everybody indeed would say it was a lie. Be that as it may. It is not my purpose to defend my assertion against opponents, *neque thesin meam publico colloquio defendere conabor.*[70] And what is the case I am arguing with God? If it were about the emperor's beard—if she were to have changed her mind, if she would gladly retract every word which works along with my melancholy to fashion the horror—what then? Then it would merely follow that she had brought a nemesis upon her own head, that it is evident she had confused her person with the eternal relationship to God which is implied in the responsibility of duty, and with that she would have shown how insignificant she is. The case has been carried to a higher court; I have bestowed upon her every possible ideality; I could not, either for her sake or for mine, desire here again to come to such close quarters with the comic.

April 5. Morning.

YES, I was quite right; I got today the declaration and the last will and testament legally confirmed by . . . my little confirmand—for that is exactly the way she impresses me, the little miss that she is. And yet she does not want to act, she seems rather to want to incite me to become an adorer. In the case of anybody else I should say that this is the beginning of a little coquetry; of her I dare not and I will not say it, not even think it. But it is one of the most ludicrous things I have experienced. I am, as I have most deeply felt, much too old in comparison with her, but by such behavior she makes me indeed so disproportionately old that I am involuntarily prompted to think of an old schoolmaster[71] who *ex*

[70] Except for the *neque*, this is the conventional formula with which the student began his academic dissertation for a degree.

[71] The Danish editors say that this was Michael Nielsen, head of the so-called School of Civic Virtue in which S.K. studied and later taught. I only know that he had a high regard for this teacher.

cathedra made the following speech to a pupil: "If you come to me again this way, you really will get one upon the ear . . . and I really believe you will get it right away."

This then is the consequence of my ideal conception of duty. If it might be made clear to me that in the strictest sense I had a duty towards all men, I should be the most worried person in the whole land. I have an ideal conception of every relationship of duty, and inasmuch as my independent position brings it about that I have not entered into any, the conception still has the primitiveness characteristic of childhood, the enthusiasm proper to youth, an anxiousness attributable to melancholy, which makes the conception itself perhaps the best thing I have, but also constrains me to the most reckless exertion.

Why should she then bring laughter into this relationship? If she really didn't care for me, well then, I am all ready for the journey; I have been religiously broken and contrite, and I may be so again when I assume the responsibility, but I am not to be broken erotically. If this is her serious meaning, then let one come straight out with it, let one say it becomingly, let one do honor to oneself in all that one does in this respect; but let not one be peevish and strike out backwards, for thus one only makes everything ridiculous. Even in her behavior there is, perhaps against her will, a recognition of me, for it is like a sort of insubordination. She must surely know that she possesses just as much power as I, and the person who possesses the power does not behave like this.

April 5. Midnight.

A POSSIBILITY[72]

LONGBRIDGE gets its name from its length, for as a bridge it is long, though as a road the length of the bridge is not very considerable, of which one can convince oneself by crossing it. Then when one is standing on the other side, in Christianshavn, it seems as though the bridge must after all be very long, for it seems as though one were far, very far away from Copenhagen. One notices immediately that this town is

[72] Upon the assumption that all of the entries registered on the fifth of the month at midnight are in some sense autobiographical, P. A. Heiberg developed from this entry the convincing theory that the sin which later tormented S.K. is here anonymously confessed—that in his youth he had been led in a state of intoxication to a brothel. I am sceptical only of Heiberg's notion that S.K., like the bookkeeper, insanely imagined he had begotten a child. See Heiberg, *En Episode i S.Ks. Ungdomsliv,* Copenhagen, 1912. The Journal for the year 1843 (IV, 63, 65, 132, 133, 147, 149) contains the first hints of this story.

not a capital or royal residence, one misses in a sense the noise and traffic in the streets, one feels as though one were out of one's element when one is out of the bustle of meeting and parting and hasting on, in which the most disparate interests assert for themselves an equal importance, out of the noisy sociality in which everyone contributes his part to the general hubbub. At Christianshavn, on the other hand, there prevails a quiet repose. There people do not seem to be acquainted with the aims and purposes which prompt the inhabitants of the metropolis to such noisy and busy activity, do not seem to be acquainted with the diversities which underlie the clamorous movement of the capital. Here the ground does not move, or rather shake, beneath one's feet, and one stands as securely as any stargazer or dowser could wish to stand for the sake of his observations. One looks about in vain for that social *posciamur,*[73] where it is so easy to go with the others, where every instant one can get rid of oneself, every hour can find a seat in the omnibus, surrounded on all sides by conductors, where one feels so deserted and imprisoned in the quietness which isolates, where one cannot get rid of oneself, where on all sides one is surrounded by nonconductors. In certain quarters there are streets so empty that one can hear one's own footfall. The big warehouses contain nothing and bring in nothing, for though Echo is a very quiet lodger, yet in the way of business and rent no owner is the better for it. In the populous quarters life is far from being extinct, and yet it is so far from being loud that the quiet human murmur suggests to me at least the buzzing of summer out in the country. One becomes sad as soon as one enters Christianshavn, for memory is sad out there among the empty storehouses, and in the overpopulated streets the sight is sad where the eye discovers only an idyl of poverty and wretchedness. One has crossed the salt water to get here, and now one is far, far away, in another and remote world where dwells a race which deals in horseflesh, where in the only square there stands a solitary ruin, ever since that conflagration which did not, as pious superstition recounts in other instances, leave the church standing while it consumed everything else, but consumed the church and left only the prison standing. One is in a poor provincial town where the only reminder of the vicinity of the capital is the presence of suspicious characters and the special vigilance of the police; everything else is just as it is in a provincial town: the quiet hum of humanity, the fact that they all know one another, that there is a shabby fellow who at least every other day does duty as a drunkard, and that there is a lunatic known to everybody, who shifts for himself.

[73] Horace, *Odes,* I, 3, 2.

So it is that several years ago there might have been seen at a definite hour of the day at the southern extremity of Water Street a tall, thin man who walked with measured tread back and forth along the pavement. The strangeness of this promenade could scarcely escape anybody's attention, for the distance he traversed was so short that even the uninitiated must observe that he neither was out on business, nor was taking a constitutional like other people. Those who observed him often could discern in his walk a symbol of the power of custom. A sea-captain, accustomed on shipboard to promenade the length of the deck, marks out on land a distance of equal length and walks mechanically back and forth—so did this wayfarer, or bookkeeper, as the people called him. When he had reached the end of the street one observed in him the converse of an electric shock, the tug of custom in him: he came to a halt, swung about, turned his eyes again to the ground, and then marched back, and so on.

He was known naturally in the whole quarter, but in spite of the fact that he was crazy he never was exposed to insult; on the contrary, by the inhabitants of the neighborhood he was treated with a certain deference. This was due in part to his wealth, but also to his beneficence and to his advantageous appearance. His face, it is true, had that monotonous expression so characteristic of a certain sort of lunacy, but the features were fine, his figure erect and handsome, his dress was scrupulous and even elegant. His lunacy was very plainly exhibited only in the forenoon between eleven and twelve o'clock, when he walked out along the paved way between the Børnehus Bridge and the end of the street. The rest of the day he doubtless was dangling after his luckless preoccupation, but his aberration did not show itself in this way. He talked with people, made longer excursions, took an interest in many things; but between eleven and twelve o'clock one could not at any price get him to stop walking, to go on farther, to make a response to a questioner, or even so much as to return a greeting, though at other times he was courtesy itself. Whether this hour had some special significance to him, or whether, as sometimes occurs, he was actuated by a bodily disorder of regular recurrence, I never was able to learn while he was alive, and after his death there was no one from whom I could seek more precise information.

Now although the inhabitants of the neighborhood almost reminded one by their attitude towards him of the behavior of the Indians towards a lunatic, whom they venerated as a wise man, they perhaps privately had conjectures about the cause of his misfortune. It not infrequently happens that a man reputed to be shrewd betrays by such conjectures quite as much disposition to madness, and perhaps more puerility, than any lunatic can be charged with. The so-called shrewd people are often stupid enough to believe everything a madman says, and often stupid enough to believe that everything he says is madness, although no one is more cunning than a lunatic often is in hiding what he wants to hide, and although many a word of a crazy man contains a wisdom which a wise man need not be ashamed of. Hence it is perhaps that the same notion which regards the governance of the universe as being determined by a grain of sand or a mere accident is considered valid in psychology; for it is the same notion when one descries no deeper cause for insanity but regards it as easily explicable by nothing, just as mediocre actors think that to play the part of a drunken man is the easiest job—which only is true when one can be sure of a mediocre audience. The bookkeeper was shielded from ridicule because he was loved, and the conjectures about him were so securely preserved in silence that actually I never heard more than one. Perhaps the neighbors had no more concealed under their silence; that is a view I too can adopt, and I am not disinclined to do so, for fear my obstinate suspicion that they privately had many conjectures should betray in me disposition to puerility. The conjecture was that he had been in love with a queen of Spain; and this obviously was wide of the mark since it did not account for one of the most remarkable traits, his decisive predilection for children. In this way he did a great deal of good, actually consuming his fortune in doing it; hence he was sincerely loved by the poor, and many a poor woman instructed her children to greet the bookkeeper deferentially. But in the morning between eleven and twelve he never responded to a greeting. I have often seen a poor woman pass him with her child and greet him in the most friendly and deferential way, as did the child too, but he did not look up. When the poor woman had gone by I saw her toss her head. The situation was touching, for his benefactions were in a very characteristic and curious sense entirely gratis. The pawnshop takes six per cent on a loan, and many a rich, many a fortunate, many a mighty man, and many a middleman between them and the poor, will sometimes take usury on the gift, but in the case of the bookkeeper a poor woman was not tempted to be envious of him, or dejected because of her wretchedness, or cowed by the poor-rates, which the poor do not pay in money but work out by a bended back and a mortified soul, for she had the feeling that her "noble and generous benefactor" (to use the expression of the poor) was more unfortunate than she—than she who got from the bookkeeper the money she had need of.

But he was not interested in children merely as an opportunity for doing good; no, he was interested in the children themselves, and that in a very singular way. The moment he saw a child, at any time but the hour between eleven and twelve, the monotonous expression of his face became mobile and reflected a great variety of moods, he made up to the child, engaged it in conversation, and all the while regarded it with such close attention that he might have been an artist who painted children's faces only.

This is what one saw in the street, but one who saw him in his apartment might marvel still more. One frequently gets an entirely different impression of a person seeing him in his home and in his chamber than when one sees him elsewhere. And this is not true only of alchemists and others who busy themselves with occult arts and sciences, or of astrologers, like Dapsul von Zabelthau,[74] who in his sitting-room looks like other people, but seated in his observatory has a high peaked cap on his head, a mantle of gray callimanco, a long white beard, and talks with a dissembled voice so that his own daughter cannot recognize him but takes him for a bugaboo. Ah, one not infrequently discovers an entirely different sort of change when one sees a person in his home or his chamber, and then compares him as he here appears to be with what he appears to be in public life. Such was not the case with the bookkeeper, and one only saw with astonishment how serious his interest in children actually was. He had collected a considerable library, but all the books had to do with physiology. Among them were to be found the most costly copper engravings, and along with them whole series of his own drawings, including faces drawn with the precision of portraits, then a row of faces connected with one original in a sequence which showed how the likeness constantly grew less, though a trace of it always remained; there were faces executed in accordance with mathematical formulae, others which illustrated by a few clear lines how a slight alteration in the proportions completely altered the total impression; there were faces constructed according to physiological observations, and these in turn were checked by other faces sketched in accordance with a hypothetical assumption. In all of these what interested him particularly were the similarities attributable to family relationship in successive generations as seen from the point of view of physiology, psychology and pathology. It is perhaps to be regretted that his works never saw the light of day; for it is true he was a lunatic, as I learned on closer acquaintance, but a lunatic is by no means the worst observer when his fixed idea becomes an instinct for prying things out. A curi-

[74] In Hoffmann's story, *Die Königsbraut.*

ously interested observer sees a great deal, a scientifically interested observer is worthy of all honor, an anxiously interested observer sees what others do not see, but a crazy observer sees perhaps most, his observation is more intense and more persistent, just as the senses of certain animals are sharper than those of man. Only it goes without saying that his observations must be verified.

When he was thus occupied with his passionate investigation (which generally speaking was at all times except between the hours of eleven and twelve) many people would suppose that he was not crazy, although it was precisely then his lunacy permeated him most completely. And as underlying every scientific investigation there is an *x* which has to be sought for, or (regarded from another side) as the thing which prompts the scientific investigation, which is an eternal presumption seeking to corroborate its certainty by observation; just so did his anxious passion have an *x* which it sought, a law which would determine precisely the degree of resemblance in racial inheritance and thus enable one to reach an exact conclusion; and so too did he have a presumption to which his imagination lent a dolorous certainty that this discovery would confirm some dolorous fact concerning himself.

He was the son of a subordinate government employee living in modest circumstances. At an early age he got a position with one of the richest merchants. Quiet, retiring, rather shy and embarrassed, he attended to his business with an intelligence and punctuality which soon led the head of the house to discover in him a very useful man. He employed his leisure time in reading, in studying foreign languages, in developing his decided talent for drawing, and in making a daily visit to the house of his parents, where he was the only child. So he lived on without knowledge of the world. He was employed as accountant, and soon he was in receipt of a considerable salary. If it be true, as the Englishman says, that money makes virtue, it is certain also that money makes vice. However, the young man was not tempted, but as year after year went by he became more and more a stranger to the world. He himself hardly noticed this because his time was always fully occupied. Only once did a presentiment of it dawn upon his soul, he became a stranger to himself, or was like one who pulls himself up and vaguely recalls something he must have forgotten, though without being able to comprehend what it was. And something indeed he had forgotten, for he had forgotten to be young and to let his heart delight itself in the manner of youth before the days of youth were past.

Then he became acquainted with a couple of clerks who were men of the world. They soon were aware of his shy embarrassment but had so much respect for his ability and knowledge that they never did anything to make him conscious of his lack. Sometimes they invited him to take part with them in a little gaiety, in short excursions, or at the theater. He did it and liked it. His companions on the other hand were doubtless none the worse for his company, for his shyness put a wholesome check upon their merriment, so that it did not become wanton, and his purity imparted to their very amusements a nobler character than perhaps they were accustomed to. But shyness is not a power able to maintain its position and assert itself, and whether it was that the sadness which sometimes seized a man unacquainted with the world then revolted against him, or whatever other cause there may have been, at all events an excursion in the forest ended with an unusually sumptuous dinner party. Frolicsome as the two clerks already were, his shyness became only an incentive to them, and the painful sense of it on his part became an incentive to him, which had a more and more powerful effect the more they were inflamed by wine. Then the others led him with them, and in his over-excitement he became an entirely different man—and he was in bad company. So then they visited one of those places where, strangely enough, one gives money for a woman's despicableness. What occurred there even he himself did not know.

The following day he was out of sorts and dispirited; sleep had obliterated the impression, yet he remembered enough not to want to seek again the society of these friends, whether it was reputable or evil society. If he had been diligent before, he now became all the more so, and the pain he felt for the fact that his friends had so misled him, or for the fact that he had had such friends, made him even more retiring, and to this the death of his parents contributed.

On the other hand, the esteem in which he was held by the head of the house increased with his efficiency. He was a man much trusted, and they had already begun to think of giving him a share in the business when he fell ill and was sick unto death. At the moment when he was closest to it and was about to set foot upon "the solemn bridge of death" there suddenly awoke in him a remembrance, a remembrance of that incident which till then had not existed for him in any real sense. In his remembrance of it that occurrence assumed a definite form which brought his life to an end along with the loss of his purity. He recovered, but when he left his couch with health restored he took with him a *possibility,* and this possibility pursued him, and he pursued this possibility in his passionate investigation, and this possibility brooded in his silence, and this possibility it was that set in manifold motion the features of his face when he saw a child—and this possibility was that another being owed its life to him. And what he sought so anxiously, and what made him old when he was barely a man in years, was the unfortunate child, or the query whether there was such a child; and what made him a lunatic was the fact that every obvious way to discovery was cut off from him, inasmuch as the two who had been his destruction had long ago journeyed to America and disappeared; and what made his lunacy so dialectical was the fact that he did not so much as know whether his notion was a result of his illness, a fevered imagination, or whether death had actually come to the aid of his memory with a recollection of reality. Behold, it ended therefore with his wandering silently with bowed head along that short path between the hours of eleven and twelve, and with his wandering the rest of the day along the prodigious detour of the desperate windings of all possibilities, to find if possible a certainty, and then the thing to be sought.

However, in the beginning he was quite capable of attending to the business of the office. He was as precise and punctual as ever. He scanned the ledger and the letter-books, but now and then it came to him in a flash that the whole thing was labor lost, that there was something quite different he ought to be scanning; he closed the yearly statement of accounts, but in a flash this appeared to him a jest when he thought of his prodigious accountability.

Then the head of the firm died, leaving great wealth, and as he had loved the bookkeeper like a son, being himself without children, he made him heir to a fortune as if he had been a son. Thereupon the bookkeeper closed the account and became a man of science.

Now he had *otium*. His anxious remembrance might not perhaps have become a fixed idea if life had not inserted one of those casual circumstances which sometimes turn the scale. The only kinsman he had left was an old man, the cousin of his deceased mother, whom he called Cousin *κατ' εξοχήν*. This was an old bachelor to whom he betook himself after the death of his parents, and in whose house he dined every day, continuing this practice even after he had ceased to be in business. The cousin took delight in a certain sort of equivocal wit which (as psychology easily explains) is more often heard from old men than from the young. It is certain that when all hath been heard and most of it forgotten a simple open-hearted word in an old man's mouth may acquire a weight it otherwise does not have, it is also certain that an equivocal expression, a careless word, in the mouth of one stricken in years may easily have a disturbing effect, more especially when one is so much disposed to infection as the bookkeeper was. Among the recurrent witticisms to which the cousin repeatedly returned there was one standing joke, namely, that no man, not even a married man, could know definitely how many children he had. This was a way the cousin had, who for the rest was a good fellow, what one calls a boon companion, fond of a merry party, but the equivocal jest and his pinch of snuff he couldn't get along without. So there is no doubt that the bookkeeper had heard the cousin go through his whole repertoire a number of times, with that equivocal jest included, but without comprehending it or in any real sense hearing it. Now on the other hand it was aimed steadily at his sore spot and was calculated to wound him where he was weak and suffering. He would fall into one of his reveries, and when the cousin's jest should have given spice to the conversation it was the accidental touch which developed the elasticity of his fixed idea so that it established itself more and more securely. The silence of the reserved man and the wit of the loquacious cousin worked together upon the unfortunate until at last the understanding seriously resolved upon a change of masters because it could not endure serving with such housekeeping, and the bookkeeper exchanged understanding for lunacy.

In the capital there is traffic and tumult in the streets, at Christianshavn there prevails a quiet repose. There people do not seem to be acquainted with the aims and purposes which prompt the inhabitants of the metropolis to such noisy activity, do not seem to be acquainted with the diversities which underlie the clamorous movement of the capital. It was at Christianshavn the poor bookkeeper dwelt; there, in the practical sense of the word, he had his home, there, in the poetical sense, he was at home. But whether it was along the specialized historical path of investigation he sought to penetrate to the origin of that reminiscence, or whether it was by the prodigious detour of ordinary human observation that he sought wearily, with only the support of deceptive hypotheses, to transform that *x* into a known quantity—he did not find what he sought. It seemed to him sometimes that the object of his search might be very far off, sometimes that it was so near to him that he was sensible only of his own contrition when the poor thanked him on behalf of their children for his lavish gifts. It seemed to him as if he were dispensing himself from the performance of the most sacred duty, it seemed to him the most horrible thing that a father should give alms to his own child. Hence he would have no thanks, lest this gratitude might be a curse to him, but for all that he could not cease to give. And seldom have the poor found a benefactor so "generous and noble" and received help on such favorable terms.

An intelligent physician, viewing the case in a more general light, would of course have been able to remove from his mind this possibility which was the origin of all the rest; and even if, accommodating himself to the sick man's fancy in order to venture another method of cure, he had admitted this as a dolorous certainty, he still would have been able by his knowledge as a physician to remove the deduction from this certainty through a sequence of so many possibilities to so remote a distance that no one would be able to descry it . . . except the crazy man, who perhaps would only be the more deranged by such treatment. Such various effects has possibility. It is used as a file: if the body is hard, the sharp edge can be filed off; but if it is soft in temper like a saw, the teeth of the saw only become sharper by filing. Every new possibility the poor bookkeeper discovered sharpened the saw of anxiety with which he was sawing alone and from the bite of which he himself was suffering.

I often saw him over there when he wandered along the waterfront, and I saw him also on other occasions; but once I encountered him in a coffee house of that neighborhood. I soon learned that every fourteenth day he came there in the evening. He read the papers, drank a glass of punch and talked with an old ship's captain who came there regularly every evening. The captain was well up in the seventies, white-haired, with a wholesome complexion and unimpaired health; his whole person showed no indication that except as a sailor he had been much tossed about in the world, and doubtless this impression was correct. How these two got to know one another I never learned, but it was a coffee-house acquaintance, and they saw one another only in that place, where they talked with one another, now in English, now in Danish, now in a mixture of both. The bookkeeper was an entirely different man, he looked so roguish one could hardly recognize him as he entered the door with an English greeting which gave cheer to the old sailor. The captain's eyes were not of the best, with advancing years he had lost the capacity for judging people by their appearance. This explains how the bookkeeper, who was in his fortieth year and here looked much younger than he did elsewhere, could make the captain believe he was sixty years old and could maintain this fiction. In his youth the captain had been, as a sailor can be in all decency, a jolly good fellow, but doubtless in all decency, for he had such a worthy air and his whole nature was so lovable that one could vouch for his life and for his smartness as a sailor. He never tired of telling tales about dance-halls in London and larks with girls and then about India. Thereupon they drank to one another in the course of the conversation, and the captain said, "Yes, that was in our youth, now we are old—but I should not say 'we,' for how old are you?" "Sixty," replied the bookkeeper, and again they drank to one another. — Poor bookkeeper, this was the only compensation for a lost youth, and even this compensation was the effect of contrast with the all too serious brooding of insanity. The whole situation was so humoristically planned, the deceit about the sixty years supported by the use of the English language was so profoundly thought out with a view particularly to the humorous effect, that it impressed upon me how much one can learn from a lunatic.

Finally the bookkeeper died. He was ill several days, and when death came in earnest and he now was about to tread in earnest the dreadful bridge of eternity, the possibility vanished, it had been nothing but a delirium; but his works did follow him, and with them the blessing of the poor, and there remained also in the souls of the children the remembrance of how much he had done for them. I followed him to the interment. I chanced to be driving back from the grave along with the cousin. I knew that the bookkeeper had made a will and that the cousin was far from being covetous. I therefore took the liberty of saying that there was something very sad in the fact that he had no family of his own which could inherit what fortune he might leave, in the fact that he had not been married and left no children. Although the cousin was really affected by the death, more so than I could have expected, and on the whole produced a more favorable impression than I had foreboded, he could not refrain from saying, "Yes, my good friend, no man, not even the married man, can know definitely how many children he leaves behind him." To me the redeeming feature was that this was an adage, which perhaps he was hardly conscious of repeating, the pitiful thing was that he had such an adage. I have known criminals in prison who were really reformed, had really got an impression of something higher, and whose lives bore witness to it, yet to whom it would occur that in the midst of their serious talk about religion the most abominable reminiscences were mingled, and that in such a way that they were not aware of it at all.

Longbridge gets its name from its length, for as a bridge it is long, though as a road the length of the bridge is not very considerable, as one can convince oneself by crossing it. When one is standing on the other side, in Christianshavn, it seems as though after all the bridge must be very long, for it seems as though one were far, very far away from Copenhagen.

April 6. Midnight.

How disappointing when a person is concerned about only one single thing and nothing occurs that has any reference to it. In the street there is plenty of life, in the houses there is movement and bustle and noise, but about my affair not a single word is heard. Thus it is a thread dealer sits in his little shop on a side street waiting for customers and rarely hears a footfall—in East Street the stores are full of people. But then the thread dealer does not have to pay so high a rent as the rich merchant in East Street. That is true, but on the other hand I am subject to as great taxes and exactions as any married man, and yet nothing happens that concerns me.

If the actress knew her rôle, had memorized it perfectly, with animation in her voice, in her bearing, was only waiting for the cue—but the prompter had fallen asleep, and she could find no means of awakening him!

If one saw that the telegraph was erected on the other side of the world, it was functioning and the first words were legible, but then a mist descended, and except by means of the telegraph nothing could be learned, and what one wished to know was as important as the salvation of one's soul!

If the noble steed knew why he was saddled, knew that now she would come, the royal maiden, the cavalier, the steed's pride, and therefore he puffed, panted, stamped his hoofs, bidding defiance with his strength, that it might please her with a voluptuous shudder to control his fiery metal—but the ostler went away and did not come again, and then he came again, but the cavalier was not with him, and yet the knightly trappings were not taken off, and the mighty steed was distressed at missing the breath in his nostrils and the joy of the leap and the satisfaction of obeying the hint of the royal cavalier!

If Scheherazade had invented a new story more entertaining than any previous one, if she had put all her trust in this tale, that it would save her life and not merely postpone the sentence of death, in case she were to succeed in telling it as thrillingly as she could at this instant—but she was not summoned at twelve o'clock, and one o'clock drew near, and she feared she might have forgotten it or forgotten how to tell it!

* * *

LAST night I had the good fortune to converse with a couple of very clever ladies. It all went off very brilliantly, and I almost believe that my presence inspired the clever women. They were ladies of fashion, and I—well, I am a man of the world, that is to say, I am intelligent and depraved. What wonder then that such clever people are in sympathy with me! It is so luxurious to try one's hand at a gallantry which is fashioned out of effeminacy and witty intelligence, the auspices are so favorable when a party to the excursion is a man from whom in case of need one can draw back and say, "No, God forbid, we do not, of course, approve of his shabby conduct, but after all he is so clever." So on that occasion I learned much about what essentially is required for a happy erotic understanding; I learned that when a man is not clever enough to follow the emancipated spirit in her lofty (I would say gadding) flight, it is a cross, and *penible* in the highest degree to be tied in this fashion, indeed such an alliance is really invalid. No more was said, but I have no doubt that my heroines, being so sure of their own cleverness, were willing also to invert the proposition and express their sympathy with one who was tied to such a girl, or rather to prompt him to cut the matter short and seek a cleverer mate. A hint was also dropped which doubtless was meant for me and obligingly meant. O silence, silence, how thou canst put a man in contradiction with himself! So then they were proclaiming to me an indulgence, making a favorable appraisement of my conduct. That one woman dare thus offend another woman, and in this case a girl the latchet of whose shoe she is not worthy to unloose! If I had been emperor, they would have been banished straightway to a desert island. Now it is a nemesis upon me that my outward existence, though it is not known to many, contributes in a measure to confirm somebody in this odious aristocratic cleverness. If only I were free and did not have in mind the consideration that an authentic interpretation of my conduct might be a dangerous precedent for her—verily, if the maiden who sorrows or causes me sorrow wishes to place a man in the field as a martial contingent to fight for the good cause of love, let her set me free, and *pro virili* I shall hold up the banner. Come on then, ye clever ones, with your disdainful witticisms! A good cause stretches the bow taut and hits most surely the mark. That true love should be held in such slight honor! Yes, I feel indeed that I could make good use of an unhappy love affair, it comports well with my existence. If only I were free in giving expression to my love, if I were rejected but yet in formal possession of my love, if only I were not afraid that by acknowledging its significance for me I might suddenly unsettle her who must be supported by precisely the contrary notion. Then I would say, "Yes, I am the effeminate male (for man I dare not suffer myself to be called), the wretched manikin, who could not manage to love more than once, the narrow-minded wretch who was stupid enough to take seriously that pretty word about the first love, and could not regard it as a coquettish nosegay which experienced or half-experienced young ladies bandy about teasingly at the tea-table. One might after all have a little compassion upon me; I myself feel what a pitiful figure I cut, especially in these times when even girls die as pathetically as Falstaff falls in the battle against Percy[75]—and arise again vigorous and nubile enough to toast a fresh love. Bravo!"[76] — And by this speech, or rather by a life which is a justification for speaking thus, I am inclined to believe (if such a thing is at all possible) that the one man may benefit the other, to believe that I should have benefited my highly esteemed contemporaries more than by writing a paragraph in the System. What we imperatively need is that the pathological factors in life are posited absolutely, clearly, legibly and forcibly, that life does not become, like the System, a peddler's cart containing a little of everything, so that everything is to be done up to a certain point, even the most foolish thing of all, that of believing up to a certain point, that people do not lie but are ashamed, do not lie in such a way that, erotically speaking, they die romantically of love and are heroes, but do not remain standing (or lying) in that position, but arise again and go further, and become heroes in the daily chronicle of news, and go further and become frivolous, witty, like the heroes they laugh at in the comedies of Scribe.[77] Just try to think the thought of eternity into such a confusion! Think of such a man at the Day of Judgment hearing God's voice, "Hast thou believed?"—and then the reply, "Faith is immediacy,[78] the immediate is not what one should stop with, that is what they did in the Middle Ages, but since Hegel one goes further. One must admit, however, that it is immediacy, and that immediacy *is*—but wait for another boon." My old schoolmaster[79] was a hero, a man of iron—woe, woe unto the lad who could not answer yes or no to a plain question! And if at the Day of Judgment one is no longer a lad, still God in heaven can count as a schoolmaster. Just to think that this paragraph-madness, this curriculum-craziness, this systematic slithering has so got the upper hand that in the end one would like to instruct God with all brevity in the newest philosophy. If God won't do it, I think then that the trumpeting angel will take his trumpet and smite such a Privatdocent upon the pate so that he will never be a man again.

[75] Shakespeare's *Henry IV*, Part I, Act V, Scene 4.

[76] The exclamation here translated "Bravo!" is "Peteheia!," taken from Holberg's comedy, *Jeffe paa Bierget*, Act I, Scene 6.

[77] Especially in the comedy called "The First Love," which is dealt with at length in the first part of *Either/Or*.

[78] There is a similar passage in *Fear and Trembling* (Oxford edition, p. 98). An entry in the Journal (I, A 273) shows that S.K. had in mind Schleiermacher rather than Hegel. Cf. *Glaubenslehre*, 3rd ed., pp. 177 *ff.*, where faith is clearly regarded as immediacy.

[79] Here obviously the reference is to Michael Nielsen.

But he who bungles in one thing bungles in all, and he who sins in one point sins in all. If only you clever ones knew how comic is the cleverness you admire. If only you knew—not how bad a seducer is, but what a comic personage. If you knew how detestable, but also how ludicrous it is that love, the loftiest thing in earthly life, should be regarded as merely the invention of sensuality, no more than the rut of the beast, or a plaything for wit and a social diversion for clever people! But you do not know that all this is merely theme for vaudeville, that your social cleverness is nothing but fiddle-faddle.[80] Suppose that a woman, beautiful as the mistress of a god and clever as the Queen of Sheba, were to offer to squander *summa summarum* of her hidden and manifest charms upon my unworthy cleverness; suppose that the same evening a comrade were to invite me to drink wine with him and clink glasses and smoke tobacco *studenticos*[81] and enjoy the ancient classics—I should not hesitate long. "What vulgar taste!" someone cries. Vulgar? I do not descry the vulgarity. I take it that along with love and the eternal element in love, all this beauty, and the gift of cleverness as well, is of infinite worth; but without this, a relationship between man and woman, which yet essentially would express this, is not worth a pipe of tobacco. I take it that when from this one separates love, and from love (mark well!) the eternal element, one can only speak correctly of what is left over, which amounts after all to the same thing, whether one talks like a midwife who talks without beating about the bush, or like an extinct soul which, being "burnt out to sheer spirit"[82] cannot comprehend natural impulse. It is comic that the action in the vaudeville turns upon the sum of 4 s. 8 d., and so too it is comic that Don Juan has 1003 loves, for the number simply proves that they have no value. Hence one should be sparing in the use of the word love. Language has only the one word, and nothing is more sacred. One should not be shy of employing if need be the expressive term, as the Bible and Holberg do; but above all one should not be so excessively spirituelle as to think that the spirituelle is the constituent factor, for it constitutes anything but an erotic relationship.

But to maintain a prescriptive right in an unhappy love affair, to become happy in the highest sense by means of it, to make significant what to me appeared senseless when in Prussia they established an order of merit for those who had taken part in the war of liberation, and likewise an order for those that remained at home, to enrich this with a

[80] *Prysings og Klatteryps,* a phrase from Heiberg's *Recensenten og Dyret.*
[81] Holberg, *Erasmus Montanus,* Act II, Scene 1.
[82] Baggesen, *Min Gjenganger-Spøg, Danske Wærker* (1845), VI, p. 135.

beautiful meaning, to wit, that he who had remained at home [understand unmarried] was happy by reason of his order, happy by reason of his [unhappy] love, although in the star upon his breast one more clearly perceives the cross [of marriage renounced] than in that of the more fortunate, although he wears the order[83] (as that other is called in Prussia) "for good will"—that I well perceive would be a task to engage the enthusiasm of one who knows how to be content with the idea, with oneself and with the cognizance of heaven. Let them then fall at his right hand, the individuals who perished battling for an unhappy love, they rest in honor, they deserve a burial inscription and a monument, but he must not bury the dead for fear he might be distracted from his task. Let them then arise again, the seemingly dead who come to life by the application of the usual remedies, let them take delight again and yet again in stabbing for the ring in the cake, let them find everything restored to them now that they are thriving mistresses in their own house, let them when they are fully restored find themselves happy in being raised up with the best of care into a third marriage, let them mumble in unison over the fragments of a love story, and dribble life away in connubial intercourse—but he must not be willing to take time to behold it for fear he might be delayed.

My vow of silence makes me strong in monologues; but even a digression like this brings me only the more definitely back to her. When the fatherland is pressed by war and a woman can afford to equip a ship, that must be glorious, it seems to me. Such never will be my lot, but she, she is able to launch in the sea a warship which will fight for a good cause.

April 7. Morning.

TODAY a year ago. She is intractable. She breaks the engagement, and breaks the engagement, and yet doesn't break it. Heavens and earth, if the match is to stand thus, if we are to break it off—well then, we may as well begin tomorrow.

April 7. Midnight.

How is it with the wish? Might I not after all wish to have another, wish to find indemnification in a new love? Well, if a man who holds a cane in his hand were as certain that he is actually holding it in his hand as I am certain that there is not a thought of this in my soul, he would be pretty sure. But the passion of the wish, is this entirely unchanged?

[83] The Iron Cross.

It is difficult to test oneself with regard to a possibility, it is as if, without daring to use the voice, one were to test whether one has a strong voice. Many a time, and hitherto in vain, I have speculated how to find a way of testing myself with regard to possibilities.

However, I still believe that the passion is the same, and if it should be changed, I am certain that a hint, the merest hint of a more definite possibility will be enough to make the wish more burning than ever; for actually it was with the rupture of the engagement that for the first time I can say of myself in every sense and from every point of view as was said of Phaedria, *amare coepit perdite.*[84]

In one way everything is in readiness, there is lacking only approval on the part of the idea, and the consent of the thought-context, notwithstanding I have sought in all quietness and still continue to seek every turn that can be given to this question. Hardly can any stage manager know with greater assurance that the change of scene is all prepared when he rings the bell than I know it. I have a standing account with a merchant for a complete set of furniture, my chambers are put in order, everything is calculated for a wedding—if only the moment comes, the bell rings, and the change of scene is accomplished in the twinkling of an eye.

Distrustful of myself, I have arranged my personal existence entirely like that of a married man. Punctuality and orderliness prevail everywhere. Darius or Xerxes (it is indifferent which) had a slave who reminded him to make war on the Greeks. Since I dare not confide in anybody, I must be content with having my reminder within myself. In my whole existence I express incompleteness—there is a memento. Whatever I buy, I buy in double quantity, my table is set for two, the coffee is served to two, when I ride I always ride as if I had a lady beside me. In so far as in these night hours I live rather differently, it is not just because this life pleases me so much.

And in case the whole thing comes to nothing after all, I regret nothing. I would not omit the least item; it is a matter of honesty which has the utmost seriousness for me, that if ever the thing might be done, my reckoning must be exact to the last farthing.

April 8. Morning.

TODAY a year ago. War has been declared. When one has to fight it is important to use self-restraint, above all no precipitancy. Admission to a menagerie costs 3 s., later it is reduced to 1 s. A fine edition of a

[84] He began to be desperately in love. Quoted from the *Phormio* of Terence, 82.

new book costs a pound; if one is not precipitate, there comes out subsequently a cheap edition, and the book after all is the same. When one has to fight one must be alert to seize the opportunity, and must know where the opportunity is. At an antiquarian's or at second hand one buys at half price. When the dancer alights from her carriage she carefully hides her feet with her cloak lest anybody might admire these pretty feet. Not for ten pounds would she do differently, and yet everybody knows that it costs only 3 s. (or for persons of rank 8 s.), and with that she dances before one in silk slippers, etc.

The mood I am in is abhorrent to me; all the frosty intellectuality which I had forever banished from this relationship she has forced back into it. It shall not be for long.

Today I entered her room with a skip, remained standing, hat in hand, assuming an easy conversational attitude, kissed her hand in passing with courteous and officious politeness, and hastened into the salon, where I knew there was company, because it was an anniversary occasion in the family. It was an opportune chance. Sarcasm, satire and coldness make a poor showing under four eyes, there must be some company present if this is to be effective.

A lady in the company was so kind as to invite us for the following evening. Usually I leave all such things to her, but in this case I hastened to accept in the most cordial terms, with thanks on behalf of both of us. It was quickly decided, and the terms in which I expressed myself were so flattering, that if my little confirmand were to have said a word against it, she would have disgraced herself. She did not do it.

When I was leaving her and had said farewell and was halfway out of the door I suddenly turned around and said to her, "Listen, it is quite true, don't you think we ought to break it off?" Thereupon I swung about and parted with a wave of the hand.

April 10. Morning.

TODAY a year ago. Last night I was bored beyond words; but what will a man not do for his fiancée, that she may have a chance to go out in society . . . and that one may get her to be a little bit courteous.

She understands me very well, that I can see. In case it really were to come to a breach I had the situation well in hand.

Today we had to go to the Exposition and take a promenade and pay calls. It all goes capitally. With the utmost courtesy I keep her at a distance from me, although we are seen together more than we commonly are. There is some advantage in being regarded as malicious: I can be pretty sure not to be treated superciliously when we are out together, she easily gets to feel that she is *de trop*. Why did she provoke me![85] Of course no third party notices her embarrassment, for I constantly draw her into the conversation: "It is as my sweetheart says, only yesterday she said it." A look from her is enough, and I proceed: "But for God's sake, my sweet girl, canst thou not remember, it was yesterday—no, wait a bit, I am not any too positive of that, it was four days ago, just four days ago. Canst thou not remember?" etc. She understands very well why I said four days.

But my mood is past, there is something ominous in the whole thing. An old man has said that it is never well to let that which is to be regarded as holy appear in a ludicrous light. It is true enough that a young girl is not a holy object, and yet she was something like that to me. Verily I did not torment her by requiring her to behave like an ideal, I only wanted her to sit still while I was concerning myself all too deeply about the relationship.

I hope, however, she will soon get over this childhood's malady, there is still so much good understanding between us that I venture with confidence to read aloud to her from an edifying work. A third party would perhaps find it suspicious that I who am capable of behaving as I do should want at the same time to be a religious character. To scorn cleverness and everything but solemn plain downright seriousness is easy enough for one who has nothing else. But such judgments are of no help to me. In a spiritual sense the same thing is true of individuals which is true of sentences: a sentence which consists only of subject and predicate is easier to construe than a period with subordinate and intermediate clauses. The fact that there was a man who *couldn't* behave thus towards his lady explains nothing therefore, whereas if there were one who could, and in a situation similar to mine would not do it, and that on valid grounds, the case would be applicable. I hold to the idea. She is comic. Essentially this is what I would express. And I believe I do her more justice than if in an erotic relationship I were presumptuous enough to reprimand her formally. I must constantly possess the saving grace of indifference, it is the aesthetic idea which judges between us.

But if this were to develop in her a spirit of defiance, it might cost me dear. However, I do not know how else to act.

[85] One naturally thinks of the great provocation registered on April 2; but a few lines below the indication of "four days ago" seems rather to point to the entry of April 7 and the threat of breaking the engagement.

April 10. Midnight.

ONCE there was a man who said to me, "I have suffered something so terrible that I never have dared to speak of it to anybody." Most people will dismiss this utterance perhaps a bit hastily as an exaggeration. And yet if they were right in thinking it an exaggeration, the man too may have been right in another way. For when it came to an explanation it appeared that the object of terror was a mere insignificance, but the fact that it had so affected him that he did not dare to confide it to anybody may well have caused him to suffer terribly.

Today I read in the newspaper about "a young girl of superior station" who had put an end to her life by suicide. If only this girl had considered what deadly anguish she might cause another person, I believe she would have desisted. But how could it occur to her to be prudently careful of me? And now not to dare to inquire of anyone, but only with countless starts and jumps and turns, in the careless language of conversation, to fish for information! If on the whole my path is strewn with thorns, these accidental commotions are like a thorn hedge in which I am stuck fast. I am constantly seeing ghosts, in chance utterances, in verse, in mystifications. It is a nemesis upon me that I am so adept at this.

It is now already a fortnight since she received my confidential communication. During all that time I have not seen her in Hauser Square. — Agitated as the sea may be, and wherever in all the world one may be upon the sea, the compass always points to the north. But upon the sea of possibility the compass itself is dialectical, and the variation of the magnet furnishes no reliable indication.

April 12. Morning.

TODAY a year ago. She finds herself on rather a fasting diet—and not without dismay, as I can well observe. She would not be averse to yielding a little, but she cannot prevail upon herself to do it. Yes, that's the way of it, she has trumped too early and quite in the wrong place. What, in view of my behavior these last days, would have been a rather justifiable retort came like a capricious shower. — True, I wage war for the sake of peace, and yet it tortures me to think of the final goal of the war, the crisis when she gives up. That will pain me, for I do not desire a victory over her. As long as we fight it is undetermined which is the stronger, but when she surrenders as the weaker one I do not desire to be present. I am proud myself, and in my relationship to her I am prouder on her account than on mine.

April 13. Morning.

TODAY a year ago. It all went capitally. For that I have to thank her good genius, and I have done so silently. Yesterday afternoon during my fencing hour the mask fell off just as I was making a pass, the adversary had raised his saber and was not able to stop it, so I got one on the head. The whole thing was of little importance, some blood flowed, a piece of plaster was applied to it, and I went home. But what happens? Yesterday evening rather tardily she gets an exaggerated account of it, and as I failed to make my appearance although I had promised to come, she becomes anxious. The shedding of blood, the tension between us, or our broadsword play, and perhaps a little love, united to make her sleepless. It is just as I have always said, in the course of one sleepless night a person can be incredibly changed. Today she came in haste to my apartment with her father. She showed a distress that must move the hardest heart. — So all went well. We were spared having me conquer, and mortal danger helped us to understand one another.

So much lovableness, such a girl, and with that such a little miss! But I gladly give twenty pounds to the poor out of gratitude for escaping so luckily the awkwardness of the capitulation. She looked at me now and then in such a way that I understood she had something on her heart to say. But I talked about the dangerous wound and about the coincidence that it was a mask that fell off. At that she laughs, although there was a tear in her eye. Then I say, "Yes, you may well laugh at me for being thus unmasked." Then she says, "Oh, what foolishness, you know very well what I mean." And I, "Yes, you mean that I should challenge him again and declare that it doesn't count when the mask falls off." And then we talked of other things.

Thereupon she goes home, and I watched her as when she returned from her singing lesson, and yet she now walks differently, there is a reckless happiness in her gait.

O Death, I believe they do thee injustice. What significance thou art able to impart to life when even such a little reminder produces such an effect!

April 14. Midnight.

THE method must be changed. When an examining magistrate would examine sharply he makes the environment as inquisitorial for the accused as possible: the murderer he seats beside the murdered man; him who is afraid of the night he awakens at cockcrow. For me there is an environment where my examiner is able to bring me very close to a confession, as close I think as it is possible to bring me. That is in a church. Today, contrary to my custom, I went to the Church of the Holy Trinity.[86] Farsighted as a bird is she, and unfortunately she has a high conception of my talent for observation. She fixed her eyes upon me and could very well see that I saw. I was standing in the narrow aisle on the right; she came from the church door, went directly across in front of the choir and was about to be shut into a pew on the opposite side. She looked and then nodded her head. I hastily withdrew my glance, turned the pages of the hymn-book as though I had lost the place, and by this movement brought about a shake of my head. Ah, I feared that in this greeting there was concealed a hope. When I looked up another glance was exchanged; she seemed to have understood the movement of my head, and thereupon she nodded again. Ah, her expression was entirely different, it was as though she required of me only an admission, having given up hope. I had found the place and was now joining zealously in the singing, and as a chorister sometimes does I lifted up my head with the voice and then let it sink, a movement like that of a man who bids at the auction and says, "Yes." Then the priest entered and we were separated. I did not watch her as she departed, and I left the same way I came, not a foot-breadth out of the path. A Pythagorean could not be more fearful of stepping on the ground than was I of taking, as they say, one step.

So I have talked then! No, I have not talked, I have not even done anything I could avoid doing. This ought not to have been in a church, she should not have tried to move me from what I once regard as my duty. But in a church I am so readily tempted to regard the matter eternally, and viewing it eternally I can willingly tell the truth, but not in time, at least not yet. She can perhaps be saved for life, she is not to bid farewell to it because I do. I do not think that she is sufficiently developed religiously to be capable of conceiving what it means to make such a break with existence, which is even more decisive for a woman than for a man. To wish to proceed along that path in union would be to repeat that dreadful incongruity which already I contemplated with dread during that two-months period of horror, that in union we should mourn an unhappy love. That cannot be. What likeness is there between her sorrow and mine, what fellowship between guilt and innocence, what kinship between repentance and an aesthetic sorrow over existence, even if that which awakens repentance is the same thing as that which causes her sorrow? I can sorrow in my way; if she is to sorrow, she

[86] This meeting with Regina is circumstantially recounted in the Journal, IV, A 97. See my *Kierkegaard,* p. 252.

must do it on her own account. A girl can subject herself to a man in many things, but not in ethical matters; it is unethical for her and me to sorrow thus in union. Along that path how is she ever to come to the point of sorrowing religiously, if she is to leave unresolved the ethical problem of my conduct towards her, when it is over the consequence of this she would sorrow? If only I might be a woman for half a year in order to learn how it is she is differently fashioned from man. I know very well that there are examples of such conduct on the part of women, I have them psychologically at my fingertips, but in my eyes all these characters were failures. I can make no sense out of my view of life if I myself am to have the experience that one individual is wasted upon another, and wasted she is if things go on this way.

As soon as she has begun to venture in the narrow way which leads to a religious view of life she is lost to me. A woman may possess passion as strong or even stronger than that of a man, but contradiction in passion is not a task for her, as for example the task of giving up this wish and retaining it at the same time. If she labors in a purely religious way to give up this wish, she is transformed; and then if ever there were to come an instant for its fulfilment, she would no longer understand it.

And yet perhaps I am talking quite irrationally, perhaps my construction of her is planned on too great a scale. Perhaps the religious movement of infinity is not within the compass of her individuality. Her pride had not energy enough to raise her temporally to a higher power. If she had been absolutely proud, this, humanly speaking, would not have happened. Perhaps therefore religiousness in her does not accomplish the complete revolution of infinity. Her religious eternity is possibly not the eternal decision but an indefinite extension of time. So eternity has dwelt with her, comforted her, as when in Homer's descriptions a god or a goddess hastens to the help of one of his heroes. She believed it was the decision of eternity, she believed it was her death, she believed all was lost; but behold, instead of waking to this eternal decision she became weary of fruitless wishing, weary of the fruitless act of renunciation, and fell gently asleep in eternity, while time passed, and she awoke and belonged again to life. Then there would even be a question of a new engagement, a new love.

This indeed was what I desired, thus she is free in fact. I have thought of three possibilities: that through pride she might be raised to a higher power in temporal existence; that through an illusory resignation she might attain a new love; or that she might become mine. Every unseemly possibility whereby she might indeed become free, but in such a way that she would lose in my eyes, I have not been willing to think.

The first possibility must be discarded; for if even now, after receiving my confidential communication, she has not got further along, she is not proud in the sense requisite for constructing the unusual character upon this foundation.

The last possibility is only a wish, which encounters moreover this difficulty, that she will have remained at the point for it only in case she had not begun at all upon the religious way but had kept herself in a state of feminine naïveté. No sooner has she begun to sorrow religiously than the wish vanishes like the evening sun when the moon begins to shine in its splendor, or like the moonlight before the break of day. Double illumination and double reflection a woman cannot deal with, her reflection is only single. If she would give up the wish, then reflection is the conflict between the life fostered by the wish and the death exacted by resignation; to will both at once is impossible to her, or perhaps even so much as to understand such a thing.

So there remains the middle possibility: the slumber of illusory resignation, repose upon an eternity, while time passes and again she opens her eyes and awakens to new life. If this comes to pass, then no human life has been wasted upon me. The girl who once in the illusion of sorrow felt, alas, that she was a superfluous flower in life, felt, alas, like the poor little bird which could not be taken into consideration when a greater was in question, seems now in this way to be taken into consideration. So let the scientists teach us that existence is waste on an enormous scale, let whosoever will talk about a love which demands sacrifices, if the situation is as I here think it, the girl becomes in my eyes a capitalist, and providence effects a highly economic conversion of her funds. It has been said that Denmark is the only state which possesses a private fortune, because it has the toll of the Sound. It appears to me that on the smaller scale of the world of private persons she in like manner becomes an exception among women. Marriage is like the ordinary revenue of the State, but then at the same time she possesses the mortgage on my life and has the interest on it. But it is well at all events that she has not done this for my sake or because I begged her to do it. — This, it seems to me, looks very inviting. Her existence acquires more importance than mine. That cannot have had great importance for her, since in such case there must have come about one of the situations constructed *en gros,* and that would have resulted in costing me dear.

Yet even when I think the thing in this purely hypothetical way there is still a ticklish point left over. For what is it she is to do? what is it one may expect to happen? Oh, yes, I know full well, she is to do what perhaps is preached in more than one church. The religiousness of infinity is perhaps not always preached where in other respects people are precise about the categories. Nor is it always Christianity these people preach when, without a trace of hypocrisy, they use the sacred name and the Biblical expression, for the movement of thought may be entirely pagan. That in which she is expected to find comfort is not the real religiousness. As seen from that point I should vanish from before her eyes as an atom, as a mere occasion like the sale of Joseph, until she should win the eternal; but with that there would be no question of a new love. No, what she is supposed to be healed by is a practical wisdom permeated by a sort of religiosity, a not altogether unseemly composition of a bit of aesthetics, a bit of religion and a bit of practical philosophy. My life-view is different, and with all my might I compel myself to hold to the categories and to hold them fast. This is what I *will,* what I require also of everyone whom I admire, of everyone I am in any real sense to recognize, that by day he should think only of the categories of his life and dream of them by night. I judge no one; he who is busy judging others *in concreto* is seldom true to the categories. It is the same as in the case of one who for the proof that he is serious has to rely upon the testimony of another; such a man is not serious, for seriousness, first and last, is self-assurance. But every existence which wills something is thereby indirectly a judgment, and he who wills the categories judges indirectly one who does not will them. I know too that even when a man has only one step left to take he may stumble and let go of his category; but I do not for this cause believe that I shall let it go and be saved in twaddle, I believe that it would hold on to me and judge me—and in this judgment there again would be the category.

But what power she has over me! To gratify her every wish, to employ the days in giving her joy, that indeed is a pleasure, had I been permitted to do it; but my thought which is my very life and the loss of which is my spiritual death—if that is to be taken from me! I have long since cancelled as unessential all the differences between men, but what keeps me in life is the belief that there is equality for all in the matter of willing, that in this respect the same thing may be required of all. And yet by the merest hint hardly divined she has brought me to the pass (as a third party would say) of treating decorously that equivocal resignation. And why? Because I in my turn cannot exist spiritually unless she may exist in the same spiritual apprehension. From this one perceives how dangerous it is for a thinker to be in love, not to say married, and to hear daily the reasonings of a woman. Ought the thinker perhaps to be neither the one thing nor the other, or ought he perhaps to be both? — Oh, yes, here you have a real man who resigns himself up to a certain point, and then in turn consoles himself up to a certain point! But no, be still, thou passion, which would stir my mind to rebellion, though there is good reason for it. For that which to the point of desperation I require of myself—not as something extraordinary but simply as the right thing—I cannot endure to see confused with something different, I cannot chaffer.

But have not I myself furnished the occasion for such a thing? I have in fact labored to the end that she may become free. Quite true; but I have left the thing so dialectically to her decision that she can do what she will. I thought I owed it to myself that I should incur no responsibility. Perhaps in the first period of horror it might have been possible to bring about a milder decision; but I should have been thinking of my own, not of her welfare, had I done anything in that direction. She perhaps would not have comprehended how in that way she became dependent upon me and instead of being respected was wasted. So the thing was put in such a way that she had plenipotentiary authority to act in the strength of religious infinity. Thereby I was bound forever and never would quite recover myself. If she chooses the other, I have guessed wrong.

What consoles me is that infinite reflection is not essentially a thing for women. Hence that rather doubtful sort of resignation may keep a woman just as beautiful. If she falls in love, that is a help to me so far as I can be helped, but whatever she does I cannot but try to make something beautiful out of it. It would be a bitter consolation for me if I am helped and she too, but in my heart I must say of her, "This existence is a renunciation of the idea."

And to what end all my cares and plans and efforts? What do I accomplish? Nothing. But not for this cause will I cease, precisely for this cause I will not cease, for when one does everything and it is of no avail, one can be sure one is acting with enthusiasm. Therefore I do not disdain this nothing, any more than the widow disdained to cast her two mites into the treasury of the Temple. This nothing in the way of accomplishment is a great deal in the way of suffering, as a lonesome man will understand. For when agony has convulsed the bowels and the body trembles, there is a friendly hand which supports the patient's head until the fury of the pain is calmed; or when the groan alarms and pain wrings the heart which is about to burst if it is that of a woman, there is a compassionate woman who loosens the stays until she breathes again; but the lonely man dare not even abandon himself to the physical relief which agony is for passion.

But there is no time yet to sorrow on my own account, for the dialectic difficulty of my position is shown also by the fact that it signifies two entirely different things, facing the alternative of sorrowing on my own account or sorrowing on account of her and her family. However, I will try to find out what would be the most beautiful form for a new attachment. The most beautiful would be that before she was engaged to me she had been in love with another and that this love might now awaken again, supported perhaps by the self-reproach she might feel at having given me the preference.[87] Thus her association with me would be an episode, she would not be falling in love anew but returning to her first love, and her association with me would perhaps have taught her to find this more beautiful than ever. Bravo, bravo, that will do! In case my pen were a living being—but it is only a steel pen—but in case it were a bird which came with this leaf in its beak, if it could have any joy in my gratitude, how I should thank it! — But the misfortune is that about this I know nothing. And yet there cannot be imagined a more reliable informant to whom I could appeal than she is. But why keep it secret? And why so zealous to hold me fast? The answer to this would make clear to her a responsibility towards the unknown individual and towards me. Have I then taken her by surprise? Far from it, I made the case clear to myself at an early date. If I have taken her by surprise, it must be by reason of the caution with which I sought to avoid it. Assuming this to be the case, all is well again. She feared me more than she loved me. So when the debates began about breaking the engagement she brought up again the forgotten experience, and the painfulness of it has been the prompting of her despair. — So it is then. If this comes about, she is helped, i.e. she has helped herself, and I am helped because she is free, and helped because she has not become less beautiful. She owes nothing to me, for she has not followed any advice of mine, since I have given none, and in this direction could not have given it. If she owes me anything, some little compensation for all the suffering, it is this, that I have not been meddlesome enough to want to advise her. I owe nothing to her directly, for I have not begged her to do anything

[87] Before this book was written Regina had in fact become engaged to Fritz Schlegel, who had been her schoolteacher, and to whom she was all but engaged, as she told S.K. when he wooed her. But from the first S.K. had contemplated this possibility, and regarded it as "the most beautiful" solution—although upon the news of it he was not able to restrain his anger.

for my sake, and she cannot by any means be supposed to have done this for my sake. Indirectly I owe her much, but the debt is essentially grounded in my personality, which precisely upon the hypothesis here assumed desires to acknowledge it.

All this is capital—if only it were not a hypothesis. It is a capital hypothesis, if only as a hypothesis it were not so frail.

It lacks five minutes to two o'clock, my working time is over. I shall think of her passionately from midnight on, but not a minute beyond this stroke of the clock. It is necessary to hold out, and after two o'clock every thought of her is a temptation, a fraud against her, for there must be some sleep to maintain passion in the long run, which is what I will to do. — The difference between thin beer and the strong beer or ale the English drink is not that the latter foams, for the thin beer too can foam and foam just as strongly, but its foaming is over in a moment—on the other hand the foam of the heavy beer lasts.

April 15. Morning.

A YEAR ago today. So then the weather became fair, indeed serene. One starts out for the country at an early hour in search of freedom and beauty, but the weather is uncertain, so one sits in the carriage speculating whether it might not be possible to wrest from the changeable condition a fairer aspect so that one might be content with it—and then the sun itself grows weary of the capricious inventions of the scurrying clouds and of the inconstancy of the showers, and it bursts forth in all its splendor, so it is settled that the weather is serene. How could I fail to appreciate duly the fact that now it has been settled by her, my sun, that the season of showers is past?

The feminine immaturity which gave vent to utterances a bit feverish is now as though forgotten. I dare to believe that I am loved. It never occurred to me indeed that she might be in love with another, but she seemed to me to lack the consolidation which embellishes the soul and permeates it by its beauty. The sight of it now affords me an experience of joy comparable to the dreadful experience of seeing a man who has taken poison and observing that it begins to take effect.

And the pain occasioned by the fact that she could behave so preposterously invests her with a gentleness I had not divined. And the fact that she is sensible of my pain—how much that proves! How fortunate that death came between us! If we had fought longer, if by our own efforts a settlement had been reached between us, however amicably, it would still have been precarious. I fear only that she takes the whole thing too much to heart. To relegate it completely to oblivion might cause her to suffer in silence, and if I make a reference to it, she at once is agitated, even though I do it as good-humoredly and as jestingly as possible. Is it perhaps precisely because of this jocular tone?

April 17. Morning.

TODAY a year ago. The misfortune is that she has no religious postulates. In this respect I have been beating the air. Yet she wanted to fight with me, she has not exactly been vanquished by me, but the dread she experienced that night has taught her to understand herself. She regards it as a defeat, even though she finds herself happier than before. Here the thing for her is the freedom of infinity as over against me. For for the moment she has idealized me, and now by this little misconception she disparages herself. If only there does not succeed to this a weakness, a blind devotion towards me which I cannot and will not understand. I do not want to be worshiped. I do not believe that unfaithfulness on her part would wound me so sorely as this annihilation of herself, as it seems in my eyes to be. I am proud, and so ought everyone to be in relation to other men; let him be humble before God, and that in every respect, but not humbled under the personality of another man. Truly, there is a kind of devotion which if it holds fast to me would compel me to repel it—terrible as it may be to say so. If it is unseemly for lovers to squabble, there is also a devotion which in a religious sense is a terrible responsibility.

April 18. Midnight.

So then there is nothing for me to do except to keep calm, for to accomplish anything with regard to another love which I know nothing about is impossible. So the reflections I have registered above are in vain, and so too a good part of my sympathetic expectation for her and the trembling for myself.

What then is the good of shrewdness? But I am anything but shrewd. If in a certain sense I am the shrewdest in my circle, in another sense I am perhaps the stupidest of all. Nothing I have heard or read has struck me so pointedly and personally as a saying about Periander.[88] It is said of him that he talked like a wise man and acted like a maniac.

[88] The story of Periander is told in the entry of May 5, midnight.

That this saying applies aptly to me is proved by the fact that I accept it with the most passionate sympathy, and yet it has not the slightest influence to change me for the better. This way of appropriating it is quite *à la* Periander. Within my postulate I am shrewd, but the postulate for my action is so ideal that it turns all my shrewdness into foolishness. If I could learn to discount my postulate, my shrewdness would make a good showing. If I could be shrewd in this way, I should have been married long ago. To get one's wish fulfilled and to get thanked for it into the bargain as for an act of charity,[89] and then to arrange matters as if one were essentially in possession of one's freedom, that would have been shrewd, and I should have been regarded as an estimable man who does not break his plighted word, a prodigy of a husband who is faithful to his wife and does honor to a girl; for my ideal postulate presumably does not do her honor, and the fact that I would prefer to spend everything and set heaven and earth in commotion rather than sneak into the honorable estate instituted by God and so sneak through life is enough presumably to prove that I have no honor.

My wish, which aims higher than to see her free, my wish, which is the culmination of the divine madness in my soul, must now, I suppose, be relinquished. But I will not relinquish it. As soon as I am set at liberty and dare to act it would still be possible that my nature might inflame the wish in her. Suppose this possibility, contingent upon a remote possibility, is infinitely remote, yet I will not let it go and will not renounce it. Only an official certainty that she is free and is another's—only with this is the wish dead. But until then it shall not visit me piteously as a fleeting fancy now and then, but it shall be held in high honor as the highest passion in my synthesis.

True enough, sadness is the grace which accompanies sorrow, as despair accompanies it as a fury; but one first shrieks in pain before one dares to be sad. To become sad at once is sometimes an indication of a base soul.

So sleep well, my girl; he who promised thee faithfulness can do no more than he does. So sleep well, my dear child, as I almost might say, for my solicitude is almost like that of a father who desires to see his daughter engaged. Behold, this is sadness. But I will not be sad, I will hold out with thee, I will hold out though I become an old man—if nothing happens in the meantime. I do not call back the night watchman who stands on the lookout for the fulfilment of expectation.

[89] Regina's father pleaded with S.K. that it would be an act of charity for him to return to her.

April 20. Morning.

TODAY a year ago. When an examining magistrate has perhaps been sitting for a long time reading documents, hearing testimony, confronting witnesses, exploring localities—just as he sits there in the chamber he suddenly sees something. It is not a man, a new witness, it is not the *corpus delicti,* it is a something, and he calls it "the course of events." As soon as he sees the course of events, he, the examiner, has all he wants.

I have noted in myself that there was disquietude in my whole being, that something dreadful was in the wind, I did not sleep at all the whole night, and now I see—alas, not the course of events, but the course to destruction. She is devoted to me in a measure which fills my whole being with dreadful foreboding; and yet she is lovable in my eyes and touches me profoundly, but this devotion and the agitation it causes me are a torment. Even if I were a different man I could not understand this devotion, and I cannot devote myself in this way. And think of me who am intensely reserved! And she hardly knows me! What an incongruity! I acquire power over her, and she has none at all over me. Is such a relationship a marriage? It is like a seduction. Do I then wish to seduce her? Abominable thought! And is there not a higher sort of seduction which is worse than that of lust?[90] She says she has never felt happier than now, she cares about nothing but her ecstasy. Is it on my part compatible with love to see such an incongruity? And I know for myself that I am intensely reserved. Yes, to be sure, I have seen that by my practice in dissimulation I am able to conceal my reserve. But her devotion becomes exigent, it turns my being inside out. True enough, she does not comprehend this in the least; but I know it, and what am I to do?

That misunderstanding has done irreparable harm. Perhaps she had inwardly intended to fight seriously. And there is no limit to the expression of devotion when once it begins to express itself directly. It is as when a person first begins to complain of his sufferings: soon the true expression no longer suffices to move the hearer, and so, without being conscious of it, he stealthily interjects untruth. That misunderstanding does irreparable harm. If I look serious, she thinks it is because of our strife. And to think that such is not the case at all, but it is my reserve which makes me gloomy! Ah, it is enough to drive one mad!

Today she bade me sit on a chair. I did so without suspecting anything. She retreated a few steps, then approached and fell upon her

[90] As exhibited in "The Diary of the Seducer" in *Either/Or.*

knees. Doubtless there was a little coquetry in this, but essentially it was an expression of sadness, and for all that an expression of beatitude (yes, I may call it that), an insane beatitude at having found the correct expression for her passion. That instant I laid hold of her and lifted her up. He who has committed a crime casts his glance around the room, suspicious of every corner, he directs it through the window to the neighbor's house, and the agony of conscience makes him sharp-sighted. I cannot say how dearly I would have paid for a certainty that no one had seen it, or how dearly I would have paid not to have seen it myself. Have I demanded this? Truly, she has never understood me. I myself have never bowed the knee before any man, perhaps I might do it before her if the situation required it, but for her personality and mine the situation ought never to occur. For me, such a thing is not a foolish prank, an exaggerated gesture; if I had done it, I should count no insult so intolerable as to have it regarded as such. Another instance of my pride.

I know very well that a girl is different from a man, but yet I shall never forget that act, it has produced a madness in my blood, a confusion in my brain, an anguish in my reserve, a despair in my resolution, and above all a humming in the ear of presentiment which is harbinger of the extremest ill.

April 22. Midnight.

As one who is sickly and accustomed to a certain medicine must have the pain-killing drops with him wherever he goes, so, alas, must I have with me everywhere a brief summary of my story of suffering, so that I may orient myself in the whole situation—orient myself in the matter I have thrashed out by myself, in a way quite different from that in which a pupil thrashes out his lesson with the teacher. If I happen suddenly to think of it (suddenly means in this instance that half a day has elapsed since the last time I recited the lesson), there occurs then the most dreadful crisis. Psychically this in a measure corresponds with a slight return of apoplexy as a bodily ailment.[91] In an instant I become dizzy, my thought cannot quickly enough catch hold of something solid in the complication, and it seems to me as if I were a murderer. There is nothing to be done except with the utmost effort to renounce all thought about it as a religious temptation—then the instant is past, and again I understand what hundreds and hundreds of times I have recited.

[91] This analogy was familiar to S.K., who was subject to attacks resembling the falling sickness. This whole passage (if it can be regarded as autobiographical) reveals more plainly an abnormal psychosis than does any page of the Journal.

— Or I suddenly reflect how much I have suffered, and the thought comes so suddenly that the superintendent of reflection cannot hasten quickly enough to the spot, and I am completely overwhelmed. This happened to me yesterday. I was sitting in a coffee house reading a paper, when suddenly that idea awakened in my soul, so suddenly that I burst into tears. Fortunately there was no one present, but I learned to be more cautious.

April 24. Morning.

TODAY a year ago. I am a lost wayfarer, I am like one who has come into a strange land where people talk a different language and have other customs. If my suffering were that the strangers behaved towards me with nationalistic pride, that would be well enough. But such is not my case. She is very far from making any demand upon me, in her illusion she sees only her illusion, and she is infatuated with it. She is happy, she says, and I believe that in a certain sense she is happy. She is lovable and busies herself with her love like a child which is left to its own devices but is joyful and happy in its pastime. One could sit and look at her and grow old and still look. There is only one inconvenience, and that is the fact that I am the object of this love. All that preceded that little *altercatio* and which in my eyes was of such great importance, namely, the ideal impression to which I, who myself bow under the ideal, sought to direct her attention, has not moved her in the least. In this respect she is, as it were, unsusceptible. But the conflict, my altered behavior, death's intervention, is changing her nature, she displays an amiability at which I sadly wonder and which makes me an enthusiast for her. And what does this mean then? It means that she is totally unreceptive of the motives which I count the highest. There is a difference of language between us, a world between us, a distance which now is revealed in all its painfulness.

April 25. Midnight.

PATIENCE!

April 26. Morning.

TODAY a year ago. So it is upon this reef I am to be wrecked! I have never humbled myself before anyone, neither have I wished to exalt myself. My notion about the relationship of man to man is for everyone to get his deserts, and that's enough. Generally speaking, I have not had a great deal to do with people in an intimate sense, my spiritual existence has preoccupied me too much for that. Now I have been humiliated. And who is it that humiliates me? It is a young girl, and it is not by her pride, for we should get ourselves out of that all right, but it is by her devotion.

Fortunately she is not to remain with me always. No, never shall that be! Possibly she may imagine it, but I do not understand it, and it is a question after all of her happiness. And if we are united, it will at last come to the point where she begins with consternation to suspect what I ought to have prevented.

To maintain my reserve in her presence is easy enough—perhaps it is precisely on this account I feel humiliated.

What for me is the nerve of my spiritual existence, namely, equality in human relationships, she does away with. She cares nothing for this infinite passion for freedom; she has conjured up her illusion, and that suffices her. I too think that one may love, that one may sacrifice everything for one's love; but whether I am to see good days, or whether I am to adventure my life, the deepest breath of my spiritual existence I cannot forego, I cannot sacrifice, for that is a contradiction, since without that I do not exist. And of this breath she feels no need.

Yet precisely now I feel that I love her, that I love her more deeply than ever, and yet I dare not, I (*nota bene*) who as her fiancé am bound to love her.

April 27. Midnight.

I HAVE no inclination to make any entry, and there is nothing whatever to register. In this town the night watchmen show by their cry that they are on their beat. Why all this crying? In England they go along in perfect silence and put a ball in the box, and the inspector sees in the morning that they have been on the beat and have not slept.

April 28. Morning.

TODAY a year ago. If only she might put up some resistance against me. When I am fighting it is easy for me, and even when I am to live in peace I wish that he I am to keep peace with were equally strong or stronger than I. The more blindly she is devoted, the more responsibility falls upon me. And I am afraid of the responsibility—and why is that? It is because I then have myself to deal with, and of this strife I always am afraid. In case God Himself were a man of some sort, whom one might have outside oneself and talk to and say, "Let's hear now what you've got to say, and you'll have a chance to see how it strikes me"—in that way one would get off easily. But this is the reason God is stronger than anybody, the strongest of all, that He does not talk that way to a man; the man He would briefly engage in conversation he takes under custody in such a way that through the man himself He speaks to the man. Their conversation is not a *pro* and *contra* as of persons outside of one another, but when God speaks He uses the man himself to whom He speaks, He speaks to the man by means of the man himself. Therefore it is He possesses might and can crush a man any moment He will. In case the situation, for instance, were this, that God has spoken once for all, in the Bible, for instance, then, so far from being the mightiest, God would be in the tightest fix, for one can readily dispute such a thing, if one is free to oppose to it one's own opinion. But such an assumption is an airy fancy which has no basis in fact, for God does not speak thus. He speaks directly to every separate individual, and the instant He speaks to him He uses the individual himself in order through him to say to him what He would say to him. Hence it is a weak point in the structure of the Book of Job that God appears in the clouds and also appears as the most accomplished dialectitian; for what makes God the terrible dialectitian He is, is precisely the fact that one has Him at very much closer quarters, and therewith the softest whisper is more blissful, and the softest whisper is more terrible, than seeing Him enthroned upon the clouds and hearing Him in the thunder. Hence one cannot argue dialectically with Him, for all the dialectical power in the soul of the man concerned God uses against this man.

When an individual fears God he fears what is more than himself, and after this fear comes the fear of oneself, and the *angustiae* of this fear is responsibility.

The more she devotes herself, the more unhappy I become. Is this a happy engagement? And what indeed is her happiness? From my point of view it is the happiness of infatuation, of illusion. But Socrates says that the greatest misfortune is to be under an illusion.

April 29. Midnight.

THE question remains whether I might not convey to her a mitigated notion of my character. If she thinks of me at all, as there seems to be a sad probability she does, I can well see what in all human probability she might need. The explanation given of my conduct was about as follows: I was to a certain degree a depraved man, but yet not entirely bad, I had good points too; I had indeed loved her but was lacking in seriousness, and then there was my instability, I could not keep a resolution; I regarded her indeed as an amiable girl, but I did not find in her a spirit with which I could be happy; it is handsome of her therefore to submit to her fate, it is magnanimous of her to be reconciled to the girl who one day is to enthrall me with a greater power, "for one thing is certain, that though he were to find a girl more *spirituelle,* he will find none that loves him so dearly. This he himself must surely admit, and in view of that he surely has repented of his conduct, even if he is too proud to alter anything." — A repentant individual who is too proud to alter anything he has done amiss! What then in God's name is repentance?

To think of being obliged to help one by such an explanation, in which every sentence is meaningless, and as applied to me is also untrue! I am either exceedingly depraved, a hypocrite, indeed, if not loathsomely enslaved by self-deception, or else I am as chivalrous a soul as the best of them. I do not lack stability in keeping a resolution, least of all when the criterion is a young girl who doesn't quite know what a resolution is. I have never regarded her as amiable, have never altered my opinion of her a tittle. I have not *found* anyone more *spirituelle* or intellectual, since I do not seek for feminine intellectuality but beg to be excused. Her magnanimity is a trump entirely misplaced, for I have no intention of enacting "A Story of Everyday Life"[92] and engaging in the business of barter. It is true that I repent, but just as certain it is that I wish to alter everything.

By the aid of this explanation I am making pretty progress: I step out of the determinants of infinity—and become comic. Not in the eyes of everyone, to be sure, for there are several poets in whose eyes I still am a hero. Verily, one would hardly suppose that an eternal and righteous God had discovered the ethical, but that a theatrical tailor had bunglingly patched something together. And this is the standard which is applied even by poets to their heroes—for the sake of showing that they themselves are heroes. But Scribe is the smartest of them all. In his works one reads or hears lines which bring to confusion the whole of existence, as if comedy were not played before men, even before madmen, but before "distracted June-bugs," and yet these lines are so trippingly composed in a conversational tone that it all seems a matter of course. A married woman is depicted and by the author is regarded as both sensible and worthy, as one in fact who champions the good cause, a case of true love between a young girl who is under her protection and

[92] The title of a novel (*Verdagshistorie*) by Fru Gyllembourg, in which one of the principal characters exchanges his lady-love with a friend.

a young man who has had recourse to her on this account. I do not recall the lady's name, so we may call her Madam Scribe. So then to the wooing swain she said, "Have you reflected that the girl has no fortune?" "Yes, I have considered that." "She has only a dowry of 20,000 francs." "I know it." "And yet you are ready to keep your word!" "Yes." "Truly, this heroic courage captivates me completely in your favor."[93] What a satirist Scribe is without knowing it. I thought I was with Master Jackel. The young swain is brought under a brilliant illumination: he gets the girl and 20,000 francs—and becomes a hero. But such a hero is as comic as a tailor's child named Casear Alexander Bonaparte Appleclump; and a poet who nominates such heroes seems to me as foolish as the tailor who had his babe thus baptized.

However, it is my duty to do everything that might seem to be serviceable, whether or no it is profitable to her as a matter of fact. What I have sought to do hitherto has proved futile. If she had been a religious personality in the proper sense, that would have been dreadful for me. But I have not sought counsel from flesh and blood.

My common sense is furious as it shudders at the motley, that is, at becoming a hero *à la* Scribe. But so much for that. I am thinking of her, I behold her in convalescence, I behold the possibility of a happy issue. Well, I submit to the discipline. Truly this girl is designed for my humiliation. Though no one understands this, though few would understand it if I were to tell of it, I understand it, understand it excellently.

When Pericles'[94] legitimate children were alive he promulgated a law that no one might be accounted an Athenian citizen who was not born of parents who were both Athenians. Many suffered by reason of this law. Then came the pest and all of Pericles' children died. His grief was so great that when he stepped forward to lay a wreath upon the head of the last he burst into tears before the eyes of all, a thing which had never before been seen. He had only illegitimate children left, so Pericles urged that the law be rescinded. It is harrowing: Pericles weeps —and Pericles does one thing one day and the opposite thing the next. But it is affecting to read Plutarch: he says that the Athenians indulged his desire; they believed that the gods had wreaked vengeance upon him, and that men therefore ought to treat him indulgently.

Pericles was a great man, he could keep a resolution; he never went into society after he had resolved to devote himself to the service of the

[93] In Scribe's comedy *Oscar*, which was played in the Royal Theater at Copenhagen the year before this book was published, the lines are better than S.K. remembered them.

[94] The story is told by Plutarch, "Pericles," 36.

State. It is easy for me in this comparison to feel my lowliness; but would that I might be sensible of the indulgence which indulges me by letting me comprehend that I ought to misrepresent my existence! But have I not constantly misrepresented it? True, but this misrepresentation was such that, if she took it into consideration, it might produce something great in her. This misrepresentation, whatever it may effect, will not be an aid to greatness. And she honored the first method far more highly than this.

April 30. Morning.

TODAY a year ago. She does not any longer foam over in the expression of her devotion. Perhaps the whole thing was a transition. But I have seen that terrifying tableau, and I shall never forget it.

My melancholy has triumphed after all.

May 1. Morning.

TODAY a year ago. Is it possible? She was provoked by an inattention on my part. I do not deny that it was an inattention. She almost challenges me. Now or never. It is well that the word separation came up between us in that little *altercatio*. It always makes it easier to bring the word out again.

I will not run away from the thing. It is not to have good days I would be separated from her, but because I cannot do otherwise. If I cause her pain, I cannot, I dare not, exempt myself from the sight. I wish to get through with the thing as soon as possible, I believe that this is best for her. However, I also am willing to do differently and shall show respect for every argument.

At this moment she is the stronger. So now the matter is started. My sentence upon her is brief: I love her, I have never loved any other, and will not. I desire to stop with this and not go farther—so I venture to say this, but yet I have strength to get me a new love. My fault is that I ventured in where I do not belong. What I have made of myself with all my passion proves to be a delusion, but now I cannot make myself over again. She does not understand me, nor I her. From the first time I saw her and while she was my object in the form of hope I could imagine her dead without losing my composure. I should have felt pain, perhaps all my life long, but eternity would promptly have been at hand, and for me eternity is the highest. Only thus can I understand that people love one another. In the consciousness of eternity, in the infinite, each of the partners is free, and this freedom they both possess while they love one another. This higher existence does not concern her at all. Is then this relationship of ours a foundation for a marriage? Is a husband then a pasha with three horsetails? By such a union I become unhappy, I feel apprehensive with regard to my deepest existence. If now I could, if I were morally compelled to go through with this, well then, what further, what of her happiness for which I am to risk all this? Am I then to stake everything upon a fond illusion? If only anyone could assure me that she would be happy—but to be in an illusion, is that to be happy? But if once she has given herself up, I have the responsibility.

That these are premises for a life sentence it is easy to see. Whether it applies to two or to one, I dare not say; the sentence upon me is the more certain. But is it not then unreasonable to make two unhappy when one is enough? Yes, it would be all right if only I could see how it is to be understood that I can make her happy.

May 2. Midnight.

But does not my soul conceal a secret wrath against her? I do not deny it. I have no liking for this direct expression of feeling. Let one keep silent and act within oneself. I do not like to talk about dying of love. And if the speaker, without any womanly resignation, does not hesitate to place upon the conscience of a melancholy man the burden of murder, as if this were faithfulness, genuine faithfulness which outdoes Charlotte Stiegliz,[95] who indeed took her own life, but because she felt that she was a burden and had a womanly sense of the situation; I do not deny that, if it were another person who did it, I should require existence to let us have a view of the case as a false alarm, it would satisfy my wrath (if it were another person) to have it publicly acknowledged that these strong words and noble oaths are neither more nor less than a bad attack of belching (with reverence be it said), a little fit of the hiccups, occasioned perhaps by a surfeit of novel-reading, that these death-thoughts are dreams, not such as Shakespeare's Juliet has, but as Greta has in Wessel's comedy[96] after eating peas. I should require this of existence because what I myself eternally respect is not to be made ridiculous, and he who truly and seriously respects it is not to be made ridiculous because a girl mimics the same words.

I am bound by no oath, on the contrary I am set at liberty, and that upon a condition very unusual, by the fact that I am a scoundrel, for

[95] Née Willhöft, who on the 29th of December, 1834, took her own life in the hope of rousing her husband from a state of apathy.

[96] *Love Without Stockings,* Act I, Scene 2; cf. Act V, Scene 4.

usually such a person is put in confinement. I uttered not a word about death when the dread of death pierced my soul, and I still am of the same opinion, that if I actually die, I have no need to say it, I have not invited anyone to view me as a melodramatic hero. This, however, has little to do with the case, if only I might in myself be found faithful. For whether a man has appearances in his favor or appearances against him, time is and remains a dangerous enemy. Impulses from without help only for a little while, and in the end this is deceptive. If a man is to hold out, it must be by his own strength, and not even this avails if his religiousness does not day by day suck eternity into the temporal resolution. Every man who truly has remained faithful must therefore thank God for it. This is the sharpest, the most difficult perhaps, but also the most inspiring discrimination, that namely which determines what a man properly can say that he has to thank God for and nobody else. To have appearances against one always helps to illuminate this distinction; but everyone makes it, as language itself does, the only question is *how*. It is this "how," not new phrases, terms and expressions, which makes the thing clear. — Yesterday I saw a drunken woman on the street; she fell down, the boys laughed at her, then she got up again without anybody's help and said, "I am woman enough to get up by myself; but that I thank God for, and nobody else—no, nobody else!" When this distinction concerns a man absolutely there is something humiliating for him in the fact that, so far from making new discoveries, a drunken woman says the same thing. And yet there is something indescribably joyful and touching in the fact that even a drunken woman says the same thing. How it is said is every man's responsibility; but I wish only to lead my life where every man can lead his—if he will.

A life which would labor for the idea I can understand; apart from that it is impossible for me to sympathize essentially with anyone, be he happy or unhappy.

This does not hold good with respect to her. No renunciation of the idea has yet taken place, and therefore I abhor any thought of this in connection with her as an affront to her. If it takes place, I crave only the indulgence that I may be able to refrain from thinking of it. What is death? Only a little halt on the path one has definitely chosen, if one has remained faithful to the idea. But a rupture with the idea signifies that one is taking a wrong direction.

May 4. Morning.

TODAY a year ago. Twice already in two days I have introduced that terrible word in the course of conversation. There is a great difference between the displacement of a warship in the ocean and a nutshell, and this difference is outwardly visible. It is not the same with words. The very same word may imply even greater differences, and yet the word is the same. This word has not yet been uttered between us with pathos, but it recurs again and again, in connection with various topics, in order to explore the feeling it evokes. — From what I have observed till now I might almost be tempted to believe that the thing will be got over more gently than I dared to hope.

As for my part, I have assumed the responsibility for this step. As I regard it, this means that I am making another person unhappy. I cannot get off more cheaply when I act on my own responsibility. The issue may show that in reality I estimated my responsibility at too high a figure. But thus it is I have resolved to act. I have pictured to myself the worst, so reality cannot terrify me. What I suffer within my own mind where everything is in confusion and perturbation, what I suffer from the thought of her pain, from the thought that I shall never overcome this impression, since my whole structure has been made to totter, since my view of life, of myself, of my relation to the idea has failed to pass muster, and I never can erect any new structure without being reminded of her and of my responsibility—this is my share in this, the lion's share, or rather the sorrow is so great that there remains more than enough for us both.

May 5. Midnight.

A SCHOOL EXERCISE

PERIANDER[97]

PERIANDER was a son of Kypselus of the Heraclidian race, and he succeeded his father as tyrant of Corinth. It is said of him that he always talked like a wise man and constantly acted like a maniac. It is very strange, and a continuation, as it were, of the madness of Periander, that he who characterized him by this clever saying did not himself know how significant it was. The rather shallow author who vouches

[97] The entry of April 18, midnight, shows that S.K. detected some similarity between himself and Periander. But here, if this story is in any sense his story, it is his father we must discover in Periander, while he is the exiled son, and the brother is Peter Kierkegaard. But his exile from home was voluntary and mitigated by an ample allowance, ending in complete reconciliation; the father's guilt was not so great, and it was deeply repented. The fact is, S.K. was not the man to spoil a good story by making of it an allegory; and the remoteness of this analogy shows the necessity of caution in dealing with the stories about "Solomon's Dream," "A Possibility," etc.

for it[98] introduces in his simplicity the wise observation in the following way: "It is very extraordinary that the Greeks could have reckoned among the wise men such a fool as Periander." But a fool (*un fat*—such is the moralizing author's term) Periander was not. It would have been different if he had said that there was another Periander, Periander of Ambracia,[99] with whom possibly he was confused, or that there were only five wise men, or that historians had rather discordant notions, etc. So the gods understood the saying about Periander better, for in their wrath they so led him through life that they brought down the wise words as a mockery upon the head of the tyrant, who by his deeds brought his own words to shame.

When he became tyrant he distinguished himself by leniency, by justice towards the lowly, by wisdom among people of understanding. He kept his word and gave to the gods the statue he had promised, but it was paid for by women's jewels. Bold were his undertakings, and this was his saying: "Diligence accomplishes all things."

But beneath the leniency smouldered the fire of passion, and the word of wisdom concealed, until the moment arrived, the madness of his actions; and the bold undertakings gave proof of powers which remained the same in the transformed man. For Periander was transformed. He did not become another man, but he became two men, who could not be contained in the one man. These two were the wise man and the tyrant. That is to say, he became a monster. The occasion of his transformation is variously related. But this is certain, that it was only an occasion, for otherwise we cannot understand how he could be so changed. However, it is related that he had lived in criminal relations with his mother Gratia—surely before he had yet heard his own fine saying: "Do not that which you have to keep secret."[100]

And this is a saying of Periander's: "It is better to be feared than to be lamented."[101] He acted in accordance with this saying. He was the first who maintained a bodyguard and altered the government as the tyranny required, and ruled as tyrant over bondsmen, himself bound by the power he could not get rid of; for he himself said: "It is just as dangerous for a tyrant to lay down his command as to be deprived of

[98] The Journal (V, A 45) shows that S.K. had been reading Fenelon in a German translation, *Lebensbeschreibungen und Lehrsätze der alten Weltweisen,* 1748.

[99] Some Greek authors held that he, not the tyrant of Corinth, was one of the Seven Wise Men. Diogenes Laertius, I, 98.

[100] Diogenes Laertius, I, 98—but there it reads: "Disclose not what should be concealed."

[101] Stobaios, *Florilegium,* III, 79: "Hide thy misfortune lest thou give joy to thine enemies."

it."[102] He also got out of this difficulty by a clever device which subsequently will be described, and not even death subjected him to revenge —his name was inscribed upon an empty tomb. That this must be, Periander understood better than anyone, for he said: "Ill gain is father of a bad bargain." "A tyrant," said he, "must have good will as a bodyguard, and not armed soldiers." Therefore the tyrant Periander was never secure, and the only refuge he found safe enough in death was an empty tomb in which he did not lie. This thought would have been expressed in a way evident to all if upon the empty tomb had been put the following inscription: Here RESTS a tyrant. The Greeks, however, did not do this. More placable, they permitted him in death to find peace in the motherly bosom of his native earth, and wrote upon the empty grave words which sound more beautiful in verse, but mean substantially this: Here Corinth, his native land, holds hidden in its bosom Periander the rich and wise. But this is untrue inasmuch as he does not lie there. A Greek writer composed another inscription, intended rather for the beholder, that the inscription might remind him "not to grieve because one never attains one's wish, but to accept with joy the dispensation of the gods, reflecting that the spirit of the wise Periander was quenched in despondency because he was unable to accomplish what he would."

This must suffice concerning his end, which teaches posterity about the wrath of the gods what Periander did not learn from it. The narrative recurs again to the occasion which led to the madness of Periander, which from that moment increased year by year to such a degree that he might have applied truly to himself a saying which, so it is said, a desperate man thousands of years later placed upon his escutcheon: "The more lost, the less repentant."[103]

As for the occasion, we will not attempt to decide whether it was that a rumor circulated about his criminal relations with his mother, so that he was mortified that people knew he "had done what one dared not mention"; or whether the occasion was an enigmatic response from his friend Thrasybolos, tyrant of Miletus, who indicated by sign lan-

[102] Diogenes Laertius, I, 98. In 97 are to be found the three following sayings, and also the two inscriptions, the latter being the invention of this author.

[103] The Journal (IV, A 26) shows that S.K. had in mind Leibnitz's account of a Baron Andrè Taifel, who on his shield had a satyr and the above motto in Spanish: *Mas perdido y menos arrepetido*. The Danish editors remark that Juan de Thaspis y Peralta of Villamediana (1622) was hopelessly in love with the queen of King Philip IV, and at a tourney where she was present he had painted upon his shield a devil surrounded by flames with the same motto.

guage[104] which, though not understood by the messenger (like the message of Tarquinius to his son)[105] was well understood by Periander as a hint for the guidance of a tyrant; or finally whether the occasion was despair at having killed with a kick his beloved wife Lyside to whom he had given the name of Melissa. This we cannot decide. Everyone of these occurrences by itself would be sufficient: the ignominy of dishonor for the proud prince; the temptation of the significant enigma for the ambitious man; the torture of guilt for the unhappy lover. In union they would little by little have the effect that wickedness altered the understanding of the wise man, and exasperation deluded the soul of the ruler.

But when Periander was altered his fortune changed too. The proud saying, that it was better to be feared than to be lamented, fell upon his own head, upon his life of despair, and fell upon him in death. For he was lamented. It was lamentable even that he had uttered such a word, lamentable that the gods, who are the stronger, worked against him, whereas the deeper he sank in perdition, the less he understood in penitence their anger.

Melissa was a daughter of Prokles, tyrant in Epidauros. When the mother was slain, her two sons, Kypselos and Lykophron, the one seventeen years old and the other eighteen, fled to their maternal grandfather in Epidauros. There they remained some time, and when they returned to Corinth Prokles took leave of them by saying, "Do you know, children, who it is that killed your mother?" Upon Kypselos this saying made no impression, but Lykophron became silent. On returning to the paternal house he never deigned to reply to his father. At that Periander became exasperated and drove him away—and then learned (when by many questions he succeeded in prodding the memory of Kypselos) what it was Lykophron concealed under his silence. His wrath now pursued the outcast, and he commanded that no one might espouse the cause of the persecuted fugitive, who went from house to house until finally some friends took him in. Then Periander had it proclaimed that whoever offered hospitality to Lykophron or even spoke to him should die. Now no one dared have anything to do with him, so that he must perish of hunger and wretchedness. Periander himself was moved and went to him when for four days and nights he had had neither meat nor drink. He invited him to be ruler in Corinth and

104 With his cane he struck off the highest spikes of grain, as Tarquin did the poppy-heads. Diogenes Laertius, I, 100.

105 S.K. used as the motto for *Fear and Trembling* (cf. the Journal, IV, A 122, 126) the story of Tarquin's message to his son at Gabii.

lord of all his treasures, since he had now learned well what it is to defy his father. But Lykophron answered nothing. Finally he said, "Thou thyself art deserving of death, for thou hast transgressed thine own commandment and spoken to me." Exasperated by this, Periander banished him to Corcyra, and his wrath was turned against Prokles, whom he vanquished, took captive and deprived of Epidauros.

Periander had now become an old man. Weary of power, he sought to lay it down. But, as he had said, "It is just as dangerous to lay down a tyranny as to be deprived of it," and from the tyrant one learns that it is also difficult to get rid of it. Kypselos was unfitted to rule, upon him not even the saying of Prokles had made an impression. So Lykophron was to succeed to the power. Periander sent a messenger to him, but to no effect. Finally he sent his daughter, that the obedient might persuade the disobedient and by her mild temper lead the erring one back to reverence for his father. But he remained in Corcyra. Then finally they decided to treat with one another, not as a father and son treat with one another in love, but like mortal enemies. They decided to exchange residences. Periander was to dwell in Corcyra and Lykophron was to be ruler in Corinth. Periander was about to start upon the journey, but the people of Corcyra had such a horror of him, and understood so well the intolerant spirit of the father and the son that they resolved to murder Lykophron, for they hoped that then Periander would not come. They did so, but by this they were not saved from Periander, who ordered three hundred of their children to be carried away and violated. But the gods prevented this, and Periander took it so to heart that he was unable to avenge his son that he resolved to put an end to himself. He summoned two young men and showed them a secret passage. Thereupon he commanded them to meet there the following day and slay the first man they encountered, burying him immediately. When these had gone he had five others summoned and gave the same order, namely, that they were to wait at the passage and when they saw two young men they were to murder them and bury them at once. Then he had twice that number summoned and ordered them in the same way to slay the five whom they would meet and bury them on the spot where they were cut down. Then came Periander himself at the hour appointed and was murdered.

May 6. Morning.

TODAY a year ago. It goes better and better. The word is acquiring more and more pathetic significance for us. She seems calm. God grant that she may be so. If only a little earlier I had understood myself as I now do! When that little *altercatio* broke out, that would have been the moment for it. Being egged on, she herself perhaps would have broken the engagement and have suffered nothing.

My soul is weighed down, my mind is oppressed, my hope is like a lifeboat with too many people in it on a tempestuous sea.

But he who has another to be concerned about finds no time to feel his own pain, and the dreadful terrors of imagination greatly outweigh those of reality. The incongruity between us shows itself again here and does her a new injustice. Her actual pain, though she feel it never so acutely, her lamentable outcry, though it were never so violent, is nevertheless weak in contrast with the inventiveness of my fantasy, even though I see nothing.

May 7. Morning.

TODAY a year ago. She does not reach a decision suddenly. And suddenness perhaps would be the most dangerous thing for her. The practice has got along so far that it is almost like a dress rehearsal. If it should come off as well in actuality, I demand nothing more, although in another sense it will be a bit inexplicable to me.

For my part, I have a feeling of homesickness for myself. It is distracting to have imagination and reality so much at odds. The distress my imagination causes me is dreadful. What if, in a way as tragic as it is comic, I should again find reality easier! Oh that I might be permitted to retain my imaginations! With them I am accustomed to wrestle.

Yet it comforts me to be eyewitness to everything. Even though she were to die, I want to be an eyewitness to it. Reality, after all, is not the torture possibility is.

May 8. Morning.

TODAY a year ago. The same situation repeated, the decision as near as it can be in a rehearsal—yet it is a rehearsal which is not without passion on her part. She seems, however, to understand that what was too grave a matter for jest must be serious. She is without any vehemence. That is the good part of it. It must come about today.

When the merchant stands at the extremest point of the harbor and sees his ship with its rich cargo imperilled by the sea, and resigns himself to the loss, and goes away, saying to himself, "It is thine own fault that thou didst not insure it"—would it be a joy to him perhaps if a sailor were to come running after him, saying, "One can see the ship again, it has not gone down," and he were to turn around, and the sailor were to take the spyglass to look out there and were to say, "Well, now it is gone again"?

True, she means to me much more than a merchant vessel and its cargo. That the whole affair may mean as little as possible to her is my wish, my most heartfelt wish; but even if she were to receive laughingly the letter which she will receive today, even if she were to regard it as glad tidings that she now is liberated from a burden—would it were so, but even if it were so, it would not help me. What I have experienced in my inward man, the fact that I have stood upon the extremest point of possibility and seen the extremest horror—the consequence of having stood there and seen that sight will pursue me. I have no wish to wound her, if I mean enough to her to be able to wound. I humble myself under the relationship and under my guilt, and thus it is I would part from her. From the rehearsals I believe I have seen enough to know that the horror of reality will be such that I should be shirking something by not beholding it.

I wrote her a letter in these terms:

"In order not to put more often to the test a thing which after all must be done, and which being done will supply the needed strength—let it then be done. Above all, forget him who writes this, forgive a man who, though he may be capable of something, is not capable of making a girl happy.

"To send a silk cord is in the East capital punishment for the receiver; to send a ring is here capital punishment for him who sends it."[106]

Now that it has been done I totter like a drunken man, I can hardly walk, cannot collect myself. Indeed there is nothing to collect. These moments are like a hyphen between two words.

What happens? Great God, she has been in my room while I was out. I find a note composed with the passion of despair, she cannot live without me, it would be her death if I were to leave her, she conjures me for God's sake and for the sake of my salvation, by every pious remembrance which binds me, by the holy name which I rarely take upon my

[106] On the date of August 24, 1849 (four years and more after the publication of "Quidam's Diary"), S.K. wrote in his Journal (X^5, A 149, p. 162): "I wrote to her and sent back her ring." The note is found verbatim in "The Psychological Experiment." "I intentionally let it be purely historical [i.e. not personal], for I have spoken of it to no one, not a single soul, I who am more silent than the grave. If she were to see this book, I wished expressly that she should be reminded of it [and of her responsibility for the months of horror which followed]."

lips, because doubt has prevented me from appropriating it, although for this very cause I have greater reverence for it than anything else.[107]

So then I am married to her! What else does a marriage mean but a religious expression and a religious sanction given to an engagement. The thing is done. There are two powers which bind me and bind me indissolubly: that of God, and that of a dead man with whom there is no disputing.[108] There is a Name which will bind me forever, although all my thought only descries it afar. That too she has laid under sequestration. Wipe out these powers, and I no longer exist; and if I exist, I am bound, and in these thoughts I shall think uninterruptedly of her who has laid these powers under sequestration.

Erotically she is at fault, that is certain. A girl has no right to employ such means. The fact that she employs them shows essentially how little understanding she has of them. I truly would not dare to employ such means. He who employs them against another binds himself just as tight as he would bind another, lest it should ever result that he had used in vain these holy means. But she has unlimited credit on the score of the capital account of my wrong.

But what folly to go up to my room! Someone may get to know that on that day she was in my room, and perhaps does not know that I was not at home. So perhaps her honor is now compromised. And I who have been so vigilant lest any indignity of the sort might dare to approach her! It is hard enough that it should appear as if I rejected her. I should be only too glad to have it appear that she rejected me. The terror of responsibility cheapens considerably the direct erotic sufferings.

And where did she go when she left my room? Perhaps she ran away in a delirium of despair at not being good enough. Good enough! That, I believe, is the only thing that is not in question. O death, who gave thee permission to exact usury? Art thou not a worse usurer than the most bloodthirsty Jew, worse than the most bloodless miser, when thou dost but threaten, or but torture one by the fear of death?

So then the terminus for our separation is postponed—if for no other reason, because her honor is involved, and because the whole thing has assumed a dreadful form: I have a human life upon my conscience, and an eternal responsibility. But what is to be my relation to her? A re-

[107] See my *Kierkegaard,* pp. 218 *ff.* She conjured him by the name of Christ and by the memory of his deceased father.

[108] When his father was dead, and his comrades thought he would give up the study of theology he had pursued halfheartedly because his father wished it, S.K. replied, "Oh, you see I can't any longer put the old man off with fibs."

ligious point of unity is nonsense. That we two should sorrow in common is crazy, seeing that I am the guilty one, and she the sufferer. What an absurdity to have to be at one and the same time father-confessor and a murderer, to have to be the one who crushes and the one who compassionately raises up!

No! She shall not fail to see me, I have no mind to run away from anything. If she has foolishly fixed me for life in this relationship, fastened me by a bond which she is able to bind but cannot loose, it may go ill with her, I shall manage to hold out. However, it does not follow from this that she is to become mine and I hers; but if she believes she can make some impression upon me, if she has an argument which I perhaps have not considered, I do not shirk anything.

We are separated, but I shall do what a man can to help her. So take hold of me with all thy might, thou mighty power, thou counterfeiter, who art truth's changeling, but not to be distinguished from it in deceit. Give me strength for two months—that is the period, not a day more; but for that time, punctually and conscientiously, give me strength. Transform all anguish in my breast to nonsense upon my lips, all pathos to twaddle when it comes to expression. Take away, take it away, conceal every look, every feeling, every hint of a feeling, which might please her, hide it so surely that no truth may glimmer through the deceit. Refashion me, let me, when I sit by her, sit like a nodding Chinese idol, with a senseless smile upon my lips, encompassed by the incense fumes of noodledom.

I went to see her. She was calmer than I had expected. — A pair of secret lovers have need of caution to conceal their mutual understanding. We are openly lovers, and yet in this case too caution is needed to conceal *our* understanding.

So tomorrow begins the last struggle, the period of horror. I have of her no impression at all. Religion, which has always preoccupied me, has preoccupied my thought to desperation, and will preoccupy me as long as I am able to think, she has won over to her side. Perhaps it was a wild combat in which she knew not what means to employ, and so hit upon this. Be that as it may, I am bound to treat it with respect. What I shall venture to do now is to wrench myself from her if possible, to confuse her picture of me to sheer nonsense, and bewilder her thoroughly. Every counter-argument shall be treated with respect. I know well enough what these arguments will be. All sympathy for me must be destroyed, and at the same time she must be run to a standstill by reflection. In all human probability, she will experience with me the worst suffering, and humanly speaking she will not be disposed to begin the thing over again the moment I leave her. — One becomes almost calm when it is a question of action, though it be the most desperate thing one proposes to do, and that in the most difficult form, namely, in the form of time and the long run. But if I cannot be calm, I might as well not begin such a work.

May 8. Midnight.

Now all is quiet, not in the sense in which it holds that quiet is attained by a passion which is stronger than the noisiest outbursts. No, it is quiet in the sense of the dealer when he says that corn is quiet, there is no demand; quiet in the sense in which one speaks of a village as quiet, because it is uneventful and no event is to be expected, where nevertheless the usual things occur, the cocks crow on the dunghills, the ducks splash in the pond, and the midday smoke rises from the chimneys, and Morten Frandsen hurries home, and all is in movement until the peasant shuts his door and looks out into the quiet night, for till then there was no quiet. Quiet, not in the romantic sense in which one uses the word in speaking of a house which by its close reserve suggests some mystery, but as one uses it in the homely sense of a house where the tranquil members of the family are severally employed about their own affairs, and where everything occurs as it is wont to occur; quiet as one uses the word with regard to "the quiet of the land,"[109] who all the week long attend to their business, cast up their accounts, shut their shops, and on Sundays go to church.

The more I think upon this quiet, the more my being is transformed. The hope of any passionate decision has been given up, the whole affair will pass off quietly. But to me this quiet, this security, appears like the slyest subterfuge of existence. Ah, when quiet is an endless nothingness, and precisely as such is the form of possibility for an infinite content, then, then indeed I love it, for then it is the element in which spirit lives, and is of richer content than any change of dynasties or any world events. Therefore I love thee, thou quiet among the graves, for the dead sleep there, and yet this quiet is the form for the eternal consciousness of their works! Therefore I love thee, thou quiet of the night, when the inmost character of nature betrays itself more clearly than when it loudly proclaims itself in the life and movement of all things! Therefore I love thee, thou quiet of the hour of spiritual exercise here in my chamber, where no sound and no human voice sets limits to the infinity

[109] Psalms 35:20. In Danish and in German it is a familiar phrase to designate the simple people who are despised and oppressed by the rich, but beloved of God.

of thought and of the thoughts, to which Petrarch's words[110] apply: "The sea has not so many creatures in its waves, never did the night behold so many stars in the vault of heaven, there dwell not so many birds in the forest, nor are there so many blades of grass in the field and meadow, as every night my heart has thoughts!" Therefore I love thee, thou solemn quiet before the battle, whether it be the quiet of prayers which are not uttered aloud, whether it be the watchword which is whispered, thy quiet signifies more than the tumult of battle! Therefore I love thee with shuddering, thou quiet of the desert; thou art more terrible than all that happens or has happened! Therefore I love thee, thou quiet of loneliness, rather than all that is multifarious, because thou art infinite!

But this vegetating quietness, which is like a spell cast upon human life, where time comes and goes, and is filled with something, so that there is no sense of lack, for all rivers run into the sea, and yet cannot fill the boundless sea, but this and that can for men fill up their time—this is foreign to my soul. And yet it is this I must try to become familiar with. Down there in the village dwells pretty Mary. She too had a love affair; now the pain is past, now the musician scrapes the violin, and Mary treads the dance with a new lover. No! No! That brings my whole being to confusion! Let infinity separate us; my hope was that eternity would unite us. Come, death, and preserve her for eternity; come, madness, and put all aside for the time being, till eternity removes the seal imposed by the probate court; come, hate, with thine infinite passion; come, proud distinction, with thy withering wreath; come, godly fear, with thine imperishable blessedness; come one of you and take her whom I cannot take—but not this, not the pottering triviality of the temporal. — If this comes to pass, then I deceive her, then I must deceive her. I steal her picture as my imagination loves to represent it, I shall gaze upon it, but it shall not remind me of her, as hitherto it did when I decided to forego the anesthetic relief of remembrance, for now it is only remembrance.

Alas, when we separated my understanding taught me that I must be prepared, yea, that I might venture to expect it. Now—now it seems to me so difficult, if this were to occur.

However, will it actually occur? I know not. But this I know, that I owe it to her to adapt myself to anything that is possible for me. And this is possible, to give her, or seek to present (and for me the decisive thing is not whether in all human probability I shall accomplish any-

110 Rime I, Sestina 7.

thing), a more lenient interpretation of my conduct, an interpretation which to me is more distasteful than the bold lie I employed when I hoped that in an infinite sense it would be advantageous to her.

May 12. Midnight.

TODAY I saw her. It was at noon, just outside King's Garden. She was coming out, and I was walking on the farther side of the street, directly opposite. It really was my intention when I started out from home to go into the garden; if such had not been my intention, I would not have gone a step out of my way to encounter her. But this strictness is not much more than a reminiscence of a bygone method, when with ascetic abstinence from every even the remotest interference, and with self-torturing cruelty, I recognized infinity in her. Accordingly I had never occasion to take advantage of the favor of a chance encounter. So we met. She had seen me a little in advance and so was prepared, but possibly also in some agitation. What a task for the observer! To have half a minute to see—to see what was to be the subject of reflection for many hours! And with that to have to look out for oneself and be mindful to take into account what impression the sight of me might make. A movement passed over her face—was it an indication of suppressed pain, or was it the transition to a smile? I have never known a girl, or indeed any person, in whom the preliminaries to weeping and laughter were so exactly alike as in her. And in this case the contraries were not so strongly pronounced; for a suppressed laughter can be observed in the movements of the muscles of the neck, and suppressed weeping by the heaving of the bosom, but here the dubious movements lay between contrasts less extreme, and moreover there was no time to look. The movement might have been accounted for by the fact that she gasped for breath, in such a way, however, that I did not see her as she opened her mouth, but as she closed it. — One could lose one's wits by wanting to torture anything out of such an impression, and yet that is what I want to do. When one hears the church clock and counts the strokes, it does not follow that one knows what the hour is, for on account of the transmission of the sound to a distance one may fail to hear the first strokes, and so be in error at the beginning of the count.

She had the appearance of being in even vigorous health—a bit pale, but I dare never ascribe to this pallor essential significance, for the sight of me might produce it. But I dare to rejoice at her wholesome appearance—or might it be a false appearance, that the air has given her the semblance of health? What can a hasty doctor say? A hasty doctor I am not, properly speaking, it is not I that pass hastily through the patient's room, it is the patient who runs past me so hastily; and a doctor I am not, rather it is I that am the patient.

May 15. Morning.

TODAY a year ago. I have often laughed at a lover of whom it was told me that he had another coat which he kept hung in his lady's house, which he put on when he visited her, in order not to wear out the new coat. Now I no longer laugh at it. I too have another coat, not hanging in her apartment, but outside in the corridor. There I put it on and discard every expression of my love, every hint of my sympathy, every tempting little wish, which, if our relationship were secure, would be fain to delight her with insignificant expressions of love. When I have the coat on, then begins a continual twaddle, beating about the bush, constantly mixing up the physical and the moral, confounding all things with one another, constantly chatting about our engagement, and our engagement, and things like that.

It is an agonizing punishment I suffer, as agonizing as if the scene were in Tartarus, to have to sit thus making mouths at myself. But so it must be. By this course of action our whole relationship, when the moment comes again to break off, will have no attraction for her, not even the fascination of the dreadful, but she will be sick and tired and disgusted, as one is tired of orange juice because one has taken medicine with it. If later she should be able by herself to bestow ideality upon the relationship, she is quite a different individual than I supposed, and is far from standing in need of me.

May 16. Midnight.

As I have said, the whole thing is likely to pass off quietly. Yesterday and the day before I had a talk with my friend, who is very well informed, and who tortures me in a spirit of true friendship, though at the same time he obliges me with all sorts of information, without referring to her except under fictitious names. And his friendship is unchanged. First he wanted to distress me with the suggestion of mortal danger to her, now he pipes a different tune, he would if possible incite me by stirring up in me a little jealousy—but then she must be in a pretty good state of health. I possess in this man an incalculable advantage. He it is I now shall make use of. Today the comedy began. As he sat talking, in the midst of his narrative, I arose, embraced him heartily and said with pathos, "Now I understand you. Oh, what a fool I am that I did not recognize in you a friend! Do not deny it, you are speaking of her, of her whom, alas, I made unhappy, and whom yet I loved, to whom many a time I have wished to return, but I cannot, no, I cannot; honestly speaking, my pride has too much power over me." My friend was rather taken aback. It must be pretty embarrassing when one is sitting in friendly converse, and with artless Christian malice would torment a man, then to be folded in friendship's embrace. As if a robber who met a traveller on a remote path and was just on the point of falling upon his prey, were to feel himself tenderly embraced and were to hear these affecting words: "O kindly fate, which hast sent me a guide when I had gone astray; O thou my benefactor, the precious representative of humanity in these lonely places," etc. It might well be possible that the robber would fall into embarrassment. So at least did my friend. I know very well that she must occasionally seek information about me. This I do not know from him, but because there is another who has been very nimble in getting news to carry to her; and my friend stands much closer to her.

He became now in a way my friend. It goes without saying, however, that I do not trust him beyond the threshold. On the other hand, it suits him well to believe that he has me in his power, and that I am still so much concerned about her that he can find pleasure in torturing me. First I wanted with his help to open a correspondence with her. I declared in the most dramatic manner that I did not dare to see her and therefore must write. That I have seen her no one knows, and it would hardly occur to her to say it. This plan, however, was rejected. Then he promised to see to it that there should come into her hands several letters which I am to write to a third person. As a precaution I have used three sorts of ink, so that there might be a little difference in the color, since the dates are different.

So with combined forces the thing is going ahead. He has no objection to her marrying again, because he believes this will irritate me, and he perceives that I possibly may be of some help to him in this direction.

An author (I forget who it is) has said that honesty is the most durable thing—only not with reference to pleasing women. I really believe too that truth does not make a woman happy; I would not say by any means that a lie does, but some sort of little untruth. The jealousy he is scheming for is my affair. *Non enim est in carendo dificultas, nisi quum est in habendo cupiditas,* says Augustine.[111] Well, it is true that I desired her, yes, that I desire her; but the fact that there was no

[111] *De doctrina Christiana,* III, 27.

external impediment shows that there was something higher which constrains my wish. This higher thing is the idea. Along with that I desire her . . . infinitely; without that, I hold to that which is higher than either of us. My preoccupation is therefore a different one, that regarded essentially (for regarded from the point of view of actuality and chance it may be that I accomplish nothing) I with these letters am writing her a letter of separation which puts infinity between us, that with these letters, regarded essentially, I have contributed my part (verily not with a sympathetic wish) to acquire some lightness in the life which heavily distresses me.

May 19. Midnight.

By this time she has presumably received my letters. The interpretation of the relationship does not fail to mention repentance and contrition. This "accommodation" is what distresses me most. In the case of every other deceit I have had at all events an ardent spirit, because the reason for it and the impulse to it was the hope that she would collect herself in an infinite sense. This time I am in low spirits, and yet this time perhaps I shall exert a much greater influence over her than by all I labored to do when by tearing myself from her I became more tightly bound to her. My repentance and contrition are of course expatiated upon in many words, and of course the upshot of the many words is that now it cannot be undone; I repent of the past, I wish to undo it, but I cannot, no, I cannot, but I have a will to do it if only my pride would let me, otherwise I would, etc. Repentance used to be recognized by the fact that it acts. In our age it is perhaps less exposed to such misapprehension. I do not believe that either Young,[112] or Talleyrand, or a more recent writer,[113] are right in saying of language that its purpose is to conceal thought, for I believe that its purpose is to assist and confirm people in refraining from action. What in my eyes is nonsense will perhaps produce a great effect, and perhaps the majority of my more intimate acquaintances will say, if they read these letters, "Well, now at last we have understood him."

It is pretty hard. One would fain enjoy the reputation of not being publicly regarded as a Bedlamite. To that in fact I too attain. I really believe that whatever I might say, if only it were not the truth or my sincere opinion, I should be regarded even as sagacious, whereas by doing the other thing I should be absolutely bringing about my depor-

[112] *Love of Fame,* II, verse 208: "And men talk only to conceal the mind."

[113] S.K.'s own pseudonym, Vigilius Haufniensis, author of *The Concept of Dread,* Danish edition of the *Works,* Vol. V, p. 415.

tation. If I were to speak thus: "I took this decisive step because I felt myself hampered, because I must have my freedom, since the *libido* of my desire embraces a world and cannot be satisfied with one girl"—then the chorus responds: "There's a lot of sense in that. Hail to thee, thou enlightened man!" Were I on the contrary to say, "She was the only one I have loved. Had I not been certain of that when I left her, I should never have had the courage to leave her"—then the chorus cries, "Off with him to the madhouse!" If I were to say, "I was tired of her" —then says the chorus, "There we have something one can understand." But if I were to say, "Then I do not understand it, for one dare not denounce a relationship of duty because one is tired of it"—the cry then is, "He is mad!" If I were to say, as the most recent construction would, "I repent it, I would fain undo it, but I cannot, no, I cannot, my pride will not permit it, no, I cannot"—then the judgment of the chorus is, "He is just like the rest of us, and like the heroes in French poetry." If on the contrary I were to say, that nothing, nothing could so satisfy my pride as to undo it, that nothing, nothing would so assuage the cold fire of revenge which demands redress—then the response is, "He is delirious, don't listen to him. Away with him to the madhouse!"

Mundus vult decipi—there could hardly be a more precise description of my relation to the environment which I may call my world. I believe too that in a broader sense it is the best thing that has been said about the world. The speculative philosophers therefore should not rack their brains to fathom what it is the age requires, for from of yore this has always been the same, namely, to be led by the nose. If only one utters some nonsense and drinks to the health of mankind *en masse,* one becomes, like Peer Degn,[114] loved and respected by the whole community. It is not different now, and everyone who sets himself down before the eyes of all to ponder how he might discover what the age requires, has substantially discovered it already. In that respect everybody can serve the age, whether it be understood as a whole nation, as humanity in general, as all the generations to come, or as a smaller group of contemporaries. I serve the sympathetic by being a scoundrel. There is no doubt that I satisfy their requirement. I myself profit by it too, and in a certain sense I find this public estimation quite desirable. To be a paragon of virtue, the normal type of intelligent man, is for one thing very embarrassing, and for another thing . . . very problematical. On the other hand, I am not persecuted either. That too is desirable, lest I should draw a false inference and think well of myself because I was persecuted in the world.

[114] Holberg's comedy, *Erasmus Montanus,* Act I, Scene 4.

With regard to other people I have never hesitated to follow my guardian angel by yielding to a certain innate bashfulness about the good that is in me, and a rather melancholy distrust of myself—that is to say, by deceiving in such a way that perhaps after all I am always a little better than I seem.[115] I have never been able to understand it in any other way but that every man is essentially thrown back upon himself, and that apart from this there is either vicarious authority such as that of an Apostle[116] (the dialectic definition of which I cannot comprehend, though in reverence for that which has been handed down to me as sacred I refrain from drawing any conclusion from my non-knowledge) . . . or else mere patter. It is perfectly true that he who cannot shave himself may very well sit down and employ others to accommodate his hair and beard; but in the world of spirit this is nonsense. Nevertheless it is esteemed a part of seriousness to be straightway at hand to exert an influence upon others, without for this wanting to be an Apostle (how humble!)—and without being able for all that to define in what way one differs from or resembles such a figure (how senseless!). Everybody wants to work for others. This is the conventional theme of the patriotic or moral address, where it is easier to understand; but it is also a conventional feature of the rhetorical form of the religious address. I do not doubt that it is found in the printed instructions for preachers, and one hears it often enough, except when one listens to an individual who has himself been tried by experience and knows how to speak, and knows whereof to speak. If the sermon is about preparing the way of the Lord, the first topic has to do with the duty of every Christian to do his part in spreading Christianity—"not only we priests, but also everybody," etc. That is *charmant*. "Not only we priests." Here one feels at once the lack of middle terms to determine whether a priest is an Apostle, and if not, how he differs from such a figure, and in what respects he is like him. The ecclesiastical points of dispute about ordination increase the difficulty, and the principal middle term is thrust into the background by decisions within the undecided. So then, "not only we priests." That to which "not only" refers is not given, and then follows the apodosis with all the seriousness of exhortation: "Give heed, my dear hearers, to what I say: it is not only I and we priests who should labor thus, but you should all labor thus!" How? Yes, this is the

[115] At a later date, and in a very personal passage, S.K. proposed the anxious query "whether a man has a right to let it be known how good he is."

[116] Here we see that S.K. was already awake to the problem upon which his attention was riveted two years later by "the case of Adler." See my translation of *The Point of View*. There is also much in this entry which presages the *Unscientific Postscript*.

only thing that is not made clear in this serious address—if that can be called serious which is not serious in its thought-content. Now the first topic is finished; the priest wipes off the sweat, and the hearers do likewise, at the mere thought that they have thus become missionaries. The orator begins again. One hopes to get a little more light on the subject; but, lo, the next topic is, that everyone should prepare within himself the way of the Lord. This of course is the way one ought to speak, and upon this point one can construct a whole life-view. One understands that the individual has to do with himself essentially, and that the business of accomplishing something is accidental, cannot be assumed by anyone in advance, and cannot be ascribed to oneself, and only as seen retrospectively in eternity can it be seen as it is, essentially as God's bounty, and accidentally the deed of the individual. For in fact existence, and providence within it, is something more than the simple sum of all the deeds of individual men. A man must have his absolute thought *in mente* wherever he fares. When it is lacking, a man is at fault in two ways: he beguiles people into dreams, and he works injustice to the sufferer. For in fact that first topic requires success of every man. It is easy enough to talk about a thing which inexperienced and indolent natures especially like to hear; but it is senseless to *require* it, because success does not depend upon freedom but is the boon of providence—and suppose now that one were to have ill success. If on the contrary it is understood that the individual has to do essentially with himself, then it will also be understood that he so exists in order that his life, his word, may *possibly* have significance for others. "Possibly," because in the first place it is the affair of providence, and secondly the power exercised by the example, the teacher, is not direct. At this point then a speaker might begin, inverting the topics, somewhat in this fashion: "Not even I, though it may seem so, can essentially do more than attend to myself. Do not let yourselves be captured by an illusion." But ordinarily the address is planned in exactly the opposite way. One appeals to the example of John the Baptist; but John is not directly a paradigm, he is set apart (*ἀφορισμένος*)[117] for a special work, and hence middle terms are needed. Moreover, one must always be cautious in employing world-renowned figures, for these possess a completely rounded character which makes it easy to contemplate them, but as easy to misunderstand. Every figure which is to be employed must in its dialectic structure be clear to thought, otherwise it is merely a jest to propose him as a paradigm.

I have pondered much over this, seeing that I am an existing person, and so must put to use ethically what is said. When one elects to do

[117] cf. Acts 13:2.

differently, elects to teach or to learn, but leaves out the crises of realization, one may have much to talk about, I dare say, many words of instruction, and may find tranquillity, I dare say. From what I have thought on this subject I have come to the conclusion that I do a man the most good by deceiving him. The highest truth with respect to my relationship to him is this, that essentially I can do him no good—this is the expression for the deepest yearning of sympathetic pain, which only by living in a mare's nest one can abstain from having an experience of, but is also an expression of the loftiest enthusiasm for the equality of all men. And the most adequate form for this truth is that I deceive him—for otherwise it would be possible for him to make a mistake and learn this truth from me, and by this he would be deceived, that is, by believing that he had learned it from me. I know well that the plurality, were I to initiate them into my doubtful process of thought, would smile at me and reprehend my levity, for the infatuating is taken to be the serious. That cannot disconcert me without making me guilty of an inconsistency, and that cannot come to pass, seeing that I have no desire to confide in anybody, and am not likely to make the mistake of supposing that I ought to go forth to proclaim this parsimonious closeness instead of being close myself. For let man be close, then God alone is openhanded.

I have learned this best, but also in the hardest way, through my relationship to her, in which yearning sympathy constantly desired to make her an exception, and in which I have wished to the point of desperation to be everything for her, until I learned in pain that it is infinitely higher to be nothing for her. It comforts me that in my relationship to her I never fancied that I was a teacher or was called upon to say a few admonishing words. Though the wisest man were to devote six hours a day to a person, and were to devote six more to consider how he might do it best, and were to keep this up for six years, he would be a deceiver, if he ventured to say that *essentially* he had done him good. And for me at least, this thought is the deepest source of enthusiasm. Language, arts, handicrafts, one man can teach another, but in an ethico-religious sense one man cannot essentially benefit another. Hence it is beautiful and it is uplifting to give expression to this by the extremest effort of deception, for a deception under ethical responsibility is anything but an easy matter, and it is always able to hold its own with the admonishing word. It comforts me now, when all the subsequent things have occurred, that she never stood to me in the relation of pupil, which might have been upsetting to her. What I have uttered I have uttered as if it were to myself I was talking, and I made neither gesticulations nor applications. If she appropriates it, she does it of her own accord, not relying on "his word and gown."[118] It is convenient enough to jump into an omnibus and ride around and say a few admonishing words, there may be something pretty implied in the wish to do it, but it is stupid to be capable of teaching that "a man can do nothing whatever," and then at the same time to be capable of ascribing to a few admonishing words such a prodigious effect. To God is due the thanksgiving of wonder and admiration for the effects. For each man is to look to himself in life, in eternity there will be time to see what God brought out of this. And this applies not only to the conspicuous influence of single individuals, but to the slightest fraction of effect ascribable to the most insignificant man.

So it is I have sought to understand existence. He who has understood it in the same way will surely behave in the same way, and above all will constantly express himself so cautiously, and in the form of deceit, that he may avoid the danger which everybody in our time, down to the most insignificant newspaper reporter, must be aware of, namely, that there are a few men who have conceived the desperate idea that the thing directly uttered is the truth, and that it is their task to sally forth into the world, etc. But to sally forth into the world may well be left to the knights errant; the true seriousness is attentive to every danger, and to this among others, that one may in bona fide become an unreasoning pupil, a thing which is best prevented by employing contradiction as the form of presentation. In my view no one (with exception of such authoritative individuals as the Apostles, whose dialectical position I do not comprehend) has been more serious than he[119] who clad his thought in the form of jest, and who loved so sympathetically his fellow men, and no one who has so profoundly admired the Deity. So let the chroniclers tell of kings who introduced Christianity; my notion is this, that a king can introduce a better breed of sheep, and railways; but Christianity and spirit (ethically understood) not even an emperor need put himself to the trouble of introducing—that is to say, in the essential sense.

A change is now being effected in my relationship to her. Till now I have remained perfectly quiet and respected the infinity in her. Now I come out with an explanation. This I regard as a deceit. In the earlier period the form was deceit, and the content was interest for the infinity in her. Thus my quietness, my silence, my self-effacement, was the form in which deception expressed an infinite interest in her. Now it is different. What I say, I do not mean; but neither do I mean that the form of

[118] A phrase from Heiberg's "Kong Salomon og Jørgen Hattemager," *Poetical Works,* Vol. V, p. 73.

[119] Socrates.

deceit adequately clothes my real meaning. Whether in reality it influences her, is not to the point. I have to do only with the essential, and the essential point is that this is my intention and purpose. The explanation I give, that I repent but cannot undo what I was at fault in doing, is sheer nonsense. For in case I am unable to allege reasons why I cannot undo it, I ought never to talk about my repenting, least of all allege pride (i.e. that I will not) as the reason, for that simply is making a fool of her. Therefore until now I have never represented myself as repentant, although in fact I am repentant and have repented of entering into that relationship, and I am humiliated by the fact that I cannot undo it, precisely as my pride prompts me to do, since now it is broken by the experience that I, who have had an almost foolhardy conception of what the will can accomplish, must here writhe at the thought of something which I will, and will passionately, but cannot do. Why I cannot (that being something implied in my relation to the idea—until that is changed or I am) it is impossible for me to tell her in such a way that she could understand it; but this precisely is the reason why I have never said to her that I repented. Such was the intention of my conduct. But to repent, and to allege pride as the impediment to the expression of repentance, is *lèse-majesté* against God. How anybody can understand it and find it plausible, I cannot conceive; but then in turn most people would say the same about my way of regarding it.

Perhaps for the first time I am doing something which I myself regard as senseless. I have done many things which the plurality perhaps would regard as senseless; but that has not disturbed me, since this might also be because the plurality has not understanding enough to think the thing out, nor courage enough to venture out to the extreme positions where I lead my life. I have done many things, too, which I myself have afterwards perceived to be foolish, and although repentance when it makes inspection has no respect for excuses, there is yet a sort of comfort in the fact that when I did the thing I did not know that it was senseless. Unqualified as I am to comprehend such problems as the future of humanity as a whole, or what it is the age requires, I have absolutely collected myself within myself. When the rights of the case seemed to me doubtful, I have been accustomed to pronounce my name aloud to myself and say, "One may die, one may be unfortunate, yet one can preserve sense in one's life, and faithfulness to the idea." Now that is no more. And who is at fault for it? Another would perhaps say, "It is she, under whose slipper you still remain." That, however, I would not say, for I fain would refrain from such senselessness as this, that another is at fault for the fact that I get into a scrape. I will say rather that I myself am at fault, the fault is mine, it lies in my weakness, and the difficulty is that my understanding vouches to me for it that my conduct may be beneficial to her in a finite sense, while my sympathy would prefer to love her in an infinite sense. This relationship has humiliated me, and now, whether she reads my letters or no, whether they have an effect upon her or no, she now triumphs over me in a way which makes me despondent.

May 21. Midnight.

THERE is nothing new under the sun, says Solomon. Well, that may be so, but it is worse when nothing happens at all. By this consideration alone I assure myself of the absurdity of seeking any confidant. Of course if my pain were rich in episodes, in changes of scenery and decoration, it then would be interesting. But my suffering is boring. In fact I am still constantly engaged in expounding this nothing, and the scenery is unalterably the same.

If I were to travel in order to make time move, *per mare tristitia fugens per saxa per ignes*[120]—but it cannot be done. I must still keep perfectly quiet. A journey, which she would easily get wind of, might possibly upset her and prompt her to entertain an illusion, namely, that I, after a certain length of time in foreign parts, had become changed. But time must be dealt out to her as stingily as possible; and I only wish that a providence would often bring our paths together, for she is the better for seeing me, and so having opportunity to assure herself that I am here and live here unchanged, that I am not sitting in a foreign land —possibly thinking about her and getting homesick. If I were to make a journey, I ought to have gone away long ago, giving out a false report of the duration of my journey, and coming back suddenly. Perhaps it would have occurred to her that this suddenness had something to do with her, until she saw that it had nothing to do with her—that possibly might have been good for her. The time for such a thing has passed.

The clock just now struck one. This disconsolate indication of time! For twelve strokes are many, one notes that time is indicated, and even two is a number to be counted; but one is suggestive of eternity. If there be such a thing as an eternity of punishment, and the unfortunate man who suffers it were to make complaint to someone, how surely one would turn away from him, for not only is he unhappy, his suffering is boring—if it were not boring one might show him sympathy.

[120] Horace's *Letters,* I, 1, 46.

For my part I crave nobody's sympathy. God in heaven is not disgusted by the boring. They say that it is a duty to pray, that it is profitable to pray, that there are three grounds for it, maybe there are even four. I have no intention of taking away from anybody his grounds, he is more than welcome to retain them, if only I may retain the thought of *daring* to pray, as something, so inspiring that, in a deeper sense than did Plato and Aristotle,[121] one can say that wonder is the beginning of knowledge. With respect to this matter I have no confidence in many arguments and sixteen grounds; perhaps it would be better, with a view to the prosperous classes (for the poor, the unfortunate, the simple classes, have no such difficulty about prayer) if a regulation were introduced making it cost something to get permission to pray—then there might be a run on it. If it is true of earthly love that it seeks privacy, it is even more true of prayer that it prefers loneliness and to be as much hidden as possible, in order that it may neither be disturbed itself, nor annoy others by its emotional character. There is not the least need of having witnesses to it, and they don't help any. A prince who travels incognito can at any moment put off his incognito; and it seems to me likewise that the outward semblance of the man of prayer is an incognito, which he cannot indeed put off in order to become an object of worldly admiration, but which he can lay aside when in the act of prayer he is raised to the infinite by wondering at God, by wondering at the fact that God is the only one who does not grow tired of listening to a man. And in turn this holy wonder will prevent the man of prayer from reflecting whether he is getting what he prays for. It is not a pretty love affair where one is looking out to see if it pays, and even if he sees that it pays capitally, it is not a happy love affair. Prayer was not invented to bring suit against God, but it is a favor graciously granted to every man, and which makes him more than a nobleman. But if one understands with wonder, yea, with a wonder which shipwrecks his understanding, that prayer is a favor, then it is apprehended that arguments are not necessary at all, for it is only the doubtful that is recommended by arguments. Every extraneous reflection has *eo ipso* the effect of nullifying prayer, whether it be a reflection which looks from the corner of the eye to temporal advantage, or a reflection upon the individual himself and his relation to others—as if a man were so serious that he could not pray within and for himself, but must come forward and do the whole congregation good by his intercession and by his example as a man of prayer. Thus there are men also who cannot speak except be-

121 Plato (in *Theatetos,* cap. 11) and Aristotle (in *Metaphysics,* I, 2) affirm that wonder is the beginning of philosophy.

fore a general assembly, and Madame Voltisubito cannot ride unless she hears the whip crack.[122]

Ah, but for her! If she will not in herself understand, but would rather seek temporal consolation! It is hard on a man who has not dissevered his soul in dissolute concern for Tom, Dick and Harry, or for the whole human race, to dare only in loneliness to express his concern for himself, and not to dare to do all that, which to be sure is in a higher sense a mere nothing, but which nevertheless is some assuagement for sympathy.

May 22. Morning.

TODAY a year ago. Laughter, after all, is the best means for exploring. She joins in the laughter, but then she can endure no more, her laugh breaks. So then after all she has no infinity of passion, but has it only to a certain degree. Then I shudder, for I know what is about to come, there will come prayers and tears until again she is weary; but my twaddle has not grown weary, it goes on indefatigably.

To be pricked where the most delicate nerves are located is dreadful, but still more dreadful it is not to dare to change an expression while that is happening, but to have to sit perfectly calm and continue to chat.

Only for ten minutes today was I serious. I propose to behave in the same way every eighth day. I said to her calmly, "Hold up, break it off, thou canst not hold out with me in the long run." But with that passion flames up most hotly, she declares that she would prefer all this to not seeing me. This is only a passionate outburst, and its very vehemence indicates to me that my line of action will be conducive to setting her afloat.

May 25. Midnight.

REMEMBER her—I dare not. Had death separated us as it separates lovers, had she broken with me, then I should have dared to remember what was beautiful and lovable, to remember every instant which was a happy one for us. When spring burgeons in youthful vigor I should remember her, when the leaf gives its shade I should repose in the memory of her, in the evening when the summer mists collect I should see her image, by the quiet lake, when the reeds rustle, when the skiff approaches, I should imagine that I was about to meet her, until the monotonous waves would rock me away into remembrance, at the shop

122 From Heiberg's *Recensenten og Dyret* ("The Reviewer and the Beast"), Scene 16—but there it is said of Madame Voltisubito that she cannot *sing* without hearing the crack of the whip.

of my old pastry cook I should seek a trace of her, and often, often deceive myself by the thought that I was going to her. But I dare not. There is no change of seasons for me, as in me there is no change. Remembrance does not blossom in my hand, it is like a judgment on my head, or like an enigmatic sign the significance of which I do not know. Did Adam dare to remind Eve, did he dare when he beheld thistles and thorns before his feet, did he dare to say to Eve, "No! It was not like this in Eden. Ah, dost thou remember?" Did Adam dare? Still less do I.

May 27. Midnight.

FORGET her?—that is impossible. The whole structure of my life has collapsed. I was melancholy, but in this melancholy I was an enthusiast, and that disconsolate thought of my youth, that I was good for nothing, was perhaps only a form of enthusiasm, because I required an ideality under the weight of which I sank. This secret I wished to keep within myself, and within this secret a glow, which indeed made me unhappy, but also indescribably happy. Early, all too early, I thought I had perceived that the enthusiasm found in the street and in the market is of a kind I should not wish to have part or lot in. So I desired to make my exterior cold and heartless, so as to have no fellowship with an enthusiasm which was deluding or self-deluded. That was a proud idea, such as might occur to a melancholy man. But though people were to cry against me loudly as an egoist, I was not willing that anyone should get the better of me. All this is brought to confusion, I am disarmed. I have been taken prisoner by the appearance I sought to conjure up. I have in fact treated a person shabbily. And although I have a different understanding of it, and although I am certain—as certain as that the sun rises in the east—that whatever I do I shall always have enthusiasm on my side—I cannot make any man understand me.

Providence has taken me captive. The idea I cherished of my existence was a proud one, now I am crushed. I know well enough that I can hide it from others, but I have lost the real pith of my existence, the secure stronghold behind the deceitful appearance, I have lost what I shall never regain, what I myself must prevent myself from regaining, for my pride is still left, but it has had to *referre pedem,* and it has the task, among other things, of never forgiving myself. Only religiously can I now understand myself before God, in relation to men misunderstanding is the foreign language I speak. I desired to have it in my power to be able to express myself in the common tongue any moment I would, now I cannot.

Ah, blessed is an understanding with God, but the fact that by providence or by my own act I am so surrounded by misunderstanding that I am constantly forced back to the lonely understanding with God has also its peculiar pain. Who would hesitate to choose a confidential relationship? But my choice is not free. I am aware of freedom in my choice only when I surrender myself to necessity, and in surrendering to it forget it. I cannot say, "To whom should I go but unto Thee," for I cannot go to any man, since one cannot confide oneself to the intimacy of misunderstanding; I cannot go to any man, for I am a prisoner, and misunderstanding, and misunderstanding, and misunderstanding again, are the iron bars before my window; and I do not elect to go to God, for I am compelled. But then comes the instant of understanding, and then it is blessed again after all that there are iron bars before the windows, for this brings it about that the understanding cannot be a deception, cannot be something traditionally acquired, a result at second hand, and that it cannot be some sort of chatty babbling—for to whom am I to talk?

My idea was to construct my life ethically in my inmost being, and to conceal this inwardness under the form of deceit. Now I have been forced farther back within myself, my life is constructed for me religiously, and so much farther back in inwardness that with difficulty I reach actuality.

Who would ever think of assuming an air of importance directly before the face of God? But my situation is as if God had chosen me, not I God. There is left to me not even the negative expression of being something of importance, namely, that it is I who come to Him. If I will not submit to bearing the smart of necessity, I am annihilated, or have no place to exist except among men in misunderstanding. If I bear the smart of necessity, then there will come about the transformation.

I shall never recover my loss, it may be long enough before I learn to bear it. As I go about amongst men putting my best foot forward, it seems to me as if my lost pride passed me by as if in the look of another I could read that he condemned me as one who had lost pride and honor. Then like a desperate man I could wish to run in among men to grasp my lost shadow, to claim it again, to revenge myself, to console myself with revenge, until I should sink down exhausted. Yea, woe to the woman whose glance might move me in such a way! Upon a woman at least one can take revenge. I know that there are horrible thoughts which may find place in the man who discovers a stone of stumbling in a situation due to nature. How was it that Richard III could overwhelm the woman[123] who was his sworn enemy, and transform her into a lover? And why, I wonder, did he do it? Was it state policy? Can we also ascribe to state policy the scorn with which he reflects upon the facility of victory? Was it to prove to himself that he was fit to be a king, when with the lust of despair he dwells upon his own deformity? No, it was hatred of existence. With the power of spirit he would mock at nature which had made mock of him, he would turn it into ridicule along with its invention of love and of love for the beautiful; he who had been wronged, he the cripple, he the man of despair, he the devil, would prove that he, in spite of language and natural law, could be loved. So he learned, so he discovered, that there is a power which has upon women a sure effect, namely, untruth and lies, when they vibrate with the flame of wild enthusiasm, with the unwholesome heat of lust, and yet with the icy coldness of the understanding, as we are bidden to cool the best wine with ice. He himself hated, and yet he generated love, even though woman does not love such a man, but feels disgust at him, and only in dizziness and stupefaction sinks into his arms. There is such an evil spirit, and it offers big earnest money, the presentiment of superhuman powers, and it tempts by illusion, as if a mad revenge were the true way to rescue one's pride and to avenge one's honor. And the way must be hard, even if it is possible, the way back across the yawning abyss which also in time separates good and evil, the transition from being supernatural in greatness through the power of evil, to being nothing, nothing whatever, less than nothing, in repentance.

"What is honor?" says Falstaff,[124] "Can honor set a leg? No. Ergo it is an imagination, it is a painted scutcheon." No, this ergo would be a crazy inference; for even if honor can do nothing of all these things when one wins it, yet when it is lost it can do the opposite, it can amputate an leg and an arm, yea, it can maltreat a man worse than they do in Russia, and send him to Siberia. If it is able to do that, it is surely no mere imagination. For go to the battlefield and consider the fallen, go to the soldiers' hospital and consider the wounded—never didst thou find there a dead man, never a mutilated man, so maltreated as he whom honor made away with.

Then comes understanding again within the iron bars. Where then is the field of honor? It is wherever a man falls with honor. But the man who, rather than slink through life with honor, preferred to lose honor and to give it all to God, he also falls upon the field of honor. If we are

[123] Anna, whose husband had been murdered by Richard. Shakespeare's *Richard III,* Act I, Scene 2.

[124] Shakespeare's *Henry IV, Part I,* Act V, Scene 1.

to expect a new heaven and a new earth, so also we must have a new honor. So then if I fall where no one dreams a field of honor can be, even if I am buried in the unconsecrated ground alotted to the dishonored, yet in case an individual, who perhaps passed by my grave with other thoughts, were suddenly to halt and address to me this funeral oration, "How comes it that this man lies here? Can one without infamy lie among the dishonored? And he indeed lies here with honor" — I demand no more than that. I will conceive the case clearly and more decisively than the crisis of my life illustrates it. Take Mary Magdalene, suppose that no one was privy to her shame, that she could have sneaked through life with honor, and in death could have sneaked out of the world with a myrtle garland upon her brow—it seems to me that by her courage she won a very different honor, it seems to me that in death she lies without the myrtle garland more illustrious than with it.

So it seems to me also that after all he did not lose his honor who admitted that he had begun what he could not finish, it seems to me that he preserved his honor better than if he had taken at a good bargain what he would give everything he had to possess, than if he had sneaked through life as a girl's benefactor, when not even to himself he dared admit that he was the more modest figure he alone desired to be, instead of holding the girl at a high valuation when in a spirit of youthfulness she overvalued herself, and holding her at a high valuation when in distress she far undervalued herself, and holding her at the highest valuation as her deceiver, when for the lowest price he might have been her husband; it seems to me that the benediction of gratitude pronounced upon him would have been like a mockery, and that the revered name which then would have designated his relationship to her would have been an abomination, but that the severest condemnation of language and of wrath pronounced upon his conduct would have been a reparation of honor.

May 30. Morning.

TODAY a year ago. Could it be possible that she might conquer and get her wish? Let us see. What I cannot get over is that my whole view of life, which is not snatched vainly from the air but is essential to my individuality, can no longer pass muster. I cannot be happy, she cannot be happy, a marriage our relationship cannot become. She cannot be happy—what is the meaning of that when she herself so passionately desires this thing? But what good does passion do when it is questionable whether she understands herself? Her passionateness simply shows that she has not enough freedom of thought to entertain another point of view. If we separate, and I employ force to break away, she will become unhappy. But in that case there is nothing to give color to the notion that she is happy, and so her unhappiness and my guilt make sense. But if by remaining with me she becomes unhappy, it is nonsense; and then when passion is over with because the inciting opposition is no more, what then? — Our relationship cannot become a marriage. Why not? Because in my melancholy I am morbidly reserved. That I knew in the beginning, and I believed that the task was to conceal it. It was in this way I understood the matter, but such a situation is not marriage. But if she is willing to put up with being married to me with the left hand, as it would be substantially? But I will not put up with it, for as I now see it this would be an affront to her. Is one to ask then only whether one can put up with something, and not ask what this something is, whether it is true, whether it is beautiful, whether it is in conformity with the idea? About this she asks nothing—she who once was proud. This shows that she is too passionate to have any judgment. — For a marriage the wedding ceremony is requisite. What is a wedding? It means taking an oath which is mutually binding. But for a mutual obligation surely mutual understanding is requisite. But she does not understand me. What then is my oath? Nonsense. Is it a wedding? No! It is a profanation. Though we were wedded ten times, I should not be wedded to her, whereas she would be wedded to me. But if she does not concern herself at all about this? Is one then only to ask for one's passionate wish, and not at all about the idea? Is one to believe merely in one's passion, and have not the least faith or trust in the thought that he whom one loves, as one says, may mean well, although he is not of the same opinion? Does not this demonstrate her passionateness and the contradiction implied in it? Precisely in the act which is to bind us most inwardly together I perceive a divine protest against the whole thing. At the moment of the wedding we do not become united, but I learn to know what I knew beforehand, that we are separate. Is this a wedding? Or am I wedded to her for the reason that she dwells in my house, and because I desire no other woman? In that case I am essentially wedded to her now, for after all she does abide with me, and I shall know well how to honor myself and her by seeking no new love—as though I had weighed and rejected her, as she doubtless imagines, showing again by this that she does not understand me, and showing also that in her passion there smoulders a hidden pride.

A woman after all is a marvellous being, and love a strange power! I cannot give up loving her, and yet her faithfulness is of a dubious sort. To love as she does at this moment, is that a difficult art? No, it is weakness. Is it beautiful? No, it is unfree. Is it a power? No, it is impotence. Is it altruistic? No, it is self-love. Is it faithfulness? No, it is innate craftiness. And yet when it is a woman who does this, then. . . . But no, I do not believe I should think thus in the case of any other; but when she does it, she does it in such a way, or I see it in such a way, that she loses nothing in my eyes. She employs every device against me, and it never occurs to her to hint by a single word that she could believe me and therefore would yield, that she will resign and thereby give me my freedom, that she will despise me and on these terms let me go. In a way we have exchanged rôles, for in a certain sense she is the strong one and I the weakling, inasmuch as I am constantly fearful on her account. And truly, one against one, I should not be a match for her; but the misfortune is that I am more than one, inasmuch as I have the category and the idea on my side. A hero therefore I am not capable of becoming, for it is not my victory I seek, but that of the idea, and I am willing to be brought to naught. So when I have conquered and the thing is decided, I shall not say like Pyrrhus, "One more such victory, and I am done for," for this victory is conclusive.

June 3. Midnight.

So then I am on the lookout. If I were to say this to another person, it doubtless would require explanation; for it is easily understood that the pilot coasting the shore, that the watchman on the pinnacle of the tower, that the lookout at the bow, that the robber in his lair, are on the lookout, since there is something to peer at—but he who sits alone in his chamber, what can he be peering at? And he who expects that everything (i.e. the insignificant affair which nobody else perhaps would heed) will pass off quietly, is in fact peering at nothing. What wonder then that this strains his soul and his head; for to look at something is good for the eyes, but to look at nothing is a strain on them. And when for a long while the eye looks at nothing, it sees at last itself, or its own faculty of seeing—so it is that the emptiness around me forces my thought back into myself.

So I begin again from the start to examine the dialectical difficulty of my expectation. The culmination of my life, that almost mad wish, the utmost effort and the last longing of my enthusiasm is that the whole thing might be made good. I have held my soul upon this supreme point.

I feel indeed that now by the weight of the temporal I am at times dragged down from that point. So then, new exercises. From this wish the paths diverge: the wish is one thing for her and another for me. Autopathically I must wish that she might become another's. For my person in its egoism this is the easiest way out. Sympathetically I do not wish this, unless it were to come about in a way that is inconceivable by a return to a first love;[125] for otherwise it is a temporal healing which is not the highest. On the other hand, for her to be infinitized in a religious sense would be and is the highest, and that too I must wish, although, autopathically understood, such an existence would be a heavy burden for me. It would not be difficult for her to find a religious way out. She has nothing to reproach herself with, she can live in blissful friendship with the eternal, she can die quietly and placidly in God, "as mild and gentle as the cradle-babe dying with mother's dug between its lips."[126] For me such an existence on her part would be a condemnation to penitence *in perpetuum*. As the next best thing to being religiously infinitized, my sympathetic wish would be that she might be raised to a higher power in temporal existence, become something great and uncommon in the world. If this were to occur my life again would be laid under embargo. — The catastrophe of horror hardly needs to be again brought up, it may be regarded as a thing of the past.

In spite of this long scala, there is sense and meaning in my existence. What I have done hitherto, until these last letters, is consistent. I have kept entirely quiet, mute, as if nothing were going on. What an effort it has cost me, only he can know who comprehends my sufferings, no one else. How truly does Heiberg say in a masterly novel:[127] "However strong one's reasons may be for regarding a person as inwardly unhappy and broken-hearted, yet if he looks composed, cheerful and merry, all our reasons are put to flight, and we believe rather what we see than what we know." — We have often laughed at the bear which struck its master a fatal blow to chase a fly away. This is indeed comic, but the situation can be made to appear profoundly tragic. Suppose that the bear was aware what the consequence would be if it exerted all its force as it alone could, suppose then that it saw its master tormented and that it must sit still and repress itself so as not to make everything worse. This might be trying and very difficult, for it knew that it could easily kill the fly.

[125] As in fact it had already come about in the case of Regina.
[126] Shakespeare's *Henry VI, Part II,* Act III, Scene 2.
[127] J. L. Heiberg, *Poetiske Skrifter,* Vol. VII, p. 109.

The art of the actor consists in seeming to be deeply moved when he is untroubled (if he is really troubled, it is a fault); the art of the reserved man consists in seeming to be untroubled although he is deeply moved. If he is not deeply moved and shaken, his art = 0, and he is not reserved.

June 5. Morning.

TODAY a year ago. I might in fact get along without the marriage ceremony, and plan for an erotic union such as we have examples of.[128] She is willing to put up with anything—but shall one not raise any question about what it is one is willing to put up with? The situation is so desperately topsy-turvy that I could easily entice her to seduce me. But though she believes now (alas, in her pain!) that I can readily find a finer girl, or though she believes (alas, in her delusion!) that I so easily could forget her and find in other ways new and ever new joy in the world, she ought then also to believe that I rate my honor so low that for a fancy I would be willing to forfeit what never can be regained. For honor I shall never acquire again, or as the last thing of all, sooner will she acquire a new love. But to live outside of wedlock, whether she would put up with it or not, whether she could rely upon my faithfulness or not, is from an ideal point of view an indignity. And she might die, and she might bring down upon my conscience a murder, and she might curse me, and she might abhor me, and she might write an epigram upon my melancholy when she is consoled by a new love, and I am unaltered in that place where she imagined herself to be. But no indignity shall be put upon her—least of all in such a way that I thereby become a knight.

If there were any man I could turn to, I would go to him and say, "Oh, please, please supply a little meaning for me in my bewilderment." The most dreadful meaning is not so dreadful as meaninglessness, and this is the more terrible the more meaninglessly it smiles.

* *
*

Laughter explores in all directions, and by its aid and under its false flag I introduce everything into the conversation, in order that my reflection may inspect the thought-paths in her soul and her powers of

[128] In the year 1847 S.K. made an astonishing entry in his Journal (VIII, A 251) which reveals that he had seriously thought of taking Regina as his concubine, but had rejected it as an indignity to her—though at this later date the false assertion of Jürgensen that Hamann, whom he so greatly admired, had lived with his wife without being wedded to her, seemed to him to "give a little different turn to the matter."

resistance. I perceive this much, that she does not possess the proper ideal conception of what it is to sorrow. In a finite sense she is in sound health, and after all it is by the finite she must be saved. She must be brought to the point of being disgusted with the whole thing, then we part, then she lays her down to sleep, then she sleeps it out, and then she is saved again for time. It is not with the powers of ideality she has to fight, she has a finite hope to which she holds fast, and my presence helps her. The fact that I am here and must look on, gives her an importance in her own eyes which she will not have when I am gone.

If I were not sure of myself that I suffer more than she does, and that the worst awaits me when I have to do only with myself, I could not hold out. However, it goes on, and one can become accustomed to every suffering. What I shuddered at as at entering a fiery furnace, I am becoming accustomed to. I am so extraordinarily successful in bosh and drivel that at home I have to make the opposite motions in order that the whole thing may not dissolve in galimatias. If she had infinity in her soul it would be an easy task for her to be magnanimous towards me (Oh, invidious situation!), to give me my freedom, to take the pain and get a religious equivalent for it, and so to make me her debtor, a debtor in respect to magnanimity. These terms have been offered her, I did not dare to refuse them to her; but verily it would have been upon me a terrible punishment. What does all her anger and contempt amount to in comparison with magnanimity!

June 5. Midnight.

NEBUCHADNEZZAR[129]

(Daniel)

1. RECOLLECTIONS of my life when I was a beast and ate grass, I, Nebuchadnezzar, to all peoples and tongues.

2. Was not Babel the great city, the greatest of all the cities of the nations? I, I Nebuchadnezzar, have built it.

3. No city was so renowned as Babel, and no king so renowned through Babel, the glory of my majesty.

4. My royal house was visible unto the ends of the earth, and my wisdom was like a dark riddle which none of the wise men could explain.

5. So they could not tell what it was I had dreamed.

[129] If this is in any sense autobiography, it must be understood as a fantastic description of S.K.'s religious conversion, which he persisted in ascribing to his experience with Regina. See *The Point of View,* Oxford edition, p. 83.

6. And the word came to me that I should be transformed and become like a beast which eateth the grass of the field while seven seasons changed over me.

7. Then I assembled all my princes with their armies and disposed that I should be forewarned when the enemy came as the word indicated.

8. But no one dared approach proud Babel, and I said, "Is not this proud Babel which I have built?"

9. Now there was heard a voice suddenly, and I was transformed as quickly as a woman changeth color.

10. Grass was my food, and dew fell upon me, and no one knew me who I was.

11. But I knew Babel and cried, "Is not this Babel?" But no one heeded my word, for when it sounded it was like the bellowing of a beast.

12. My thoughts terrified me, my thoughts in my mind, for my mouth was bound, and no one could perceive anything but a voice in likeness as a beast's.

13. And I thought, Who is that Mighty One, the Lord, the Lord, whose wisdom is like the darkness of the night, and like the deep sea unfathomable?

14. Yea, like a dream which He alone understandeth, and the interpretation of which He hath not delivered into any man's power, when suddenly He is upon one and holds one in His powerful arms.

15. No one knoweth where this Mighty One dwelleth, no one could point and say, "Behold, here is His throne," so that one could travel through the land till it was said, "Behold, here is the confine of His dominion."

16. For He dwelleth not on the confines of my kingdom as my neighbor, neither from the uttermost sea unto the confines of my kingdom like a bulwark round about.

17. And neither doth He dwell in His Temple, for I, I Nebuchadnezzar, have taken His vessels of gold and vessels of silver, and have laid His Temple waste.

18. And no one knoweth anything of Him, who was His father, and how He acquired His power, and who taught Him the secret of His might.

19. And He hath no counsellors, that one might buy His secret for gold; no one to whome He says, "What shall I do?" and no one who says to Him, "What doest thou?"

20. Spies He has not, to spy after the opportunity when one might catch Him; for He doth not say, "Tomorrow," but He saith, "Today."

21. For He maketh no preparations like a man, and His preparations give the enemy no respite; for He saith, "Let it be done," and it cometh to pass.

22. He sitteth still and speaketh with Himself, one knoweth not that He is present until it cometh to pass.

23. This hath He done against me. He aimeth not like the bowman, so that one might flee from His arrow; He speaketh with Himself, and it is done.

24. In His hand the brain of kings is like wax in the smelting oven, and their potency is like a feather when He weigheth it.

25. And yet He dwelleth not on earth as the Mighty One, that He might take from me Babel and leave me a small residue, or that He might take from me all and be the Mighty One in Babel.

26. So did I think in the secrecy of my mind, when no one knew me, and my thoughts terrified me, that the Lord, the Lord was such as that.

27. But when the seven years were past I became again Nebuchadnezzar.

28. And I called together all the wise men that they might explain to me the secret of that power, and how I had become a beast of the field.

29. And they all fell down upon their faces and said, "Great Nebuchadnezzar, this is an imagination, an evil dream! Who could be capable of doing this to thee?"

30. But my wrath was kindled against the wise men in the whole land, and I had them cut down in their folly.

31. For the Lord, the Lord possesseth all might, as no man doth possess it, and I will not envy Him his power, but will laud it and be next to Him, for I have taken His vessels of gold and vessels of silver.

32. Babel is no more the renowned Babel, and I, Nebuchadnezzar, am no more Nebuchadnezzar, and my armies protect me no more, for no one can see the Lord, the Lord, and no one can recognize Him,

33. Though He were to come, and the watchmen were to give warning in vain, because already I should have become like a bird in the tree, or like a fish in the water, known only to the other fish.

34. Therefore I desire no longer to be renowned through Babel, but every seventh year there shall be a festival in the land,

35. A great festival among the people, and it shall be called the Feast of the Transformation.

36. And an astrologer shall be led through the streets and be clad like a beast, and his calculations shall he carry with him, torn to shreds like a bunch of hay.

37. And all the people shall cry, "The Lord, the Lord, the Lord is the Mighty One, and His deed is swift like the leap of the great fish in the sea."

38. For soon my days are told, and my dominion gone like a watch in the night, and I know not whither I go hence,

39. Whether I come to the invisible land in the distance where the Mighty One dwelleth, that I might find grace in His eyes;

40. Whether it be He that taketh from me the breath of life, that I become as a cast-off garment like my predecessors, that he might find delight in me.

41. This have I, I Nebuchadnezzar, made known to all peoples and tongues, and great Babel shall carry out my will.

June 7. Midnight.

When I was a child a little peat fosse was my all in all. The dark tree-roots which protruded here and there in the profound obscurity were vanished kingdoms and lands, where every discovery was as important to me as are antediluvian remains to the scientist. There was eventfulness in plenty, for if I threw a stone, what prodigious movements it caused, the one circle greater than the other, until the water again stood still; and if I threw the stone in another fashion, the movements were different from these and in themselves were enriched by many diversities. I lay by the edge and looked out across the surface, seeing how half-way out the wind first began to ripple the water, until the rippling waves vanished among the rushes on the opposite side. Then I climbed up into the willow which leaned out over the fosse, sitting on the extremest branch I could reach and weighing it down a little so that I might stare down into the obscurity. Then came the ducks swimming to strange lands and climbing the small tongue which jutted out from the land and formed with its rushes a bay where my boat of driftwood lay. But if then there flew out of the woods and over the water a wild duck, it awakened by its cry obscure memories in the heads of the tame ducks, so that they began to flap their wings and fly wildly along the surface—then it awakened also a longing in my breast, until again I stared myself into contentment with my little peat fosse.

So it always is, so compassionate is nature, so rich: the less one has, the more one sees. Take for example a book, the most mediocre that has been written, but read it with the passionate feeling that it is the only one thou wilt read, then out of that book thou dost read all things, i.e.

as much as there was in thee, and more thou didst never get out of any book, though thou wert to read the best.

The period of childhood is now long past, hence on the score of imagination I have less to contribute—so greatly am I changed. But the object of my contemplation has not become very great in proportion to advancing age. There is *one* person, one only, about whom everything turns. Upon that girl I gaze and gaze until I produce out of myself what perhaps I should never have managed to see, though I had seen ever so much, for it would not follow that by seeing much my inwardness would have become transparent to me. If she had been uncommonly talented in spirit, she never would have had such an influence upon me. She is just enough for me as a responsibility, and the responsibility again is mine, and yet it is she who by this responsibility brings out before consciousness my inwardness. I was far too much, and much too definitely developed for her to influence me by imparting anything, nor was she equipped to enrich me in a spiritual sense with new content. But, in the last resort, for understanding oneself one has to be in the right situation. This she has helped me to reach by responsibility. From this point of view all my suffering is directly favorable to me. The searching quietness of responsibility teaches one the necessity of helping oneself by force of spirit. Achievement, action, activity, which so often are praised, and deservedly, may easily have, however, an admixture of distraction, so that one does not get to know what one is capable of by force of spirit, and what part the manifold external impulses play; by them one is also spared many terrors, which do not get time to reach one; but being spared does not mean to overcome them or to understand oneself. By the responsibility she will help me further, for I shall not be through with the thing when she is. Suppose she were to become the wife of another man, and I free; with that I am not through with it, I still should have left the possibility that it suddenly might dawn upon me (perhaps owing to the guidance of some thinker, perhaps by a casual word, which sometimes has such great power)—that it suddenly might dawn upon me that a marriage might have been constructed out of our relationship. Precisely because in such a case I should not have the sympathetic dread on her account, pain will grip me again, but then autopathically. What then will responsibility be to me? It will be my comfort, and precisely in the responsibility I shall learn to know myself.

As viewed from this standpoint of self-understanding, I comprehend very well that as a man I am far from being paradigmatic, I am rather a sample man. I indicate with fair precision the temperature of every mood and passion, and while I produce my own inwardness, I understand these words: *homo sum, nil humani a me alienum puto.*[130] But in a humane sense no man can fashion himself after me, and least of all in a historical sense am I a prototype for any man. I am rather a man such as might be needed in a crisis, an experiment which existence uses to feel its way before it. A man half as reflective as I, would be able to acquire significance for many, but precisely because I am wholly reflective through and through I acquire none at all.

As soon as I am outside my religious understanding I feel as an insect must feel when the children play with it, for existence seems to have acted just as mercilessly with me. As soon as I am within my religious understanding I understand that precisely this has absolute significance for me. That which in the one case is horrible jest, is in the other sense the deepest seriousness.

At bottom, seriousness is far from being a simple thing, a simplex, but is a compositum; for the true seriousness is the unity of jest and seriousness. Of this I can best convince myself by contemplating Socrates. If in accordance with one of Plato's interpretations[131] we ingeniously explain Socrates as the unity of the comic and the tragic, it is quite right, but the query remains, Wherein does this unity consist? It cannot be a question of a new kind of poetry or anything of that sort; no, the unity consists in seriousness. Socrates then was the most serious man in Greece. His intellectuality stood in absolute proportion to his ethical nature (where this is not the case one can be serious about trivialities), his comic sense was precisely as great as his ethical pathos; his seriousness was hidden in jest, hence he had freedom in it, and to be serious he did not need the least outward support (which always detracts from the specific worth of seriousness).

In the case of an immediate existence it is important not to see the contradictions, for with that immediacy is lost; in the existence of spirit the important thing is to hold out and to endure the contradictions, but at the same time to hold them off from oneself in freedom. Hence the narrow-minded seriousness is always afraid of the comic, and rightly so; but the true seriousness itself invents the comic. If this were not so, stupidity would be the privileged caste with relation to seriousness. But seriousness is not mediation—that is a poor jest and a new motive for the comic. Mediation has no place in the existence-sphere[132] of freedom,

[130] From the *Hautontimorumenos* of Terrence, 77.

[131] In the *Symposium,* cap. 39, Plato lets Socrates propound the view that the tragic poets must also be comic.

[132] Here, where for the second time we encounter this word, it may be said that S.K.'s thought is more aptly rendered by "existence-spheres" than by "stages," which commentators use far too commonly, for no better reason than that it is conspicuous as the

and only in a ludicrous way, coming from metaphysics, can it intrude into the sphere where freedom is constantly in process of becoming. Seriousness fathoms the comic, and the greater the depth out of which it fetches itself up out of this sphere, so much the better for it; but it does not mediate. What it seriously wills it does not regard as comic inasmuch as it wills it, but for all that it is well able to see the comic side. Thus it is the comic purifies the pathetic, and conversely the pathetic lends emphasis to the comic. Accordingly that comic construction will be the most annihilating which is so fashioned that indignation is latent in it, though no one observes this for laughter. *Vis comica* is the most dangerous weapon and therefore is entrusted only to the hand of him who has a pathos which completely corresponds to it. The man who could thus make a hypocrite truly ridiculous would be able also to crush him by his indignation. On the other hand, the man who would employ indignation, and does not possess the corresponding *vis comica,* will easily fall into declamation and become himself comic.

But here I sit and forget her! No, certainly not; for the unity of the comic and the tragic concerns me closely. My belligerent understanding has often wanted to whirl the whole thing away in laughter, but precisely out of this whirlwind has my tragic passion developed more strongly. Thus it is that I understand myself better, and understand that I have held fast to seriousness. If it had not been so from the beginning, if step by step I had not seen the comic, and under its supervision preserved the tragic, then if it turns out that she becomes another man's wife, presumably a certain passionateness (which is not seriousness in spite of its vehemence) would have got the better of me, or else laughter (in a way that is unbecoming in its separation from the pathetic). For this is comic, that I am a scoundrel, and she the one who will die—now that the situation is inverted. But this shock I can well endure, for from the very beginning my pathos is saved. My pathos has not its origin in her or her vehement outburst, but is my soul's inwardness. Hence transformation cannot make me its plaything, for I hold fast to the idea, and the comic from without has no power over me. The fact that I believed everything, every word of hers, as seriously as a person possibly can, is not at all comic. Whether she did not mean it, has nothing to do with the case; whether like Jacob von Thyboe[133] she says, "We have reconsidered that," makes no difference whatever. True, if I had believed it

title of this book. But even in this book S.K. was thinking of spheres which coexist and in part overlap, rather than of stages which in the sequence of time one completely surmounts.

[133] Heiberg's comedy of that name, Act III, Scene 5.

merely in virtue of her, because she said it, if I had believed it merely in reliance upon her trustworthiness, I should then be comic, and in a certain sense I should have been comic from the beginning. But I believed her because she stood in an ethical relationship to me, so that it was my duty to believe, it is I who have given her word the weight of eternity for me, because I showed respect to the relationship; never have I relied "upon her word and gown" in planning my life. Hence I have seen the comic from the very beginning, and just for this reason I cannot to all eternity become comic. I can produce the comic any moment I will, but I will not, and this will controls my pathos, so that it is not vehement and blind and thereby comic.

So the matter stands, even in case that "if" comes to pass. I am and remain unchanged.

June 11. Midnight.

TODAY I saw her. But this seeing is of no great service to me, for I dare not believe what is commonly accounted the surest thing, my own eyes. But today circumstances favored me. I was walking with another man when we met her. I knew that he was not acquainted with her. As we were approaching I said to him, "How suffering the girl looks!" That maybe was an untruth, but what will a man not do to get ocular demonstration? He replied quite apathetically, "It doesn't seem so to me at all." It is an odd thing to talk to a person in such a way; I doubt if ever in his life he will chance to say a word to me which is so important, although for him it had no importance at all. It didn't stop there, however, for we had something to talk about and therefore walked back and forth in the street, and half an hour later she returned by the same path from a shop. While she was passing us (which she could not avoid doing, because there was no side street, and she had seen us too late) I called his attention to her again, and when she had passed I said, "You really are right, she looks blooming." He replied, "Yes, that's what I said; but I cannot conceive why you concern yourself about it." It is an odd thing to talk to a person in this way; I doubt if he ever will make a remark which touches me so closely, and yet he thought nothing much about it. I explained to him that it was one of my diversions to pay attention to peoples' exterior in order to infer their interior condition. So I was quite ready to concede to him that the last time she looked well, but I was convinced that in the course of her walk something must have occurred which produced this effect, for the first time she looked unwell. He became a bit angry and maintained that he could read faces as well as I, and that both times he had seen one and the same thing. I stood as upon hot coals, lest I might have compromised myself; but to save myself from the snares of imagination when in loneliness it would distress me with the fear that he might have noticed her particularly and would later learn to know that it was she, I then risked the utmost: "Well, we shall soon have the case decided. Do you believe you could recognize her again, for I am not sure that I could, although I looked at her more attentively than you did. Let us go together and procure some information about her." "Evasions," said he, "evasions merely for the sake of carrying the point. How should I recognize her again, since I only looked at her cursorily, though I saw enough to vouch for what I have said." It is an odd thing to talk to a person in this way; for I doubt if he ever will utter a word which so relieves my concern as does this word, which he uttered however only for the sake of getting the better of me. This is like an official survey. The person I walked with was truly an impartial man. So I dare to believe it. — When one must thus steal up to a thing, one appreciates it the more. — To steal up to a pleasure is natural enough, but not to dare to be concerned, to walk in the path of concern as though it were a forbidden path—and now if the result had been that she looked unwell, I should have had to steal up to that.

June 12. Morning.

TODAY a year ago. If then a marriage could be constructed in spite of my morbid reserve,[134] this union is my wish. Quite certainly, even though I cannot at this moment decide in how far it is purely erotic, or has an admixture of emotion prompted by her pain in conjunction with my pride, which in a sense she has on her side. So I might indeed try to imagine that my break with the idea was praiseworthy, since it was for her sake; without concerning myself about her, I might take her at her passionate word, and thus have as much as possible of the joy I wished for myself and which is always in her possession—and thus be unrepentant and free from all difficulties and terrors. When I look away from the idea, I seem to be very well off with this. And now when she not only will put up with everything, but will thank me for it as for a charitable deed, consequently—I cannot endure this confusion. Where can my weary thought find a place to repose? Circumstances

[134] In his Diary, Quidam gives only this remote hint of the reason which S.K. in his Journal alleges as the principal impediment to his marriage, namely, the impossibility of making to Regina a clean breast of his father's guilt and of his own *vita ante acta*. Perhaps this is the only serious omission in Quidam's version of the story.

change, and my head swims. It was my wish that she might become mine, it is my pain to relinquish it; it was my duty to remain in the relationship, it is enough to consume one's strength that I have broken a relationship of duty—but, God in heaven preserve my understanding, save me from one thing, let me not become her benefactor; I cannot live without having some sense in my life, I must have a little, it may be little enough. Let me become her murderer, if so it must be; I understand then that I have pressed forward where I ought not to have ventured, when I make an effort I can understand that it is a heavy punishment inflicted upon me, and the thought-life in me can again draw breath—but to be her benefactor! No, that is impossible. Avaunt, crazy senselessness with thy smiling phyz, make me miserable, but so that there is some sense in it, but beatify me not in nonsense. If I cannot do it though it is my wish, if I cannot do it though it is my duty, there is nothing more to be said, the rest is not only of the evil but of insanity.

Happen what may, though I fall dead today, it is after all not so terrible to go hence with a homicide upon my conscience, as to live as her benefactor. There must be a fault on her part: such terms should never have been offered me. This implies an insult to us both, for it is as if she said "Thou dost not love me, thou hast no regard for thy duty, but after all thou art miserable enough to let thyself be moved, and I am weak enough to will this."

Perhaps she suffers for the fact that her breast is burdened by suppressed sighs, that she cannot weep; so does my consciousness suffer for the same cause, that it cannot manage to take breath, but groans with suppressed thoughts and perishes in meaninglessness. As a fish when it lies upon the beach gasps in vain for the sea wherein it can breathe, so do I gasp in vain for sense and meaning.

* *
*

She suffers, it is evident, and he who sees it is I. No one else has a notion of what is going on between us. When anyone is present my bearing is as it always was. She remains quiet, and I keep watch with a hundred eyes over every word that is spoken, lest suddenly there might come an explosion. She would find relief by talking to somebody, but it would merely have a cooling effect, and the worst symptoms perhaps would come over her in loneliness; she is much better off in holding out with me.

A casual utterance may cause the worst disturbance of all. When one is keeping everything in check by one's calculations, suddenly somebody may let fall a remark which, without having any intention of the sort, touches one sensibly. Yesterday we were at a dinner party. There was talk at table about engagements. A lady remarked that "engaged persons always lose weight." How strikingly applicable! For her and for me it was a harrowing truth. When I already was trying to distract attention from this subject, in order that no further application of this dictum of experience might be made, a gentleman continued it: "But in requital people commonly become fat when they are married." Poor girl! I however retained sufficient composure to adjoin, as lightly as a heavily armed man can, "But yet there are instances of the contrary," and mentioning the name of a man which was enough to produce laughter, I said "He has been married three times, and yet is thinner than I." People were pleased to laugh. She had time to collect herself. But such a torture destroys both soul and body.

Moreover, she is and remains without resignation. She underbids and underbids, but to conceive the problem sympathetically does not occur to her. When she is willing to cast herself away like a slave, like a naught, like a burden, it appears to her that she is carrying resignation to extremes. God knows that in a way the thing is carried to very much greater extremes than I can bear to see it. On the other hand, she either cannot or will not understand what she ought to do, and that she tortures me in an unjustifiable way, for there never has been any dispute about her loveliness, and then too such conduct confirms me in my resolution, precisely out of solicitude for her.

What I fear most of all is that in her imagination she has concocted something great out of me. If that be so, then this humiliation of herself is the worst of all misfortunes. Here I have found a limit for my deceit. If in the form of bosh I were to talk about my insignificance, it would only confirm her in such an imagination, if she has it. Therefore, just as every eighth day I seriously challenge her to break the engagement, so too I have opened to her a little communication with my inmost thought with regard to this last hazard. Next to becoming her benefactor I rank the absurdity that I might be something great and disdain her. This communication is opened only for an instant, for as soon as I have said that she is always plenty good enough, the bosh begins again. I comfort myself in this respect by the thought that when I have forsaken her she will find the opinion confirmed by everyone that it was no great loss. With regard to my heartlessness in treating her thus, it is to be hoped that she will also find confirmation in everybody's condemnation of me.

It would be splendid if she could be brought to the point, or herself get the notion, of breaking the engagement. She would thus be spared the humiliation. I throw out hints of it, for with a whole voice and full passion I dare not talk of it, for thus she would discover how much she concerns me, and so would try all expedients over again. Hence I must talk with half a voice and a fictitious passion.

June 14. Midnight.

In the Middle Ages people saved their souls by repeating the rosary a certain number of times. If I could save my soul by repeating to myself the story of my sufferings, I should have been saved long ago. If my repetition is not always prayerful—oh, yet preferably it ends in the consolation of prayer. In this she aids me in a singular way. If I were not to maintain myself in the passion of action, if this were past and I quiet, i.e. if in repose I dared to reflect upon the whole situation, then I would say that she has done me a good turn for the fact that in my humiliation at seeing her subject herself to me I find all the more joy in subjecting myself to a higher Power. Her misfortune was that she had nothing higher than a man. As the Scripture says that an idol is nothing in the world, so it may well be that I shall end by being nothing, because to her I was an idol.

But how strange the whole thing was, the situation is so dialectically illusive that any instant it might, as it were, escape me, so as to seem as if I had not left her because I loved her but because I loved myself! I find everything just as I wished it, her whole environment just as I had imagined it from first impressions. It suits me like nothing else, I might travel the world around and perhaps not find a situation so propitious for me. If another step is required before marriage, namely, a rational deliberation, then I venture to bear witness on my own behalf that I thoroughly tried out myself beforehand. Only I did not wish to offend her by reconnoitering. I find her rather different from what I had imagined, a little scene helps us, and she becomes in my eyes more lovable than ever—and then, behold, the whole difficulty comes from my side. But then perhaps I am light-minded? All my deliberation about her situation and that of her family before ever I took the step is proof to the contrary, and I dare testify on my own behalf that I entered into the relationship with an entirely honest will, convinced that I knew wherein the problem consisted, and perhaps a bit proud of being able to resolve it, by mastering my reserve and keeping it to myself—and, lo, precisely this is my downfall, not meaning by this that I cannot do it, but that this is not the solution of the problem. After that little incident her devotion becomes more and more unrestrained in its expression, and becomes proof to me that my reserve means absolute incompatibility, that her union with me would be a *mésalliance* for her, even if she does not understand it so. That such is the state of the case is my pain, and yet for all that I cannot give up my reserve. I have employed fifteen years to form a life-view for myself and to attain proficiency in it. It is a life-view which stirred my enthusiasm and was entirely in accordance with my nature, and so I cannot suddenly be made over. I cannot even tell her that I wish such a thing, because such a wish is an undetermined determinant which cannot presume without great light-mindedness to dispose of her life. In proportion as she has struggled with all her might to show her devotion she has labored against herself with all her vital power.

And now I see clearly that my melancholy makes it impossible for me to have a confidant, and I know well that what the wedding ceremony exacts of me is that she should be precisely this. But this she never has been, and could not be even if I were to open myself ever so thoroughly, for we do not understand one another. This is due to the fact that my consciousness has one more register than hers. In the lower court of appeal, which properly is the sphere of everyday life and what is called reality, in that court where she essentially has her life, as surely the majority of men have, I am more than a little queer. Only by a long detour do I become again secure and composed like other men. I am not actually crazy, for I am perfectly capable of looking after myself, I have need of no confidant, I burden no one with my unhappiness, and it does not disturb me at all in my work. My melancholy searches in every direction for the dreadful. Then it grips me with its terror. I cannot and will not flee from it, I must endure the thought; then I find a religious composure, and only then am I free and happy, as spirit. Although I have the most enthusiastic apprehension of God's love, I have also an apprehension that He is not a dear old grandpapa who sits in heaven and indulges people, but that in time and in temporal existence one must be prepared to suffer everything. It is my conviction that it is only a Judaizing reminiscence, a petty particularism in Christianity, or habitual cowardice and indolence, to think that one enjoys a special relationship to God and is exempted from such things. Bustling spiritual and worldly expedients for keeping the terror away are a disgust to me, because these expedients have no understanding of what the terrible is. True, he who is busy in willing to be or has become something in this finite world does well to keep the terror away, and he is compelled to do so lest it should transform his aim into nothing and prevent him from attaining the imagined greatness. But he who wills in a religious sense must have a receptive attitude to the terrible, he must open himself to it, and he has only to take care that it does not stop halfway, but that it leads him into the security of the infinite. This comes about little by little through the instrumentality of the particular terror. He becomes familiar with it, familiar with the thought that what he most fears will happen to him, but he also becomes expert in drilling this thought into conformity with his assurance of God's love. So the thought visits him perhaps off and on, but it lasts only a minute, that very instant he is religiously oriented in it, and the thing disturbs him no more. But then comes another terror, and he does not prate about it to men, but attends to his business, and in this case too he succeeds, etc.

If she had become mine, I am convinced that I should have stood beside her with the thought that one of us would die before night, or with some similar foreboding. I vouch that neither she nor anyone else would have observed it in my looks. Within myself too I should have been composed, but religiously composed, and yet I should have had the thought all the same. Lo, this is a deceit. In case I had a confidant, I would make this inquiry of him: "Is it not a shame for a man who is melancholy to torture his wife with his melancholy ideas?" And he would reply, and with him perhaps all men: "Yes indeed, a man ought to repress himself and thereby show that he is a man." "Very well," I would answer, "that is what I can do, I can look like a smiling hope; and yet it is precisely upon this I have come to grief, for it is a deceit which marriage does not tolerate, whether the wife in question understands it so or not." And the misfortune is that I believed this was the task, until I learned to perceive that the wedding is a divine protest against it.

As for talking with a confidant, that I cannot do. A confidant will not think my melancholy idea so passionately as I do, and so will not understand that for me it is a religious starting-point. In order to live in intimacy with another person it is requisite, either that one has not such thoughts, that one's world of consciousness ends with the "systematic," hardly Greek and still less Christian, board fence, "the outward is the inward and the inward is the outward";[135] or else that such thoughts are not too stoutly held to yield to what one calls reasonable grounds. For most men have a fractional conception of the deceitful appearance of life; but then experience and probability come along and rivet the loose ends together, and so they attain security and have reasonable grounds for it. I know all about that. An elderly woman once got the idea that she would be buried alive. She confided in me. Quite naturally she had

[135] It was in these terms S.K. formulated the Hegelian thesis which he began to attack in *Either/Or*.

thought out three precautionary measures, but as she was distressed by melancholy, her distress had naturally taken all three away from her again, i.e. she could imagine the possibility that they might not suffice. Had she not been melancholy, she would have remained blissful in the assurance that there are such prudential rules and priceless truths which are able to secure something for a person in the finite. Then I had to help her to become blissful in galimatias; for as I perceived that the infinite would perhaps put her to complete confusion, I chose the finite. I myself had once been worried by the same idea and so was bountifully supplied with prudential rules. This abundance had not helped me, for my melancholy had taken it from me, until I found comfort in the infinite. I suggested to her then the fourth and the fifth precautionary measures which she had not dreamt of, and she has never ceased to thank me; but I have never known whether I should laugh or weep at it.

If then I were married and my wife were my confidant—what then? I will suppose that it was that old woman's melancholy idea which worried me, and that it was in the period of suffering, before I had got myself into perfect training. So then I would talk and initiate her into this idea. Then as a matter of fact she would likely laugh, for it would be inconceivable to her how a person could get such ideas. Now in case my melancholy were not constantly the starting point for a religious satisfaction, in case it were an empty whim or crotchet from which nothing resulted, then perhaps this innocent laughter would be precisely the most healing medicine, for a lovable youthfulness has also a great power. But the religious satisfaction is to me of more value than all youthfulness, and therefore this would not help me, except to the point of sadly rejoicing in her happiness, which nevertheless I do not covet. But talk I must, for the easiest thing for me is to keep silent. So she would surely become concerned, and then she would make trial of the reasonable grounds. Suppose then she thinks out five precautionary measures which should take the wind out of my sails. The whole thing is so clear to me that I should like to hear her voice to convince myself that I have done right in preventing myself from hearing it. So she would enumerate the five precautionary measures, and then would say, "And finally thou hast me, who would then do everything for thee, trust me, I promise that it shall not occur, everything shall be done, as if the salvation of my soul depended upon it—so be joyful again." It seems to me that this situation must be enough to make the stones weep. The poor wife! She has suggested everything she could think of. If I were to oppose her, she would believe that I have no confidence in her as being what she would seem to be, and this grieves her. And on the other hand, this then is the dialectic that is to bind me. Even the simplest objection, which would occur to everybody, that she might in fact die before me, she would not understand; for just because it is essentially characteristic of her to look forward to everything happy, and that it is in this "immediate" hope and faith and confidence she has her security in life, she would be speaking from the bottom of her heart were she to say, "How couldst thou think that? I know now why the notion of my dying before thee is so momentous to thee," etc. She would again make the stones weep by her genuine and heartfelt emotion; but on the other hand, this is the dialectic which is to bind him who for fifteen years, day and night, has practised himself in wrestling dialectically with thoughts, as an Arab manages his steed, as a juggler plays with sharp knives. What would be the end of it? That I could not bear to see her distressed, could not find it in my heart to let her go off with the mortification of thinking that I had no confidence in her. And what then? Why then I would let a day intervene, and then I would assume my disguise of deceit, would look as friendly as possible and say to her, "Yes, my dear, it is just as thou didst say. It is true, I have thee, and thou hast convinced me, if not by thy reasons, at least by what thou didst say about thyself." And then she looks so happy and delighted, she who is the joy of my eyes—and I have deceived her. And this I cannot endure, because in her place I could not endure it, and because I will and must love her as greatly as myself, which I do only by leaving her. In relation to other people a deceit is permissible, for they are not tied to me, and not divinely installed as my confidants; and if they are tired of me, they can go, as she cannot, if one day she obscurely comprehends the incompatibility. — The question whether I really was composed when I talked to her thus is not to the point, for if I was composed, it would have been within myself. In this instance the incompatibility shows itself again. A melancholy idea cannot acquire for her the significance that it becomes the starting point for a religious satisfaction. If she has one opinion about a theatrical piece and I another, if the difference of opinion proved perhaps that I am an aesthetic critic and she anything but that, this by no means constitutes an incompatibility, and if it came to that, I would gladly give up my opinion for her sake. But the strange ideas of melancholy I do not give up; for these, which perhaps a third person would call crotchets, which she perhaps would sympathetically call distressing fancies, I call pulls—if only I follow them and hold out, they lead me to the eternal certainty of the infinite.

In my loneliness therefore these ideas are dear to me, even though they affright me; they have the utmost importance for me and teach me, instead of congratulating myself and rendering mankind blissful by peerless discoveries in the religious field[136]—instead of this they teach me to my own abasement to discover as it were, and with endless contentment to be satisfied with, the very simplest things. — In the concept of godly fear it is surely implied that He is to be feared, and if it is dangerous for a man's soul to make God a despot, it is also dangerous for his religion to make Him a subject in reduced circumstances; and if it would be alarming to a man's soul if God were shut up in eternal silence, it is also dangerous to audit speculatively God's accounts and to prance[137] prophetically through world history. Why is it indeed that in remote places where half a mile separates the little huts there is more godly fear than in the noisy town, that sailors have more godly fear than the inhabitants of the market town[138]—why indeed unless it is because such men experience something, and experience it in such a way that there is no escape? When at night the tempest rages and the hungry cry of the wolf is ominously heard therein,[139] when in peril upon the sea a man has saved himself upon a plank, that is to say, must be rescued by a straw from certain destruction, also when no one can send a message to the next hut because no one will venture out at night, and one can spare oneself the trouble of shouting—then one learns to possess one's soul in patience, relying upon something else besides night watchmen and the police and the distress-gun of the life-saving station. In the great cities both men and buildings are crowded too close together. If one is properly to receive a primitive impression, there must either be an event, or one must have another way, as I have in my melancholy. If not, there is danger that the total outcome may be as follows: he had been young and still recalls many pleasant experiences of that time,

[136] This again is aimed at Grundtvig. Where I say "prance," S.K.'s expression is more picturesque: *ride Herredage ind* refers to the gay parade of lords which inaugurated the Danish Parliament before the democratic reform.—A reference to Pastor Grundtvig was planned for in the first notes which sketched the forthcoming work (*Papirer,* V, B 97, 16): "I am not at all a religious individual, I am a capitally constructed possibility of that; I discover primitively the whole religious catastrophe, but when I would apprehend the religious patterns my philosophic doubt comes in. It is dreadful to feel the religious need so deeply, and yet to have such doubt. Yet I will hold out, as soon as I am through with my relationship to her, then is the moment to throw myself absolutely into the thing, I will not run away, will not seek company with a yodelling saint who when he contemplates world history yodels half in Norwegian: 'It is so marvellous.'—The comic." cf. V, B 102 (4).

[137] Aimed at Pastor Grundtvig.

[138] Playing upon the name of Copenhagen (*Kjøbenhavn*—market harbor); S.K. was wont to deride the capital of Denmark as a market or provincial town.

[139] On his visit to Sæding on the Jutland heath where his father was born S.K. was profoundly impressed by the loneliness of the life and by the strong characters produced by its rigorous poverty.

many joyful days, then he was married, and all went well, only one time he was seriously ill, and at once a messenger went for the doctor, one fetched in haste whoever could be found, and so came Professor D., and one learned to know in him a very careful physician, who therefore became the family doctor; also in Pastor P. one found a serious spiritual guide, of whose deep religiousness and genuine piety one was more thoroughly convinced than of one's own religiousness, for which one valued him more and more and more highly from year to year; then one learned to know several like-minded families, attached oneself to them, and then died. And why should it not be a pretty thing to have had a happy youth and to remember it, why should it not be a joyful thing to have learned to know Professor D. and Pastor P.—but is this then the maximum when all is said and done? If so, I would prefer not to incommode either the professor or the pastor, but to have heard the howl of the wolf and to have learned to know God.

In love stories the messenger whom the lover employs is often a dwarf, a deformed person, an old crone. Who could believe it was a love message? So for me my melancholy ideas are messengers from my first love, from what always must remain my only love. They terrify me, but they have never had permission from the sender to destroy me, to enfeeble my spirit, to let me become burdensome to others. Whether this is some time to occur, I do not know, whether it shall occur soon or late, I do not know, but this I know, that these messengers have led me on to the most blissful certitude—and so it may be the same with promotion, "whether one came limping or came hobbling, without glamor of pleasing appearance."[140] Even at this very instant the thought overwhelms me that I have been able to hold out. Oh, in loneliness I never have wished for death. I do not understand how men can suddenly become torpid enough to wish for death. For me on the contrary, the more it grows dark around me, the more I wish to live, in order to hold out by myself, to see if my enthusiasm was an empty word or a power, whether it was the strong drink which foams of itself or penny beer, which foams indeed—but by a foreign admixture. And if a man can understand how dreadful it might be for one who fights to become a king to think of the inopportune arrival of death just when he was nearest the goal, then I can understand that he whose life was troubled to the core, that he who had no confidant at his side and no *impressa vestigia* before his feet regards it as of the utmost importance for him that death may not come and render it impossible to get to know whether

[140] Baggesen, *Danske Waerker,* Vol. VIII, p. 140.

along that path he might press on, or whether he was infatuated by an illusion, whether his resolution which renounces declamation was just as completely fudge as that of the declaimers.

June 18. Midnight.

AM I guilty? Yes. How? By the fact that I began what I could not carry to completion. How is it thou dost understand it now? I understand now why it was impossible for me. What then is thy guilt? That I did not understand it earlier. What is thy responsibility? Every possible consequence that may follow in her life. Why say "every possible," for this seems an exaggeration? Because here there is no question about an occurrence and its consequences, but about an act and about ethical responsibility, against the consequences of which I dare not arm myself by being courageous, since in this courage consists precisely in laying myself open to them. What may serve as thy excuse? That my individuality as a whole disposed me to conduct which on all hands I find confirmed and which, were I to seek a confidant, I should find corroborated: "that a melancholy person should not worry his wife with his sufferings, but should keep them closely to himself like a man." What is thy comfort? That while recognizing this guilt I have likewise a presentiment of a divine governance in the whole affair. Precisely because I have considered the matter to the best of my ability and have acted as honestly as I could by virtue of this recognition, precisely for this reason I perceive a co-operation which led me on to a point where I understood myself as perhaps I never could have done in any other way, but also taught me this in such a way that I shall not become arrogant. What is thy hope? That it may be forgiven—if not here, at least in eternity. Is there no hitch with regard to this forgiveness? Yes indeed, there is the fact that I have not her forgiveness; and she is and remains a court of first resort which cannot be ignored. Her forgiveness cannot indeed justify me eternally, any more than a man's implacability can injure anybody but this man himself, but her forgiveness is part and parcel of the divine juridical procedure. Why hast thou not her forgiveness? Because I could not make myself comprehensible to her. It would indeed have been far easier for me if only I could have secured that and been exempted from the dreadful hovering in which I find no foothold but by assuming the utmost possibility of responsible obligation. No question was asked thee about the easiest or the hardest, for a man may choose the wrong even when he chooses the hardest—so then, why dost thou not possess it? Because I could not get it. When I dissolved my engagement to her by my letter I made request for that. This she would not understand and therefore compelled me to employ the only means left for rescuing her, namely, to put the misunderstanding of deceit between us. My continuation in this course showed me that the deceit itself really expressed the truth, that she did not understand me. Her opinion of me was that I had more inclination for the world, that I wanted to have my freedom because the relationship was too narrowing for me. Precisely because this was her opinion it offended her pride, and therefore she was reckless in employing every expedient. To win me back again she had to rely essentially upon bringing me back to my duty and touching me sympathetically. If at that juncture I had talked plainly and said, "The maintenance of this relationship is my own wish"—then I would not have been allowed to say more, but she would have exulted somewhat in this fashion: "O my dear, thou dost not know how happy thou hast made me. It is thine own wish. Ah, I had given up hope of it and had learned to content myself with something less until it might again become thy wish; but now all is well, indeed it is splendid. It is thy wish and my wish, so every obstacle is removed." What does that mean? It means that she does not understand me. So I did not elect to make myself understood, but understandable to her, for she could understand that I was tired of her, that I was a deceiver and a twaddler. Her salvation depended upon my holding fast to this. But what then would it signify if I were suddenly to beg for her forgiveness? It would sound like making a fool of her. The word forgiveness uttered between *us* puts everything upon a religious basis. To trick her out of an expression of forgiveness is not what is required of me. If I were to talk, I must admit my fault, but also, if the thing is to be serious, she must be able to understand my justification. As soon then as the talk began she would confine herself to understanding the first half, and thereupon understand nothing of the rest, that is to say, she would misunderstand the first part as well. If I could have been comprehensible to her in my whole construction, and her forgiveness could thus be something more than a situation in comedy, her conduct towards me would have been so shocking that she rather would have been in need of my forgiveness, and so I did enough with that letter. But as the case then stood, every utterance of mine could only contribute to make the two months still longer, for she would be led thereby to become more and more vehement in her attack—although without gaining anything. Hence the few serious words I stealthily mingled with the confusion are what I most have to reproach myself for. So then I have no forgiveness. An official forgiveness between two persons who do not understand one another is an empty ceremony and as questionable as a written contract made between two persons of whom one can neither write nor read writing. The great reciprocal security of having a written rather than a verbal agreement vanishes in a double way: he who cannot read writing has nothing to rely upon but what he has heard, and whether it stands written as it was read to him he does not know; the other has the onus of vouching for both, although the document should be mutual. Before I can have real forgiveness she must be able to put herself in my situation, otherwise her forgiveness is like a written declaration by one who cannot read writing, indeed her forgiveness is still less than that, because the man who cannot read writing can nevertheless understand very well what the question is about, but forgiveness by one who cannot or will not understand what the question is about is just as meaningless as a grant made in response to a petition by one who does not know what the petitioner asked. Lo, it is for this reason I have no forgiveness. I believed that I did her more honor by not getting such a thing out of her by craft, I have done what I thought I owed to her, or rather the thing was done for her sake: forgiveness has been made as difficult for me as possible. My break with reality was of such a sort that it is a simple consequence from it that a genuine forgiveness on her part is unthinkable, for this would define me as in continuity with reality.

This is the position of the case in time. As for eternity, it is my hope that we shall be comprehensible to one another,[141] and that there she will forgive me. In time it remains a dialectic sting in my pain, which wounds me in many ways, inasmuch as it brings to confusion my life-view, as well in the direction of sympathy as in the direction of deceit. There is something alarming in the thought that a deceit, be it ever so pious and well meant, should have the ascendancy, and there always remains open the possibility that the deceit may acquire an epigrammatic power to satirize. The most poetical act is also the most ethical. On her part it would be the most poetical thing to remain devoted to me or to remain true to herself in her love, and this would also be the most terrible revenge upon me. Every prosaic revenge makes *eo ipso* my responsibility lighter, because it is less ethical.

How consistent existence is! There is nothing true in one sphere which is not true in the other. What a deep responsibility, that the laws of existence are such that everyone must serve them whether he will or no. The Governance which requires placability of every man knows also how to revenge itself, for precisely when the individual would revenge

[141] In his plan for this work S.K. noted: "Nearly all the entries in the last part at midnight shall deal with meeting again in eternity." Cf. *Papirer,* V, B 97 (34).

himself the case becomes easiest for the guilty one; and on the other hand, when the offended man chooses to be placable, Governance lays the emphasis of revenge upon this gentleness. Caesar performed many glorious deeds, but if there were recounted only one single word he is reputed to have said, I should admire him: "Cato deprived me of my most beautiful victory, for I should have forgiven him."[142]

What I demand of existence is that it would let it become clear to me whether I was ensnared in an illusion or loved faithfully, more faithfully perhaps than she. How long I am to hold out is not known. If the age of oracles has long ago vanished, there is yet one thing about which the simplest and the profoundest man when talking of it must talk enigmatically, and that is time. It undoubtedly is the most difficult enigma, and is also to be accounted the profoundest wisdom,[143] to arrange one's life as if today were to be the last one has to live, and at the same time the first in a series of years.

June 19. Morning.

TODAY a year ago. Yet these tears which torture themselves out of her eyes, torture out the possibility of impossibilities from my brain. Even though it be a superfluous ceremony, I cannot help it. So I shout out into the world if anyone were to hear me: "I make my bid, I bid half my life for half a year of happiness with her, I bid it for a fortnight, I bid it for the marriage day—does not the hammer fall?"

No! — But I must to work. He who has a life sentence is employed in labors dangerous to life. So it is also with me and with my labor.

Today there fell from her lips the most remarkable line I have ever heard from any actress. In a sense it was a shot straight at the heart. In target shooting, when a shot falls in the center, the umpire first takes the precaution to ascertain whether it was not an accidental shot, a shot in the air, a shot without aim, a gun which perhaps went off without anybody firing it. She said to me that she really believed I was mad. But then upon examination it proved to be a wild shot; and there is perhaps no word of hers which more plainly proves to me our diversity. Yes, it is true, a melancholy man is in a certain sense mad, but it requires a great deal of dialectic and a great deal of pathos to comprehend this

[142] Plutarch, "Caesar," 54: "I grudge thee thy death, Cato, for thou didst grudge me the chance of saving thee."

[143] Bias, one of the Seven Wise Men of Greece, is said to have recommended, "to measure one's life as though one had both a short time to live and a long time." Diogenes Laertius, I, 87.

madness. One who makes this remark pretty much as one might say of a man ridiculously dressed, "Oh, he's mad," proves *eo ipso* that he has not a trace of a presentiment as to what madness really is. The whole thing was a false alarm. It was a quick-tempered outburst which in its precipitancy didn't know what else to say. And a little quick-tempered she is now and then. She says that I am malicious, not kind. That she said again yesterday. Such a thing is desirable as an incitement to my palaver, which at once seized upon it. "Yes, I see that now. We understand one another. The thing is perfectly simple. Thy declaration is pretty much to this effect: 'So help me God, the undersigned declares, I do indeed feel esteem, do utter and subscribe esteem' . . . or what was it I wanted to say? It was in fact esteem thou dost not feel, I am getting all muddled, in romances the lovers always have esteem—so then what thou wouldst say is, 'I feel no esteem, genuine love cannot be conceived without esteem, therefore' etc. That as thou dost perceive, can be argued in two ways. For when esteem and love combine against a man, then good night, Ole. On the other hand, either by the help of esteem or of love one can get out of the fix quite well. For if one will consider what esteem properly is"—here I was interrupted. She cannot help laughing when I am thoroughly launched upon the sea of galimatias. This comforts me. At bottom she suffers from this less than I who in a desperate way must work her loose.

June 24. Midnight.

Not even what I write here is my inmost meaning. I cannot so far trust myself to paper, although in the writing I see my meaning. Think of what might happen! The paper might get out of my hands, a fire might break out where I dwell and I be left in uncertainty whether it was burned or whether it existed, I might die and so leave it behind me, I might become insane and my inmost thoughts fall into the hands of a stranger, I might become blind and not be able to find it, not know whether I was holding it in my hands without asking another, and not know whether he lied, whether he read what was written there or something else for the sake of inquiring into my affairs.

I can remember it, however, and more swiftly than the briefest fraction of an instant passes. Lessing[144] was wrong after all when he said that the swiftest thing, swifter than sound or light, is the transition from good to bad. For still swifter than that is the *zugleich,* the "at once." Transition itself is a time, but that which is at once is swifter

[144] "D. Faust," Collected Works (Leipzig 1841), Vol. I, pp. 365 *ff*.

than any transition. After all, transition is a determinant of time, but the haste with which that is present which once was and never is forgotten, this haste, in spite of the fact that the thing is present, is the swiftest of all things, for it is so swift that its being gone was only a delusion.

June 20. Morning.

TODAY a year ago.

I bid my whole life for the wedding day; and indeed we are two who bid. No, that we are not, for she is willing to strive but would also have a future. Naturally she must not leave her honor and pride in the lurch. The hammer does not fall.

Day before yesterday the small talk kept on indefatigably as usual. We talked about my discharge, "and that would be the wisest thing she could do, if I might advise. The consequence would be that I should come back like a wet dog." This advice she received with a laconic "Indeed!," to which she added, "No, I don't trust thee over the threshold." I can see from this what a poor opinion she has of me after all, and what a mistaken overestimate she has of the importance of her personal presence. That is lucky. But then, just as the small talk was going on at its best, she burst into tears. He who is in desperate danger always possesses supernatural powers, and therefore my mien remained entirely unchanged. Thereupon she said, "Let me weep, it is a relief." All torture is forbidden by law, but verily this is a dreadful torture. But I must show respect for the argument—only not in such a way that it disturbs me. And there is also a comfort in the fact that I did not shirk the sight of a thing from which ordinarily a man in my position who is about to appear in a despicable rôle would be inclined to excuse himself. Then the small talk got started again, and the whole thing certainly signifies not so much to her as to me.

Not to dare to utter a serious word!—for it would be crazy for me the guilty one to admonish or console. But is it not also crazy for me to sit here and look on? But one good thing about it is that it furnishes her with an incitement, even though it be against her will, to come out with such utterances. When I am away she would hardly do it, and perhaps would feel no impulsion to do it.

Suppose a third person had been a witness of this situation! Suppose that one who never did anything else but write riddles and one who had grown old in guessing riddles were to combine and make a guess which of the two suffers most, upon whom it makes the deepest impression! Tell me then, thou man of wide experience, about a whirlwind which brought existence to confusion—yet I have seen a confusion where it was as if the tumult would not harken to a rower of honest will. Talk about a dead calm which reduced all effort to despair—yet I saw a dead calm where a lover labored and labored and almost became the murderer of his beloved, not for maliciousness, not by accident, but in conformity with his most honest conviction.

June 30. Midnight.

WHAT is my life but a striving after wind? My existence is nothing but *molimina,* useless effort; I cannot return to myself. Whether in time that ever shall come about, I do not know. And if I become free, so that again I can collect myself, I shall have trouble enough in separating from me the heterogeneous, which after all I do not wish to separate. If I become free, then in my close reserve there will still remain the distress that she has become changed.

So it is a mussel lies on the seashore; it opens its shell in search of nutriment, a child sticks a twig into it, so that it cannot shut. Finally the child grows tired of the play and would pull the twig out, but there remains a splinter. And the mussel shuts its shell; but deeply within its shell it suffers and cannot get the splinter out. That there is a splinter, no one can see, for the mussel has shut itself, but that it is there, the mussel knows.

But away with despondency. It is a fraud against her and is essentially foreign to my soul. If the Jewish high priest was forbidden to rend his garments as a sign of mourning, because this was too passionate and strong an expression, so also am I forbidden to be despondent, because it is too apathetic and too weak. But the fact that for an instant I have become despondent shows me that for the first time in my life I have trusted my common sense against her. What it might say to me I have always known, but I have not been willing to hear it. The impression of that meeting has given my common sense the predominance.

Yet sympathy reduces me at last to beggary. I am like that Englishman who got into pecuniary embarrassment although he had a five-hundred-pound note in his hand—but nobody could change it in the village where he was. But should the expression of sympathy be comparable to exchanging a coin of great value and paying it out in small bits? I supposed that sympathy was like that shilling in Fortunatus's purse,[145]

[145] In Tieck's "Fortunat," *Works,* Vol. III, p. 133.

one constantly gives it out whole, and one constantly has the whole left, and if one would convert it into change, the magic vanishes. Behold, this consoles me.

July 2. Morning.

TODAY a year ago. An eyewitness of my situation would say to me, "Thou dost not know what love is, seeing thou dost behave thus." Maybe, but this much I know, that I am acquainted with its pain. Its pleasures I am acquainted with also, but at a distance, at a very great distance. If it were possible, if only it were possible—I should wipe away every tear from her eyes, ah, as schoolchildren do, so that no one shall see that they have wept. Then the pain is forgotten, more than forgotten. Swiftly, by the omnipotence of love, as swift as the growth of the plant which is tended by fairies, she develops, more charming than ever, by her own force, by the burgeoning power of love, and by my breath upon her, and by the word which is whispered in her ear; then I take her upon my arm and rush out with her through the world—so far at least I understand love. But precisely this understanding I have of love might easily make me lose my understanding and go mad. Never in all my life until now have I felt the temptation of suicide. But the anguish of sympathy!—and with that to be the guilty one! This contradiction has just such an effect upon my soul as when in a physical sense a man's joint is twisted out of its natural position. But what would be the use of suicide? Yes, it would prevent her from being mortified, for then she could live on as mine, if she would. But suppose one day she were to get to know it—that would be still more terrible. If she had understanding, she surely would perceive that she never ought to have brought me to this extremity. And so I would have made her guilty. And by such a step I perhaps would have determined her whole life, so that in finite existence she would not seek healing where properly she must seek it.

Spiritually speaking, she does not suffer so much. She is not so much exhausted as she is tired, with a little touch of feeling bored. Humanly speaking, this does not surprise me, for she has no confidant, and I am untiring in nonsense.

The days are numbered. Suppose she were now to fall ill before the last day had come. Suppose that in the delirium of fever she were to betray what was passing between us. Her closest kindred would believe that this was imagination—and I who knew that it was reality! And then when she recovered and we had to begin all over again.

July 3. Midnight.

WHEN shall we see one another again? In eternity. So there is time enough for reaching an understanding. When does eternity begin? What language is spoken there? Or is perhaps none spoken? Might there not be a little interim? It is continually bright daylight in eternity? Might there not be a morning twilight when one would find understanding in intimacy? What is the judgment of eternity? Is the judgment complete before eternity begins? How is eternity represented? Like the wide horizon where one sees nothing. So it is represented in the picture of the grave: the mourner sits in the foreground and says, "He went hence into the beyond." But in the wide horizon I see nothing at all. So neither do I see her. This is impossible! I must see her. Is this no argument? Or is it a better argument, that whether I will or no, I must see her? Suppose she had forgotten me. Can we then see one another? Suppose she had not forgiven me. Then indeed she had not forgotten me. But can we then see each other? Suppose she were standing beside another. When she stands thus in time, I am in the way, and therefore I will withdraw. But if I stood in her way in eternity, whither shall I go away? Is time then stronger than eternity? Has time power to separate us eternally? I supposed that it only had power to make me unhappy in time, but must let me go as soon as I exchange time for eternity and am where she is, for eternally she is with me. If so, what then would time mean? It would mean that we two did not get a chance to see one another yesterday evening; and if she were to get another man, it means that we did not get a chance to see another yesterday evening because she was out somewhere else. And who was at fault? Yes, the fault was mine. But would I or could I now act otherwise than as I did, if it is assumed that the first thing had come about? No! I regret the first. From that moment I acted in accordance with the most honest premeditation and with all my might, as I also did in the first act, until I perceived my error.

But does eternity talk so lightly about guilt? Time at all events does not; it still will go on teaching me what it has taught me, that a life is something more than a yesterday evening. But eternity will also heal all sickness, give the deaf hearing, the blind sight, and the deformed man bodily beauty, and so it will also heal me. What is my sickness? Melancholy. Where is the seat of this sickness? In the power of imagination, and possibility is its nutriment. But eternity takes away the possibility. And was not this sickness hard enough for me to bear in time, that I not only should suffer but become guilty through it? The deformed man has after all only to bear the pain of being deformed, but how dreadful if being deformed made him guilty!

So then, when for me time has come to an end, let my last sigh be to Thee, O God, for my soul's blessedness, the next to the last for her, or let me for the first time be again united with her in the last sigh.

July 6. Midnight.[146]

TODAY I saw her. How strange a chance! A thunder shower obliged me to take refuge in the shop of my old pastry cook, where I had not been since those days of waiting: *erat in eo loco vicinio tonstrina quaedam.*[147] Such a barber shop is the nearest equivalent, said the teacher, to what we know as a coffeehouse. *Eo sedebamus plerumque dum illa rediret.* The shower was soon over, the air mild and inviting, everything refreshed and rejuvenated. If I had not been absorbed in recollections, I scarcely would have stayed so long. The old pastry cook came out to greet me and entered into conversation. Everything combined to benumb my senses. I sat in my old seat and sometimes cast my eye out of the window—then she came walking by. She was walking with another young girl, both engaged in lively conversation, she merry and hale and happy. Was she coming perhaps from her singing, my beloved songstress? Is she taking up her singing again? Is the song merely a different one?

Would that for half a year I might be transformed into a woman in order to understand her nature! The scale I apply is perhaps too great.

It seems like old times, she goes to her singing, she comes away from it, joyful as she used to be. But there is no one waiting for her. Here in the coffeehouse there is in a sense no one, but perhaps elsewhere. After all, one often hears of a girl overcoming pain and falling in love again. And in this case indeed the situation precisely prompts some such course, for in fact I was not her lover but a deceiver. One often hears

[146] We note with surprise that there is no entry for July 5, midnight. We have reason to expect some such story as celebrates every other fifth day. And in fact S.K. designed to deal here with the theme of Abelard and Heloise (*Papirer,* V, B 124, 5). It is strange that he omitted this theme, for he had contrived to transform both of these characters into the likness of himself and Regina: "But some day I must use Abelard. He must be entirely modernized. The conflict in his soul must not be between the authority of the Pope and the Church, and his knowledge, but between sympathy in him which fain would uphold the constituted order. And then Heloise:" philosophically (V, A 177); "Heloise was not only in love with Abelard but doted on him, was proud of his fame, and jealous of his philosophic honor" (V, A 31).

[147] See the entry for January 8.

also that a girl could not live without a man, and it was true, only it turned out to be not that man but another.

Thus we are back in the old situation, with an alteration, and I remain unaltered in it. I can truly say, "I remain," etc., but it is not easy to say what I remain. I assume that she has become another's, but what then do I remain? And yet not thus! I cannot thus let her go! That almost crazy wish to see the relationship reestablished is now resolved into another like it, that if she is to become another's, this other might be her first love. Thus she has not broken with the idea and not lost my esteem. True enough, what does she care about losing my esteem? But she should not think thus, for my view is more considerate of her than is that of any other. Though all the rest of the world has another view, that is merely a signal for battle. But the misfortune is that I know nothing at all about such an earlier love. However, it must be remembered that I was too much absorbed in myself and too much occupied ethically to learn to know about such a thing. So it might be possible. It is a bit of a satire upon me if something of the sort was the case and I remained unaware of it. She did not feel called upon to say anything, and perhaps my reserve influenced her in this way. So it might be possible. Would it were also actual! And if it were actually so, how lucky I did not know it. Perhaps I might have taken the affair too lightly, and the event would not have assumed for me the importance it has assumed.

What do I remain? Yes, that is not easy to say. But in case it were not I myself that had experienced this history, and another were to relate it, I should believe that he was talking about me, so perfectly does it fit my case.

With her I should less than ever be able to talk if she were to become the wife of another. Am I to modify the deceit a little and seek a mutual understanding based on the fact that so does Jack and so does Gill and so do they all? That indeed would be a new untruth, for I am entirely unchanged and it has never occurred to me to think of any other girl.[148] Might I speak with the passion of truth and be satirical against my will? She herself is at fault for a part of the confusion, for she disturbed the erotic by playing false in the religious sphere. She would not rest satisfied with the erotic, with being loved or not loved, and what for her was the logical consequence of this, but she grasped at the religious sanction and became for me in responsibility a gigantic figure. Notoriously it has brought about a war between great powers that a prince sent back a king's daughter; for me my strife was still more ter-

[148] The last two sentences are S.K.'s correction of the printed text. *Papirer,* V, B 122 (5).

rible when I rejected her, for it was God who had betrothed her to me. So I have regarded the case. But the dreadful seriousness transforms the erotic into something almost comic; for, thinking pathetically, I might say that though she had been as ugly as original sin, as ill tempered as the day is long, yet for me she would have had the same significance—but this is speaking entirely unerotically. And whose fault is it that I must speak thus? It is hers who transformed an erotic relationship into a religious.

Only when I am silent can I keep my soul pathetically behind the deceit of the comic, or behind the cover of the pretense that I have long forgotten the whole thing.

July 7. Morning.

TODAY a year ago. Let us see. My philosophy of life was that under my reserve I concealed my melancholy. It was my pride that I was able to do that, it was my determination to keep that up with all my might. I have come to wreck. Upon what? Upon the incompatibility of individual disposition and upon the wedding as a protest in virtue of that. What is it that confounds my life? That to me the maxim becomes meaningless: *ultra posse nemo obligatur*. What is my guilt? That I have ventured upon an undertaking I could not achieve. What is my fault? That I have made a person unhappy. In what way unhappy? In possibility—in such a way that I have a murder upon my conscience in consequence of her utterance and by virtue of possibility. What is my punishment? To endure this consciousness. What is my hope? That a merciful Governance will in actuality make this punishment less by helping her. What does my understanding say about her? That there is not exactly any probability of the worst. What consequence has this for me? None at all. An ethical obligation cannot be discharged by any calculation of probability, but only by assuming the utmost possible limit of responsibility.

* * *

I went to her. I approached her with an unusual appearance of gladness and declared that it was possible to do as she wished. It is easy to explain that so long as one is fighting, even if one is capable of understanding what sympathy enjoins, one can forget this consideration precisely because one is fighting. When one has conquered, sympathy commonly awakens most powerfully. I thought I ought to make trial of this extremest possibility, that maybe she, being moved to sympathy at having conquered, might resolve to give me my freedom. No! she accepted this declaration, but without a word in the direction of sympathy. She even accepted it rather coldly. I am glad of that, for it proves that she is tired of the thing.

I went away. At noon I returned. An absolute resolution bestows calmness, the resolution which has gone through the dialectic of fear makes one unafraid. Coldly and decisively I announced to her that it was over. She wanted to abandon herself to the most vehement expression of passion, but for the first time in my life I spoke in a tone of command. It is dreadful to take that bold step, but it was the only thing. Though she had come near dying before my eyes I should not have been able to alter my resolution. My inflexibility helped her, and what was the rashest undertaking went off in due order. One more effort still she made to move me sympathetically. It was without effect. Finally she begged me to think of her sometimes. Perhaps she meant nothing much by it, but I in my turn meant it seriously.

So it is over. If she chooses to cry, I choose the pain; and one grows tired of crying aloud, perhaps she already is; for me the turn of pain will come and come again.

What does my understanding teach me with respect to her about the use I made of the two months? She will not sorrow dangerously. In part, her passion is not very dialectic in inwardness; in part, no one will be able to provide her with so favorable a situation as she has had—for affrighting me the guilty one, for moving me by her suffering. The concern of a sympathizer cannot give such emphasis to the pain as my presence did. Reflection will not easily get a hold on her, for she has now gone through a considerable course of it. What she herself may hit upon will not be much in comparison with what I already (to the point of disgust) have perfected her in. She will not be able to arouse in herself any sympathy for me, and if there is a little left, it will soon be quenched. It will never occur to her to ask whether she might have something to reproach herself with. Perhaps she will fall ill, as one who has read too strenuously for examination falls ill after the examination is over. Of such a sickness one might die, but from this there follows no certain inference as to the *propter hoc.* — So far as I am concerned, she, by driving me to extremes, has helped me to withdraw my personality as far as possible out of her. If she, tired of the whole affair, were to find herself a new love, not only will I be extraneous to it, but so will be every picture of me, for she has none, at least none which has a trace of truth.

July 7. Midnight.

Lo, now I leave off for this time. My dormant period of repose with reference to her now begins. I have my discharge. The third of January[149] the disquietude begins again. When one is discharged the command is: right face—left about—march! That is a bit satirical, for my misfortune is that I cannot do either right face, left about, or march.[150]

The period of disquietude is the half year, which returns again and again until I become free. It is well that it was not a whole year, for then I should have had a sorrow-year in the sense that one has a church-year—the instant I was through with the old I should have to begin with the new.

An old woman used to say of the watchman when he shouted, "There is a man who is lost." And indeed the man who is lost also shouts. So I in the period of disquietude am a shouter, a man who has lost his way.

My resolution, in faithfulness to her, is to remain faithful to the ideas and to my spiritual existence with all my might, that by experience I might be convinced that it is the spirit which giveth life, that the outward man may perish and the spirit triumph, the creature groan and the spirit exult, that I might become comforted and become joyful in spirit, renouncing all the consolations of finiteness, that I might hold out and not let the magniloquence of words end in the pettiness of deeds, and not make a deposition in high phrases and contradict myself in the deeds of finiteness. I should have been more complete if I could have remained faithful to her, it would have been something greater if my spiritual existence had had the accompaniment in daily life of marriage, and I should have understood life more surely and more easily. This is first in the order of precedence. Next comes what I do. If she were to bleed to death in useless passion, if she were not to be saved by a help which is nearer than I know of, or at least comes near enough when it is needed, then I must so labor that my existence may count for two. If she helps herself in another way, my labor is superfluous.

Suppose there was a book which was already printed and could not be reprinted, and there was no opportunity to make corrections in it, but in the list of *errata* there stood a phrase which surpassed in significance what stood instead of it in the text—it might be satisfied to stand among the *errata*, but to stand there with its great significance. Suppose there was a weed which was separated from the useful plants, so it stood in

149 Note that this was the date of the first entry.

150 In his youth S.K. entered the Royal Guard, and after a few days was discharged as unfit for military service.

fact apart, was in fact a weed, was in fact ashamed—but suppose its name was *Der stolze Heinerich.*

Here ends the diary for this time. It deals with nothing. But not in the same sense as the diary of Louis XVI, the alternating contents of which are said to have been: one day, "At the chase"; the second day, "*Rien*"; the third day, "At the chase." It contains nothing; but if, as Cicero says, the easiest letter is the one which deals with nothing, it is sometimes the hardest life which deals with nothing.

EPISTLE TO THE READER

from

Frater Taciturnus

My dear Reader,

In case thou hast any technical competence, thou wilt instantly perceive that the figure which here is conjured up is demoniac in a religious direction, i.e. with an approach to it. How honestly, how copiously indeed, he does his part by talking to enable thee to see him (*loquere ut videam*), no one knows better than I, who often exhausted, often bored, have been tempted to let him alone and lose patience, which means the same thing—whence also, by observing the stars and reading the future in coffee grounds, by virtue of my inspiration as a scald and my falcon eye, I make public the peerless prediction that of the few readers of the book two-thirds will fall away before they are half way through, which may also be expressed in this wise, that they will stop there and throw away the book for boredom.

Inasmuch as he stands upon the extremest dialectic pinnacle, one must be capable of reckoning with infinitesimal quantities if one would make observations upon him. No one for a round sum (be it never so great, if only it is round) can purchase entrée to his dialectic performances, and hence in such case one would do well not to consider it worth the trouble to make observations upon a manikin like this. And yet for all that there may be some significance in observing him, because in aberrations one can make a study of the normal, and always can learn this much, if nothing else, that religion is not a thing to be poohpoohed, or something for stupid people and unshaven striplings, seeing that it is the most difficult of all things, although absolutely accessible to all—which in itself is a difficulty for the understanding, like the contradiction that the same water at the same place is so shallow that a sheep can wade it, and so deep that an elephant can swim.

The girl I have represented quite generically (as a special characteristic I have only let her lack religious presuppositions), and this I have done intentionally, in order that she might the better illuminate him and teach him to exert himself. It would require frightful exertions, it might perhaps even be impossible, to lift a small object with a jackscrew, or with a ship's derrick to hoist half a pound—and so I have reflected that if it were to come to a misunderstanding, it should be a thorough one.

However, the erotic and the erotic relationship is of minor concern to me. Essentially I employ it for orientation in the religious sphere, in order that one may not get all mixed up and suppose that religion is the first immediacy,[1] a bit of one thing and another: instinct and natural impulse and youthfulness in which, by the addition of a little dose of spirit, fermentation has begun. — The girl is what one rightly calls a nice girl.[2] In novels and in the drama, and that properly only in the fifth act, "such a girl" makes a man happy; in the fifth act of reality she does the best she can for him; in the psychological experiment she is unable to make him happy, not because she cannot do it (for she can), but because she cannot get to that point—hence they make one another un-

[1] Four years later S.K. formulated clearly the thought that "faith is a second immediacy," "immediacy after reflection." *Papirer,* VIII, A 649, 650.

[2] [The following footnote is by Frater Taciturnus.]

The female figure is indicated of course merely by the general lines of its contour: a very young and lovable girl within the aesthetic circumference of naïveté. Here I give a sketch of her, for otherwise she would not be presented in her entirety. I have him constantly *in mente,* yet with due regard to the psychological probability that, in spite of his influence, she will not get beyond the limits of aesthetic naïveté. *In the period of the engagement* she is at first reserved. His singular character and unerotic demeanor must surely make a strange impression upon a young girl, she gets tired of it, she turns up her nose at it and "puts the chair outside the door" for him. Then comes a little incident, and she is softened; she puts the chair forward and begs him to sit down, while she performs the prettiest little roguish genuflection with the utmost charm. He is a sorrowful hero as lover and cannot understand it, in no situation does he so much resemble the immortal knight of the sorrowful countenance as when thus seated. Now he wants to leave her, she adjures him by God and by everything holy that in her distress she can think of, she brings a note to him herself, she has no notion there might be anything out of the way in that. She displays all her lovable sympathy, which was ready to content itself with any conditions, and this lovable sympathy is the resignation of naïveté. In on other way is she able to express herself, and even if one were to require illogically a trace of the resignation of reflection, his deception and his desperate behavior in carrying it out absolutely prevent the genesis or the expression of any reflective sympathy. Thus she is lovable through and through, yet with only so much elasticity, if one were to measure it, that the psychological probability of a new love is posited, although psychologically the pattern of it might be variously conceived.—*After the period of the engagement* she does nothing at all. Even when the psychological probability points most dangerously at him, as on the occasion of the meeting in church, it is not posited as a reality (but at the same time it is far from being a psychological impossibility), for his passion perceives everything, in this instance in spite of the distance. But even if he saw aright, the whole thing would have been a little whim of hers, perhaps a little kindness, perhaps because it then occurred to her that she had been too severe with him, a little whim *ad modum* that genuflection above mentioned. But he who had undertaken in relation to her to want to abolish fate and chance has naturally qualified himself to be constantly led by the nose, just as he was by several utterances about her future [i.e. that she would die, etc.], which he to his own misfortune drew out of her, and by which she did not mean a great deal when she uttered them, whereas he feels eternally bound in rehearsing them to think of everything they imply.

happy. By equipping her differently I should merely have prevented my chief character from being adequately illuminated. By her lovableness she did him considerable service, more than any maid-of-all-work could, and that in itself is saying a good deal for a generic girl in a psychological experiment, for there she is out of place.

As a lover, the male figure would hardly get on in the world. His attitudes and his fidelity are so grandiose, so unpractical, and so awkward, that one might be tempted to ask in the words of a French writer, I think it is,[3] whether he became mad because he was faithful to the girl, or whether he was faithful to the girl because he was mad; for as a lover he is mad. If he really existed, and if I were capable of bestowing flesh and blood upon the figure in the experiment, if he lived in our time and with his introversion manifested in his external appearance and not disguised by deceit, it would be a comedy complete. How droll it would be to see such an owl, troglodyte, cave-dweller, come sneaking out, after listening to men's romantic talk, and lay claim to be an unhappy lover of the first rank! He would have the street urchins following him, that is perfectly certain. Such an anachronism in the nineteenth century!—when everybody knows that the unhappy lovers are like those serpents with seven heads which Lineus proved to be nonexistent,[4] a mere cobweb of the brain. To take seriously all that which everybody knows about loving only once, making one another happy; and to act in virtue of it with the utmost expenditure of exertion, in such a way as only in a very young man might be pardonable, and that only for half a day; to work oneself to death in such an empty ceremonious service which aims at introducing ways and customs which are entirely antiquated—that indeed would be rich material for laughter. It is a matter of course that just as one learns languages in one's childhood, so also in one's youth one lays up provision for a whole lifetime, including a little store of pretty phrases and exalted turns of expression wherewith one serves oneself and others throughout life and is sociable in friendship and friendly in society and constantly friendly. That the phrase lasts through a whole life is quite natural, all the more because it performs a rather various service, is rather fantastically dressed up for youth in its happiest day, is a pleasantry when mamma says it, a witticism in the mouth

[3] In reality it was Börne, *Gesammelte Schriften,* Vol. I, p. 77: "Braucht man ein Pariser zu sein um zu fragen: hat Herr Ulrich den Verstand verloren, weil er seine Frau so treu liebt, oder hat er sie so treu geliebt *weil* er den Verstand verloren?"

[4] *Systema naturae* (12th ed., 1776), Vol. I, 1, p. 358. Lineus mentions among fabulous "dracones" a "hydra" which an earlier author had seen in Hamburg and describes as *"non naturae sed artis opus eximiam."*

of the old man; but that love has the same imperishable quality (not to speak of an unhappy love) betrays a negligent upbringing; I at least would say with Pernille,[5] "I give thanks in my grave to my parents that I was differently brought up." Who indeed in these days would buy, as they did in the old days, one umbrella for a lifetime, or a silk dress, a thoroughly good piece one can wear as long as one lives, or a serviceable cloak for eternity? One may willingly admit that the quality perhaps is not what it was in the case of that Chinese satin, one may willingly admit that the owner does not treat her clothes with the care which was shown for that Chinese satin, but the advantage of being able to procure the dress three or four times over, and the advantage of being able to treat one's clothes negligently, is after all very obvious. This wisdom must not be regarded as peculiar to elect individuals, fortunately (to the glory of our century) it is common among men. Hence, as rarely as one sees a cloak of Chinese satin, just so rarely does one see an unhappy lover. And then for this man to want to be an unhappy lover (although perhaps he isn't), to stake his honor upon it in fact, that is simply in sheer madness to want to take the world by the nose; the only insanity higher than this would then be that he supposed he was not the only one, but that there was a whole tribe of such people. Don Quixote believed, as is well known, that he was a knight errant. But this was not by any means the culmination of his madness. Cervantes is more profound. When Don Quixote was cured of his illness, and the Licentiate already began to hope for the recovery of his reason, he wanted to test him a bit. He talks to him about various things and suddenly intermingles with them the news that the Moors have invaded Spain. "Then," said Don Quixote, "there is only one way of saving Spain." "What is that?" asked the Licentiate. Don Quixote will not tell him, only to His Catholic Majesty the King of Spain will he reveal his secret. Finally Don Quixote yields to the Licentiate's prayer, and he under oath of silence and with the gravity of a father-confessor receives the confession of the renowned knight: "The only way is for His Catholic Majesty to issue a summons to all knights errant." To be oneself a knight errant is, if one will, the act of a semi-lunatic, but to populate the whole of Spain with knights errant is verily *delirium furibundum*. In this respect my hero is more reasonable, for he has so understood the age that he remains the only knight of unhappy love.

The erotic, as was said, is of minor concern to me. I have used it as Constantine Constantius attempted to do in a work entitled "Repetition"

[5] Holberg, *Jacob von Tyboe*, Act III, Scene 2.

(Copenhagen, 1844), but he without success because he remained within the aesthetic. The collision that through a girl a man becomes a poet and therefore cannot become her husband lies within the aesthetic. The collision is one which can arouse concern only in a young man, and I do not understand why Constantine concealed from the young man what every practitioner knows, that the collision can be resolved without the least difficulty: he marries her, and so does not become a poet. That in fact is what he fears, he does exactly the opposite, and thereby perhaps become a poet. If not every girl can make a man a poet, it is certain that every female can prevent a man from becoming such if he marries her. That I vouch for—and especially and best of all the girl who was by way of making him a poet. For the poet's intercourse with the muse is exceedingly different from the marriage relationship, and muses, as well as whatever other fanciful beings are associated with them, do well to keep themselves at a distance; and as there is nothing so embarrassing for a being having flesh and blood as to be a muse, the object of adoration will do everything to prevent him from becoming a poet, and second every attempt on his part to become a real husband. This whole collision is the sort of thing that might have been invented by my hero, something he had happened to think of to show civility to the girl. With this it is not my intention to disparage the young man, for in his youthfulness he might have had the best of intentions. My hero on the other hand could not entertain such a fancy, he was far too much developed for that. All the better, i.e. all the more strongly, does the misunderstanding reveal itself.

Fortunately my hero does not exist outside of my thought-experiment. He cannot be exposed to ridicule in real life. This in itself is fortunate enough, but still more fortunate it is for me that it cannot be my task to dispute with him or to dialecticize him out of his dialectic difficulty. Such a person as he in actual existence would be a handful for a *doctor seraphicus* and a *doctor contradictionum* combined into one, and in the end they would perhaps be unable to accomplish anything. Whatever they might hit upon, he would answer, "I have thought of that myself; now you have only to listen"—and with that he would develop the dialectic objection until little by little he had brought out of it a variation in his favor. Neither would it be of any use to affright him with pathos, for he is also man enough to give expression to the most opposite pathetic point of view.

It is therefore by no means my purpose in what I have written to convince him, but to remark upon something true in him and in much that he says. I let him pass for what he is, an enthusiast, and an enthusiast of a peculiar sort—not only for the reason that he arrives a few centuries too late. It has been well said by Börne[6] that "the individual enthusiasts are related to one another like the sharers in a tontine insurance policy—in proportion as they die off, the share of the survivors is greater." What wonder then that as an enthusiast he is uncommonly enthusiastic, since the whole capital with accrued and compound interest fall to him. Yet it is not only in this degree he is an enthusiast of a peculiar sort, but also for the fact that he is not an enthusiast in the form of immediacy but in the form of deceit, under which he lives freely in his enthusiasm. This is a new expression for the degree of his enthusiasm, and it proves that his is the highest sort. An immediate enthusiast (and to this class belong substantially all known examples) will either press on jubilantly through all human opposition and plant the banner of victory, or he will weigh upon existence by his suffering, i.e. in spite of all his enthusiasm the enthusiast cannot get along without the world. My hero has no desire for this. On the contrary, he would conceal his enthusiasm by an exterior the very opposite to it, and is so sure of his cause that he does not even have a mind to utter it, or, as he thinks, does not dare to.

I let him pass for what he is, and I go on to the matter I am concerned with. I will discuss it by directing attention to definite points, and in this I always have him *in mente*.

§ 1.

WHAT IS UNHAPPY LOVE, AND WHAT IS THE VARIANT FORM OF IT IN THIS EXPERIMENT?

In unhappy love poetry has from immemorial times possessed a foil for its happy love. If, as someone has said, it was a mother at the sick-bed of her child who invented prayer, which indeed is precisely apt for such a sufferer, so one might almost suppose that unhappy love was the invention of poetry. But then it is only fair that poetry should come to the aid of unhappy love, and it is not asking too much to expect that it would do so willingly.

Now it is characteristic of unhappy love that, love being assumed, there is a power which prevents it from expressing itself happily by the union of the lovers. Nothing is easier said than this, but from this trivial statement the distance is as long as the diameter of the earth's orbit to being a poet who fills this nothing by his divine pathos and his creative breath. Without pathos no poet. Pathos is primary, but the next thing,

[6] *Gesammelte Schriften*, Vol. III, pp. 241 *ff*.

standing in an essential and absolute relation to that, is to excogitate a profound opposition. If one were to enumerate all the obstacles to love's happiness, there would be, as on the scale of a thermometer, a plus and minus series. Beginning with the insignificant obstacles, one would reach a point where the change occurred and everything became different. For one can think of obstacles of such a sort that one might say "The task of love is to overcome them." If a poet makes choice of such obstacles as constituting unhappy love, he is no poet, but is a satirist against his will. So then it must not be in the lover's power to remove the obstacle.

So the case stands, or rather, so it remained standing many years ago. Our later age has the general fault of limping on both sides: neither believing in love as an absolute passion, nor choosing obstacles of prime quality. People offer to compound with the creditors, and they agree to it—and the article "unhappy love" drops out of circulation, and instead of it there remains "tolerably happy love," there remains equality and *eins Bier* for everybody.

Poetry deals with immediacy and cannot therefore think an ambiguous situation. If for a single instant it is put in doubt whether the lovers are solvent *qua* lovers, are absolutely ready within themselves for the union of love—a single doubt of this sort, and with that poetry turns away from the guilty one and says, "To me this is an indication that thou dost not love, hence I cannot have anything to do with thee." And in this poetry does well, if it would not become a ludicrous power, as in these latter times it often enough has been through a mistaken choice of its task.

Without passion no poet, and without passion no poetry. If then one is to press out beyond the limitations of poetry, and if this exodus is not to mean that one is lost in common sense and pitiableness, it must come about by virtue of a higher passion. To take passion away from poetry and make up for this loss by decoration, charming rural scenery, much acclaimed sylvan picnics, enchanting theatrical moonlight, is perdition, just as it is to make up for the worthlessness of a book by the elegance of the binding, which properly is of no interest to readers, but at the most to bookbinders. To take away passion from the lines of a play, and to make up for that by letting the orchestra scrape a little, is a prostitution of poetry and is comic, just as though in real life a lover, instead of having pathos in his breast, were at the decisive moment to have a music box in his pocket.

Only when to the passion of poetry there is added a higher passion have we the ambiguous situation of which we are speaking here. The task then becomes dialectic in itself, and this never can or should be the task of poetry. It is true that unhappy love, for example, has its dialectic, but it does not have it in itself but outside itself. That which in itself is dialectic contains the contradiction within itself. On the other hand, the task of the poet is simple, because the contradiction comes from without. Left to himself, the unhappy lover must be happy. To the poet this is a certainty, but the misfortune is that outside there is a power which would hinder it. In poetry therefore love does not relate itself to itself but to the world, and this relationship determines whether it is to become unhappy. As soon therefore as the sonorous note of passion ceases to sound from a single source, as soon as there is conflict in passion itself, yea, even if a higher passion announces its presence by a new sonorous note, as soon as one senses in it the concurrent sound of ambiguity, the poet can no longer deal with it. If the passion is love, this must be undialectic in itself if poetry is to see in the man an unhappy lover. If the passion is patriotism, this must be undialectic in itself, and if the hero sacrifices an erotic relationship by virtue of his patriotic passion, he is not called an unhappy lover, but is named after the passion which is undialectic in him. Thus the patriotic hero in his enthusiasm for his fatherland does not relate himself to himself but to the world about him, including a relationship of love and a relationship of patriotic piety. Thus it is that poetry must understand it. The aesthetic hero must have his opposition outside himself, not within himself. The fact that this is not the case with Hamlet is perhaps precisely the trouble with him. But of this more hereafter.

To return to unhappy love. If one will observe the outstanding figures among those unhappy ones, the men and women whom song and legend have rewarded with renown, one will at once perceive that the passion is immediate and the opposition is from without—pretty much as the priest in pronouncing the banns of betrothal thinks only of external impediments why they may not lawfully be joined together, for he too does not reflect that in the lover's own passion there might be a contradiction, for in that case he might like the poet feel prompted by a poetic vocation to say of the guilty one that he does not love. Petrarch sees Laura united to another; Abelard does not feel separated from Heloise by his clerical order (for love is the absolute passion), he is separated by Fulbert's wrath, and, alas, by his cruelty; Romeo does not feel the family hatred as the separating factor, as if through filial piety towards his father it became active in him, it is the family feud which objectively separates him from Juliet; Axel feels no scruple of conscience on account of the close kinship, and Valborg understands only that they love one another, it is the Church which separates them by its external power. Take away the impediments, and those lovers would have been the happiest of all lovers.

In our time unhappy love makes a sorry figure. One sees Romeo and Juliet but does not know quite what to make of it, at the most it is the gallery that really weeps, and moreover it is to Shakespeare rather than to Romeo and Juliet one sacrifices a tear, and at the theater one feels oneself in an almost painful situation. This is due quite simply to the fact that love, like all passion, has for the existing generation become dialectic. One cannot comprehend such an immediate passion, and even the grocer's apprentice could tell Romeo and Juliet astounding truths. It might seem then as if this inconvenience could be obviated by introducing the modern apprehension into the play and bringing it to consciousness, so that the public would not feel entirely foreign in the theater but would recognize itself at least in the grocer's apprentice. The misfortune is that this would be of no avail, for in that case the apprentice, a jejune philosopher, a director of sanitation, or whatever other representative of common sense one would cite, must come off victorious. For the seamy side of the matter is that this is precisely the truth. If this were to occur, Romeo and Juliet would not only seem foreign to the spectators, but they would lose all esteem in their eyes as stiff-necked persons whose death was not tragic but well merited for contumacy against reason. Shakespeare, it is true, has opposite points of view represented in his drama, but his definite pathos makes him just as secure in dealing with them as Romeo and Juliet were undialectic in their passion.

So when men disdain poetry and yet have no higher passion, what consequence may follow from that? Naturally, that one runs wild in half-thoughts and is beatified by conceit and self-delusion, and becomes the most boastful but not the most judicious, the generation which above every other is full of promises and lies[7]—a thing which could easily be proved a priori. Whereas now one almost never hears tell of an unhappy lover, there is all the more competition in the claim to have been such a thing, to have suffered—even more than once—what those unhappy ones suffered, but also to have overcome these sufferings, etc., etc., etc. Poetry can make no use of such people; it demands an essential expression for what one essentially has suffered, and is not satisfied with the asseverations of a few female friends that they had witnessed her sufferings, nor with the testimony of a clergyman, even if he had a

[7] These are the speculative philosophers, who promise so much and perform so little. The choice of words to describe them is obviously determined by the ear: *den skydesomste men ikke den skjødsomste, den lovende og lyvende Slægt.*

speculative eye and had gone through the requisite development. Oh, tempting fruits for a comic poet! And if some day he comes, my only concern is lest he himself, enchanted by the sight of the inexhaustible theme, might die of laughing, and so be prevented from accomplishing anything. Precisely a poet would be an apt figure for the leading rôle in such a comedy, precisely Scribe, e.g., is comic in spite of his perhaps peerless talent, and comic for the fact that he has not understood himself, that he would be a *poet,* and yet has forgotten that poetry and passion are inseparable, and comic for having satisfied the age as a *poet* —the whole thing is comic in the sense of Aristophanes. Scribe's entire existence is a contradiction like that which is so often found in his plays. I will take for example *La Cameraderie,* his drawing-room piece, the masterly effect of which one cannot sufficiently admire. Here is described the base accord among a lot of ugly customers who in all sorts of despicable ways know how to push themselves forward by their effrontery; but a young advocate despises these ways, he therefore becomes the object of ill-natured and lying persecution—what comes of it? A young lady is so good as to take an interest in him, she is not unpracticed in intrigue, she succeeds completely, and the advocate comes to honor and high estate. So the result is that one coterie triumphs over the other, one intrigue gets the better of the other. Just as the rubric "unhappy love" went out of use, and instead of two opposites we got one single sort, "the tolerably happy love," so too has the opposition, honesty/dishonesty, virtue/baseness, gone out of use, and we get one sort, the tolerably honest, or the pretty nearly honest.

Now that love itself has become dialectic, poetry must give it up; for the fact that it has become dialectic signifies: first, that the poet cannot get at his task, cannot get to the point of beginning, because the introduction is such that the issue is critical; second, because there is no assurance whatever that the issue will be happy if only all outward obstacles are cleared away; and finally, because in case of death there is no assurance whatever that it is a heroic death for love's sake and for passion, since he dies perhaps of a fever incurred from catching cold.

If then the fact is brought to consciousness that love has been given up as an absolute passion, poetry must give it up, and where the carcass is, there will the vultures be gathered together—here in the form of novelists, feuilleton writers, hermaphroditic tragi-comic poets who do not definitely know whether they want to be authors of tragedy or comedy and hence are neither the one nor the other, for without passion no poet, not even a comic poet. If poetry is to continue to exist, it must discover another passion which is just as legitimate a subject of poetry as love was. It would not be difficult to show that no such substitute exists because of the peculiar synthesis of the erotic. However, I will not develop this theme here, but neither will I require any man to believe that I can do it, seeing that I do not do it. Yet there are also other passions which in the eyes of poetry are legitimate. But the same thing which weakens men's faith in love, namely, a lack of a sense for the infinite, will also weaken faith in the other passions. Forsaken then by poetry men will work their way down in finiteness till they get to politics in the bad sense. If politics is conceived with the passion of infinity, it will of course be able to furnish heroes such as there were in old times when people also believed in love. In the world of infinity it holds good that he who offends in one thing offends in all; for he who has a sense for infinity has a sense for every infinity. The same reflection which has demolished love will also demolish the infinite passion of politics. The heroic man in such an age is the man who wants to labor for a finite aim, is ready, he says, to sacrifice his life for it, perhaps through an inadvertence actually comes to that, and through a new inadvertence is canonized as a hero. Such a figure, however, is quite unserviceable for poetry (unless he were to be used as the sausage maker is used by Aristophanes), he is unpoetic and contradicts himself. It is quite consistent of politics that in our day it does not prompt its votaries to enthusiasm for sacrifice, since it prompts no enthusiasm at all. With enthusiasm the sacrifices would come of themselves. It is a contradiction to sacrifice one's life for a finite aim, and such conduct is in the eyes of poetry pure comedy, just as it is to dance oneself to death, or to want to walk with spurs when one is bow-legged and trip over them and depart this life—rather than give up wearing spurs. Oh, tempting theme for a comic poet! He shall not lack material, for politics does not lack servitors. An apt figure for the principal rôle might be a politician who in spite of all his shrewdness wants to be enthusiastic, wants to be a sacrifice, but is not willing to sacrifice himself, not willing to fall, but would himself be witness to the applause, and hence cannot get to the point of falling, and perhaps in the last resort is the only man who stands in his way—an enthusiast who has no inkling of what enthusiasm is. His pathos would culminate in this sentence, which inconceivably enough was not long ago posted in a public place: "I would sacrifice my life, no one shall say that I do not possess heroic courage, but this blind courage is not the highest, therefore I restrain myself"—and continue to live; therefore I restrain myself and let another less important person fall in my stead. *Plaudite.* It is natural that a shrewd politician is shrewd enough to perceive (what is hidden from simpler minds) how important his life is for the state, that if he lives long no one will come to want; but enthusiasm this is not. All enthusiasm is a consequence of the passion of infinity, where this great man and that for all their shrewdness vanish as a thing of naught. God help poetry! By the aid of politics it is put on a diet of bread and water. Already Aristotle has divided men into θεόλογοι, φιλόσοφοι, πολίτικοι. Politicians come last—not to speak of the politicians of finiteness, who renounce the passion of infinity, they come last of all, or rather trailing on behind—that always makes pretty thin beer. There is no enthusiasm in believing in oneself, still less in believing in one's bit of shopkeeper-shrewdness; all enthusiasm is a consequence either of faith in one's passion or, more deeply, of faith in a providence which teaches one that even the death of the greatest man is a mere jest for a providence which has legions of angels in reserve, and that therefore he shall walk resolutely to his death, leaving his good cause to providence and his posthumous fame to the poet. As one rarely sees an unhappy lover in our time, so it is just as rare to see a martyr in the world of politics; but on the other hand there is a general competition about, "The devil take me if I'm not willing to be that, yes, to have been that, if one did not perceive that it is greater," etc.; and politics has innumerable hosts of titular heroes and volunteer martyrs, not under arms but *inter pocula.* They all have that magnanimous willingness for heroic death, but with an equally heroic wisdom have perceived "that it would be better on the whole, for the community; that one owes it to mankind to live . . . and carouse." There is still one step left, and that is a veritable *ne plus ultra*—this is when such a life-assuring generation of parlor-politicians conceives that it is an injustice on the part of poetry not to choose its heroes among the worthy contemporaries. But it does poetry an injustice, or rather, it had better not stir it up too far, lest the thing end with its taking by the collar the first sausage maker that comes to hand and making him a hero *à la* Aristophanes. In no other way can poetry show its enthusiasm for swearing and bluffing at the card table.

So it seems as though the age of poetry were past, and especially tragedy. A comic poet will lack a public, since not even the public can be in two places at once—on the stage and in the audience. Moreover the comic poet has his stronghold in a pathos which lies outside the play, and he proves by his existence that the age of poetry is past. He who would set his hope upon a speculative drama serves poetry only in so far as he serves comedy. If a wizard or a sorcerer were to bring such a thing to pass, if by the support of a thaumaturge (for a dramaturge would not suffice) it were to satisfy the requirement of the age as a *poetic* work, this event would indeed be a good motif for a comedy, though it would attain the comic effect through the medium of so many presuppositions that it would not become popular.

That the age of poetry is past signifies essentially that immediacy is no more. Immediacy is not entirely devoid of reflection; as poetry conceives it, it has a relative reflection by having its opposition outside itself. But only then is immediacy really at an end when the immediate infinity shall be grasped by an equally infinite reflection. That very instant all tasks are transformed and made dialectic in themselves; no immediacy is permitted to stand by itself or exposed merely to strife with another power, but must strive with itself.

To return to the subject of love. When love is not secure in itself, this means that it is not simply a given fact, as in poetry, having its obstacles outside itself, but finds its obstacle within itself. There thus presents itself a task which every poet must discard, but which nevertheless is very important. It is a problem which can be conceived in various ways, and one of these I have chosen in my psychological experiment. There love is assumed, no obstacle is to be seen, on the contrary there is peace and security, a dead calm favors it. But in the fact that it has to be introduced into the infinite reflection it stumbles upon difficulties. Thus the difficulties do not arise from collision with the world, but from the fact that love has to reflect itself in the individuality. The problem is so dialectic that the fact of love encountering in itself a stumbling block may tempt one to affirm that it is not love. In fact, if this is not a religious collision, the problem has no existence whatever except as prattle; for poetry is glorious, religion still more glorious, but what lies between them is prattle, no matter what talent is wasted upon it.

Love then encounters a stumbling block, or so it seems to the individual, and he says to himself that his is an unhappy love. I express myself very dubitatively and do not for my part possess the passion of my knight but am trying to understand him. The poet would now ask him, "What is the obstacle, is it cruel parents who must be mollified, is it a family feud which must be conciliated, is it a papal dispensation which must be obtained, another man who must be done away with, or (alas, I have reason to feel sorry for myself and for my poverty) is it a mite I must throw to thee, art thou in need of money in order to be happy? Very well (unless thou dost prefer to be in one of the first four cases), I will make thee unhappy but a hero. The man in question answers, "No." Then the poet turns away and says, "Well, my dear friend, then thou art not in love." Poetry is willing to do everything for love, willing to beautify the happy, willing to chant the praises of the unhappy, but in its amiable naïveté it must know one thing surely, namely, love, lest when it has done everything, it might suddenly discover that was all in vain, because there were other obstacles.

In order to hold the problem fast one must continually perform double-movements.[8] No one who is unable to do that can see the problem at all, and good luck to him if he has not also lost his pleasure in poetry. But if a man can do it, then he knows also that the infinite reflection is not something heterogeneous to him but is the transparency of immediacy to itself.

If it be assumed that love has happily passed through the infinite reflection, then there is something else, there is religion; if it comes to grief by the way, it comes to grief upon the religious. Perhaps this may not be perceived at once, because often enough under the name of infinite reflection one thinks of finite reflection. In comparison with every finite reflection immediacy is essentially the higher, and it feels offended at the assumption that it has to deal with such a thing. The poet understands this very well, and for this reason the obstacles come from without, and tragedy consists precisely in the fact that such obstacles as these have in a sense the power to triumph over the infinity of immediacy; and only Philistines and hermaphrodite poets think otherwise. But an infinite reflection is infinitely higher than immediacy, and in it immediacy relates itself to itself in the idea. But this phrase, "in the idea," denotes a God-relationship in the widest circumference, and within this circumference there is a multiplicity of more definite determinants.

In immediacy there is the idea, the poet in fact sees it, but it does not exist for his hero, or he in his relation to it is not related to himself. Precisely on this account he is not free in his passion. Freedom indeed does not mean that he is to give up his passion, but freedom means that he uses the passion of infinity whereby he might give it up in order to hold it fast. Such a thought the poetic hero is quite unable to think, and the poet does not allow him to think it, for that very instant he ceases to be a poetic figure.

So in the infinite reflection freedom is won—a freedom which may be affirmative of love or negative. In my experiment I have chosen protestation against the immediate passion of love, and with this the double-movement is clearly visible. At one and the same time he is holding fast to his love, encounters no opposition from without, where

[8] This word had already been used in *Fear and Trembling* and was to crop up again in the *Postscript*.

on the contrary everything smiles favorably and threatens to be transformed into horror if he does not follow his wish, threatens him with certain loss of honor, with the death of the loved one—so at one and the same time he is holding fast to his love, and yet in spite of all that he will not, he cannot realize it.

The situation is so dialectic that one must not be in too much of a hurry, for that would only produce confusion. But if it is true that the time of immediacy is past, then the thing is to win the religious, nothing intermediate is of any avail. And for the man of whom it is true that the time of immediacy is past the most difficult dialectic movement will be popular, though I am very willing to concede that in any other case my experiment is far from being of a popular character. People generally believe that what makes a presentation of thought unpopular are the many technical terms of scientific phraseology. That however is an entirely extrinsic sort of unpopularity, which scientific speakers have in common, e.g. with sea-captains, who also are unpopular because they speak a jargon, and by no means because they speak profoundly. Therefore time and again the phraseology of a philosophy may penetrate even to the common man, proving that its unpopularity was only extrinsic. A "systematic" handicraftsman may be unpopular, but he is not intrinsically unpopular, because he does not attach much thought to the exceedingly strange things he says (and, alas, this is a very popular art); Socrates, on the other hand, was the most unpopular man in Greece, precisely because he said the same thing as the simplest man, but attached infinite thought to it. To hold on persistently to one thought, to hold on to it with ethical passion and intrepidity of spirit, to see the essential duplicity of this one thought without loss of equanimity, and at one and the same time to see in it the deepest seriousness and the highest jest, the deepest tragedy and the highest comedy, that at all times is unpopular for everyone who has not comprehended that the time of immediacy is past. But what is intrinsically unpopular is not a subject to be learned by rote. But of this more hereafter.

So this is the problem I have propounded to myself: a story of unhappy love where love is dialectic in itself and in the crisis of the infinite reflection acquires a religious aspect. One easily sees that this presents a different problem from that of any other type of unhappy love; one sees this easily when one sees both of the contrasted sides, otherwise one sees perhaps neither of them.

§ 2.

MISUNDERSTANDING EMPLOYED IN THIS EXPERIMENT AS THE TRAGIC AND COMI-TRAGIC PRINCIPLE.

When Claudius says[9] that misunderstanding is essentially due to the fact people do not understand one another, in this naïve humor which simulates immediacy, there lie hidden the distinctions which on being educed characterize the tragic and the comic; and hence this naïve pronouncement takes on a different significance according as one or the other of these opposite passions gives emphasis to it. The tautology in this saying may be an incitement to the comic as well as to the tragic passion. In itself, however, the saying is simply humorous. So Socrates might well have said ironically in the indeterminate situation of a colloquy, "By the gods, it is very strange, dear Polos, that we do not understand one another; there must be some misunderstanding." An enthusiast would exclaim tragically, "Oh, misunderstanding! Oh, that we are not able to understand one another!" Viewed from the uniting point of the comic and the tragic the saying would not be humorous but profound. That is to say, a misunderstanding being posited between two people, they will not be able so long as they misunderstand one another to allege any other ground for it but misunderstanding. If the ground of misunderstanding is given, the *discrimen* of the misunderstanding is resolved. Hence the two might well continue to misunderstand one another, but yet understand one another fundamentally.

Now misunderstanding exists wherever the heterogeneous is brought together, but observe that it must be a heterogeneity such as does not exclude a relationship, for otherwise there is no misunderstanding. It can therefore be said that at the bottom of misunderstanding lies an understanding, i.e. a possibility of understanding. If impossibility is present, misunderstanding is not. But along with the possibility there is misunderstanding, and dialectically seen it is both comic and tragic.

Poetry cannot deal with this duality; it must employ misunderstanding either comically or tragically. To this extent it is justified in putting the ground of misunderstanding in an external factor with the removal of which the parties to the misunderstanding understand one another. For if the misunderstanding is implicit in the very relationship of the heterogeneous parties to one another, the relationship is dialectic, and the misunderstanding is just as comic as it is tragic. On the other hand, when it is an external factor which separates the two in misunderstand-

[9] *Sämmtliche Werke des Wandsbecker Bothen,* Vol. III, p. 91: "Die Missverständnisse in der Welt kommen gewöhnlich daher, dass einer den andern nicht versteht."

ing, these two, essentially conceived, are not persons who misunderstand but who understand, as one sees when the external factor is removed.

Not to multiply examples and comparisons, I remark merely that when poetry employs misunderstanding in connection with an unhappy love it places the misunderstanding in a fatal event, a mysterious occurrence, a wicked or foolish individual who by his interference puts misunderstanding between the two. Poetry must know that it is thoroughly assured of the possibility of real understanding, for otherwise it cannot begin at all. Take away therefore that event, that occurrence, that individual, and they understand one another, for the obstacle has merely the effect of keeping them from getting to that point. A misunderstanding such as that is not at the same time comic and tragic. The reference of the misunderstanding is plain, and what makes it tragic in the case of unhappy love is the fact that the content of love is given in the lovers' passion. Take from the two the substantial content, and then the misunderstanding is comic, the parties who misunderstand one another are precisely by the misunderstanding revealed in their emptiness, and the laughter visited upon them is the judgment by which existence is propitiated and appeased.

The fact that these two opposites exist at once is too dialectic for poetry. Even though romantic poetry puts the comic and the tragic together, it does so in the form of contrast, and at the utmost it finds a unity which is not furnished by poetry but is vaguely sensed as the negative unity of a particular philosophy of life. But this is not the same as being at once comic and tragic; on the contrary, the contrast is the separating factor which by the same pressure whereby it thrusts down the burlesque lifts up the lyrical. — In immediacy one of the two is regularly present, and the highest form of cohesion it knows is that when one has been the other follows. In the "Phaedon"[10] this succession is beautifully expounded by Socrates, and that in a situation which made it perspicuous in the instance of a sense impression, the impression of the agreeable and the disagreeable, for one could see him sitting there and rubbing with delight the leg from which the fetter was removed and by its removal gave him delight, whereas it pained him when it was there; and he thought it would have been a task for Aesop to compose a fable about how the gods, when they were not able to unite those contending powers in any other way, had tied them together at their extremities. It is true that with this Socrates admits that the agreeable and the disagreeable do not exist at one and the same time, but for

[10] Cap. 3—the same chapter which tells how Socrates had Criton lead away the wailing Xanthippe.

his ironic consciousness they have a negative unity. The contrasts of poetry likewise merely resolve one another. Socrates' death therefore could never be conceived by poetry. Here everything is complete, and yet poetry would only be able to see the one side, in this case of course the tragic side. At the utmost it would be able to produce a comic contrast, though this perhaps is not easy. One cannot deny that Xanthippe constitutes a comic figure with her screaming and noise-making, and that her behavior recalls many a shrewish widow's contrite advertisement of the deceased, neither can one deny that Socrates very ironically lets a comic light fall upon the scene when one beholds Xanthippe transported out of doors with all her tenderness and the screaming emotion which for many years had been saved up and hidden away for this solemn moment; but this contrast would be rather unjust and inadequate. Perhaps it would be better to form a fantastic chorus of a certain class of philologists whose "tear-compelling" observations about this paragon of virtue and his martyr-death form a good contrast to Socrates' whole view of the case. But with that the historical reality would disappear. Even Socrates' friends are farther along than poetry can go; for Phaedon himself says[11] that as a witness to the event he was in a strange condition, an uncommon blending of joy and sorrow, in fact that those present laughed at one moment and wept at another, especially Apollodorus. And what of Socrates himself? The fact that those present laughed *at one moment* and wept *at another* shows that they had not completely understood him. Socrates in fact exemplifies a duality which poetry cannot express. If poetry would take the pathos of tragedy in order to depict Socrates as suffering like a martyr, it had better beware, for in fact he does not suffer, he already had conceived the drollery in the fact that such an 'ἀτοπός τις[12] comes to his end by being executed. Poetry cannot interpret him comically, for the fact that he himself has thought of all the comic in the situation proves precisely that he is not comic, and if ever there was a man who was not comic, it was Socrates. A tragic death as a hero is something simple, and that is what poetry loves; but if it gets an inkling at the same time that the man himself assumes that the case might also be comic, poetry must declare itself insolvent.

Before I bid farewell to poetry I must make still another observation about misunderstanding when it is employed aesthetically. Poetry may also employ misunderstanding in such a way that it applies to a single individual just because he has no point of connection with one person

[11] *Phaedon,* cap. 2.

[12] A lazy fellow. So it was that Socrates several times described himself.

or more who misunderstand him. This may be either comic or tragic, according to the quality of the situation and the character of the passion involved, but it cannot be at once comic and tragic, because there is lacking the point of connection which would combine the parties to the misunderstanding in a unity, or whereby they combine in such a way that they at once hold together and yet fall apart in misunderstanding, yet cannot separate because there is this connection, and the fact that this connection is there makes the relationship at once comic and tragic. — It is tragic when an enthusiast talks to a race of old fogies and is not understood; but it is tragic only because there is no point of unity between them, for the old fogies pay no attention to the enthusiast. *Gulliver's Travels* is comic by reason of an imagination which verges upon madness, but the effect is merely comic, and it is comic because the content of qualitative passion is not present in the misunderstanding, even though in the poet the passion exists, for without passion no poet, not even a comic poet. If the misunderstanding has to do merely with things of no importance, it remains an idle jest. Life is rich in examples. A deaf man enters a hall while the meeting is going on, he does not want to disturb it and therefore he opens the big folding doors very slowly. Unluckily the door possesses the property of creaking. This he cannot hear, he thinks he is doing so well, and by his slow movement he produces a protracted creak; the people become impatient, one of them turns and cries "Hush." He thinks that possibly he has moved the door too rapidly, and its creaking continues. This situation is a jest, and hence neither comedy nor tragedy can make anything out of it. Yet there is in this case a point of union remotely suggested: he does not want to make a disturbance, the meeting does not want to be disturbed, and he disturbs it. By the addition of a little more emotion and other such elements we get the many situations in which one knows not whether to laugh or weep. This is the tragi-comic, in which, since no essential passion is involved, neither the comic nor the tragic is essentially present. In the comi-tragic they are both involved, and the spirit dialectically infinitized sees both aspects in the same thing all at once.

Now for my experiment. I have brought together two heterogeneous individualities, a male and a female. Him I have treated as impelled by the intensity of the spirit towards the religious, her I have kept in aesthetical categories. Here there is plenty of room for misunderstanding so soon as I posit a point of unity, that is, that they are united in loving one another. Here the misunderstanding is not referable to any third party, as though they understood one another and were separated by a foreign power. No, ironically everything favors their misunderstanding, there is nothing to hinder them from talking with one another intimately, but precisely with that the misunderstanding begins. If I now remove the passion, it is all an ironical situation with Greek *Heiterkeit*; if I posit passion, the situation is essentially tragic; if I contemplate it, I declare that it is at once comic and tragic. The heroine of course cannot see it thus, she is far too immediate for that. If she sees the comic side at all, this according to the law of succession must occur at a later moment, when her own laughter would make her comic, for to laugh at a real error proves that one has fallen into a new error, and by laughing thus one is no more healed than "he is free who doth his chains deride."[13] The hero indeed is promptly aware of the presence of the comic, which is what saves him from being comic, but for all that he is not able to see the thing as I see it who am the experimenter and have planned it all. This is due to the fact that he is in a state of passion, and the degree of his passion is showed best by the observation that because he is aware of the comic he confirms his pathos. He is in a state of passion. If I were to say to him, "Try to get out of it," he immediately would fall into another passion and say that it would be behaving basely towards the girl. So he is quite able to see the comic element in the relationship, and he can also see the misunderstanding, but he regards this view of it as a factor of subordinate importance, and out of it he develops his passion with more and more pathos. The conjunctive particle in their misunderstanding is that they love one another, but in their heterogeneity this passion must express itself in ways essentially different, and so the misunderstanding does not have to come from without but develops between them in the relationship itself. The tragedy is that two lovers do not understand one another, the comedy is that two who do not understand one another should love one another. That such a case might occur is not unthinkable, for indeed love itself has its dialectic, and even if it is a thing unheard of, an experimenter surely has plenary power to experiment. When the heterogeneity is presented as I have presented it, both parties have a right to say that they love. Love has an ethical and an aesthetic side. She says that she loves, and she possesses that love aesthetically and understands it aesthetically; he says that he loves, and he understands it ethically. So both of them love, and they love one another, and yet it is a misunderstanding. The heterogeneous is kept apart from other species by category, and so the misunderstanding is not like that of novelistic barter and exchange or of reconsideration within the aesthetic categories.

[13] Lessing, *Nathan der Weise,* Act IV, Scene 4: "Es sind nicht alle frei, die ihrer Ketten spotten."

The male figure in the experiment therefore sees the comic, but not as a hardened observer sees it. He sees the comic and is thereby confirmed in the tragic. That is what interests me especially, for thereby the religious is illuminated. By force of spirit to see at once the comic and the tragic in the same thing is the culmination of paganism. In the loftier passion which out of this unity elects the tragic, religiousness has its beginning, I mean the religiousness for which immediacy is a thing of the past—and indeed it is assumed that in our age it is for all men a thing of the past, so they say. As an animal, man has two legs (extremities), and likewise the comic and the tragic are extremities necessary for movement in the case of one who would exist by virtue of spirit after having given up immediacy. And one who has only one of these legs and yet would be spirit by virtue of spirit is ridiculous, however great a genius he may be. In the equable proportion between the comic and the tragic is to be found the condition for the proper gait; the disproportion can therefore be described here as lameness, bowleggedness, clubfootedness, etc. — My knight's misfortune is that when he is about to collect himself in religiousness he becomes dialectic at the extremest point. About this more is to be said in another paragraph. Here I say only that he does not become dialectic by reason of the fact that out of the comic and the tragic he grasps the tragically higher passion (for in that case I could make no use of him), but he becomes dialectic in the last expression of this very passion. Except for this I could make no use of him whatever; for precisely in this there is discoverable a demoniac trait approximating the religious.

In order to illuminate the experiment I will examine the structure of it.

By the form of the project the duality is exhibited. In the morning he remembers actuality, at night he deals with the same story, but now as it is permeated by his own ideality. So this ideality is not an illusory anticipation which has not yet seen actuality, but it is an act of freedom after actuality. This is the difference between the aesthetic and the religious ideality. The aesthetic is higher than actuality before actuality, that is to say, in illusion; the religious is higher than actuality after actuality, that is, by virtue of a God-relationship. The duality is expressed. A poet or a lover may have an ideal conception of the loved one, but he cannot at the same time be conscious in actuality how far this is true, or be conscious in actuality how far it is not true. This contradiction is endurable only to the new ideality which comes after actuality.

So the story begins twice. I have allowed half a year to intervene, and I assume that during that time he has lived in a kind of stupor, until passion suddenly awakens on the third of January. Other interpretations might be advanced, my choice is made with a view to the general plan.

The two individualities are related to one another conversely. The critical point for her occurs in actuality, but he, who is essentially without any practical experience of the other sex, does not see this clearly, and only by theoretical exertion does he attain a presentiment of something of the sort. Shakespeare has said somewhere, I do not remember where, and I cannot quote, but it was something to this effect:[14] The very instant before the healing of a violent disease, at the instant of convalescence, the fit is most violent; and every evil is at its worst when it takes its leave. The critical point for her, when the healing properly begins, is the moment when she has ventured everything to hold him fast, and when he thereupon, quite consistently from his point of view, ventures upon the extremest measures to fight himself free from her. The instant she felt the pain most deeply was the instant when, psychologically considered, her recovery began. His picture therefore fades even while he is present, and from the time of the separation it becomes more and more a recollection of the past. It is actuality which must help her. In the time of actuality he is strongest because he has only her as an actuality. On the other hand, the moment he sees her again, not in actuality but in the illumination of his own ideality, she is transformed into a gigantic figure. What he did in actuality, namely, the deceit whereby he actually profited her (for the relationship is so dialectic that fundamentally the deceit is her truth, i.e. what she can best understand), he cannot hold fast in her presence as he evokes her in his thought. In order to believe in the importance of the deceit he has to stand in actual relation to her and actually see her. Hence his critical moment occurs on the third of January the year following, for he has to be healed religiously, and in this regard her actuality disturbs him, he must have her ideally. Having misunderstood one another from the beginning, the misunderstanding continues after the separation and precisely then displays itself clearly. At the very moment when she is about to forget him and is well along in convalescence, and he has become unimportant to her, at that very moment she has become to him most highly important,

[14] cf. *Papirer,* V, B 148, 8. The reference here is to *King John,* Act III, Scene 4:

> Before the curing of a strong disease,
> Even in the instant of repair and health,
> The fit is strongest; evils that take leave,
> On their departure most of all show evil.

just because he does not see her. When he sees her, is with her, talks to her, he is in possession of his understanding and is strong; but as soon as he himself constructs her he loses his understanding, dare not believe in it, and the religious must more definitely work itself out. A specter is always terrifying, and that is what she is for him. But what a difference between a young girl for whom his understanding is a match, and an ideal form which advances to meet him terrifyingly, and against which his understanding is of no avail! His individuality was ethico-religiously planned. This is what he is to become. She helps him also, but not by her actuality. Herein consists also the significance of his melancholy. His melancholy is the condensation of possibility. But when it signifies something of that sort, then of course all the talk about a young girl's cheerfulness and the tendency of marriage to disperse melancholy is an idle tale, for it should not be dispersed. On the contrary, the clouds should grow still darker before his soul, then he will be on the way to recovery. This she is unable to perceive, and she always acts in a manner consistent with her perception. Neither is he able to see it, for if he could, he would not receive the *coup de grace* in the way it falls with the most certain stroke by the force of his own guilt and of her peril.

The idea requires that he catch sight of her again, but in such a way, be it observed, that he does not see an actuality, for by that he would not be helped. Hence I have let him see her again several times. But these encounters were peculiar affairs. As he views the case, from his standpoint he is entirely consistent in holding the opinion that the infinity in her ought not to be troubled by intervening with half-measures. One can see at once that he is preoccupied with himself, and not with her as an actuality outside himself, for if he were thinking objectively of her, the deceit would again be in place. So then, lest he might trouble the infinity in her, he bewitches himself into a dreadful state of extinction or decease. From his standpoint this is just as energetic an expression of his love as was her vehemence, viewed from her standpoint. On both sides this of course was the most preposterous way they could behave to one another.

So then, he sees her again. But just because he holds himself like a departed spirit in order to be serviceable to her, he has prevented himself from obtaining a single direct impression. With this he is in the way of becoming normal, his aberration consists in the fact that he nevertheless concerns himself passionately about her. He never gets hold of any occurrence relating to her, or into direct connection with any such thing, never gets any certainty, but continuing passionately to concern himself about her, he picks up every report, even the most unimportant items, and he does not get a great deal more out of his dialectic exertions.[15] That is to say, he becomes more and more absorbed in himself.

So far as the meetings are concerned, they actually prove nothing to him. The inferences he draws, nobody but he would draw; and the paleness he sees I don't believe in at all, at all events I have many other explanations. That it was the third time he saw her in Hauser Square on a Thursday, no one else in his place would have discovered, still less would infer from a fortuitous circumstance what he infers. Even the encounter in church is nothing to rely upon, and actually he learns nothing at all. He notices this himself, but consistently with his standpoint he does not credit his understanding—and this to do honor to her, out of his pride in her. But at the same time something else comes to pass in him, he is more and more religiously absorbed in himself. If he had entered into conversation with her, he again would have been in possession of his understanding, and the religious progress would have been hindered. This he himself does not see, he acts as he does in order to sustain her. — The meetings therefore correspond to his psychic situation, and the contact with actuality whereby he merely grazes it tangentially in a direction away from it keeps him in the state of hovering suspense in which the religious must consolidate itself. He poetizes her now, but he does so by virtue of a religious ideality which comes after actuality. As a lover by virtue of an ideality which comes before actuality sees beauties in the loved one which are not there, so he, with the high-strung passion of repentance, sees terrors which do not exist. — Herein one perceives the good and uncommon qualities which distinguish him, but also the demoniac trait, the fact that he cannot attain rest and repose in the final religious resolution, but is kept constantly under tension. She decides his fate, he says, and that is true; but the untruth is that she is deciding it still, for it is decided. The fact that he remains *in suspenso* is at once a passionate expression of his sympathy

15 [Note by Frater Taciturnus.] How exhausting such exertions must be I can see from the fact that it is exhausting even to construe the thing in thought without forgetting his dialectic difficulty at a single point, a single comma. In the entry of February 13, midnight, instead of the dialectic prolixity we find there, these words would have been enough: "The physician's report is to the effect that on the whole she is in good health." Of the few readers of this book the hasty ones have noticed nothing here, and even of the few discriminating readers perhaps only a single individual has asked, "How did he get such a direct report? He must indeed have asked somebody! And, after all, his tense passion did not prevent him from doing what in the form of possibility he must regard as the most dreadful thing." [The translator cannot suppress his surprise that Frater Taciturnus did not observe how Quidam got this direct report without asking anybody.]

and the demoniac trait.[16] He ought to remain *in suspenso,* or at the apex of the wish, as he expresses it, but at the same time, in view of the fact that the decision is passed, he ought to possess his religious resolution in peace, and not let the decision remain dialectic by reason of her. But just because he is not like this, he illuminates by his hovering and aberration many a religious problem—though one must remember that his "lines" are the expression of an individual passion. — He had energy enough to maintain his deceit, energy enough to choose the religious, and up to the last instant, or in the utmost extremity of religious passion, he remains dialectic. It is as though there were a possibility that he would plan his life differently if he were free from the whole thing. Precisely here lies the daimonia, that because of a possibility vaguely sensed of healing for her, he would not relate himself to himself in the religious idea, but would conceive of her in aesthetic categories, and would defraud the ethical a little bit, as though he, if he were guilty, were less guilty because he got out of the scrape safely, less guilty even by reason of the fact that she perhaps was at fault in her treatment of him. But of this more in another place.

The heterogeneity between the two individualities is now to be shown in its decisive aspects. Heterogeneity will cause the relationship to be inverted constantly, as the reader will have observed in the book itself.

1. *He is closely reserved/she cannot possibly be so.*

Why can she not be so? All close reserve is due to a dialectic reduplication which is quite impossible for immediacy. The language of immediacy is easily pronounced, like a language rich in vowels; the language of reserve is a language only in silence, or at the most it is like the language which places four or five consonants before a vowel. Because she is immediate in this degree, attestation of devotion is quite rightly the medium through which she gives expression to her passion, after having for a long while been overwhelmed by him and suffered injustice, and thereupon been precipitated into a little incident. Upon this devotion his reserve runs aground, that is to say, he is so much more dialectical that he perceives the incompatibility.

16 [Note by Frater Taciturnus.] So must every step be regarded which he takes to help her. But in the last, which he himself regards as a weakness, he is sublime in his suffering, inasmuch as at the instant when the understanding must say that everything seems to be good, he collapses from pure sympathy at the thought of her being healed only in a finite sense.

Reserve, however, may signify various things. His reserve is essentially a form of melancholy, and again the melancholy in his case is the condensed possibility which must be gone through with in the experience of a crisis if he is to become clear to himself in the experience of the religious. As for his melancholy, there is no passage where he declares what its content is. I have so represented him intentionally, partly because I only needed reserve as the limit, as the limit of understanding which posits misunderstanding, and partly because not even he could say what its content is. His reserve is in fact neither more nor less than the condensed anticipation of the religious subjectivity. The religious subjectivity has one dialectic factor more than all actuality has—not as anterior to actuality but as subsequent to it. He can therefore perfectly well exist in actuality, and he is assumed to have done so, but his reserve is a presage of a higher life. It follows therefore as a matter of course that such categories as "the outward is the inward and the inward is the outward"[17] are, when applied to religion, the inventions of Münchausens who have no understanding of religion, which I, an enthusiast for the understanding, can very well have without being religious. In these spheres they do just as much good as one who (to recall an old saying) sticks his tongue out of the window to get a taste of the weather.

His reserve therefore has for the time being no content, but it is there as the limit, and it holds him fast, and for the time being he is melancholy in his reserve. The most abstract form of close reserve is that which encloses itself. The psychologist knows well that the reserved man, although he can tell, and tell with ease, what *made* him reserved, does not tell and cannot tell what *makes* him reserved. Reserve therefore one hardly can take away from the reserved man, and properly he must be healed religiously in himself. This is the most abstract form of reserve when it is the anticipation of a higher life in the condensation of the possibility. Hence he never says what is the content of his reserve but only that it is a fact. From this standpoint of possibility one can strive after religious transparency, and this is what he must do. But this he does not know, and least of all does he suspect that the path of his development passes through the horror of giving up his relationship to her because of the incompatibility. If he had not found in himself strength for the desperate resolution, if he had not acted without understanding what significance his act had for himself, or rather without understanding anything else but that it was his own destruction, if he

[17] Which S.K. ascribed to Hegel and repudiated in *Either/Or*.

had not found strength for this act in sympathetic enthusiasm for her welfare, whether she understood it then or not, she would have conquered—and he would have been lost. The developing process of reserve would have been halted, he would have taken active steps with regard to his close reserve, would have closed it off,[18] hidden it as a fixed idea in his inward parts, perhaps in the quiet form of madness, perhaps even in the form of guilt, for these are the two essential forms of the consolidated reserve. — He had her life upon his conscience, that helped him and will help him. She had upon her conscience his whole spiritual existence—a thing she never dreamed of.

In order to throw light upon his reserve I have introduced in the diary passages in which he gropes as it were after an expression for his own reserve. He never expresses himself directly but indirectly. These expressions must therefore be understood indirectly. One of them is called "A Possibility,"[19] his decisive category, which therefore must be followed to the extreme limit. In the end it appears that the sense of guilt was a vain imagination, a feverish dream. He is groping here after the notion of sin. If he had had a real sin upon his conscience, if I had conceived him thus, it would have been far easier to clarify him out of it; but then the whole plan would not have turned out as I would have it.

2. *He is melancholy/she is light-hearted.*

But if his melancholy is of a sort that ought to be checked, then that is up to her, for then she could help him, as he himself declares so ardently. But it is not so. He does not know that this melancholy signifies something different. Although he himself is brought to naught, the smart of sympathy on her account still prevails, and he resolves to leave her, without any presentiment that precisely this must be of help to him. On the whole, his concern for this girl is pure fanaticism, in itself ludicrous, tragic because of his suffering, comic for the fact that he does the thing in the craziest way.

There is a difference between melancholy and melancholy. There is a melancholy which in the case of poets, artists, thinkers, is a crisis, and on the part of women may be an erotic crisis. So the melancholy of this lay figure of mine is a crisis anticipatory of the religious experience. If I take for example an artist, his melancholy, this critical melancholy, does not straightway express itself in lamentation that he is no good as an artist. Far from it. Sometimes it is a suspicious sign that the sufferer

[18] The modern psychological term is repression, and for what follows the modern psychologist would use the word subliminal or subconscious.

[19] The entry for April 5, midnight.

is thus aware what ails him, a sign that perhaps his sufferings are only warmed-over sufferings. No, this melancholy may cast itself upon anything, the most insignificant thing, and only when the man's essential destiny is determined is it evident that this was the secret of his melancholy. But the crisis must come later in the case of the religious man, that is to say, for the sort of religion in which immediacy has been overcome. This is because of the many postulates which this case exacts: he must be aesthetically developed in imagination and must be able to conceive the ethical with primitive passion in order to be properly offended at it, so that the pristine possibility in the religious man may break its way out in this catastrophe. Therefore melancholy must have accompanied him through the previous stages.

So it is with the personality represented in my experiment. It is precisely the horror of the situation which is to be of help to him. This he does not dream of, he thinks only of her and of his sufferings from a sense of guilt. His sympathy for her prompts him to enthusiastic punctiliousness in venturing the utmost. He leaves her—but not to give her up, rather to hold out in the hope that in the end this might be of help. This he will not say to her, for the hope is uncertain and insecure, it would be an affront to her to put her off with such a hope. This is entirely consistent, it is this that must help, but he knows not how. One word exchanged between them, and his development would have been disturbed.

The consequence will naturally be that in the mean while she reconsiders the situation. That is as it should be. His path does not point that way, and everything is so prepared for him that he may become a normal individual. — So it is I have planned the experiment, making it at once comic and tragic.

If she had conquered, he would have been lost. Even though her lightheartedness (which after all is a security which steadily depreciates) had been capable of making him a happy husband, this is not what he ought to be. But of this he does not dream, and he only feels deeply his misery for the fact that he is incapable of being what every man is capable of—of being a husband.

He has her life upon his conscience, she has had upon her conscience his whole personality, and of course did not dream of it.

3. *He is essentially a thinker/she is anything but that.*

The word "thinker" sheds a rather comical light upon him, for only the fact that he was busied with thoughts serves to explain that, as the experiment assumes, he had been able to live on without the least experience of the world and especially of the other sex. If he had had such knowledge, especially of the latter sort, the experiment could not have been carried out, for one does not have to look far to see what he had to do, and especially how one ought to treat the terrifying pronouncements of a young girl, which are most duly honored by taking as a rule of life an old verse:

Cantatur haec, laudanter haec,
Dicunter, audientur;
Scribuntur haec, leguntur haec,
Et lecta negliguntur.[20]

In the experiment therefore there falls upon him, as the reflection of his lack of knowledge of the world, a rather ludicrous light, but on the other hand his inexperienced veneration for the other sex has something touching about it, and at the same time a certain pungency as an epigram upon worldly knowledge.

To say that he is a thinker does not mean that he reads many books and purposes to ascend the cathedra as *Privatdocent*. That sort of a thinker could well unite divers activities and so attain mediation. He on the contrary is essentially a self-thinker, and that in the sense of always having to have the idea on his side in order to exist. This preoccupies him with all the passion of a self-thinker, not with the affected assumption of solemn responsibility characteristic of the *Privatdocent*.

The girl has life and light for her part, with which she is graciously clothed. She has no objection to his studies though they were to include Syro-Chaldaic, but she cares not a pin for learned subjects, which in her is an amiable trait and not without charm. But what preoccupies him is not the Syro-Chaldaic tongue nor the Eleamitic; no, it is the very life itself in which he has his existence.

Consequently they cannot understand one another. What preoccupies him absolutely is entirely beyond her ken, and if he were to speak of it, she would be no more concerned about it than if he talked of Sennacherib and Shalmaneser. She requires nothing of the sort from him, and on her part this is an amiable trait, especially if her task had been the opposite of what it was, so that in order to be serviceable to him she should not concern herself about such things. Naturally she does not apprehend in the least that the things she requires of him and the things she dispenses him from have no weight in comparison with the ideas, and that not to express the idea is a thing which not only disturbs him but a thing which he regards as disparaging to her.

[20] Quoted in the Journal, IV, A 22.

So it is he thinks. And he is capable of thinking that he may have a murder upon his conscience, but not to express the idea is something he is incapable of thinking. What a maiden's honor is means for the thinker consistency and idea, and for a self-thinker it means to hold fast to it in life. If he has her honor upon his conscience, she in turn has had upon hers his thought-existence. Naturally she had no inkling of it.

4. *He is ethico-dialectic/she aesthetically immediate.*

From each of these standpoints the conception of suffering is entirely different. He cannot understand what her suffering essentially is, if there is any involved in losing possession of another person; she does not understand in the least what his suffering essentially is, namely, a sense of responsibility and guilt.

So they both become unhappy, and each has done the best thing for the other by way of becoming unhappy—he by severing the relationship, she by laying a murder upon his conscience. In fact he would have had that burden all the same, but nevertheless she did it.

5. *He is sympathetic/she is innocently self-loving in the sense of immediacy.*

The unsightly form of self-love is always recognizable by the fact that it involves reflection. In her nothing of this sort is discernable, but rather the instinct of self-preservation, which several Greek philosophers[21] have regarded as a moral principle. Their mistake was that as a principle this involves reflection. She is without reflection, hence this self-love is not an unseemly thing and is an indication of healthiness.

Notwithstanding the partiality he commonly shows in his interpretation of her, he nevertheless does her in a way an injustice by saying that she has not a trace of resignation. Not that the dictum is unjust, for it is quite true, but the reason for it is that she has no notion what it means —and that may be an indication of healthiness, but at the same time it may perhaps indicate an erotic modesty. Moreover he hinders her from getting a notion of it. He employs deceit to hide his own sufferings, so that she may not be moved sympathetically. But then he forgets to take into account the deceit which in fact prevents her from becoming aware of the promptings of sympathy. But just as there is a contradiction here, his position here is also so dialectic, so ambiguous, that one might assume he was just as loath for her sake to see her sympathetically moved as for his own sake he was loath to have a vigorous expression of her

[21] Chrysippos and other Stoics, according to Diogenes Laertius, VII, 85.

magnanimity. This, however, he himself perceived, for he says that he had proposed to her an opportunity to give him his freedom, as in fact he did, but it does not follow that at this point he was purely sympathetic, but rather that he was subjecting himself to what he considered a duty. Inasmuch as he made this proposition he is saved from becoming demoniac in the direction of the evil, but he is by no means purely religious, that is as yet only a possibility. The misfortune is that she will not understand him and only takes advantage of every new discovery of his feeling to cast herself upon him with her devotion.

It is sympathy for her (in the form, be it noted, which is consonant with his individuality, for his sympathy of course cannot talk in her idiom) which inspires him to take the step he otherwise would hardly have ventured to take. I might have left it at that, but in order to throw light upon him I allow the thought to enter his mind, and reality seemed to favor it, that the thing will end after all in a perfectly natural way by her becoming again freely at ease through a *restitutio in integrum.*[22] Here it will appear whether he is sympathetic, or rather, since his disposition is by nature sympathetic, it will appear that he now almost suffers more than before because she seems to him to lose in ideality. His sympathy appears here in all its strength and in the way it must show itself in a thinker to whom idea-existence is the one and only thing. If he had possessed knowledge of the world and of the other sex, he would have got off more easily—supposing he was willing to make use of that knowledge.

So then he breaks off, and the wedding ceremony serves the strange purpose of being the separating factor. Misunderstanding appears again in the subsequent period. She, as was said above, was already on the way to recovery when he left her, and she recovers gradually; he suffers most afterwards. He is the active party, she the passive sufferer, so it seems; but in reality the inverse of this is true: he is the passive sufferer who would not venture to do what she did, to lay such a heavy responsibility upon another person. She thinks that he has affronted and mortified her by breaking the engagement, and yet he had affronted her only by beginning the thing. His fault is (apart from beginning it) that he applied too high a standard, and this precisely is his title to honor. He is guilty, she is entirely innocent, he thinks. This, however, is not true: if he is to blame for having begun, she too is to blame for taking advantage of the ethical side of the relationship so as to bind him to herself, and for venturing to take a step the consequences of which she

[22] I.e. her engagement to another.

neither dreams of nor can calculate. He sees the comic side of the situation, but he sees this passionately, so that out of the situation he chooses the tragic side (this is the religious trait which explains the ability I am unable to understand of seeing both factors in equilibrium); she sees the tragic side, and sees it so clearly that she makes it comic. He produces no outward effect whatsoever, except what every male could accomplish just as well, namely, that a girl "wants to die," etc., he cannot even make a girl unhappy; she produces an immense effect. Upon this she does not reflect at all, for she thinks that if she had been permitted to make him happy, she then would have been doing something. Nor does he think of the consequences for him, for he must think that he has crushed her. He is sure of one thing, that it is the ruin of the girl to be united to him; perhaps the girl is shrewder in holding the opinion that she could make good use of him. She is sure of being able to make him happy; and yet, as has been shown, this would absolutely have been his ruin. He makes a fool of himself by his humble veneration; she makes a fool of herself by her great words.

But how was it after all that he began such a thing? This, I believe, I have indicated clearly. He begins with a whole life-view which he had formed. I have to make out of him an approximation to a religious individuality, and hence this life-view of his must be an aesthetic-ethical one in illusion. So it is too, and it is quite natural that this must have satisfied his individuality. He sees the girl, gets an erotic impression, and no more than that. She becomes a part of his existence, and he is not willing, as he says, to affront her by learning to know more definitely about her. One perceives at once the fanatic enthusiast, and an enthusiast he is to become, but in another sphere. So time passes, he forms his resolve, but the erotic factor has not received due attention. Then he is in for it, and he conceives the situation ethically, whereas the religious possibility is constantly the deepest thing in his soul, as it already was in his first life-view, without his knowing it. The ethical now becomes clarified to him in reality, and he comes to grief. The offense he did her was not in breaking off, but it was that with such a view of life he wanted to be in love. The stages were arranged thus: an aesthetic-ethical life-view in illusion, with the dawning possibility of the religious; an ethical life-view which condemns him; he sinks back within himself—and there he is where I would have him.

I have now quite briefly made the circuit around my experiment. Round about it I am constantly moving; for I can well grasp the unity of the comic and the tragic, but I cannot conceive whence he gets the new and higher passion which is religiousness. Might it be the ethical which by its negative pressure helps him past the metaphysical (for that is where my place is) into the religious? I do not know.

The result of the whole process of misunderstanding is that after all they do not love. But this cannot be affirmed at the beginning, and each still retains a share of the factors of love. He fails to love because he lacks immediacy, in which love first has its place. If he could have become hers, he would have become a spirit who would have done everything to indulge her wishes, but not a lover. But if he lacks immediacy, he has the ethical, for which she has no understanding and no interest. She does not love; that is to say, she has the impulses of immediacy and perseverance in them, but in order to love she must also have resignation, so that it may become clear that she does not love herself.

With this the experiment is finished; but in another sense, even in this prolonged development of it, it is not finished or brought to an end. (As to the reason for this, more will be said later.) If I were to assume that what he had a presentiment of, and what in itself was probable enough, did actually occur, namely, that she fell in love anew—what then? Why then he possibly might have got over his aberration. I constantly put myself in his place and clearly perceive that he is not to be helped as I in such a case would long ago have helped myself. I have no mind to contend about that, I would only experiment. His aberration consists in permitting himself to be disturbed by her reality so that he cannot collect himself in the act of repentance, and so cannot attain peace in repentance because she makes this act dialectical for him. (About this more later.) As soon therefore as she is out of the way he will have only himself to deal with, and repentance unimpeded will acquire the ideality he has need of, without being disturbed by a pathetic passion which stimulates him to action or by comic visions which he himself does not produce. To definitely bound an individuality and set down the mathematical answer to the given problem is the task of great systematic thinkers who have such a broad field to hurry over. To allow him to exist in all his possibility is what interests the experimenter. Therefore, even if I were to relinquish this point of view, I can very well imagine that he might still become dialectic again. If this were to occur, he is in the way of becoming demoniac. It is not the dialectical which makes a person demoniacal, far from it, but it is persisting in this state.

The reader who is acquainted with the little book by Constantine Constantius[23] will perceive that I resemble in a way that author but yet am

[23] I.e. S.K.'s own work, *Repetition.*

very different, and he who experiments ought always to fashion himself in conformity with the experiment.

§ 3.

THAT TRAGEDY FEELS GREATER NEED OF HISTORICAL REALITY THAN DOES COMEDY; AND ABOUT THE DISAPPEARANCE OF THIS DISTINCTION IN THE "EXPERIMENT."

I have often reflected upon the fact that the tragic poets, in order to be sure of making an impression upon the audience, to win for the play their confidence and trust, and their tears for the performance of it, rely upon the fact that their hero had performed great deeds, even though the poet does not confine himself to history. That this is a fact surely no one will deny or be inclined to appeal against me to Lessing, since Amelie Galotti is the exception which proves the rule, and there are many utterances of this author[24] which show that he viewed the case precisely in this way. The almost universal practice is to use historical material, and, with considerable reservation, to understand it in the Aristotelian sense, regarding the poet as a greater philosopher than the historian, because he shows how a thing ought to be, not how it is.[25] On the other hand, the comic poet has no need of such historical support. He gives his characters just what names he will, he lays the scene where he will, and if only the comic ideality is present, the people are sure to laugh. And conversely, he gains nothing by using Harlequin and Pierrot if he only knows how to use them as names.

Is this because men are more inclined to see the weak points of people than to see their greatness? Is it because it is more natural to laugh at something without a sufficient guarantee than to weep over it, considering that a fool will laugh at nothing? Or is the reason perhaps this, that the light-armed comedy hastens past the ethical to the unconcerned position of metaphysics and wants only to arouse laughter by making the contradiction manifest, and that tragedy on the other hand, heavy-armed as it is, remains mired in the ethical difficulty that though the idea triumphs the hero is destroyed—which is rather discouraging to the auditor in case he would like to be a hero, and it would be something of a satire upon him if he reflects that he has nothing to fear for his life since it is only the heroes that die.

[24] In Lessing's *Hamburgische Dramaturgie* much is said about the relation of tragedy to history, e.g. I, 14, 19, 23, 88, 91.

[25] Aristotle's *Poetic*, cap. 9.

However, be the reason what it may, the thing that I am interested in is not the reason but the fact that tragedy seeks support in the historical. This means that poetry does not believe itself capable by itself of awakening ideality in the auditor, does not believe that it is present in the auditor, but in the historical—that is to say, poetry expects to derive it from history.

With regard to the comical, on the contrary, it never occurs to the poet to want to appeal to history or to support the comic figure by the aid of history; for the auditor says quite rightly, "Show him to us as comic, and we will cheerfully make thee a gift of the historical."

But does it then help one to believe in greatness to know that it was historical? No, not at all. This knowledge only helps one into an illusion which beguiles by the material fact. What is it I know historically? It is the material fact. Ideality I know by myself, and if I do not know it by myself, I do not know it at all; all historical knowledge is of no avail. Ideality is not loose cash which can be transported from one person to another, or something which is thrown into the bargain when one buys a big consignment. If I know that Caesar was great, I must know what greatness is, and this is what I behold, otherwise I do not know that Caesar was great. History's report that reliable men assert this, that there is no risk involved in the acceptance of this opinion, that it must be regarded as certain that he was a great man, that the outcome proves it, is all of no avail. To believe ideality on the word of another is like laughing at a witticism not because one understands it but because another man said that it was witty. In that case the witticism might essentially be left just as well unuttered in the presence of a man who laughs out of belief in and respect for another person, for such a man would laugh with the same emphasis.

The reader will easily see from the title of this section that it is not my intention to remain in the aesthetic sphere but that I would proceed to the religious. What the tragic hero is in the aesthetic sphere, that the religious pattern (I am of course thinking only of pious men etc., not of Christ) is for the religious consciousness. The poet in this case is an orator. Here again recourse is had to the historical. The pattern is presented, and now, says the orator, it is certain because it is historic, and the believing congregation believes everything, even that the orator knows what he himself is saying.

In order to grasp ideality I must be able to resolve the historical in the ideality, or to do what a pious expression says of God, "let light shine upon it." On the other hand I do not enter into the ideality by repeating the historical rigamarole. One therefore who in a given case cannot just as well grasp the conclusion *ab posse ad esse* as he can grasp the conclusion *ab esse ad posse* does not grasp the ideality in that given case. He feeds only upon imaginations. Ideality as the animating principle is as a matter of course not historical. What can be historically transmitted to me is a congeries of data which are not idealities, and so the historical is always raw material which he who appropriates it knows how to resolve in a *posse* and assimilate as an *esse*. There is therefore nothing more foolish in the religious field than to hear the common sense question asked when something is taught, "if the thing actually happened thus, for if so we would believe it." The question whether it actually happened thus, whether it was so ideal as it is represented, can only be tested by ideality, but this does not come conveniently bottled in history.

I have become conscious of this by composing the story of suffering which I have carried out in my experiment. Ah, if I were a renowned author, a reading world which is industrious in believing, indefatigably industrious, would be in a fix, for it would be concerned about the book and ask, "But then is this also actually so?—then we will believe it." What is it that it will believe? That it is actually so. Well, along that path one gets no further. In case an orator takes no account of this, he may perfectly well be able to make a profound impression upon his hearers but will also turn into a satire upon himself what Socrates says of eloquence, that it is a deceitful art.[26] The more he emphasizes that it is historical, and therefore etc., the more he deceives; and if it is a small living he has, so that it is not worth while talking of the money he gets, it is just as certain that he gives out fudge, perhaps a great deal of fudge —alas, for scanty pay. Such a historizing orator only does his part to make the learners unintelligent. For intelligence asks about two things: (1) is that which is said possible? (2) can I do it? But it is unintelligent to ask about two things: (1) is it actually so? (2) has my neighbor Christopherson done it, has he actually done it? And faith is the ideality which resolves an *esse* into its *posse,* and then draws the conclusion inversely with passionate ardor. If the object of faith is the absurd,[27] it is not the historic which is believed, but faith is the ideality which resolves an *esse* into a *non posse*—and then *will* believe it.

In order to secure the religious paradigm more thoroughly the religious is kept strictly apart and conceived exclusively in the pathetic categories of immediacy. Here the situation of the orator is like that of

[26] Plato, *Gorgias,* cap. 57.
[27] Here emerges a theme which was to become prominent in the *Postscript.*

the poet with his tragic hero. He dare not permit the comic to appear. Therefore the hearer knows definitely that this is seriousness, and if it is seriousness, he can well enough believe it. But suppose now that this seriousness were jest. Religious seriousness is, like religion itself, the higher passion which issues from the unity of the comic and the tragic. This I know precisely for the reason that I myself am not religious and have reached this standpoint (that of the unity of the two) without leaping over any preliminary stage and without finding the religious in myself. — If such be the case, the historical need not incommode itself, for it never can be of any assistance in reaching an ideality, least of all a dialectic ideality. If I were a reliable man, the prospect would be pretty bad for a reading world which cannot learn beforehand to know whether the thing is jest or earnest. I would be required to give an explanation—there is some compensation after all for not being responsible.

They secure the religious just as they do the theatrical piece by the result—and my experiment in fact is not finished. So there is no result. — "I beg a highly respected and intelligent public to consider what it means to publish a book without any result. Fortunately no one reads it since it is by an obscure author." Thus a reviewer would talk, in spite of the fact that I have besought him so imploringly to abstain—not to abstain from saying this, for if finally he has to talk, it makes no difference what he says. So then the result, which every bustling reader might reasonably require to have at his disposition in advance, does not come at all. Oh, that these considerations which I present here might make up a little for this lack.

Poetry depends upon the commensurability of the outward and the inward, and therefore it shows the result in the realm of the visible. The result is right there to be grasped. However, a little prudence is not out of place, for the result has the same dialectic as ideality. The religious lies in the inward sphere. In this case the result cannot be shown outwardly. But what does the orator do? He vouches for the result. Such a security must be regarded as satisfactory from every point of view—by serious and positive people.

The aesthetic result is in the realm of the outward and can be shown. It can be shown, and even by the nearsighted it can be seen by the aid of an opera glass that the hero conquers, that the magnanimous man falls in battle and is carried home dead (of course not all at the same moment), etc. This precisely is the defect of the aesthetic production. — The ethical result is already less visible, or rather it is demanded with such swiftness that one has not time to look around before it is there.

So when I make abstraction from everything else and think only of the ethical, I demand with ethical propriety to see the good triumph with infinite swiftness and to see punishment overtake the evil with infinite swiftness. Now this cannot be represented, at least not in five acts, and hence the aesthetic and the ethical have been combined. The ethical thought as a totality has been retained, and the infinite swiftness slowed down by aesthetic categories (fate—chance), and then in the ethical thought as a totality is to be seen at the end a world-order, divine governance, providence. This result is aesthetic-ethical and hence to a certain degree can be seen outwardly. This result nevertheless is precarious, for the ethical cannot show respect for the aesthetic in any other way than by regarding a union with it as a *mésalliance*. (It is surely for this reason that Boethius is so wroth at poetic representations, in Book I, cap. 9; for this reason surely that Solon prohibited theatrical plays as a deceit; for this reason surely that Plato wished to exclude poets from his state.) The ethical inquires only about guilty/not guilty, it is man enough to hold its own with anybody, it has no need of anything outward or visible, not to speak of anything so ambiguously dialectic as fate and chance, or of the judgment of any formal tribunal. The ethical is proud and says, "When I have passed judgment nothing more is needed." That is to say, the ethical desires to be separated from the aesthetic and from the outwardness which is its imperfection, it desires to enter into a glorious alliance, and that is with the religious.

The religious then plays, though in a higher sphere, the same rôle as the aesthetic; it spaces out the infinite swiftness of the ethical, and development can take place; but the scene is laid in the interior, in thoughts and the mind which one cannot see, not even by the aid of a telescope. The principle of the spirit is that the outward and visible (the glory of the world or its wretchedness, an outward result or the lack of it for the agent) exist in order to test faith, and hence not to deceive, rather that the spirit may be put to the test by setting all this at zero and withdrawing itself. The outward counts neither one way nor the other—and for one thing the result remains in the inward sphere, and, secondly, it is constantly deferred.

The aesthetic outcome is in the outward sphere, and it is this outward which provides assurance that the outcome is there; one sees that the hero has triumphed, has conquered the land, and then we are through with it. The religious outcome, indifferent to the outward result, is only assured in the inward sphere, that is, in faith. Indifferent to the outward which the aesthetic needs (that there must be great men, great objects, great events, so that it is comic when ordinary people are involved, or two shillings and eightpence) the religious is commensurable for the greatest man that ever lived and for the most abject, and equally commensurable; commensurable for the wealth of nations and for a farthing, and equally commensurable. The religious is simply and solely qualitatively dialectic and disdains quantity in which the aesthetic man discovers his task. Indifferent to the outward which the aesthetic needs for the result, the religious disdains such things and proclaims to each and every man that he who believes that he is perfected (that is to say, imagines it, since such a thing cannot be believed, because faith precisely is infinity)—has lost.

And now the orator who deals in results, what does he do? He does everything he possibly can to deceive the hearers. But the orator is "positive." Quite so—he also takes money for what he says, and this of itself is enough to inspire people with a certain confidence in him; for in case a man were to lay out money or to lose his reputation in order to speak the truth, what confidence could one have in him, indeed he contradicts himself, for might that be the truth which did not procure for a man money, reputation and similar things?

In case one were to say that to swim is to lie upon dry land and flounder about, everybody would regard him as mad. But to believe is exactly like swimming, and instead of helping a man to get to his feet on dry land the orator should help him to get out upon the deep. So then if one would say that to believe is to lie upon dry land and go through the motions, he says the same thing as the above, only people perhaps do not notice it.

What is said here about the lack of a result in the religious sphere may also be expressed thus: the negative is higher than the positive. How lucky to be an obscure author when one experiments with such thoughts! An author of repute would be put to embarrassment, for because of his repute the positive people would presumably perceive at once that this was a positive result he had reached, and his positive repute would become still greater. Positive people, or (to indicate by the definite article more definitely what I mean) the Positives, have a positive infinity. That is quite so, a "positive" is finished, and when we hear that, we also are soon finished with them. Here we have result in superabundance. If one would seek enlightenment from Hegel the Master about what is to be understood by a positive infinity,[28] one learns much, with prodigious pains one succeeds in understanding him—the only thing a laggard perhaps does not understand is how a live man or a man

[28] *Die objective Logic,* I, Book I, § 2, cap. CC: "die affirmative Unendlichkeit."

in a living body becomes such a being that he can be tranquillized by the positive infinity, which ordinarily is reserved for the Deity and eternity and the deceased. Consequently there is no other way I can understand the thing but by supposing that a result is missing which the negative ones who are not finished might *en passant* look forward to eagerly, wondering if long after the System has been finished[29] astronomy might discover on those distant stars higher beings who could make use of it. It must be left to the higher beings what they will make out of it, but for men it would be the part of prudence not to be too positive, for this really means to be made a jest of by existence. Existence is cunning and possesses many means of enchantment to catch rash adventurers, and he who is caught, yea, he who is caught, out of him is not made exactly what could be called a higher being.

For a finite being—and that after all is what man is (cf. Balle's *Lesson Book*)[30]—the negative infinity is the highest attainable, and the positive is a precarious assurance. Intellectual existence, especially for the religious man, is not easy, the believer lies constantly out upon the deep and with seventy thousand fathoms of water under him. However long he may lie out there, there is no assurance that little by little he will find himself lying upon land, stretched out at his ease. He may become calmer, more accustomed to his position, and find a sense of security which loves jest and the joyous mind—but up to the last minute he lies above a depth of seventy thousand fathoms.[31] If immediacy is done away with, as in fact everybody loudly requires, then this situation comes about. There are to be enough difficulties in life for everybody. Let the poor feel the hard pressure of poverty and anxiety about a livelihood, he who elects a spiritual existence by virtue of the religious will have the comfort, which I well understand he needs, of knowing that he too suffers in life and that before God there is no respect of persons. For to become "positive" does not procure for any man personal respect in God's eyes, even though this has been accounted wisdom since the time Speculation took charge of religion by taking its life.

This I have understood well in spite of the fact that I myself am not religious, but at least I do not presume to take religion by force and

[29] In other places S.K. reproached the System for the fact that it was not "finished"—and he affirmed that until it was finished it was not a system.

[30] S.K. often refers humorously to this schoolbook of his childhood. In this instance he doubtless has in mind cap. 8, § 1: "Notwithstanding no man knows at what time he shall die, it is certain nevertheless that all men who till the world's end live upon earth, must one day die, because all are sinners."

[31] Johannes Climacus developed this theme in the *Postscript,* especially in Part I, § 2, cap. 2—that is, Vol. VII, pp. 217 *ff*.

merely try to understand with the cunning of an observer the object I experiment with. The religious seeks no support in the historic, still less than does the comic, and for a higher reason; it presupposes the unity of the tragic and the comic in passion, and with a new passion or with the same it chooses the tragic, and this situation again makes every historic support meaningless; it is never finished,[32] at least not in time, and hence only as a delusion can it be so represented. So then, in case a man who had been steadily listening to an orator who talked of things religious[33] were to go to him and say, "Are you, sir, of the opinion that I now have faith, seeing that I have been listening to you so steadily?" Perhaps then the orator, in an access of what is called good nature, sympathetic concern, for which one receives thanks in letters to the editor, might reply, "Why, certainly that is my opinion. Only do not fail to hear my addresses, and come to me freely if again you are assailed by doubt," etc. My experimental observation (devoid of all good nature and sympathetic concern) prompts me to the opinion that he would have done better to reply, "My dear man, would you make fun of me? I dare not even vouch for my wife, yea, not even for myself, for I lie constantly above a depth of seventy thousand fathoms of water."

If only now no one would tempt me, promise me perhaps gold and forests green, the favor of maidens and the applause of reviewers—but then require an answer to the question whether my experiment is a real history, whether at the bottom of it there is something real. Why, yes, certainly there is something real at the bottom of it—namely, the categories. However, for an unknown author the temptation is not so great, everyone will easily see that the whole thing is a prank—which nevertheless it is not, for it is an experiment. Tragedy has the interest of reality, comedy has the disinterestedness of metaphysics, but the experiment lies in the invisible unity of jest and earnest. The dialectic tension between form and content and between content and form prevents any immediate relationship to it, and in this tension the experiment avoids the honest handshake of earnestness and the rollicking fellowship of jest. The experiment constantly addresses the reader as "you," to indicate a ceremonious distance. The poetic hero would arouse enthusiasm by his triumph, would distress one by his sufferings (would have the

[32] Accordingly S.K. habitually spoke of himself as "*becoming* a Christian."

[33] The reader will hardly fail to observe the satire involved in speaking of the preacher as "the orator." This is a presage of the terrible satire he launched against the clergy the last year of his life.

interest of reality), the comic hero would awaken laughter, the *quidam*[34] of the "experiment" desires nothing of the sort, without making any demands he is in every way "at your service," he cannot annoy you, for in this respect also he is "at your service," willing to be ignored without any risk whatsoever on your part, and that all the more because it is absolutely indeterminable whether one who paid attention to him gained anything by it or suffered damage from it.

§ 4.

REPENTANCE DIALECTICALLY PREVENTED FROM COMING TO A HEAD; AND THAT THE LAST CONFINE BETWEEN THE AESTHETIC AND THE RELIGIOUS LIES IN THE FIELD OF PSYCHOLOGY.

Poetry can make no use of repentance, for as soon as it is posited the scene is transferred to the inward man. And the System of course can make no use of it whatever, for the System has to be finished, the sooner the better, it is unimpeachable[35] only when it is finished, and in order to get finished it takes pains to be rid of repentance. The Systematic abbreviation of the pathological factors of life is simply ridiculous if it claims to have anything but a metaphysical significance. The System is therefore merely metaphysics, and that is all right, but it is not a system which embraces existence, for in that case the ethical must be included in it, and to abbreviate the ethical is to make a fool of it.

On the Systematic "gliding track" (as the *quidam* of the experiment expresses it) the thing goes on as follows: § 17. Repentance; § 18. The Atonement; §—. System Finished—concluding with some hints to the bookbinder about how it is to be bound: in half calf it is metaphysics, in full calf it is the System. So then one does not linger over repentance. No one, not even the man whose business requires the utmost haste, has cause to complain that "one paragraph need not be an eternity." I on the other hand propose to linger a little instant over repentance. An experimenter has more time.

The demoniac trait in the *quidam* of the experiment is essentially this, that he cannot withdraw himself in repentance, that at the extremest point he remains stuck in a dialectic relationship to reality (see above). It is well known that Juno sent a gadfly to persecute Latona[36]

[34] As S.K. gives him no name, we have to use this Latin word, meaning "a certain one," and call him Quidam.

[35] A play on words: this word is *Angerlos* (literally, "free from repentance"), whereas in the next clause *Angeren los* means "rid of repentance."

[36] It was not Leto but Io whom Hera pursued with a gadfly.

so that she could not give birth to her child—so is the girl's reality a gadfly, a perhaps, which teases him, a nemesis of reality, life's envy, which will not let him get away and thereby get absolutely into the religious.

When repentance is treated less systematically, i.e. more effectively, one generally has one's eyes opened to get the atonement brought forward all the same. This may be all very good, but existential difficulties lie also in another quarter. When repentance is posited, guilt must be presumed as clear and well ascertained. But the difficulty arises precisely when guilt becomes dialectic. Therefore I said before that if the *quidam* of the experiment had had an actual sin, it would have been far easier to clarify him out of it, for then one would have been able to avoid the dialectical.

It makes no difference to the experiment whether such a case occurs rarely or not at all. It might be possible, however, that this dialectic situation occurs very frequently but comes to nothing at all. For the strictly normal occurs perhaps solely in textbooks and lectures of men who do not exist at all in themselves, nor know how to peer into life and into other men.

The experiment has made the existential position as dialectic as possible. He may have a murder upon his conscience, or the whole thing may be wind; he has this burden for the fact that a young girl lays it upon him, and if there should be a little galimatias in this, then he has no murder upon his conscience. What is to determine this? Reality. But reality takes a little time, and when I experiment I am not in a hurry like the Systematic writer of a paragraph. How does he exist all this time? It is a thing to drive repentance to despair. With me the case is different, for I sit at my ease, cheerfully employed with my calculations, and look out over the tragic and the comic: the tragic girl who dies, and the comic sinner who becomes a murderer, the tragic sinner who suffers, and the comic girl who lives. "A word is a word, and a man is a man," but the proverb applies only to men, who ought therefore to be prudent about talking of death. For it is true indeed, as a deceased man said of death, that it recognizes no class nor age; but from this it does not follow that we are to believe everybody's word.

The dialectic reader will observe at once that there is a difficulty which the *quidam* of the experiment did not take into account, or at least not sufficiently. By means of a deceit he would cunningly take away from her every impression of him she might have had. This deceit he carries out, but he forgets to reckon its consequences. He is sturdy enough to defy the terrors of reality, but he has not the strength to maintain the rôle when it reacts upon himself. He is superior to reality, as he shows in carrying out the deceit, for he shuns no argument she advances but persists in his course. By reason of the deceit, however, the argument becomes different from what it otherwise would have been. The moment the deceit is effective he is in fact misleading the girl and inciting her to express herself unsympathetically. She has no suspicion that he suffers, she must suppose that he is bent upon seeing the end of the engagement and so triumphing over her. So there is nothing to restrain her utterances. To this extent it is his own fault that the situation becomes so terrible as it does. Only it must be remembered that he attempted a milder solution before he had recourse to the deceit. But the fact that he himself by the deceit contributes to make everything more terrible for him, and hence the fact that he did not gain deceitfully any advantage for himself but only discomfiture, is for me a very important factor in the experiment. In an external sense he has conquered, the power with which reality challenges him does not prevail against him—but then a half year later he begins it all over again within himself, wounded as he is by that experience, and now he must give in. This precisely is what illuminates the religious situation. The religiousness which is fetched directly from reality is a dubious religiousness; it may be that aesthetic categories are employed and worldly wisdom acquired; but when reality has not been able to crush an individual and he falls by himself, the religious factor is clearer.

In this fact then, which he does not sufficiently observe, I see again the unity of the comic and the tragic. The comic feature is not that he is a braggart, for then it must have been reality which made him bite the dust, but it is the fact that he survives the crisis of reality and then falls in conflict with himself. It is a problem for aesthetics to let one who imagines he is something become manifest in the face of reality as nothing. But if in the first instance the aesthetic has conceded that in reality he is great, it has then no superior power over him and must recognize him as a hero—but then the religious says, "Tut, tut, let us look a little more closely to see how it stands with him." I am concerned about this in a thoroughly Greek way. I imagine the blissful gods creating such a man for the sake of enjoying a dialectic pleasure in observing him. They give him powers to deal with reality, but they give him also an inward disposition by which he gets into trouble. He really is capable of great deeds, but so soon as he has performed them the event is reduplicated within himself, and he topples over. And I imagine the gods saying to one another, "After all, we must have some sport for ourselves alone, and here is a thing which is not for the goddesses, who do not comprehend it and, if they did comprehend it, would not behold it without pity. This is not something to laugh at, like the inventions of a poet whom we honor with the guerdon of our laughter, and it is not a thing to weep over, as we do when the case deserves it, but this is a solemn pleasure, the dialectic pleasure of beholding equilibrium. He cannot complain of us, for indeed we have made him great, and it is we gods alone, in fact, who see at the same moment his nothingness."

The *quidam* of the experiment does not see it thus, for in his passion he holds fast by faith to the Deity, and in his own annihilation he does not see as I do the unity of the comic and the tragic, and no more than that, but he sees his own resuscitation, he sees himself fall, not before reality but by God's hand, and therefore resuscitated. Speaking religiously, I might express myself in a different way, even though I speak in what to me is a strange tongue: Providence, which is infinitely concerned about every man, endows an individual with uncommon powers of dealing with reality; "but then," says Providence, "lest he might occasion too much harm I confine this power in melancholy and thereby hide it from him. What he is capable of he shall never learn to know, but I want to make use of him. He shall not be humbled by any reality, to that extent he is treated with more partiality than other men, but in himself he shall be sensible of annihilation as other men are not sensible of it. First in that position, and only there, shall he understand me, but then also he shall be certain that it is I he understands." As an experimenter I can well understand this, but not otherwise, for I am not tranquillized by passion but by dispassionateness.

So then repentance has become dialectic for him and remains so, because he must wait to be informed by reality what wrong he has actually done. The dialectic reader will of course be able to adduce many examples of such dialectic repentance, I would merely suggest one. David has resolved that Uriah shall be got rid of by the crafty means the Bible records so that Bathsheba may be his. I assume that he has sent a messenger with secret orders to the commander of the forces, I assume that it takes a messenger three days to reach the camp. The historic reality is a matter of indifference in this case. What happens? When David the very night the messenger departed would seek repose in sleep he does not find it, but horror awakens, it grips him, and he sinks down in repentance—in the next paragraph comes "The Atonement." No, halt! That same instant David perceives that it might yet be possible to prevent the murder. A swift messenger is sent out, and David remains behind. I assume that in this case five days are required for the return of the messenger. Five days—how much is that? Indeed it is not so much as a clause in the paragraph, at the most it is a particle, a "meanwhile" which is merely the beginning of a sentence. But five days might very well turn a man's hair gray. After all, there is a great difference between having wanted to be a murderer and being one. David is now in dialectic suspense, and the experimenter who would describe his condition can have use for very many paragraphs. — Meanwhile everyone will easily see that this is a far easier case than that of my experiment. After all, David wished to make himself guilty of a murder, but the *quidam* of the experiment wished precisely to save life, inspired by pure sympathy he ventures the utmost, and, behold, he gets a murder upon his conscience, or rather he gets into the dialectic embarrassment here described. This also is more dialectic than David's situation, because the comic element absolutely cannot emerge in David's case. It might have been an alleviation for David if he had succeeded in preventing Uriah's actual death, but a jest it never could have become. On the other hand, the *quidam* of the experiment may almost become ludicrous if he does not parry with the idea.

Here the dialectic form of repentance is this: he cannot get to the point of repenting, because it is as though it were still undetermined what he is to repent of; and he cannot find repose in repentance, because it is as though he ought constantly to be doing something, undoing what was done, if that were possible. The fact therefore that he yields to this is the demoniac trait in him; he ought to fix his attention merely upon the possibility and withdraw repentance from it entirely. Insofar as he is kept *in suspenso* for the first reason (that it is not yet determined what he is to repent of) he is ironic; insofar as it is for the other reason (that he constantly must be doing something) he is purely sympathetic. — There is still another factor, a third factor, in his situation as a penitent. In the System a man repents once for all in § 17 and goes on to § 18. But for the existing man, if healing is to come about, the moment must arrive when one lets the act of repentance go. This for an instant has a deceptive resemblance to forgetfulness. But to forget one's guilt is a new sin. Here lies the difficulty. To hold the guilt fast is the passion of repentance, and proudly, enthusiastically, it disdains the prate of forgetfulness about the alleviation it offers, and its deep concern makes it suspicious of itself. And the *quidam* of the experiment even thinks that by holding on to the sense of guilt he does honor to the girl —a seductive thought precisely for the reason that she is pretty. To let go of repentance, to put it at a distance, so that one does not have it equally near every instant, is a necessity for healing. Such a dialectic labor of treading water is not noticed when everything goes off so smoothly as when § 18 follows upon or out of § 17.

SUPPLEMENT.

A SIDE GLANCE AT SHAKESPEARE'S HAMLET.

Börne has written a brief critical appreciation of *Hamlet*.[37] It is only a concluding utterance of his which concerns me, and I do not know whether he attached as much importance to it as I do. In general, such writers as Börne, Heine, Feuerbach, etc., have great interest for an experimenter. They are for the most part very thoroughly informed about the religious, i.e. they know definitely that they want to have nothing to do with it. This is a great advantage over the "Systematic" writers who, without knowing in what the religious properly consists, undertake to explain it, at one moment deferentially, at another superciliously, but always incompetently. An unhappy, a jealous lover can know about love as well as a happy one, and so too one who is offended at the religious can in his way know about the religious just as well as the believer. Therefore, since our age furnishes few examples of men who in a great sense are believers, one has reason to be glad that there are some right clever men who are scandalized at religion. If a person, wishing to have something definitely explained, is so fortunate as to find one man who in the seventeenth-century sense is a strict believer, and a scandalized man in the nineteenth century, who both say the same thing (that is, the one says, "It is thus and so, that I know full well, therefore I do not want it," and the other says, "Thus and so it is, therefore I believe it," and these "thus and sos" agree completely), then one can confidently bring his observations to a conclusion. Two such consonant witnesses are more trustworthy than such as lawyers deal with.

Börne says of "Hamlet," "It is a Christian drama." This to my thinking is a peculiarly good observation. I would alter it only by saying "a religious drama," and then would say that its fault is, not that it is a religious drama, but that it did not remain such to the end, or rather that it ought not to be drama at all. If Shakespeare will not give Hamlet religious postulates which conspire against him to produce religious doubt (wherewith the drama should properly end), then Hamlet is essentially a victim of morbid reserve, and the aesthetic demands a comic interpretation. His great plan of being the avenger ("to whom ven-

[37] *Gesammelte Schriften* (Hamburg, 1829), Vol. II, pp. 172-98. The "concluding utterance" is on p. 197: "Hamlet is a Christian tragedy."

geance belongeth,"[38] says Hamlet) he has conceived. In case one does not see him at the same instant sink under the weight of this plan (wherewith the scene becomes introspective and his unpoetic scruples, viewed psychologically, are a remarkable form of dialectic repentance, inasmuch as repentance comes as it were too early)—if this does not take place, one demands resolute action, for he has only to deal with outward circumstances where the poet puts no difficulties in his way. If the plan holds good, Hamlet is a dawdler who doesn't know how to act; if the plan does not hold good, he is a sort of self-tormentor who torments himself for and by wanting to be something great—and neither of these alternatives is tragic. Rötscher[39] quite rightly regards Hamlet as a case of morbid reflection. Rötscher's explanation is capital, and it has at the same time another interest for one who wishes to see how even "Systematic" writers are compelled to employ existence-categories.

If Hamlet is kept in purely aesthetic categories, one must see to it that he has demoniac strength to carry out such a resolution. His scruples are in this case of no interest at all; his procrastination and delay, his postponement and his self-deceitful pleasure in renewing his purpose when at the same time there is no outward hindrance, merely abase him, so that he does not become an aesthetic hero, and so becomes nothing at all. If he is conceived religiously, his scruples have great interest, they insure that he is a religious hero. People have sometimes had an entirely external conception of the religious hero; especially in the Middle Ages, for example, there lived perhaps many a man who had for the Church the same enthusiasm a Roman had for his country and became a tragic hero for the sake of the Church as the Roman did for his country, and then was regarded as a religious hero. That is, by the help of purely aesthetic categories he passed his final religious examination. No, the religious is in the interior, and therefore in this case scruples have essential importance.

If Hamlet were to be interpreted religiously, one would either have to let him conceive the plan and then let the religious doubt take it from him, or else (the alternative which to my thinking illustrates better the religious, for in the first case there might possibly be mingled also doubt as to whether in reality he was capable of carrying out the plan) one must bestow upon him demoniac strength to carry out his plan resolutely and vigorously and then let him collapse within himself in the religious experience, until he should there find peace. A drama can of course never

[38] An allusion to Rom. 12:19, "Vengeance belongeth unto me, saith the Lord," and Heb. 10:30, both being quoted from Deut. 32:35.

[39] *Die Kunst der dramatischen Darstellung* (Berlin, 1844), pp. 99 *ff*.

be made out of this, a poet cannot use this theme, which would have to begin with the last phase and let the first glimmer through it.

About a single point one may have a doubt, a difference of opinion, and yet agree with one opinion which has been the opinion of one, two and three centuries, that Shakespeare stands unapproached—in spite of the progress the world is supposed to have made—and that one can learn from him, and learn the more the more one reads him.

§ 5.

ABOUT THE HERO. ABOUT SUFFERING. TRAGEDY WOULD PURIFY THE PASSIONS BY FEAR AND PITY. THAT THE PITY OF THE SPECTATORS VARIES IN CORRESPONDENCE WITH THE VARIOUS WORLD-VIEWS.

The aesthetic hero is great for the fact that he *conquers,* the religious hero is great for the fact that he *suffers.* It is true that the tragic hero also suffers, but in such a way that he at the same time triumphs in the outward world. It is this triumph which exalts the spectator, whereas he has tears for the dying man. If the *quidam* of the experiment were to have been a kind of aesthetic hero, he must have been such in a demoniac sense (in the direction towards evil), and he might thus have become a hero; for the aesthetic is not so material that it essentially gives attention only to the shedding of blood or the number of murders in order to determine accordingly whether one is a hero. It has regard essentially to passion, only it is unable, because it is not emancipated from the external, to press on to that merely qualitative act of determination which is reserved for the religious, where a farthing counts for just as much as empires and kingdoms. If then he were to have been a hero, he must have acted by virtue of this reflection: "I see the idea of my existence brought to naught by this girl, *ergo* she must be got rid of, over her destruction passes my path to a great goal." It is not at all difficult to construct for him one or another splendid ideal which he would desire to realize. One might then see him attain the goal and see the world-order bring upon him a nemesis. Above all he must be egotistically sure of himself, and this, one would perceive, accounted for his intrepidity and explained how it was he became supernatural—not like the religious man who becomes so by making sacrifices, but as the man who is demoniac in the direction of evil becomes so by demanding sacrifices. But above all he must not be, as in the experiment he actually is, a sympathetic nature, for then the aesthetic cannot comprehend his collision; and above all he must not, as in the experiment, regard it as a matter of prime importance that he manages to suffer more than she does and is assured, as he wishes to be, that even the step he takes will not be the girl's destruction but his own. The *quaedam*[40] of the experiment lies essentially within the aesthetic sphere. The uncommon qualities which constitute an aesthetic heroine would in this case be: to have within herself sufficient ideality to hold fast to love, and through this strength which preserved love to be raised to something extraordinary and so to constitute herself a nemesis upon him. A girl of such quality of course I could not use in the experiment, where the important thing is to illuminate him and have the unity of the comic and the tragic as law for the construction. I chose therefore a girl of a more ordinary sort. His sympathetic nature has to be illuminated from all sides, and hence I had to have a feminine figure which is able to make the whole situation as dialectic as possible for him, and among other things is capable of putting him to the torture of seeing her, as he expresses it, break with the idea, although after all she does nothing more (if she does that) but to get for herself, *sine ira et studio* and without loss of her loveliness, a new cavalier for the dance of life. For if a person cannot get the one, then a person takes the other, without making any fuss about ideas, and precisely for this reason remains lovable. Such an event anybody could have foretold to him, but in his case that does no good. Of course like every girl she had the possibility of becoming something great, and there were moments during their engagement when I expected I might be able to bow before her in reverence. For I who am an observer, and hence *poetice et eleganter* a sort of public watchman, have great joy in bowing and have never envied Napoleon his greatness but have on the other hand envied the two chamberlains who opened the door for him their good fortune of being the only ones to throw open the folding doors, bow profoundly, and announce, "The Emperor!" For the sake of her relationship to the experiment I could not represent her thus, and it is in proportional relationships I find my dialect satisfaction. How they chanced to begin, the fatality which compelled each of them, is not my interest. The moment I went into that I should be essentially influenced by his passion, and that would be the end of my equilibrium. As soon as I put passion aside and regard each one separately and the fate of each, I must say of *him* that he is the one who suffered most. He it was who began it and by beginning it offended her, inasmuch as he did not comprehend the specific peculiarity of a feminine existence. He began it, and hence his suffering was deserved. About *her*

[40] The feminine form, which of course in this case refers to "the girl."

I must say that she is the one to whom life does the greatest injustice in the experiment, inasmuch as in having to do with him she always appears in a false light from the moment he prevents her by the deceit from expressing what sympathy there may well have been in her. Do what she will, even though she were to choose to remain true to him, a comic light falls upon her because she has her existence in the deceit. This injustice he feels acutely, yet he behaves with sympathetic passion from his point of view, and it is one of the sources of his suffering that from his standpoint he does his utmost and yet does the maddest thing, because they have no standpoint in common, are not adjacent angles. Neither from his standpoint nor from hers is there any give and take: on the one hand feminine loveliness, charm—on the other spiritual existence by virtue of the dialectic. His most desperate efforts are of no avail, do not bridge the disparity, for feminine loveliness makes a claim which demands precisely what he lacks. In this his suffering consists. On the other hand, the opposite point of view might be maintained, that in relationship to feminine loveliness a spiritual existence by virtue of the dialectic might ask like the mathematician, "What does that prove?" This, however, he does not do, for he is not in equilibrium of spirit but in passion, and therefore concerns himself about the first (her legitimate claim) and chooses here his suffering.

Of suffering he has a plenty; but the aesthetic, by reason of the externality which is its element, has its own thoughts about suffering. Aesthetics says quite rightly that suffering itself has no significance and no interest, and only when suffering is related to the idea is it concerned with it. This is an incontrovertible truth, and hence it is quite right of aesthetics to reject such sufferings as toothache and gout. But when aesthetics has to explain to itself more precisely what it means to be related to the idea, it again must become evident, as was shown incidentally in § 1, that it is only an immediate relationship which concerns aesthetics, in other words, that suffering must come from without, be visible, not having its origin and expression in the individual himself. Accordingly this view has been ably presented by accomplished writers on aesthetics and has become common property, accessible even to the lowliest newspaper scribbler, that not every suffering has aesthetic interest, for example; sickness has not.

This is altogether right, and the result of such reflections is that the aesthetic hero by reason of his quantitative differentiation must preeminently be in possession of the requisites for conquering, must be in good health, in full vigor, etc., so that the difficulty comes from without.

I recall a little polemic[41] which was carried on in Germany where the one side appealed to the Greeks and the Greek aesthetic against a play in which someone had used blindness as a tragic motif, and the other side replied by appealing to the *Aedipos* of Sophocles. Perhaps the appeal might have been made with more reason to the "Philoktet," which in a way constitutes an exception to the universal aesthetic rule, yet in such a way that it cannot by any means upset it but rather must itself fall.

This then is an established fact for aesthetics. When I now take leave of aesthetics I do away with its externality but retain the just principle, that only such suffering has interest as stands in relation to the idea. This remains true to all eternity. When a relationship to the idea is not visible in suffering, it must be rejected in the aesthetic field and condemned in the religious. But since the religious is only qualitatively dialectic and is commensurable for everything, and equally commensurable, every suffering may therefore *eo ipso* acquire interest, precisely for the reason that everyone may acquire a relationship to the idea.

A great deal has been said about poetry reconciling one with existence; rather it might be said that it arouses one against existence; for poetry is unjust to men by reason of its quantitative estimate, it has use only for the elect, but that is a poor sort of reconciliation. I will take the case of sickness. Aesthetics replies proudly and quite consistently, "That cannot be employed, poetry must not become a hospital." That is quite right, so it must be, and it is only a bungler who would attempt to treat such subjects aesthetically. In this situation when people have no religion they are in a dilemma. Aesthetics culminates in the end by regarding sickness in accordance with the principle enunciated by Friederick Schlegel: "*Nur Gesundheit ist liebenswürdig.*"[42] So too poetry must speak (when compelled to make answer to people—though the people are at fault in compelling it, as will be indicated later); if it would not degenerate into snivel and whining drama, it must say, "Wealth alone is lovable, or it is the *conditio sine qua non* of making use of my figures—unless I were to compose an idyl, but even here it is not poverty."

[41] Between L. Börne and the *Tübinger Literaturblatt* with regard to Ernst v. Houwald's tragedy, *Das Bild.* See *Börne's Gesammelte Schriften,* Vol. II, pp. 132 *ff.*, 161 *ff.*, especially on Sophocles' "Aedipos in Colonos," pp. 165 *ff.*

[42] "Health alone is lovable." From "Lucinda," p. 20, in *Reclams Universalbibliothek,* No. 320.

It is true that poetry, hospitable and kindly as it is, invites everyone to lose himself in it, and in this way to be reconciled, but nevertheless it posits distinctions and concerns itself only with the privileged sufferings, and thus demands more of the man who is tried by the unprivileged sufferings of life, requires of him more strength in order to lose himself in poetry. And with this poetry has already undermined itself, for it cannot be denied that he who is able to lose himself in poetry in spite of the unprivileged sufferings is greater than he who does the same thing but does not suffer in the same way, and yet poetry must say that it does not find such a person a fit subject for its treatment, notwithstanding he is great.

So soon as one takes leave of poetry, which like a friendly power of divine origin is far from wishing to offend anyone and does its best to reconcile, so soon as I transport the aesthetic principle from the securely hedged meadows of poetry into the field of reality such a principle as that health alone is lovable is simply that of a despicable man. Such a man is despicable because he is devoid of sympathy, and because he is cowardly in his egoism.

In this dilemma, when what one has learned from poetry does not reconcile one with reality, the religious makes its appearance and says, "Every suffering is commensurable for the idea and so soon as the idea is present it has interest, otherwise it is culpable, and that through the sufferer's own fault. Whether the suffering consisted in not being able to see one's great plans realized or in being a hunchback, has nothing whatever to do with the case; whether it consisted in being deceived by a faithless lover or in being so unhappily deformed that even a good man cannot refrain from laughing when he sees it and no one therefore could fall in love with it, has nothing whatever to do with the case."

Thus it is that I as an experimenter have understood the religious. But what is the idea-relationship here in question? Naturally it is a God-relationship. Suffering is in the individual himself, he is no aesthetic hero, and the relationship is with God. But here we must draw the rein, for otherwise the religious becomes so mettlesome that it goes straight to the opposite extreme and says, "The lame, the cripples, the poor are my heroes, not the privileged classes," which would be unmerciful of the religious, which yet is mercy itself.

That such is the case with suffering as viewed from the religious standpoint I know from the fact that I can confront two men who say the same identical thing. Feuerbach, who pays homage to the principle of healthy-mindedness, says that the religious existence (more particularly the Christian) is a constant history of suffering; he begs us merely to consider Pascal's life, and that is sufficient. Pascal says exactly the same thing: "Suffering is the natural state of the Christian, just as health is that of the 'natural' man"; and he was a Christian and spoke out of his own experience.[43]

A passion narrative also stands in relation to a reader, just as the aesthetic production does. (Only take notice of the dialectic difficulties which were emphasized in § 3 and brought to mind in the form of the experiment). About the relation of tragedy to the auditor we have the word of Aristotle the father of aesthetics: *δι' 'ελέου καὶ φόρου περαίνουσα τὴν τῶν τοιούτων παθημάτων κάθαρσιν.*[44] Just as in the foregoing passage I removed from aesthetics is externality and retained in the religious sphere its principle, so too may these words be retained, but they must be understood more precisely. Aristotle's meaning is clear enough. He assumes emotional susceptibility on the part of the auditor, and tragedy stimulates this by *φόβος* and *'έλεος*, but this in turn takes away the egoistic from the individual thus affected, so that he loses himself in the suffering of the hero, forgetting himself in him. Without fear and pity he would be sitting like a clod in the theater, but if he gets no further than to fear for himself, he sits there as an unworthy auditor.

This is not difficult to understand, but it is already implied here that the fear and pity must be of a definite sort, and that not everyone who knows fear and pity is able to behold a tragedy. The purely "natural" man has no fear at all for that about which the poet is concerned, so he feels at the play neither fear nor sympathy. Let him see a man walk a tightrope between the towers of Rosenborg Castle, and then he will fear, or with a man who is hung he will feel sympathy. The spectator of tragedy must have an eye also for the idea, then he sees the poetic, and his fear and pity are purified of all egoistic ingredients.

But the religious man has a different conception of what awakens fear, and therefore his sympathy is in another place. The aesthetic man is not concerned with sickness and poverty, he has no sympathy for these sufferings, he feels no solidarity with them, as Börne somewhere

[43] Feuerbach, *Das Wesen des Christenthums,* 2nd ed., p. 91; *"Die christliche Religion ist die Religion des Leidens."* Cf. p. 425, where the words of Pascal are quoted (*Vie de B. Pascal, écrite par Madame Périer, sa soeur,* in *Pensées de Pascal,* Paris, 1849, p. 40): "Sickness is the natural state of the Christian."

[44] The purification of such conditions of soul accomplished by pity ('έλεος) and fear (φόβος). From Aristotle's *Poetics,* cap. 6.

says,[45] he himself is in sound health and does not wish to hear about sickness. But all healing art, that of poetry as well as that of religion, is only for the sick, since it is exercised through fear and pity. The last clause Börne should not have uttered, for in this case the aesthetic is already qualified by relation to reality, and so it is narrow-mindedness or obduracy not to be willing to know anything of it. When the aesthetic is confined to its pure ideality, one has nothing to do with such things, that is true, and the poet offends no one. It is a mistake therefore on the part of the religious man to be angry with poetry, for poetry is and remains lovable. With the spectator the case is different when he is aware that such things exist. It is of course stupidity or cowardly obduracy to wish to be unaware that poverty and sickness exist because for one's own part one is in good health; for even if the poet does not point this out, yet anyone who has thought two healthy thoughts about existence knows that the next instant he may be in this case. It is not wrong of the spectator to want to lose himself in poetry, this is a joy which has its reward, but the spectator must not mistake the theater for reality, nor himself for a spectator who is nothing else but a spectator at a comedy.

Fear and pity again are operative in the religious sphere to purify these passions. But here the fear has become different, and so also has pity. The poet does not want the spectator to fear what vulgar men fear, and he teaches him to fear fate and to pity the man who suffers under it—yet the object of this pity must be great and quantitatively conspicuous.

The religious man begins at another place, he would teach the auditor not to fear fate, not to be absorbed in pity for him who falls before it. All such things have for him acquired less importance, and hence too he sees, as the aesthetic man does not, all men, great and small, equally exposed to the blows of fate. But then he says, "What thou art to fear is guilt, and thy pity must be for him who falls in this way, for only this is danger. Yet thy pity must not run wild, so that for concern about any other man thou dost forget thyself." He will teach the auditor to sorrow, as does the parish clerk, a lowly servitor under orders, a humbly proud right reverend high priest when with inward emotion he proclaims "that we should sorrow for our sins"[46]—a thing which of course

[45] "What concern to us is a woe occasioned by blindness! *We* have our good eyes, *we* see all around us, nothing of the sort can happen to *us*." *Gesammelte Schriften,* Vol. II, pp. 144 *ff*.

[46] In the Danish Prayer Book, "the prayer to be read before the service" by the parish clerk contains the phrase, "that I may learn from the sermon to sorrow for my sins."

the parish clerk would not dare to say to his reverend superiors, the *Docents* in the pulpit. Fear and pity are to be aroused by the matter presented, and these passions also should be purified from egoism, not however by absorbing oneself in contemplation, but by finding within oneself a God-relationship. For the poet says, "This is egoism, that in seeing the tragic hero thou canst not forget the blow of fate which struck thee; this is egoism, that in seeing the hero thou dost become as timid as a tailor who dreads to go home." — "But to dwell upon thine own guilt," says the religious man, to fear for thine own guilt, is not egoism, for precisely thereby is man in a God-relationship!" Fear and pity are for the religious man a different thing, and they are purified not by turning one's mind outward but by turning it inward. The aesthetic healing consists in the fact that the individual by gazing dizzily into the aesthetic disappears from his own eyes like an atom, like a mote, which is simply part and parcel of man's lot in general, the lot of all mankind, disappears like an infinitely small element of sound in the spherical harmony of existence. The religious healing consists on the contrary in transforming the world and the centuries and the successive generations and the millions of contemporary men to an evanescent distraction, in transforming jubilation and acclaim and aesthetic hero-worship to a disturbing distraction, the notion of being "finished," to a juggler's illusion, so that the only thing remaining is the individual himself, the single individual, placed in his God-relationship under the rubric: Guilty?/Not guilty?[47]

Such is the religious position, according to the results I have reached as an experimenter. But for my own part I do not see it thus, for in the relation between the aesthetic and the religious I see again the unity of the comic and the tragic which the two of them constitute when they are brought together. Thus in poverty I see the tragedy that an immortal soul suffers, and the comedy that it all turns on two shillings. I go no farther than the unity of the comic and the tragic in the equilibrium of life. I have a surmise that if I were to go farther and were to begin upon the religious, I should get into the difficulty of discovering that it was doubtful whether I am not guilty—hence I keep out of it. I am not one who is offended at the religious, far from it, but neither am I religious. The religious interests me as a phenomenon, and as the phenomenon which interests me most. Hence it is not for the sake of men in

[47] "The individual," says S.K., "is my category." Nowhere has he expressed his doctrine of the individual more eloquently than here, but he expressed it more fully in the "Two Notes" appended to *The Point of View*, pp. 105 *ff*. in my translation published by the Oxford University Press.

general but for my own sake I am sorry to see religiousness disappearing, because I want to have material for my observations. This I do not hesitate to say, and moreover I have plenty of time to make observations on the religious, for an observer always has time enough. It is different with the religious man. When he talks it is only a monologue. Being concerned solely about himself, he talks aloud—that is what preaching is. If there is somebody listening, he knows nothing of his relationship to this man, except this, that he owes him nothing, for what he has to accomplish is to save himself. Such a right reverend monologue, which bears witness in a Christian way when by its emotion it moves the speaker, the witness-bearer, because he is speaking about himself, is what is called a sermon. World-historical perspectives, systematic results, gesticulation and wiping the sweat from the brow, strength of voice and vigor of fist, along with the deliberate employment of the same in order to *accomplish* something, are aesthetic reminiscences which do not know even how to accentuate properly fear and pity in the Aristotelian sense. For world-historical perspectives are no more apt to arouse fear than are systematic results, and strength of voice does not shake the soul, and pounding the pulpit and wiping away the sweat arouse at the most only sensuous pity for the sweater. A religious orator who is not moved within himself and talking about himself but about everything else is thinking of Geert Westphaler.[48] Geert could talk about everything, knew much, and was very perfectable, so that he might perhaps have reached the point of knowing everything, one only thing he did not learn to know, that he himself was a *Schwatzer*. Yet Geert is blameless, for he did not give himself out to be a religious orator.

The religious orator who through fear and pity purifies these passions does not perform the amazing exploit of rending the clouds asunder in the course of his address, so as to display the heavens opened, the Judgment Day at hand, with hell in the background, himself and the elect triumphing—he performs the more simple, the more artless, the more lowly feat, which one would think so very easy: he lets the heavens stay closed, recognizes in fear and trembling that he himself is not "finished," and he bows his head while the discourse pronounces judgment upon thought and heart. He does not perform the amazing exploit which upon his next appearance might give him a claim to be hailed with acclamation, he does not thunder with the intent that the congregation might at least be kept awake and might be saved by *his* discourse—he performs the more simple, the more artless, the more lowly feat, which one might think so very easy: he lets God keep the thunder and the

[48] In Holberg's comedy of that name.

might and the glory; he talks in such a way that though everything were to go amiss he is sure nevertheless that there is one auditor who is seriously moved . . . the speaker himself, that though everything were to go amiss there was nevertheless one auditor who went home fortified . . . the speaker himself, that though everything were to go amiss and everybody were to stay away there was nevertheless one who in the difficult complications of life longed for the edifying moment of the address . . . the speaker himself. He is not lavish in dispensing the abundance of the mouth and of information, but is niggardly in his use of the funds of edification, providing economically that the admonitions obligate him before they go on to somebody else, that the comfort and truth do not depart from him . . . in order to be communicated the more lavishly. "Hence," says the religious man, "wert thou to see him all by himself in a lonely place, forsaken of all and convinced that he had accomplished nothing by talking, though thou wert to see him there, thou wouldst see him just as deeply moved as ever, if thou wert to hear his discourse, thou wouldst find it as powerful as ever, without deceit, without calculation, without striving after effect, thou wouldst comprehend that there was one person whom it must edify . . . the speaker himself. He will not grow weary of talking; for attorneys and orators who have a worldly aim, or a worldly sense of self-importance with relation to an eternal aim, grow weary when they cannot count upon their fingers what they accomplish, if existence does not cunningly deceive them with the illusion that they are accomplishing something, but the religious orator has always as his principal aim . . . the orator himself.

So it is (as I have convinced myself by experimentation) that the religious man would work through fear and pity for the ennobling of these passions. Every other way of going about it brings things to confusion by proposing semi-aesthetic categories: by making the orator aesthetically self-important, and by helping the auditors to become dizzy by losing themselves in something universal.

SUPPLEMENT.

THE SELF-INFLICTED SUFFERINGS—SELF-TORTURE.

Viewed aesthetically, every *heautontimorumenos*[49] is comic. Different ages produce different types of this ailment. Our age does not fall behind in this respect, for it is as though the whole generation were worrying itself with the fixed idea that it is called to some extraordinary task,

[49] The comic Greek title of a well known Latin comedy by Terence. It means self-tormentor.

as if at any instant there might come a delegation from the council of the gods with a summons to take their place in the assembly; for so much is certain, that being confidentially charged with looking after the future of the whole human race, it is as though every instant, like Hermann v. Bremenfeldt,[50] it must be up and off to whisper in God's ear what is the right thing for Him to do. And how deplorable it was too that Hermann v. Bremenfeldt never got a chance to talk with the Kurfürst of Saxony! It has, moreover, like all who suffer from fixed ideas, a great propensity to see espionage, persecution, everywhere, and just as rheumatic people notice drafts on all sides, so does it notice pressure everywhere, the abuse of power, and it knows how to explain in a way satisfactory to itself the feeble evidences of life in public spirit, not by the fact that its strength is only superficial and imaginary, but by the pretense that it is cowed by the governments, pretty much as when an idle busybody[51] explains why he gets nothing accomplished all day, not by the fact that he is idle, but by the many affairs which overwhelm him. But enough of this.

Precisely because it is aesthetically correct to say that all self-torment is comic, one is psychologically justified in using the comic probe before treating self-torment by another method. Of course one does not at once get the patient to laugh at his fixed idea, but by the employment of analogies one approaches nearer and nearer. If he laughs easily and heartily, one may be able perhaps to take him off his guard. How the method is carried out in detail can only be understood in actual practice, but in practice there is nothing more ludicrous than to see religious categories employed with profound and stupid seriousness where one ought to employ aesthetic categories with humor and jest. — The *quidam* of the experiment has, without knowing it, gone about the thing very correctly. With prodigious passion he conceives the plan of making his whole love-relationship appear a prank in the girl's eyes. What I have to laugh at from my standpoint is his prodigious passion—apart from this he is in the right. Danger to life is not always at hand because a person cries, "Murder!" If the *quaedam* of the experiment had been suffering tragically, she would have prevented him from getting an opportunity to employ the deceit. She would have collected herself within herself and held back. These are always the dangerous phenomena. Instead of that she went directly to the opposite extreme by

[50] Holberg's comedy *The Political Tinker,* Act I, Scene 5: "I should like to see the Kurfürst of Mayence and whisper something in his ear he would thank me for."

[51] The reference is to a comedy by that name (*Den Stundesløse*) by Holberg, Act I, Scene 6.

opening her mouth as wide as possible and tormenting herself by wanting to be an unhappy lover on a big scale. But precisely this indicates that a comic treatment is correct; for a woman who is an unhappy lover on a big scale keeps silent. If she had been depicted in religious categories, she would not have acted as she did; in that case she would have feared for herself, and therefore would have feared most the responsibility she incurred by making the thing as difficult for him as possible, not only by her personality, but by an erotic fraud which lays an attachment upon the ethical and the sense of duty. — If the *quidam* of the experiment had understood with equilibrium of spirit what he was doing, he would have been quite a different man. But his troubled passion made him tragic in the employment of the deceit, and I see the unity of the comic and the tragic precisely in the fact that he does the right thing, but not for the reason he supposes, namely, that in his sympathetic enthusiasm he might have strength to tear away from her a real love-attachment. No, the comic thing is that his tragic foolhardiness triumphed for the reason that her love-attachment does not draw many fathoms of water.

The reason why the aesthetic consistently treats all self-torment as comic can be easily perceived, just because it is logically consistent. Aesthetics keeps the hero in an undamaged state by reason of the direct proportion between strength and suffering (the one within, the other from without). It therefore regards every inward direction of thought as desertion, and not being able to have the deserter shot it makes him ridiculous.

I now leave the aesthetic and go on to the religious. As an experimenter I merely set the categories in motion in order to behold at my ease what they require, without concerning myself with the question whether anybody has done it or can do it, whether Tom let it alone because he was weak, Dick because he was too shrewd, Harry because he saw that the others let it alone and that he also could let it alone and become loved and esteemed, seeing that he didn't want to be better than others—in short, without believing the life insurance wisdom, the gist of which is that when one sheep goes to the water the other does too, what the one ass does the other does too.

The religious does not consist in a direct proportion between strength and suffering, but in the inwardness where man relates himself to himself. The fact that "self" is emphasized here suffices to show that in the religious sphere self-torment is regarded differently, but it does not suffice, says the religious, to justify the fact that individuals who have their whole existence in the aesthetic jumble things up and that the religious orators, in spite of all their phrases and holy words, have no pure categories.

If self-torment as viewed aesthetically is comic, as viewed religiously it is culpable. A religious healing of this ailment is not attained by laughter but by repentance, by the recognition that self-torture is a sin like other sins.

But whereas the aesthetic, precisely because it has nothing to do with the inward, universally dismisses self-torment as comic, the religious is unable to do the same. The fear of the religious individual is precisely fear of and for himself; the religious healing consists first and chiefly in awakening this fear, and from this one can easily see that the thing becomes more difficult. But how does the individual manage to fear himself without *by himself* discovering the danger in which he is? A crafty religiosity, I admit, goes about the thing in a different way. It says, "One must not court danger, our Lord can easily send it when it is needed." That is easily said, but it will not do to say amen and end with that, for the saying is ambiguous. In spite of the religious expression, "our Lord" (instead of which one might prefer to say "our Saviour" in order to speak more religiously, as though the religious consisted in certain words and phrases)—in spite of this the categories are half aesthetic. Although the saying sounds religious, the individual is viewed only in an external relationship to God, not in an inward relationship to himself. The saying comes about to this: "Our Lord can well bring danger and misery to thy house, indeed He can take away thy fortune, thy loved one, thy child, and He will surely do this when it is serviceable to thee—*ergo,* since He has not done this, there is no danger." This is aesthetics with a spurious religious gilding.

Religiously viewed the greatest danger is that a man does not discover, is not always discovering, that he is in danger, even if he had money and the handsomest girl and lovely children and was king of the land or one of the simple folks free from all care.

That, as I have remarked, is easily said, but one must not say amen and end there, for then one deceives. This is evident when one considers the speech more closely. Here then we have a man, a perfect Pamphilius of fortune (this name is admirably suited to such a religious speech), tenderly nursed and coddled, without having acquaintance with fear, who is edified by the consideration that our Lord . . . if. Oh, what a lucky favorite of the aesthetic, who in addition to aesthetic *Heiterkeit* obtains a religious guarantee! Every man, however, has to start with a thing called imagination; so then our lucky man learns by hearsay of the existence of poverty and misery in the world. So then he is willing to give and be praised for it. But imagination is not satisfied by this. It depicts to him suffering in the most terrible forms, and at the instant when it is most terrible of all the thought strikes him and a voice says to him, "This might also happen to thee." If he has any chivalrous blood in him he says, "Why should I be exempted any more than others?" (Tieck has dealt with this theme somewhere in a novel,[52] where a rich young man despairs over his riches, not in spleen, but out of sympathy for men.) The speech had nothing to say about this, and yet here lies the boundary between the aesthetic obduracy which would know nothing about the existence of misery, and the religious exaltation through suffering. About their being such a parting of the ways, that one does not buy oneself off by paying the poor-rate and giving a little something besides, nothing is said in the speech—and our Pamphilius ought to be joyous until our Lord, if it were to be found needful, might send danger. What is the orator doing here? He is deceiving. Instead of getting him launched into danger, he helps him to hide from life in a religious illusion. Every effort to obstruct receptivity for the fact that one is in danger is aesthetically misleading in the direction, not of poetry, but of aestheticism as it is when it has relation to reality, that is, it leads to hardening of the heart.

In case the speaker is rather more of a religious orator, he moves with ease in this difficulty and helps the hearer into it. He talks with light religious humor about fate and reverses of fortune—our lucky Pamphilius becomes a bit apprehensive, and the orator has not deceived him. Then he edifies by referring to the security of faith, and in his enthusiasm the religious orator shouts to himself and to the other, "A religious man is always joyful." This is the proudest word uttered anywhere in the world, in case it is true that no one, no one upon earth or in heaven, knows so well what danger is, and what it is to be in danger, as does the religious man, who knows that he is always in danger. He therefore who can say in one breath that he is always in danger and always joyful utters at once the most disconsolate and the most high-spirited word that can be uttered. And I who am only an observer, *poetice et eleganter* a public watchman, count myself fortunate in venturing to bow before such a man; but, to speak of myself in my categories, I would say that, if the gods have denied me the great gift, that which is infinitely higher than all I am capable of, they have bestowed upon me a far more than ordinary sagacity in sizing people up, so that

[52] The reference is perhaps to Belshazzar in "Der Alte vom Berge" (*Schriften,* Vol. XXIV, pp. 173 *ff.*), but there is no "young man" in this passage.

I neither take off my hat before I see the man, nor take it off before the wrong person.

There is many a man who has always been merry and yet stands so low that even aesthetics regards him as comic. The question is whether he has not been joyful in the wrong place. And where is the right place? It is . . . in danger, above seventy thousand fathoms of water, many, many miles from all human help, there to be joyful—that is great! To swim in shallow water along with the bathers is not the religious.

It is now easily seen what the religious must mean by self-torment. The thing is to discover *by oneself* the whole possibility of danger, and *by oneself* to discover every instant its reality (this the aesthetic man would call self-torment, and the aesthetic lecture with spurious religious gilding would keep one from it), but the thing is at the same instant to be joyful. In what then does self-torment consist? It consists in halting halfway. It does not consist therefore in the first stage above mentioned, but it consists in the fact that one is not able to press through to joy. And this is not comic, says the religious, nor does it exist in order to draw aesthetic tears, for it is culpable, and one *shall* press through. Everyone who does not get through is himself to blame for it. Here there are no hardhearted fathers as for the unhappy lover in the plays, there is not the superior force of the enemy before which the hero falls in the tragedy, here there is no betrayal by the person one trusted most, so that the man of distinction is caught in the trap, here there is only one who can be the betrayer . . . the man himself, and next to him, but infinitely far behind, the orator who would lead one to leave it alone, whereas the one and only thing he can do is to help one to get out upon the deep where there are seventy thousand fathoms of water, and when this has come to pass and he perceives that he can do no more, can render no further help to one whom he loves more dearly than his life (as one is able to love in the fable of the play), but only discovers in this distress that he himself has one hundred and forty thousand fathoms under him, there is, however, one thing he still can do, he can shout to the loved one, "In case thou dost not become joyful, know thou, know thou assuredly that it is thine own fault."[53]

Even though it be the opinion of many (supposing they were to give attention to what is here set forth) that such an orator must be regarded as a public nuisance, and that it would be the silliest thing of all to pay him for making one unhappy, yet this is not my opinion. Gladly would I pay him, and unembarrassed I would accept pay for it, if I could be

[53] S.K. had once the poignant experience of hearing an acquaintance cry out from the deep in which he was about to disappear, "It is all my own fault."

such as he, but not with the understanding that I was rewarding him or being rewarded, because money is incommensurable with such instruction, and it is not of so much worth that one ought, as Socrates did, to lay accent upon it by not being willing to receive it.

So much for self-torture. It is extremely simple, everyone knows it; and precisely in this I see again the unity of the comic and the tragic, when I consider that *everyone* knows what a man *is,* and I the observer know what everyone is.[54] For this is not aesthetic-comic for the reason that it is more than a direct proportion (for the comic consists in the disproportion between an imaginary possibility and reality). Dietrich Menschenschreck[55] is comic because his courage is an imaginary possibility and therefore dissolves his reality into nothingness. But the possibility here in question is a real possibility; man can, says religion, become the highest because he is planned for the highest. It is tragic that he is not this, but comic that he is this nevertheless, for that possibility planned by God Himself cannot be obliterated. Thus everyone knows that a man is immortal, the "observer" knows what everyone *is,* and yet everyone is and remains immortal. So the man's immortality was no imaginary possibility like the courage of D. Menschenschreck; and on the other hand, he who in all the terrors of time and custom, and in spite of their cunning, keeps the faith in immortality ever present to him does not become more immortal than every other man.

The *quidam* of the experiment is something of a self-tormentor. His first movement is good and correct, but he remains absorbed in the outcome, he does not get back quickly enough to joy in order to repeat this movement again. However that moment in which I have depicted him is also his crisis, it may perhaps go easier with him in case he is sensible enough to regard a whole life as appropriately spent in such a course of instruction, is ready to put up with being a dawdler among those who are quickly "finished," a backward child among those who go infinitely

[54] [Note by Frater Taciturnus.] In spite of my usual reluctance to hear anything from the gentlemen of the press, the reviewers, I could almost desire it in this instance—if, so far from flattering me, they were to take the ground and express it bluntly to my face, that "what he says everybody knows, every child, and the educated infinitely more." If only the fact is established that everybody knows, then my standpoint is all right, and I shall surely make a go of it with this thing of the unity of the comic and the tragic. If there was somebody who didn't know it, I might be jerked off my balance by the thought that possibly I could impart to him the needed information. What preoccupies me so much is precisely what the educated are saying in our time, that everyone knows what the highest thing is. This was not the case in paganism, not in Judaism, not in the seventeen centuries of Christianity. Hurrah for the nineteenth century! Everyone knows it. What progress over those ages when only a few knew it. Might a just balance perhaps require one to reply that to redress matters there is no one who does it?

[55] In Holberg's comedy of that name, Scene 20.

further. — That the girl assists him to get out upon the deep there can be no doubt, and viewed from my standpoint his whole relationship to her is a fortunate relationship. For the man is always fortunate in love who gets a girl who is precisely calculated to develop him. Thus Socrates was happily married to Xantippe. In the whole of Greece he would not have found her match; for that ancient grand-master of irony had need of such as she in order to develop himself. Hence if Xantippe has often had to hear herself ill spoken of in the world, I believe on the contrary that she has the triumph of asserting that the supreme head of irony, who rises head and shoulders above the mass of mankind, owed no one so much as he owed to Xantippe's housekeeping, the arena in which Socrates maintained ironically his disputation *pro sumis in ironia honoribus*[56] and thereby disputed himself into the ironic competence and equipoise by which he overcame the world. — So likewise is this girl perfectly suited to him, as was required in the experiment. She is lovable enough to move him, but weak enough to abuse her power over him. The first of these qualities binds him, the last helps him to get out upon the deep, but also saves him. If the girl had been more characterized by spirit and less by feminine loveliness, if she had been very magnanimous, she would have said to him as he sat pursuing his deceit, "My dear, thy cunning distresses me. I do not understand thee, and I do not know whether thou art frivolous enough to want to desert me, or whether thou art hiding something from me and art perhaps better than it seems. But be this as it may, I perceive that thou must have thy freedom; I am fearful on my own account if I were not to give it to thee, and I love thee too dearly to refuse it to thee. So take it, without any reproaches, without anger between us, without thanks on thy part, but with the consciousness on my part that I have done the best I could." If this had come to pass, he would have been crushed, he would have sunk to the ground in shame, for with his passion he can endure all evil treatment when he knows that he is the better one, but he would not have been able to forget that he was a debtor to such magnanimity, the greatness of which he would discover with demoniac keenness of sight. This would have been an injustice to him, for from his standpoint he too had meant well. In the experiment he is not humbled by a human hand but by God.

He who has inclination and capacity to calculate experimentally with categories without having need of a theatrical scene, meadows, many

[56] For the highest honors in irony. The phrase is constructed in conformity with the formula which describes the academic disputation for the doctor's (or master's) degree. Cf. Diogenes Laertius, II, 37, for an appreciation of Xanthippe's influence.

personages, "and then some cows," will perceive how many new constructions might be made at this point by altering him or her a little to see what would follow for him and for her, how he might have been altered so as to crush her (if, e.g., he had cruelly made her responsible for his life and perhaps terrified her so that she never got over it), as in the experiment he is quite unable to do; or how both might have been constructed with a view to both of them being crushed (if, e.g., he had not had religious postulates and perhaps, being driven to despair by his pride, had ended by celebrating their union with a suicide), instead of both being helped as they are.

Readers of romances of course make other and greater demands. They think that when everything turns upon two people it must be tiresome, as indeed it is if it does not also turn upon the categories. If the categories are involved, one person alone can be entertaining, and 6,477,-378,875 people couldn't turn upon more than the categories. A reader of romances is of course only interested when there is something doing, as one says on seeing a riot. But suppose now that the riot turned upon nothing, then after all there was nothing doing.

§ 6.

TO REPENT NOTHING IS THE HIGHEST WISDOM. — THE FORGIVENESS OF SIN.

In conformity with such negative rules of conduct as, to admire nothing,[57] to expect nothing, etc., we have the negative rule, to repent nothing, or (if one would prefer to use another word which perhaps ethically has not so disturbing an effect) to regret nothing. The secret of this wisdom really lies in the fact that they have embellished an aesthetic principle to make it look like an ethical principle. Aesthetically understood it is quite true from the ethical point of view that the free and noble spirit should not set so much store by the aesthetic in all its compass that it regrets anything. So if one has become poor, it is said rightly that to regret nothing is the highest wisdom, which means, to act in virtue of the ethical. This principle then means, to cut the bridge of the past behind one, in order to be able constantly to act at the instant. If with the best deliberation thou hast conceived a plan, and the outcome seems to show that the plan was a poor one, then the thing is to regret nothing and to act in virtue of the ethical. It is undeniable that much time is wasted in this world by such a looking backward, and to that extent the principle may be praiseworthy.

[57] The *nil admirari* which Horace made proverbial. *Letters,* I, 6, 1.

But if the plan was not made with the best deliberation, if there was fraud in it, what then? Is it then also the proper thing to regret nothing in order to suffer no delay? It depends upon what delay one might be fearful of. In case it is delay and prevention from sinking deeper and deeper that one fears, then the best thing would be to shout, "to regret nothing," and to understand the word of the poet, *nulla palescere culpa,*[58] as inculcating the impudence which does not blush at guilt; but then the principle is in the highest degree unethical. There are, however, many men who dash through life with the haste of dread. There is nothing they fear more than the dialectic, and when they say, "to repent nothing" with reference to the past, they might with as much justification say, "to deliberate nothing" with reference to the future. So it is not without wit that a cunning fellow in one of Scribe's comedies says that as he had never made any plan, neither had he suffered the distress of seeing it fail. Womenfolk also often act thus without deliberation—and come out of it very well. In another way a wise man sometimes acts without deliberation and by force of despair to attain his end. When one is stumped by something and does not know which way to turn, when everything has become deadly relative as if one were being smothered, it may be expedient to act suddenly at a single point merely to stir up life in all that dead clot. An examining magistrate, e.g., when the understanding is brought to a halt and everything seems equally probable, suddenly aims his interrogation at a single individual, not because he has the most reason to suspect him, for a definite suspicion is precisely what he lacks—he follows this trace passionately, and sometimes a light flashes out, but at another spot. When one does not know whether one is sick or well, when this situation begins to be nonsense, one does well to venture upon something desperate. But notwithstanding one acts without deliberation, there is a sort of deliberation after all.

Otherwise the rule is to endure the dialectic tension, with deliberation as the antecedent and with repentance as the consequent term. Not till a man in deliberation has exhausted the dialectic does he truly act, and not till in repentance he has exhausted the dialectic does he truly repent. Hence it seems inexplicable that the mighty thinker Fichte could assume that a man of action has no time to repent,[59] and all the more strange because this energetic and (in the noble Greek sense) candid philosopher had a high conception of man's actions as being only in the inward sphere. Perhaps it is to be explained by the consideration that on account

[58] Horace's *Letters,* I, 6, 1—in which context it means not to have any guilt to blush for.

[59] *Die Bestimmung des Menschen* (1800), *Werke* (Berlin, 1845), Vol. II, p. 311.

of his energy he did not notice (at least in an earlier period) that this inward action is essentially passive, and that therefore a man's highest inward action is repentance. But to repent is not a positive movement out to or on till, but a negative movement in at, not a doing but a letting something befall one.

There are three existence-spheres: the aesthetic, the ethical, the religious. The metaphysical is abstraction, there is no man who exists metaphysically. The metaphysical, ontology, *is* but does not *exist;* for when it exists it is in the aesthetic, in the ethical, in the religious, and when it *is* it is the abstraction of or the *prius* for the aesthetic, the ethical, the religious. The ethical sphere is only a transitional sphere, and hence its highest expression is repentance as a negative action. The aesthetic sphere is that of immediacy, the ethical is that of requirement (and this requirement is so infinite that the individual always goes bankrupt), the religious sphere is that of fulfilment, but note, not such a fulfilment as when one fills a cane or a bag with gold, for repentance has made infinite room, and hence the religious contradiction: at the same time to lie upon seventy thousand fathoms of water and yet be joyful.

Inasmuch as the ethical sphere is a transitional sphere (which however one does not pass through once for all), and as repentance is its highest expression, repentance is also the most dialectic thing. So no wonder one fears it, for give it a finger and it takes the whole hand. As Jehovah in the Old Testament visits the iniquities of the fathers upon the children in subsequent generations, so does repentance go constantly further back surmising objects for its investigation.[60] In repentance is the tug of this movement, and for that reason the movement is reversed. The tug signifies precisely that the difference between the aesthetic and the religious is that between the inward and the outward. This infinitely annihilating power of repentance one can best perceive in the fact that it is sympathetically dialectic. One seldom gives heed to this. I would not speak here of such pitiable instances as that of wanting to repent of a single act and then be a fine fellow again, or wanting to have done it and to have people believe one's assertion to this effect, notwithstanding every such utterance is proof sufficient that the resolver, the assertor, the believer have no conception of what repentance means. But even more competent treatises on repentance overlook its dialectic side in the direction of sympathy. An example to illustrate this. A gambler is brought to a halt, repentance seizes him, he gives up all gambling; notwithstanding he was close to the abyss, repentance holds him back, it

[60] It was characteristic of S.K. that he felt obliged to repent the sin of his father.

seems to succeed, and now while he is thus living in retirement, possibly saved, he sees one day that they have dragged up from the Seine a dead man, a gambler such as he had been, and this gambler had nevertheless, as he knew, striven against his vice, had fought a desperate fight to resist his inclination. But my gambler had loved this man, not because he too was a gambler, but because he was a better man. What then? There is no use in consulting romances and novels, but even a religious orator would perhaps break off my narrative a little earlier and let it end with my gambler going home shocked by the sight and thanking God for his own salvation. Halt! We should first have a little explanation, a judgment pronounced upon the other man. Every existence which is not devoid of thought is *eo ipso* engaged indirectly in passing judgment. If the other had been a hardened sinner, my man might well conclude that he did not want to be saved. But the other man was not that. Now my gambler is a man who has understood the old saying, *de te narratur fabula,*[61] he is no modern fool who believes that everyone should court the objective and monstrous task of being able to patter something which applies to the whole human race, only not to himself. So then, what judgment shall he pronounce? For he cannot forbear to pass judgment, this *de te* is for him the most sacred law of existence because it is the covenant of humanity. If a religious orator, who to make up for the lack of ability to think is able at least to prate, were to be so deeply moved by human sympathy that he wished to help him with half-categories, my gambler is mature enough to see through the delusion—so that he must fight his way through. He stands at the decisive instant, he has to pass judgment with the humble expression of the doctrine of predestination (for the proud expression has its place in the aesthetic with spurious religious gilding) if he has hope for his own salvation. He who has no sympathy but has hydrophobia finds it of course unreasonable to take another man's fate so much to heart; but not to do so is unsympathetic, and it is guiltless only insofar as the reason for it is stupidity. Existence after all must have a law, the ethical world order is not a hurly-burly where one comes out well from the maddest enterprise, the other badly from the best. But now for the judgment. It is not meant here of course that he is censoriously inclined and feels compelled to condemn as a hen is to lay eggs. But he cannot himself be saved by an accident, that is mere thoughtlessness, and if he says of the other that he sank in spite of his good will, then he himself sinks; and if he says that the other did not want to be saved, then he shudders, because after

61 Horace, *Satires,* I, 1, 69, 70.

all he saw the good in him, and because this would seem as though he made himself out a better man.

I have intentionally pushed the case to extremes. By means of the dialectic of repentance in the direction of sympathy every man who is not stupid must at once run aground. Although I am not a gambler, this phenomenon is enough for me—in case I am not an angel. Though I have ever so little guilt upon my conscience, yet if I have merely a little bit of thought in my brain, all small talk about rescue exchanged by Tom and Harry, breaks like a thread until one finds the law of existence. A man who indefatigably goes through life relying upon the category that he is not a criminal but neither is he pure, is of course comic, and one must help the aesthetic to get him extradited if he has hidden in the religious sphere in order to have a part in that, and must help to have him delivered over to comic treatment.

It is very droll to see an author who, though he is not observant of the dialectic of repentance in the direction of sympathy, is observant of something resembling it, namely, the expression of sympathy—to see such an author heal this suffering by making the sickness still worse. Börne, seriously, and not without a certain emotion at the thought of how easily in a little town one becomes a misanthrope or even a blasphemer and a rebel against the wise governance of Providence, declares that in Paris the tabulated statistics of suffering and crime contribute to heal people by the impression they make, as presumably they have contributed to make Börne a philanthropist. Yes indeed, the tabulated statistics are a precious discovery, a glorious fruit of culture, a characteristic contrast to the antique *de te narratur fabula.* Thus Schleiermacher[62] says enthusiastically that knowledge does not disturb religion, and that the religious man does not sit in security under a lightning-rod and mock at God; but by the help of tabulated statistics one laughs at the whole of existence. And just as Archimedes sat absorbed in his calculations and did not notice that he was put to death, so, I think, does B— sit, and does not notice. . . . But what am I saying? Oh, far from it! Such a sensitive soul as B— will notice quickly enough when death comes so near to him, but so long as one is oneself saved from misfortune (for from sin B— can assuredly save himself by means of an un-Socratic ignorance) one owes one's luxurious living to the possession of means whereby one holds the horror at a distance. To the poor indeed one can shut one's door, and if someone were to perish of hunger, one

62 "Ueber die Religion," *Sämmtliche Werke* (1843), Vol. I, p. 219.

can find out from the statistical works how many die each year of hunger—and one is comforted.[63]

An experimental psychologist has no use for tabulated statistics, but neither does he need such an immense concourse of people.

As an experimenter I have again propounded a problem for the religious man, the forgiveness of sin. To set immediacy and the forgiveness of sins cheek by jowl, in an immediate relationship, is a thing which might naturally occur to many people, they could also talk about it, they

[63] *A note by Frater Taciturnus, in which Börne's words are quoted in German. I have translated the German also, but S.K.'s comments are distinguished by being enclosed in brackets. The "tribune of the people" referred to in the note is of course Menenius Agrippa, who uttered the famous parable (so like St. Paul's) about the dependence of the several members of the body upon one another. The passage in quotation marks ("Good God, how great everything is in Paris . . .") is quoted from Heiberg's comedy, "The Danes in Paris," Act II, Scene 4.*

As a notable example of the sort of mystification whereby sympathy is confused with egoism, I will transcribe the passage from Börne's *Collected Works* (Hamburg, 1829), Vol. VII, p. 96. He talks about the danger of living in small towns, and then continues: "Great crimes so seldom occur that we declare them free acts, and the few who are guilty of them we piteously condemn. [This is unnecessary, however, if people are not egoistically cowardly or very stupid. And divine justice does not let itself be overawed like a court martial by a mutiny which procures pardon for all because all cannot very well be executed.] . . . But it is entirely different in Paris. [That is to say, there they believe in the saving power of mutiny.] There the weaknesses of men appear as the weaknesses of humanity [Yes, hit it hard! Mankind, especially when B— is talking, is a fictitious entity which without embarrassment can be treated as *canaille,* for doubtless B— is not embarrassed by the difficult question of how the race results from the individuals and their reciprocal relations.]; crimes and misfortunes [the one as well as the other] appear as beneficent diseases which cast upon individual members the ills of the whole body so as to preserve it. [And B— imagines he is persecuted as a demagogue! He is so aristocratic that he here evidently derides the speech of the tribune of the people about the whole body suffering when one member suffers.] We recognize there [in Paris] the natural necessity of evil ['Good God, how great everything is in Paris, there is not a single thing like the ordinary, it is all like our spring festival at Copenhagen (*Dyrehavstiden*) exactly.']; and necessity is a better comforter than freedom. [Especially for him who has ceased to sorrow and therefore has no need of comfort.] When a suicide occurs in a small town, how long it will be talked about, how much logic they will chop over it! [Yet I believe that people will be finished with it sooner than logic can be brought into this wisdom. Poor Paris! For is it not also true that a poor rascal who hides in the human swarm like an urchin under his mother's skirts and writes something in which he is not, like others, wittily diverting but instructive has the same fate as the suicide, no attention being paid to him.] . . . But if one reads in Paris the official reports of the suicides that have occurred . . . how so many kill themselves for love, so many on account of poverty, so many for bad luck at cards, so many because of ambition—then one learns to regard suicide as a disease [indeed as a beneficent disease, according to the foregoing], just as the cases of death from apoplexy or consumption occur every year in the same constant proportion!" And when one has learned this one has become a philanthropist, a man of piety, who neither mocks God nor revolts against His wise dispensation. [For piety has its dwelling in Paris, and Börne exercises the cure of souls!]

might also induce others to believe that they had experienced something of the sort, they might even prompt others to want to do the same and to want to have others think that they had done it. Why not? The only difficulty with this is that it is an impossibility. With respect to the bodily gait one does not have it so much one's own way, and if someone were to say that he walked on one arm, or even to say that everybody did so, people would soon discover that it was a false report, but a reporter has freer scope in dealing with the things of the spirit.

An immediate relation between immediacy and the forgiveness of sin means that sin is a single separate thing, and that this single thing forgiveness takes away. But this is not the forgiveness of sin. Thus a child does not know what the forgiveness of sin is, for a child believes of itself that fundamentally it is a nice child, "if only that thing had not occurred yesterday," and forgiveness takes that thing away. But if sin is something radical (a discovery due to repentance, which always precedes forgiveness), this means precisely that immediacy is viewed as invalid, but if so viewed it is practically abolished ("resolved").[64]

But how does one manage to exist by virtue of such an idea, if it is a little more concretely understood? — For to patter something is not difficult. I perceive indeed that speculative minds and prophetic seers who contemplate the whole future of mankind will regard me at the most as a seminarist who perhaps might be capable of writing a catechetical commentary to a textbook for primary schools. It may be so, but after all that is something. If only the seminarists in turn will not exclude me from their society because they know infinitely more, and if only in the end, if I were content to be a schoolchild, the enlightened seminarist and the world-historically concerned parish clerk would not say, "It is a thoroughly stupid boy, he asks such foolish questions." To me this matters very little, I am taken up only with the thought of some day approaching in conversation that wise man of Greece whom I admire, that Greek wise man who laid down his life for what he had understood, and would gladly risk his life again to understand more, since he regarded it as the most dreadful thing of all to be in error. And I am

[64] The word is ambiguous. *Hæve, ophævnet* (like the German *heben, aufgehoben*) means originally "to lift," but then "to remove," "to abolish." In the Hegelian terminology it means that the antitheses (and the factors they contain) are "resolved" in the synthesis. But it comes in the end to the same thing, for what is thus "resolved" is practically abolished for the thinker who has attained the lofty height of the synthesis. In the long note by S.K. which follows, the word "existence" is his battlecry against Hegelianism. Unfortunately there are *two* words here which have to be so translated, *existere* and *Tilvaerelse* (the latter being equivalent to the German *Dasein*). But though they are different words, they are closely related, and both are key-words in the so-called Existential Philosophy which Jaspers and Heidegger profess to derive from S.K.

confident that Socrates would say, "Certainly that is a difficult problem about which thou dost inquire, and it has always surprised me that so many could believe they understood such a doctrine, but still greater is my surprise that not a few of them have understood far more. With these latter, would that I might fall into conversation, and although it is not usually my custom to defray the cost of a banquet and pay the musicians, I nevertheless would have saved my pennies for such a purpose, in order to be initiated into their high—not merely superhuman but superdivine—wisdom. For Gorgias and Polos and Thrasybolos and the other Sophists who in my time had their shops in the market-place at Athens were only superhuman after all, were on a par with the gods, but from these men who outdo the gods and for this very reasonably receive not only money but adoration, from these men one might be able to learn much."

The thing that is difficult about the forgiveness of sin (if it is not to be determined on paper what it is, or by the living word in asseverations made at one moment with joyful emotion, at another with tears) is to become transparent to oneself to such a degree that at no point does one exist by virtue of immediacy, indeed even to such a degree that one has become another man—for otherwise the forgiveness of sin amounts to the same thing as my standpoint: the unity of the comic and the tragic.

But since immediacy is something simple (but also in the highest degree composite), it follows that by this one difficulty (i.e. that immediacy is abolished) as well as by the other which resembles it (that it is even abolished as sin) the signal is given for the question most *difficile,* which comprises all in one: how immediacy is to come back again (or whether the fact that immediacy is abolished for the individual signifies that he does not exist at all),[65] what difference there is between

[65] [Note by Frater Taciturnus.] Whereas one reads hundreds of times that immediacy is abolished, one does not see a single remark about how one is to contrive to exist in this fashion. From this one possibly might conclude that the writers are making fun of us, and that they themselves go on quietly existing by virtue of immediacy, and along side of that live by writing books about immediacy being abolished. Perhaps after all the System is not so difficult to understand, but what makes it so difficult to appropriate is that the writers have leaped over all middle terms: how it is that the individual suddenly becomes a metaphysical *Ich-Ich,* whether that is practicable, whether it is permissible, whether the whole of the ethical has not been cast to one side, whether the eternal truth of the System has not as its assumption (in the direction of the existential, the psychological, the ethical, the religious), for lack of another introduction, a necessary little lie, and whether the heavenly text of the System has not for its explanation rather paltry notes which along with an equivocal tradition dispense the initiates from thinking anything decisive even in the most decisive passages. An "immediate" genius can become a poet, artist, mathematician, etc., but a thinker surely must know his relation to human existence, lest he become an un-German (by means of "pure being," which is an

this second immediacy and an earlier one, what is lost by it and what is gained, what it is the first immediacy can do which the second dare not do, what it is the first immediacy loves which the second dare not love, what is the certainty of the first immediacy which the second does not possess, etc., for this is a very prolix subject. In another sense it is a subject easily exhausted when one has no dread of living in error but has the modern foolhardiness in thinking that if only one says the thing, he is that—just as in a fairy-tale[66] one by uttering a certain word becomes a bird.

Although I am not generally inclined to make wishes, and am by no means disposed to believe that the fulfillment of the wish would do me any good, yet for all that I could wish that a man with Socratic precision would let such an existing figure [i.e. a person who exists in virtue of the second immediacy] come into being before our eyes, so that we could see him as well as hear him. It is far from being my notion that by reading a narrative of such a thing a hundred times I should get one step further along, unless I were myself to approach that position by suffering. Praise be to the righteous rule and the just scale which does not let one acquire in mortal danger and with the utmost effort what another thoughtlessly sleeps into possession of by stupidity.

But the problem itself, the idea of the forgiveness of sin, lies outside the scope of that task which the experiment set itself, for its *quidam* is no more than a demoniac figure in the direction of the religious, and the problem surpasses both my understanding and my talents. I shall not avoid it with the excuse that this is not the proper place, as though it were only the place I lacked, or the time perhaps, or space on the paper, inasmuch as my way of thinking is this, that if once I myself had understood it, I could well enough find the place and the time and the space for the presentation of it.

"un"thing) in spite of all the German books he reads. He must surely know whether it is ethically and religiously justifiable to shut himself in metaphysically, to be unwilling to respect the claim existence has, not upon his many beatifying thoughts, not upon his imaginary *Ich-Ich,* but upon his human *thou,* no matter whether existence invites him to delight and joy and pleasure, or to horror and trembling, for in thoughtlessness to be unobservant of either is equally hazardous. And if he is able thoughtlessly to overlook this, make an experiment with such a thinker, set him down in Greece: he will be laughed to shame in that elect land, so happy in its beautiful situation, happy in its rich language, happy in its inapproachable art, happy in the joyful disposition of its people, happy in its beautiful maidens, happy first and last in its thinkers, who sought and strove to understand themselves, and to understand themselves in existence, before they tried to explain existence as a whole.

66 "The Story of Califf Stork," W. Hauff, *Sämtliche Werke* (1840), Vol. V, pp. 14 *ff.*

CONCLUSION

MY dear reader! — But to whom am I speaking? There is perhaps not a single reader left. My case is inversely like that of the noble king whom the message of sorrow taught to make haste, whose swift ride to the side of the beloved one in danger of death the immortal ballad[1] has made immortal, when it sings of the hundred swains who followed him from Skanderborg, of the fifteen who rode with him across Randbøl Heath, but when he crossed the bridge at Ribe their lord was alone. Pretty much so it is with me, but for the opposite reason, that enthralled by the one thought I have not budged from the spot, and all have ridden away from me. Maybe at the beginning the benevolent reader held in his swift courser and supposed it was an ambling steed I rode, but as I did not budge from the spot, the horse (i.e. that of the reader, or, if one will, the knight) became impatient, and I remained behind all by myself—a non-rider, or a *Sonntagsreiter,* from whom all ride away.

That being the case, there is no reason whatever for haste, I have plenty of time for myself and can, undisturbed and without incommoding others, talk to myself about myself.

The religious man, according to my view, is the wise man. But he who imagines he is a religious man without being that is a fool, and he who sees one side of the religious is a sophist. Of these sophists I am one, and even if I were capable of eating up the others, I should nevertheless not become fatter—which is not inexplicable as in the case of the lean kine in Egypt, for in the matter of religion the sophists are not fat kine but lean herring. I see the religious on all sides, but what makes me a sophist is that I do not become a religious man. The least in the sphere of religion is greater than the greatest sophist. My pain at this deprivation the gods have assuaged by granting me many a fine reflection and arming me with a certain degree of wit, which will be taken from me in case I employ it against the religious.

The sophists can be assigned to three classes. (1) Those who start with the aesthetic and obtain an immediate relationship with the religious. In this case religion becomes poetry, story. The sophist himself is enthusiastic about religion, but poetically enthusiastic; in this way he is willing to make every sacrifice, even to stake his life, but for all that he does not become the religious man. When he enjoys the maximum of

[1] A legend of Queen Dagmar.

esteem he confuses himself and permits himself to be confused with a Prophet and an Apostle.[2] (2) Those who start with an immediate ethic and come into immediate relationship with the religious. For them religion becomes a positive doctrine of duty, whereas in truth repentance is the highest work of the ethical, and that is definitely negative. The sophist remains untried by the experience of infinite reflection, is a paragon of virtue in a positive abridgment. This is the source of his enthusiasm, and he honestly finds joy in making others enthusiastic in the same cause. (3) Those who put the metaphysical in an immediate relationship with the religious. Here religion becomes history, a thing which is finished—and the sophist is finished with religion and at his maximum becomes discoverer of the System. — What the sophists are admired for by the human throng is that they magnanimously refuse to be concerned about themselves in comparison with the poetic intuition in which the one loses oneself, in comparison with the positive endeavor to attain the goal which beckons the second, in comparison with the prodigious result the third attains by putting together finished facts. But the religious consists precisely in being religiously concerned about oneself infinitely, and not about visions; in being concerned about oneself infinitely, and not about a positive aim, which is negative and finite, because the infinitely negative is the only adequate form for the infinite; in being concerned about oneself infinitely, and so not thinking oneself finished, which is negative and perdition. — This I know, but I know it in equilibrium of spirit and therefore am a sophist like the others, for this equilibrium is an offense against the holy passion of the religious. But this equilibrium in the unity of the comic and the tragic, which is the infinite concern about oneself in the Greek sense (not the infinite religious concern about oneself), is not without significance as throwing light upon the religious. In a certain sense I am far more remote from the religious than are the three classes of sophists, who have all made a beginning at it, but in another sense I am closer to it, because I see more clearly where the religious is, and also do not make the mistake of laying hold of something amiss, but miss it by not laying hold of it.

So it is I understand myself. Contented with the lower thing, hoping that some day the greater thing shall be granted to me, busied with the occupations of the spirit, in which every man, it seems to me, must have plenty to do for the longest life, even if it were composed exclusively of the longest days. — I rejoice in existence, rejoice in the small world which is my environment. Some of my countrymen are maybe of the

[2] S.K. was doubtless thinking of Grundtvig especially, for Adler had not yet swum into his ken.

opinion that Copenhagen is a tiresome town and a small town. It seems to me on the contrary that, refreshed as it is by the sea on which it is situated, and without being able even in winter to dismiss the recollection of its beech forests, it is as favorable a place as I could desire to dwell in. Big enough to be a great city, small enough to have no market price set upon men, where the tabulated comfort one has in Paris that there are so and so many suicides, where the tabulated joy one has in Paris that there are so and so many persons of distinction, cannot penetrate disturbingly and whirl the individual away like foam, so that life acquires no significance, consolation lacks its day of rest and joy its holy day, because everything dashes off into space without content—or too full of it. — Some of my countrymen find the people who dwell in this town not vivacious enough. It does not seem so to me. The speed with which in Paris thousands form a mob around one person may indeed be flattering to the one about whom they collect, but I wonder if that makes up for the loss of the quiet mind which permits the individual to feel that after all he too has some importance. Precisely because the individuals have not totally fallen in price, as though it took a dozen to make one man, and because fortunately the people are too indocile to comprehend the half-hour erudition which only flatters the desperate and the blind, precisely for such reasons is life in this capital so entertaining for him who knows how to find in men a delight which is more enduring and yields bigger dividends than getting a thousand men to acclaim one for half an hour. Its defect is perhaps rather that one individual dreams of foreign lands, a second individual is absorbed in himself, a third individual is narrow-minded and separatist, etc., and so all these individuals prevent themselves from taking what is abundantly proffered, from finding what exists in abundance when it is sought. He who is not willing to undertake anything, might nevertheless, if he had an open eye, lead a life rich in enjoyment merely by paying heed to others; and he who has also his own work to do, would do well to take heed that he be not too much imprisoned by it. But how pitiable if there were many who miss what costs nothing, no entrance fee, no expenses for banquets, no dues to one's society, no inconvenience and trouble, what costs the rich and the poor equally little and yet is the richest enjoyment, who miss an instruction which is not obtained from a particular teacher but *en passant* from any person whatsoever, from conversation with someone unknown, from every accidental contact.[3]

[3] S.K. practised what he here preaches, for it was one of his most characteristic and most endearing traits that he was accustomed to chat in the street with all sorts and conditions of men.

That upon which one in vain has sought enlightenment from books is suddenly illuminated by a flash of light at hearing one serving-maid conversing with another; an expression which one has tried in vain to torture out of one's own brain, in vain has sought in dictionaries, even in the "Dictionary of the Society of the Sciences," this one hears in passing—a raw soldier utters it, and does not dream what a rich man he is. And as he who walks in the great forest, amazed at it all, sometimes snatches a branch, sometimes a leaf, sometimes stoops to pluck a flower, now listens to the note of a bird—so does one walk in the midst of the human throng, amazed at the marvellous gift of speech, snatches now one and now another expression from a passer-by, rejoices in it and is not ungrateful enough to forget to whom he owes it; so one walks in the midst of the human throng, sees now one expression of a mental state, now another, learns and learns and becomes only more avid of learning. So let no one be deceived by books, as though the humane were of such rare occurrence, so let no one read of that in the newspapers, where the best part of the saying, the most lovable, the little psychological trait, is sometimes not preserved.

Some of my countrymen are of the opinion that their mother tongue is hardly capable of expressing difficult thoughts. This seems to me a strange and unthankful thought, as it also seems to me strange and exaggerated to be so zealous for one's language that one almost forgets to rejoice in it, to assert so zealously its independence that the zeal almost seems to indicate that one already feels one's dependence, and that in the end excitement is derived from the strife of words rather than refreshment from the joy of the language. I feel myself fortunate in being bound to my mother tongue, bound perhaps as few are, bound as Adam was to Eve because there was no other woman, bound because it has been impossible for me to learn any other tongue, and hence impossible to be tempted to look down proudly and haughtily upon the tongue to which I was born. But I am also glad to be bound to a mother tongue which is rich in original idioms, which expands the soul and delights the ear with its softer sounds; a mother tongue which does not puff and groan when it is held in the toils of a difficult thought (for which reason some think that it is incapable of expressing it), for it makes the difficulty easy by uttering it; a mother tongue which does not sound strained and panting when it is confronted with the unutterable, but employs itself with it in jest and earnest until it manages to utter it; a language which does not find at a remote distance what is near, nor seek in a profound abyss what lies close to hand, because it is on such good terms with the object that it passes in and out like a fairy, and like a child comes out with the happiest expression without quite knowing it; a language which is vehement and emotional when the right lover knows how to incite manfully the feminine passion of the language, is self-confident and victorious in the strife of thought when the right ruler knows how to lead it, is supple as a wrestler when the right thinker will not let go of it and will not let go of thought; a language which if it seems poor in a single instance, is nevertheless not so, but is disdained as a false lover disdains an unassuming maiden who possesses in reality the greatest worth and above all is not sophisticated; a language which is not lacking in expressions for the great, the decisive, the conspicuous, yet has a charming, a winning, a genial preference for the nuances of thought, for the qualifying term and the small talk of humor and the thrill of transition and the subtlety of inflection and the concealed luxuriousness of modest affluence; a language which understands jest quite as well as earnest—a mother tongue which binds its children with a chain, "easy to bear . . . yes, but hard to break."[4]

Some of my countrymen are of the opinion that Denmark lives by consuming the memory of its ancient greatness. This seems to me a strange and ungrateful opinion to which no one can assent who would prefer to be friendly and joyful rather than sullen and refractory—the only thing which consumes. Others are of the opinion that a peerless future awaits Denmark; some who think themselves undervalued and unappreciated also comfort themselves with the thought of a better generation to come. But he who is fortunate in the present generation and is quick in inventiveness when the issue is to be satisfied with this has not many moments free for peerless expectations, and no more than he grasps at them is he inclined to be disturbed by them. And he who thinks that he is unappreciated by his contemporaries uses a wondrous argument in predicting a better generation to come. Even if it were true that he is unappreciated, and even if it is true that he would be recognized in a better age which would praise him, it is nevertheless unjust and a proof of prejudice to say of this later age that it is better because it thinks better of him.[5] There is no such great difference between one generation and another; precisely the generation he censures finds itself in the position of praising what an earlier generation of contemporaries failed to appreciate.

[4] Quoted from St. Blicher, *Trækfuglene,* No. 11, pp. 23 *ff.* — I cannot of course translate adequately such a passage as this in which S.K. gives proof of the fact, now generally conceded, that he was at once the "lover," the "thinker," and the "ruler" who more than anyone else contributed to make the Danish language great.

[5] If the argument is a bit lame, what wonder, seeing that S.K. himself lived in expectation of a better age which would appreciate him?

Some of my contemporaries are of the opinion that to be an author in Denmark affords a poor livelihood.[6] They do not merely mean that this is the case with such a questionable author as I am, who have not a single reader, and only a few who get as far as the middle of the book, and of whom therefore they are not thinking in passing this judgment; but they mean that it is the case even with distinguished authors. Now this land is only a little one. But in Greece was it so mean a position to be a magistrate, notwithstanding it cost money to be one?[7] Suppose it were so, suppose it were to continue to be so, and that in the end it were to be the lot of an author in Denmark to pay a certain sum yearly for the labor of being an author. Well then, what if it were possible for foreigners to say, "In Denmark it is a costly thing to be an author, there are therefore no heaps of them, but then in turn they have not what we foreigners call catch-pennies, a thing so unknown in the realm of Danish literature that the language does not even possess an expression for it."

In case it were thinkable (as I do not assume) that there was one reader who had held out and so had got to the point of reading this Conclusion (a thing I could not have imagined, and, if I had, I would not have written this), and in case he were to talk to others about what he had read, perhaps some of my countrymen would have said, "Pay no attention to such an author, do not listen to him, he is a seducer." And one of these "some" would perhaps have continued thus: "Generally one thinks of a seducer in connection with women, and even in this connection he is commonly depicted secretive and sly, with a demoniac passion. But this is not the most dangerous sort of seducer, even in relation to women. No, if I am to imagine the most dangerous sort, I picture to myself a young man with much imagination and intellectuality. He desires no woman's favor, and this indifference is not a cover for a secret passion, far from it, he aspires after no girl, but he is a fanatic. He does not dance with the girls—in this respect he is far behind—but he seeks out a place in the cabinet adjoining the ballroom or a corner in the drawing room. When the young girls are a little tired of dancing, or when the dusk of evening falls and labor reposes and thought would flutter, there he sits, now is his time. Then they listen to his talk, and by his power of imagination he allures them on into seduc-

[6] As S.K. himself thought and often said—and says here, for what follows is an ironic complaint.

[7] The Greek magistrates were not paid, but they were not obliged like the Romans of a later time to lay out large sums to entertain the people with games. S.K. said of himself that he had to "lay out money" to produce his books. As a matter of fact he received from his publishers much more than he paid them, yet not enough to support him, and in this sense it cost the Greek magistrates money to hold office.

tive ideals, and while he talks, the expectation of their aspiring souls and the urgency of presentiment he stretches to a higher pitch. He himself asks for nothing, and again they seek the pleasure of the dance, again they return to their occupations, but privately they ponder over the lofty thoughts he uttered, and they long to imbibe again the benumbing delusion. He himself remains unchanged, for his joy is only the longing of speech and thought for the ideal. And when he falls silent it seems to him as if there were a profound sorrow in his heart, in his melancholy it seems to him as if he were an old man whom speech like a child leads through life. Thus the young girls harken to him, and little by little they are seduced, they seek in vain for what he described, seek it in vain in him, seek it in vain in themselves, and yet they long for his talk and grow old by hearing it. And when a little earlier the old aunt said to the girls, 'Beware, little children, do not listen to him, he is a seducer,' they smiled and said, 'What, he! Why, he is the best man, and in his intercourse with us so circumspect, so reserved, as if he did not see us, or as if he were sorry for us, and what he says is so beautiful, oh, so beautiful!' A poet may be such a seducer. This author of course does not possess powers of this sort, just as he does not aspire after women, but yet in another sphere he is a seducer. Essentially he has nothing to say, is far from being dangerous, it is not for this that I warn against him, for as a profound philosophical friend said to me, 'He who regards him with a genuine speculative glance sees with half an eye that he, himself deceived by life from being merely an observer, has become not a deceiver but deceit itself, the objective deceit, the pure negation.' Only at a time when men's spirits are so profoundly moved that the rule, 'He that is not with is against,' applies with double force, only in an age when the individuals, keyed up by the great crisis and the great decisions which confront them, might so easily be harmed, even by the most insignificant things, only in such an age could one be tempted to waste a word by giving warning against him, if that after all is necessary. He is in another sphere a seducer. Arrayed in jest, and by reason of that deceptive, he is inwardly a fanatic. So there he sits, close to the place where the company is assembled, so he prefers the quieter moment when the ear of the inexperienced youth eagerly drinks in the false teaching. Himself intoxicated by dreams and rendered strong by vain imaginations, as quiet as an observer, he would delude everyone into the belief that the individual possesses an infinite importance, and that this is the significance of life. Therefore do not listen to him, for he wishes, without any evil intention, to seduce you in a period of ferment to accept the undivided legacy of Quietism, with the idle notion that everyone should look after himself. He would induce you to shirk the great tasks which require united strength but also provide abundant reward for all. Behold, this he has not understood because he lacks objectivity and positivity. His existence is sheer optical illusion, his speech is as powerless and impotent as that of a ghost, and all his views are only, as the poet[8] would say, 'Pearly hues upon the ancient gate, and like snow at the end of summer.' But ye who are alive and are the children of the age, do ye not observe that existence trembles, hear ye not the martial music which beckons, are ye not sensible of the haste of the instant such as the hand of the clock is unable to follow? Why this roaring, unless something is seething in the depths? Why this dreadful anguish, unless it is a sign of pregnancy? Therefore believe him not, nor listen to him, for I suppose that in his jesting and tiresome way which he takes to be Socratic he would say that from the anguish one cannot directly conclude that delivery is at hand, since it is with anguish as it is with nausea, which is worse with an empty stomach. Nor does it follow that everyone who has pains in the belly is therefore in parturition, it might also be tympanitis; *item,* nor that everyone who has a pain in the belly is therefore in parturition, it might also be something quite different, as Suetonius reminds us when he says of a Roman emperor,[9] *vultus erat nitantis.* So do not concern yourselves about him, let him not trouble you, he has not been able to legitimate himself as a plenopotentiary authority for the age, he is not man enough to hit upon the very least thing the age might require, he is not capable of making any single proposal or of stepping forth with positive seriousness and with an attitude of distress to face the great task of the moment. But do not incite him to anger, for then he might possibly become dangerous, let him go for what he is, a scoffer and a fanatic *in uno,* a Philistine *in toto,* a deceiver, the pure negation. If ye do that, then he is no seducer."

Ah, what luck that there is no reader who reads the whole thing through! And if so be, the injury done a man by leaving him to shift for himself, when that is the only thing he wishes, is like the Wise Men of Gotham punishing the eel by throwing it into the water. *Dixi.*

[8] Baggesen, "My Ghost," *Danske Waerke* (Copenhagen, 1845), Vol. VI, p. 135.
[9] Of Vespasian, cap. 20.

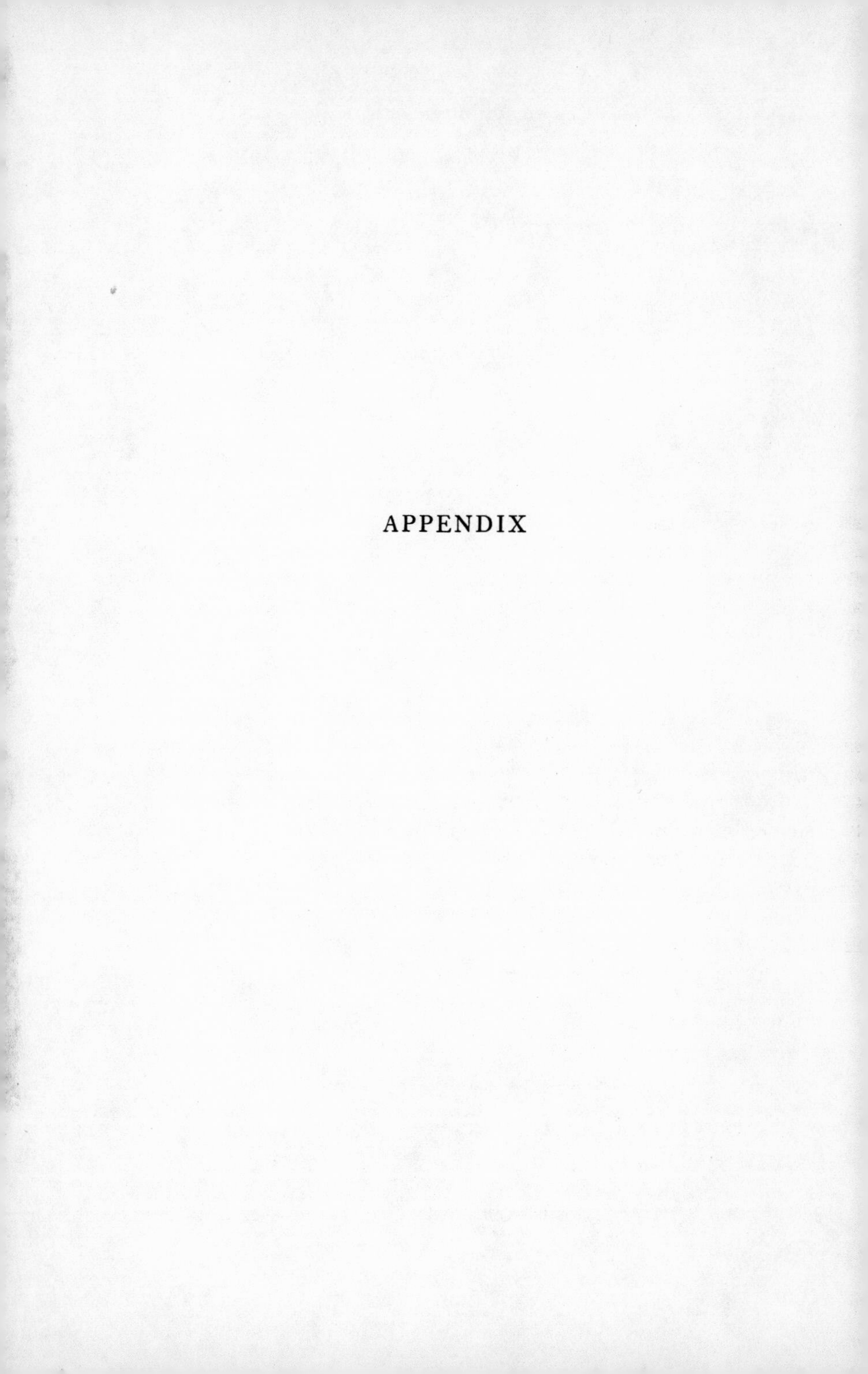

APPENDIX

ORATORY

OR

SOMETHING ABOUT THE OCCASIONAL ADDRESSES OF THE CLERGY

by

JOHANNES DE SILENTIO

(with constant reference to Aristotle's "Rhetoric")

WHAT I am here about to say might perhaps best be regarded as an introduction to a book, and if it is so regarded I desire in the next place to have it conceived of as the blurb on the dust cover which is not bound up with the book. The resolution to write it is in fact my own, otherwise I might give it up as an unwelcome task, but he who put this into my mind is Magister S. Kierkegaard, who expressly required it of me. For he has the intention of trying his hand on several discourses of this sort, and his wish was that this undertaking might need no introduction. Yet in bringing out the book he is afraid of seeing it subjected to the criticism of reviewers, and by connecting this introduction closely with his undertaking he fears that the book for all its unimportance might acquire a wrong kind of importance by means of this introduction which seems to invite criticism, and that this possibly would have the effect that the book might get too many readers, and, worst of all, not one uncritical reader. But this would be a sorry mistake. For, as it is required of a good speaker that he himself be his severest critic, so it is required of the good hearer or reader, though he were the cleverest head of all, that he renounce criticism. In relation to religion, the choice of the parson or of the book is perhaps not of so much importance as the deliberate and resolute choice to want to let oneself be edified. Therefore, without wishing in the following utterance to proclaim indulgence for the speaker, I am convinced that he who will let himself be edified, even if he were to hear perhaps a mediocre parson, or to read perhaps a mediocre book—that man will be edified. . . .

The manifold political, philanthropic, social, artistic, literary, Italian-Danish, Danish-Italian, Scandinavian, etc., conflicts which are carried on in our time I leave entirely out of account. But if one considers the field of *learning,* and of *theological* learning especially, one is aware of a continual skirmish going on, whether it be that speculation seeks to take possession, by force or by guile, of the material of theology, or whether it be that theology seeks to shun an impudent familiarity as one would shun drinking brotherhood with the hangman. No decisive battle seems yet to have been waged. But all the same the struggle more or less clearly has captivated the attention of many, and among the devotees of theology the more distinguished men are entering this conflict because they think that strength is needed here, and the high prelates who keep watch over the whole joyfully fix their attention upon one or another distinguished man with a view to bringing him to the point where the danger is.

I assume that as a matter of fact it is precisely the more capable and distinguished men who, as teachers in the universities or in whatever other learned way it may be, sustain the conflict at these points—so the rest of us are safe, the studious youth will not be led astray, for the distinguished men defend the good cause and teach youth the truth.

The studious youth on the average cannot of course be accounted so highly gifted as these distinguished men, but for this reason the life-task of these students as subordinate clergy will be far easier to perform. I assume hypothetically that the danger really lies here, and that this contentious age, vigilant and alert to the scientific strife, safely leaves the easier tasks (assuming hypothetically that the other is harder) to the less gifted.

Of the subordinate servants of the Church (I mean the parsons, for I am not thinking here of the gravediggers, etc., and between parsons there should after all be only a relative distinction)—of these subordinate clergymen people think that they cannot require so much scholarly culture as of the docents in the university; and that is quite as it should be. But when with this they forget what properly is required of the Church's teachers, confusion results. For because not so much scholarly culture is required, there might all the more, along side of this more modest culture in exact learning, be required something else, which would make the demands upon the parson just as great as those upon the professor, and hence he would not continue to be evaluated in proportion to his relationship with the university for the reason that it was to this honorable institution he owed his youthful training as a student. If scientific scholarship is overestimated, not only the students but the clergy are ranked according to a possible relation to this maximum of being able to become or to be a theological professor. . . . But is there any justification for this conclusion, that a man who is not quite capable of being a professor but comes close to it would *eo ipso* be a distinguished servant of the Church?

So people see the *scientific danger*; but in the field where the man less strictly trained and less gifted has to put out at interest what he has learned, has to put it to use, has to make the sublime pronounceable, has to give a definite answer to a simple question, assume a definite position at the point where, as he heard from his professor, even learning wavers, and without daring to secure his position by showing his scholarly disdain for someone as not sufficiently learned (tasks which are all of them readily perceived to be the easiest)—in that field there is no danger!

Let us, however, make an experiment. Let us take a fairly competent theological professor whose lectures from a scholarly point of view are worthy of respect. Now we will make the experiment—he is asked to give an edifying lecture. . . . He can't do it. It is not impossible that the learned professor will himself admit this, and that thereupon everyone, every clergyman who hears him, every deferential layman, will humble himself under the following dignified remark: "I can do it all right; it is not that I can't do it, but the congregation can't follow me." That I am quite ready to believe; it is precisely upon this I found my conclusion: so then he can't do it. Socrates, for example, was not great because he could talk so that nobody could understand him, nor because he could talk so that the sophists understood him, but because he could talk with everybody in such a way that everybody understood him, and in such a way, be it noted, that he constantly said the same thing. . . .

So then, the reason the professor gave seems to me a vain utterance, well devised to save his skin. It is perfectly true that the professor should be proud of his scholarly knowledge, that he should say of it, "I do not want to make a fool of myself or of them, as though it were possible in half an hour to convey to everyone what costs me with my superior talents time and diligence year in and year out, and hence I disdain all dabbling at popular instruction." That is quite right. It is perhaps to be wished that men of scholarship would sometimes talk that way in all seriousness. But in case the professor is not hide-bound, he will add: "On the other hand, there are different tasks, such as that of delivering an edifying discourse, a sermon, which I feel the need of hearing just as the simplest man does, and for that I have not the gifts and am not trained for it; but I understand very well that it may take the whole time and diligence of a distinguished man just as scholarly learning does mine." . . .

THREE DISCOURSES
ON IMAGINED OCCASIONS

Published separately to "accompany" the Stages. *Here the translator reproduces as a specimen only one-third of the first discourse, "On the Occasion of a Confession."*

BY

S. KIERKEGAARD

Copenhagen 1845

[April 29]

DEDICATED

TO THE MEMORY OF

MY DECEASED FATHER

MICHAEL PEDERSEN KIERKEGAARD

PREFACE

NOTWITHSTANDING this little book (of occasional addresses, as they might be called, although the occasion is lacking which creates the speaker and gives him *authority,* or the occasion which creates the reader and makes him a *learner*) is entirely uncalled for, and so in its unimportance is entirely without excuse, is without support from any external circumstance, and so is helpless in its detailed development, it is nevertheless not without hope, and above all not without a cheerful confidence. It seeks that individual whom I with joy and gratitude call *my* reader—or it does not even seek him: regardless of time it waits in quietness for that right reader to come as a bridegroom and bring the occasion with him. Each does his part, so it is the reader who does most. What really counts is appropriation. Hence the book's *joyful surrender*. Here there is no worldly mine and thine to separate, and to forbid one to appropriate what belongs to his neighbor. For admiration after all contains a little envy and so is a misunderstanding, and censure, however justified it may be, contains after all a little resistance and so is a misunderstanding, and recognition in the mirror is only a fleeting acquaintance and so is a misunderstanding, but to behold rightly and not be willing to forget as the impatient mirror does, that is appropriation, and appropriation is the *reader's* still greater, his triumphant *surrender*.

S.K.

—inasmuch as without purity no man can see God, and no man takes notice of God without becoming a sinner.

In case the seeker seeks what lies outside him, as something external, something which is not within his power, then the thing sought is in a particular place. If only he finds the place where it is, then indeed it is well with him, then he grasps it, and his seeking is at an end. So it is that everyone knew once in his early youth that there were so many beautiful things in existence, but the place he did not know definitely. Ah, even though many a man has forgotten this childish wisdom, I wonder if all have therefore become wiser, and he too, I wonder, who instead of that beautiful unity of fullness has gained the duplicity of doubt and half-heartedness in resolution![1]

In case it is assumed that the seeker himself is able to do nothing at all to find the place, he is then a wisher. So was everyone once in earlier youth. Ah, even though many a man has changed, I wonder if all therefore have truly changed for the better, and he too, I wonder, who instead of the uncertain wealth of the wish has gained the certain wretchedness of mediocrity!

When the wisher sees his wish fulfilled he is struck with wonder, as already by being a wisher he was in wonderment. So was everyone once in his early youth—not easily allured, as they say unjustly of the young, into foolish enterprises, but easily allured into blissful and unrestrained abandonment to wonder, the honest requittal which the wisher scrupulously keeps in store for the instant of fulfilment. Ah, even though many a man has lost this impetuous haste to render like for like, as he has also learned to think meanly of the wish, is therefore this higgling honesty which does not thoroughly wish and does not thoroughly wonder, and in this fashion renders like for like, is this a gain? — He who wishes also seeks, but his seeking is blind, not so much with respect to the object of his wish as with respect to the fact that he does not know whether he is approaching it or receding.

Now among the many goods there is one which is the highest, which is not to be defined by its relation to other goods, since it is the highest, and this the seeker knows without having a definite conception of it, for precisely as the Unknown it is the highest—and this good is God. The other goods have names and designations, but where the wish breathes most deeply, where this Unknown seems to show itself, there is wonder, and wonder is the sense immediacy has of God and is the beginning of all

[1] In his preparatory notes S.K. says of this formula, which was to be repeated eleven times, "Here is the place for a little rhetoric."

deeper understanding. The seeking of the wisher is blind, not so much with respect to the object (for this in fact is the Unknown) as with respect to the question whether he is approaching it or receding—all at once he is startled, the expression of wonder is worship. And wonder is an ambiguous state of mind which comprises fear and bliss. Worship therefore is mingled fear and bliss all at once. Even the most refined and rational worship of God is blissfulness in fear and trembling, confidence in the face of mortal danger, frank-heartedness in the consciousness of sin. Even the most refined and rational worship has the fragility of wonder, and it is not directly the greatness of the power and the wisdom and the performance which determines the magnitude of the God-relationship; the most potent is in the deepest impotence, the most pious sighs out of the deepest sense of need, the mightiest is he who rightly folds his hands.

The wonder of the wisher answers to the Unknown and so is entirely indeterminate, or rather infinitely determinable, may be just as loathsome as it is ludicrous, may be just as bewildered as it is childish. When the forest darkens at the evening hour, when at night the moon loses its way among the trees, when in the forest the wonders of nature lurk for their prey, and then suddenly the pagan sees a wondrous effect of light which grips him, then he sees the Unknown, and worship is the expression of wonder; when the knarled tree-trunk forms a deceptive shape which is unknown to him, which resembles a human being and yet again in his amazement has only a supernatural resemblance, then he comes to a halt and worships; when in the desert he sees a track which does not belong to any man or to any being known to him, when the power of solitude impregnates his soul with wonder, then in this track he sees that the Unknown has been here, and he worships; when the sea lies still and inexplicable in its profundity, when wonder gazes dizzily down into it until it is as though the Unknown were rising up, when the waves of the sea roll monotonously towards the shore and overwhelm the soul by the power of uniformity, when the rush whispers before the wind and whispers again and so must desire to confide something to the listener—then he worships. — If the wonder defines itself, then its highest expression is that God is the inexplicable All of existence, as this is sensed by the presentiment of imagination, in the least things and in the greatest, everywhere. What once was the content of paganism is experienced again in the repetition of every generation, and only when it has been outlived is that which was idolatry reduced to a careless existence in the innocence of poetry. For poetry is idolatry refined.

In case it is assumed that the wisher himself is able to contribute something to the finding of what is sought, then he is a striver. With that both the wonder and the wish are about to encounter their test. Often deceived, since in fact the scope of wonder, precisely because it had a direct relationship to the Unknown, comprised the loathsome as well as the ludicrous, the bewildered as well as the childish—wonder, often deceived, would look ahead and no longer walk blindly. The direct relationship is thus at the very first instant a broken relationship, without being however a breaking through to its object. It is broken by the fact that the way comes between as a determinant, whereas for the wisher there is no way. When the seeker does not walk blindly, he then does not wish only, he strives; for striving is precisely the way to the thing sought. So was everyone once in his earlier youth, high-soaring in purpose; ah, even though many a man has now learned to remain on the ground, I wonder if they therefore have all become wiser, he too, I wonder, who instead of the flight of a bird has gained the stooping gait of a four-footed beast! So was everyone once in his earlier youth, reckless in daring; ah, and even though many a man gave it up, I wonder if they all therefore became wiser, he too, I wonder, who instead of the race of recklessness after an uncertainty has gained the safety of the pedestrian upon the highway of mediocrity! So was everyone once in his earlier youth, undaunted; ah, and even though many a man learned to tone down his demands, I wonder if they all therefore became wiser, he too, I wonder, who was surfeited by fortune's favors, or he who from his environment learned pettiness, or he who in bondage to custom learned contentment! Oh, truly it is wise not to talk of fortune if one knows how to utter a holier name; but if not, it was indeed a misfortune that fortune vanished from human life, that it became weary of giving and taking, became weary of man who defrauded it of its wonder.

But in the world of freedom where in fact all striving has its source and all striving its life, there wonder meets one upon the way. The striving has various names, but that which is after the Unknown is directed toward God. The fact that it is toward the unknown means that it is infinite. Then the striver comes to a stop, he sees the deceptive track of a monstrous being which exists when it is past, which is and is not; and this being is fate, and the striving is like going astray. Worship is again the expression of wonder, and its scope comprises the loathsome as well as the ludicrous, the bewildered as well as the childish.

In case it is assumed that the seeker can do everything to find the thing sought, then the magic is done away with, wonder is forgotten, there remains nothing to wonder at. And then, the next instant, the thing sought is nothing, and this is the reason why the man was capable of doing everything. So was everyone once at the turning point of youth, when he became an eternity old; ah, and even though many a man comforts himself with the thought that he has not experienced this horror, I wonder if they therefore have all become wiser, he too, I wonder, who was still a youth at the age of an old man! So it was with everyone once, in bidding farewell to youth, that life came to a stop and he was undone; and even though many a man brags of his youthfulness, I wonder whether he therefore too was wiser who defrauded the years and eternity of their rights and whose highest wisdom was to make a frivolous answer to the most serious question!

There was a time in the world when men, weary of wonder, weary of fate, turned away from the external and found that there was no object of wonder, that the Unknown was a naught and wonder a fraud. And what once was the content of life returns in the repetition of the race. Though someone were to deem himself wise in saying that there are superseded forms which were done with thousands of years ago—it is not so in human life. And thou, my hearer, surely art not disposed to think that I would waste thy time recounting great events and mentioning queer names and being prosaically self-important in the contemplation of humanity as a whole. Ah, no, if it is true that he is defrauded who only gets to know a little, I wonder if he too is not defrauded who got to know so much that he appropriated nothing at all! Man advances slowly. Even the most glorious knowledge is after all only a presupposition. If one would augment the presuppositions more and more, he is like the miser who heaps up money for which he has no use. Even what is worthy of being valued highly, a happy upbringing, even that is only a presupposition, much time elapses before it is appropriated, and a whole lifetime is not too much if one would appropriate it. Ah, in case he was defrauded whose upbringing was neglected, I wonder then if not also he was defrauded who remained unaware that it was a presupposition, a treasure entrusted to him, a sacred heritage which should be acquired, who without more ado laid hold upon it and deemed himself to be what he had the name of being. If the better men have sometimes sighed because the thing sought was so far distant, thou surely, my hearer, hast comprehend that there is also another difficulty, that there is an illusion of knowledge which deludes the soul, that there is a security in which one is knowing . . . and yet deceived, that there is a remoteness from all decision where one without dreaming it is lost. Let terror seize its prey—ah, this security is a more terrible monster! Let the distress of poverty reduce to starvation—is it better to perish of over-abundance? It was harrowing when wonder let go of a man and he despaired of himself, but just as harrowing it is that one can know of this, can know far more, and not have had this experience, and most harrowing that one may know everything and not have made a start with the least thing. And if it is so, ah, let me begin over again; return, thou youth, with thy wish and thy lovable wonder, thou wild striving of youth with thy recklessness and thy shudder before the unknown, seize me, thou despair which breaks with the wonderful and with the wonder of youth, but quickly, quickly, if it be possible, if I have wasted my best years without experiencing anything, teach me at least not to become indifferent, not to seek consolation with others, so terror at the last may be the beginning of my healing; however late it may be, this at all events is better than to live as a liar, deceived, not by what might seem calculated to deceive, and therefore, alas, horribly deceived—deceived by much knowledge.

So then, wonder was a thing of the past, it is a thing of the past; so it was said at one time, and so now the despairer speaks and repeats it in despair, and repeats it mockingly, and would comfort himself by mockery while this wounds others, as if all mockery were not a two-edged sword! But thou, my hearer, knowest that the discourse precisely now stands at the threshold of wonder. Hence the discourse has no wish to take thee by surprise, nor would it deceive thee by an optical illusion in the lightning flash of thought when everything is reversed, nor would it carry thee away in an amazed confusion. He who actually has experienced the foregoing easily sees through the confused medley of remembrance, and in case he has not experienced it, then to hear or to read a discourse will be of dubious benefit to him. But thou who thyself art in a state of wonder, thou knowest surely that this wonder came into existence when once that first wonder was consumed by despair. But where might there be found a worthier object of wonder than when the seeker with his wishing and striving, the desperate man about to perish in despair, suddenly discovered that he was the thing sought, that the misfortune is that he stands there and loses it![2] For take the wisher as he sits and dreams, call to him and say, "Thou hast the thing wished for"; stop the striver as he rushes along the way, stop him and say, "Thou hast the thing striven for"; break through the despair, that the desperate man may comprehend that he has it—ah, what emotion he feels when he is overwhelmed with wonder, and again at the same instant a second time overwhelmed because he loses again as it were the thing sought! The glory of the wish and the striving of recklessness do not a second time awaken wonder, this is prevented by the long hyphen of despair; but that the object of his search is a given fact, that it is in the possession of him who stands there in misunderstanding and loses it—this awakens the wonder of the entire man. And indeed what stronger expression is there for wonder than that the wonderer is as it were changed, as when the wisher changes color, what stronger expression than this, that he *actually* is changed! And so it is with this wonder which changed the seeker, so it is with this wonder, that this thing of seeking became something different, yea, the very opposite: that to seek signifies that the seeker himself is changed. He does not have to find the place where the object of his search is, for it is right beside him, he does not have to find the place where God is, he does not have to strive towards it, for God is right beside him, very near, near on every hand, omnipresently near, but the seeker has to be changed so that he himself becomes the place where God truly is.

[2] Perhaps no one needs a note at this point, but I confess that for my part I had to read to the end of the chapter before it was clear to me why the thing must be lost the instant it was found. The statement with which this chapter begins is hardly apprehended as an insoluble dilemma at that point, where it is not even emphasized by italics: "without purity no man can see God—no man takes note of God without becoming a sinner." But gradually we are made to feel the dilemma, and at the end of this selection, where the same statement is repeated in italics, we are brought close to the perception that the dilemma is after all not insoluble, that the sinner who loses God the instant he finds Him, on learning that he is a sinner, may be in the way of becoming pure so that he may see God.

However, wonder, which is the beginning of all deeper understanding, is an equivocal passion which comprises fear and bliss. Or was it not fearful, my hearer, that the object sought was so near thee that thou wast not seeking God but God was seeking thee; was it not fearful that thou couldst not move without being in Him, and not be so unobserved but, lo, thou wast in Him, nor flee to the uttermost bounds of the world but that He was there and at every place on the way, nor hide thyself in the abyss but that He was there and at every place on the way, nor say to Him, "Only an instant," seeing that He also was in the instant when thou didst say this; was it not fearful when the playfulness of youth and the immaturity of despair became seriousness at the instant when that which thou didst once point at and aspire after and of which thou didst say that it did not exist then came into existence, yea, was in existence everywhere about thee and embraced thee on every hand! But was it not blissful that the hand of the mighty could block thee up in the darkest hole and yet not shut out God; was it not blissful that thou couldst fall into the deepest abyss where one can see neither sun nor stars and yet can see God; was it not blissful that thou couldst go astray in the solitary wilderness and yet at once find the way to God; was it not blissful that thou couldst become an old man who had forgotten everything and yet never forgets God because He cannot become something by-gone, that thou couldst become dumb and yet call upon Him, blind and yet see Him, deaf and yet hear Him, that He would not say as men do, "Only an instant," because He was in the instant the instant He said it! — But he who leaves out fear, let him look well to it that he does not also leave out the finding. It is so easy, or if someone would prefer to say the same thing in another way, it is so hard to find God that people even go to the trouble of proving that God exists and find a proof necessary. Let the labor of proof be hard, especially let it cause trouble to him who is expected to understand that it proves something; the thing has become easy for the prover, for he has taken his position outside, he does not treat with God, but his is a treatise about God. If on the contrary this thing of seeking should signify that a man himself is to be changed, then let the seeker look well to himself. One has to learn wonder from a child and fear from a man; that is at all events a preparation, then comes fear enough when God comes and renders proofs superfluous. Or is this perhaps courage that one remains unconscious of danger, that the prover sits unchanged and proves and proves that the Omnipresent exists, the Omnipresent who therefore also at the instant of the proof sees through the prover—without however having any scientific opinion about the utility of the proof? Might the Omnipresent actually become like a rare freak of nature the existence of which the scholar proves, or like an irregular star which people observe at intervals of hundreds of years, the existence of which therefore requires a proof, especially for the intervening centuries in which it is not visible?

But the true wonder and the true fear one man cannot teach the other. Only when they constrict and expand the soul, thine, precisely thine, thine alone in the whole world, because thou art alone with the Omnipresent, only then do they truly exist for thee. Though an orator had the eloquence of an angel, and though he had an aspect which could strike the bravest heart with terror, so that thou didst fall, as the expression is, into the profoundest wonder at his eloquence, and horror seized thee upon hearing him; it is not this wonder and not this fear which helps. It applies to every man, the least and the greatest, that neither an angel, nor legions of angels, nor all the terrors of the world, can instil the true wonder and the true fear, but they well may make him superstitious. The true wonder and the true fear is there only when he, precisely he, be he the meanest or the greatest of men, finds himself alone with the Omnipresent. The greatness of power and wisdom and performance does not directly determine the magnitude of the God-relationship. Or did not the magicians of Egypt perform almost as great signs as Moses? Suppose they had been greater—what inference could be drawn from that? None, no inference at all with respect to the God-relationship. But Moses feared God, and Moses wondered at God, and fear and wonder, or the fear in wonder together with its bliss determines the magnitude of the God-relationship.

It is true, as the understanding says, that there is nothing to wonder at, but precisely for this cause is wonder secure—because the understanding vouches for it. Let the understanding condemn what is transitory, let it clear the ground, then wonder comes in the right place, in ground that is cleared, in the changed man. Everything appertaining to that first wonder the understanding can consume; let it do so, in order that enigmatically it may help one to wonder, for it is indeed enigmatical, since it conflicts with the judgment of the understanding concerning itself. But if a man gets no farther, let him not accuse the understanding, nor let him be triumphant because it has been victorious. In case a prince sends a general against a foreign land, and that general conquers it, and thereupon himself takes possession of it as a rebel, then there is indeed no reason for accusing him because he conquered it, but neither is there any reason to be triumphant, since he himself retained it. And so, if a man by his understanding is victorious over what was pretty indeed yet also childish, then let him not accuse the understanding; but if the understanding ends by making a rebellion, then let him not be triumphant. But the wonder is in the changed man.

As here is described, so it was once with every man at the instant of decision when the sickness of the spirit struck in and he felt himself imprisoned, imprisoned forever. Ah, though many a man comforts himself with the thought that he has avoided this danger, I wonder if he too was wiser who shrewdly and cravenly defrauded himself when he thought he was defrauding God and life! So it happened once to everyone, when it was all over with jest and illusion and diversion; ah, and though many a man boasts defiantly of his unconcernedness, I wonder if he therefore was wiser whose life ran riot in parasitic growth because he was not bound! So it happened once to everyone; ah, and even though many a man flatters himself that he had a more advantageous lot, I wonder if therefore he became wiser who, being unbound, did not know that just for this cause he was unfree!

When the thing sought is assumed to be given, seeking signifies that the seeker himself is changed so that he becomes the place where the object of the search can truly be. And the thing sought was in fact given, it was so near that it was as though again it were lost, without the certainty that it is lost—how a man loses ground! What a distance separates him from that time when he wished, when he recklessly dared, when the thing sought was far off, when self-complacency boasted defiantly that it did not exist—and now it has come so near that it is lost, and the loss dates back to a distant past! The seeker was to be changed; ah, and he was changed—how a man loses ground! And the changed state in which he is we call sin. So the thing sought *is,* the seeker is the place, but changed, and changed from having once been the place where the object of search was. Ah, now there is no wonder, no ambiguity! The state of the soul when it comprehends this is fear and trembling in the guilty one, its passion is sorrow over remembrance, its love is repentance in the man of perdition. My hearer, was it not thus? The discourse does not mean to take thee by surprise, it possesses no authority to extort from thee any confession of sin. On the contrary, it cheerfully acknowledges its impotence in this respect, it is willing to say to a man that not all the eloquence of the world is capable of convincing him of his sin, but then also it would remind him not to fear the eloquence of sinners but the omnipresence of the Holy One, and still more to fear escaping from it. If a man is to understand his sin essentially, he must understand it because he remains alone, he alone, precisely he alone with the Holy One who knows all things. Only this fear and trembling is the true sort, only the sorrow which the remembrance of God awakens in a man, only the repentance His love fosters. Though an orator had a voice like the thunder of heaven, though he had an aspect which struck men with terror, though he understood how to accuse with his eye, and then as thou wast sitting there, my hearer, he pointed to thee and said, "Thou, thou art a sinner," and though he did it with such power that thine eyes sought the ground, that the blood retreated from thy cheeks, and perhaps for a long time thou didst not recover from the impression—then thou didst know surely that he by his behavior transformed the scene into a booth at the fair where he performed his juggler's tricks, and thou didst deplore that he disturbed thee from finding the stillness. Fear and trembling before an abomination, before a pious debaucheé, is not the true fear and trembling. As it is truly said that a man is not to seek his peace in another man lest he build upon the sand, so it is true also that he is not to rely upon the notion that it is the business of any other man to convince him that he is a sinner, though another may well remind him of his own responsibility to God, if he does not discover it himself. Every other understanding is distraction. And it is mere jest if I were to judge thee, but this is seriousness if thou dost forget that God will judge.

So then, the object of the search is given, God is near enough; but no man can *see God without purity,* and sin is precisely impurity, and *therefore no man can take note of God without becoming a sinner.* The first is an inviting word, and the glance of the soul is upward towards the height where the goal is; but at the same instant there rings out the other word which indicates the beginning, and this word is a depressing word. And such is the case with him who would understand sin for himself.

So here the discourse arrives at the beginning. The beginning does not come about through wonder, but verily neither does it come about through doubt, for he who doubts of his guilt makes a bad beginning, or rather he continues what with sin was badly begun. "What comes with sin goes with sorrow,"—this surely applies to sin itself: it goes with sorrow. Sorrow is therefore the beginning, and trembling is the vigilance of sorrow. The deeper the sorrow, so much the more does a man feel himself to be nothing, less than nothing, and this precisely for the reason that the sorrower is the seeker who begins to take note of God. It has always been said, even in paganism, that the gods do not sell the highest things for naught, that a divine envy which prompts the divinity to set store upon itself determines the conditions of the relationship—how might not then this thing of an individual man becoming aware of God, how might it not have its requirement? And this requirement is that a man become a sinner. And yet this is not, if I may say so, a courtesy man shows to God, that His holy presence reduces the individual to a sinner; no, the individual was a sinner, but he became such only by God's presence. He, however, who seeks to understand himself in the consciousness of sin before God does not understand this as a general proposition that all men are sinners, for it is not upon this generality the emphasis falls. The deeper the sorrow, so much the more does a man feel himself as nothing, as less than nothing, and abatement of self-esteem is a sign that the sorrower is a seeker who begins to take note of God. In a worldly sense it is said that he is a poor soldier who does not hope to attain the highest rank; in a godly sense the reverse is true: the less one believes in oneself, not as man in general or as being a man, but of himself as an individual man, not with respect to talents, but with respect to guilt—so much the more distinct will God become in him. We would not increase guilt in order that God may become greater, but we well may increase the knowledge of guilt. And as the magistrate who sleeplessly watches over justice sometimes employs spies who themselves are guilty, so is everyone whom the Holy One employs himself a debtor, sometimes even a debtor in the strictest sense, a guilty man, so that the Holy One is concerned both for the salvation of the guilty one and about saving others by means of him.

INDEX

INDEX

Inasmuch as the themes here referred to are commonly continued, perhaps through many pages, the customary indication of this is not necessary